Get the eBook FREE!
(PDF, ePub, Kindle, and liveBook all included)

We believe that once you buy a book from us, you should be able to read it in any format we have available. To get electronic versions of this book at no additional cost to you, purchase and then register this book at the Manning website.

Go to https://www.manning.com/freebook and follow the instructions to complete your pBook registration.

That's it!
Thanks from Manning!

Praise for the Second Edition

A thorough manual for learning, practicing, and implementing MongoDB with real-world examples.

—Jeet Marwah, Acer Inc.

A must-read to properly use MongoDB and model your data in the best possible way.

—Hernan Garcia, Betterez Inc.

Awesome! MongoDB in a nutshell.

—Hardy Ferentschik, Red Hat

Provides all the necessary details to get you jump-started with MongoDB.

—Gregor Zurowski, independent software development consultant

This book is going beyond the ordinary information. If you want to be successful with your deployment and development of NoSQL databases, you have to read this book.

—Jürgen Hoffmann, Red Hat

For online information and ordering of this and other Manning books, please visit www.manning.com. The publisher offers discounts on this book when ordered in quantity.

For more information, please contact

    Special Sales Department
    Manning Publications Co.
    20 Baldwin Road
    PO Box 761
    Shelter Island, NY 11964
    Email: orders@manning.com

© 2025 Manning Publications Co. All rights reserved.

No part of this publication may be reproduced, stored in a retrieval system, or transmitted, in any form or by means electronic, mechanical, photocopying, or otherwise, without prior written permission of the publisher.

Many of the designations used by manufacturers and sellers to distinguish their products are claimed as trademarks. Where those designations appear in the book, and Manning Publications was aware of a trademark claim, the designations have been printed in initial caps or all caps.

∞ Recognizing the importance of preserving what has been written, it is Manning's policy to have the books we publish printed on acid-free paper, and we exert our best efforts to that end. Recognizing also our responsibility to conserve the resources of our planet, Manning books are printed on paper that is at least 15 percent recycled and processed without the use of elemental chlorine.

The author and publisher have made every effort to ensure that the information in this book was correct at press time. The author and publisher do not assume and hereby disclaim any liability to any party for any loss, damage, or disruption caused by errors or omissions, whether such errors or omissions result from negligence, accident, or any other cause, or from any usage of the information herein.

Manning Publications Co.	Development editor:	Rebecca Senninger
20 Baldwin Road	Technical editor:	Christopher Dellaway
PO Box 761	Review editor:	Kishor Rit
Shelter Island, NY 11964	Production editor:	Kathy Rossland
	Copy editor:	Keir Simpson
	Proofreader:	Melody Dolab
	Technical proofreader:	Doug Warren
	Typesetter:	Tamara Švelić Sabljić
	Cover designer:	Marija Tudor

ISBN 9781633436077
Printed in the United States of America

MongoDB 8.0 in Action, Third Edition

BUILDING ON THE ATLAS DATA PLATFORM

AREK BORUCKI

MANNING
SHELTER ISLAND

*In memory of my dear parents, Ela (1942–2014) and
Bogumił (1938–97) Borucki. Your wisdom and support shaped my path,
and your presence lives on in my heart and memories.
To my beloved wife, Kasia Jakubów, for your endless love, patience,
and encouragement. Your unwavering support means everything to me.
And to my dear friend Juergen Schaecher, whose influence sparked my journey
with MongoDB—thank you for setting me on this path.*

brief contents

PART 1 A DATABASE FOR MODERN WEB APPLICATIONS 1

- 1 ■ Understanding the world of MongoDB 3
- 2 ■ Getting started with Atlas and MongoDB data 14
- 3 ■ Communicating with MongoDB 34
- 4 ■ Executing CRUD operations 57
- 5 ■ Designing a MongoDB schema 92
- 6 ■ Building aggregation pipelines 121
- 7 ■ Indexing for query performance 140
- 8 ■ Executing multidocument ACID transactions 180
- 9 ■ Using replication and sharding 196

PART 2 MONGODB ATLAS DATA PLATFORM 241

- 10 ■ Delving into Database as a Service 243
- 11 ■ Carrying out full-text search using Atlas Search 262
- 12 ■ Learning semantic techniques and Atlas Vector Search 302
- 13 ■ Developing AI applications locally with the Atlas CLI 335
- 14 ■ Building retrieval-augmented generation AI chatbots 358
- 15 ■ Building event-driven applications 384
- 16 ■ Optimizing data processing with Atlas Data Federation 430
- 17 ■ Archiving online with Atlas Online Archive 437

18 ■ Querying Atlas using SQL 449
19 ■ Creating charts, database triggers, and functions 459

PART 3 MONGODB SECURITY AND OPERATIONS 479

20 ■ Understanding Atlas and MongoDB security features 481
21 ■ Operational excellence with Atlas 507

contents

preface xviii
acknowledgments xx
about this book xxii
about the author xxvi
about the cover illustration xxvii

PART 1 A DATABASE FOR MODERN WEB APPLICATIONS..1

1 ■ Understanding the world of MongoDB 3

1.1 Examining the document-oriented data model 4

1.2 Scaling data horizontally 6

1.3 Exploring the MongoDB ecosystem 8

Learning the core MongoDB server features 9 ■ *Learning MongoDB Atlas concepts 9*

1.4 Enhancing the TCMalloc version 11

1.5 Discovering MongoDB Query API 11

2 ■ Getting started with Atlas and MongoDB data 14

2.1 Setting up your first Atlas cluster using Atlas CLI 15

Installing the Atlas CLI 15 ■ *Creating an Atlas account 15 Creating an organization 16* ■ *Creating an Atlas project 17 Creating a MongoDB Atlas cluster 18* ■ *Navigating the Atlas user interface 19*

viii

2.2	Loading a sample data set 19
2.3	Adding an IP address to the project access list 20
2.4	Creating a user 21
2.5	Establishing a connection to MongoDB through MongoDB Shell 21
2.6	Managing data with databases, collections, and documents 23

*Working with dynamic schema 23 ▪ Working with databases 25
Working with collections 26 ▪ Working with documents 31*

3 Communicating with MongoDB 34

| 3.1 | Interacting via MongoDB Wire Protocol 35 |
| 3.2 | Discovering mongosh 35 |

*Connecting to MongoDB Atlas 36 ▪ Connecting to self-hosted deployments 36 ▪ Performing operations 36 ▪ Viewing mongosh logs 38 ▪ Running scripts in mongosh 38
Configuring mongosh 40 ▪ Using .mongoshrc.js 42*

3.3	Playing with MongoDB Compass 43
3.4	Connecting using MongoDB drivers 45
3.5	Using the Node.js driver 45
3.6	Employing Python drivers 49

PyMongo 49 ▪ Motor 51 ▪ PyMongo vs. Motor 53

| 3.7 | Integrating Ruby drivers 53 |
| 3.8 | Learning Mongoid 55 |

4 Executing CRUD operations 57

4.1	Connecting to mongosh for CRUD operations 58
4.2	Inserting documents 58
4.3	Updating documents 61

Using update operators 62 ▪ Updating many documents 63

| 4.4 | Updating arrays 64 |

Adding elements to an array 64 ▪ Removing elements from an array 66 ▪ Updating array elements 67 ▪ Updating using array filters 68

| 4.5 | Replacing documents 70 |

- 4.6 Reading documents 71
  - *Using logical operators 72* ▪ *Using comparison operators 74*
  - *Working with projections 75* ▪ *Searching for null values and absent fields 76*
- 4.7 Performing regular-expression searches 77
- 4.8 Querying arrays 78
- 4.9 Querying embedded/nested documents 81
  - *Querying on a nested field with dot notation 82* ▪ *Matching an embedded/nested document 83* ▪ *Querying an array of embedded documents 83*
- 4.10 Sorting, skipping, and limiting 84
  - *The sort operation 84* ▪ *The skip operation 84* ▪ *The limit operation 85*
- 4.11 Deleting documents 85
- 4.12 Using bulkWrite() 86
- 4.13 Understanding cursors 88
  - *Using manual iteration 88* ▪ *Returning an array of all documents 89*
- 4.14 Employing MongoDB Stable API 89

5 ▪ Designing a MongoDB schema 92

- 5.1 Organizing the MongoDB data model 93
  - *Determining the workload of the application 93* ▪ *Mapping the schema relationship 95* ▪ *Applying a design pattern 97*
- 5.2 Embedding vs. referencing 98
- 5.3 Understanding schema design patterns 101
  - *Approximation pattern 102* ▪ *Archive pattern 102* ▪ *Attribute pattern 103* ▪ *Bucket pattern 104* ▪ *Computed pattern 105* ▪ *Document Versioning pattern 106* ▪ *Extended Reference pattern 106* ▪ *Outlier pattern 107* ▪ *Polymorphic pattern 108* ▪ *Preallocation pattern 109* ▪ *Schema Versioning pattern 110* ▪ *Subset pattern 111* ▪ *Tree pattern 112*
- 5.4 Schema validations 113
  - *Specifying JSON schema validation 114* ▪ *Testing a schema validation rule 115* ▪ *Modifying schema validator behavior 117* ▪ *Bypassing schema validation 118*
- 5.5 MongoDB schema antipatterns 119

6 Building aggregation pipelines 121

- 6.1 Understanding the aggregation framework 122

  Writing an aggregation pipeline 123 • *Viewing the aggregation pipeline stages 124* • *Using $set and $unset instead of $project 127* • *Scenarios for $set and $unset operators 128* • *Scenario for the $project operator 129* • *Saving the results of aggregation pipelines 129*

- 6.2 Joining collections 131

  Creating a MongoDB view using $lookup 132 • *Using $lookup with $mergeobjects 133*

- 6.3 Deconstructing arrays with $unwind 134
- 6.4 Working with accumulators 136
- 6.5 Using the MongoDB Atlas aggregation pipeline builder 137

7 Indexing for query performance 140

- 7.1 MongoDB query planner 141

  Viewing query plan cache information 141 • *MongoDB plan cache purges 145*

- 7.2 Supported index types 145

  Creating single field indexes 146 • *Understanding compound indexes 151* • *Using multikey indexes 156* • *Using text indexes 158* • *Creating wildcard indexes 160* • *Geospatial indexes 162* • *Hashed indexes 164*

- 7.3 Dropping indexes 165
- 7.4 MongoDB index attributes 165

  Partial indexes 165 • *Sparse indexes 166* • *Time-to-live indexes 167* • *Hidden indexes 169*

- 7.5 Understanding index builds 170

  Monitoring in-progress index builds 171 • *Terminating in-progress index builds 172*

- 7.6 Managing indexes 172

  Discovering the $indexStats aggregation pipeline stage 172 • *Modifying indexes 173* • *Controlling index use with hint() 174* • *Using indexes with $OR queries 174* • *Using indexes with the $NE, $NIN, and $NOT operators 175* • *Ensuring that indexes fit in RAM 175* • *Sorting on multiple fields 176* • *Introducing covered queries 177*

- 7.7 When to not use an index 177

8 Executing multidocument ACID transactions   180

- 8.1 WiredTiger storage engine   181
  *Snapshots and checkpoints 181 ▪ Journaling 182
  Compression 182 ▪ Memory use 182*

- 8.2 Single-document transaction   182

- 8.3 Defining ACID   183

- 8.4 Multidocument transactions   184
  Differentiating the Core and Callback APIs 184 ▪ Using transactions with mongosh 185 ▪ Using transactions with the Callback API 187

- 8.5 MongoDB transaction considerations   194

9 Using replication and sharding   196

- 9.1 Ensuring data high availability with replication   197
  Distinguishing replica set members 197 ▪ Electing primary replica-set member 200 ▪ Understanding the oplog collection 201

- 9.2 Understanding change streams   206
  Connections for a change stream 207 ▪ Changing streams with Node.js 209 ▪ Modifying the output of a change stream 210

- 9.3 Scaling data horizontally through sharding   211
  Viewing sharded cluster architecture 212 ▪ Creating sharded clusters via Atlas CLI 214 ▪ Working with a shard key 216 Choosing a shard key 216 ▪ Using a shard-key analyzer 217 Detecting shard-data imbalance or uneven data distribution 222 Resharding a collection 222 ▪ Understanding chunk balancing 224 ▪ Administrating chunks 225 Automerging chunks 228

- 9.4 MongoDB 8.0 sharded cluster features   229
  Embedding config servers in sharded clusters 230 ▪ Moving unsharded collections seamlessly between shards 230 Fragmentation 231 ▪ Faster resharding 231 Unsharding collections 232

- 9.5 Managing data consistency and availability   233
  Write Concern 233 ▪ Read Concern 235 ▪ Read Preference 237

PART 2 MONGODB ATLAS DATA PLATFORM 241

10 Delving into Database as a Service 243

10.1 Shared M0 and Flex clusters 244

10.2 Dedicated clusters 247

Atlas clusters for low-traffic applications 248 ▪ Atlas clusters for high-traffic applications 249 ▪ Autoscaling clusters and storage 249 ▪ Customizing Atlas cluster storage 251

10.3 Atlas Global Clusters 253

10.4 Going multiregion with workload isolation 254

Adding electable nodes for high availability 256 ▪ Adding read-only nodes for local reads 256 ▪ Using analytics nodes for workload isolation 256

10.5 Using predefined replica set tags for querying 257

Routing queries to analytics nodes 258 ▪ Isolating normal application secondary reads from analytics nodes 258 Routing local reads for geographically distributed applications 258

10.6 Understanding the Atlas custom Write Concerns 259

11 Carrying out full-text search using Atlas Search 262

11.1 Implementing full-text search 263

11.2 Understanding Apache Lucene 265

11.3 Getting to know Atlas Search 267

Learning Atlas Search architecture 268 ▪ Using Atlas Search Nodes 269 ▪ Atlas Search indexes 270

11.4 Building an Atlas Search index 274

11.5 Running Atlas Search queries 278

Using the $search aggregation pipeline stage 279 Executing the $searchMeta aggregation pipeline stage 294

11.6 Learning Atlas Search commands 297

11.7 Using Atlas Search Playground 298

12 Learning semantic techniques and Atlas Vector Search 302

12.1 Starting with embeddings 303

Converting text to embeddings 305 ▪ Understanding vector databases 308

- 12.2 Using embeddings with Atlas Vector Search 309

  Building an Atlas Vector Search index 310 ▪ Selecting a Vector Search source 310 ▪ Defining your Vector Search index 312 Creating an Atlas Vector Search index 314

- 12.3 Running Atlas Vector Search queries 315

  Querying with embeddings 316 ▪ Using prefiltering with Atlas Vector Search 320

- 12.4 Executing vector search with programming languages 322

  Using vector search with JavaScript 322 ▪ Using vector search and prefiltering with Python 323 ▪ Using vector search with prefilters in Ruby 325

- 12.5 Using Atlas Triggers for automated embeddings creation 326

- 12.6 Workload isolation with vector search dedicated nodes 331

- 12.7 Improving Atlas Vector Search performance 331

13 ▪ Developing AI applications locally with the Atlas CLI 335

- 13.1 Introducing local Atlas clusters 336

- 13.2 Creating an Atlas cluster locally with Atlas CLI 337

  Configuring Docker 338 ▪ Building your first local Atlas cluster 340

- 13.3 Managing your local Atlas cluster 341

  Stopping, starting, checking, and deleting your local cluster 341 Loading a sample data set 344

- 13.4 Diving into a local Atlas cluster 346

  Displaying processes 349 ▪ Executing into the container 350

- 13.5 Creating search indexes 352

  Executing full-text search locally 352 ▪ Executing vector search locally 355

14 ▪ Building retrieval-augmented generation AI chatbots 358

- 14.1 Gaining insight into retrieval-augmented generation 359

- 14.2 Embedding LangChain in the RAG ecosystem 360

- 14.3 Introducing the MongoDB Atlas Vector Search RAG template 362

14.4 Getting started with AI chatbots 362
Describing LangChain capabilities 363 ▪ Starting with the LangChain CLI 364

14.5 Creating an AI-powered MongoDB chatbot 364
Setting up a new application 365 ▪ Inserting embeddings into MongoDB Atlas 367 ▪ Creating an Atlas Vector Search index 374 ▪ Testing a chatbot with LangServe 376 Communicating programmatically with a chatbot 381

15 Building event-driven applications 384

15.1 Understanding event-driven technology 385

15.2 Examining the concepts of stream processing 387
Differentiating event time and processing time 387 Using time windows 388

15.3 Starting with Atlas Stream Processing 388

15.4 Exploring Atlas Stream Processing 390
Discovering Atlas Stream Processing components 390 Understanding Atlas Stream Processing capabilities 392

15.5 Structuring a stream processor aggregation pipeline 394
Taking a deep dive into the $source aggregation stage 395 Using the stream processor $validate aggregation stage 400 Viewing all supported aggregation pipeline stages 400

15.6 Mastering Atlas Stream Processing 402
Adopting new stream processor methods 402 ▪ Using the Atlas CLI with stream processing 402 ▪ Creating your first stream processor 404 ▪ Learning the anatomy of a stream processor 406 Setting up a streams Connection Registry 419 ▪ Ensuring persistence in stream processing 420

15.7 Controlling the stream processing flow 425
Capturing the state 425 ▪ Using a dead-letter queue 425

15.8 Securing Atlas Stream Processing 426
Discovering new roles 427 ▪ Learning new privilege actions 427 Protecting network access 427 ▪ Auditing events 427

16 Optimizing data processing with Atlas Data Federation 430

- 16.1 Querying Amazon S3 and Azure Blob Store data via the Query API 430
- 16.2 Learning Atlas Data Federation architecture 432
- 16.3 Deploying an Atlas Federated Database instance 433
- 16.4 Limitations of Atlas Data Federation 434
- 16.5 Charges for Atlas Data Federation 435

17 Archiving online with Atlas Online Archive 437

- 17.1 Archiving your data 438
  Seeing how Atlas archives data 438 ▪ Deleting archived documents 440
- 17.2 Initializing Online Archive 440
- 17.3 Connecting and querying Online Archive 444
- 17.4 Restoring archived data 446

18 Querying Atlas using SQL 449

- 18.1 Introducing the Atlas SQL interface 450
- 18.2 Connecting to the Atlas SQL interface 451
  Enabling the interface 451 ▪ Accessing the interface 452
- 18.3 Querying MongoDB using SQL 453
  Aggregation pipeline Atlas SQL syntax 453 ▪ Short-form Atlas SQL syntax 454 ▪ UNWIND and FLATTEN with Atlas SQL 455

19 Creating charts, database triggers, and functions 459

- 19.1 Visualizing data with Atlas Charts 460
  Using natural language to build visualizations 462
  Using billing dashboards 465
- 19.2 Atlas Application Services 466
  Triggering server-side logic with Atlas Database Triggers 467
  Writing Atlas Functions 474

PART 3 MONGODB SECURITY AND OPERATIONS 479

20 Understanding Atlas and MongoDB security features 481

20.1 Understanding the shared responsibility model 482

20.2 Managing authentication 485

*Choosing an Atlas database cluster authentication method 486
Integrating with HashiCorp Vault 487 ▪ Choosing the authentication method 488*

20.3 Handling authorization 488

*Understanding the principle of least privilege 489
Differentiating Atlas user roles 489 ▪ Using MongoDB RBAC 490*

20.4 Auditing Atlas 492

20.5 Encrypting data in Atlas 495

*Encrypting data in transit 495 ▪ Encrypting data at rest 496
Managing encryption keys yourself 496 ▪ Encrypting during processing 497*

20.6 Securing the network 500

*Using an IP access list 500 ▪ Peering networks 501
Using private endpoints 502*

20.7 Implementing defense in depth 503

21 Operational excellence with Atlas 507

21.1 Crafting backup strategies and practices 508

Discovering Atlas backup methods 508 ▪ Restoring an Atlas cluster 512

21.2 Inspecting the performance of your Atlas cluster 516

*Finding slow queries 516 ▪ Improving your schema 520
Using native MongoDB diagnostic commands 521*

21.3 Alerting and logging 524

Setting alert conditions 524 ▪ Logging in Atlas 526

21.4 Upgrading your Atlas cluster 527

index 531

preface

My journey with MongoDB has been both extensive and deeply immersive. As a MongoDB Champion, I have had the privilege of participating in numerous MongoDB events and training sessions, contributing to the development of certification-exam questions, and have also been a speaker at various conferences, sharing my expertise and real-world experiences.

Professionally, I work as an SRE/DevOps engineer, managing some of the most complex and largest-scale deployments in Europe. One of my most significant experiences involved managing one of the continent's largest MongoDB farms, with clusters that exceeded 100 TB. Each cluster consisted of 130 nodes and implemented microsharding, a technique that allows multiple MongoDB processes to run on the same host. These clusters were not just massive in scale but also mission-critical, responsible for handling passenger flight information. The need for lightning-fast search capabilities made MongoDB an indispensable part of these high-stakes operations. Through this hands-on experience, I used many of MongoDB's advanced features, which I explore in detail throughout this book.

This journey also introduced me to MongoDB Atlas, the fully managed Database as a Service (DBaaS). It was in this high-pressure environment that I first recognized the power and convenience of Atlas, especially in reducing the operational overhead of managing massive clusters. Atlas's ability to handle scaling, backup management, and performance optimization with minimal intervention was a game-changer.

Beyond working with large-scale enterprise applications, I have seen MongoDB thrive in the startup ecosystem. One such project involved a customer relationship management (CRM) system, in which MongoDB proved its value not only in scalability but also in agility and performance. This experience, however, also highlighted the challenges of running self-managed MongoDB instances, particularly the complexity of replicating collections from MongoDB to Elasticsearch to enable full-text search capabilities. It was through overcoming these challenges that I truly appreciated the built-in capabilities of MongoDB Atlas, which offers full-text search natively, eliminating the need for such complex integrations.

This book is a culmination of my hands-on experience, real-world challenges, and deep technical insights. My goal is to provide a comprehensive guide to MongoDB, whether you are building a small application or managing a multiterabyte enterprise system. I cover not only best practices and technical optimizations but also strategic insights to help you make the right architectural decisions for your needs.

I invite you to join me on this journey as we delve into MongoDB's capabilities and unlock its full potential together.

acknowledgments

First and foremost, I want to express my deepest gratitude to my wife, Kasia Jakubow, for her unwavering support and patience throughout the journey of writing this book. Her encouragement and understanding made this project possible.

I am also incredibly grateful to the production team at Manning for their guidance and assistance in bringing this book to life. A special thank you to Jonathan Gennick for giving me the opportunity to write this book and believing in my vision. My sincere appreciation goes to Rebecca Senninger for her invaluable feedback and meticulous review of the manuscript.

Heartfelt thanks to technical editor Chris Dellaway, a fellow MongoDB Champion, for his review and insightful tips that greatly enriched the content of this book. Chris has worked professionally with MongoDB databases since 2016 and currently holds four MongoDB certifications. In recognition of his significant contributions to the MongoDB community, Chris was honored with the MongoDB 2023 William Zolo Award for Community Excellence.

I would also like to extend my gratitude to the team at MongoDB for their support throughout this process. Special thanks to Rachelle Palmer and Rita Rodrigues for supporting my book idea and backing me along the way. My appreciation also goes to Veronica Cooley-Perry for her outstanding coordination of the workflow, ensuring that everything stayed on track. Bree Grosshandler deserves recognition for creating the beautiful images that complement this book so well.

Huge thanks to technical proofreader Doug Warren and to everyone involved in the technical review process at MongoDB, including Asya Kamsky, Rita Rodrigues, Joel Lord, Manuel Fontan, Sigfrido Narváez, Eoin Brazil, and Ger Hartnett. Your insights and expertise were invaluable in refining the technical aspects of this book.

To all the reviewers: Advait Patel, Akshay Phadke, Alain Lompo, Alankrit Kharbanda, A.J. Bhandal, Anandaganesh Balakrishnan, Andres Sacco, Asaad Saad, Eddú Meléndez Gonzales, Ganesh Swaminathan, Giampiero Granatella, Giuseppe Catalano, Jaume López, Kalai Chelvi Erudia Nathan, Kim Lokoy, Leonardo Gomes da Silva, Matteo Rossi, Maulik Modi, Maurizio Bonifazi, Mihaela Barbu, Oscar F. Gil C., Peter Szabo, Piti Champeethong, Rajasekhar Reddy Genupula, Richard Meinsen, Rohan Pasalkar, Shantanu Kumar, Simon Verhoeven, Venkata Yanamadala, and Vinicios Wentz. Your suggestions helped make this book better.

To each and every one of you, I extend my sincere appreciation. Your contributions made this book what it is, and I am truly grateful.

about this book

This book provides a comprehensive guide to MongoDB version 8.0 and the MongoDB Atlas data platform, covering everything from fundamental concepts to advanced techniques for building, scaling, and optimizing modern web applications. You will learn how to use different types of indexes for query optimization, scale data horizontally using sharding, and use advanced features such as full-text search, vector search, and change streams to enhance search capabilities, real-time analytics, and event-driven architectures in AI-powered applications.

Who should read this book

This book is for developers who want to build scalable applications with MongoDB and MongoDB Atlas DevOps and SRE professionals who are responsible for database deployment, monitoring, and scaling; data architects seeking to design efficient database schemas and optimize query performance; and engineers working with AI applications, full-text search, event-driven architectures, or real-time analytics.

How this book is organized: A road map

The book is divided into three parts:

- Part 1 provides an overview of MongoDB:
  - *Chapter 1*—Introducing MongoDB, document-oriented data modeling, and the flexible schema. This chapter lays the groundwork for understanding how MongoDB structures data differently from relational databases.
  - *Chapter 2*—Getting started with Atlas, setting up clusters, and managing data. You learn how to deploy a MongoDB instance quickly using Atlas and explore its essential features.

- *Chapter 3*—Connecting to MongoDB using MongoDB Shell (`mongosh`), Compass, and various programming language drivers. This chapter covers different tools and methods for efficient interaction with MongoDB.
- *Chapter 4*—Executing create, read, update, and delete (CRUD) operations, scripting with mongosh, and working with time-series collections. Hands-on examples demonstrate how to manipulate and query data effectively.
- *Chapter 5*—Designing schemas, embedding and referencing data, and validating schema structures. This chapter is a journey into data modeling strategies to ensure optimal database performance and maintainability.
- *Chapter 6*—Building aggregation pipelines for data processing and optimization. You explore how to transform and analyze data using MongoDB's powerful aggregation framework.
- *Chapter 7*—Indexing strategies, performance tuning, and query execution analysis. This chapter focuses on improving query performance through strategic indexing and query optimization.
- *Chapter 8*—Understanding atomicity, consistency, isolation, and durability (ACID) transactions in MongoDB and best practices for multidocument transactions. Learn how MongoDB handles transactions to ensure data consistency across multiple operations.
- *Chapter 9*—Replication for high availability and horizontal scaling with sharding. This chapter examines the fundamentals of data distribution and replication to enhance fault tolerance and scalability.

- Part 2 covers the Atlas developer data platform:
  - *Chapter 10*—Exploring MongoDB Atlas as a DBaaS and its developer-centric tools. This chapter provides insights into Atlas's managed features and shows why it simplifies database operations.
  - *Chapter 11*—Implementing full-text search using Atlas Search and Apache Lucene. You learn how to use search indexing to build fast, scalable search applications.
  - *Chapter 12*—Using Atlas Vector Search for AI-driven applications and similarity search. This chapter explains how vector-based search enhances AI applications with semantic retrieval.
  - *Chapter 13*—Using the Atlas command-line interface (CLI). The CLI enables local development and testing of AI applications by allowing you to spin up a local Atlas cluster, load data, and perform both full-text and vector searches, enabling rapid iteration without cloud deployment.
  - *Chapter 14*—Building retrieval-augmented generation (RAG) AI chatbots with LangChain and MongoDB. Learn how to develop intelligent chatbots that retrieve and generate relevant responses dynamically.
  - *Chapter 15*—Developing event-driven applications with Atlas Stream Processing. You see how to process real-time data streams and trigger database-driven events.

- *Chapter 16*—Querying Amazon S3 and Azure Blob Storage using the MongoDB Query API, which enables seamless access to distributed data. Explore the architecture of Atlas Data Federation, deploy a federated database instance, and understand its limitations and pricing model.
- *Chapter 17*—Archiving aging or infrequently accessed data with Atlas Online Archive for seamless storage optimization. Initialize the archive, apply archiving strategies, connect and query archived data, delete archived documents, and restore data when necessary.
- *Chapter 18*—Querying Atlas using SQL and integrating business-intelligence (BI) tools. This chapter is a guide to using SQL-based queries in MongoDB and connecting it to BI platforms.
- *Chapter 19*—Creating Atlas Charts, database triggers, and serverless functions. This chapter walks through MongoDB Atlas's visualization and automation capabilities for data-driven applications.

- Part 3 covers security and operations:
  - *Chapter 20*—Securing your data with Atlas. This topic involves managing authentication and authorization, enforcing least-privilege access, integrating with HashiCorp Vault, and configuring encryption in transit, at rest, and during processing. Strengthen network protection through IP access lists, virtual private cloud (VPC) peering, and private endpoints.
  - *Chapter 21*—Achieving operational reliability with Atlas. This topic involves implementing robust backup strategies, monitoring performance, and tuning your cluster. Restore data, identify slow queries, optimize schema design, configure alerts, analyze logs, and manage cluster upgrades effectively.

About the code

This book contains many examples of source code in numbered listings and inline with normal text. In both cases, source code is formatted in a `fixed-width font like this` to separate it from ordinary text. Sometimes, code is also **`in bold`** to highlight code that has changed from earlier steps in the chapter, such as when a new feature adds to an existing line of code.

In many cases, the original source code has been reformatted; we've added line breaks and reworked indentation to accommodate the available page space in the book. In rare cases, even this was not enough, and listings include line-continuation markers (➥). Also, comments in the source code were removed from the listings when the code was described in the text. Code annotations accompany many of the listings, highlighting important concepts.

All source-code examples, command-line scripts, and supplementary materials referenced throughout this book are available in the companion GitHub repository at https://github.com/arekborucki/MongoDB-in-Action.

The repository is organized by chapter, and each directory contains practical materials aligned with the book's content. It serves as a hands-on companion for exploring

MongoDB and the Atlas developer data platform in real-world contexts. The repository includes the following, among other things:

- Code examples written in JavaScript (Node.js), Python, and shell scripts
- Aggregation pipelines, indexing strategies, and query optimization examples
- Use cases for Atlas Search, including autocomplete, fuzzy search, and synonym mapping
- Atlas Vector Search samples demonstrating similarity search and AI-driven retrieval
- Real-time stream processing examples using Atlas Stream Processing
- Data life-cycle management using Online Archive and Data Federation
- Backup and restore utilities, including snapshot creation, point-in-time recovery, and cluster restoration
- DevOps tools for performance tuning, schema validation, and automation workflows
- Monitoring, alerting, and diagnostic scripts for managing MongoDB Atlas clusters

This codebase is updated continually to reflect new MongoDB 8.0 features and enhancements in the Atlas platform. It provides a practical reference for professionals who are building reliable, scalable applications in the cloud.

You can get executable snippets of code from the liveBook (online) version of this book at https://livebook.manning.com/book/mongodb-in-action-third-edition. The complete code for the examples in the book is also available for download on the Manning website at https://www.manning.com/books/mongodb-in-action-third-edition.

liveBook discussion forum

Purchase of *MongoDB 8.0 in Action, Third Edition*, includes free access to liveBook, Manning's online reading platform. Using liveBook's exclusive discussion features, you can attach comments to the book globally or to specific sections or paragraphs. It's a snap to make notes for yourself, ask and answer technical questions, and receive help from the author and other users. To access the forum, go to https://livebook.manning.com/book/mongodb-in-action-third-edition/discussion.

Manning's commitment to our readers is to provide a venue where meaningful dialogue between individual readers and between readers and authors can take place. It is not a commitment to any specific amount of participation on the part of the author, whose contribution to the forum remains voluntary (and unpaid). We suggest that you try asking the author some challenging questions lest their interest stray! The forum and the archives of previous discussions will be accessible on the publisher's website as long as the book is in print.

about the author

AREK BORUCKI is an SRE/DevOps expert specializing in MongoDB, NoSQL, Kubernetes, and cloud platforms. He builds scalable, high-performance systems for mission-critical workloads. As a MongoDB Champion and co-author of official MongoDB and Atlas certification exams, he shares his expertise through training, technical content, and regular talks at global events like MongoDB.local and the Data on Kubernetes Community. His interests include real-time analytics, performance tuning, automation, observability, and AI-driven distributed systems. He helps teams apply best practices to deliver efficient, resilient infrastructure.

about the cover illustration

The figure on the cover of *MongoDB 8.0 in Action, Third Edition*, titled "Le Bourginion" (a resident of the Burgundy region in northeastern France), is taken from a book by Louis Curmer published in 1841. Each illustration is finely drawn and colored by hand.

In those days, it was easy to identify where people lived and what their trade or station in life was by their dress alone. Manning celebrates the inventiveness and initiative of the computer business with book covers based on the rich diversity of regional culture centuries ago, brought back to life by pictures from collections such as this one.

Part 1

A database for modern web applications

Imagine that you're running an online store with millions of products and thousands of customers shopping at the same time. In a traditional relational database, you might start to hit performance walls as your data grows. Tables get larger, queries slow, and scaling vertically (adding more CPU or RAM) becomes expensive and limited.

MongoDB was designed to solve these problems. Unlike relational databases that rely on rigid schemas, monolithic architectures, and JOIN-heavy queries, MongoDB embraces a flexible, document-oriented model and is built from the ground up to scale horizontally. JOINs, although powerful, create tight coupling between tables, making horizontal scaling across distributed systems much more difficult. MongoDB prevents this problem by storing related data together in rich, self-contained documents. Need more capacity? Add another server. MongoDB's automatic sharding takes care of distributing your data across nodes, allowing your system to grow with your users.

Have you ever tracked your food delivery in real time, received a personalized product recommendation while shopping online, or collaborated with teammates in a shared document editor? If so, you've experienced the power of modern web applications—and chances are that MongoDB was working behind the scenes.

Today's applications are built to be fast, flexible, and evolving. They collect and process enormous volumes of data, from user preferences and chat messages to product catalogs and sensor readings. Traditional relational databases, with their rigid schemas and limited scalability, often struggle to keep up with the pace and diversity of these demands.

MongoDB takes a different approach. It's a document-oriented database designed for the modern web. Instead of storing data in fixed tables with rows and columns, MongoDB stores information as flexible, JSON-like documents that naturally map to how developers think and code. This design makes it possible to build and iterate on applications rapidly without being held back by schema changes or performance bottlenecks.

In this first part of the book, you'll dive into the world of MongoDB and see how it powers cloud-native applications. Chapter 1 introduces the document data model and shows how MongoDB enables flexible, schema-agnostic development. You'll also learn about MongoDB Atlas, a fully managed database service that lets you run MongoDB clusters in the cloud with ease.

Chapter 2 guides you through your first hands-on experience with Atlas: spinning up a cluster, importing data, and making your first queries. Chapter 3 introduces the tools you'll use to interact with MongoDB, from the `mongosh` shell and MongoDB Compass to programming-language drivers like Node.js, Python, and Ruby.

In chapter 4, you'll learn how to create, read, update, and delete documents—the core operations that power every database application. Chapter 5 shifts focus to schema design and data modeling. You'll explore different approaches to structuring documents and linking related data, whether through embedding or referencing.

Chapter 6 introduces aggregation pipelines, a powerful feature that allows you to transform and analyze data within MongoDB. You'll see how to group, filter, reshape, and even output data from your collections using declarative pipeline stages.

Next, chapter 7 dives into indexing, which is a critical topic for performance. You'll learn about various index types and see how to use them to speed your queries. Chapter 8 explores multidocument atomicity, consistency, isolation, and durability (ACID) transactions, showing how MongoDB ensures data consistency in complex operations.

Finally, chapter 9 turns your attention to scaling and resilience. You'll discover how MongoDB ensures high availability through replication and scales horizontally using sharding, letting you handle massive volumes of data across distributed systems.

Whether you're building your first MongoDB app or looking to master the foundations, this part of the book gives you the tools and understanding to start strong.

Understanding the world of MongoDB

This chapter covers

- Analyzing the document-oriented data model
- Breaking down MongoDB sharded cluster components
- Exploring the core features of the MongoDB server
- Understanding Atlas and its key features
- Taking a first glance at full-text search and vector search

The landscape of database technology is undergoing a significant transformation, ushering in an era of next-generation databases designed to meet the evolving demands of modern applications. These cutting-edge systems offer unparalleled flexibility, scalability, and performance, challenging traditional paradigms and setting new standards for data management.

In this book, I explore MongoDB, the next-generation NoSQL database, and its vast potential. MongoDB is a versatile, flexible, and scalable document database suitable for a wide range of applications. It supports scaling out and includes features like secondary indexes (e.g., faster lookups in e-commerce), range queries (e.g., chat applications), sorting (e.g., ordering search results), change streams (e.g., real-time updates in stock trading apps), aggregations (e.g., analytics dashboards), and geospatial indexes (e.g., Uber Maps), making it a powerful tool for developers. MongoDB Atlas, on the other hand, is a managed MongoDB Database as a Service (DBaaS) that operates across multiple cloud platforms. Atlas enhances MongoDB's core server capabilities by adding features such as full-text search for ranking, relevance, wildcard, fuzzy, or faceted search; vector search (pivotal in supporting retrieval-augmented generation applications and generative AI); stream processing; SQL interface; and more, offering advanced search and real-time data processing functions.

With built-in security, automated backups, and seamless scalability, Atlas simplifies database management while ensuring high availability. This makes it a good choice for startups and large enterprises looking to build reliable, data-driven applications.

1.1 Examining the document-oriented data model

In modern software development, objects that encapsulate data and methods are central, representing real-world entities such as customers, invoices, and flights. These objects are ephemeral during program execution and must be stored permanently for future use—a process known as *persistence*. Persistence ensures that the state of objects is maintained across program runs, allowing for ongoing interaction with stored data.

Document databases cater to this need by enabling direct storage of objects without significant data transformation, simplifying the persistence process. They support intuitive querying by allowing data to be filtered and aggregated directly through objects, aligning with object-oriented programming principles. It's important to note, however, that MongoDB is versatile and equally suited to functional programming, as it accommodates various programming paradigms effectively.

Unlike traditional relational databases that use a strict schema, document databases offer flexibility in data organization to optimize storage and retrieval for specific operations. Traditional relational databases are well suited to applications requiring complex, precise transactional operations, such as financial systems, in which data integrity and consistency are paramount. They are defined by a schema that describes all functional elements (such as tables, rows, and relationships), providing a high degree of control but requiring data to be formatted to fit into a structured table model. By contrast, document databases like MongoDB operate on a flexible schema basis, meaning that they do not require a predefined structure for data before it is stored. This flexibility allows each document to store data in a dynamic structure that can include fields and data types that vary from one document to another, significantly enhancing data access efficiency by allowing the co-location of related data. This flexible schema architecture makes these databases ideal for scenarios requiring rapid development and the ability to scale and adapt data structures on the fly, such as content management systems, e-commerce platforms, and real-time big data analytics. By embedding related data as arrays or nested documents, document databases reduce the need for separate tables, streamline data management, reduce reliance on separate storage structures, simplify access through fewer read operations, and lower overall data retrieval costs.

MongoDB uses Binary JSON (BSON), a binary-encoded serialization of JSON-like documents, to store objects. Although BSON maintains the lightweight, easy-to-use characteristics of JSON, it extends these capabilities by supporting data types that are not available in standard JSON, such as dates and binary data. This enhancement enables MongoDB to handle more complex data structures effectively.

It's important to note that although the way a document is represented can differ across programming languages, most languages offer a data structure that aligns well with the concept of a document. Structures like maps, hashes, and dictionaries are commonly used, providing a flexible means to organize and access data in the form of key-value pairs. These structures naturally support the organization and access of data in key-value pairs, a format that MongoDB uses efficiently to facilitate data manipulation and retrieval across various applications. A simple document containing a book title might look like this in JavaScript:

```
{ "title": "MongoDB 8.0 in Action" }
```

This example is straightforward; most documents in MongoDB are more complex, typically containing multiple key-value pairs, arrays, and nested documents. This structure allows storage of structured information in a way that's both efficient and easy to access. Storing more information within a single document can reduce read operations, improve query performance, and simplify data retrieval. Following is an example of a MongoDB document with arrays and nested documents.

Listing 1.1 A MongoDB document with arrays and nested documents

```
{
  "_id": 1,
  "title": "MongoDB 8.0 in Action",
  "publisher": "Manning Publications",
  "status": "Available",
  "focusAreas": [
    "MongoDB Database System",
    "Atlas Platform"
  ],
  "publicationYear": 2025,
  "additionalDetails": {
    "embeddedDocument": {
      "description": "A comprehensive guide to mastering
MongoDB 8.0, including working with the Atlas
Platform and learning the latest features"
    }
  }
}
```

As we've seen, MongoDB stores data in flexible, JSON-like documents. To interact with this data, the MongoDB Query API (previously known as MongoDB Query Language) can be used, which provides an effective and versatile way to perform all database operations. The Query API is designed to be intuitive, allowing you to naturally express queries that can range from the very simple to the highly complex. In later chapters, we will dive into this language, examining its syntax and capabilities in detail. For now, let's look at three introductory examples of queries in MongoDB:

- Finding a book by title:

```
db.books.find({ "title": "MongoDB 8.0 in Action" })
```

This query would return the document(s) in which the title field is `"MongoDB 8.0 in Action"`.

- Updating the publisher of a book:

```
db.books.updateOne(
   { "title": "MongoDB 8.0 in Action" },
   { $set: { "publisher": " Manning Publications Co" } }
)
```

This operation changes the publisher field of the matching document to `"Manning Publications Co"`.

- Removing documents based on publication status:

```
db.books.deleteMany({ "status": "out of print" })
```

This command deletes all documents in the books collection that have a status of `"out of print"`.

These queries illustrate the fundamental principles of the Query API design: its directness and effectiveness in data manipulation. Through these examples, we see how this query language facilitates precise data querying and updating with minimal complexity. This introduction paves the way for a deeper dive into its capabilities, highlighting its role in efficient database operations and setting a foundation for the detailed exploration to follow.

1.2 Scaling data horizontally

Data sets for applications are growing rapidly, driven by more bandwidth and cheaper storage, leading to applications managing large volumes of data, often in terabytes. This growth challenges developers to scale their databases by scaling up, upgrading to bigger servers with inherent cost and physical limits, or scaling out (partitioning data across multiple machines), adding more servers to a cluster for a more cost-effective and scalable solution, albeit with increased management complexity.

MongoDB is optimized for scaling out, using its document-oriented model to distribute data efficiently across multiple servers. MongoDB's document-oriented model is well suited to distributing data because each document is self-contained, meaning that all necessary information is stored in one place, reducing the need for the complex joins between data that are common in relational databases. As a result, MongoDB can efficiently manage and allocate data across servers, facilitating easy scaling. Because documents don't rely on others to function or fulfill queries, the system can quickly retrieve data from the appropriate server, enhancing performance and scalability.

Figure 1.1 illustrates this scaling-out approach. The process that implements this approach is known as *sharding*. Sharding distributes data across multiple machines, automating data balancing and load distribution to simplify the management of data scalability. This method allows MongoDB to handle large datasets and high-throughput operations by partitioning data into shards, each of which can be hosted on different servers. Adding new machines to accommodate growing data needs is seamless with MongoDB, which intelligently redistributes data across the cluster.

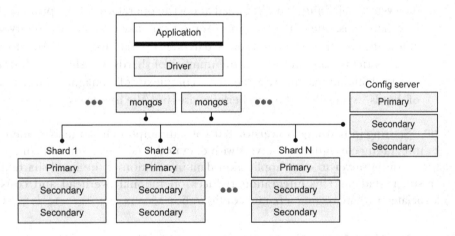

Figure 1.1 MongoDB's sharding architecture enables horizontal scaling by distributing data across multiple servers. (Image © MongoDB 2024 CC BY-NC-SA 3.0)

As shown in figure 1.1, the architecture surrounding a sharded MongoDB cluster involves several key components:

- *Application and driver*—The application interacts with MongoDB through a driver, which is responsible for connecting to the appropriate MongoDB instances. The driver communicates with mongos to route queries to the correct shard.
- mongos *(query routers)*—mongos routers are responsible for distributing client queries to the correct shards by using metadata from config servers. They support high availability and scalability through the deployment of multiple mongos

instances. If a proxy or load balancer is between the application and the mongos routers, configuring it for client affinity is essential. Client affinity, or *sticky sessions,* ensures that a load balancer or proxy directs a client to the same backend server for all requests. In this setup, after a client connects to a specific mongos router, all subsequent requests are routed to that same instance, ensuring session consistency. For shard-level high availability, you can add more mongos instances on the same hardware where they are already running or embed mongos routers directly at the application level. Adding more mongos routers can lead to performance degradation due to frequent communication with config servers. To avoid this situation, I recommend keeping the number of mongos routers below 30.

- *Config servers (replica set)*—These servers store the metadata required to manage the sharded environment, such as the layout of the shards and the location of data within the shards. Operating as a replica set, they ensure redundancy and high availability of this crucial metadata.
- *Shard (replica set)*—Within the sharded cluster, each shard is essentially a replica set that acts as a single data partition. These shard replica sets ensure data redundancy and availability, handling read and write operations. If the primary server in a shard fails, one of the secondary servers can take over as the primary server automatically, ensuring continuous database operations. MongoDB does not have a strict maximum limit on the number of shards in a sharded cluster, but practical limitations can arise due to the complexity of managing a large number of shards, especially as the number increases into the hundreds.

TIP Starting with MongoDB version 8.0, you can simplify cluster management by integrating configuration servers with data nodes (shards). You can configure a config server to store application data in addition to the usual sharded cluster metadata. This integration reduces operational overhead and costs associated with managing separate configuration servers.

1.3 Exploring the MongoDB ecosystem

MongoDB is a general-purpose database that provides a broad range of features. It's available as a Community Edition (a free version designed for developers and small teams looking to explore MongoDB's capabilities without the cost of a full-fledged commercial license) and MongoDB Enterprise Advanced (which offers operational and security enhancements, including encrypted and in-memory storage engines, authentication and authorization using OpenID Connect (OIDC) and OAuth 2.0, as well as auditing capabilities). MongoDB Enterprise Advanced also includes entitlements to use comprehensive management tools such as Ops Manager and Enterprise Operator for Kubernetes. It's available on MongoDB Atlas, a fully managed cloud service that not only simplifies database setup, scaling, and management but also enhances the core MongoDB server with exclusive features for cloud environments.

1.3.1 Learning the core MongoDB server features

Here's an outline of some essential MongoDB features, available in MongoDB Community Edition, Enterprise Edition, and MongoDB deployed in Atlas:

- *Indexes*—MongoDB provides support for generic secondary indexes, along with specialized indexing options such as unique, compound, geospatial, and text indexes. It also supports secondary indexing on hierarchical data structures, including nested documents and arrays, thus empowering developers to model their data optimally according to the specific needs of their applications.
- *Aggregation framework*—Aggregation operations process data records and return computed results. Aggregation operations group values from multiple documents together and can perform a variety of operations on the grouped data to return a single result. The framework provides features similar to SQL's GROUP BY, related operators, and basic self-joins; it also allows data reshaping.
- *Change streams*—Applications can use change streams to subscribe to all data changes on a single collection, a database, or an entire deployment and react to them immediately. Because change streams use the aggregation framework, applications can also filter for specific changes or transform the notifications at will.
- *Special collections and indexes*—MongoDB features time-to-live (TTL) indexes for automatically expiring data, capped collections for maintaining recent data like logs, and partial indexes to index only documents that meet specific criteria, enhancing efficiency and saving storage space.
- *Time-series collections*—Applications can use these collections to manage time-stamped data efficiently, optimizing both storage and retrieval processes for information that changes over time, such as metrics, device data, and application logs.

1.3.2 Learning MongoDB Atlas concepts

The contribution of Atlas to the robustness of MongoDB is invaluable. It enables data distribution among leading cloud service providers, such as Amazon Web Services (AWS), Microsoft Azure, and Google Cloud Platform (GCP). Atlas has built-in automation mechanisms for optimizing resources and workloads. It includes a comprehensive security suite to protect data integrity and privacy; it also offers advanced tools for backup and restoration, ensuring data resilience and effortless recovery capabilities.

Over the past few years, Atlas has evolved from merely a DBaaS to a comprehensive suite of features and services designed to support the entire application development life cycle, significantly expanding the capabilities of the core MongoDB server. These capabilities, accessible through the unified MongoDB Query API, include

- *Atlas Search*—Built on industry-leading Apache Lucene. Atlas Search is an embedded full-text search in MongoDB, including abilities like custom scoring and facets to provide fast, relevant searches for users.

- *Atlas Vector Search*—Supports storing vector embeddings alongside unstructured data, enabling their use in semantic searches. These embeddings, generated by machine learning models such as OpenAI and Hugging Face, can be indexed in Atlas for applications like retrieval-augmented generation (RAG), recommendation engines, dynamic personalization, and other advanced use cases.
- *Atlas Stream Processing*—Allows for the processing of complex data streams using the same data model and Query API as in Atlas databases.
- *Atlas Online Archive*—Enables automatic archiving of infrequently accessed or historical data from MongoDB Atlas collections to low-cost cloud storage, while still allowing it to be queried in place using standard MongoDB queries. Helps reduce storage costs without impacting access to valuable historical data.
- *Atlas SQL Interface*—Enables the use of existing SQL knowledge and familiar tools to query and analyze Atlas data. The Atlas SQL Interface uses mongosql, a dialect compatible with SQL-92 and designed for the document model.
- *Atlas Database Triggers*—Enables the execution of server-side logic whenever changes occur in a connected MongoDB Atlas cluster. Triggers can be set up for specific collections, whole databases, or the entire cluster.

Figure 1.2 illustrates the high-level architecture of Atlas.

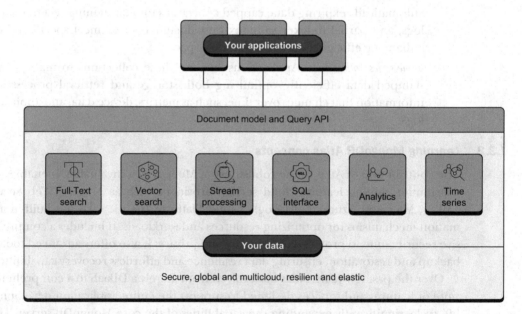

Figure 1.2 High-level architecture of the MongoDB multicloud Atlas data platform, with key components such as the Document Model and Unified Query API, as well as foundational features like security, global multicloud capabilities, resilience, and elasticity. MongoDB supports diverse functionalities like full-text search, vector search, stream processing, SQL interface, analytics, and time series, all of which integrate with your applications and data across various environments. (Image © MongoDB 2024 CC BY-NC-SA 3.0)

A detailed discussion of the Atlas Developer Data Platform and all its features is available in part 2 of this book.

1.4 Enhancing the TCMalloc version

MongoDB 8.0 uses an enhanced version of TCMalloc, which relies on per-CPU caches rather than per-thread caches to minimize memory fragmentation and improve the database's resilience under heavy workloads. TCMalloc, short for *Thread-Caching Malloc*, is a high-performance memory allocator designed to optimize memory management in multithreaded applications. Unlike traditional memory allocators that often face contention between threads, TCMalloc provides each thread its own cache of memory blocks. This method not only accelerates memory allocation and deallocation but also reduces memory fragmentation. The shift to per-CPU caching in the MongoDB 8.0 update further increases efficiency, especially in high-concurrency environments, by aligning memory allocation more closely with individual CPU core operations, thereby enhancing overall performance and stability during intense workloads.

1.5 Discovering MongoDB Query API

The MongoDB Query API is the primary method for interacting with data in MongoDB. It offers a flexible, efficient way to query documents, allowing you to apply filters, projections, and sorting to retrieve the exact data you need. You can use the Query API to perform queries in MongoDB in two main ways:

- *Create, read, update, and delete (CRUD) operations*—Basic operations that enable the creation, reading, updating, and deletion of data in MongoDB. These operations are crucial for the management of data stored in databases (explained in chapter 4).
- *Aggregation pipelines*—An advanced querying technique that processes data through a multistage pipeline. This method facilitates complex data aggregation, transformation, and analysis operations, supporting sophisticated queries and data processing tasks (explained in chapter 6).

The MongoDB Query API allows you to execute the following:

- *Dynamic queries*—Interact with your MongoDB data by using tools like MongoDB Shell (`mongosh`) and Compass GUI for MongoDB or MongoDB drivers.
- *Data reshaping*—Modify and compute data using powerful aggregation pipelines.
- *Document joins*—Combine data from several collections using aggregation pipeline operators like `$lookup` and `$unionWith`.
- *Geospatial and graph-based queries*—Handle location-based queries with `$geoWithin` and `$geoNear`, or explore graph data relationships using `$graphLookup`.
- *Full-text search*—Use MongoDB and Apache Lucene full-text search capabilities with the `$search` stage in aggregation.
- *Vector search*—Perform approximate nearest neighbor queries and apply prefilters like `$eq` and `$gte` using the `$vectorSearch` aggregation pipeline stage.

- *Stream processing*—Manage and process real-time data streams with the `$source` stage for continuous data ingestion and processing.
- *Time-series analysis*—Query and aggregate timestamped data with time-series collections.
- *Index creation*—Enhance the performance of your MongoDB queries by using indexes specifically designed for them.

Summary

- In modern software development, objects representing real-world entities need to be stored permanently for future use via a process called persistence. Document databases like MongoDB simplify this process by allowing direct storage of objects without significant data transformation, supporting intuitive querying.
- Unlike traditional relational databases with strict schemas, document databases like MongoDB offer a flexible schema, allowing dynamic structures with varied fields. This flexibility makes them ideal for rapid development and scalable scenarios, such as content management systems and real-time analytics, streamlining data management and reducing retrieval costs.
- MongoDB uses BSON to store objects, extending JSON with data types like dates and binary data. This extension allows it to handle complex structures effectively. Most programming languages offer compatible structures like maps or dictionaries, which MongoDB uses for efficient data manipulation and retrieval.
- To interact with this data, you can use the MongoDB Query API, which is effective and versatile for all database operations. The Query API is designed to be intuitive, making it easy to express both simple and complex queries.
- MongoDB is optimized for scaling out, using its document-oriented model and sharding to distribute data across multiple servers. Sharding automates data balancing and load distribution, simplifying scalability management and allowing MongoDB to handle large datasets and high throughput. Adding new machines is seamless, as MongoDB intelligently redistributes data across the cluster.
- MongoDB is a general-purpose database available as a free Community Edition and as MongoDB Enterprise Advanced, which offers enhanced security, operational tools, and management capabilities. Enterprise features include encrypted storage, OIDC and OAuth 2.0 authentication and authorization, auditing, Ops Manager, and Enterprise Operator for Kubernetes.
- MongoDB Atlas, a fully managed cloud service, simplifies MongoDB setup, scaling, and management while adding exclusive cloud features. Over the past few years, Atlas has evolved from a DBaaS to a full platform, significantly expanding the core MongoDB server's capabilities with a comprehensive suite of features and services for the entire application development life cycle.

- MongoDB 8.0 introduces a new version of TCMalloc that uses per-CPU caches instead of per-thread caches. This change helps reduce memory fragmentation and enhances the database's ability to handle heavy workloads effectively.
- The MongoDB Query API is the primary method for interacting with MongoDB data. It allows flexible, efficient querying of documents through filters, projections, and sorting to retrieve the specific data you need. You can use the Query API to perform queries in MongoDB in two main ways: CRUD operations and aggregation pipelines.

Getting started with Atlas and MongoDB data

This chapter covers

- Discovering the Atlas platform and its command-line interface
- Loading a sample data set into your MongoDB Atlas cluster
- Getting started with the MongoDB shell (`mongosh`)
- Managing data with databases, collections, and documents
- Examining time-series and capped collections

In this chapter, we will take our first steps with MongoDB Atlas and delve into data management within a MongoDB deployment. We will explore the concepts, features, and techniques for storing data in MongoDB.

Part 2 of this book gives you a more comprehensive understanding of MongoDB Atlas. For now, our focus is on taking the first steps to build the first MongoDB Atlas cluster using the Atlas command-line interface (CLI). Building this cluster is essential because it allows us to conduct practical exercises and gain a deeper understanding of MongoDB concepts, providing a hands-on experience that illustrates the platform's capabilities and benefits in real-world applications.

2.1 Setting up your first Atlas cluster using Atlas CLI

The quickest way to establish a MongoDB Atlas database cluster is to use the Atlas CLI. This interface, designed specifically for MongoDB Atlas, enables programmatic interaction with the Atlas platform, including features like Atlas Search and Vector Search, right from the terminal. It uses concise, intuitive commands, permitting the execution of database management operations in mere seconds.

Additionally, there's the option to load a sample MongoDB Atlas data set via the Atlas CLI, which will be useful during exercises. Let's do that now!

2.1.1 Installing the Atlas CLI

In this section, you'll install the Atlas CLI using Homebrew, a versatile package manager available for both macOS and Linux, including the Windows Subsystem for Linux (WSL). To begin, open your terminal—whether it's the Terminal in macOS, a Linux terminal, or the Windows Terminal in WSL. Next, execute the following command in your terminal to download and initiate the Homebrew installation script:

```
/bin/bash -c "$(curl -fsSL https://raw.githubusercontent.com/Homebrew/install/HEAD/install.sh)"
```

This command fetches the latest Homebrew installer from its official GitHub repository using `curl` and executes it with `bash`, setting up Homebrew on your system. When Homebrew is installed, you can easily proceed with installing the Atlas CLI by using the command

```
brew install mongodb-atlas
```

This command will install Atlas CLI on your workstation. If you want to explore alternative methods of installing the Atlas CLI, you can use Yum for Red Hat–based systems, Apt for Debian-based systems, or Chocolatey for Windows, or you can install it within a Docker container. To check how to do it, see the official MongoDB documentation at https://mng.bz/RwEn. If you prefer manual installation, downloading the binary files directly is also an option. Detailed instructions on all these methods are available in the MongoDB official documentation.

Also, you can download the Atlas CLI directly from https://www.mongodb.com/try/download/atlascli, which provides the latest versions for all supported platforms.

2.1.2 Creating an Atlas account

To create an Atlas account, execute the Atlas CLI command `auth register` in your terminal. To register and log in to Atlas, you can use one, and only one, of these options: an email account, a GitHub account, or a Google account.

TIP If your company uses federated authentication, you should use your company's email address.

When you use `atlas auth register`, you are redirected automatically to the Atlas user interface, where you need to select the login option and follow the onscreen steps. After creating an account in Atlas, you can log in.

Authentication to an Atlas account is achieved by executing the Atlas CLI `login` command and following the instructions that appear in the terminal:

```
atlas login
```

Now that you have an account and are authenticated to that account, you can move on to create an organization.

2.1.3 Creating an organization

Your next step is creating an Atlas organization, which serves as a top-level container to manage multiple projects under a single umbrella. An organization can contain multiple projects and serve as the primary account level. Under this setup, it is possible to apply identical billing settings and implement uniform alert settings across all projects within the organization.

To create an organization, use the command `atlas organizations create`, and assign a name to the organization you want to create.

TIP Don't provide sensitive information such as personally identifiable information (PII) or protected health information (PHI) for the Organization, Projects, Clusters, Databases, and Collections names.

I'm using Manning Publications as my organization, and you can replace it with your name:

```
atlas organizations create "Manning Publications"

Organization '65d70b45e4d5f96f787075c3' created.
```

This command creates an organization with a unique organization ID. Typically, you can consider your company to be an "organization." In most cases, one organization is sufficient. To check your organization ID, execute

```
atlas organizations list
```

This command displays your new organization ID. You will need that ID in the next step.

You can save your commonly used Atlas connection settings as profiles for easy access. Profiles keep the organization IDs, project IDs, and (optionally) API keys for use in future Atlas CLI sessions. Profiles help streamline your workflow.

Run the `atlas config set org_id <your organization ID>` to set the organization ID in your default profile. This will save you time; you can specify a profile instead of using the `--projectId` and `--orgId` flags with each Atlas CLI command that you use in this book:

```
atlas config set org_id 65d70b45e4d5f96f787075c3

Updated property 'org_id'
```

Now my Atlas Organization ID is saved as a profile. The Atlas CLI stores profiles in a configuration file called `config.toml`, in a location that depends on the operating system.

> **NOTE** If you're using Windows, the `config.toml` file is located in the `%AppData%/atlascli` directory. If you're using macOS, the file is in `/Users/{username}/Library/Application Support/atlascli`. For Linux users, it's in the `$XDG_CONFIG_HOME/atlascli` directory (or `$HOME/.config/atlas` if `XDG_CONFIG_HOME` is unset).

2.1.4 Creating an Atlas project

Next, you'll need to set up a project within your Atlas organization, where your deployments will be organized. In MongoDB, a *deployment* refers to an instance of your database environment that includes servers, storage, and configuration settings. Each deployment is linked to a specific project, allowing individual settings for monitoring, backup, and automation. Projects within the same organization are grouped under the same billing settings to streamline cost management.

Use the command `atlas project create`, naming the project MongoDB 8.0 in Action:

```
atlas project create "MongoDB 8.0 in Action"

Project '65d70c5bc9b5633e80a9c998' created.
```

Now use the command `atlas project list` to display your new project and assign the project's ID to the profiles:

```
atlas config set project_id 65d70c5bc9b5633e80a9c998
Updated property 'project_id'
```

This operation updates the property `project_id` in the profile configuration. If you want to verify the settings of your default profile, run the command

```
atlas config describe default
```

> **TIP** The Atlas CLI also supports environment variables. `MONGODB_ATLAS_ORG_ID` sets the organization ID for commands, and `MONGODB_ATLAS_PROJECT_ID` sets the project ID.

NOTE Settings stored in environment variables override those in profiles. Projects or organizations specified with the `--projectId` and `--orgId` flags take precedence over the profile and environment variables.

2.1.5 Creating a MongoDB Atlas cluster

Now is the time to create a MongoDB Atlas cluster for performing exercises, starting with the free tier. (I show you how to upgrade to a paid tier in chapter 9.) Let's name this cluster `"MongoDB-in-Action"`. Execute `atlas cluster create` with the appropriate flags. The cluster is deployed in the Google Cloud Platform (GCP) central U.S. region, but you can also choose Amazon Web Services (AWS) or Microsoft Azure as the provider:

```
atlas cluster create "MongoDB-in-Action" --provider GCP \
--region CENTRAL_US --tier M0
```

TIP You don't need to provide your own GCP credentials; MongoDB Atlas handles the infrastructure provisioning using its own credentials. You need only specify your desired provider.

If cluster creation is successful, you see the following message:

```
Cluster 'MongoDB-in-Action' created successfully.
```

The creation of the cluster may take around 5 minutes. You can verify the success of the cluster's creation with the command

```
atlas clusters list

ID                        NAME               MDB VER  STATE
65d71a7dc9b5633e80ae89ba  MongoDB-in-Action  8.0.4    IDLE
```

The visible MongoDB version is the current version at the time I wrote this book. In free clusters, you cannot choose the MongoDB version you want to install. Atlas upgrades free clusters to the newest MongoDB version after several patch versions become available for that version.

Also, you can access the Atlas UI to check the cluster. Figure 2.1 shows the MongoDB Atlas interface highlighting the `"MongoDB-in-Action"` cluster, along with options for managing the deployment and its data.

NOTE If you encounter problems while creating an Atlas cluster or if the process takes a long time, check the website https://status.mongodb.com. This website provides real-time information about the operational status of MongoDB services, including Atlas. It shows whether outages, maintenance events, or performance degradations are occurring across MongoDB services.

Loading a sample data set 19

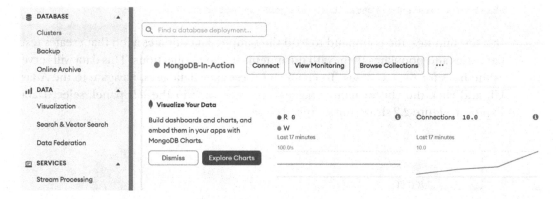

Figure 2.1 This MongoDB Atlas interface displays the active database deployment named `"MongoDB
-in-Action"`, with direct access to options such as Connect, View Monitoring, and Browse Collections. The left
sidebar shows an expanded navigation menu, highlighting key sections: Database (Clusters, Backup, and Online
Archive), Data (Visualization, Search & Vector Search, and Data Federation), and Services (Stream Processing).
The interface also includes a Visualize Your Data prompt for exploring MongoDB charts, which allows you to build
dashboards using your application data. Real-time cluster metrics, such as read/write operations and active
connections, are displayed in the monitoring panel on the right. (Image © MongoDB 2025)

2.1.6 Navigating the Atlas user interface

Atlas helps you find what you need quickly by organizing key functionality in clearly defined sections on the left side of the screen. This structure is designed to make navigation more intuitive and to help you access important features faster. Here's a quick overview of how the main areas are grouped:

- *Database*—This section is where you'll find all the main database tools. It includes functions such as managing clusters, checking performance, browsing data, running queries, making backups, and using Online Archive.
- *Data*—Here, you get tools for working with your data. You can create charts (with Atlas Charts), search using Atlas Search or Vector Search, and run queries across sources with Data Federation.
- *Services*—This section is for automation and processing data as it happens. It includes real-time stream processing, triggers to run actions automatically, and migration tools to move your current setup to Atlas.
- *Security*—Here, you can manage who has access and how your data is protected. It covers settings for projects, identity and access management (IAM), audit logs, and extra security features.

2.2 Loading a sample data set

Import a sample data set into the new cluster named `"MongoDB-in-Action"`. The sample data set is readily available in MongoDB Atlas for use. To execute the import, run the following Atlas CLI command:

```
atlas clusters sampleData load "MongoDB-in-Action"
```

In a few minutes, the command to load the sample data initiates a job that creates test databases and populates them with documents in their collections. This data will serve as the basis for the exercises. To check out these new databases, navigate to the Atlas UI, and click the cluster name `"MongoDB-in-Action"`; in the left panel, select Data Explorer. Figure 2.2 shows the sample data set.

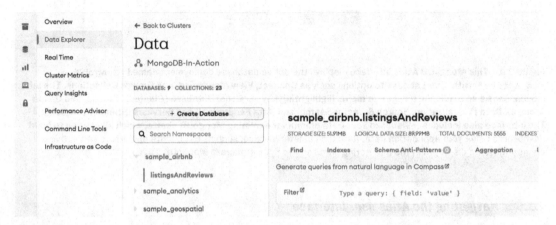

Figure 2.2 This MongoDB Atlas UI displays the `listingsAndReviews` collection within the `sample_airbnb` database, following the loading of the sample data set. The right panel shows key details such as storage size, logical data size, total documents, and index count. On the left, the navigation panel is expanded, showing options including Overview, Data Explorer, Real Time, Cluster Metrics, and Query Insights, enabling you to explore, monitor, and manage your cluster in depth. (Image © MongoDB 2025)

2.3 Adding an IP address to the project access list

It is essential to add your current IP address to the Atlas project access list to enable communication with the cluster using `mongosh`. Do that using this command:

```
atlas accessList create --currentIp
```

After adding your IP address to the Atlas access list, you see the following response:

```
Created new IP access list.
```

This command adds your current IP address to the Atlas access list. You can also use the Network Access page in the Atlas UI to manage and configure this setting.

If you want to display the IP addresses added to the Atlas project access list, use the following command:

```
atlas accessList list
```

This command displays the IP addresses that have been added to the Atlas project access list.

2.4 Creating a user

It's time to create the first user in the MongoDB database, who will be named `manning`. Atlas has authentication enabled by default to ensure secure access. When creating this user, I will assign them the `atlasAdmin` role. This role grants the user administrative privileges on all databases on the server, allowing them to perform any administrative action, such as managing other users and roles and executing any commands across databases. You can learn more about the roles and their permissions in chapter 20. Run the following command using the Atlas CLI:

```
atlas dbusers create --role atlasAdmin --username manning

? Password: ************
Database user 'manning' successfully created.
```

Now you can check whether the user has been created via the Atlas CLI:

```
atlas dbusers list

USERNAME    DATABASE
manning     admin
```

This command displays the user and the admin database where the user was created.

> **TIP** To enhance security, employ the principle of least privilege by assigning specific roles that grant only the necessary permissions for each task. This approach minimizes security risks and prevents unauthorized actions. In MongoDB Atlas, customize user roles instead of assigning broad administrative privileges like `atlasAdmin` for all users.

2.5 Establishing a connection to MongoDB through MongoDB Shell

In subsequent steps, you'll need `mongosh`, the MongoDB shell. It is a Read-Eval-Print Loop (REPL) environment built on JavaScript and Node.js, created for engaging with MongoDB deployments on Atlas, on-premises, or on any other remote host. `mongosh` facilitates the testing of queries and direct interaction with your MongoDB database's data. You can install `mongosh` using a single simple `brew` command:

```
brew install mongosh
```

If you prefer an alternative method, you can download `mongosh` directly from the MongoDB official website at https://www.mongodb.com/try/download/shell. This page provides the latest version of `mongosh` for Windows, Linux, and macOS.

After installing, you can verify the installation of mongosh by checking its version. Enter the following command in your terminal:

```
mongosh --version
```

Next, for database use and connection to the new cluster with mongosh, obtain the connection string from the Atlas CLI:

```
atlas clusters connectionStrings describe \
"MongoDB-in-Action"
```

After executing the command, you will see your connection string. Mine looked like this:

```
STANDARD CONNECTION STRING
mongodb+srv://mongodb-in-action.fpomkk.mongodb.net
```

> **NOTE** Your connection string will be different. Copy your connection string from the console before moving on.

With your connection string, connect to the MongoDB cluster using the mongosh command. The command uses the manning database user created in section 2.4. After entering the command, you're prompted to input the password to secure the connection; see listing 2.1.

> **TIP** An atlas setup option automates the creation and authentication of your Atlas account, sets up one free database, loads sample data, adds your IP address to your project's IP access list, creates a MongoDB user, and allows you to view your connection string. I recommend that you execute these operations step by step to understand how the process works before going the automatic route.

Listing 2.1 Connecting to a MongoDB deployment with mongosh

```
mongosh "mongodb+srv://mongodb-in-action.fpomkk.mongodb.net" \
--apiVersion 1 --username 'manning'
Enter password: ************
```

After logging in to the MongoDB Atlas cluster using mongosh, use the command show dbs to display the databases created during the loading of the sample data set:

```
[primary] test> show dbs
sample_airbnb          52.77 MiB
sample_analytics        9.63 MiB
sample_geospatial       1.24 MiB
sample_guides          40.00 KiB
sample_mflix          114.69 MiB
```

```
sample_restaurants         8.03 MiB
sample_supplies            1.07 MiB
sample_training           50.58 MiB
sample_weatherdata         2.63 MiB
admin                    336.00 KiB
local                      5.71 GiB
[primary] test>
```

> **TIP** If you're unsure about the Atlas CLI command you want to execute, use `atlas --help`. It displays all the possible options.

Table 2.1 briefly describes the new databases.

Table 2.1 Description of databases

Database	Description
`sample_airbnb`	Contains details on Airbnb listings
`sample_analytics`	Contains training data for a mock financial services application
`sample_geospatial`	Contains shipwreck data
`sample_guides`	Contains planetary data
`sample_mflix`	Contains movie data
`sample_restaurants`	Contains restaurant data
`sample_supplies`	Contains data from a mock office-supplies store
`sample_training`	Contains a MongoDB training services data set
`sample_weatherdata`	Contains detailed weather reports

2.6 Managing data with databases, collections, and documents

MongoDB structures data into a hierarchy consisting of three levels. At the highest level, we have databases. Inside databases are collections, which hold documents. Documents contain different types of data: strings, numbers, and dates, as well as other documents nested within them. By contrast, relational databases have databases, which contain tables. Tables hold rows, and these rows are made up of columns that store various types of data. Figure 2.3 illustrates how MongoDB structures data in a hierarchy and compares it with relational database structures.

2.6.1 Working with dynamic schema

MongoDB's dynamic schema approach offers a flexible way to store data, allowing the structure of documents within a collection to evolve. Unlike traditional relational databases that require predefined schemas before data insertion, MongoDB adapts to data's natural diversity. This flexibility facilitates rapid development and iteration, as changes to the data model do not necessitate a restructuring of existing data. It's particularly beneficial for applications dealing with heterogeneous data types or rapidly

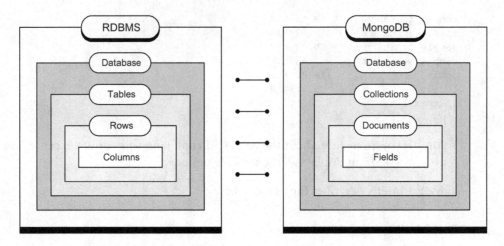

Figure 2.3 The terminology differences between relational databases and MongoDB
(Image © MongoDB 2024 CC BY-NC-SA 3.0)

evolving data sets. Both of the following documents, for example, could be stored in a single collection:

```
{ "title": "MongoDB 8.0 in Action" }
{ "name": "MongoDB 8.0 in Action" }
```

Storing dissimilar documents in the same MongoDB collection, however, can lead to several technical challenges and inefficiencies:

- Queries on collections with heterogeneous document structures can be slower because MongoDB has to scan a wider variety of document shapes, making index use less efficient. When documents are homogenous within a collection, MongoDB can optimize query execution and index use, leading to significantly faster query response times.
- MongoDB allows for schema validation at the collection level. If a collection contains various types of documents, applying comprehensive validation rules becomes complex or impossible.
- Handling diverse document structures within a single collection complicates application logic. The application must constantly discriminate between document types, leading to convoluted code and increasing the likelihood of bugs.
- Aggregation pipelines that operate on collections with mixed document types can become unnecessarily complex, as they may require additional stages to filter and process different document shapes.

To avoid these problems, best practices suggest taking the following actions:

- *Separate documents by type.* Store documents with similar structures in the same collection. This approach aligns with MongoDB's design philosophy, optimizing performance and simplifying database and application design.
- *Consider the document structure carefully during the schema design phase.* Designing documents with future queries in mind can help you choose how to split documents into collections.
- *Use MongoDB's schema validation features at the collection level to ensure data integrity and consistency.* This approach is more straightforward when each collection contains only one type of document.
- *Periodically review the database schema, and refactor collections as necessary.* This may involve migrating documents to new collections as the application evolves and requirements change.

2.6.2 Working with databases

In MongoDB, databases hold collections of documents. When you first save data for a database in MongoDB, it automatically creates the database if it doesn't already exist.

To select a database to use or create, in mongosh, issue the use <db> statement. The use command changes the current database context represented by the global variable db. By default, db is set to the test database when you start mongosh, as in this example:

```
use booksData
db.books.insertOne({"title": "MongoDB 8.0 in Action"})
```

The use booksData command sets the current database context to booksData, allowing you to interact with collections in this database. The insertOne() operation creates the database booksData and the collection books if they do not already exist.

You must observe some database naming restrictions:

- Database names are case-sensitive in MongoDB. An additional restriction is that case cannot be the only difference between database names. You can't use two databases with names like booksData and BooksData, for example.
- For MongoDB deployments running in Windows, database names cannot contain any of the following characters:

  /\. "$*<>:|?

- For MongoDB deployments running on UNIX and Linux systems, database names cannot contain any of the following characters:

  /\. "$

- Database names cannot contain the null character.
- Database names cannot be empty and must have fewer than 64 characters.

Some databases are created during the cluster creation process and are reserved for MongoDB's internal use. These databases include

- `admin`—The primary function of the admin database is to house system collections along with user authentication and authorization information. This encompasses administrator and user credentials, such as usernames, passwords, and roles. Access is granted exclusively to administrators, who possess the authority to create, update, and delete user accounts and assign roles.
- `local`—Each instance of `mongod`, the MongoDB server process, maintains a unique local database containing data essential for replication and other data specific to that instance. The local database is not subject to replication, meaning that its collections are not replicated across instances.
- `config`—The config database is primarily used internally; it contains session information and in-progress index build metadata. In sharded clusters, it stores information about each shard.

2.6.3 Working with collections

Collections are analogous to tables in relational databases. If a collection does not exist, MongoDB creates the collection when you first store data for that collection (as with a database). The `insertOne()` and `createIndex()` operations create their respective collection.

MongoDB offers the `db.createCollection()` method for explicitly creating a collection with different options, such as capped or time-series, defining the maximum size or document validation rules. If these options are not specified, you don't need to create the collection manually; MongoDB automatically generates new collections upon initial data storage for those collections.

Collection names must start with either an underscore or a letter. They cannot

- Start with the `system` prefix, which is reserved for internal purposes
- Contain the null character
- Contain the `$.` or be an empty string (such as `""`)

If the collection name contains special characters, such as underscores, you need to use the `db.getCollection()` method to access the collection in `mongosh`.

Let's log in to the MongoDB deployment using `mongosh` in the Atlas cluster, look at the collections created there, and examine some available collection methods. The following listing shows methods that can be useful for working with MongoDB deployments.

Listing 2.2 Connecting to a MongoDB deployment and inspecting collections

```
mongosh "mongodb+srv://mongodb-in-action.fpomkk.mongodb.net" \
--apiVersion 1 --username 'manning'
Enter password: ************
```

Managing data with databases, collections, and documents

Switch to the `sample_mflix` database using the `use` method, and list the collections present in this database using the `db.getCollectionNames()` method:

```
[primary] test> use sample_mflix
switched to db sample_mflix
[primary] sample_mflix> db.getCollectionNames()
[
  'sessions',
  'theaters',
  'embedded_movies',
  'comments',
  'users',
  'movies'
]
  [primary] sample_mflix>
```

As an alternative, to display the collections from the database, use the command `show collections`. To display more detailed information about a collection, use `db.getCollectionInfos()`. This method shows the options that were set during the creation of the collection, information about permissions, and current indexes:

```
db.getCollectionInfos({name: 'sessions'})
[
  {
    name: 'sessions',
    type: 'collection',
    options: {},
    info: {
      readOnly: false,
      uuid: UUID(,0fe0efd9-4e07-4808-a0f1-c11478f9da56')
    },
    idIndex: { v: 2, key: { _id: 1 }, name: '_id_' }
  }
]
```

There is also a *namespace*, which is a combination of the database name and the collection name, separated by a dot. If you have a database named `sample_mflix` and a collection within it named `embedded_movies`, the namespace for this collection would be `sample_mflix.embedded_movies`. Namespaces uniquely identify collections within the MongoDB environment. MongoDB limits a namespace to 255 bytes.

We can display the collection `embedded_movies` namespace using the `db.getCollection()` method, as seen in the following listing.

Listing 2.3 Displaying a namespace

```
[primary] sample_mflix> db.getCollection("embedded_movies")
sample_mflix.embedded_movies
[primary] sample_mflix>
```

CAPPED COLLECTIONS

Capped collections in MongoDB are collections of a fixed size (the number of documents can also be capped) that facilitate operations with high throughput for inserting and retrieving documents according to the order of insertion. They operate similarly to circular buffers: when a capped collection reaches its size limit, it accommodates new documents by replacing the oldest documents within the collection. Capped collections ensure the maintenance of insertion order, eliminating the need for an index to retrieve documents in the order in which they were added. This reduction in indexing overhead enables capped collections to achieve greater efficiency in insertion operations.

Capped collections can be useful for tasks such as these:

- *Storing log data from high-volume systems*—Writing to a capped collection without indexes is nearly as fast as logging directly to a filesystem. The natural first-in-first-out (FIFO) feature of capped collections keeps events in sequence and manages storage efficiently.
- *Caching small amounts of data*—Caches are read-heavy, so aim to keep them in RAM or accept a minor slowdown for necessary indexing. Because the most recent data is often the most relevant, the natural ordering of capped collections (FIFO) aligns well with cache use.

Capped collections have limitations, however:

- They have a fixed size, so older documents are overwritten when the limit is reached, which can be problematic if historical data is still needed for reference or compliance.
- Individual documents cannot be deleted, and updates that change a document's size are not allowed.
- They don't support complex queries or secondary indexes, making them less flexible for certain use cases.

You can create a capped collection using the `db.createCollection()` method and setting the option `capped: true`.

> **TIP** As an alternative to capped collections, consider MongoDB's time-to-live (TTL) indexes, described in chapter 7. These indexes allow you to expire and remove data from normal collections based on the value of a date-typed field and a TTL value for the index. TTL indexes are not compatible with capped collections.

TIME-SERIES COLLECTIONS

Time-series collections are specialized collections designed to efficiently store and manage *time-series data*, which is data recorded at regular intervals, with each entry associated with a specific timestamp. This type of data is common in scenarios such as sensor readings, stock prices, server logs, and application performance metrics, where the time dimension is crucial for analysis. Storing time-series data in time-series collections, as opposed to regular collections, enhances query performance and decreases disk space use for the time-series data and its secondary indexes.

Time-series collections store data in time order by grouping related data points in buckets based on time intervals and metadata. Data points are stored together in Binary JSON (BSON) format, with multiple readings combined into a single document. This approach reduces disk use, improves query performance, decreases I/O for reading operations, and simplifies the handling of time-based data. Although nested documents can be used, this structure is most efficient with simple, flat data models.

Time-series data consists of data points arranged in a sequence, where understanding comes from observing variations over time. Typically, time-series data includes the following elements:

- *Time* when the data point was recorded
- *Metadata* that acts as a unique label or identifier for a series and rarely changes
- *Measurements* that are the data points monitored over time intervals (typically, key-value pairs that vary with time)

When you examine weather data, for example, you can identify the measurement as temperature, with the metadata being the sensor identifier and location. Another example is analyzing financial transactions, where the measurement might be the transaction amount and the metadata could include account identifiers.

To create a time-series collection, use the `db.createCollection()` method with the options described in the next listing.

Listing 2.4 Creating a time-series collection

```
db.createCollection(
"my_time_series_collection",
{
  timeseries: {
  timeField: "timestamp",
  metaField: "metadata"
}})
```

To find all time-series collections in a database, use the `listCollections` command, and apply a filter `{ type: "timeseries" }`.

Listing 2.5 Listing time-series collections in a database

```
db.runCommand( {
   listCollections: 1,
   filter: { type: "timeseries" }
} )
```

VIEWS

A MongoDB *view* is a queryable, read-only entity defined through an aggregation pipeline (described in chapter 6) applied to other collections or views. MongoDB doesn't store the contents of a view on disk. Instead, the content of a view is generated dynamically upon query by a client. Here are some example use cases:

- You can create queryable entities that show only specific fields, hiding sensitive information from certain users or applications. This helps enforce security by limiting the exposure of sensitive data.
- You can simplify complex data structures by presenting only relevant information, allowing users to work with a more concise and understandable representation of the underlying collection.
- You can encapsulate frequently used complex queries, enabling consistent and simplified access to data without requiring users to write the same aggregation logic repeatedly.
- You can combine information from multiple collections into a unified result without physically merging the data, allowing easy integration of data from different sources for analytical purposes.

To create a view, use the `db.createView()` method with the options described in this listing.

Listing 2.6 Creating a MongoDB view

```
use sample_training
db.createView(
    "aerocondorRoutesView",        // Name of the view
    "routes",                      // Source collection
    [
        {
            $match: { "airline.id": 410 } // Filter to include only routes
 operated by Aerocondor
        }
    ]
)
```

Listing 2.6 shows how to create a view that displays routes operated by Aerocondor using the `db.createView()` method. This method defines a new view named `aerocondorRoutesView` based on the `routes` collection from the `sample_training` database. The view uses a single stage in the aggregation pipeline—specifically, a `$match` stage that filters the documents to include only those in which the airline's ID is `410`, which corresponds to Aerocondor. As a result, when you query the `aerocondorRoutesView`, you retrieve all fields from the original documents that meet this condition, providing a convenient way to access routes operated by Aerocondor without altering the underlying data.

To see full details on each route operated by Aerocondor in the collection, you can use the query `db.aerocondorRoutesView.find()`.

ON-DEMAND MATERIALIZED VIEWS

An *on-demand materialized view* is a stored result of a precalculated MongoDB aggregation pipeline (using the `$merge` or `$out` stages, described in chapter 6), which is saved to and accessed from the disk. Both view types—standard and on-demand materialized view—return the result from an aggregation pipeline. On-demand materialized views offer improved read performance over regular views because they are retrieved from disk rather than calculated during the query. The performance advantage grows with the complexity of the aggregation pipeline and the volume of data aggregated. But on-demand materialized views do not update automatically and require manual refreshing to reflect changes in the underlying data. You do this by rerunning the aggregation pipeline, which writes the updated results back into the collection, allowing the view to be refreshed with the most current data.

2.6.4 Working with documents

MongoDB stores records as documents in BSON format, which is an extension of JSON that includes additional data types. These documents are grouped in collections. The maximum BSON document size is 16 MB. The maximum document size serves to prevent a single document from consuming an excessive amount of RAM or bandwidth during transmission. Documents can accommodate various data types, such as strings, numbers, arrays, arrays of documents, and nested documents. This flexibility allows the storage of diverse information within a single document, making MongoDB suitable for handling complex data models. Additionally, documents can include fields with different data types, enabling the representation of rich and hierarchical data structures.

MongoDB documents are composed of field-and-value pairs. The value of a field can be any of the BSON data types. To understand it better, let's examine an example document from our data set. The following listing shows how to display a single document using the `findOne()` method from the `grades` collection in the `sample_training` database.

Listing 2.7 Displaying a single MongoDB document using `findOne()`

```
[primary] sample_training> use sample_training
already on db sample_training

[primary] sample_training> db.grades.findOne()

{
  _id: ObjectId('56d5f7eb604eb380b0d8d8ce'),
  student_id: 0,
  scores: [
    { type: 'exam', score: 78.40446309504266 },
    { type: 'quiz', score: 73.36224783231339 },
```

```
      { type: 'homework', score: 46.980982486720535 },
      { type: 'homework', score: 76.67556138656222 }
  ],
  class_id: 339
}

[primary] sample_training>
```

This document represents a student's academic record and contains the following fields and corresponding values:

- `_id`—The unique `_id` field acts as a primary key. This field holds the value `ObjectId('56d5f7eb604eb380b0d8d8ce')`, which is a unique identifier generated by MongoDB. It consists of a 4-byte timestamp indicating the creation time, a 5-byte random value unique to the machine and process, and a 3-byte incrementing counter. MongoDB uses `ObjectId`s as the default value for the `_id` field if the `_id` field is not specified. If a document doesn't have an `_id` field at the top level, for example, MongoDB's driver includes one automatically, using an `ObjectId`. Similarly, when the `mongod` server receives a document for insertion without an `_id` field, it adds one with an `ObjectId` value.
- `student_id`—This field is set to `0`, the student's identification number.
- `scores`—This field is an array containing objects that represent different types of assessments, such as exams, quizzes, and homework. Each object within the array has two fields: `type`, indicating the type of assessment, and `score`, representing the numerical score achieved by the student.
- `class_id`—This field is set to `339`, the identifier of the class.

Documents have the following restrictions on field names:

- The `_id` field is designated for use as a primary key. Its value must be unique within the collection, cannot be changed (is immutable), and can be of any type except an array. If the `_id` field includes subfields, those subfield names cannot start with the `$` symbol.
- Field names cannot contain the null character.

Summary

- The Atlas CLI is an essential tool for setting up and managing MongoDB Atlas, streamlining the process of creating organizations, projects, and clusters. It offers a comprehensive range of commands for seamless database deployment, user management, security configuration, and maintenance.
- To enhance security, assign users in MongoDB specific roles that grant only the permissions necessary for their tasks, applying the principle of least privilege. This strategy minimizes security risks and prevents unauthorized actions.
- Sample data loading is streamlined via the Atlas CLI, enabling preparation for practical exercises within the Atlas ecosystem.

- An Atlas organization acts as a top-level container that manages multiple projects under one umbrella, serving as the primary account level. Each project within the organization can contain individual deployments—instances of your database environment, including servers, storage, and configuration settings.
- The MongoDB shell (mongosh) is a powerful interface for direct database interactions, offering a range of functionalities from basic commands to scripting.
- MongoDB organizes data in a three-level hierarchy: databases contain collections, which in turn hold documents featuring various data types, including nested documents. By contrast, relational databases structure data into databases, tables, rows, and columns.
- MongoDB's dynamic schema approach allows document structures within collections to evolve, unlike traditional relational databases, which need predefined schemas. This flexibility supports rapid development by accommodating changes without restructuring existing data, making it ideal for handling diverse and rapidly evolving data sets.
- MongoDB's capped collections are fixed-size and operate like circular buffers. They ensure high-throughput insertion and retrieval by overwriting the oldest documents when the size limit is reached.
- MongoDB offers time-series collections for storing time-series data efficiently. These collections enhance query performance and reduce disk space use by structuring writes to store data points from the same period close together.
- A MongoDB view is a read-only entity that is queryable and defined by an aggregation pipeline applied to collections or other views. Unlike stored data, the contents of a view are generated dynamically from underlying data only when queried by a client and are not stored on disk.
- An on-demand materialized view in MongoDB is a precalculated aggregation pipeline result stored on disk. It improves read performance by allowing data retrieval from disk rather than calculating it during each query, unlike standard views.
- MongoDB stores records as documents in BSON format, an extension of JSON that supports additional data types. These documents are grouped in collections, with each document having a maximum size of 16 MB.

Communicating with MongoDB

This chapter covers

- Getting an overview of the MongoDB Wire Protocol
- Customizing MongoDB Shell
- Introducing MongoDB Compass GUI
- Connecting to the MongoDB database using the Node.js driver
- Communicating with MongoDB using the Python driver
- Querying MongoDB with Ruby drivers

In this chapter, I delve into the fundamentals of interacting with MongoDB through the MongoDB Wire Protocol. I show you how to customize the MongoDB Shell (mongosh) for your development needs and introduce MongoDB Compass, a user-friendly graphical user interface (GUI). Finally, I demonstrate how to connect your applications to MongoDB using Node.js, Python, and Ruby drivers (widely used with MongoDB). By understanding these connectivity methods, you'll be better equipped to build reliable, efficient applications that communicate seamlessly with your database regardless of the tech stack.

3.1 Interacting via MongoDB Wire Protocol

MongoDB communication relies on the MongoDB Wire Protocol, the backbone for data exchange between MongoDB clients and servers. This protocol operates via a simple request–response mechanism over sockets, facilitating seamless interaction between clients and the database server. It specifies byte ordering in little-endian format: the least significant byte is stored first, ensuring efficient communication over the standard Transmission Control Protocol/Internet Protocol (TCP/IP) socket. TCP/IP is the fundamental set of protocols governing the internet, allowing multiple computer networks to interact. MongoDB typically uses port 27017 for these communications.

By employing the OP_MSG opcode, MongoDB enhances communication between clients and the database through a more flexible, structured data exchange mechanism. The OP_MSG opcode, which is part of the MongoDB Wire Protocol, is an extensible message format designed to encode client requests and server replies. This opcode enables the structuring of data into multiple sections within a single message, facilitating the concurrent processing of diverse data types and requests. This design reduces the computational and temporal overhead associated with processing separate messages, and by integrating multiple operations into a single message format, it effectively minimizes protocol overhead and maximizes throughput—particularly advantageous in environments experiencing high operational loads. The OP_MSG message structure is configured as follows:

```
OP_MSG {
    MsgHeader header;             // standard message header
    uint32 flagBits;              // message flags
    Sections[] sections;          // data sections
    optional<uint32> checksum;    // optional CRC-32C checksum
}
```

The OP_MSG structure consists of a MsgHeader header, which serves as the standard message header, followed by uint32 flagBits, an integer bitmask containing various message flags that modify message behavior. It also includes Sections, which are the main data sections of the message, and an optional uint32 checksum, a CRC-32C checksum for verifying the integrity of the message during transmission.

3.2 Discovering mongosh

For manual interactions with MongoDB, mongosh is the default client. It enables connections and communication using the MongoDB Wire Protocol over TCP/IP and presents the results (typically in a textual JSON format). mongosh operates as a JavaScript and Node.js Read-Eval-Print Loop (REPL) environment, an interactive console tailored for interactions with MongoDB deployments. This means that the entire Node.js API is available within mongosh. The key features of mongosh include

- *Syntax highlighting*—Makes input/output easy to read with color codes
- *Error messages*—Provide clear messages to help pinpoint problems in your code
- *Intelligent autocomplete*—Suggests commands/operators as you type
- *Contextual help*—Lets you access online documentation for `mongosh` commands
- *Scripting*—Enables scripting within an environment built on Node.js REPL
- *Snippets*—Allow you to save commonly used scripts for reuse and sharing

3.2.1 Connecting to MongoDB Atlas

To initiate a connection with the MongoDB Atlas cluster you created in chapter 2, use the `mongosh` command with your Service Record (SRV) connection string, credentials, and any additional options necessary for connection setup. The SRV connection string, identified by the prefix `mongodb+srv://` (as opposed to the simpler `mongodb://`), is designed to simplify and shorten the connection string. It's used by all MongoDB Atlas connection strings for its ability to discover servers within a MongoDB replica set or sharded cluster automatically, eliminating the need to specify individual server addresses manually. Here's how you might structure your command:

```
mongosh "mongodb+srv://YOUR_CLUSTER.YOUR_HASH.mongodb.net/" \
--apiVersion API_VERSION --username USERNAME --password PASSWD
```

By executing this command, you establish a connection to your MongoDB Atlas deployment. Specifying `--apiVersion` with the appropriate version (currently, 1 is the only supported version) guarantees that you use the MongoDB Stable API (chapter 4). This API lets you upgrade your MongoDB server at will and ensures that behavior changes between MongoDB versions do not break your application. The Stable API guarantees application stability, facilitating regular updates and seamless upgrades, allowing quick adoption of new features without backward-compatibility problems.

3.2.2 Connecting to self-hosted deployments

You can also use `mongosh` to establish connections to self-hosted MongoDB deployments, whether they are hosted locally or on remote servers, enabling access to your data wherever it is hosted. For deployments that demand authentication, use the `--username`, `--password`, and `--authenticationDatabase` options:

```
mongosh "mongodb://mongodb1.example.com:27017" --username book \
--password my_password --authenticationDatabase admin
```

3.2.3 Performing operations

After you connect and authenticate to the database, you can begin performing operations. To display the database you are using, type `db`:

```
> db
test
>
```

The default database, `test`, is returned:

```
To display the list of databases, type show dbs.
To change databases, use the use <db>
helper command:
> show dbs
admin                30.41 MiB
config              404.00 KiB
local                42.81 MiB
> use admin
switched to db admin
>
```

The database changes from `test` to `admin`.

> **TIP** To access a different database without changing your current database context, include the `db.getSiblingDB()` method.

Type the `help` command when you need help. The following listing shows some of the available commands in the `mongosh` console.

Listing 3.1 A snippet of help-command output

```
test> help
  Shell Help:
 use    Set current database
 show   'show databases'/'show dbs': Print a list of
all available databases.
       'show collections'/'show tables': Print a list of
all collections for current database.
       'show profile': Prints system.profile information.
       'show users': Print a list of all users for current database.
       'show roles': Print a list of all roles for current database.
       'show log <type>': log for current connection,
if type is not set uses 'global'
       'show logs': Print all logs.
... ...
 exit     Quit the MongoDB shell with exit/exit()/.exit
 quit     Quit the MongoDB shell with quit/quit()
... ...
 For more information on usage:
➥ https://docs.mongodb.com/manual/reference/method
test>
```

> **TIP** mongosh supports tab completion, which helps you find commands easily. Typing `db.[tab][tab]` shows commands for the `db` object, and `db.book.[tab][tab]` lists commands for collection objects.

> **Database methods**
>
> To see the list of database methods you can use on the `db` object, run `db.help()`; for collection-level assistance, use `db.collection.help()`. If you need more information about a particular collection-level method in `mongosh`, type `db.<collection>.<method name>`, omitting the parentheses `()`. `db.collection.countDocuments`, for example, returns this information:
>
> ```
> [Function: countDocuments] AsyncFunction {
>   apiVersions: [ 1, Infinity ],
>   serverVersions: [ '4.0.3', '999.999.999' ],
>   returnsPromise: true,
>   topologies: [ 'ReplSet', 'Sharded', 'LoadBalanced', 'Standalone' ],
>   returnType: { type: 'unknown', attributes: {} },
>   deprecated: false,
>   platforms: [ 'Compass', 'Browser', 'CLI' ], isDirectShellCommand: false,
>   acceptsRawInput: false,
>   shellCommandCompleter: undefined,
>   help: [Function (anonymous)] Help }
> ```

3.2.4 Viewing mongosh logs

`mongosh` uses Newline Delimited JSON (NDJSON) to keep records of session logs. From version 1.0.5 of `mongosh` onward, the logging format of the `mongosh` has been revised to align with the log format used by the MongoDB server. `mongosh` redacts credentials from both the command history and the logs. Reviewing `mongosh` logs is vital for diagnosing problems and understanding command usage patterns within the `mongosh` environment. These logs help identify problematic queries and operational anomalies.

`mongosh` stores the log of each session in the `.mongodb/mongosh` directory of your user profile. You can find the logs at `~/.mongodb/mongosh/<LogID>_log`.

`mongosh` saves a history of all commands you've executed across sessions. When a new command is issued, it is appended to the start of the log file. You can find the commands at

- *macOS and Linux*—`~/.mongodb/mongosh/mongosh_repl_history`
- *Windows*—`%UserProfile%/.mongodb/mongosh/mongosh_repl_history`

`mongosh` keeps up to 100 log files for 30 days and then automatically deletes log files older than 30 days.

3.2.5 Running scripts in mongosh

In `mongosh`, you can develop scripts in JavaScript for data modification or administrative purposes and package these scripts as snippets for simple distribution and management. You can run a `.js` file within `mongosh` using the `load()` method. Furthermore, the `require()` function allows the inclusion of built-in Node.js modules or external npm modules, enhancing your script's functionality. The `require()` and `load()` methods have different behaviors and availability:

- The `require()` method is used for including modules and is available in Node.js scripts, supporting modularity by allowing the inclusion of local, built-in, or external npm modules. `require()` uses the standard Node.js module resolution algorithm, starting from the current working directory of the shell.
- The `load()` method is specific to mongosh for executing JavaScript files directly. The `load()` takes an absolute path or a relative path.

Construct a script that, when run within mongosh through the `load` command, retrieves the server's uptime and the current number of open connections from a MongoDB database. This script uses the Day.js library to format the uptime into a more straightforward representation. Save the script as `mongodb-script.js`.

> **NOTE** You must include the Day.js library because it uses the `require` statement at the beginning of the script. You can install Day.js on your machine using the `npm install dayjs` command.

Listing 3.2 demonstrates the `printMongoDBDetailsSimplified` function, which retrieves and displays MongoDB server details like version, host, uptime in days, and current open connections. The function, when called, prints this information to the console.

Listing 3.2 Displaying the MongoDB server information function

```
function printMongoDBDetailsSimplified() {
  const dayjs = require('dayjs'); //
  const relativeTime = require('dayjs/plugin/relativeTime');
//
  dayjs.extend(relativeTime); //

  try {
    const adminDB = db.getSiblingDB('admin'); //
    const serverStatus = adminDB.serverStatus(); //
    console.log("MongoDB Version:", serverStatus.version);
//
    console.log("Host:", serverStatus.host); //
    console.log("Uptime:", dayjs().subtract(serverStatus.uptime,
 "second").fromNow(true)); // //
    console.log("Currently open connections:",
 serverStatus.connections.current); //
  } catch (err) {
```

- Imports dayjs for handling date and time
- Imports the relativeTime plugin for human-readable time formatting
- Activates the relativeTime plugin
- Accesses the admin database
- Retrieves MongoDB server status
- Displays the MongoDB version
- Displays host information
- Shows uptime in a human-readable format using dayjs
- Displays the current number of open connections

```
        console.error("Failed to retrieve status. Error:", err.message);
    //                                        ◀──────── Handles errors if server status
    }                                                   cannot be retrieved
}

printMongoDBDetailsSimplified();
```

After you save this function to the `mongodb-script.js` file, connect to your deployment using `mongosh`, and execute the following command to load and run the script:

```
load( "/scripts/mongodb-script.js" )
```

The script is designed to output data from your database directly to the console. On my machine, the output looks like this:

```
MongoDB Version: 8.0.4
Host: ac-5dhjxpf-shard-00-01.fpomkke.mongodb.net:27017
Uptime: 11 hours
Currently open connections: 5
```

The script shows that the MongoDB server version is 8.0.4, it's running on the Atlas host `ac-5dhjxpf-shard-00-01.fpomkke.mongodb.net`, port 27017, it has been up for 11 hours, and five connections are currently open.

You can also use `mongosh` to run a script directly from the command line, bypassing the interactive shell. To indicate the script you want to execute, add the `--file` or `-f` option to the filename. If you want to run the `mongodb-script.js` script directly from the command line using `mongosh`, for example, use the following command:

```
mongosh "mongodb+srv://YOUR_CLUSTER.YOUR_HASH.mongodb.net/" -username
    USERNAME -password PASSWD --file mongodb-script.js
```

This command connects to your MongoDB Atlas cluster using `mongosh` with the specified cluster URL, username, and password; then it automatically executes the script contained in `mongodb-script.js`. When you include the `--file` option followed by the script's filename, the command runs the script without requiring manual input or interaction in the `mongosh` interactive shell, streamlining the process of script execution against your MongoDB database. This approach is particularly useful for automated tasks or batch processing.

3.2.6 Configuring mongosh

You can customize `mongosh` to fit your specific requirements by using the config API. It's important to note that any changes you make through the config API are designed to be persistent, ensuring that your customizations are maintained across all subsequent sessions, thereby enhancing your user experience over time.

To display the current configuration in `mongosh`, run the `config` command after connecting to `mongosh`. The following listing gives you a detailed look at the output of the `config` command in `mongosh`, showcasing the various configuration settings and parameters available.

Listing 3.3 Default configuration settings and parameters in `mongosh`

```
> config
Map(12) {
  'displayBatchSize' => 20,
  'maxTimeMS' => null,
  'enableTelemetry' => true,
  'editor' => null,
  'snippetIndexSourceURLs' => 'https://compass.mongodb.com
 /mongosh/snippets-index.bson.br',
  'snippetRegistryURL' => 'https://registry.npmjs.org',
  'snippetAutoload' => true,
  'inspectCompact' => 3,
  'inspectDepth' => 6,
  'historyLength' => 1000,
  'showStackTraces' => false,
  'redactHistory' => 'remove'
}
>
```

To get a clearer idea of how to customize `mongosh`, let's look at a few examples. You can configure an external editor to be used with `mongosh`, either through the shell that initiates `mongosh` or directly within `mongosh`. To establish an editor while inside `mongosh`, use the `config.set()` command:

```
> config.set( "editor", "vi" )
Setting "editor" has been changed
>
```

This command changes the `"editor"` configuration to `"vi`. Now you can use `"vi"` for editing scripts or initiating commands from within `mongosh`. You can also modify the value of the `historyLength` setting to, say, `3000`. Increasing `historyLength` in `mongosh` to `3000` allows you to keep a longer record of commands you've used, making it easier to retrieve and reuse past commands during database management and operations:

```
test> config.set("historyLength", 3000)
Setting "historyLength" has been changed
```

To verify that your changes have been applied successfully, execute `config.get()`:

```
test> config.get("historyLength")
3000
test>
```

3.2.7 Using .mongoshrc.js

For more advanced configuration, you can use JavaScript to include custom functions and shell helpers in your `.mongoshrc.js` configuration file. Upon startup, `mongosh` examines your home directory for a JavaScript file named `.mongoshrc.js`. If it locates the file, `mongosh` reads the contents of `.mongoshrc.js` before presenting the prompt for the initial time.

A good use case for `.mongoshrc.js` is customizing the default `mongosh` prompt. By default, the `mongosh` prompt displays the name of the current database, but you can modify the prompt.

Suppose that you want to enhance your `mongosh` prompt to display not just dynamic session data but also the MongoDB version and the total number of collections within the current database. Listing 3.4 illustrates how to use the JavaScript function to customize the `mongosh` prompt. It retrieves the MongoDB version and the number of collections in the current database. Then it constructs a string that includes server uptime, document count, MongoDB version, and collection count, separating them with vertical bars and appending a greater-than (>) sign at the end.

Listing 3.4 The JavaScript function responsible for customizing the `mongosh` prompt

```
prompt = function() {
   const version = db.version();
   const collectionsCount = db.getCollectionNames().length;
   return "Uptime:" + db.serverStatus().uptime +
          " | Documents:" + db.stats().objects +
          " | Version:" + version +
          " | Collections:" + collectionsCount +
          " > ";
};
```

Enter this function into your `.mongoshrc.js` file, and then launch `mongosh`. In my database, the new prompt looks like this:

```
Uptime:122765 | Documents:1843009 | Version:8.0.4 | Collections:218 >
```

In your `.mongoshrc.js` file, you can also include scripts that automate your work, making your `mongosh` sessions more efficient. If you often work with a specific database, such as `sample_training`, you can automate the process of switching to this database every time you start `mongosh` rather than switching manually from the default `test` database to `sample_training`. The following script defines the function `switchToDatabase()`, which automatically switches the `mongosh` session to a specific database named `sample_training`.

Listing 3.5 The JavaScript `switchToDatabase()` method

```
// Script to switch to a specific database
const targetDatabase = "sample_training";
```

```
function switchToDatabase() {
 const currentDatabase = db.getName();
 if (currentDatabase !== targetDatabase) {
  print(`Switching to database: ${targetDatabase}`);
  db = db.getSiblingDB(targetDatabase);
 }
}

// Call the function when connecting to mongosh
switchToDatabase();
```

Enter this script into your `.mongoshrc.js` file, and add the name of your default database, to which you will be switched upon logging in. In this example, the database is named `sample_training`. You can modify the database name within the script as needed, of course.

> **TIP** Use the `--norc` option to prevent `.mongoshrc.js` from loading.

3.3 Playing with MongoDB Compass

MongoDB Compass is a free interactive GUI tool for querying, optimizing, and analyzing MongoDB data in a visual environment. Compass provides detailed schema visualizations, real-time performance metrics, sophisticated querying abilities, and many other features.

Go to https://www.mongodb.com/try/download/compass to download and install the most recent version of Compass. Review the requirements for your operating system to ensure that the version of Compass you download is compatible with your system.

Compass stands as a solid alternative to mongosh (mongosh is accessible from within Compass) and other command-line tools if you'd rather have a visual and interactive method of database interaction.

After installing MongoDB Compass, launch it, and connect to your MongoDB cluster. You can use the MongoDB Uniform Resource Identifier (URI) from your Atlas cluster that you created in chapter 2, as I did in figure 3.1. This figure shows the view that appears after you launch MongoDB Compass and click the Add New Connection button in the navigation sidebar on the left. This interface is designed to configure a new connection to a MongoDB deployment. It includes a field for entering the MongoDB deployment's URI, with an option to edit the connection string using a toggle switch. Below the URI field is a space to assign a name to the connection, which in this example is "MongoDB-in-Action". The interface also provides Save, Connect, and Save & Connect buttons to finalize the connection setup.

Upon connecting to your MongoDB deployment, you can explore the available databases, which are databases created by loading the default Atlas data sets (chapter 2). At the top is a query bar where you can type or generate a query. The Add Data, Export Data, Update, and Delete buttons allow you to manage and change the data within the database. You can also use mongosh directly from MongoDB Compass. To do this, click the Open MongoDB Shell button in the top-right corner.

New Connection

Manage your connection settings

URI ⓘ   Edit Connection String ⬤

```
mongodb+srv://manning:*****@mongodb-in-action.nu96v.mongodb.net/
```

Name   **Color**

MongoDB-in-Action   No Color ▾

Figure 3.1   You can connect to a MongoDB deployment with the MongoDB Compass application. Enter a MongoDB connection string in the New Connection window. (Image © MongoDB 2025)

MongoDB Compass comes with a suite of tools tailored for developers, including the Aggregation Pipeline Builder, shown in figure 3.2. This robust feature allows you to construct and configure aggregation pipelines, which are crucial for complex data processing. With an intuitive interface, you can visualize documents from a collection, add multiple stages of data processing, and see a preview of the resulting aggregated data set. The Aggregations tab in Compass offers a clear, manageable space for creating these pipelines, with helpful functions like Add Stage and additional controls for previewing. These tools give you flexibility in constructing and customizing pipelines to meet your precise data processing needs.

Figure 3.2   The Aggregations tab is where you can add various stages of data processing. (Image © MongoDB 2025)

MongoDB Compass provides a toolkit for database management that's designed to enhance productivity for developers and database administrators. Key features of Compass include

- *Create, read, update, and delete (CRUD) operations*—A user-friendly interface for creating, reading, updating, and deleting data, allowing for efficient data manipulation directly within Compass

- *Query building*—Advanced query capabilities with a visual builder that helps you craft precise queries without writing code, making data retrieval accessible and intuitive
- *Schema visualization*—A graphical representation of the database schema that helps you understand the structure and relationships within the data, as well as detect outliers and schema anomalies
- *Performance profiling*—Tools for monitoring and optimizing database performance, including visual explanations of query execution plans that help you identify bottlenecks
- *Index management*—Simplified index creation and management tools that improve query performance and suggest optimal indexing strategies
- *Real-time server statistics*—Dashboards that display real-time operational statistics and server status, providing insights into the health and performance of MongoDB deployments
- *Generative AI (GenAI) for queries and aggregation generation*—Tools that generate queries and aggregation pipelines using natural language, employing AI to interpret the prompts you provide

Overall, MongoDB Compass streamlines the process of database development and maintenance. As a GUI client, it allows for simplified data operations and analysis. Later in this book, we'll delve into mongosh and demonstrate the use of MongoDB Compass for constructing complex queries and managing aggregation pipelines.

3.4 Connecting using MongoDB drivers

A *driver* in this context is a software library that enables an application to interact with a database, providing a way to connect, execute queries, and manage data. You can connect your application to your MongoDB Atlas deployment or a self-hosted MongoDB cluster by using one of the official MongoDB libraries.

MongoDB supports a wide array of libraries, with active development and maintenance from MongoDB to incorporate new features, enhance performance, fix bugs, and implement security patches. The officially supported libraries include C, C++, C#, Go, Java, Kotlin, Node.js, PHP, Python, Ruby, Rust, Scala, and TypeScript. Community-supported libraries are also available, including Elixir for Erlang, Mongoose for JavaScript, Prisma for Node.js/TypeScript, and R for Data Science and Statistics. In this book, I focus on the Node.js, Python, and Ruby drivers, providing insights into and practical examples of these popular languages.

3.5 Using the Node.js driver

To integrate MongoDB into your JavaScript or TypeScript application, you need to use the MongoDB driver. By using the Node.js driver, you can establish connections to MongoDB deployments in different environments, such as MongoDB Atlas, MongoDB

Enterprise, and MongoDB Community, allowing your application to interact seamlessly with MongoDB databases regardless of the hosting environment.

To start, make sure you have Node.js version 16 or later and npm installed in your development environment. You can verify and install them at https://mng.bz/26jN. Then follow these steps:

1. Create a project directory named `mongodb_book_project`.
2. Open your shell, and execute the following command:

   ```
   mkdir mongodb_book_project
   ```

3. Navigate to the new directory:

   ```
   cd mongodb_book_project
   ```

4. Initialize your Node.js project by running the following command:

   ```
   npm init -y
   ```

   When this command completes successfully, you'll find a `package.json` file in your `mongodb_book_project` directory, ready for your project.

5. Execute the following command in your shell to install the driver within your project directory:

   ```
   npm install mongodb@6.5
   ```

   This command downloads the `mongodb` package and its dependencies, saves the package in the `node_modules` directory, and records the dependency information in the `package.json` file. Then you'll have Node.js and npm installed, along with a new project directory containing the installed driver dependencies.

6. Retrieve the connection string for MongoDB from your Atlas cluster.

   You can use the Atlas CLI by running the following command, which displays your connection string for your MongoDB cluster running in Atlas:

   ```
   atlas clusters connectionStrings describe "MongoDB-in-Action"
   ```

   You can also use the Atlas UI. Log in to your cluster, navigate to the Database section, click Connect, and select your driver and version in the Connecting with MongoDB Driver section. Then click the icon at the right end of the connection string to copy the string to your clipboard, as shown in figure 3.3.

Listing 3.6 shows how to perform database queries within a Node.js application and retrieve data from MongoDB, in this case finding routes originating from John F. Kennedy International Airport (JFK). It uses the Node.js MongoDB driver to establish a

Using the Node.js driver 47

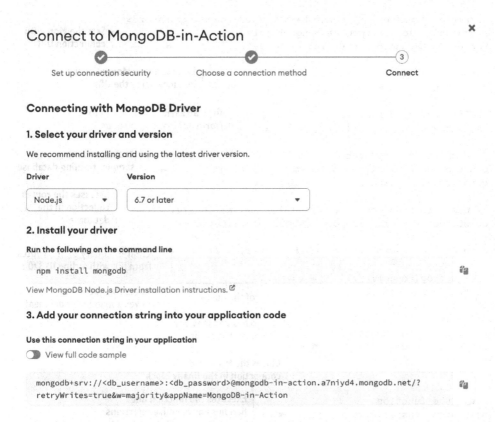

Figure 3.3 Use the MongoDB Atlas interface to connect a MongoDB database to an application using a MongoDB driver. Select your driver and version; then click the clipboard icon next to the connection string to copy the string. (Image © MongoDB 2025)

connection with a MongoDB database and interact with it. After establishing a connection through the specified URI, the script sets up a MongoClient instance and defines an asynchronous function that connects to the `sample_training` database, targeting the `routes` collection. The results of this query are logged to the console. The script ensures the proper closure of the database client, following best practices for resource management.

In your `mongodb_book_project` project folder, create an `index.js` file to house your application's code. Make sure to replace the `<connection string uri>` placeholder with the actual connection string you copied from the Atlas GUI or obtained via the Atlas CLI, and copy the following code into the `index.js` file.

Listing 3.6 Node.js MongoDB query example

```
const { MongoClient } = require("mongodb"); //   ◀── Imports MongoClient to connect to MongoDB
// Replace the uri string with your connection string.
```

```
// Example: const uri = "mongodb+srv://<username>:<password>
➥@mongodb-in-action.fpomkke.mongodb.net"
const uri = "<connection string uri>" //          ◀── Sets the MongoDB connection URI

// Create a MongoClient instance.
const client = new MongoClient(uri); //           ◀── Creates a new MongoClient instance using the URI

// Define an async function.
const run = async () => { //                      ◀── Defines an async function run to perform database operations
  try {
    // Connect to the database.
    const database = client.db("sample_training"); //  ◀── Accesses the sample_training database
    const routes = database.collection("routes"); //   ◀── Accesses the routes collection in the database

    // Query to find routes from JFK by airline ID 3201.
    const query = { src_airport: "JFK", "airline.id": 3201 };
➥//                                               ◀── Creates a query to find routes from JFK with airline ID 3201
    const route = await routes.findOne(query); // ◀── Executes the query and retrieves a matching document

    console.log(route); //                        ◀── Logs the result of the query
  } catch (error) {
    console.error(error); //                      ◀── Catches and logs any errors that occur
  } finally {
    // Close the database client.
    await client.close(); //                      ◀── Closes the MongoDB connection in the finally block
  }
};

// Call the function.
run().catch(console.error); //                    ◀── Executes the function and handles any promise rejections
```

In your terminal, execute this command to launch the application:

```
node index.js
```

This command invokes the Node.js runtime environment to execute the JavaScript code in the index.js file, initiating the processes or operations defined within it. You receive the following output in your terminal upon completion.

Listing 3.7 Single MongoDB document returned from the Node.js script

```
{
  _id: new ObjectId('56e9b39b732b6122f877fe58'),
  airline: {
    id: 3201,
    name: 'LAN Argentina',
    alias: '4M',
    iata: 'DSM'
  },
  src_airport: 'JFK',
  dst_airport: 'EZE',
  codeshare: 'Y',
```

```
  stops: 0,
  airplane: 777
}
```

With the Node.js driver for MongoDB, you can establish connections to MongoDB instances, configure user authentication, execute CRUD operations to read and write data, use promises and callbacks for asynchronous operations, optimize queries with index creation and design, apply language-specific sorting rules through collations, set up logging for MongoDB operations, and monitor server events for enhanced database management and performance.

> **MongoDB and TypeScript**
>
> Given that TypeScript is transpiled into JavaScript, you can use the MongoDB Node.js driver to develop TypeScript applications that interact with MongoDB. Using TypeScript definitions with MongoDB requires Node.js driver version 4.0 or later.
>
> The TypeScript compiler provides real-time type checking. Code editors that support TypeScript can offer autocomplete suggestions, inline documentation, and detect type-related errors. All TypeScript features of the driver are optional. Any valid JavaScript code written with the driver is also valid TypeScript code.

3.6 Employing Python drivers

Now let's delve into the Python drivers for MongoDB. Python developers have two primary options for interfacing with MongoDB, catering to different programming paradigms:

- *PyMongo*—The preferred choice for synchronous Python applications. PyMongo provides a direct, sequential mode of interaction with the MongoDB server, fitting well with applications in which tasks are executed one after another.
- *Motor*—Specifically crafted for asynchronous Python applications, integrating smoothly with Python's asyncio framework. This driver is optimal for scenarios that demand nonblocking I/O, such as in applications that have high levels of concurrency or require efficient performance under load, such as web servers and systems dealing with intensive I/O operations.

3.6.1 PyMongo

To make the PyMongo driver module available to your Python application, you must install it using `pip`. This command shows how to install the latest version of the module via the command line:

```
python3 -m pip install pymongo
```

Listing 3.8 shows a query that finds routes originating from JFK airport in Python. Note that I'm using the Stable API feature, available with PyMongo driver version 3.12 and later, to connect to MongoDB Server version 5 and later. This feature allows you to update the driver or server without worrying about backward-compatibility problems, using commands covered by the Stable API. Create a `mongodb-pymongo.py` file, and enter the following code into the file. Make sure to replace the `<connection string uri>` placeholder with the actual connection string you copied from the Atlas GUI or obtained via the Atlas CLI.

Listing 3.8 PyMongo Python driver example

```python
from pymongo.mongo_client import MongoClient       # Imports the
from pymongo.server_api import ServerApi           # required modules
from pprint import pprint

# Replace <connection_string> with your MongoDB Atlas connection string.
# Example: uri = "mongodb+srv://<username>:<password>
# @mongodb-in-action.fpomkke.mongodb.net"
                                                    # Sets the MongoDB
uri = "<connection_string>"                         # connection string

# Create a MongoClient instance specifying the Stable API version
client = MongoClient(uri, server_api=ServerApi('1'))
                                                    # Creates a
                                                    # MongoClient
# Specify the database and collection               # instance with
database = client['sample_training']                # the specified API
routes_collection = database['routes']              # version
                                      # Accesses the database
                                      # and collection

# Define the query
query = {"src_airport": "JFK", "airline.id": 3201}   # Defines the query

try:
    # Execute the query to find a document matching the query
    route = routes_collection.find_one(query)
                                                     # Executes the query
    # Check if a route is found and print the result
    if route:
        print("Found a route:")
        pprint(route)
    else:                                            # Prints the result or indicates
        print("No route found from JFK.")            # that no match was found

except Exception as e:
    # Handle any errors that occur during the query
    print(f"An error occurred: {e}")                 # Handles exceptions
finally:
    # Close the connection to MongoDB                # Closes the connection
    client.close()                                    # to MongoDB
```

In your terminal, execute this command to launch the application:

```
python3 mongodb-pymongo.py
```

Executing the command `python3 mongodb-pymongo.py` initiates the script with Python 3, activating the sequence of operations that connect to MongoDB, execute the query, manage any encountered exceptions, and close the connection. You receive the following output in your terminal upon completion.

Listing 3.9 Single MongoDB document returned from the Python script

```
Found a route:
{ _id: new ObjectId('56e9b39b732b6122f877fe58'),
  airline: {
    id: 3201,
    name: 'LAN Argentina',
    alias: '4M',
    iata: 'DSM'
  },
  src_airport: 'JFK',
  dst_airport: 'EZE',
  codeshare: 'Y',
  stops: 0,
  airplane: 777 }
```

Unlike the Node.js MongoDB driver, which relies on promises and callbacks, PyMongo uses Python's context managers for resource management and supports native coroutines for asynchronous tasks. It integrates seamlessly with Python's data types, such as rich Binary JSON (BSON) and datetime objects, and employs Pythonic syntax in its aggregation framework to enhance code readability and efficiency. PyMongo also makes handling large files with GridFS straightforward, fitting well with Python's idiomatic practices and offering a cohesive, efficient toolkit for Python developers interfacing with MongoDB.

3.6.2 Motor

The choice between synchronous and asynchronous programming depends on the specific requirements of your application. For tasks that are CPU-bound or require sequential execution without significant waiting periods, synchronous programming is sufficient and easier to implement. On the other hand, asynchronous programming is indispensable for modern web applications and services that require high concurrency and efficiency in handling I/O operations.

To make the Motor driver module available to a Python application, you must install it using `pip`. This command shows how to install the latest version of the module via the command line:

```
python3 -m pip install motor
```

Listing 3.10 illustrates an asynchronous interaction with MongoDB using the Motor library in Python, contrasting with the synchronous approach with PyMongo in listing 3.8. This example also uses the Stable API feature. To begin, create a `mongodb`

52 CHAPTER 3 *Communicating with MongoDB*

-motor.py file, and enter the code into it. Replace the <connection string uri> placeholder with the actual connection string you obtained from the Atlas GUI or through the Atlas CLI.

Listing 3.10 Motor Python driver example

```
import asyncio
from motor.motor_asyncio import AsyncIOMotorClient       Imports the
from pymongo.server_api import ServerApi                  required modules
from pprint import pprint

# Replace <connection_string> with your MongoDB Atlas connection string.
uri = "<connection_string>"
                                    Sets the MongoDB connection string
async def find_route():
  # Create an AsyncIOMotorClient instance specifying the Stable API version
  client = AsyncIOMotorClient(uri, server_api=ServerApi('1'))
                                                                Defines the
                                                                asynchronous
                    Creates an asynchronous MongoDB client     find_route function
  try:              using the specified API version
    # Specify the database and collection
    database = client['sample_training']
    routes_collection = database['routes']   Accesses the database and collection

    # Define the query
    query = {"src_airport": "JFK", "airline.id": 3201}
                                                         Defines the query

    # Execute the query to find a single document matching the query
    route = await routes_collection.find_one(query)
                                                       Executes the query
    # Check if a route is found and print the result   asynchronously
    if route:
      print("Found a route:")      Prints the result if
      pprint(route)                a document is found
    else:
      print("No route found from JFK.")
                                            Indicates whether a
                                            matching route is found
  except Exception as e:
    # Handle any errors that occur during the query
    print(f"An error occurred: {e}")
  finally:                                  Handles any errors that
    # Close the connection to MongoDB       occur during the query
    client.close()
                      Closes the MongoDB client

# Run the asynchronous find_route function
asyncio.run(find_route())
                               Runs the asynchronous find_route
                               function using asyncio.run
```

In your console, execute this command to launch the application:

```
python3 mongodb-motor.py
```

This script asynchronously queries a MongoDB database using the Motor library to find a flight route originating from JFK airport. It prints the found route or a message if no route is found, handles any errors, and closes the database connection efficiently.

3.6.3 PyMongo vs. Motor

When querying the database for routes originating from JFK airport using PyMongo, the program waits for the query to complete before moving on to the next line of code. This blocking nature ensures a straightforward, linear execution flow, making the code easier to read and debug. Synchronous programming is ideal for scripts and applications in which operations are not I/O-bound, concurrency is not a concern, or tasks need to be performed in a strict sequence. It's suitable for small-scale applications, data analysis scripts, or server-side tasks in which the load is manageable and real-time performance is not critical.

While awaiting a database response to a query initiated with Motor, the Python event loop can switch to executing other tasks. This nonblocking behavior makes handling I/O-bound operations more efficient because it doesn't waste CPU cycles waiting. Asynchronous programming shines in I/O-bound applications such as web servers, real-time data processors, and any other applications that require high concurrency. It's particularly effective for handling multiple simultaneous database operations, network requests, or long-running I/O tasks. Asynchronous code can significantly improve the responsiveness and throughput of web applications, especially those that serve a large number of clients or perform extensive I/O operations.

Asynchronous code can handle more tasks in the same amount of time than synchronous code, especially in I/O-bound applications, which makes it a better choice for scalability and handling high loads. But asynchronous programming introduces complexity due to its nonlinear execution flow. Managing this complexity requires a good understanding of `async/await` patterns and the event loop. By contrast, synchronous code is simpler to write and understand but may not use system resources as efficiently.

3.7 Integrating Ruby drivers

The Ruby driver for MongoDB is a library that facilitates interactions between Ruby applications and MongoDB databases. It provides direct mapping between Ruby code and MongoDB operations, enabling developers to execute database queries and operations directly from Ruby scripts and applications.

The Ruby driver is distributed as a gem, hosted on RubyGems. It is written entirely in Ruby and supports connections to MongoDB servers using Transport Layer Security (TLS). It offers authentication via the Salted Challenge Response Authentication Mechanism (SCRAM), supporting both SCRAM-SHA-1 and SCRAM-SHA-256, as well as X.509 authentication, all of which operate over TLS connections. This functionality requires a working Ruby `openssl` extension. To install the gem, add `mongo` to your Gemfile:

```
gem "mongo", "~> 2"
gem install mongo
```

TIP To use MongoDB Atlas, I recommend using version 2.6.1 or later of the driver. This version offers significant performance improvements for TLS connections, which are used in all Atlas connections.

Listing 3.11 shows a Ruby script that uses the `mongo` gem to connect to a MongoDB database and employs a query pattern to search for specific records within the `routes` collection. If the operation is successful, the retrieved document is printed to the console. The script is structured to handle exceptions gracefully, printing any error messages encountered. It also ensures that the database connection is closed properly.

Create a file named `mongodb-ruby.rb`, and insert the provided code snippet into it. Remember to replace the `<connection string uri>` placeholder with your actual MongoDB connection string, which you obtained from the MongoDB Atlas GUI or through the Atlas CLI.

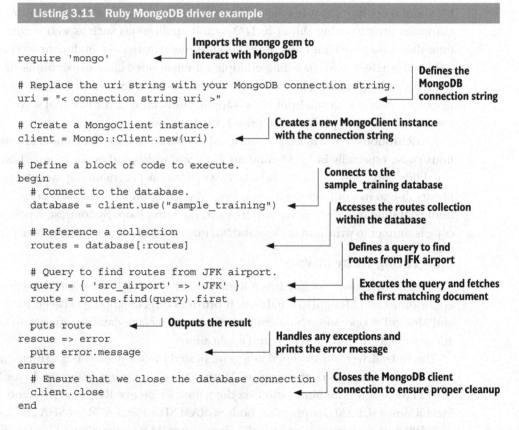

Listing 3.11 Ruby MongoDB driver example

In your console, execute this command to launch the application:

```
ruby mongodb-ruby.rb
```

The script searches for the first route originating from JFK airport and prints this route to the console. It uses the `mongo` Ruby driver to find and display this information efficiently. Thanks to seamless BSON handling within Ruby's object-oriented framework, the driver excels in serialization and connection pooling.

3.8 Learning Mongoid

For numerous applications, the basic Ruby driver serves as the optimal choice. When you need validations, associations, and advanced data modeling capabilities, however, switching to an object-document mapper (ODM) is essential.

In Rails, developers are accustomed to Active Record for database interactions. Mongoid offers a seamless drop-in replacement for Active Record, allowing you to integrate MongoDB using a familiar and natural syntax. This makes transitioning from traditional SQL databases to MongoDB straightforward while allowing you to benefit from Rails' conventions and ease of use.

> **NOTE** Given MongoDB's nature as a document-oriented database, these mappers are termed ODMs instead of object-relational mappers (ORMs).

Mongoid, the officially sanctioned ODM for MongoDB within the Ruby ecosystem, is managed by MongoDB and has some external community contributors working on it. Mongoid is bundled as a gem and hosted on RubyGems. It can be installed manually or with a bundler.

To install the gem manually, use this command:

```
gem install mongoid
```

To install the gem with a bundler, include the following in your Gemfile:

```
gem 'mongoid', '~> 8.1.0'
```

The advantages of using Mongoid ODM are

- *High-level interface*—Mongoid facilitates an elevated programming interface that uses objects, streamlining interaction with databases instead of handling the document format directly.
- *Uniform access*—Mongoid offers a uniform interface that ensures standardized data access patterns throughout an application.
- *Schema validation*—Although MongoDB does not inherently require schemas, Mongoid supports schema definitions and offers an organized method for prestorage data validation.
- *Transition ease*—If you are acquainted with ORMs from SQL database systems, you may find Mongoid more natural when you switch to MongoDB.
- *Transactional support*—Mongoid provides transactional assistance, ensuring that all operations within a transaction are completed in unison.

- *Enhanced efficiency*—By integrating caching strategies, Mongoid improves performance.
- *Code minimization*—Mongoid automates various repetitive database tasks, significantly decreasing the amount of code developers need to write and manage.

TIP For detailed documentation and helpful resources on configuring Mongoid, see https://www.mongodb.com/docs/mongoid/current.

Summary

- The MongoDB Wire Protocol is essential for client-server data exchange, offering efficient communication through a request–response mechanism over sockets, typically on port 27017.
- mongosh is a versatile client for direct MongoDB interactions, supporting features such as syntax highlighting, intelligent autocomplete, contextual help, and scripting capabilities.
- MongoDB Compass is a GUI tool offering schema visualizations, query building, index management, and performance profiling for an enhanced database management experience.
- The Node.js MongoDB driver simplifies the integration of Node.js applications with MongoDB databases, offering techniques and configurations to optimize interaction.
- You use the MongoDB Node.js driver to develop TypeScript applications that interact with MongoDB.
- PyMongo, tailored for synchronous operations in Python, facilitates direct connections and interactions with MongoDB. You can use it to execute database queries.
- Motor, the asynchronous Python driver, permits nonblocking database operations, boosting the efficiency of Python applications with concurrent database interactions.
- The Ruby driver makes it easy to work with MongoDB in Ruby by handling database connections and executing queries efficiently.
- Mongoid, the officially supported ODM for MongoDB in Ruby, improves Ruby's interaction with MongoDB.

Executing CRUD operations

This chapter covers

- Inserting documents in MongoDB
- Reading operations from MongoDB
- Updating operations in MongoDB
- Removing operations from MongoDB
- Reviewing MongoDB's Stable API

CRUD operations involve creating, reading, updating, and deleting documents. These fundamental actions form the backbone of data management systems, allowing applications and users to manipulate data effectively. Each type of CRUD operation has a specific function:

- *Create*—Adds new documents to the MongoDB database
- *Read*—Retrieves a document from the database
- *Update*—Changes details in existing documents within the database
- *Delete*—Eliminates documents from the database

CRUD operations define how applications interact with a database by managing the document life cycle, enforcing data consistency, and ensuring efficient access to stored information. This chapter covers executing these operations within MongoDB using `mongosh`, focusing on their behavior, performance considerations, and best practices for handling data modifications.

4.1 Connecting to mongosh for CRUD operations

Let's begin exploring CRUD operations. Connect to the MongoDB database in Atlas, which was established in chapter 2. Here's how you might structure your connection command:

```
mongosh "mongodb+srv://YOUR_CLUSTER.YOUR_HASH.mongodb.net/" \
--apiVersion API_VERSION --username USERNAME --password PASSWD
```

> **TIP** The `--apiVersion` parameter in the connection string ensures that your app uses a specific version of the MongoDB Stable API, even if MongoDB is upgraded to a newer version. This way, your app stays compatible, and you can safely use new features without worrying about breaking changes. The Stable API is explained at the end of this chapter.

All the examples in this chapter use the sample dataset imported into the MongoDB Atlas cluster in chapter 2, in which we established the following databases: `sample_airbnb`, `sample_analytics`, `sample_geospatial`, `sample_guides`, `sample_mflix`, `sample_restaurants`, `sample_supplies`, `sample_training`, and `sample_weatherdata`.

With the `use` command, switch to the `sample_training` database to access the `routes` collection:

```
[primary] test> use sample_training
switched to db sample_training
[primary] sample_training>
```

4.2 Inserting documents

Inserts are fundamental operations for adding data in MongoDB. MongoDB offers the `insertOne()` and `insertMany()` methods for inserting documents into a collection. To insert a single document, use the `insertOne()` method, as shown in the following listing.

Listing 4.1 Inserting a single document

```
[primary] sample_training> db.routes.insertOne({
  airline: { id: 410, name: 'Lufthansa', alias: 'LH',
  iata: 'DLH' },
  src_airport: 'MUC',
  dst_airport: 'JFK',
```

```
  codeshare: '',
  stops: 0,
  airplane: 'A380'
})

{
  acknowledged: true,
  insertedId: ObjectId('661998a755d788cb7662a3ed')
}
  [primary] sample_training>
```

Listing 4.1 uses the `insertOne()` method to insert a single document into the `routes` collection. The document specifies details such as airline ID and name, source and destination airports, and airplane type. The response object from MongoDB confirms the successful insertion with `acknowledged: true` and provides the `insertedId` of the newly added document, indicating that the operation was executed and providing the document's unique identifier, `ObjectId('661998a755d788cb7662a3ed')`.

> **TIP** When inserting a document into a MongoDB collection, you can provide your own `_id field` value. This allows you to specify a custom identifier for the document instead of using the autogenerated `ObjectId`.

If you need to insert multiple documents into a collection, use the `insertMany()` method, as shown in the next listing. This method allows you to pass an array of documents to the database. It's much more efficient because it doesn't require a round trip to the database for each document inserted; instead, it inserts all documents in bulk.

Listing 4.2 Inserting many documents

```
[primary] sample_training> db.routes.insertMany([
  {
    airline: { id: 413, name: 'American Airlines', alias: 'AA',
➥iata: 'AAL' },
    src_airport: 'DFW',
    dst_airport: 'LAX',
    codeshare: '',
    stops: 0,
    airplane: '737'
  },
  {
    airline: { id: 411, name: 'British Airways', alias: 'BA',
➥iata: 'BAW' },
    src_airport: 'LHR',
    dst_airport: 'SFO',
    codeshare: 'Y',
    stops: 0,
    airplane: '747'
  },
  {
    airline: { id: 412, name: 'Air France', alias: 'AF', iata: 'AFR' },
    src_airport: 'CDG',
```

```
      dst_airport: 'JFK',
      codeshare: '',
      stops: 0,
      airplane: '777'
    }
])

{
  acknowledged: true,
  insertedIds: {
    '0': ObjectId('661a252acf6203ef2a1db277'),
    '1': ObjectId('661a252acf6203ef2a1db278'),
    '2': ObjectId('661a252acf6203ef2a1db279')
  }}
[primary] sample_training>
```

Listing 4.2 uses the `insertMany()` method to bulk-insert multiple documents into the `routes` collection. The method is efficient because it performs the insertions in a single database operation, confirmed by the `acknowledged: true` status and the listing of each document's unique `ObjectId`.

> **TIP** The number of documents you can include in a single `insertMany()` operation is constrained by the 16 MB Binary JSON (BSON) document size limit. Essentially, you can insert any number of documents as long as their combined size remains below this 16 MB threshold.

By default, MongoDB inserts documents in the order in which they are provided. If the `ordered` option is set to `true` and an insert fails, the server stops processing subsequent records. If the option is set to `false`, the server continues with the next document even if one fails, potentially reordering the documents for better performance. Applications should not rely on the insertion order when using `insertMany` with `ordered` set to `false`.

> **TIP** To check which document failed in an `insertMany()` operation in MongoDB, look at the error details provided in the operation's response. The error message will include the index of the failed document within your array of documents. This index corresponds to the position of the document that caused the failure, allowing you to identify and address the problem. For unordered operations (`ordered: false`), multiple errors may be reported, each with a corresponding index.

MongoDB limits the number of operations in each batch to the `maxWriteBatchSize`, which defaults to 100,000. This limit helps prevent problems with large error messages. If a batch exceeds this limit, the client driver splits it into smaller batches, each of which complies with the maximum size. A batch of 300,000 operations, for example, would be divided into three batches of 100,000 each.

When you are inserting large amounts of random data into an indexed field, such as with hashed indexes (chapter 7), performance may decline because each bulk insert generates random index entries, enlarging the index and possibly causing each insert to access a different entry. This situation can lead to high rates of cache eviction and replacement in the WiredTiger storage engine (chapter 8), reducing performance because the index updates occur on disk rather than in cache. You have two options for enhancing performance with bulk inserts of random data:

- Consider dropping the index before the insert and re-creating it afterward.
- Insert the data into an unindexed collection and create the index postinsertion, allowing for an organized, memory-sorted index.

> **NOTE** Dropping an index before large bulk inserts can significantly boost write performance by reducing insertion overhead. This boost, however, comes at the cost of slower reads and potential query disruptions. This approach is best suited to scenarios with planned downtime or systems that experience long periods of low activity, allowing the index to be dropped and rebuilt safely without affecting the read workload. To minimize risks, estimate rebuild time, schedule operations during low-traffic windows, and monitor system resources carefully. Always test and coordinate thoroughly to ensure a smooth process.

If the insertOne() operation successfully inserts a document, it adds an entry to the oplog collection. (I explain oplog in chapter 9.) Conversely, if the operation fails, no entry is made. Similarly, if the insertMany() operation successfully inserts one or more documents, an entry is added to the oplog for each document inserted, whereas failed inserts do not appear in the oplog.

4.3 Updating documents

After you store a document in the database, you can make modifications with various update methods. These methods include updateOne(), updateMany(), and replaceOne(), in which the initial parameter serves as the filter. This filter identifies the documents targeted for updates based on specified criteria. Filters range from simple, such as {"_id": MyNumber }, which targets a specific document via its MongoDB ObjectID, to complex queries that target multiple documents based on diverse criteria. When you use updateOne() or replaceOne(), only a single document is updated or replaced, even if the filter matches multiple documents. Specifying an empty filter {} updates the first document returned in the collection, but it is worth verifying which document will be selected in such cases, as this behavior depends on the query execution.

In methods such as updateOne(), updateMany(), and replaceOne(), the second parameter is a document that outlines the desired changes to the document(s). Optionally, a third parameter can specify additional options.

If upsert: true is specified and no documents match the filter, updateOne() or updateMany() creates a new document using the filter criteria and the specified update modifications.

> **TIP** To avoid multiple upserts, make sure that the filter field(s) are uniquely indexed.

CHAPTER 4 *Executing CRUD operations*

> **WARNING** Document updating can modify or replace existing documents. Whereas `replaceOne()` swaps the current document with a new one, `updateOne()` modifies the existing document based on the supplied changes.

4.3.1 Using update operators

Often, only specific parts of a document require updates. Update operators like `$set` and `$inc` enable precise and atomic modifications to a document.

Suppose that you are managing flight details in a `routes` collection. If an airline changes the aircraft type for a specific route, you can use the `$set` operator to update the `airplane` field. If British Airways decides to switch from a Boeing 747 to an Airbus A380 on the LHR-to-SFO route, for example, the `$set` operator would update the airplane field from `"747"` to `"A380"`. If American Airlines needs to add a stopover at Phoenix for the DFW-to-LAX route, the `$inc` operator increments the `stops` field from 0 to 1. To update the aircraft type on a specific route, you can use the `$set` operator with the `updateOne()` method. The following listing shows these examples.

Listing 4.3 Using the `$set` operator

```
db.routes.updateOne(
    { "airline.id": 411, "src_airport": "LHR",
➥"dst_airport": "SFO", "airplane": "747" },
    { $set: { "airplane": "A380" } }
)
```

The command uses an `updateOne()` method with a specific filter to locate the document that needs updating in the MongoDB `routes` collection. The filter `{ "airline.id": 411, "src_airport": "LHR", "dst_airport": "SFO", "airplane": "747" }` targets a specific flight by its airline ID, departure airport, destination airport, and current airplane model. Then the `$set` operation `{ $set: { "airplane": "A380" } }` updates the `airplane` field to `"A380"` for this route.

> **NOTE** The `updateOne()` method in MongoDB arbitrarily updates one of the matching documents if multiple documents fit the query criteria and no specific sort order is applied. This behavior can be unintuitive because it does not specify which document will be updated when multiple matches occur. To target a specific document accurately, I advise using unique identifiers in your query, ensuring a predictable update.

> **TIP** The `$set` operator allows you to modify the values of any field in a document except `_id`. If the field specified by the `$set` operator does not exist, the operator creates it.

Another useful operator is `$inc`. The following listing shows how to adjust the number of stops on a specific route by using the `updateOne()` method with the `$inc` operator.

Listing 4.4 Using the `$inc` operator

```
db.routes.updateOne(
    { "airline.id": 413, "src_airport": "DFW",
"dst_airport": "LAX", "stops": 0 },
    { $inc: { "stops": 1 } }
)
```

The command uses the filter `{ "airline.id": 413, "src_airport": "DFW", "dst_airport": "LAX", "stops": 0 }` to identify the specific flight based on airline ID, departure airport, destination airport, and current number of stops (0). Then the `$inc` operation `{ $inc: { "stops": 1 } }` increments the `stops` field by 1 for this route, effectively changing the number of stops from 0 to 1.

> **TIP** The `$inc` operator modifies the value of an existing key or creates a new one if the key does not exist. This operator is particularly useful for incrementing or decrementing numerical fields within a document, making it ideal for applications such as updating inventory levels and for any scenario that involves changeable numeric values.

When choosing between MongoDB's `$inc` and `$set` operators, select `$inc` for numeric updates to benefit from its fast, low-overhead operations. Use `$set` for broader updates or new fields, keeping an eye on performance, especially if these changes increase document size or require movement within the database. Table 4.1 lists the update operators available in MongoDB.

Table 4.1 MongoDB update operators

Name	Description
$currentDate	Sets a field to the current date as a `Date` or `Timestamp`
$inc	Increments or decrements a field by a specified amount
$min	Updates only if the specified value is less than the current value
$max	Updates only if the specified value is greater than the current value
$mul	Multiplies the value of the field by the specified amount
$rename	Renames a field
$set	Sets the value of a field in a document
$setOnInsert	Sets a field during insertion, not affecting updates
$unset	Removes the specified field from a document

4.3.2 *Updating many documents*

The `updateMany()` method modifies all documents in a collection that meet the specified filter criteria, applying the provided update rules. In your `sample_training.routes` namespace, which stores information about various airline routes, the `updateMany()` method can be particularly useful for bulk updates across multiple documents. If you need to update attributes such as airplane models, airport codes, or even airline details across a large number of routes, `updateMany()` streamlines this process by applying the changes to all relevant documents at the same time. This ensures data consistency and efficiency in managing the route information within your collection. The `updateMany()` method operates under semantics similar to those of `updateOne()`, with the notable distinction being the effect on multiple documents rather than one.

> **TIP** To ensure the smooth execution of the `updateMany()` operation in production, thoroughly validate the filter beforehand. Using incorrect or insufficient filters can lead to unintended updates and potential chaos in the database. Before using it, execute a `find()` method to verify whether the filter accurately selects the desired documents.

> **NOTE** If a failure occurs in updating one of the documents, `updateMany()` still attempts to update the other documents that meet the criteria. The operation does not roll back changes if one document fails; the updates done before the failure are retained, but any matching documents after that are not updated. As a result, partial updates can occur: some documents are updated successfully, while others are not.

4.4 Updating arrays

MongoDB provides a variety of array operators that are extensive and powerful for manipulating documents that contain array fields. These operators enable functionalities such as adding elements to an existing array, removing elements from an array, modifying existing elements, and creating a new array. For example, if you have a data set with airline `routes`, and you want an array called `prices` to list the prices of the different classes, you can use MongoDB's `$push` operator to add the prices dynamically.

4.4.1 Adding elements to an array

The next listing uses the `$push` operator with `updateOne()` to add a price for a specific class to a flight.

Listing 4.5 Using the `$push` operator

```
db.routes.updateOne(
    { "airline.id": 413, "src_airport": "DFW", "dst_airport": "LAX" },
    { $push: { "prices": { class: "business", price: 2500 } } }
)
```

This operation adds the price for the business class to the `prices` array for the specified flight. If the `prices` array doesn't exist, MongoDB creates it.

Updating arrays

If you want to add more prices for other classes or update existing prices, you can use the `$push` operator combined with the `$each` modifier to append multiple values to an array field at the same time:

```
db.routes.updateOne(
    { "airline.id": 413, "src_airport": "DFW", "dst_airport": "LAX" },
    { $push: { prices: { $each: [{ class: "economy", price: 800 },
    { class: "first", price: 2000 }] } } }
)
```

This command appends each of the specified price entries to the `prices` array for the specified document, efficiently adding multiple prices for different classes in one operation.

You can also use the `$push` operator with the `$each`, `$sort`, and `$slice` modifiers if you want to add new classes such as `"premium economy"` or `"luxury"` to the prices array in a MongoDB document. Here's how you can update the array dynamically to include these new entries:

```
db.routes.updateOne(
    { "airline.id": 413, "src_airport": "DFW", "dst_airport": "LAX" },
    {
        $push: {
            prices: {
                $each: [
                    { class: "premium economy", price: 1100 },
                    { class: "luxury", price: 3000 }
                ],
                $sort: { price: 1 }, // Sorts prices in ascending order
                $slice: -3 // Keeps the last 3 entries
            }
        }
    }
)
```

TIP Use the `$slice` modifier only if you want to prevent the array from growing larger than a specific length, effectively maintaining a top *n* list of items.

The following listing shows the content of the document after the update. You can verify the changes using the `find` command.

Listing 4.6 The content of the document after an array update

```
db.routes.find({ "airline.id": 413, "src_airport": "DFW",
"dst_airport": "LAX" })
[
    {
        _id: ObjectId('661a252acf6203ef2a1db277'),
        airline: { id: 413, name: 'American Airlines', alias: 'AA',
iata: 'AAL' },
```

```
            src_airport: 'DFW',
            dst_airport: 'LAX',
            codeshare: '',
            stops: 1,
            airplane: '737',
            prices: [
                { class: 'first', price: 2000 },
                { class: 'business', price: 2500 },
                { class: 'luxury', price: 3000 }
            ]
        }
    ]
```

This result confirms that the document has been successfully modified to include the new classes and prices. You can use $addToSet, shown in the next listing, to ensure unique entries in an array field in MongoDB and prevent duplicates in the array.

Listing 4.7 Using the `$addToSet` operator

```
db.routes.updateOne(
    { "airline.id": 413, "src_airport": "DFW", "dst_airport": "LAX" },
    {
        $addToSet: {
            "prices": {
                class: 'economy plus', price: 1200
            }
        }
    }
)
```

The $addToSet operator attempts to add a new object with class `'economy plus'` and `price: 1200` to the `prices` array of the specified document. This object is added only if an identical object—the field names and their values—doesn't already exist in the array. If an object with the same field names but different values is added, it will be treated as a unique entry and included in the array. This ensures that only fully identical objects are prevented from being added, maintaining unique entries. This behavior contrasts with the $push operator, which adds the specified value to an array whether or not the value already exists, potentially leading to duplicates.

4.4.2 Removing elements from an array

You can also remove a specific element from an array in MongoDB, such as `{ class: 'first', price: 2000 }`. Typically, you use the $pull operator for this task, as shown in the following listing. The $pull operator allows you to specify the condition of the element to remove, matching the object you want to delete from the array.

Listing 4.8 Using the `$pull` operator

```
db.routes.updateOne(
    { "airline.id": 413, "src_airport": "DFW", "dst_airport": "LAX" },
```

```
    {
        $pull: {
            prices: {
                class: 'first',
                price: 2000
            }
        }
    }
)
```

This operation removes the object `{ class: 'first', price: 2000 }` from the `prices` array if it exists. The `$pull` operator is effective for selectively deleting elements from an array that match a specified condition.

Listing 4.9 shows the `$pop` operator in MongoDB, which removes either the first or the last element of an array within a document. This operator is helpful when you need to remove elements from the end or the beginning of an array without specifying exact values.

Listing 4.9 Using the `$pop` operator

```
db.routes.updateOne(
    { "airline.id": 413, "src_airport": "DFW", "dst_airport": "LAX" },
    {
        $pop: {
            prices: 1 // Removes the last element from the 'prices' array
        }
    }
)
```

In this example, specifying `1` with `$pop` removes the last element from the `prices` array. If you want to remove the first element instead, you would use `-1`.

4.4.3 Updating array elements

When you modify arrays with numerous elements, the process becomes slightly more complex if you need to alter specific items. You can target a specific item's position or use the positional operator (`$`) to update matching elements. In arrays, indexing starts at zero, allowing elements to be targeted as though their numerical index was akin to a document key:

- *Direct indexing*—This method is straightforward if you know the exact index of the element in the array you want to update. Suppose that you want to update the price of the second class (index 1) in the prices array:

  ```
  db.routes.updateOne(
      { "airline.id": 413, "src_airport": "DFW", "dst_airport": "LAX" },
      { $set: { "prices.1.price": 3500 } }
  )
  ```

68 CHAPTER 4 *Executing CRUD operations*

This operation sets the price of the second element, – `class: luxury` (assuming that the array elements are indexed from 0), in the `prices` array to `3500`.

- *Positional operator (`$`)*—This method is useful when you don't know the exact index of the element but can specify a condition that uniquely identifies it within the array. This approach is often recommended for dealing with elements that need to be identified dynamically:

```
db.routes.updateOne(
    {
        "airline.id": 413,
        "src_airport": "DFW",
        "dst_airport": "LAX",
        "prices.class": "luxury" // Condition to identify the element
    },
    {
        $set: { "prices.$.price": 4500 }
➥// Using the positional operator to update the price
    }
)
```

This command replaces the price of the `"luxury"` class within the `prices` array with `4500`, where the condition `"prices.class": "luxury"` is met.

NOTE If the specified field price does not exist within an array element that matches the condition (such as `"prices.class": "luxury"`), MongoDB automatically adds the `price` field to that element and sets its value to `4500`. This action occurs because the `$set` operator in MongoDB not only updates existing fields but also creates new fields in document elements where they are missing, ensuring that the specified update is applied correctly.

4.4.4 Updating using array filters

Another option involves the `$[<identifier>]` operator, commonly known as the *filtered positional operator*. This operator offers a powerful capability in MongoDB for pinpointing array elements that satisfy specified conditions defined by `arrayFilters`. When employed alongside the `arrayFilters` option, the `$[<identifier>]` operator is structured as follows:

```
{ <update operator>: { "<array>.$[<identifier>]" : value } },
➥{ arrayFilters: [ { <identifier>: <condition> } ] }
```

Starting with MongoDB 5.0, update operators process fields in documents with string-based names in lexicographic order, whereas fields with numeric names are processed in numeric order.

Suppose that you want to update the price of the `business` class for the flight from DFW to LAX operated by American Airlines (airline ID `413`) in your MongoDB document. You can use the `$[<identifier>]` operator with `arrayFilters` to achieve this goal, as shown in the following listing.

Listing 4.10 Using the `$[<identifier>]` operator with `arrayFilters`

```
db.routes.updateOne(
    { "airline.id": 413, "src_airport": "DFW", "dst_airport": "LAX" },
    {
        $set: {
            "prices.$[elem].price": 2600
        }
    },
    {
        arrayFilters: [
            { "elem.class": "business" }
        ]
    }
)
```

Listing 4.10 updates a document in the `routes` collection, targeting a specific route with the airline ID `413` that departs from `"DFW"` and arrives at `"LAX"`. Then, within this document, it modifies the price of the `business` class to `2600` using the `$[elem]` filtered positional operator along with the specified array filter.

The identifier `elem` used with the `$[<identifier>]` filtered positional operator acts as a placeholder that refers to specific elements within an array: elements that match the conditions specified in `arrayFilters`. This setup enables selective updating of array elements that meet defined criteria, focusing the update actions on those specific elements without affecting others in the array. Table 4.2 lists the array operators available in MongoDB.

Table 4.2 MongoDB array update operators

Name	Description
`$(update)`	Placeholder that updates the first element that matches the query
`$[]`	Placeholder that updates all array elements that match the query
`$[<identifier>]`	Placeholder that updates all elements that match the `arrayFilters` condition
`$addToSet`	Adds elements to an array only if they do not exist in `set`
`$pop`	Removes the first or last item of the array
`$pull`	Removes all array elements that match a specified query
`$push`	Adds an item to an array
`$pullAll`	Removes all matching values from an array

4.5 Replacing documents

The `replaceOne()` method in MongoDB replaces a single document within a collection that matches a specified filter with a new document. This method provides a way to replace the existing document with a new one rather than modify specific fields within the document. One common use case for `replaceOne()` is when you need to update a document with a new set of data, such as when you receive fully updated or corrected information or make a major change in the document structure. Instead of updating each field individually, you can replace the entire document with the new data.

> **NOTE** The new data must be a full representation of the document. If you need to preserve existing fields from the original document, `replaceOne()` is not the right option. In such cases, you should use an update operation such as `updateOne()` or `updateMany()` to modify only the necessary fields.

Listing 4.11 shows how to modify the structure of a document in MongoDB's `routes` collection with the `replaceOne()` method, replacing a document that matches the specific filter `{ "airline.id": 412, "src_airport": "CDG", "dst_airport": "JFK" }` with a new document structure.

Listing 4.11 Replacing a document in MongoDB

```
db.routes.replaceOne(
    { "airline.id": 412, "src_airport": "CDG", "dst_airport": "JFK" },
    {
        flight_info: { airline: "Air France", flight_number: "AF 007" },
        route: { from: "CDG", to: "JFK" },
        aircraft: "Boeing 777",
        status: "Scheduled"
    },
    { upsert: true }
)
```

If `upsert` is set to `true` and no documents match the filter, `replaceOne()` creates a new document based on the replacement document.

To verify the `replaceOne()` method you just executed, use a filter that specifically targets key fields that were part of the updated document structure. The reason to use a different filter, such as `{aircraft: "Boeing 777", status: "Scheduled"}`, rather than the one used in the `replaceOne` method is to ensure that the new document structure is reflected correctly in the database:

```
db.routes.find({"aircraft": "Boeing 777", "status": "Scheduled"})
[
    {
        _id: ObjectId('661a252acf6203ef2a1db279'),
        flight_info: { airline: 'Air France', flight_number: 'AF 007' },
        route: { from: 'CDG', to: 'JFK' },
        aircraft: 'Boeing 777',
```

```
        status: 'Scheduled'
    }
]
```

When using the `replaceOne()` method in MongoDB, you replace the entire document except for the `_id` field, which is immutable. The replacement document may have different fields from the original document. If the `_id` field is included in the replacement document, it must match the current value of `_id` in the document being replaced. If `_id` is omitted, MongoDB retains the original `_id` of the document automatically, ensuring continuity of the document's identity even as its content changes completely.

> **NOTE** If a different `_id` is supplied, the replacement operation will fail. MongoDB enforces the immutability of the `_id` field, and any attempt to change it will result in an error.

> **TIP** Avoid replacing the entire document when you're updating only a few fields. Replacing a whole document to update one or two fields can cause scalability problems. As documents grow, sending entire documents across the network leads to unnecessary traffic and bloats the oplog. Using `updateOne()` with operators like `$set` is more efficient for updating specific fields than using `replaceOne()` is.

4.6 Reading documents

The `find()` method in MongoDB executes queries. It retrieves a selection of documents from a collection, which can range from none to all documents within the collection. It accepts an optional filter parameter that specifies which documents to retrieve. If you don't provide a filter, all documents in the collection are returned.

To fetch all documents from the `sample_training.routes` collection without any specific query filter, you can run the following command in `mongosh`:

```
use sample_training
db.routes.find()
```

This command is equivalent to the following SQL statement, retrieving all documents from the `routes` collection:

```
SELECT * FROM routes
```

To find documents that meet a specific equality condition, include the condition as a `<field>:<value>` pair in the query filter document.

To find all documents in which `src_airport` equals `'LHR'`, run the command with the following filter:

```
db.routes.find({ src_airport: 'LHR' })
```

The find command returns all routes departing from Heathrow and is equivalent to the following SQL statement:

```
SELECT * FROM routes WHERE src_airport = 'LHR'
```

It returns all documents from the `routes` collection where the source airport is `'LHR'`.

When the `find()` method is called, it returns a cursor that points to the resulting documents rather than to the documents themselves. This cursor can be iterated automatically, but it also allows manual control if necessary. By returning a cursor, the design optimizes memory use because it fetches data on demand rather than loading everything into memory at the same time. This lazy loading improves performance, especially when you're working with large data sets, and provides greater flexibility in how applications handle the query results.

> **TIP** When you execute `db.collection.find()` in mongosh, it automatically iterates the cursor to display up to the first 20 documents. To continue viewing more documents, you can type `it` to iterate further.

In version 8.0, MongoDB introduces the `defaultMaxTimeMS`. This parameter enables you to specify a default time limit in milliseconds for individual read operations to complete. To set `defaultMaxTimeMS` for your deployment, run the following command on the admin database, replacing `5000` with the desired time limit in milliseconds:

```
db.adminCommand(
    {
        setClusterParameter: {
            defaultMaxTimeMS: { readOperations: 5000 }
    // Example value: 5000 milliseconds (5 seconds)
        }
    }
)
```

To view the current value for `defaultMaxTimeMS`, run the following command on the admin database:

```
db.adminCommand( { getClusterParameter: "defaultMaxTimeMS" } )
```

By default, `defaultMaxTimeMS.readOperations` is `0`, meaning that no default query timeout is set. If no default query timeout is set, the query runs until it returns a result or fails. If a query exceeds the set time limit, it terminates, and an error is returned, indicating that the operation exceeded the maximum time limit.

4.6.1 Using logical operators

Listing 4.12 demonstrates using a compound query to retrieve routes from the `routes` collection in which Charles de Gaulle is the source airport, along with other specified

Reading documents

criteria. A *compound query* combines multiple conditions using logical operators such as AND and OR to filter the results more precisely. This query finds routes for which the source airport is "CDG" and the destination airport is "JFK".

> **Listing 4.12 Using logical operators**

```
db.routes.find({ "src_airport": "CDG", "dst_airport": "JFK" })
```

TIP In MongoDB, a comma-separated list of expressions implicitly acts as an AND operation.

You can use the $or operator in a compound query to combine conditions with a logical OR. This allows the query to select documents that meet at least one of the specified conditions. Here's an example:

```
db.routes.find({
    $or: [
        { "src_airport": "CDG" },
        { "dst_airport": "JFK" }
    ]
})
```

This query checks for documents in which the source airport is CDG or the destination airport is JFK, retrieving any that match either condition.

You can use logical operators for more complex queries and combine them with query selectors to refine your search criteria. In the following query, the $or operator specifies conditions on different fields, enhancing the specificity of the database search:

```
db.routes.find({
    $or: [
        { "src_airport": "CDG", "airline.name": { $ne: 'American Airlines' } },
        // Routes from CDG not operated by American Airlines
        { "dst_airport": "JFK", "airplane": { $ne: '777' } }
        // Routes to JFK not using a 777 airplane
    ]
})
```

This query filters for routes departing from CDG that are not operated by American Airlines or that are arriving at JFK not on a Boeing 777, targeting more specific travel options. Table 4.3 presents MongoDB's logical operators.

Table 4.3 Logical operators for querying documents

Name	Description
$and	Combines query clauses with a logical AND to return documents that match both conditions
$not	Inverts the query expression's effect, returning documents that do not match the expression

Table 4.3 Logical operators for querying documents (*continued*)

Name	Description
$nor	Combines query clauses with a logical NOR to return documents that fail to match both clauses
$or	Combines query clauses with a logical OR to return documents that match the conditions of either clause

4.6.2 Using comparison operators

The following listing shows how to use find() with the query operators within a query filter document to conduct intricate comparisons and evaluations. If you want to find documents in which src_airport is 'MUC', 'JFK', 'LHR', or 'DFW', use the $in operator.

Listing 4.13 Using the $in and $nin operators

```
db.routes.find({ src_airport: { $in: ['MUC', 'JFK', 'LHR', 'DFW'] } })
```

Similarly, you can exclude documents for those airports by using the $nin operator. Here's how you can write the query:

```
db.routes.find({ src_airport: { $nin: ['MUC', 'JFK', 'LHR', 'DFW'] } })
```

To further expand on the use of query operators for fine-tuned filtering in MongoDB, the $not operator negates a condition. Here's how you can implement the $not operator in a query:

```
db.routes.find({ "airplane": { $not: { $regex: '^7' } } })
```

In this query, the $not operator is used with $regex (explained in section 4.7) to exclude all routes in which the airplane model starts with '7'. This typically includes models such as 737, 747, and 777, commonly used by various airlines. This kind of query is beneficial when you want to filter out a series of similar entries based on a pattern in one of the fields, providing a clearer demonstration of the power and flexibility of using $not for pattern negation in MongoDB queries. Table 4.4 presents the available query selectors in MongoDB.

Table 4.4 Query selectors for document comparison

Name	Description
$eq	Finds values that match a specified value
$gt	Finds values that are greater than a specified value
$gte	Finds values that are greater than or equal to a specified value
$in	Finds matches for any of the values specified in an array

Table 4.4 Query selectors for document comparison (*continued*)

Name	Description
$lt	Finds values that are less than a specified value
$lte	Finds values that are less than or equal to a specified value
$ne	Finds all values that are not equal to a specified value
$nin	Finds no matches among the values specified in an array

In a compound query, you can establish conditions for several fields in the documents of a collection. Typically, these conditions are linked through a logical AND, meaning that the query selects only documents that satisfy all specified criteria.

4.6.3 Working with projections

To control which fields are returned in the matching documents from a MongoDB query, you can use projections to specify exactly which fields should be included in or excluded from the result set. Projections allows you to tailor the query results by selectively retrieving only the necessary fields, thereby optimizing data retrieval and reducing network overhead.

Let's look at a couple of examples. To retrieve only the airline name, source airport, and destination airport from the routes collection, you can specify a projection that includes these fields, as shown in the next listing.

Listing 4.14 Using projection

```
db.routes.find(
   {},
   { "airline.name": 1, "src_airport": 1, "dst_airport": 1, "_id": 0 }
)
```

Here, the first parameter of the find method means that no filtering criteria are applied, so all documents are considered.

The second parameter of the find method, { "airline.name": 1, "src_airport": 1, "dst_airport": 1, "_id": 0 }, specifies the projection. Setting the value to 1 for a specific field tells MongoDB to return this field for each document that matches the query.

On the other hand, setting it to 0 (as in _id: 0) indicates that the specified field (in this case, _id, which is included by default in all MongoDB documents as a unique identifier) should be excluded from the query results. Setting the value to 0 tells MongoDB not to return this field. This setting is useful when the unique identifier is not needed in the output, simplifying the data returned.

> **TIP** Although it is common to use 1 or 0 to include or exclude fields, using true or false is also possible and serves the same purpose.

If you want to exclude certain fields from the results, such as `codeshare` and `stops`, use a projection that sets these fields to 0:

```
db.routes.find(
   {},
   { "codeshare": 0, "stops": 0 }
)
```

This projection excludes the `codeshare` and `stops` fields from the results by setting them to 0. These specific fields aren't included in the output documents returned by the query. Other fields, including the default `_id` field, are included in the results unless they are explicitly excluded.

4.6.4 Searching for null values and absent fields

Different query operators in MongoDB treat `null` values differently, offering various approaches to handle the presence or absence of data in a collection. Understanding these differences is crucial for querying documents effectively, especially when you're dealing with incomplete or optional fields. Let's look at a few examples of executing queries in mongosh.

QUERYING FOR NULL OR MISSING FIELDS

To find documents in which a specific field, like `codeshare`, is explicitly `null` or does not exist in the `routes` collection, run

```
db.routes.find({
   "codeshare": null
})
```

This query returns documents in which the `codeshare` field is present and its value is `null` or `missing`.

QUERYING FOR NON-NULL AND EXISTING FIELDS

To find documents in which a `codeshare` field exists and is not `null`, run

```
db.routes.find({
 "codeshare": { $ne: null, $exists: true }
})
```

This query returns all documents in which the `codeshare` field exists and its value is not `null`.

QUERYING FOR FIELDS THAT DO NOT EXIST

To find documents that do not contain a specific field, such as `codeshare`, run

```
db.routes.find({
   "codeshare": { $exists: false }
})
```

This query returns documents in which the `codeshare` field does not exist.

QUERY USING TYPE CHECK FOR NULL

To find documents in which a field, like `codeshare`, contains a `null` value, meaning that its value is stored as BSON Type Null (type 10), differentiating it from nonexistence, run

```
db.routes.find({ codeshare: { $type: "null" } })
```

This query returns documents in which the `codeshare` field has the BSON Type Null.

Table 4.5 lists the available MongoDB element operators.

Table 4.5 Element operators

Name	Description
$exists	Filters documents based on the presence of the specified field
$type	Chooses documents based on the type of a specified field

4.7 Performing regular-expression searches

The `$regex` operator in MongoDB enables you to perform regular-expression searches, pattern-matching strings within queries. To use `$regex`, you can structure your query in one of the following ways:

```
{field: {$regex: /pattern/, $options: 'options'}}
{"field": {"$regex": "pattern", "$options": "options"}}
{field: {$regex: /pattern/options}}
```

Available options for additional operators are

- `i`—Case insensitivity
- `m`—Multiline matching, treating start (`^`) and end (`$`) anchors to match line beginnings and endings
- `x`—Extended regex to ignore whitespace within the regex pattern
- `s`—Allows the dot (`.`) to match newline characters
- `u`—Unicode support, though redundant, as MongoDB's `$regex` defaults to Unicode Transformation Format (UTF)

Suppose that you want to find all routes within the `routes` collection that are operated by airlines with `Air` in their names, irrespective of case sensitivity. You can accomplish this by executing the following MongoDB query:

```
db.routes.find({
  "airline.name": {$regex: "air", $options: "i"}
})
```

This query matches any airline name that includes `"Air"`, such as `"Air France"`, `"Air Burkina"`, `"Helvetic Airways"`, or `"American Airlines"`.

Or maybe you need to identify all routes departing from airports whose codes start with B or C. This query is particularly useful for conducting regional analysis or managing routes in certain geographic areas:

```
db.routes.find({
"src_airport": { $regex: "^[BC]", $options: "i" }
})
```

This query uses a regular expression to find routes in which the source airport codes begin with B or C, such as BKO for Ouagadougou Airport and CEK for Chelyabinsk Airport.

Suppose that you're tasked with analyzing flight routes to international airports, often distinguished by a three-letter code ending in X (such as LAX and PHX). These airports tend to be large and usually are situated in major cities. To streamline your analysis, you decide to use the `$regex` operator to identify all routes heading to these prominent airports. Here's how you can structure your query:

```
db.routes.find({
"dst_airport": { $regex: "X$", $options: "i" }
// Matches destination airport codes ending with 'X'
})
```

This query checks for destination airport codes that end with X, using `$regex` with the pattern `"X$"`, where $ signifies the end of the string. This ensures that only airport codes ending in X are matched regardless of case due to the `"i"` option for case insensitivity.

These examples demonstrate the flexibility of the `$regex` operator in querying text fields within MongoDB documents, enabling sophisticated pattern matching and filtering based on specific conditions.

> **TIP** MongoDB provides an enhanced full-text search solution called Atlas Search (described in part 2), which includes its own `$regex` operator. From MongoDB version 8.0, full-text search is also available in MongoDB Community Edition.

4.8 Querying arrays

In this section, we use documents with arrays from the `customers` collection, which are located in the `sample_analytics` database. This database was created during the import of sample data in chapter 2. A sample document from the `customers` collection contains the following data:

```
{
  _id: ObjectId('5ca4bbcea2dd94ee58162a68'),
```

```
    accounts: [ 371138, 324287, 276528, 332179, 422649, 387979 ],
    tier_and_details: {
      '0df078f33aa74a2e9696e0520c1a828a': {
        tier: 'Bronze',
        id: '0df078f33aa74a2e9696e0520c1a828a',
        active: true,
        benefits: [ 'sports tickets' ]
      },
      '699456451cc24f028d2aa99d7534c219': {
        tier: 'Bronze',
        benefits: [ '24 hour dedicated line', 'concierge services' ],
        active: true,
        id: '699456451cc24f028d2aa99d7534c219'
      }
    }
}
```

In MongoDB, you can easily find documents based on the presence of a specific value within an array by using a simple query. If you want to check whether the accounts array contains the number 371138, for example, you can use a straightforward query:

```
db.customers.find({
accounts: 371138
})
```

This query searches for all documents in the customers collection in which the accounts array includes the account number 371138.

If you want to find a document containing the specific array, such as [371138, 324287, 276528, 332179, 422649, 387979], the filter must match this array exactly:

```
db.customers.find({
 accounts: [371138, 324287, 276528, 332179, 422649, 387979]
})
```

This query returns documents in which the accounts array matches the provided sequence exactly, including the order of the elements. But if the query filter is changed to include only a subset of these numbers

```
db.customers.find({
accounts: [371138, 324287, 276528]
})
```

the revised query doesn't find any documents unless it finds one whose accounts array matches the array [371138, 324287, 276528] in that order and with no additional elements. MongoDB treats arrays in a query for exact matches as requiring the exact sequence and complete list of elements specified in the query.

If, instead, you want to find documents in which the accounts array contains all the specified numbers regardless of their order, you can use the $all operator, as shown in listing 4.15. This operator allows you to find documents that include all specified elements but may include other elements and in any order.

Listing 4.15 Using the `$all` operator

```
db.customers.find({
accounts: { $all: [371138, 324287, 276528] }
})
```

This query returns documents in which the `accounts` array contains all the numbers `371138`, `324287`, and `276528`, regardless of the order or the presence of additional numbers in the array. This is useful for more flexible querying when the exact order and completeness of the sequence are not critical.

To perform a query on the `accounts` array in the `customers` collection to find any account number greater than `300000`, use the following example:

```
db.customers.find({
   accounts: { $gt: 300000 }
})
```

This query uses the `$gt` operator to search for documents in which at least one element in the `accounts` array is greater than `300000`. This is a useful way to filter documents based on conditions applied to individual items within an array.

Use the `$elemMatch` operator to define multiple conditions for the elements of an array, ensuring that at least one element within the array meets all these conditions, as the following listing shows.

Listing 4.16 Using the `$elemMatch` operator

```
db.customers.find({
accounts: { $elemMatch: { $gt: 300000, $lt: 400000 } }
})
```

The query searches the `customers` collection for documents in which at least one number in the `accounts` array is greater than `300000` and less than `400000`. It uses the `$elemMatch` operator to ensure that the specified conditions are met by at least one element in the array.

If you want to find a particular item in the array, you can do so by indicating its index using this syntax:

```
db.customers.find({
'accounts.1': 324287
})
```

This corresponds to the second item in the array, as array indexes start counting from `0`.

You can also combine several conditions in a query to find documents that meet all your criteria. In this example, using `.0` targets the first element of an array:

```
db.customers.find({
  "tier_and_details.0df078f33aa74a2e9696e0520c1a828a.active": true,
  "accounts.0": { $gte: 300000 }
})
```

This query checks for documents in which the account with the key `0df078f33aa74a2e9696e0520c1a828a` in the `tier_and_details` map is active and the first item in the `accounts` array has a value of `300000` or more. In MongoDB, array indices start at `0`, so `accounts.0` refers to the first item in the `accounts` array.

TIP When you use dot notation to query, enclose both the field and any nested fields within quotation marks.

You can use the `$size` operator to query for arrays by number of elements. The following listing demonstrates how to do this.

Listing 4.17 Using the `$size` operator

```
db.customers.find({
accounts: { $size: 6 }
})
```

The query uses the `$size` operator to filter and retrieve documents from the `customers` collection in which the `accounts` array field contains exactly six elements. This is crucial for applications that need to enforce or validate specific array lengths within document structures.

TIP The `$size` operator supports only exact matching; it does not allow range queries or comparison operations directly on the array size.

Table 4.6 shows the array operators available in MongoDB.

Table 4.6 Array operators

Name	Description
$all	Matches arrays containing all elements specified in the query
$elemMatch	Selects documents in which elements in the array field match all specified $elemMatch conditions
$size	Selects documents in which the array field has a specified size

4.9 Querying embedded/nested documents

MongoDB offers two methods for querying embedded documents. The first method involves using dot notation to query fields within nested documents. The second method requires matching the entire embedded or nested document. Let's discuss both approaches.

Recall the appearance of the document from the `routes` collection that we created in this chapter and then modified. It looks like this:

```
[
  {
    _id: ObjectId('661a252acf6203ef2a1db277'),
    airline: { id: 413, name: 'American Airlines', alias: 'AA',
      iata: 'AAL' },
    src_airport: 'DFW',
    dst_airport: 'LAX',
    codeshare: '',
    stops: 1,
    airplane: '737',
    prices: [
      { class: 'business', price: 2600 },
      { class: 'luxury', price: 4500 }
    ]
  }
]
```

4.9.1 Querying on a nested field with dot notation

To use the dot-notation approach to find documents containing the airline name `"American Airlines"` and airline ID `413`, your query should look like the following listing.

Listing 4.18 Using dot notation

```
db.routes.find({"airline.name": "American Airlines", "airline.id": 413})
```

This query specifically targets documents in which the airline's name is `"American Airlines"` and the airline's ID is `413`. It uses dot notation to access the nested `name` and `_id` fields within the `airline` object. Dot notation is used because the airline is an embedded document within the `routes` collection. By using dot notation, the query precisely filters for conditions within this nested structure. The approach effectively narrows the search to entries that match the specified airline criteria exactly, ensuring more accurate data retrieval.

Suppose that you want to find routes offering tickets priced below `3000`. In this scenario, you can use dot notation to target the `price` field nested within each `prices` document of the route records. Your MongoDB query might look like this:

```
db.routes.find({ "prices.price": {$lt: 3000}})
```

In this query, `prices.class` and `prices.price` with `$lt: 3000` directly target the `price` field within the `prices` array, searching for values less than `3000`. This pattern is useful for filtering arrays of nested documents based on specific conditions within those documents.

TIP When using dot notation in queries, enclose both the field and nested field in quotation marks.

4.9.2 Matching an embedded/nested document

The second method to query embedded or nested documents in MongoDB involves matching the entire embedded document exactly. This method uses a query filter in which you specify the field and the complete nested document as the value.

The following query filter is derived from the airline embedded document. To select all documents in which the `airline` field exactly matches `{ id: 413, name: 'American Airlines', alias: 'AA', iata: 'AAL' }`, your query should be structured like this listing.

Listing 4.19 Using a nested document

```
db.routes.find({
"airline": { "id": 413, "name": "American Airlines",
↳"alias": "AA", "iata": "AAL" }
})
```

This query returns documents with an airline embedded document that exactly matches the provided structure and field order.

WARNING MongoDB cautions against using exact matches for embedded documents because such queries demand a complete match, down to the order of fields. If even one field is omitted, removed from the document, or reordered, the query won't work. It's generally better to use the dot-notation approach for more flexibility and reliability.

4.9.3 Querying an array of embedded documents

If you're looking to query nested fields in an array without knowing their exact index position, you can concatenate the name of the array with a dot (.) followed by the name of the field inside the nested documents:

```
db.routes.find({
  "prices.price": { $gte: 1000 }
})
```

The query searches the `routes` collection for documents in which any `price` field within the `prices` array is greater than or equal to `1000`. It uses dot notation to access the `price` field across all elements in the array without specifying their indices, allowing the query to evaluate every object in the `prices` array.

The following example selects all documents in which the first element in the `prices` array meets a specific condition on the `price` field. This query accesses the `price` field of the first item in the `prices` array:

```
db.routes.find({
  "prices.0.price": { $gte: 650 }
})
```

In the query, the `.0` in `prices.0.price` indicates that you are specifically targeting the first element of the `prices` array and searching for documents in which the price of this initial class is greater than or equal to 650.

To use the `$elemMatch` operator to specify multiple criteria on an array of embedded documents so that at least one embedded document satisfies all the specified criteria, you can construct a query like this:

```
db.routes.find({
  prices: {
    $elemMatch: {
      class: 'business',
      price: { $lt: 3000 }
    }
  }
})
```

The query uses the `$elemMatch` operator to find documents in which at least one element of the `prices` array is a business class with a price below 3000. This operator ensures that the specified conditions are met in the same array item.

4.10 Sorting, skipping, and limiting

In MongoDB, you can use the `sort`, `skip`, and `limit` operations to manage and navigate query results efficiently. These operations are crucial for handling large data sets, ensuring that data is presented in meaningful order and optimizing data retrieval for pagination.

4.10.1 The sort operation

The `sort` operation organizes the documents in the result set according to specified fields. It can be set to ascending (1) or descending (-1) order. If you want to view flight routes sorted by the number of stops, you could use

```
db.routes.find().sort({"stops": -1})
```

This query sorts the routes based on the number of stops in descending order.

4.10.2 The skip operation

The `skip` operation omits a specified number of documents from the beginning of the result set. It's particularly useful for implementing pagination. If you want to skip the first five routes and start displaying from the sixth, use this query to jump over the first five documents:

```
db.routes.find().skip(5)
```

4.10.3 The limit operation

The `limit` operation restricts the number of documents returned by the query, ideal for controlling the size of data returned. To limit the output to 10 routes, use

```
db.routes.find().limit(10)
```

This query returns only the first 10 documents of the result set.

These operations are often combined to facilitate detailed data retrieval strategies, especially in applications that require data pagination. The query

```
db.routes.find().sort({"stops": -1}).skip(10).limit(5)
```

sorts the routes by the number of stops, skips the first 10 sorted routes, and limits the output to the next 5 routes, effectively providing a means to paginate sorted data.

4.11 Deleting documents

The deletion process is straightforward but must be handled with care to avoid removing unintended data. To delete a single document that matches specific criteria, you can use the `deleteOne()` method. This method removes the first document that matches the query. The following listing shows how to delete the route document for American Airlines flying from DFW to LAX.

Listing 4.20 Using the `deleteOne()` method

```
db.routes.deleteOne({
  "airline.id": 413,
  "src_airport": "DFW",
  "dst_airport": "LAX"
})
```

This command finds the first document in the `routes` collection that matches the airline ID (413) and the specified route from "DFW" to "LAX" and then removes it from the collection.

If multiple documents match the same criteria (such as multiple flights on different days), you could use the `deleteMany()` method to remove all matching documents at the same time.

Listing 4.21 Using the `deleteMany()` method

```
db.routes.deleteMany({
  "src_airport": "MUC",
  "dst_airport": "LAX"
})
```

This command removes all documents that fit the specified criteria, which is particularly useful for batch deletions when you're updating or clearing out specific routes or flight data.

It's worth mentioning the existence of the `db.collection.findOneAndDelete()` method in MongoDB. This method deletes a single document based on specified filter criteria and returns the deleted document. The method is useful when you need to delete a document and also retrieve the details of the deleted document. When executed, `findOneAndDelete()` deletes the first document that matches the filter criteria, influenced by the `sort` parameter. If no matching document is found, the operation returns `null`. This method ensures atomicity on single documents, meaning that the deletion is fully completed or not performed.

> **TIP** Always have an up-to-date backup of the database to restore it in case of loss. The methods for backup and restore are in chapter 21.

> **When performing delete operations**
>
> Be specific with your query criteria to avoid unintentionally deleting more documents than intended. It's a good practice to use a `find()` query with the same criteria to review which documents will be affected before executing `deleteOne()` or `deleteMany()`.
>
> Consider implementing logical deletes (using a status field to mark documents as inactive) instead of physical deletes for critical data that may need to be retained or audited later.

4.12 Using bulkWrite()

MongoDB enables you to perform write operations in bulk. The `bulkWrite()` method allows you to perform bulk insert, update, and delete operations. Bulk-write operations in MongoDB are either ordered or unordered:

- In ordered operations, MongoDB processes the operations sequentially. If an error arises during the execution of any write operation, MongoDB halts further processing of subsequent write operations in the list.
- When dealing with an unordered list of operations, MongoDB has the potential to execute these operations in parallel, although this behavior isn't assured. If an error emerges during the processing of a write operation, MongoDB persists in processing the remaining write operations in the list.

Executing an ordered list of operations on a sharded collection typically incurs slower performance compared with executing an unordered list because with an ordered list, each operation must wait for the preceding operation to complete.

By default, the `bulkWrite()` function conducts operations in an ordered manner. To designate unordered write operations, you can set `ordered: false` in the options document.

`bulkWrite()` supports the following write operations:

- `insertOne`
- `updateOne`
- `updateMany`
- `replaceOne`
- `deleteOne`
- `deleteMany`

Each write operation is passed to `bulkWrite()` as a document in an array.

With the release of MongoDB 8.0, the new `bulkWrite` command allows you to perform multiple insert, update, and delete operations on various collections in a single request. The existing `db.collection.bulkWrite()` method is limited to modifying only one collection per request.

Following is an example of the `bulkWrite` command. To specify each collection in the command, use a namespace (database and collection name).

Listing 4.22 Syntax of the `bulkWrite` command in MongoDB 8.0

```
db.adminCommand({
    bulkWrite: 1,
    ops: [
        // Insert operation for sample_training.routes
        {
            insert: 0,
            document: {
                airline: { id: 413, name: 'American Airlines',
 alias: 'AA', iata: 'AAL' },
                src_airport: 'DFW',
                dst_airport: 'LAX',
                codeshare: '',
                stops: 0,
                airplane: '737'
            }
        },
        // Insert operation for sample_analytics.customers
        {
            insert: 1,
            document: {
                accounts: [371138, 324287],
                tier_and_details: {
                    '0df078f33aa74a2e9696e0520c1a828a': {
                        tier: 'Bronze',
                        id: '0df078f33aa74a2e9696e0520c1a828a',
                        active: true,
                        benefits: ['sports tickets']
                    },
                    '699456451cc24f028d2aa99d7534c219': {
                        tier: 'Bronze',
                        benefits: ['24 hour dedicated line'],
                        active: true,
```

```
            id: '699456451cc24f028d2aa99d7534c219'
          }
        }
      }
    }
  ],
  nsInfo: [
    { ns: "sample_training.routes" },    // Namespace for routes collection
    { ns: "sample_analytics.customers" }
 // Namespace for customers collection
  ]
})
```

In listing 4.22, the `bulkWrite` command inserts documents into two collections, `sample_training.routes` and `sample_analytics.customers`, as specified in the `nsInfo` array. This demonstrates how `bulkWrite` can handle operations across multiple collections in a single request.

4.13 Understanding cursors

Read operations that retrieve multiple documents do not directly provide all documents matching the query at the same time. Because a query may match a large number of documents, these operations yield a cursor. This cursor points to the documents that meet the query criteria and retrieves documents in batches, which helps minimize memory use and network bandwidth. Cursors are versatile, can be finely tuned, and support various methods of interaction to suit different scenarios. The `find()` method directly returns a cursor.

You can use a variety of cursor paradigms to retrieve data. Most of these paradigms enable you to access the results of a query one document at a time, effectively hiding the complexities of network and caching operations. Different use cases require different access methods, however, and some paradigms call for collecting all matching documents directly in process memory.

To start with cursors, you typically execute a query like `db.routes.find()`, which returns a cursor. The cursor does not immediately return all documents; it allows you to fetch the documents in batches. You can store this cursor in a variable:

```
const cursorVariable = db.routes.find()
```

Then you can use the cursor to iterate over the documents as needed.

4.13.1 Using manual iteration

In `mongosh`, you can iterate over query results manually by defining a function that uses a cursor to fetch documents one by one. This method gives you fine-grained control over the iteration process, allowing you to perform additional operations between document retrievals. Here's an example:

```
async function manualIteration() {
  const cursorVariable = db.routes.find()
```

```
  // Loop while there are documents available in the cursor
  while (await cursorVariable.hasNext()) {
    // Log each document to the console as it's fetched
    console.log(await cursorVariable.next())
  }
}

// Call the function to perform the iteration
manualIteration()
```

The `manualIteration` function uses the `hasNext()` method, which returns `true` if additional documents are available in the cursor. The `next()` method retrieves the next document in the sequence.

4.13.2 Returning an array of all documents

Using the `toArray()` method, you can fetch all documents matched by a query into memory at the same time. This method is straightforward, but you should use it with caution on large data sets due to potential memory constraints:

```
async function fetchAllDocuments() {
  // Create a cursor for all documents in the 'routes' collection
  const cursor = db.routes.find({})

  // Use toArray to convert the cursor to an array of documents
  const allValues = await cursor.toArray()

  // Output all documents to the console
  console.log(allValues)
}

// Call the function to execute the fetching process
fetchAllDocuments()
```

> **WARNING** Mixing different cursor paradigms, such as using `hasNext()` and `toArray()` together, can lead to unexpected results.

4.14 Employing MongoDB Stable API

MongoDB offers a Stable API feature, which ensures that applications maintain consistent behavior despite updates to the MongoDB server. By using the Stable API, you can specify which version of the MongoDB API your applications are targeting. This specification allows MongoDB to handle requests in a way that is compatible with the version of the API the application expects, thereby avoiding potential incompatibilities that might arise from updates in the database software. Key features of the Stable API include

- *API version specification*—Defines the `apiVersion` parameter in database connection settings. This parameter instructs the MongoDB server to adhere to the specified API version's protocols and behaviors.

- *Backward compatibility*—Maintains backward compatibility by preserving the behavior of older API versions, even as new versions are released. This feature is essential for legacy applications that rely on specific database behaviors.
- *Isolation from deprecations*—Targets a specific API version so that applications are insulated from deprecations and removals in newer MongoDB versions, which might otherwise necessitate code refactoring.

When connecting to a MongoDB server, the driver typically operates with the default behavior unless specified otherwise. By explicitly setting the apiVersion in the connection settings, developers instruct MongoDB to apply the Stable API, as in this example:

```
mongosh "mongodb+srv://YOUR_CLUSTER.YOUR_HASH.mongodb.net/" \
--apiVersion API_VERSION --username USERNAME --password PASSWD
```

This setting ensures that all operations performed by the driver adhere to the behaviors and functionalities of the specified API version, regardless of any new changes or deprecations in the latest MongoDB server versions.

Currently, API version 1 is the only supported version. Table 4.7 lists the commands you can use with this version.

Table 4.7 Commands available with Stable API

Command	Stable API version	Added to Stable API version(s)
abortTransaction	1	MongoDB 5.0
Aggregate (with limits)	1	MongoDB 5.0
authenticate	1	MongoDB 5.0
collMod	1	MongoDB 5.0
commitTransaction	1	MongoDB 5.0
count	1	MongoDB 6.0, 5.0.9
create (with limits)	1	MongoDB 5.0
createIndexes (with limits)	1	MongoDB 5.0
delete	1	MongoDB 5.0
drop	1	MongoDB 5.0
dropDatabase	1	MongoDB 5.0
dropIndexes	1	MongoDB 5.0
endSessions	1	MongoDB 5.0
explain	1	MongoDB 5.0
find (with limits)	1	MongoDB 5.0
findAndModify	1	MongoDB 5.0
getMore	1	MongoDB 5.0
hello	1	MongoDB 5.0
insert	1	MongoDB 5.0

Table 4.7 Commands available with Stable API (*continued*)

Command	Stable API version	Added to Stable API version(s)
`killCursors`	1	MongoDB 5.0
`listCollections`	1	MongoDB 5.0
`listDatabases`	1	MongoDB 5.0
`listIndexes`	1	MongoDB 5.0
`ping`	1	MongoDB 5.0
`refreshSessions`	1	MongoDB 5.0
`update`	1	MongoDB 5.0

Summary

- `insertOne` and `insertMany` enable you to add new documents to MongoDB databases.
- Read operations include advanced query capabilities, allowing for effective data retrieval through the use of the `find()` method, which supports detailed query filters and options to precisely define the documents to be retrieved.
- Update operations include the `updateOne` and `updateMany` commands, offering precise adjustments to existing documents. You can use operators such as `$set`, `$inc`, `$push`, and `$unset`, which allow specific modifications to document fields, ranging from updating existing values to adding elements to arrays.
- Remove operations use the `deleteOne` and `deleteMany` methods, focusing on the secure removal of documents while preserving database integrity.
- Arrays use operators like `$push`, `$pop`, `$addToSet`, and `$pull` to efficiently structure and modify array data within documents. This functionality is crucial for dynamic data handling and organization in MongoDB.
- Starting in MongoDB 8.0, the `bulkWrite` command enables multiple insert, update, and delete operations across several collections in a single request, unlike the `db.collection.bulkWrite()` method, which modifies only one collection per request.
- Cursors in MongoDB streamline the process of navigating large data sets, enabling efficient data retrieval by accessing documents one at a time.
- The Stable API feature in MongoDB ensures compatibility across server versions and consistent API behavior.

Designing a MongoDB schema

This chapter covers

- Exploring MongoDB's flexible schema capabilities
- Understanding principles of effective schema design
- Applying schema design patterns
- Implementing schema validation techniques
- Recognizing schema design antipatterns

In database management, MongoDB stands out due to its flexible schema nature, offering a flexible, dynamic approach to data organization. Unlike traditional relational databases, which require a predefined schema to structure data, MongoDB allows documents within a collection to have different fields and data types. This flexible schema not only handles evolving requirements smoothly but also easily accommodates structured, unstructured, and semistructured data, as each document inherently carries its own schema.

The absence of an explicit schema does not eliminate the need for thoughtful data modeling. Designing an effective MongoDB schema is crucial for optimizing the performance, scalability, and maintainability of applications. Proper schema design involves understanding the relationships between data entities, considering query patterns that efficiently support applications, and anticipating how data will evolve. By carefully modeling a schema in MongoDB, you can ensure efficient data retrieval and use the full potential of the database's capabilities, ultimately leading to robust, scalable, and efficient applications.

5.1 Organizing the MongoDB data model

MongoDB is built to let you adjust your schema on the fly without downtime, making it highly adaptable as your data needs evolve. I still advise you to design your data model before deploying at production scale, however, to ensure that your data remains well organized and performs efficiently. This involves four key steps:

1. Determine the workload of your application.
2. Map the relationships among objects in your collections.
3. Implement design patterns.
4. Create indexes to optimize query performance. (Chapter 7 describes indexes.)

Suppose that you are designing a schema for an airline route management system, which is needed for managing and querying flight route data. This application supports various operations, such as adding new routes, searching existing flight routes, updating details of specific routes, and retrieving comprehensive information about specific routes. Understanding these operations will help you tailor the database schema to meet the system's needs effectively.

5.1.1 Determining the workload of the application

The initial step in the proposed schema design process is comprehending the workload your application will handle, focusing on the most common operations it performs. This understanding enables you to tailor your schema to support these operations efficiently by using multiple performance optimization strategies—such as optimizing index use, applying proven schema design patterns, avoiding common antipatterns, and refining queries—to reduce unnecessary database calls. When considering your application's workload, account for both current functionalities and potential expansions.

Construct a table listing the essential queries your application must execute, considering the following aspects:

- *Action*—The user action that triggers the query
- *Query type*—Whether the query is a read or write operation
- *Information*—The document fields involved in the query
- *Frequency*—How often the query is executed
- *Priority*—The criticality of the query to the application's functionality

Table 5.1 presents an example workload for an airline route management system. It details the user actions that trigger these queries, the type of operation (read or write), the specific fields involved, their frequency of execution, and their priority.

Table 5.1 The workload necessary for an application

Action	Type	Information	Frequency	Priority
Add new route.	Write	`flight_id`, `airline(id, name, alias, iata)`, `src_airport`, `dst_airport`, `airplane`, `stops`, `codeshare`	150 per day	High
Search flight routes.	Read	`src_airport`, `dst_airport`	22,000 per day	High
Update route details.	Write	`flight_id`, `src_airport`, `dst_airport`, `airline(name, alias, iata)`	100 per day	Medium
Check route information.	Read	`src_airport`, `dst_airport`, `airplane`, `stops`	40,000 per day	High

> **Differentiating between relational and document databases**
>
> When designing a schema for a document database like MongoDB, it's important to understand the differences compared to traditional relational databases. With MongoDB, you have the freedom to add and change the data structure on the fly, which can make it easier to develop and scale your application because you're not locked into an initial design:
>
> - *Relational databases:*
>   - You must define the schema of the table before inserting data.
>   - Data from multiple tables often needs to be joined to meet the requirements of your application.
>   - Updating the schema if necessary can be a painful process, involving potential downtime and complex migrations.
> - *Document databases:*
>   - The schema can evolve as your application's needs change.
>   - The flexible data model lets you store data in a way that matches the way your application accesses it, reducing the need for joins. This approach improves performance and reduces the strain on your system.

It's also important to emphasize that in NoSQL databases like MongoDB, the data model should be designed based on how the data will be displayed and accessed rather than on how it is logically connected. This shift changes the design paradigm and pattern, focusing more on performance and ease of access than adherence to strict relational structures.

5.1.2 Mapping the schema relationship

In the airline route management system, you need to determine the best ways to organize and access data related to airlines, airports, and flights. Begin understanding the frequent queries and operations your application manages.

When mapping relations between data entities, three primary types of relationships are generally used to structure data:

- *One-to-one relationships*—This relationship can exist within a single document or between two documents, with each document or subdocument corresponding uniquely.
- *One-to-many relationships*—In this setup, a single document or a specific field within a document (such as an embedded array) can relate to multiple other documents or subdocuments. This is common in hierarchical data structures when one parent document contains multiple child documents or entries.
- *Many-to-many relationships*—You can model this relationship by using arrays of references in each related document, allowing multiple documents to be associated with multiple other documents. This relationship often requires more complex querying and indexing strategies.

In MongoDB, the preferred strategy for managing related data is embedding it in a subdocument. Embedding allows your application to retrieve necessary information through a single read operation, thus avoiding unnecessary $lookup operations (described in chapter 6). In some cases, however, using a reference to link to related data in a different collection may be more appropriate. Follow the steps in the following sections to map schema relationships accurately within your database.

IDENTIFYING RELATED DATA IN YOUR SCHEMA

Begin by analyzing how data elements interact. Examine the relationships between airlines and their routes, as well as the connections between airports and routes. This foundational understanding will guide the structuring of your database schema:

- *Airline-to-routes relationship*—One-to-many. Each airline operates multiple routes, establishing a clear one-to-many relationship.
- *Airports-to-routes relationship*—Many-to-many. Airports serve as both departure and arrival points for various routes, creating a many-to-many relationship.

CHOOSING WHETHER TO EMBED RELATED DATA OR USE REFERENCES

To determine the best data structuring method for your airline route management system, consider the specific scenarios for which embedding or referencing is more beneficial. Embedding stores related data within a single document, which can improve read performance by retrieving all necessary information in one go when that data is frequently accessed together. By contrast, referencing links related data stored in separate documents through identifiers, reducing duplication and supporting data consistency, though it may require additional queries to fetch all related details:

- *Embedding*— Airline information can be embedded in route documents when one airline operates many routes. Embedding airline information in each route document is advantageous for read performance, as it eliminates the need for joins when you're querying routes by airline details. For airlines within routes, because airline data (such as name and alias) is typically small and frequently accessed with route information, embedding this data directly in route documents can reduce read operations.
- *References*—Each airport serves as the departure and arrival point for multiple routes, creating a many-to-many relationship. Handling this relationship using references is effective due to the complex interconnections between airports and multiple routes. Using references is advantageous, especially given that airport data, such as facilities and services, can be extensive and infrequently modified. Also, referencing provides an advantage: detailed airport information may not be frequently accessed and can be cached if necessary, enhancing performance and efficiency.

CREATING SAMPLE DOCUMENTS IN COLLECTIONS

Create sample documents as follows:

- For the `routes` collection, embed `airline` information directly within each document. This method improves performance by reducing the queries needed to retrieve connected data. Although this approach leads to data duplication, it is manageable because airline information rarely changes, and the additional storage required is not a significant concern. Here's an example of a document in the `routes` collection:

```
{
  "_id": ObjectId("56e9b39b732b6122f877facc"),
  "flight_id": "FL123",
  "airline": {
    "id": 410,
    "name": "Delta Airlines",
    "alias": "2B",
    "iata": "ARD"
            },
  "src_airport": "JFK",
  "dst_airport": "LAX",
  "codeshare": "",
  "stops": 0,
  "airplane": "ATP"
}
```

- For `airports`, use a separate collection to avoid data duplication and simplify updates to airport information. This separation ensures that changes to airport details do not affect the routes. Here's an example document for the `airports` collection:

```
{
    "_id": "JFK",
    "name": "JFK International Airport",
    "location": {
       "city": "New York",
       "country": "USA"
    },
    "facilities": ["Wi-Fi", "Lounge", "VIP Services"]
}
```

This structure organizes the `routes` collection to provide details for most route-related queries while maintaining detailed airport information in a separate `airports` collection. This approach ensures that the data management strategy is efficient and adheres to best practices for schema design.

5.1.3 Applying a design pattern

Schema design patterns are structured approaches to refining your data model based on your application's specific access patterns. These designs enhance performance and simplify the schema by optimizing the storage and retrieval of data.

Before applying schema design patterns, you must identify the primary challenges your schema faces, such as write performance, read performance, or data duplication. Understanding these challenges helps you select the most beneficial pattern. The design patterns for an airline route management system are

- *Subset*—Instead of embedding or referencing the full airport document, each route in the `routes` collection can store a small subset of key airport information—such as the name and location—that is most frequently accessed. This pattern is useful when only a portion of the data is frequently accessed. Applying this pattern can minimize the sizes of the documents retrieved, enhancing read performance.

  It's important to realize that this pattern introduces a toll on updates. You may have to update the `routes` collection if there are updates to the `airport` collection, which can increase maintenance efforts:

```
{
    "_id": ObjectId("56e9b39b732b6122f877fa35"),
    "flight_id": "FL123",
    "airline": {
       "id": 410,
       "name": "Delta Airlines",
       "alias": "2B",
       "iata": "ARD"
    },
    "src_airport": {
       "code": "JFK",
       "name": "JFK International Airport"
    },
    "dst_airport": {
```

```
            "code": "LAX",
            "name": "Los Angeles International Airport"
        },
        "airplane": "CR2",
        "stops": 0
    }
```

- *Computed*—Use computed fields in the `airports` collection to reduce CPU use by precomputing values at write time. This prevents costly calculations at read time, optimizing query performance and sparing CPU resources. You can include a field like `total_flights`, which is computed to reflect the total number of flights associated with each airport. This approach helps centralize important metrics at the airport level, facilitating more efficient data management and retrieval. It is particularly valuable in scenarios in which data requires frequent aggregation or calculations, enhancing the application's performance and responsiveness:

```
{
    "_id": "JFK",
    "name": "JFK International Airport",
    "location": {
        "city": "New York",
        "country": "USA"
    },
    "facilities": ["Wi-Fi", "Lounge", "VIP Services"],
    "total_flights": 3500    // Computed field representing the
 total number of flights from/to this airport
}
```

By applying these schema design patterns effectively, you can ensure that your flight data management system achieves enhanced performance and reduced complexity, providing scalable, efficient, and high-performing operations as your data and user base grow.

5.2 Embedding vs. referencing

In MongoDB, you have the option to embed related data within a single document or structure. These schemas are typically referred to as *denormalized* models, which use the capabilities of MongoDB's rich document format. Figure 5.1 shows an example of embedding.

Embedded data models enable applications to store related data in the same document structure. Consequently, applications might perform fewer queries and updates to carry out routine operations. Consider using embedded data models in the following cases:

- Entities have a "contains" relationship, such as a contacts document that includes an address.
- Entities have a one-to-many relationship in which the many (child) documents are consistently accessed or displayed within the context of the one (parent) document.

```
{
    _id: <ObjectId1>,
    username: "123xyz",
    contact: {
            phone: "123-456-7890",         ⎤ Embedded
            email: "xyz@example.com"       ⎦ subdocument
    },
    access: {
            level: 5,                       ⎤ Embedded
            group: "dev"                    ⎦ subdocument
    }
{
```

Figure 5.1 A MongoDB document with embedded subdocuments for contact information and access details (Image © MongoDB 2024 CC BY-NC-SA 3.0)

Generally, embedding enhances the performance of read operations by allowing the retrieval of related data in a single database operation. Embedded data models also enable the updating of related data through a single atomic write operation.

> **NOTE** Embedding large documents or multiple documents may result in bloated documents with loads of information that is unlikely to be accessed together, which may end up exceeding the max Binary JSON (BSON) size. In MongoDB, documents must be smaller than the maximum BSON document size, which is 16 MB.

In certain situations, it is advisable to store related information in separate documents, usually in different collections or databases. Generally, opt for normalized data models in the following scenarios:

- The reference entity is frequently accessed on its own.
- Embedding could lead to data duplication without offering significant read-performance benefits that justify the duplication.
- You need to represent complex many-to-many relationships accurately.

Figure 5.2 illustrates the use of MongoDB's `ObjectId()` to reference documents in two collections.

To join collections, MongoDB offers the following aggregation stages, providing sophisticated methods for integrating data across collections:

- `$lookup`—This stage performs a left outer join to another collection in the same database, allowing you to combine documents based on a join condition similar to relational databases.
- `$graphLookup`—Introduced for complex aggregations, this stage facilitates recursive lookups, enabling the exploration of relationships within data sets that have a hierarchical or graphlike structure.

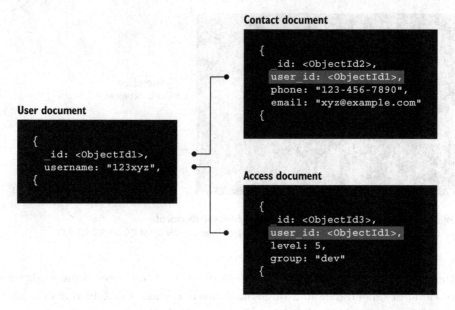

Figure 5.2 MongoDB can reference documents between collections. (Image © MongoDB 2024 CC BY-NC-SA 3.0)

MongoDB applications can relate documents using either of two methods, which cater to different data management needs:

- *Manual references*—This method involves storing the `_id` field of one document in another document as a reference. The application must execute a second query to fetch the related data. This approach is simple and effective for many scenarios.
- `DBRefs`—These references link one document to another using the `_id` field of the first document, the collection name, and optionally, the database name, among other fields. `DBRefs` are particularly useful for referencing documents spread across multiple collections or databases. Resolving `DBRefs` requires using additional queries to retrieve the linked documents, ensuring data consistency across complex structures.

Consider an example with two collections: `routes` and `airports`. Each route document may include a reference to an airport document using a `DBRef` to dynamically represent either the source or the destination airport:

```
{
  "_id": ObjectId("56e9b39b732b6122f877fa35"),
  "flight_id": "FL123",
  "src_airport": {
    "$ref": "airports",
    "$id": "JFK",
    "$db": "airportData",
```

```
        "YourExtraField" : "Can be anything"
    },
    "airline": "Delta Airlines",
    "airplane": "Boeing 737",
    "stops": 0
}
```

`DBRefs` can contain additional fields beyond the required ones. The order of fields in the `DBRef` matters, and you must use the preceding sequence when using a `DBRef`.

5.3 Understanding schema design patterns

Every schema design pattern comes with its own set of use cases and tradeoffs in terms of data consistency, performance, and complexity. Certain schema design patterns are geared toward enhancing write performance, for example, whereas others are optimized for better read performance. Figure 5.3 shows various schema design patterns for different applications.

	Catalog	Content management	Internet of Things	Mobile	Personalization	Real-time analytics	Single view
Approximation	✓		✓	✓		✓	
Attribute	✓	✓					✓
Bucket			✓			✓	
Computed	✓		✓	✓	✓	✓	✓
Document versioning	✓	✓			✓		✓
Extended reference	✓			✓		✓	
Outlier			✓	✓	✓		
Polymorphic	✓	✓		✓			✓
Preallocated			✓			✓	
Schema versioning	✓	✓	✓	✓	✓	✓	✓
Subset	✓	✓		✓	✓		
Tree and graph	✓	✓					

Figure 5.3 The suitability of different schema design patterns for various use-case categories. The right pattern balances data consistency, performance, and complexity. (Image © MongoDB 2024 CC BY-NC-SA 3.0)

The set of rules dictating the exclusive design pattern for any particular application type is flexible. Focus on patterns commonly associated with your specific use case, but don't disregard alternative ones that might be relevant. Tailor your application's data schema to fit your unique data access patterns. Next, we'll examine the schema design patterns shown in figure 5.3.

5.3.1 Approximation pattern

The Approximation pattern is particularly valuable when data changes frequently and precise calculations are not required. Estimating values instead of computing them exactly each time can improve efficiency and reduce write-intensive operations. A common example is tracking page views on a website. Instead of updating the view count in the database with every page load, which can be highly write-intensive, the application can estimate this number using techniques such as sampling. Because precise tracking of every single view is not always necessary, updates can be aggregated and written to the database at fixed intervals, such as every X minutes or hours, significantly reducing the write workload by replacing thousands of updates with a much smaller number of batched writes. This method reduces the strain on database resources by lessening the frequency of write operations, making it ideal for high-traffic environments in which exact counts are less critical than overall trends. The following document illustrates how estimated values can be stored to reduce the frequency of database writes when tracking page views:

```
{
  "page_id": "12345",
  "estimated_views": 1500,
  "sampling_rate": 0.05,
  "last_updated": "2024-04-20T12:00:00Z"
  // This document estimates page views to reduce database writes.
}
```

Advantages of the Approximation pattern are

- Reduces databases write operations
- Maintains statistically valid figures

Disadvantages of the Approximation pattern are

- Does not represent precise numbers
- Requires applications to implement the pattern

5.3.2 Archive pattern

The Archive pattern is useful for managing large volumes of data; it separates active data from historical data that does not need to be accessed frequently, improving the performance and manageability of the database by reducing the size of the collection. The pattern involves moving older data to a separate collection or an external storage solution. One of the most common approaches is archiving documents to blob storage like Amazon S3, which is cheap. This reduces the load on the primary collection, decreases index sizes, and improves query performance by ensuring that frequently accessed data remains efficiently searchable. Consider an application that logs user activities:

```
{
  "log_id": "abc123",
  "user_id": "98765",
  "activity": "login",
  "timestamp": ISODate("2024-05-12T10:00:00Z"),
  "status": "active"
}
```

The `logs` collection records all activities, but over time, old logs can be archived to keep the active collection performant. Typically, only logs from the past 30 to 90 days are actively used for troubleshooting, auditing, or compliance purposes. Logs older than this period become less relevant and can be moved to an archive to reduce the size of the active collection.

Advantages of the Archive pattern are

- Active collections remain small and performant by offloading older data.
- Archived data can be stored in less expensive storage solutions, reducing overall costs.
- Index sizes are reduced.

TIP MongoDB Atlas Online Archive can be useful for implementing the Archive pattern, helping you manage infrequently accessed data by moving it to a more cost-effective storage solution automatically while maintaining access for queries when necessary. Read more about Online Archive in chapter 17.

5.3.3 Attribute pattern

The Attribute pattern is useful when you are handling documents that have many similar fields and a subset of fields is rare, appearing in only a few documents (such as specific products on an e-commerce site). To sort or query these specific fields efficiently, use indexing (chapter 7). This involves creating an array of objects, each of which contains two attributes—a key and a value—enabling the construction of efficient indices for these unique fields.

Let's see how the document structure looks before we apply the Attribute pattern. Rare attributes are stored as separate fields, leading to a schema with many `null` values for attributes that are not relevant to most products:

```
{
  "product_id": "98765",
  "name": "Laptop",
  "price": 1200,
  "in_stock": true,
  "special_offer": "10% off",
```

```
    "warranty_years": 3,
    "processor_generation": null,
    "custom_rgb_lighting": null,
    "touchscreen_support": null,
    "military_grade_certification": null
}
```

When you apply the Attribute pattern, rare attributes are stored as an array of key–value objects, making the document structure more flexible and reducing the need for multiple indexes. This approach helps you manage attributes that appear infrequently across documents without inflating the schema:

```
{
    "product_id": "98765",
    "common_attributes": {
      "name": "Laptop",
      "price": 1200,
      "in_stock": true
    },
    "rare_attributes": [
      {"key": "special_offer", "value": "10% off"},
      {"key": "warranty_years", "value": 3},
      {"key": "processor_generation", "value": "13th Gen"},
      {"key": "custom_rgb_lighting", "value": true},
      {"key": "touchscreen_support", "value": false},
      {"key": "military_grade_certification", "value": "MIL-STD-810G"}
    ]
}
```

Advantages of the Attribute pattern are

- A reduced number of required indexes
- Simplified query writing and generally faster query execution

5.3.4 Bucket pattern

The Bucket pattern is effective for managing streams of documents that generate large volumes of time-series or event-driven data, such as sensor readings. Before you apply the Bucket pattern, store each sensor reading as an individual document, leading to many small documents. The structure might look like this:

```
{
    "sensor_id": "abc123",
    "timestamp": ISODate("2024-04-20T08:00:00Z"),
    "value": 22.5
}
{
    "sensor_id": "abc123",
    "timestamp": ISODate("2024-04-20T08:05:00Z"),
    "value": 22.7
}
```

```
{
  "sensor_id": "abc123",
  "timestamp": ISODate("2024-04-20T08:10:00Z"),
  "value": 22.9
}
```

To manage this structure, you can segment data based on a specific value, such as a day, creating buckets of data. In the case of sensor readings, you might create one document for every 100 readings or one document per day, storing all relevant data within these documents:

```
{
  "sensor_id": "abc123",
  "date": "2024-04-20",
  "readings": [
    {"time": "08:00", "value": 22.5},
    {"time": "08:05", "value": 22.7},
    {"time": "08:10", "value": 22.9}
  ]
  // Grouping sensor readings by day to manage large data volumes.
}
```

Advantages of the Bucket pattern are

- Decreases the total count of documents within a collection
- Enhances the performance of indexes
- Facilitates easier access to data by using preaggregation

TIP Time-series collections automatically implement the Bucket pattern, making them suitable for most applications that require time-series data to be organized in buckets.

5.3.5 Computed pattern

If reads occur more frequently than writes, it's efficient to precompute certain data. In an online store, for example, each product might have user ratings. Instead of calculating the average rating each time a product page is accessed, you could compute the average when new ratings are submitted and stored with the product details. This way, the stored average is displayed quickly, enhancing performance, especially when product views significantly outnumber rating updates. Ratings can be updated individually as they come in or in batches if slight delays are acceptable:

```
{
  "product_id": "321",
  "product_name": "Wireless Headphones",
  "ratings": [
    5, 4, 5, 3, 4
  ],
  "average_rating": 4.2,
```

```
    // Average rating is pre-computed whenever new ratings are added.
}
```

Advantages of the Computed pattern are

- Decreases CPU use by reducing the need for repeated calculations
- Simplifies query writing and generally speeds query execution

5.3.6 Document Versioning pattern

To manage the retention of past document versions in MongoDB, the Document Versioning pattern is a functional approach. Use this pattern when you need to maintain historical versions of documents for purposes such as auditing, rollback, or analysis. It involves storing each update as a separate document version, enabling full history tracking without altering the original data:

```
{
  "document_id": "456",
  "version": 3,
  "content": "Latest content here.",
  "previous_versions": [
    {
      "version": 2,
      "content": "Older content here.",
      "date_modified": "2023-12-01"
    },
    {
      "version": 1,
      "content": "Original content here.",
      "date_modified": "2023-11-01"
    }
  ],
  // Each document update is stored as a new version,
  maintaining a history of changes.
}
```

Advantages of the Document Versioning pattern are

- Simple to integrate
- Applicable to new and existing systems
- Performance-effective queries for the latest document version

Disadvantages of the Document Versioning pattern are

- Requires twice as many write operations

5.3.7 Extended Reference pattern

The Extended Reference pattern avoids repetitive joins by embedding key data from the referenced collection, such as user data (names, email addresses, roles, and so on), directly in posts to reduce database load. This method is effective if such data seldom changes.

It's important to consider how often duplicated data updates and whether embedding provides sufficient details for front-end display without joins. You can make updates to duplicated data during the update query or later, in batches:

```
{
  "post_id": "789",
  "content": "Check out these new features!",
  "user": {
    "user_id": "555",
    "name": "Alex",
    "email": "alex@example.com,
    "role": "admin"
  },
  // User details are embedded in the post to avoid joins and
  improve read performance.
  "timestamp": "2024-04-20T15:00:00Z"
}
```

Advantages of the Extended Reference pattern are

- Improved performance when a lot of JOIN operations occur
- Faster reads and fewer overall JOINs

Disadvantages of the Extended Reference pattern are

- Data duplication

5.3.8 Outlier pattern

The Outlier pattern manages documents that significantly differ from the norm, ensuring that they do not hinder the performance of standard queries. If a document in a collection contains a far larger array than is typical, for example, you might choose to store it in a separate collection or apply specific indexing strategies to it.

This approach prevents such documents from affecting query performance on the rest of the documents, maintaining system responsiveness and efficiency. Consider a sensor data schema where documents typically contain a small array of readings:

```
{
  "sensor_id": "xyz987",
  "readings": [
    {"time": "09:00", "value": 19.5},
    {"time": "09:05", "value": 19.7}
  ],
  "date": "2024-04-20"
}
```

Occasionally, a sensor might generate a significantly larger number of readings, creating a performance bottleneck. In such cases, you could identify a threshold for an outlier document (such as a document containing more than 1,000 readings) and store any readings beyond this threshold separately. To indicate additional data storage, you can include a Boolean field:

```
{
  "sensor_id": "xyz987",
  "readings": [
    {"time": "09:00", "value": 19.5},
    {"time": "09:05", "value": 19.7}
    // up to threshold
  ],
  "has_extra_readings": true,
  "date": "2024-04-20"
}
```

The additional readings are stored in a separate collection, clearly linked to the original document:

```
{
  "sensor_id": "xyz987",
  "date": "2024-04-20",
  "extra_readings": [
    {"time": "09:10", "value": 20.1}
    // additional readings...
  ]
}
```

This approach prevents large volumes of sensor readings from affecting query performance on the rest of the documents, maintaining system responsiveness and efficiency.

Advantages of the Outlier pattern are

- Prevents a few documents or queries from determining an application's solution
- Focuses on typical use cases while accommodating exceptional scenarios

Disadvantages of the Outlier pattern are

- Typically optimized for specific queries, which may result in poor performance for ad hoc queries
- Relies heavily on application code for implementation

5.3.9 *Polymorphic pattern*

The Polymorphic pattern in MongoDB allows you to store documents with similar but not identical structures in the same collection, improving query efficiency and reducing the need for separate collections for each data type. In a sports-tracking application, for example, you can store documents for different types of athletes—such as tennis players and soccer players—in a single collection. Each document type might have different attributes specific to the sport, but common attributes such as name and age are maintained. This approach eliminates complex joins and makes querying across different sports straightforward, as all athlete documents are in one place. Then queries can differentiate based on a `type` field or other sport-specific attributes contained within each document, as in this example:

```
{
  "athlete_id": "78910",
  "type": "tennis_player",
  "name": "Alice Smith",
  "age": 25,
  "tennis_specific": {
    "ranking": 15,
    "hand": "right"
  }
  // Tennis specific attributes are stored along with common attributes.
}
{
  "athlete_id": "78911",
  "type": "soccer_player",
  "name": "Bob Johnson",
  "age": 22,
  "soccer_specific": {
    "position": "forward",
    "goals_scored": 30
  }
  // Soccer specific attributes are stored along with common attributes.
}
```

Advantages of the Polymorphic pattern are

- Queries can be executed within a single collection.
- The pattern is easy to implement.

5.3.10 Preallocation pattern

The Preallocation pattern is useful when you already know how your documents will be structured, but you'll be filling in the details later. An example application is a yearly planner for a classroom. At the beginning of the academic year, you can create a document for each student, with sections for each month and placeholders for assignment grades and attendance records. As the year progresses and assignments are graded, you fill in the predetermined sections with the specific details. Initially, your document structure could look like this:

```
{
  "student_id": "12345",
  "name": "John Doe",
  "academic_year": "2024",
  "monthly_records": {
    "January": {"attendance": [], "grades": []},
    "February": {"attendance": [], "grades": []},
    // Other months follow the same structure.
  }
```

```
    // Structure is pre-allocated, details to be filled
    in as the year progresses.
}
```

As data becomes available, you incrementally update the preallocated fields:

```
{
  "student_id": "12345",
  "name": "John Doe",
  "academic_year": "2024",
  "monthly_records": {
    "January": {
      "attendance": ["2024-01-03", "2024-01-10", "2024-01-17", "2024-01-24"],
      "grades": [90, 85, 88, 92]
    },
    "February": {
      "attendance": ["2024-02-07", "2024-02-14", "2024-02-21"],
      "grades": [88, 91, 87]
    }
    // Additional months filled in similarly.
  }
}
```

This approach streamlines data management by clearly defining the structure in advance and simplifying subsequent updates.

Advantages of the Preallocation pattern include

- Design simplification when the document structure is known in advance

Disadvantages of the Preallocation pattern include

- Simplicity versus performance

5.3.11 Schema Versioning pattern

The Schema Versioning pattern uses a `schema_version` field in documents to manage different schema versions within the same collection. This field tracks the schema version to which each document conforms, starting with version 1 for documents that lack this field.

Subsequent schema changes increment this version number. Application logic reads the `schema_version` to handle documents appropriately based on their version, allowing previous and current versions of documents to coexist in the same collection. This setup streamlines managing schema updates and maintaining data consistency over time. The pattern allows previous and current versions of documents to exist side by side in a collection:

```
{
  "document_id": "456789",
  "schema_version": 2,
  "name": "Product XYZ",
```

```
  "price": 199.99,
  "new_feature": "Improved battery life",
  // The schema_version field indicates the version of
  the schema this document follows.
}
```

As the schema evolves further, newer documents may include additional fields, and their schema_version would reflect these updates:

```
{
  "document_id": "789012",
  "schema_version": 3,
  "product_details": {
    "name": "Product XYZ Pro",
    "price": 249.99,
    "features": ["Improved battery life", "Wireless charging",
    "OLED display"],
    "availability": {
      "status": "In stock",
      "quantity": 150
    }
  },
  "warranty_period_years": 2,
  "release_date": "2024-05-01"
  // schema_version indicates the document adheres to the
  latest schema with expanded details.
}
```

Advantages of the Schema Versioning pattern are

- No downtime is needed during schema migration.
- Future technical debt is reduced.

Disadvantages of the Schema Versioning pattern include

- Two indexes might be needed for the same field during migration.

5.3.12 *Subset pattern*

The Subset pattern optimizes the size of the working set by storing only the most frequently accessed data directly in the main document and less frequently accessed data in separate documents. This method reduces the load on the database during common queries.

In a social network application, for example, you might store only a user's most recent posts directly in their main user profile document. Older posts could be stored in a separate document or collection. This ensures that the user profile loads quickly, as it contains only the most relevant and recent data. The link between the user's profile and their older posts is maintained, allowing for easy access when necessary. Here's an example:

```
{
  "user_id": "112233",
  "name": "Emily White",
  "recent_posts": [
    {"post_id": "p100", "content": "Exciting news today!",
 "date": "2024-04-18"},
    {"post_id": "p101", "content": "Loved the weather!",
 "date": "2024-04-17"}
  ],
  "older_posts_link": "posts_archive/112233",
  // Only recent posts are stored in the main document,
 older posts are referenced.
}
```

Advantages of the Subset pattern are

- The overall size of the working set is reduced.
- Disk access time for the most frequently used data is shorter.

Disadvantages of the Subset pattern are

- You are required to manage the subset.
- Pulling in additional data requires additional trips to the database.

5.3.13 Tree pattern

The Tree pattern in MongoDB represents hierarchical relationships within a single document. This approach is particularly useful for data structures (such as organizational charts) in which relationships are defined hierarchically.

Before you use the Tree pattern, hierarchical relationships often require references or joins between multiple documents, making queries more complex and less efficient. An employee document before you apply the Tree pattern might store references to other employee documents separately:

```
{
  "employee_id": "2001",
  "name": "Alice Johnson",
  "position": "Regional Manager",
  "reports_to_id": "1001",
  "direct_reports_ids": ["2002", "2003"]
  // References require joining multiple documents
to resolve relationships.
}
```

When you use the Tree pattern, hierarchical relationships are encapsulated within a single document, eliminating the need for joins. A document for an employee might include a field named `reports_to`, which is an array containing the names or IDs of the people to whom they report:

```
{
  "employee_id": "2001",
```

```
    "name": "Alice Johnson",
    "position": "Regional Manager",
    "reports_to": [
      {
        "employee_id": "1001",
        "name": "Sarah Gold"
      }
    ],
    "direct_reports": [
      {
        "employee_id": "2002",
        "name": "Bob Smith"
      },
      {
        "employee_id": "2003",
        "name": "Linda White"
      }
    ]
    // Hierarchical relationships are encapsulated within the document.
}
```

This pattern simplifies the data model and enhances query performance by keeping all related information in a single document.

Advantages of the Tree pattern include

- Avoiding multiple JOIN operations increases performance.

Disadvantages of the Tree pattern include

- Updates to the graph need to be managed in the application.

> **TIP** If you'd like to learn more about MongoDB data modeling, visit MongoDB University, and take the Schema Design Patterns course at https://mng.bz/5vQ1, explore the official documentation at https://mng.bz/64XD, or read the blog post at https://mng.bz/oZ2r.

5.4 Schema validations

To prevent unintended schema changes, you can create schema validation rules. In MongoDB, the schema is flexible, allowing documents within a collection to vary in terms of fields and data types. After you set up a schema for your application, you can implement schema validation to prevent unexpected schema modifications and incorrect data types.

Schema validation is extremely useful for established applications with well-defined data structures. Here are some specific examples:

- For a users collection, make sure that the password field is stored exclusively as a string. This validation prevents the possibility that passwords will be saved in an unexpected format, such as an image.

- For a `flight routes` collection, validate that the `flight_id` follows a specific format (such as `"FL"` followed by numbers), ensure that `airline.id` is a positive integer, and confirm that airport codes in `src_airport.code` and `dst_airport.code` are valid and correspond to actual airports.

- For an `airport` collection, ensure that the `total_flights` field is maintained as an integer. This validation is important for accurately representing the total number of flights operating from or arriving at the airport.

5.4.1 Specifying JSON schema validation

The JSON schema is a standard format for defining the structure, data types, and constraints of JSON documents. It ensures data consistency and validity by enforcing rules on the fields stored in a collection.

Let's look at how to perform schema validation for documents in a `routes` collection. You can specify a collections schema validation using the `validator` object during the creation of a collection using the `db.createCollection()` method, as well as to an existing collection using the `collMod` command.

To modify an existing `routes` collection to include schema validation, use the `collMod` command. Listing 5.1 shows how you can structure this command to implement the validation rules. To execute this command, permissions such as `dbAdmin` on the `sample_training` database or `dbAdminAnyDatabase` need to be appended to the user's role. MongoDB roles are discussed in chapter 20.

Listing 5.1 Example schema validator

```
db.runCommand({
   collMod: "routes",
   validator: {
      $jsonSchema: {
         bsonType: "object",
         required: [
"flight_id",
            "airline",
 "src_airport",
 "dst_airport"
],
         properties: {
            flight_id: {
               bsonType: "string",
               pattern: "^FL\\d+$",
               description: "must be a string starting
with 'FL' followed by numbers"
            },
            airline: {
               bsonType: "object",
               properties: {
                  id: {
                     bsonType: "int",
                     minimum: 1,
```

```
                    description: "must be a positive integer"
                }
            }
        },
        src_airport: {
            bsonType: "object",
            properties: {
                code: {
                    bsonType: "string",
                    description: "must be a valid airport code"
                }
            }
        },
        dst_airport: {
            bsonType: "object",
            properties: {
                code: {
                    bsonType: "string",
                    description: "must be a valid airport code"
                }
            }
        }
    }
  },
  validationLevel: "moderate",
  validationAction: "error"
})
```

The `$jsonSchema` operator matches documents that satisfy the specified JSON schema. The validation rule dictates that documents must include specific fields such as `flight_id`, `airline`, `src_airport`, and `dst_airport`, with detailed conditions for each.

The `validationLevel` set to `moderate` means that this validation applies to new documents and to updates on existing documents that already comply with the validation rules. Existing documents that do not match the rules, however, are not required to pass validation unless they are modified. This approach allows for the gradual enforcement of schema rules without disrupting existing data that may not comply.

The `validationAction` set to `error` means that MongoDB will reject any insert or update operation that does not meet the defined validation rules. If a document fails validation, the operation is not executed, and an error is returned.

5.4.2 Testing a schema validation rule

Let's attempt to add an invalid document to the `routes` collection, to which we recently added schema validation rules. The following `insertOne()` method tries to insert an incorrect document into the collection:

```
db.routes.insertOne({
    flight_id: "XYZ123", // flight_id should start with "FL"
    airline: {
        id: -410, // airline.id must be a positive integer
```

```
      name: "Delta Airlines",
      alias: "2B",
      iata: "ARD"
   },
   src_airport: {
      code: "JFK",
      name: "JFK International Airport"
   },
   dst_airport: {
      code: "999", // dst_airport.code must be a valid code
      name: "Unknown Airport"
   },
      airplane: "CR2",
      stops: 0
})
```

MongoDB rejected the document due to validation failures, returning the following error:

```
{
   "MongoServerError": "Document failed validation",
   "Additional information": {
     "failingDocumentId": "ObjectId('6624dbc6cf6203ef2a1db280')",
     "details": {
       "operatorName": "$jsonSchema",
       "schemaRulesNotSatisfied": [
          {
            "operatorName": "properties",
            "propertiesNotSatisfied": [
              {
                "propertyName": "flight_id",
                "description": "must be a string starting
 with 'FL' followed by numbers",
                "details": [
                   {
                     "operatorName": "pattern",
                     "specifiedAs": {
                        "pattern": "^FL\\d+$"
                     },
                     "reason": "regular expression did not match",
                     "consideredValue": "XYZ123"
                   }
                ]
              },
              {
                "propertyName": "airline",
                "details": [
                   {
                     "operatorName": "properties",
                     "propertiesNotSatisfied": [
                        {
                          "propertyName": "id",
                          "description": "must be a positive integer",
                          "details": [
```

```
                    {
                      "operatorName": "minimum",
                      "specifiedAs": {
                        "minimum": 1
                      },
                      "reason": "comparison failed",
                      "consideredValue": -410
                    }
                  ]
                }
              ]
            }
          ]
        }
      ]
    }
  ]
}
```

The errors occurred because the `flight_id` did not start with `"FL"` and contained the incorrect format, and the `airline.id` was not a positive integer, as required. Consequently, MongoDB returned an error message detailing these validation failures, including descriptions of the specific schema rules that were not satisfied.

5.4.3 Modifying schema validator behavior

You can specify how MongoDB handles documents that violate validation rules. When a document operation fails to comply with validation rules, MongoDB can do the following:

- Deny any insert or update operation that breaches the validation rules, which is the standard setting
- Permit the operation while noting the violation within the MongoDB log

Rejecting nonconforming documents helps maintain schema consistency. Nonetheless, you might choose to allow invalid documents in some situations, such as during data migrations involving older documents created before schema definitions were in place.

`validationAction` determines how MongoDB handles invalid documents. This setting can be configured to either of the following:

- `error`—This is the default setting. MongoDB will reject any operation that attempts to insert or update documents in a way that violates the validation rules.
- `warn`—MongoDB allows the operations to proceed, but it logs a warning message for any violation. This can be useful for tracking compliance without disrupting ongoing operations, such as during a gradual schema enforcement phase or in a development environment.

When `validationAction` is set to `warn`, you can check the MongoDB logs for related warnings using the following command in the MongoDB Shell (`mongosh`):

```
db.adminCommand(
   { getLog:'global'} ).log.forEach(x => { print(x) }
)
```

NOTE This example is not available on the free/shared Atlas tier.

5.4.4 Bypassing schema validation

In certain cases, you may have to override a collection's schema validation rules. When you're restoring data from a backup into a collection that is governed by validation rules, for example, there's a chance that older documents from the backup won't comply with the newer validation criteria.

Bypassing schema validation can be managed on a per-operation basis. If you choose to bypass schema validation when inserting an invalid document, any subsequent updates to that document must also bypass schema validation or ensure that the document meets the existing validation criteria. You can bypass validation using the following commands and methods:

- `findAndModify` command
- `insert` command
- `update` command
- `$out` and `$merge` aggregation stages

Suppose that you want to insert a document that does not comply with schema requirements. Perhaps the `flight_id` does not start with `"FL"` or the `airline.id` is less than 1. Instead of modifying the document to meet the schema criteria, you can bypass the validation as shown in this example:

```
db.routes.insertOne(
   {
      flight_id: "12345",   // Does not meet schema requirements
      (should start with 'FL')
      airline: {
        id: 0,   // Does not meet schema requirements
      (must be a positive integer)
      },
      src_airport: {
        code: "JFK"
      },
      dst_airport: {
        code: "LAX"
      }
   },
   { bypassDocumentValidation: true }   // Bypasses the schema validation
);
```

The option `bypassDocumentValidation: true` allows you to insert a document, even though fields such as `flight_id` and `airline.id` violate the schema's rules. By using this option, you temporarily disable validation for this particular operation.

Bypassing these rules is necessary sometimes, although it carries the risk of introducing invalid documents into the collection. Various commands, including insert and update, allow you to bypass these rules. If you want more information about schema validation in MongoDB, see the official documentation at https://mng.bz/nZNg.

5.5 MongoDB schema antipatterns

You should avoid antipatterns when working with MongoDB. Recognizing antipatterns can help you prevent performance problems and maintain the efficiency of your database. Here are some key antipatterns:

- *Massive Arrays*—Storing large, unbounded arrays in documents can cause inefficient queries and performance degradation. Break such data into separate collections, or use pagination strategies to manage large data sets more effectively.
- *Bloated Documents*—Overloading documents with excessive data that is not frequently accessed together can slow read operations. Keep documents lean by including only data that is commonly accessed together to ensure efficient read performance.
- *Massive Number of Collections*—Creating too many collections, especially if many are rarely used, can degrade performance. Consolidate your schema design into fewer, more efficient collections whenever possible.
- *Unnecessary Indexes*—Maintaining indexes that are rarely used or redundant consumes memory and can slow write operations. Regularly review and remove indexes that do not contribute significantly to query performance.
- *Separating Data Accessed Together*—Storing related data in separate documents or collections can lead to frequent joins and complex queries. Embed related data in a single document to simplify and speed read operations.

In part 2 of this book, I show you how to identify these problems quickly using the Atlas Performance Advisor. This tool helps you spot and resolve schema design antipatterns, ensuring that your database operates efficiently.

Summary

- MongoDB's flexible schema design allows a flexible and dynamic data structure. Unlike traditional databases that need a fixed schema, MongoDB lets documents in the same collection have varied fields and types. This adaptability is beneficial for projects with evolving or unclear data needs.
- Although MongoDB is a flexible schema, effective data modeling is still crucial. Proper MongoDB schema design enhances performance, scalability, and maintainability. It requires understanding data relationships, predicting query patterns, and planning for data evolution.

- When designing a schema for MongoDB, it's crucial to recognize its flexibility compared with that of traditional relational databases. MongoDB allows dynamic changes to the data structure, enabling easier development and scalability, and its data model should be designed based on data access patterns rather than logical connections, emphasizing flexibility and scalability.
- Schema planning involves determining workloads, mapping relationships, and implementing design patterns that cater to specific application needs.
- MongoDB offers various schema design patterns, including Approximation, Archive, Attribute, Bucket, Computed, Document Versioning, Extended Reference, Outlier, Pre-allocation, Polymorphic, Schema Versioning, Subset, and Tree.
- Schema validation allows you to set rules for your fields, including permitted data types and value ranges. When your application schema is defined, schema validation ensures that there are no unexpected changes or incorrect data types.
- After you add schema validation rules to a collection, by default, if an insert or update operation results in an invalid document, MongoDB rejects the operation and does not save the document to the collection. Alternatively, you can configure MongoDB to accept invalid documents and log warnings when schema violations occur.
- Bypassing schema validation is required in some cases, though it carries the potential risk of adding noncompliant documents to the collection. Several commands—such as `insert`, `findAndModify`, and `update`—provide the `bypassDocumentValidation: true` option, which skips these validation checks when necessary.
- Avoid certain antipatterns when working with MongoDB, including Massive Arrays, Bloated Documents, Massive Number of Collections, Unnecessary Indexes, and Separating Data Accessed Together.

Building aggregation pipelines

This chapter covers

- Exploring the MongoDB aggregation framework
- Setting up and using aggregation pipelines
- Describing aggregation pipeline stages
- Joining MongoDB collections using `$lookup`
- Using the MongoDB Atlas aggregation pipeline builder

The MongoDB aggregation framework is a powerful tool for processing and analyzing data within MongoDB. It allows you to create complex data transformation and aggregation pipelines to perform operations such as filtering, grouping, and transforming data efficiently. This framework is essential for extracting meaningful insights from large data sets, making it a crucial component for developers and data analysts working with MongoDB. Also, the aggregation framework supports full-text search and vector search capabilities in MongoDB Atlas.

With the aggregation framework, you can construct multistage pipelines that process data in a sequence of steps. Each stage performs an operation on the data and passes the result to the next stage. This approach allows sophisticated data manipulation and analysis, providing flexibility and performance beyond simple queries. Whether you need to calculate averages, sum totals, organize data by categories, or generate reports, the aggregation framework offers the capabilities you need to handle these tasks effectively. Another benefit is that when a complex transformation is broken into more manageable parts, the entire process becomes easier to understand, maintain, and debug. The framework supports a wide range of operators and expressions, enabling you to perform complex calculations and transformations.

6.1 Understanding the aggregation framework

If you know how a production line works in a factory, the aggregation pipeline will be quite familiar. In a factory, each station in the production line performs a specific task, and the product moves from one station to the next. Similarly, in the aggregation pipeline, each stage performs a specific operation, and the output of one stage becomes the input for the next stage:

```
[ { <stage> }, { <stage> }, { <stage> }, { <stage> }, ... ]
```

Aggregation operations handle multiple documents and return computed results. You can use them to do the following:

- Generate business reports (rollups, sums, and averages)
- Perform full-text search and fuzzy search (chapter 11)
- Conduct vector search in data sets (chapter 12)
- Present up-to-date business dashboards
- Mask sensitive data securely
- Join data from different collections on the server
- Perform data discovery and wrangling
- Conduct large-scale data analysis (big data)
- Execute complex real-time queries
- Analyze graphs of relationships between records
- Perform data transformation in extract, load, transform (ELT) processes
- Report data quality and cleansing
- Update materialized views with recent data changes
- Conduct real-time analytics for user insights

Table 6.1 compares SQL terms, functions, and concepts with the corresponding MongoDB aggregation operators. If you're familiar with SQL, this comparison will help you understand how to use MongoDB's aggregation framework to perform similar operations.

Table 6.1 MongoDB operators for common SQL operations

SQL terms, functions, and concepts	MongoDB aggregation operators
WHERE	$match
GROUP BY	$group
HAVING	$match
SELECT	$project, $set, $unset
LIMIT	$limit
OFFSET	$skip
ORDER BY	$sort
SUM()	$sum
COUNT()	$count, $sum, $sortByCount()
JOIN	$lookup
SELECT INTO NEW TABLE	$out
MERGE INTO TABLE	$merge
UNION ALL	$unionWith

6.1.1 Writing an aggregation pipeline

In MongoDB, you can use the db.collection.aggregate() method to execute aggregation pipelines. The documents in the collection remain unchanged unless the pipeline specifically includes a $merge or $out stage. These stages are exceptions that can write the results back to the original collection or to a new collection.

The following listing shows how to use the aggregate method in MongoDB within the routes collection, using stages such as $match, $group, $sort, and $limit.

Listing 6.1 Executing an aggregation pipeline

```
db.routes.aggregate([
  {
    $match: { airplane: "CR2" } // Filter documents where the
➥airplane is "CR2"
  },
  {
    $group: {
      _id: "$src_airport",      // Group by source airport
      totalRoutes: { $sum: 1 }  // Count the number of routes
➥from each source
    }
  },
  {
    $sort: { totalRoutes: -1 }  // Sort the results by the
➥number of routes in descending order
  },
  {
    $limit: 5                   // Limit the number of displayed
➥documents to 5
```

```
    }
])

[
  { _id: 'DME', totalRoutes: 19 },
  { _id: 'SVX', totalRoutes: 17 },
  { _id: 'OVB', totalRoutes: 12 },
  { _id: 'LED', totalRoutes: 11 },
  { _id: 'OMS', totalRoutes: 8 }
]
```

Within this aggregation pipeline

- The $match stage filters documents in the collection in which the airplane type is "CR2".
- The $group stage groups the filtered documents based on the source airport ($src_airport), calculating the total number of routes (totalRoutes) from each distinct source airport using the $sum accumulator operator.
- The $sort stage arranges the grouped data based on the total number of routes in descending order (totalRoutes), helping you identify airports with the highest number of routes.
- The $limit stage restricts the number of documents passed to the subsequent stages or returned to the client, ensuring that only the five airports with the most routes are included in the output.

6.1.2 Viewing the aggregation pipeline stages

The aggregation pipeline is composed of several distinct stages, each responsible for a specific data processing task. Combined, these stages enable complex transformations and analyses. Certain stages in the pipeline are more frequently used due to their versatility and utility in a wide range of data processing tasks. Here are the most popular stages:

- $match—Filters documents to include only those that meet specified conditions
- $group—Groups documents by a specified key and applies aggregate functions such as sum, avg, min, max, and count
- $set, $unset, $project—Reshape each document by adding, removing, or modifying fields
- $sort—Orders documents by specified field(s) in ascending or descending order
- $limit—Restricts the number of documents passed to the next stage
- $skip—Skips a specified number of documents
- $unwind—Deconstructs an array field to output a document for each element of the array
- $lookup—Performs a left outer join with another collection to include related data

Table 6.2 lists all the aggregation pipeline stages available in MongoDB 8.0. You can combine and customize these stages to create powerful data transformations and aggregations tailored to specific application needs. It's important, however, to adhere to best practices to ensure optimal performance and maintainability. Here are some recommended practices:

- *Place* `$match` *early*. Position the `$match` stage at the beginning of the pipeline to filter out unnecessary documents early, reducing the workload for subsequent stages and improving performance.
- *Prefer using* `$set` *(or* `$addFields`*) and* `$unset`. Rather than using `$project` for fields inclusion and exclusion, use `$set` and `$unset`. Use `$project` only when you need a significantly different document structure and are retaining only a few fields from the original.
- *Use indexes for* `$sort`. Ensure that the fields used in the `$sort` stage are indexed to speed the sorting process and prevent performance bottlenecks.
- *Use* `$limit` *for efficient data processing*. Use the `$limit` stage to control the number of documents processed, reducing memory use and improving query execution time, particularly in large data sets.
- *Filter arrays before* `$unwind`. Apply filtering conditions to arrays before using the `$unwind` stage to minimize the increase in document count and avoid excessive processing.
- *Optimize* `$lookup` *operations*. Ensure that the foreign field used in the `$lookup` stage is indexed in the joined collection.
- *Use* `$addFields` *sparingly*. Apply the `$addFields` stage judiciously to create or modify fields, avoiding overly complex expressions that can slow the pipeline.
- *Streamline your pipeline*. Regularly review and optimize your pipeline by removing unnecessary stages and combining stages wherever possible to streamline processing.
- *Monitor pipeline performance*. Use MongoDB's `explain()` method (chapter 7) and other performance monitoring tools to analyze and optimize pipeline performance, as well as identify and address bottlenecks.

Table 6.2 MongoDB aggregation pipeline stages available in MongoDB 8.0

Stage	Description
`$addFields`	Adds new fields to documents
`$bucket`	Categorizes documents into buckets
`$bucketAuto`	Groups incoming documents into specified buckets based on an expression, automatically adjusting boundaries for even distribution
`$changeStream`	Returns a change stream for the collection
`$changeStreamSplit-LargeEvent`	Splits change-stream events into smaller fragments returned in a change-stream cursor

Table 6.2 MongoDB aggregation pipeline stages available in MongoDB 8.0 (*continued*)

Stage	Description
$collStats	Provides statistics on a collection or view
$count	Counts documents at the pipeline stage
$densify	Creates new documents in a sequence in which some field values are missing
$documents	Returns documents from input
$facet	Runs multiple pipelines on the same data set, returning the results as separate arrays in one document
$fill	Fills in empty or missing fields in documents
$geoNear	Filters and sorts documents by distance from a given geographic point
$graphLookup	Performs a recursive search on a collection, adding a new array field to each document containing the traversal results
$group	Groups input documents by a specified identifier and performs specified calculations on each group
$indexStats	Provides statistics on the use of indexes
$limit	Passes the first *n* documents unchanged to the pipeline, where *n* is the specified limit
$listSampledQueries	Provides sampled queries for collections
$listSearchIndexes	Provides information about existing search indexes
$listSessions	Lists active sessions stored in the system.sessions collection
$lookup	Executes a left outer join with another collection in the same database, filtering in documents from the joined collection for further processing
$match	Filters the document stream, allowing only matching documents to pass unchanged to the next pipeline stage
$merge	Writes the output of the aggregation pipeline to a collection. It can perform various actions, such as inserting new documents, merging, replacing, or keeping existing documents based on specified criteria. $merge must be the final stage in the pipeline.
$out	Writes the output of the aggregation pipeline to a collection. The $out stage must be the final stage in the pipeline.
$planCacheStats	Plans cache information for a collection
$project	Restructures each document in the stream, potentially by adding new fields or removing existing ones
$redact	Restructures each document by limiting its content based on information stored within the documents themselves
$replaceRoot	Replaces a document with the specified document
$replaceWith	Serves as an alias for the $replaceRoot stage
$sample	Randomly selects documents from its input
$search	Performs a full-text search
$searchMeta	Returns various types of metadata-result documents for the search query on a collection

Table 6.2 MongoDB aggregation pipeline stages available in MongoDB 8.0 *(continued)*

Stage	Description
`$set`	Adds new fields to documents
`$setWindowFields`	Adds new fields based on a specified grouping
`$skip`	Skips the first *n* documents
`$sort`	Sorts the document stream based on specified criteria
`$sortByCount`	Groups incoming documents based on a specified expression, computes the count of documents in each group, and sorts the documents by descending count
`$source`	Defines which connection from the Connection Registry to stream data from in a stream processing pipeline
`$unionWith`	Performs a union of two pipelines
`$unset`	Removes fields from documents
`$unwind`	Deconstructs an array field in the input documents, creating a document for each element
`$vectorSearch`	Performs an ANN search on a vector in the specified field of the collection

TIP MongoDB periodically introduces new stages, so review this table with each new release.

6.1.3 Using $set and $unset instead of $project

The primary method for specifying which fields to include in or exclude from MongoDB's aggregation framework has traditionally been the `$project` stage. In earlier versions of MongoDB, this stage was the sole method for defining which fields to retain or remove. The `$project` stage presents several significant challenges, however, including the following:

- *Nonintuitive use*—With `$project`, you can include or exclude fields in a single stage but not both, except for the `_id field`, which can be excluded while including other fields. This exception makes `$project` somewhat confusing and counterintuitive.
- *Verboseness and inflexibility*—The `$project` stage tends to be verbose. To add only one field, you must explicitly list all other fields to include. This requirement leads to redundant and lengthy code, complicating maintenance and making it difficult to adapt to changes in the data model.

To address these limitations, MongoDB version 4.2 introduced the `$set` and `$unset` stages, which offer several advantages over `$project`:

- *Clearer intent*—The `$set` and `$unset` stages clarify the code's purpose, making it immediately apparent whether you are adding, modifying, or removing fields.

- *Reduced verboseness*—These stages result in more concise and readable pipelines, as you no longer need to list all fields when modifying only one.
- *Flexibility*—The stages provide greater flexibility, reducing the need for extensive refactoring when the data model changes.

6.1.4 Scenarios for $set and $unset operators

Use the $set and $unset stages when you need to keep most fields in the input documents unchanged and need to add, update, or remove only a small number of fields. This scenario is common in most aggregation pipeline operations.

Listing 6.2 shows examples of using the $set and $unset operators. In the first example, suppose that you want to exclude the codeshare and stops fields from the output documents when querying the routes collection, focusing only on the essential information about the route and airline.

Listing 6.2 Using the $set and $unset operators

```
db.routes.aggregate([
    {
        $unset: ["codeshare", "stops"] // Excludes 'codeshare'
and 'stops' fields from the output documents
    }
])
```

In this pipeline, the $unset operator removes specified fields from documents during aggregation, allowing other fields to pass through unchanged. This operator is more intuitive for retaining most fields while excluding specific ones, unlike $project, which includes fields explicitly.

If you want to enhance the documents by adding an isDirect field to indicate whether a flight is direct (has no stops) and remove the codeshare field, which is not needed for analysis, run the following pipeline:

```
db.routes.aggregate([
    {
        $set: {
            isDirect: {
                $eq: ["$stops", 0] // Sets 'isDirect' to true
if there are no stops, false otherwise
            },
            codeshare: "$$REMOVE" // Removes 'codeshare'
within the same stage
        }
    }
])
```

The $set operator adds a new isDirect field to each document. It also uses a conditional expression to check whether the stops field is 0. If it is, isDirect is set to true;

otherwise, it's set to `false`. The special variable `$$REMOVE` deletes the `codeshare` field within `$set`, making it unnecessary in the output.

6.1.5 Scenario for the $project operator

The `$project` stage is most effective when you need the output documents to have a significantly different structure from that of the input documents, and you usually should use it last to specify what fields to return to the client. The following code demonstrates the `$project` stage selectively including only the source and destination airports in the output while omitting the document ID.

Listing 6.3 Using the `$project` operator

```
db.routes.aggregate([
    {
        $project: {
            src_airport: 1, // Include the source airport
            dst_airport: 1, // Include the destination airport
            _id: 0 // Exclude the MongoDB document ID from the output
        }
    }
])
```

The `$project` stage is well suited to this task because it reshapes the output documents to contain only the necessary fields: `src_airport` and `dst_airport`. This structure significantly differs from the structure of the input documents, which contain multiple additional fields. This approach allows for a focused view of the data, omitting irrelevant details such as the `_id field`, which is not needed for specific analysis of airport routes.

6.1.6 Saving the results of aggregation pipelines

MongoDB offers two stages for saving aggregation pipeline results to a collection: `$out` and `$merge`. These stages provide different ways to store and update documents in the target collection with varying levels of flexibility and control.

THE $OUT STAGE

The `$out` stage takes the documents returned by the aggregation pipeline and writes them to a specified collection, with the option to specify the output database. The `$out` stage must be the final stage in the pipeline. This operator allows the aggregation framework to handle result sets of any size.

Listing 6.4 shows an example of using the `$out` stage during document processing in the `routes` collection. The following pipeline filters documents in which the airplane is `"CR2"`, projects the `src_airport` and `airplane` fields, and writes the results to a specified output database and collection.

Listing 6.4 The aggregation pipeline's `$out` stage

```
db.routes.aggregate([
    {
```

```
    $match: { airplane: "CR2" } // Filter documents where the
➥airplane is "CR2"
  },
  {
    $project: {
      src_airport: 1,  // Include the source airport field
      airplane: 1     // Include the airplane field
    }
  },
  {
    $out: { db: "output_db", coll: "projected_routes" }
➥// Write the results to the specified collection
  }
])
```

> **NOTE** If the collection specified by the $out operation already exists, the $out stage atomically replaces the existing collection with the new results collection when the aggregation is complete.

THE $MERGE STAGE

The $merge stage writes the results of the aggregation pipeline to a specified collection and must be the last stage in the pipeline. This stage can output to a collection in the same database or a different one, and it can output to the same collection that is being aggregated.

Pipelines with the $merge stage can run on replica set secondaries (chapter 9). Read operations for the $merge stage are sent to secondary nodes, whereas write operations occur only on the primary node.

The $merge stage creates a new collection if the output collection does not already exist. Also, it can incorporate results into an existing collection by inserting new documents, merging documents, replacing documents, keeping existing documents, failing the operation, or processing documents with a custom update pipeline. Further, the $merge stage can output to a sharded collection, and the input collection can be sharded as well. Following is an example of using the $merge stage to update documents in MongoDB.

Listing 6.5 The aggregation pipeline's $merge state

```
db.routes.aggregate([
  {
    $match: { airplane: "CR2" }
  },
  {
    $group: {
      _id: "$_id",
      src_airport: { $first: "$src_airport" },
      dst_airport: { $first: "$dst_airport" },
      airline_name: { $first: "$airline.name" }
    }
  },
  {
```

```
    $merge: {
      into: "routes",
      on: "_id",
      whenMatched: "merge",
      whenNotMatched: "insert"
    }
  }
])
```

This aggregation pipeline demonstrates how to selectively update documents in the routes collection in which the airplane field is "CR2". The pipeline consists of three stages:

1. The $match stage filters the documents to include only those in which the airplane field is "CR2".
2. The $group stage processes the filtered documents by grouping them based on _id. It retains the first occurrence of src_airport and dst_airport and extracts the airline name from the nested airline.name field, assigning it to airline_name.
3. The $merge stage writes the results back to the same routes collection. Existing documents that match on _id are updated with the new fields, and new documents are inserted if no match is found.

This method ensures efficient updates without data loss, providing precise control of the document structure.

6.2 Joining collections

Sometimes, you have to combine data from different collections, and the $lookup operator proves to be helpful in such cases. Suppose that you have a transactions collection that stores detailed transaction records, a separate accounts collection that stores account information, and a customers collection with customer details. All those collections are in the sample_analytics database. Using $lookup, you can join these collections to include detailed account and customer information directly within each transaction document. This approach is useful for generating comprehensive financial reports that display not only transaction details, such as amounts and dates, but also the associated account features and customer profiles, enhancing the data available for financial analysis and customer relationship management.

In MongoDB, the $lookup operation conducts a left outer join within the same database, bringing in documents from a joined collection for processing. This operation enhances each input document with a new array field, populated with matching documents from the joined collection. Then these augmented documents are forwarded to the subsequent stage for further processing. As of MongoDB 5.1, $lookup can also be used with sharded collections.

The $lookup stage in MongoDB employs this syntax to conduct an equality match between a field in the input documents and a field in the documents of the joined collection:

```
{
    $lookup:
      {
        from: <collection to join>,
        localField: <field from the input documents>,
        foreignField: <field from the documents of the "from" collection>,
        as: <output array field>
      }
}
```

6.2.1 Creating a MongoDB view using $lookup

You can use `$lookup` to create a MongoDB view. You create a view by applying a specified aggregation pipeline to the source collection or view. Views function as read-only collections and are computed in real time during read operations. Views must be established within the same database as the source collection. When performing read operations on views, MongoDB runs them as part of the base aggregation pipeline.

In a database named `sample_analytics`, you have collections named `transactions` and `customers`. You can create a view that enriches transaction data with customer details, defined as shown in the following listing.

Listing 6.6 Creating a MongoDB view with `$lookup`

```
// Connect to the sample_analytics database
use sample_analytics

// Create a view named 'enriched_transactions' within
➥the 'sample_analytics' database
db.createView("enriched_transactions", "transactions", [
  {
    // Lookup to join 'transactions' with 'customers' based on
➥matching account_id
    $lookup: {
      from: "customers",
      localField: "account_id",
      foreignField: "accounts",
      as: "customer_details"
    }
  },
  {
    // Extract customer details
    $set: {
      "Customer Name": { $arrayElemAt: ["$customer_details.name", 0] },
      "Customer Email": { $arrayElemAt: ["$customer_details.email", 0] },
      "Customer Address": { $arrayElemAt:
➥["$customer_details.address", 0] },
      "Customer Tier and Benefits": { $arrayElemAt:
➥["$customer_details.tier_and_details", 0] }
    }
  },
  {
    // Remove the temporary 'customer_details' field no longer
```

```
           needed after extraction
      $unset: "customer_details"
    }
])
```

The `$lookup` stage joins the `transactions` collection with the `customers` collection based on matching `account_id`, storing the result as an array in `customer_details`. Because each transaction should have at most one matching customer, the `$set` stage extracts the relevant customer fields using `$arrayElemAt`, selecting the first element from the `customer_details` array. Then the `$unset` stage removes the temporary `customer_details` field to keep the view streamlined.

To read data from the view you've created in MongoDB, you can use the `find()` method, similar to the way you would query a regular collection. Here's an example:

```
// Query the view to retrieve data
db.enriched_transactions.find().limit(5)
```

> **TIP** The view-definition pipeline cannot include the `$out` or `$merge` stage. This limitation extends to embedded pipelines used in stages such as `$lookup` and `$facet`.

6.2.2 Using $lookup with $mergeobjects

Sometimes, you have to combine and streamline information from separate MongoDB documents into a single document for each record. Using `$lookup` followed by `$mergeObjects` achieves this goal. First, you perform a join to fetch related data, and then you merge the fetched data with the original document to simplify the structure:

```
db.transactions.aggregate([
    {
        $lookup: {
            from: "accounts",              // Joining from the
            accounts collection
            localField: "account_id",      // Field from
            transactions collection
            foreignField: "account_id",    // Field from the
            accounts collection
            as: "account_details"
        }
    },
    {
        $unwind: "$account_details"        // Unwind the result
        to merge objects properly
    },
    {
        $replaceRoot: {
            newRoot: {
                $mergeObjects: ["$account_details", "$$ROOT"]
                // Merging the account details into the transaction
```

```
            }
        }
    },
    {
        $unset: "account_details"  // Remove the account_details
➥field from the final output
    }
])
```

The pipeline uses the `$lookup` stage to join the `transactions` and `accounts` collections based on the `account_id` field; then it employs `$mergeObjects` in the `$replaceRoot` stage to combine the joined documents into a single document. This process enhances the resulting documents by merging details from both collections, providing a flattened, more accessible data structure.

> **WARNING** Excessive use of `$lookup` can lead to overly complex and slow queries, complicating code management and maintenance. In such scenarios, consider an alternative approach, such as data denormalization, instead of relying heavily on collection joins. Thoughtful schema design is essential for optimizing database performance. It's worth noting that joins, including `$lookup`, can be resource-intensive operations, particularly on larger data sets, potentially affecting query execution time significantly. Thus, it's crucial to carefully evaluate the tradeoffs and performance implications before integrating joins into your database queries.

> **TIP** To combine documents from two collections, use the `$unionWith` aggregation pipeline stage. Unlike `$lookup`, which joins documents based on a common field, `$unionWith` merges entire collections into a single stream of documents.

Beginning with MongoDB 6.0, you can include the Atlas Search `$search` or `$searchMeta` stage as part of a `$lookup` pipeline to perform searches within collections hosted on the Atlas cluster. The `$search` or `$searchMeta` stage must be positioned as the first stage in the `$lookup` pipeline.

6.3 Deconstructing arrays with $unwind

The MongoDB `$unwind` operator flattens an array field in a document, creating separate output documents for each item in the array. The primary difference between the input and output documents is that the array field in the output documents contains a single item from the original array.

This transformation simplifies complex documents, enhancing readability and understanding. Also, it enables you to perform further operations, such as grouping and sorting, on the resulting documents. `$unwind` does not output a document by default if the field value is `null` or missing or the array is empty.

Consider the following document from the `customers` collection in the `sample_analytics` database:

```
{
  "_id": ObjectId("5ca4bbcea2dd94ee58162a76"),
  "username": "portermichael",
  "name": "Lauren Clark",
  "address": "1579 Young Trail\nJessechester, OH 88328",
  "birthdate": ISODate("1980-10-28T16:25:59.000Z"),
  "email": "briannafrost@yahoo.com",
  "accounts": [883283, 980867, 164836, 200611, 528224, 931483],
  "tier_and_details": {
    "b0d8ebd346824edc890898b0b2ad6e2d": {
      "tier": "Silver",
      "benefits": ["concert tickets", "sports tickets"],
      "active": true,
      "id": "b0d8ebd346824edc890898b0b2ad6e2d"
    }
  }
}
```

The `accounts` field is an array containing multiple account numbers. Here's how to use the `$unwind` operator to deconstruct this array.

Listing 6.7 Using the `$unwind` operator

```
use sample_analytics
  db.customers.aggregate([
  {
    $match: { _id: ObjectId("5ca4bbcea2dd94ee58162a76") }
  },
  {
    $unwind: "$accounts"
  },
  {
    $project: {
      _id: 0,
      username: 1,
      accounts: 1
    }
  }
])
```

When this aggregation pipeline is executed, `$match` filters the documents to include only the one with `_id` equal to `ObjectId("5ca4bbcea2dd94ee58162a76")`. `$unwind` deconstructs the `accounts` array in the matched document, creating a separate document for each account number:

```
[
  { username: 'portermichael', accounts: 883283 },
  { username: 'portermichael', accounts: 980867 },
  { username: 'portermichael', accounts: 164836 },
  { username: 'portermichael', accounts: 200611 },
  { username: 'portermichael', accounts: 528224 },
  { username: 'portermichael', accounts: 931483 }
]
```

Consider another example. The goal is to count the occurrences of account numbers within an `accounts` array across the entire collection of documents in the `customers` collection. In this scenario, `$unwind` can be valuable. The next listing shows how to use aggregation to count occurrences of account numbers within arrays in all documents in the collection, focusing on the `accounts` array.

Listing 6.8 Counting occurrences of each account number

```
db.customers.aggregate([
  { $unwind: "$accounts" },

  // Group by account number and count occurrences
  {
    $group: {
      _id: "$accounts", // Group by account number
      count: { $sum: 1 } // Count occurrences of each account number
    }
  },

  // Sort by the number of occurrences (descending)
  { $sort: { count: -1 } }
])
```

The aggregation employs `$unwind` to deconstruct the `accounts` array, `$group` to group documents by account number, and `$sum` to tally occurrences. Optionally, the results can be sorted by count in descending order.

6.4 Working with accumulators

Accumulators in MongoDB are operators used in aggregation pipelines, mainly within the `$group` and `$project` stages, to calculate data. They aggregate data by summing, averaging, or finding extremes, aiding in statistical analysis.

Now let's check the `$max` accumulator. It returns the highest value by comparing value and type, adhering to Binary JSON (BSON) comparison order. The following code demonstrates the use of aggregators in MongoDB aggregation pipelines.

Listing 6.9 Using aggregation accumulators

```
db.customers.aggregate([
  {
    $group: {
      _id: { username: "$username" }, // Group by username
      maxAccountNumber: { $max: "$accounts" } // Find the maximum
account number
    }
  }
])
```

The pipeline starts by grouping the documents by username. Within each group, it calculates the maximum account number using the $max accumulator. Finally, it returns the maximum account number for each unique username.

In the second example, I focus on the $avg accumulator. The pipeline starts by using $group, where $size counts the number of accounts per user and $avg calculates the average number of accounts:

```
db.customers.aggregate([
  {
    $group: {
      _id: null, // Group all documents together
      averageNumberOfAccounts: { $avg: { $size: "$accounts" } }
    }
  }
])
```

The pipeline calculates the average number of accounts per user in a single step by combining $size and $avg in $group.

6.5 Using the MongoDB Atlas aggregation pipeline builder

You can use the Atlas UI to manage your data through the construction of aggregation pipelines. The Atlas aggregation pipeline builder is designed mainly for creating these pipelines rather than running them. It offers a convenient method to export your pipelines for execution in a driver. Figure 6.1 shows the MongoDB Atlas user interface for managing data via aggregation pipelines.

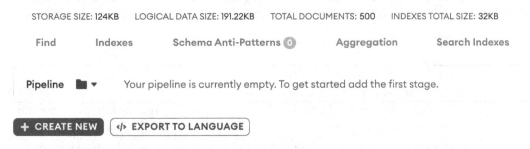

Figure 6.1 The MongoDB Atlas interface in the Aggregation tab of the `sample_analytics.customers` collection, where you can manage data by building and modifying aggregation pipelines (Image © MongoDB 2025)

This section of the interface provides tools for creating new pipelines or exporting them to code, facilitating easy integration with application codebases. It supports both building pipelines from scratch and exporting existing ones for implementation.

Figure 6.2 shows an example of creating an aggregation pipeline using the pipeline builder and exporting it to programming languages in MongoDB Atlas.

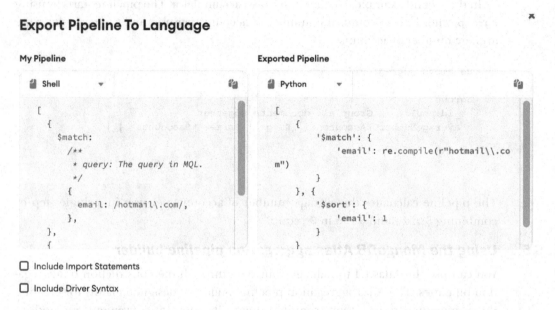

Figure 6.2 The interface shows the Export Pipeline to Language feature for a user-defined pipeline involving a match stage that filters documents by email addresses. On the left, the pipeline configuration is displayed in MongoDBs Shell (`mongosh`) syntax. On the right, the same pipeline is exported in Python syntax. (Image © MongoDB 2025)

This functionality helps developers integrate MongoDB operations directly into their application code, providing ready-to-use code snippets in various programming languages.

Summary

- MongoDB's aggregation framework lets you create complex data transformation and aggregation pipelines for efficient operations such as filtering, grouping, and transforming data.
- Operators such as `$match` filter data based on conditions, selecting relevant documents for further processing.
- The `$group` operator aggregates documents by criteria, enabling calculations such as sums, averages, and other aggregate functions across grouped data.
- The `$limit` operator restricts data set size, limiting the number of documents passed to subsequent pipeline stages or returned to the client, enhancing processing efficiency.

- The `$sort` operator arranges documents in order within a pipeline based on specified fields, facilitating data organization for analysis or presentation.
- Use `$set` (or `$addFields`) instead of `$project` for field inclusion. Use `$project` when you want a significantly different document structure and will retain only a few original fields.
- `$lookup` enables integrating data from multiple collections through left outer joins, combining related information for enhanced data analysis.
- The framework provides accumulators such as `$sum`, `$avg`, `$max`, and `$min` for performing aggregation operations such as summing, averaging, and finding extremes.
- The `$unwind` operator deconstructs arrays within documents, producing a separate document for each array element, facilitating further processing.
- MongoDB aggregation pipelines also support full-text search, fuzzy search, and vector search, enabling advanced data retrieval and analysis based on intricate search parameters.
- MongoDB Atlas provides an aggregation pipelines builder, which is designed primarily for building pipelines rather than executing them. The pipeline builder offers a straightforward method to export a pipeline for execution in a driver.

Indexing for query performance

This chapter covers

- Understanding MongoDB's query planner and execution plan
- Creating, deleting, and viewing MongoDB indexes
- Learning MongoDB index types
- Understanding the Equality, Sort, Range rule of thumb
- Measuring MongoDB index use

Over years of work, I have encountered numerous instances in which indexes were not used correctly or at all. This is suboptimal, as indexes allow efficient query performance and overall database optimization. In this chapter, I give you best practices for using indexes, rules of thumb, and methods for monitoring index use and optimization.

Indexes are special data structures that store a small portion of the collection's data in an easily traversable B-tree form. An index orders the values of specific fields, supporting efficient equality matches and range-based queries. MongoDB can also use the index to return sorted results.

Without indexes, MongoDB must scan every document in a collection to return query results. This process is very poor in terms of performance. A suitable index limits the number of documents that need to be scanned.

Although indexes improve query performance, they can negatively affect write operations. In collections with a high write-to-read ratio, indexes can be costly because each insert operation must update the indexes.

7.1 MongoDB query planner

The query planner in MongoDB is a component that analyzes various ways to execute a query and selects the most efficient execution plan. It uses indexes and other available data to minimize response times and resource use. If no index is available for a given query, the query planner performs a *full collection scan*, which involves searching every document in the collection to find those that match the query criteria. This method is typically less efficient than indexes and can significantly burden the database, especially in large data sets.

To determine the most efficient execution strategy, the query planner temporarily tests all available options during what is known as a *trial phase*. This phase is part of MongoDB's plan caching mechanism; the database evaluates the efficiency of different execution strategies under actual query conditions. The plan that demonstrates the best balance of speed and resource use during this trial is selected and cached for future use. Generally, the winning plan is the one that retrieves the most results with the least effort, effectively balancing speed and resource use. Each query shape is categorized into one of three states in the plan cache:

- `Missing`—No cache entry exists. MongoDB evaluates plans, selects a winner, and creates a new `Inactive` cache entry with the plan's work value.

- `Inactive`—This state is a placeholder. The query shape is recognized, and the work required is noted. If queried again, MongoDB reevaluates plans. A new, equally or more efficient plan replaces the `Inactive` entry and becomes `Active`. If the new entry is less efficient, it remains Inactive, updating the work value.

- `Active`—The entry is a winning plan currently used. If performance degrades or work increases, the entry may be reassessed and moved to `Inactive` if it no longer meets efficiency criteria.

7.1.1 Viewing query plan cache information

To access the query plan details in the MongoDB Shell (`mongosh`) for a specific query, you can use `db.collection.explain()` or `cursor.explain()`. These methods are MongoDB features that provide insight into how MongoDB executes a query. They can be useful for understanding performance characteristics or diagnosing problems with query efficiency. To obtain information about the plan cache for a collection, you can use the `$planCacheStats` aggregation stage.

The `db.collection.explain()` helper method accepts the `verbosity` parameter, which sets the level of detail provided by the `explain` output. The selected `verbosity` mode affects how `explain()` operates and dictates the extent of information returned. Available modes include

- `"queryPlanner"` (default)—Provides details about the chosen query plan
- `"executionStats"`—Includes all data from `"queryPlanner"` plus statistics about the execution of the query
- `"allPlansExecution"`—Offers comprehensive information, including all possible query plans and their execution statistics

For compatibility with previous versions, passing `true` as a parameter is interpreted as `"allPlansExecution"`, whereas `false` is treated as "queryPlanner".

If you want to understand how MongoDB executes a specific query, append the `explain()` method to your query, as shown in the following listing.

Listing 7.1 Appending the MongoDB `explain()` method

```
db.collection.find(
    { yourField: "value" }
).explain() // Explain the default query planner information

db.collection.find(
    { yourField: "value" }
).explain(
    "executionStats" // Explain the query execution statistics
)

db.collection.find(
    { yourField: "value" }
).explain(
    "allPlansExecution" // Explain the query execution
plan with all possible query plans
)
```

This listing returns detailed information about how MongoDB plans to execute the query. As you see in listing 7.2, the output of `explain()` includes a tree of stages, with each stage representing a specific operation in the query execution process. These stages are connected, with the lower stages accessing the collection or indexes and the middle stages processing the data retrieved from the lower stages. The top stage delivers the final results.

Listing 7.2 Execution-plan output structure

```
{
  "winningPlan": {
    "stage": "FETCH",
    "inputStage": {
      "stage": "IXSCAN",
```

```
      "indexName": "yourField_1",
      "keyPattern": {
        "yourField": 1
      },
      "indexBounds": {
        "yourField": [
          "[\"value\", \"value\"]"
        ]
      }
    }
  },
  "executionStats": {
    "nReturned": 1,
    "executionTimeMillis": 3,
    "totalKeysExamined": 1,
    "totalDocsExamined": 1
  }
}
```

In this execution plan, the IXSCAN stage scans the index yourField_1, efficiently locating the relevant keys that match the query condition { yourField: "value" }. These index keys are passed to the FETCH stage, which retrieves the actual documents from the collection. The executionStats section provides detailed insights into the query's performance. It includes the number of documents returned, which in this case is 1, indicating that one document was matched and retrieved. The executionTimeMillis field shows that the query took 3 milliseconds (ms) to execute. Additionally, totalKeysExamined and totalDocsExamined reveal how many index keys and documents were scanned during the query process, both of which are 1 in this example. This indicates efficient use of the index, minimizing the need to scan unnecessary documents.

MongoDB uses several types of stages during query execution, depending on the operation:

- COLLSCAN for scanning the whole collection.
- IXSCAN for scanning index keys.
- FETCH for fetching documents.
- GROUP for grouping documents.
- SHARD_MERGE for combining results from different shards.
- SHARDING_FILTER for removing orphan documents from shards.
- BATCHED_DELETE for deleting multiple documents in batches.
- EXPRESS for specialized stages introduced in MongoDB version 8.0. They are execution phases that allow specific queries to bypass the traditional query planning and use highly optimized index scan strategies directly. This approach is designed to enhance performance for targeted query patterns, offering faster query execution by focusing on indexed fields. The available EXPRESS stages include

- `EXPRESS_CLUSTERED_IXSCAN`—Provides optimized index scanning for queries targeting clustered indexes, enabling faster data retrieval
- `EXPRESS_DELETE`—Delivers high-performance execution for delete operations by using index optimizations
- `EXPRESS_IXSCAN`—Accelerates index scans for nonclustered indexes, improving query speed in relevant operations
- `EXPRESS_UPDATE`—Optimizes the execution of update operations, making them more efficient when interacting with indexed data

TIP To see the list of operations supported by `db.collection.explain()`, run `db.collection.explain().help()`.

NOTE You can also use the MongoDB Compass GUI to view `explain` plans.

MongoDB uses two query engines to find and return results: the classic query engine and the slot-based query engine. MongoDB automatically chooses the engine; you can't select it manually.

The slot-based engine usually offers better performance and lower CPU and memory use. If a query doesn't meet the criteria for the slot-based engine, MongoDB uses the classic engine instead. Two common pipelines that use the slot-based execution engine are aggregations with `$group` or `$lookup` stages.

To determine which query engine was used, you can examine the `explain` results for a query or check the logs. The `explain` results vary depending on the query engine. Queries executed with the slot-based engine, for example, include the `explain.queryPlanner.winningPlan.slotBasedPlan` field:

```
{
  "winningPlan": {
    "queryPlan": {
      "stage": "FETCH",
      "inputStage": {
        "stage": "IXSCAN",
        "indexName": "yourField_1",
        "keyPattern": {
          "yourField": 1
        },
        "indexBounds": {
          "yourField": [
            "[\"value\", \"value\"]"
          ]
        }
      }
    },
    "slotBasedPlan": {
      "...": "..."  // This represents internal details
➥ specific to the slot-based engine
    }
  },
```

```
    "executionStats": {
      "nReturned": 1,
      "executionTimeMillis": 3,
      "totalKeysExamined": 1,
      "totalDocsExamined": 1
  }
}
```

You can also check MongoDB logs if you want to determine which query engine was used. (You will learn how to do this in chapter 21.) Log messages have a `queryFramework` field that shows the engine used:

- `queryFramework: "classic"` means that the classic engine executed the query.
- `queryFramework: "sbe"` means that the slot-based query engine executed the query.

7.1.2 MongoDB plan cache purges

The query plan cache is purged if a `mongod` process restarts or shuts down. Also

- Catalog operations such as dropping indexes or collections reset the plan cache.
- The least recently used (LRU) replacement method removes the least accessed cache entry, regardless of state.

You also have the capability to

- Clear the plan cache for the collection manually via the `PlanCache.clear()` method
- Selectively clear specific entries in the plan cache using the `PlanCache.clearPlansByQuery()` method

TIP Beginning with MongoDB 5.0, the plan cache stores only complete plan cache entries as long as the total size of the plan caches across all collections remains below 0.5 GB. If the combined size of the plan caches for all collections surpasses this limit, new plan cache entries are recorded without debug information.

NOTE `$planCacheStats` returns the approximate size of a plan cache entry in bytes.

7.2 Supported index types

A *database index* is a specific type of data structure that enables quicker data retrieval, contributing to application efficiency. Typically, an index includes two components: the search key and the data pointer. The search key holds the value being searched, and the pointer indicates the location of the data within the database.

Figure 7.1 shows an indexed search operation within a database called `sample_mflix` for a `movies` collection. If you need to query a movie with a running time of less than

40 minutes, the index on the `runtime` field allows the system to efficiently scan blocks of data rather than individual documents.

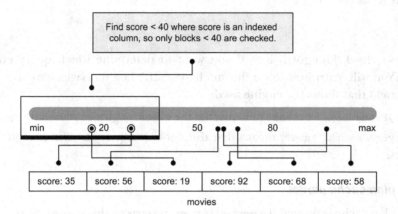

Figure 7.1 The index guides the search, allowing the system to skip entire blocks of data that don't meet the search criteria and examine only blocks that potentially contain relevant data. This optimization significantly reduces the number of operations, highlighting the efficiency of using indexed searches in managing and querying large data sets. (Image © MongoDB 2024 CC BY-NC-SA 3.0)

MongoDB automatically creates a unique index on the `_id` field when a collection is created. This `_id` index ensures that no two documents can have the same `_id` value. This index cannot be dropped.

7.2.1 Creating single field indexes

If your application frequently executes queries on specific fields, establishing an index on these fields can enhance performance. Several types of indexes cater to different data types and query requirements. This section examines the choices in detail.

Single-field indexes store and order data from a single field across each document in a collection. You can create a single-field index on any document field, such as top-level document fields, embedded documents, and fields within those embedded documents. When you set up an index, define the field for the index and the direction of sorting for the indexed values. A sort order of 1 indicates ascending order, and -1 indicates descending order. Here's how to create a single-field index on the `runtime` field in a MongoDB `movies` collection using ascending order:

```
db.movies.createIndex({ "runtime": 1 })
```

The `createIndexes` command in MongoDB creates indexes on specified fields within a collection. In `mongosh`, you can also run this command through the `helper` method. It uses the syntax `db.collection.createIndex(keys, options)`, where keys indicate the fields to index and the direction (ascending or descending), and options can specify additional properties, such as uniqueness. The index supports queries on the field `runtime`, as in this example:

```
db.movies.find({ "runtime": { $lt: 40 } })
db.movies.find({ "runtime": 410    })
```

If you want to check all the indexes currently available in the `movies` collection, execute

```
db.movies.getIndexes()
[
   { v: 2, key: { _id: 1 }, name: '_id_' },
   { v: 2, key: { runtime: 1 }, name: 'runtime_1' }
]
```

The `getIndexes()` method here reveals two indexes in the `movies` collection. The first is the default index on the `_id` field, labeled `'_id_'`, which MongoDB automatically creates for all collections. The second index is on the `runtime` field and is named `'runtime_1'`. To validate whether the query is truly using the index, you can append the `explain("executionStats")` method to the query, as the next listing shows.

> **Listing 7.3 Using the `explain()` method with the query**

```
db.movies.find({ "runtime": 100 }).explain("executionStats")
{
  explainVersion: '1',
  queryPlanner: {
    namespace: 'sample_mflix.movies',
    indexFilterSet: false,
    parsedQuery: { runtime: { '$eq': 100 } },
    queryHash: 'ADC785B0',
    planCacheKey: 'F015DF0A',
    maxIndexedOrSolutionsReached: false,
    maxIndexedAndSolutionsReached: false,
    maxScansToExplodeReached: false,
    winningPlan: {
      stage: 'FETCH',
      inputStage: {
        stage: 'IXSCAN',
        keyPattern: { runtime: 1 },
        indexName: 'runtime_1',
        isMultiKey: false,
        multiKeyPaths: { runtime: [] },
        isUnique: false,
        isSparse: false,
        isPartial: false,
        indexVersion: 2,
        direction: 'forward',
        indexBounds: { runtime: [ '[100, 100]' ] }
      }
    },
```

```
      rejectedPlans: []
  },
  executionStats: {
    executionSuccess: true,
    nReturned: 719,
    executionTimeMillis: 3,
    totalKeysExamined: 719,
    totalDocsExamined: 719
```

The `explain()` method output shows that the `runtime_1` index optimizes the search, with the `IXSCAN` stage specifically targeting the runtime field. This leads to the `FETCH` stage, which retrieves the matching documents according to the `winningPlan`. `executionStats` shows that the query successfully returned 719 documents in 3 ms, with 719 keys and 719 documents examined due to the effective use of the `runtime_1` index. The `queryHash` helps MongoDB determine whether the same query structure has been executed before, allowing the reuse of execution plans, and the `planCacheKey` considers the current state and environment of the database to determine whether a cached plan is appropriate. The complete `explain` plan is much longer and more complex, but in this chapter, I'm showing only part of the `explain` plan.

You can create an index on a field within an embedded document by using dot notation. To index the `wins` field inside the `awards` embedded document, use the following command:

```
db.movies.createIndex({ "awards.wins": 1 })
```

> **NOTE** A single collection can have no more than 64 indexes.

> **TIP** An index fully supports a query when it includes all the fields that the query needs to scan. Instead of scanning the entire collection, the query scans the index. By creating indexes that align with your queries, you significantly enhance query performance. If the index does not include all the fields the query needs, the query scans the index and then accesses the collection for the remaining fields, which can still improve performance, though not as much as when all required fields are included in the index.

USING AN INDEX TO SORT QUERY RESULTS

Because indexes hold ordered records, MongoDB can derive sorted results directly from an index that encompasses the fields used in the sort operation. If the sort operation aligns with the indexes used in the query predicate, MongoDB can use the index efficiently to perform the sorting. The following listing shows how to use the `runtime_1` index to sort and filter documents in the `movies` collection.

Listing 7.4 Using an index to filter and sort query results

```
db.movies.find(
    { "runtime": { $gt: 500 } }
```

```
).sort(
    { "runtime": 1 }
).explain("executionStats")

{
  explainVersion: '1',
  queryPlanner: {
    namespace: 'sample_mflix.movies',
    indexFilterSet: false,
    parsedQuery: { runtime: { '$gt': 500 } },
    queryHash: '059DF6AA',
    planCacheKey: '8E8D39FB',
    maxIndexedOrSolutionsReached: false,
    maxIndexedAndSolutionsReached: false,
    maxScansToExplodeReached: false,
    winningPlan: {
      stage: 'FETCH',
      inputStage: {
        stage: 'IXSCAN',
        keyPattern: { runtime: 1 },
        indexName: 'runtime_1',
        isMultiKey: false,
        multiKeyPaths: { runtime: [] },
        isUnique: false,
        isSparse: false,
        isPartial: false,
        indexVersion: 2,
        direction: 'forward',
        indexBounds: { runtime: [ '(500, inf.0]' ] }
      }
    },
    rejectedPlans: []
  },
  executionStats: {
    executionSuccess: true,
    nReturned: 21,
    executionTimeMillis: 0,
    totalKeysExamined: 21,
    totalDocsExamined: 21,
}
```

MongoDB uses the `runtime` index for an index scan (`IXSCAN`) on documents in which `runtime > 500`, optimizing match and sort operations. The forward scan matches the ascending sort order (`runtime: 1`). ExecutionStats show 21 documents returned and examined, with minimal execution time (0 ms), demonstrating efficient index use.

If MongoDB cannot use indexes for sorting, it uses a blocking sort operation, processing all documents in memory before returning results.

> **TIP** Starting with MongoDB 6.0, if a pipeline execution stage requires more than 100 MB of memory, MongoDB automatically writes temporary files to disk unless the query explicitly sets `{ allowDiskUse: false }`.

CONVERTING AN EXISTING INDEX TO UNIQUE

A *unique index* ensures that the indexed fields in a database do not store duplicate values, enforcing data uniqueness. This is beneficial because it guarantees data integrity, improves search performance by allowing faster retrieval of unique entries, and optimizes use of space by eliminating redundant data entries. To create a unique index, use the `.collection.createIndex( <key and index type specification>, { unique: true } )` method with the `unique` option set to `true`.

If a collection already has a nonunique index, and you want to convert it to a unique index, you can use the `collMod` command. This process involves several steps. If you have an existing index on the `email` field in the `users` collection of the `sample_mflix` database created with the command

```
db.getSiblingDB('sample_mflix').users.createIndex(
    { "email": 1 }
)
```

and you want to ensure that each user has a unique email, you have to convert this existing index to a unique index. The `getIndexes()` method can help you display existing nonunique indexes:

```
db.getSiblingDB('sample_mflix').users.getIndexes()
[
    { v: 2, key: { _id: 1 }, name: '_id_' },
    { v: 2, key: { email: 1 }, name: 'email_1' }
]
```

First, use the `collMod` command with the `prepareUnique` option. This command looks like this:

```
use sample_mflix
db.runCommand({
    collMod: "users",
    index: {
        keyPattern: { email: 1 },
        prepareUnique: true
    }
})
```

After you set `prepareUnique` to `true`, MongoDB prevents any new insertions or updates that would result in a duplicate email value in the `users` collection. If you try to insert a document with an email that already exists in the database, MongoDB throws a duplicate-key error, indicating a violation of the `unique` constraint.

Next, check for existing violations of what will become the `unique` constraint by running the `collMod` command with the `unique` and `dryRun` options:

```
db.runCommand({
    collMod: "users",
```

```
    index: {
       keyPattern: { email: 1 },
       unique: true
    },
    dryRun: true
})
```

This operation simulates the application of the `unique` constraint without applying it, allowing you to identify and resolve any existing duplicates in the email index. If the command returns without errors, there are no duplicate values, and you can convert the index permanently to unique. To finalize the conversion of the index to unique, run the `collMod` command again, this time removing the `dryRun` flag:

```
db.runCommand({
    collMod: "users",
    index: {
       keyPattern: { email: 1 },
       unique: true
    }
})
```

This command modifies the index on the `email` field to enforce uniqueness, ensuring that each document in the `users` collection has a unique email address. This change will help maintain data integrity by preventing future duplicates in the email field.

7.2.2 Understanding compound indexes

Compound indexes in MongoDB involve multiple fields within a document. You create these indexes by specifying several fields in the index-creation command. Compound indexes enable execution of queries that involve all the fields in the index or the fields that prefix those in the index. To create a compound index, you can use this prototype.

Listing 7.5 Compound Index prototype

```
db.<collection>.createIndex( {
    <field1>: <sortOrder>,
    <field2>: <sortOrder>,
    ...
    <fieldN>: <sortOrder>
} )
```

If your application frequently runs queries involving multiple fields, setting up a compound index on those fields can significantly enhance performance. Take, for example, a movie-analytics platform that managers use to assess films based on release year, type, and Internet Movie Database (IMDb) ratings to manage content effectively and tailor recommendations. To optimize these search operations and boost performance, you can create a compound index on the `year`, `type`, and `imdb.rating` fields in the `movies` collection. To implement this index, execute the following command.

> **Listing 7.6 Creating a compound index on three fields**

```
db.movies.createIndex(
    { year: 1, type: 1, "imdb.rating": 1 }
)
```

This command sets up the index to include these three key fields, sorting each in ascending order. Compound indexes support queries on all fields included in the index prefix, enabling fast, efficient retrievals.

An *index prefix* is any subset of the indexed fields starting from the first field defined in a compound index. For the compound index { year: 1, type: 1, "imdb.rating": 1 }, the possible index prefixes are

```
{ year: 1 }
{ year: 1, type: 1 }
{ year: 1, type: 1, "imdb.rating": 1 }
```

MongoDB can use this compound index to optimize queries involving these field combinations:

- Query by release year only:

    ```
    db.movies.find({ year: 1914 })
    ```

- Query by release year and type:

    ```
    db.movies.find(
        {
            year: 1914,
            type: "movie"
        }
    )
    ```

- Query by release year, type, and specific IMDb rating:

    ```
    db.movies.find(
        {
            year: 1914,
            type: "movie",
            "imdb.rating": { $gte: 7.6 }
        }
    )
    ```

MongoDB cannot use this compound index to optimize queries that do not contain the year field, such as querying by type alone or imdb.rating alone, because they do not match any prefix defined by the index. Those queries are not supported by the index:

```
db.movies.find({ type: "movie" })
db.movies.find({ "imdb.rating": { $gte: 7.6 } })
db.movies.find(
    { type: "movie", "imdb.rating": { $gte: 7.0 } }
)
```

The next listing shows the execution plan for a query that is not supported by a compound index, highlighting the COLLSCAN stage in the winning plan.

Listing 7.7 Example COLLSCAN stage in the winning plan

```
db.movies.find(
    { "imdb.rating": { $gte: 7.6 } }
).explain("executionStats")
{
  explainVersion: '1',
  queryPlanner: {
    namespace: 'sample_mflix.movies',
    indexFilterSet: false,
    parsedQuery: { 'imdb.rating': { '$gte': 7.6 } },
    queryHash: '5D6975B4',
    planCacheKey: 'AD7111A5',
    maxIndexedOrSolutionsReached: false,
    maxIndexedAndSolutionsReached: false,
    maxScansToExplodeReached: false,
    winningPlan: {
      stage: 'COLLSCAN',
      filter: { 'imdb.rating': { '$gte': 7.6 } },
      direction: 'forward'
    },
    rejectedPlans: []
  },
  executionStats: {
    executionSuccess: true,
    nReturned: 3472,
    executionTimeMillis: 20,
    totalKeysExamined: 0,
    totalDocsExamined: 21349
```

The output shows that MongoDB performs a full collection scan (COLLSCAN) for the "imdb.rating" query due to the lack of a suitable index. Consequently, all 21,349 documents in the collection are scanned (totalDocsExamined: 21349). No index keys were examined (totalKeysExamined: 0), leading to inefficiency in large data sets. This results in a longer execution time of 20 ms to return 3,472 results.

TIP If your collection includes both a compound index and an index on its prefix—such as { a: 1, b: 1 } and { a: 1 }—you can safely delete the index on the prefix ({ a: 1 }). MongoDB will use the compound index in all situations in which it would have used the prefix index.

NOTE A compound index can have a maximum of 32 fields.

UNDERSTANDING THE ESR RULE

The Equality, Sort, Range (ESR) rule in MongoDB is a guideline for designing compound indexes to optimize query performance. It dictates the order in which the query elements should be indexed: first by fields used in equality conditions, followed by fields used for sorting, and finally by fields used in range conditions. This ordering ensures that MongoDB indexes efficiently by quickly narrowing down the results using equality, efficiently sorting them, and then applying range filters.

Consider a query that looks for movies released in 1914, with an IMDb rating greater than 7.0, and sorts the results by the movie title:

```
db.movies.find(
    { year: 1914, "imdb.rating": { $gte: 7 } }
).sort(
    { title: 1 } // Find movies released in 1914 with
an IMDb rating of at least 7 and sort by title
)
```

To enhance the efficiency of this query, set up the following compound index:

```
db.movies.createIndex(
    { year: 1, title: 1, "imdb.rating": 1 } // Create a compound
index on the year, title, and imdb.rating fields
)
```

This index is designed according to the ESR rule. It prioritizes the equality condition on year, optimizes sorting on title, and then applies the range filter on "imdb.rating". This structure is beneficial because it allows MongoDB to effectively narrow, sort, and filter the data, using the index's sequence to match the query's needs efficiently. The following sections explore why this rule is advantageous.

EQUALITY

Equality means matching one value exactly. Consider queries that search the movies collection for documents in which the year field exactly matches a specific year:

```
db.movies.find({ year: { $eq: 1914 }})
db.movies.find({ year: 1914 })
```

Place fields that require exact matches at the beginning of the index. Index searches using exact matches reduce the number of documents MongoDB must review to complete a query. Ensure that equality tests are selective to minimize the number of index keys scanned and to filter out a significant portion of potential document matches.

SORT

Sort means organizing the results and following equality matches to reduce the number of documents to sort. This configuration allows MongoDB to perform a nonblocking sort. An index supports sorting when the fields in the query match a subset of the index keys, but only if there are equality conditions for all preceding prefix keys in the index before the sort keys:

```
db.movies.find({ year: 1914 }).sort({ title: 1 })
```

This query retrieves documents from the movies collection in which the year field exactly matches 1914.

RANGE

Range filters scan fields by matching values within a specified range rather than requiring exact matches. For more efficient queries, narrow the range, and use equality matches to reduce the number of documents scanned. Range filters can be formatted as follows:

```
db.movies.find({ year: 1914, "imdb.rating": { $gte: 7.0 } })
```

MongoDB cannot use an index to sort results if a range filter is applied to a different field. To enable MongoDB to perform an index-based sort, place the range filter after the sorting condition.

Figure 7.2 shows the execution of a query in MongoDB Compass (introduced in chapter 3) that filters the movies collection in the sample_mflix database to find documents in which year is 1914 and imdb.rating is greater than or equal to 7.

Figure 7.2 The MongoDB Compass GUI executes the query { year: 1914, "imdb.rating": { $gte: 7 } } on the movies collection. The results are sorted by { title: 1 }. (Image © MongoDB 2025)

To display the explain plan, click the Explain button, located in the top-right section of the screen next to the Generate Query button. Figure 7.3 shows the explain plan for the query executed in MongoDB Compass.

Figure 7.3 The `explain` plan for a query optimized with an index using the ESR rule in Compass. The plan contains an `IXSCAN` stage, which uses the `year_1_title_1_imdb.rating_1` index to scan and fetch documents. This stage returned two documents and examined four index keys with an execution time of 0 ms. Then the `FETCH` stage retrieves the documents with an execution time of 0 ms. (Image © MongoDB 2025)

The query performance summary provides detailed metrics on the query's execution and its interaction with the database. It shows that two documents were returned as a result of the query and two documents were examined, indicating precise, efficient query execution. The execution time was measured at 0 ms, reflecting optimal performance with minimal processing overhead.

The summary further highlights the fact that the query results were not sorted in memory, meaning that no in-memory sort operation was required and suggesting that the existing index handled sorting efficiently. Four index keys were examined, indicating the number of index entries scanned to satisfy the query conditions. The query used a compound index consisting of the fields `year`, `title`, and `imdb.rating`, as noted in the summary. Using this index significantly enhanced query performance by minimizing the need to scan unindexed data, resulting in a highly efficient operation.

7.2.3 Using multikey indexes

Multikey indexes in MongoDB are B-tree indexes that enable efficient querying of array values. When you create an index on a field that contains an array, MongoDB creates separate index entries for each element of the array. This allows MongoDB to quickly perform queries that involve elements of arrays, such as checking if an array contains a specific value or if it matches certain criteria.

MongoDB is capable of generating multikey indexes for arrays containing both scalar values (such as strings and numbers) and embedded documents. When an array includes several occurrences of the same value, the index records only one entry for that value. To create a multikey index, you can use the following prototype.

Listing 7.8 Multikey index prototype

```
db.<collection>.createIndex( { <arrayField>: <sortOrder> } )
```

Suppose that the application frequently has to identify customers based on their account numbers, which are stored in the `sample_analytics` database within the `customers` collection. To optimize this common query, consider using a multikey index. Here's a snippet of a document from the `customers` collection, demonstrating how the accounts are stored in an array:

```
{
_id: ObjectId('5ca4bbcea2dd94ee58162a68'),
username: 'fmiller',
accounts: [ 371138, 324287, 276528, 332179, 422649, 387979 ]
}
```

You can optimize search efficiency by creating a multikey index:

```
db.customers.createIndex({ accounts: 1 })
```

This command sets up an index in which each element of the accounts array is indexed individually; MongoDB stores this index as a multikey index. With the multikey index in place, searching for a customer by account number becomes more efficient. To find all customers with the account number 371138, simply run

```
db.customers.find({ accounts: 371138 })
```

This use of the multikey index allows MongoDB to locate and retrieve the relevant documents swiftly.

COMPOUND MULTIKEY INDEX

A *compound multikey index* is created on multiple fields, but only one of these fields can be an array to avoid creating an overly complex index structure. If your application frequently queries `username` (nonarray) and `accounts` (array) in the `customers` collection, create a compound multikey index . Here's how to create this index:

```
db.customers.createIndex({ username: 1, accounts: 1 })
```

This index supports queries involving these fields because it indexes `username` as a scalar and `accounts` as an array. To find all customers with the username `'fmiller'` and account number 371138, run

```
db.customers.find({ username: 'fmiller', accounts: 371138 })
```

MongoDB can quickly locate documents based on `username` and then filter results using specific account numbers.

MULTIKEY INDEXES WITH EMBEDDED FIELDS IN ARRAYS

You can create indexes on embedded document fields within arrays. When you create an index on a field inside an array, MongoDB stores that index as a multikey index. In the `sample_training` database, within the `grades` collection, you can create an index to improve the performance of queries on the `scores.score` field:

```
db.grades.createIndex({ "scores.score": 1 })
```

The following query returns documents in which at least one element in the `scores` array has a score greater than 70:

```
db.grades.find({ "scores.score": { $gt: 70 } })
```

This query uses the multikey index to find documents efficiently. MongoDB can quickly locate all documents in which any `score` field within the `scores` array is greater than 70. This eliminates the need for a full collection scan, significantly improving query performance.

The index also supports sort operations on the `scores.score` field. To sort the documents by `scores.score` in descending order, use the following query:

```
db.grades.find().sort({ "scores.score": -1 })
```

This index enables MongoDB to sort the documents efficiently based on the `scores.score` field, providing faster results for queries that require ordered data.

7.2.4 Using text indexes

In MongoDB, a standard text index is created on the entire value of a field, which means that searches must also target the full value to use the index efficiently, resulting in fast query performance. This type of index, however, does not support searches for partial values, such as those conducted with regular expressions. In such cases, MongoDB bypasses the index and performs a full collection scan, significantly slowing the search process.

Conversely, a search index, available in Atlas, requires more data storage but enables partial value searches, commonly referred to as *full-text searches*.

> **NOTE** Make sure not to confuse MongoDB's text indexes with the full-text search capabilities available in Atlas. Using Atlas Search is the recommended approach and is much better than relying on traditional MongoDB text indexes.

Let's focus on the classical MongoDB text index. The next listing shows a text index prototype. Collections can have only one text index, but that index can cover multiple fields.

Listing 7.9 Text index prototype

```
db.<collection>.createIndex(
   {
      <field1>: "text",
```

```
        <field2>: "text",
        ...
    }
)
```

The `$text` operator in MongoDB performs text search queries on content within a collection that has a text index. This operator can search for words and phrases within string fields that are indexed with a text index. It includes features such as these:

- *Case insensitivity*—By default, the search does not consider case, making it easier to find matches regardless of text case.
- *Language-specific rules*—MongoDB can apply language-specific rules for stemming and stop words (commonly ignored words such as *and*) when performing searches, improving the relevance of search results.
- *Searching on multiple fields*—You can create text indexes on multiple fields, and searches using the `$text` operator can include any or all of these indexed fields.
- *Text scoring and sorting*—Results can be scored based on the relevance to the search, allowing you to sort by how well each result matches the search criteria.

The `$text` operator has the following syntax:

```
{
  $text: {
    $search: <string>,
    $language: <string>,
    $caseSensitive: <boolean>,
    $diacriticSensitive: <boolean>
  }
}
```

Suppose that an application frequently searches for specific movies based on titles and plots. Setting up a text index on these fields enhances search capability with flexible, keyword-based queries. This type of index is useful for users who remember parts of the plot but not exact titles. Text indexes handle partial or mixed terms efficiently, improving search performance and user experience in movie databases. The following listing shows how to create such an index.

Listing 7.10 Creating a text index on two fields

```
db.movies.createIndex({
  title: "text",
  fullplot: "text"
})
```

After you set up the text index on the `title` and `fullplot` fields, the application can handle searches that include partial and keyword-based terms. The following query uses the text index to search for movies involving any title or plot containing the words *Zone* and *drinks*:

```
db.movies.find(
    { $text: { $search: "Zone drinks" } },
    { score: { $meta: "textScore" } }
).sort(
    { score: { $meta: "textScore" } }
).limit(3) // Find and sort the top 3 documents by text
➥search score for the query "Zone drinks"
```

This query searches the `movies` collection for documents that match the text search criteria `"Zone drinks"` and sorts the results by their text search score, limiting the output to the top three results. Here is one of the results documents:

```
[ {  _id: ObjectId('573a13c0f29313caabd615ad'),
    plot: "For her, there have always been two kinds of guys:
the ones you desire and the ones who buy you drinks.
➥For him, she is the woman of his dreams, the one he's been
➥waiting for. He is madly ...",
    genres: [ 'Comedy' ],
    runtime: 80,
    title: 'Friend Zone',
    fullplot: "For her, there have always been two kinds of guys:
➥the ones you desire and the ones who buy you drinks.
➥For him, she is the woman of his dreams, the one he's been
➥waiting for. He is madly in love with her and patiently waiting
➥for her to realize it. The thing is that she actually wants
➥him to buy her a drink and stay in the friend zone.",
    score: 2.0769230769230766 } ]
```

This document shows a movie titled *Friend Zone* with a plot involving characters who desire drinks and relationships. The score, which rounds to 2.08, indicates the relevance of this document to the search terms `"Zone drinks"`, with a higher score representing a closer match. This scoring helps users quickly identify the most relevant movies, enhancing user experience by prioritizing results that best match their search criteria.

You can execute more nuanced queries, such as those that search for movies that explicitly exclude certain terms. This query searches for movies that do not include *Zone* in the title or full plot but include the word *drinks*:

```
db.movies.find( { $text: { $search: "-Zone drinks" } } )
```

In this query, the minus sign (-) before `Zone` acts as a negation operator, instructing MongoDB to exclude results that contain the word *Zone*. This allows you to filter out specific movies and focus on those that include the term *drinks*.

7.2.5 Creating wildcard indexes

MongoDB supports creating wildcard indexes on a field or a set of fields. Wildcard indexes on a single field allow queries on any subfield of the indexed field, making them useful for querying fields with unknown or varying names between documents.

Wildcard indexes can be compound starting in MongoDB 7.0. A compound wildcard index includes one wildcard term and one or more additional index terms, allowing for more complex queries across multiple fields.

To create wildcard indexes, use a standard index creation command, and include the wildcard specifier (`$**`) in the index key. Here's how to create a wildcard index on a single field:

```
db.collection.createIndex( { "fieldName.$**": <sortOrder> } )
```

A compound wildcard index includes a wildcard term along with one or more additional index terms.

Use wildcard indexes when fields to be indexed are unpredictable or subject to change. Targeted indexes on specific fields usually perform better. If your collection has unpredictable field names, consider redesigning your schema for consistency. Use wildcard indexes in these scenarios:

- If field names vary among documents, a wildcard index supports queries on all possible field names.
- If embedded document fields have inconsistent subfields, a wildcard index supports queries on all subfields.
- If documents have shared characteristics, a compound wildcard index efficiently covers many queries for those common fields.

Suppose that your application frequently queries various subfields within the `tomatoes` field in the `movies` collection of the `sample_mflix` database, but the exact subfields are unpredictable or may change over time. To support queries on all possible subfields within the `tomatoes` field, create a wildcard index with the following command:

```
db.getSiblingDB('sample_mflix').movies.createIndex(
    { "tomatoes.$**": 1 } // Create a wildcard index on all
subfields of the tomatoes field in the movies collection
)
```

The wildcard index on the `tomatoes` field allows you to query on any subfield within `tomatoes` efficiently without knowing the specific subfields. This type of index is useful when the `tomatoes` field has varying subfields across documents, ensuring that any subfield can be queried. Although targeted indexes on known fields generally offer better performance, wildcard indexes provide a flexible solution for unknown or varying subfields, which is crucial for maintaining query performance in dynamic schemas.

> **TIP** You can create a wildcard index to support queries on all potential document fields. Wildcard indexes are useful for querying arbitrary or unknown field names. To create a wildcard index that covers all fields except `_id`, use the wildcard specifier (`$**`) as the index key: `db.<collection>.createIndex ( { "$**": <sortOrder> } )`.

7.2.6 Geospatial indexes

Geospatial indexes store and retrieve data efficiently based on geographic location. They involve creating an index on spatial data using a specialized structure that can quickly determine which objects or data points are within a specific area.

This type of indexing is especially valuable in applications that handle large volumes of geographic data, such as mapping applications, geolocation services, and spatial analytics. Geospatial indexing allows these applications to query and analyze data by location quickly, eliminating the need to scan extensive data sets to find relevant information.

MongoDB offers two types of geospatial indexes:

- *2dsphere*—Used for queries that interpret geometry on a spherical surface
- *2d*—Used for queries that interpret geometry on a flat plane

If your application often queries a field with geospatial data, creating a geospatial index can significantly improve performance. Some query operations mandate a geospatial index. To perform queries using the `$near` or `$nearSphere` operator or the `$geoNear` aggregation stage, create a geospatial index.

2DSPHERE INDEXES

2dsphere indexes support geospatial queries on an earthlike sphere, such as determining points within an area, calculating proximity to a point, and finding exact matches on coordinate queries. Indexed field values must be GeoJSON objects (a format for encoding a variety of geographic data structures) or legacy coordinate pairs—older formats stored as [longitude, latitude], which MongoDB converts to GeoJSON points. A simple GeoJSON point looks like this:

```
{
  "type": "Point",
  "coordinates": [40.7128, -74.0060]
}
```

This object represents a point at latitude 40.7128 and longitude -74.0060, which are the coordinates of New York City. To create a 2dsphere index, specify the `location` field with the type "2dsphere".

To create a 2dsphere index in the `shipwrecks` collection stored in the `sample_geospatial` database, use the following command:

```
db.shipwrecks.createIndex({ coordinates: "2dsphere" })
```

To find shipwrecks within a 5-kilometer radius of the coordinates [-79.9081268, 9.3547792], use the following query:

```
db.shipwrecks.find({
  coordinates: {
    $near: {
```

```
      $geometry: { type: "Point", coordinates: [-79.9081268, 9.3547792] },
      $maxDistance: 5000
    }
  }
})
```

This query returns shipwrecks close to the specified location:

```
{
  "_id": ObjectId("578f6fa2df35c7fbdbaed8c4"),
  "feature_type": "Wrecks - Visible",
  "coordinates": [-79.9081268, 9.3547792]
}
```

Longitude must be between -180 and 180, and latitude must be between -90 and 90. Use cases include finding nearby restaurants, calculating shortest routes, and identifying parks within city limits. 2dsphere indexes are always sparse and can be part of compound indexes that reference multiple location and nonlocation fields.

2D INDEXES

2d indexes support queries on data stored as points on a two-dimensional plane, intended for legacy coordinate pairs.

To find shipwrecks within a 0.1-degree radius of the coordinates [-79.9081268, 9.3547792] on a planar surface, create an index with

```
db.shipwrecks.createIndex({ coordinates: "2d" })
```

and execute the following query:

```
db.shipwrecks.find({
  coordinates: {
    $near: [-79.9081268, 9.3547792],
    $maxDistance: 0.1
  }
})
```

This query returns shipwrecks close to the specified location:

```
{
  "_id": ObjectId("578f6fa2df35c7fbdbaed8c4"),
  "feature_type": "Wrecks - Visible",
  "coordinates": [-79.9081268, 9.3547792]
}
```

NOTE 2d indexes cannot be used for GeoJSON objects; for those, use 2dsphere indexes.

When you create a 2d index, longitude must be between -180 and 180, and latitude must be between -90 and 90.

7.2.7 Hashed indexes

Hashed indexes collect and store hashes of the values of the indexed field. These indexes support sharding using hashed shard keys, which means that they use a hashed index of a field as the shard key to partition data across your sharded cluster.

Hashed indexing is ideal for shard keys with fields that change monotonically, such as `ObjectId` values and timestamps. In traditional ranged sharding, a monotonically increasing shard-key value can lead to a problem: the chunk with an upper bound of `MaxKey` receives most of the incoming writes. This behavior restricts insert operations to a single shard, negating the advantage of using distributed writes in a sharded cluster. Hashed sharding helps distribute the writes more evenly across shards, solving this problem. (Sharding is explained in chapter 9.)

To create a hashed index on a single field, set the index key's value to `"hashed"`:

```
db.<collection>.createIndex(
    {
        <field>: "hashed"
    }
)
```

To create a compound hashed index, set `"hashed"` as the value for one index key:

```
db.<collection>.createIndex(
    {
        <field1>: "hashed"
        ...
    }
)
```

> **TIP** When MongoDB uses a hashed index to resolve a query, it automatically computes the hash values using an internal hashing function. Applications do not need to calculate these hashes themselves.

Hashed indexes convert floating-point numbers to 64-bit integers before hashing. The values 2.3, 2.2, and 2.9, for example, will share the same hash key due to this conversion, causing a collision when multiple values are assigned to a single hash key. These collisions can negatively affect query performance.

To prevent collisions, do not use a hashed index for floating-point numbers that cannot be reliably converted to 64-bit integers and then back to floating-point numbers. Also, hashed indexes do not support floating-point numbers larger than 2^{53}.

> **TIP** Hashed indexes have limitations regarding array fields and the `unique` property. The hashing function does not support multikey indexes, which means that you cannot create a hashed index on a field that contains an array or insert an array into a hashed indexed field.

> **NOTE** You cannot specify a `unique` constraint on a hashed index. Instead, to enforce uniqueness on a field, you need to create an additional no-hashed index with the unique constraint. MongoDB will use this nonhashed index to ensure the uniqueness of the field.

7.3 Dropping indexes

To drop an index in MongoDB, you can use the `db.collection.dropIndex(index)` `mongosh` helper method, which removes a specified index from a collection. The `index` parameter specifies the index to drop and can be provided as either the index name (string) or the index specification document (object).

> **WARNING** Dropping an actively used index in production can lead to performance degradation in your application. To assess the potential effect before dropping an index, hide the index, and observe any changes in performance. Hidden indexes are explained in section 7.4.4.

You can also use the Atlas User Interface, shown in figure 7.4, for this purpose. The Atlas UI lets you add and drop indexes as you do with `mongosh`. To add an index, click the Create Index button to the right of the list of existing indexes.

> **NOTE** The index on the `_id` field cannot be removed.

Figure 7.4 The MongoDB Atlas IU allows you to add and remove indexes. (Image © MongoDB 2025)

To remove an index, click the trashcan icon in the Action column for the specific index. Then type the index name in the confirmation dialog box, and click the red Drop button.

7.4 MongoDB index attributes

Index attributes influence how the query planner uses an index and how indexed documents are stored. You can set these attributes as optional parameters when creating an index.

7.4.1 Partial indexes

Partial indexes index only the documents in a collection that meet a specified filter expression. By indexing only a subset of the documents, partial indexes have lower storage requirements and reduced performance costs for index creation and maintenance.

To create a partial index, use the `db.collection.createIndex()` method with the `partialFilterExpression` option. The `partialFilterExpression` option accepts a document that specifies the filter condition using various operators, such as equality expressions (such as `field: value` or the `$eq` operator); the `$exists: true` expression; the `$gt`, `$gte`, `$lt`, and `$lte` expressions; the `$type` expression; and the `$and`, `$or`, and `$in` operators.

Here, we'll see that the compound index used earlier in this chapter would look like a partial index with the `$eq` operator:

```
db.getSiblingDB('sample_mflix').movies.createIndex(
    {
        year: 1,
        type: 1,
        "imdb.rating": 1
    },
    {
        partialFilterExpression: { type: { $eq: "movie" } }
    } // Creates a partial index on the movies collection
      // for documents where type is "movie"
)
```

This command creates a partial index on the `movies` collection, indexing only the documents in which the type of field is `"movie"`. By using the `$eq` operator, the filter ensures that only documents with type equal to `"movie"` are indexed. Because the index includes only documents in which the type is `"movie"`, it requires less storage space and reduces the overhead associated with index creation and maintenance.

7.4.2 Sparse indexes

Sparse indexes include entries only for documents that have the indexed field, even if the field contains a `null` value. The index ignores any document that is missing the indexed field, making the index sparse because it does not cover all documents in a collection. By contrast, nonsparse indexes include all documents in a collection, storing `null` values for documents that do not have the indexed field.

> **TIP** Partial indexes provide a broader range of functionality compared with sparse indexes and should be preferred over sparse indexes.

To create a sparse index, use the `db.collection.createIndex()` helper method with the `sparse` option set to `true`. Here, we'll look at how the single index used earlier in this chapter would look as a sparse index:

```
db.movies.createIndex(
    { "runtime": 1 },
    { sparse: true } // Create a sparse index on the runtime field
)
```

This command creates a sparse index on the runtime field in the movies collection. The index includes entries only for documents that contain the runtime field, ignoring any documents that do not have this field.

7.4.3 Time-to-live indexes

Time-to-live (TTL) indexes are single-field indexes in MongoDB that automatically delete documents from a collection after a specified duration or at a specific time. This feature is particularly useful for managing data with a limited lifespan, such as machine-generated event data, logs, and session information. In flight search systems, for example, you can use TTL indexes to remove flight documents automatically when the flight has departed. Other examples include expiring session data after a user logs out, deleting temporary files after a certain period, and removing outdated promotional offers when they have expired.

To create a TTL index, use the createIndex() method. Choose an index field that is either the date type or an array containing date-type values. Use the expireAfterSeconds option to set a TTL value in seconds.

> **NOTE** The expireAfterSeconds value for a TTL index must be between 0 and 2147483647, inclusive.

To create a TTL index on the date field in the sample_analytics database and the transactions collection, use the following command:

```
db.getSiblingDB('sample_analytics').transactions.createIndex(
    { "date": 1 },
    { expireAfterSeconds: 31536000 } // Creates a TTL index on
➥the "date" field. Documents will expire 1 year after the
➥value in the "date" field.
)
```

This command creates a TTL index on the date field of the transactions collection in the sample_analytics database. The expireAfterSeconds option is set to 31536000, which corresponds to one year. This means that any document in the transactions collection with a date field older than one year will be deleted automatically.

SETTING EXPIRE AFTER SECONDS TO 0

You can expire documents at a specific clock time by creating a TTL index on a field that holds Binary JSON (BSON) date type values or an array of BSON date-typed objects and specifying an expireAfterSeconds value of 0. For each document in the collection, set the indexed date field to the time when the document should expire. If the indexed date field contains a date in the past, MongoDB considers the document expired.

The following operation creates an index on the transactions collection's date field in the sample_analytics database and specifies an expireAfterSeconds value of 0:

```
db.getSiblingDB('sample_analytics').runCommand(
    {
        collMod: "transactions",
        index: {
            keyPattern: { date: 1 },
            expireAfterSeconds: 0
        }
    } // Set the TTL index on the date field to expire documents immediately
)
```

MongoDB automatically deletes documents from the `transactions` collection when the documents' date value is older than the number of seconds specified in `expireAfterSeconds`, which is `0` in this case. As such, the data expires at the specified date value.

CONVERTING A NON-TTL INDEX TO A TTL INDEX

You can add the `expireAfterSeconds` option to an existing single-field index. To change a non-TTL single-field index to a TTL index, use the `collMod` database command:

```
db.getSiblingDB('sample_analytics').runCommand({
  "collMod": "transactions",
  "index": {
    "keyPattern": { "date": 1 },
    "expireAfterSeconds": 31536000 // 1 year in seconds
  }
})
```

This command modifies the existing index on the `date` field in the `transactions` collection to include the `expireAfterSeconds` option. As a result, documents with a `date` value older than one year will be deleted automatically, ensuring that the collection retains only recent data.

> **WARNING** After creating a TTL index, you may find that you have a large number of qualifying documents to delete at the same time. This substantial workload can lead to performance problems on the server. To mitigate these potential problems, consider creating the index during off-peak hours when server load is lower. Alternatively, you can delete qualifying documents manually in batches before creating the TTL index, ensuring that the index will manage only future documents and thus reducing the initial load.

TTL indexes restrictions as follows:

- TTL indexes are restricted to single-field indexes; compound indexes do not support TTL and ignore the `expireAfterSeconds` option.
- The `_id` field does not support TTL indexes.
- You cannot create a TTL index on a capped collection.
- For a time-series collection, you can create TTL indexes only on the collection's `timeField`.

- You cannot use the `createIndex()` method to change the `expireAfterSeconds` value of an existing index. Instead, use the `collMod` database command.

If a non-TTL single-field index already exists for a field, you cannot create a TTL index on the same field because indexes with the same key specification but differing options are not allowed. To convert a non-TTL single-field index to a TTL index, use the `collMod` database command.

> **TIP** If you are deleting documents to reduce storage costs, consider using the Online Archive feature in MongoDB Atlas (chapter 17). Online Archive automatically moves infrequently accessed data to fully managed Amazon S3 buckets, providing a cost-effective solution for data tiering.

> **NOTE** Beginning with MongoDB 7.1, TTL indexes can be created on capped collections.

7.4.4 Hidden indexes

By hiding an index, you can test the effects of its absence without removing it permanently. If the results are unfavorable, you can unhide the index instead of re-creating it.

Hidden indexes are not visible to the query planner and are not used to support queries. If you hide an index on the `runtime` field and notice a significant slowdown in user lookup queries, for example, you can unhide the index to restore performance without re-creating it.

To hide an existing index, use the `db.collection.hideIndex()` method. To hide and index on the `runtime` field in the `sample_mflix.movies` collection, use the following command:

```
db.getSiblingDB('sample_mflix').movies.hideIndex(
    { runtime: 1 } // Specify the index key specification document
)
```

To unhide a hidden index, use the `collMod` command or `mongosh` helper method:

```
db.collection.unhideIndex()
db.getSiblingDB('sample_mflix').movies.unhideIndex(
    { runtime: 1 } // Specify the index key specification document
)
```

These commands allow you to manage the visibility of indexes in the `movies` collection within the `sample_mflix` database.

Apart from being hidden from the planner, hidden indexes behave like unhidden indexes. A hidden index that is a unique index still enforces its unique constraint on the documents. Similarly, if a hidden index is a TTL index, it still expires documents as expected. Hidden indexes are updated with write operations to the collection and continue to consume disk space and memory. Hiding an unhidden index or unhiding a hidden index resets its $indexStats (explained in section 7.6.1), but hiding an already-hidden index or unhiding an already-unhidden index does not.

7.5 Understanding index builds

Index builds engage in an optimized construction technique that involves securing an exclusive lock on the collection at the beginning and end of the build. Throughout the rest of the construction process, it allows the interleaving of read and write operations. Index builds across a replica set or sharded cluster occur simultaneously on all data-bearing members of the replica set. The primary node mandates that a minimum number of data-bearing, voting members, including itself, complete the build. Only then is the index marked as ready for use.

Beginning with MongoDB 7.1, improvements have been made to index builds, enhancing error-reporting speed and bolstering failure resilience. Also, you can specify the minimum required disk space for index builds using the new `indexBuildMinAvailableDiskSpaceMB` parameter. This parameter halts index builds if available disk space falls below the set threshold. Table 7.1 outlines the differences in index build behavior between MongoDB 7.1 and previous versions.

Table 7.1 Mongo build behavior for different versions

MongoDB 7.1	Earlier MongoDB versions
During the collection scan phase, any index errors detected, except duplicate key errors, are reported immediately, and the index build is halted.	Delays in reporting index build errors may occur because the errors are returned toward the end of the index build, in the commit phase.
If an index build encounters an error, a secondary member can instruct the primary member to halt the index build, preventing the secondary member from crashing.	An error during an index build might lead to the crash of a secondary member.
An index build can be halted automatically if available disk space falls below the threshold specified in the `indexBuildMinAvailableDiskSpaceMB` parameter.	An index build is not halted due to insufficient available disk space.

Currently, MongoDB exclusively locks only the collection being indexed at the beginning and end of the build to safeguard metadata changes. The rest of the build process uses the yielding behavior of background builds, enhancing read–write access to the collection during construction. This approach maintains efficient index structures while allowing more flexible access.

The index build process unfolds as follows:

1 Upon receiving the `createIndexes` command, the primary immediately logs a `"startIndexBuild"` oplog entry tied to the index build.

2 The secondary members initiate the index build upon replicating the `"startIndexBuild"` oplog entry.

3 Each member casts a vote to commit the build after completing the indexing of the collection's data.
4 If no violations occur, the build continues with these steps:
   a While waiting for the primary to confirm a quorum of votes, secondary members integrate any new write operations into the index.
   b When a quorum is confirmed, the primary checks for key-constraint violations, such as duplicate keys.
   c If no violations are found, the primary finalizes the index build, marks the index as ready, and logs a `"commitIndexBuild"` oplog entry.
5 If key constraint violations occur, the index build is deemed a failure:
   a The primary logs an `"abortIndexBuild"` oplog entry and halts the build.
   b Secondaries that replicate the `"commitIndexBuild"` oplog entry complete the index build.
   c If secondaries replicate an `"abortIndexBuild"` oplog entry, they terminate the index build and discard the build task.

TIP Index builds can affect the performance of a replica set. For workloads that cannot afford a decrease in performance during index builds, consider using a rolling index build process. This method involves taking one replica-set member offline at a time, beginning with the secondary members, and building the index on that member while it is temporarily running as a standalone server outside the replica set. Rolling index builds necessitate at least one replica-set election.

NOTE If you invoke `db.collection.createIndex()` on an index that already exists, MongoDB will not re-create the index.

7.5.1 Monitoring in-progress index builds

To monitor the status of an index build operation, you can use the `db.currentOp()` method in `mongosh` (chapter 3). The next listing show the executed command that returns information on index creation operations on any number of fields.

Listing 7.11 Status of an Index build operation

```
db.adminCommand(
    {
      currentOp: true,
      $or: [
        { op: "command", "command.createIndexes": { $exists: true } },
        { op: "command", "command.$truncated": /^\{ createIndexes/ },
        { op: "none", "msg" : /^Index Build/ }
      ]
    }
)
```

7.5.2 Terminating in-progress index builds

To terminate an in-progress index build, use the `dropIndexes` command or its shell helpers `dropIndex()` or `dropIndexes()`. If an index specified in `dropIndexes` is still being built, the command attempts to halt the in-progress build. Halting an index build effectively has the same result as dropping the completed index.

> **NOTE** Do not use `killOp` (chapter 21) to terminate an in-progress index build in replica sets or sharded clusters; this can lead to inconsistent state across nodes and may require manual cleanup.

7.6 Managing indexes

Effective index management is crucial for optimizing query performance and ensuring efficient data retrieval in MongoDB. Proper handling of indexes can significantly enhance the efficiency and speed of your database operations. Always check whether the indexes in your database are appropriate and being used; if they are not used, remove them. Having too many indexes can lead to additional overhead, consuming more disk space and slowing write operations. Ensure that only necessary, frequently used indexes are maintained for optimal performance.

7.6.1 Discovering the $indexStats aggregation pipeline stage

The more indexes you have, the more work MongoDB must do when inserting a document because it needs to update each index. Indexes operate behind the scenes, making it difficult to determine whether they are being used.

MongoDB monitors use statistics for each index. To access these statistics, you can use the `$indexStats` aggregation pipeline stage. The following listing shows how to retrieve these statistics.

Listing 7.12 Displaying `$indexStats` statistics

```
db.movies.aggregate( [ { $indexStats: { } } ] )
[
  {
    name: 'year_1_title_1_imdb.rating_1',
    key: { year: 1, title: 1, 'imdb.rating': 1 },
    accesses: { ops: Long('11'), since: ISODate('2024-06-01') },
    host: 'ac-pikzgq8-shard-00-02.a7niyd4.mongodb.net:27017'
  }
]
```

The name of the index is `year_1_title_1_imdb.rating_1`. The key pattern of the index is `{ year: 1, title: 1, 'imdb.rating': 1 }`. The number of operations that have accessed the index is `11`, collected since `2024-06-01`. The host information in which the index resides is `ac-pikzgq8-shard-00-02.a7niyd4.mongodb.net:27017`.

You can also use this script to log index-use statistics across all databases, excluding the `admin`, `config`, and `local` system databases:

```
db.getMongo().getDBNames().forEach(function(dbname) {
    // Processing the database
    if (dbname !== "admin" && dbname !== "config" && dbname !== "local")
➥{ // Skip system databases
        var currentDB = db.getSiblingDB(dbname);
        currentDB.getCollectionNames().forEach(function(cname) {
            // Processing the collection
            var indexStats = currentDB[cname].aggregate([{ $indexStats: {}
➥}]).toArray(); // Use $indexStats aggregation
            indexStats.forEach(function(indexStat) {
                // Log index usage statistics
                print("Index usage statistics: " +
➥JSON.stringify(indexStat));
            });
        });
    }
})
```

For each database, the script retrieves all collection names and processes each collection. Using the $indexStats aggregation stage, it collects index-use statistics for each collection and prints these statistics to the console.

You can also use MongoDB Compass to display index statistics. Figure 7.5 shows the Compass GUI used to manage indexes in the sample_mflix.movies collection. The interface displays details about each index, including name, type, size, use, and properties.

Name & Definition	Type	Size	Usage	Properties	Status
> _id_	REGULAR	704.5 KB	2 (since Tue Dec 17 2024)	UNIQUE	READY
> title_text_fullplot_text	TEXT	14.9 MB	0 (since Tue Dec 17 2024)	COMPOUND	READY
> year_1_title_1_imdb.rating_1	REGULAR	761.9 KB	16 (since Tue Dec 17 2024)	COMPOUND	READY

Figure 7.5 Index statistics help you make decisions about index maintenance and optimization. For the sample_mflix.movies collection, the title_text_fullplot_text index is a text index that has been accessed 0 times since December 17, 2024, whereas the year_1_title_1_imdb.rating_1 compound index has been accessed 16 times since December 17, 2024. (Image © MongoDB 2025)

TIP Index statistics are reset on every mongod service restart.

7.6.2 Modifying indexes

To modify an existing index, you have to drop and re-create it. TTL indexes are an exception, however; you can modify them by using the collMod command along with the index collection flag.

Dropping an actively used index in production can lead to performance degradation. To prevent this degradation, you can create a temporary redundant index that includes the existing index keys as a prefix and a dummy field as a suffix. This approach ensures that queries can still use an index during the modification process.

After dropping the original index, re-create it with the desired modifications. When the new index is in place, drop the temporary index, ensuring that queries continue to operate efficiently. Confirm that the new index has been updated successfully by viewing the collection's indexes. This method ensures seamless index modifications without disrupting application performance.

7.6.3 Controlling index use with hint ()

Sometimes, you want to compel MongoDB to use a specific index. To do this for a `db.collection.find()` operation, use the `hint()` method. Attach the `hint()` method to the `find()` method to specify the desired index, as in this example:

```
db.movies.find(
    { year: 1914, "imdb.rating": { $gte: 7 } }
).sort(
    { title: 1 }
).hint(
    { year: 1, type: 1, "imdb.rating": 1 })
```

The `hint()` method tells MongoDB to use the specific compound index `{ year: 1, type: 1, "imdb.rating": 1 }` to execute the query. You can check it by adding `explain()` to the query:

```
db.movies.find(
    { year: 1914, "imdb.rating": { $gte: 7 } }
).sort(
    { title: 1 }
).hint(
    { year: 1, type: 1, "imdb.rating": 1 }
).explain("executionStats");
```

This approach can be useful if the index you want to use is not being selected by the query planner. If you know that a particular index will provide better performance for a specific query, using `hint()` ensures MongoDB uses that index. Also, if you are diagnosing query performance problems or want to test the effect of different indexes, `hint()` allows you to force the use of a specific index for precise control and analysis.

7.6.4 Using indexes with $OR queries

When evaluating the clauses in a `$or` expression, MongoDB performs a collection scan or, if all clauses are supported by indexes, performs index scans. For MongoDB to use indexes to evaluate a `$or` expression, all the clauses in the `$or` expression must be supported by indexes; otherwise, MongoDB performs a collection scan.

When you use indexes with `$or` queries, each clause of a `$or` can use its own index. Consider the following query on the `movies` collection in the `sample_mflix` database:

```
db.movies.find({
  $or: [
    { year: 1914 },
    { "imdb.rating": { $gt: 7 } }
  ]
}).explain("executionStats")
```

The movies collection had this index created earlier in the chapter: { year: 1, type: 1, "imdb.rating": 1 }. Because the existing compound index { year: 1, type: 1, "imdb.rating": 1 } does not fully support both conditions in the $or clause, MongoDB performs a collection scan instead of using the index. The index does not have imdb.rating as the leading field, so it cannot be used effectively for the { "imdb.rating": { $gt: 7 } } condition.

To avoid a collection scan and optimize the query performance, you must ensure that each condition in the $or clause is supported by an appropriate index. MongoDB uses indexes to evaluate a $or expression only if all the clauses are supported by indexes. To ensure that both conditions in the $or clause are supported by indexes and to optimize query performance, create an additional index for the imdb.rating condition:

```
db.movies.createIndex({ "imdb.rating": 1 })
```

This setup ensures that both conditions in the $or clause are supported by indexes, preventing a collection scan and optimizing query performance.

7.6.5 Using indexes with the $NE, $NIN, and $NOT operators

The performance effect of the $ne (not equal), $nin (not in), and $not operators depends on the index structure. Although single-field indexes may offer limited benefits, the query planner can still use multifield indexes effectively.

7.6.6 Ensuring that indexes fit in RAM

To follow best practices, ensure that random-access indexes fit entirely in RAM for fastest processing. This prevents the system from reading the index from disk.

To determine the size of your indexes, use the db.collection.totalIndexSize() helper, which provides the size in bytes:

```
var indexSizeBytes = db.movies.totalIndexSize();
var indexSizeGB = indexSizeBytes / (1024 * 1024 * 1024);
print("Total Index Size in GB: " + indexSizeGB);

Total Index Size in GB: 0.015438079833984375
```

> **TIP** You can also use MongoDB Compass to check index sizes.

> **NOTE** Indexes don't always need to fit entirely into RAM. If the indexed field increments with each insert, and most queries target recent documents,

MongoDB needs to keep only the most recent or "rightmost" parts of the index in RAM. This ensures efficient index use for reading and writing operations while minimizing RAM use.

7.6.7 Sorting on multiple fields

You can use a compound index to enable sorting on multiple fields. You can sort using all the keys in the index or only a subset, but the sort keys must be in the same order as they are in the index. The index key pattern { a: 1, b: 1 }, for example, supports sorting by { a: 1, b: 1 } but not by { b: 1, a: 1 }.

Suppose that you want to sort by `runtime` and then by `year` in the `movies` collection. First, create a compound index on these fields:

```
db.movies.createIndex({ runtime: 1, year: 1 })
```

Then use the following query to sort movies by `runtime` in ascending order and then by `year` in ascending order:

```
db.movies.find().sort({ runtime: 1, year: 1 })
```

You can also execute a query that filters documents in which `runtime` is greater than 40 and then sort the results by `runtime` in ascending order and `year` in ascending order. Here is the query:

```
db.movies.find({ runtime: { $gt: 40 } }).sort({ runtime: 1, year: 1 })
```

The index { runtime: 1, year: 1 } allows MongoDB to filter documents in which `runtime` is greater than 40 and then sort the results by `runtime` and `year`.

In the `theaters` collection, create a compound index on `theaterId`, `location.address.city`, and `location.address.zipcode`:

```
db.theaters.createIndex({ theaterId: 1, "location.address.city": 1,
➥ "location.address.zipcode": 1 })
```

Use the following code to sort theaters by `theaterId` in ascending order, then by city in ascending order, and finally by zip code in ascending order:

```
db.theaters.find().sort({ theaterId: 1,
➥ "location.address.city": 1, "location.address.zipcode": 1 })
```

MongoDB can use compound indexes to optimize sort operations. By understanding and using index prefixes, you can ensure that your queries are as efficient as possible. Ensure that the order of fields in your sort operations matches the order in your indexes to maximize performance.

7.6.8 Introducing covered queries

A *covered query* in MongoDB is one in which all the fields used in the query and the fields returned by the query are included in an index. This allows MongoDB to retrieve the results directly from the index without scanning the documents in the collection, leading to more efficient query performance.

The following code is a covered query because there is already an index, { year: 1, title: 1, "imdb.rating": 1 }, that includes all the fields used in the query filter (year and imdb.rating) and the fields returned by the query (title and year). This allows MongoDB to use the index to retrieve the results directly without scanning the documents in the collection:

```
db.movies.find(
{ year: 1914, "imdb.rating": { $gte: 7 } },
{ title: 1, year: 1, _id: 0 }
).explain("executionStats")

......
winningPlan: {
    stage: 'PROJECTION_COVERED',
    transformBy: { title: 1, year: 1, _id: 0 },
    inputStage: {
      stage: 'IXSCAN',
      keyPattern: { year: 1, title: 1, 'imdb.rating': 1 },
      indexName: 'year_1_title_1_imdb.rating_1'
......
  executionStats: {
    executionSuccess: true,
    nReturned: 2,
    executionTimeMillis: 0,
    totalKeysExamined: 4,
    totalDocsExamined: 0
```

The execution plan shows that the query used the compound index { year: 1, title: 1, "imdb.rating": 1 }. It was a covered query (PROJECTION_COVERED), meaning that all the required fields were retrieved directly from the index without scanning the documents in the collection. The index scan (IXSCAN) used the specified index to filter the results. The execution was successful, returning two documents in 0 ms, with four index keys examined and zero documents scanned.

> **WARNING** Forgetting to exclude _id is a common failure in creating a covered query. Also, multikey indexes cannot provide a covered query plan if any of the returned fields contains arrays.

7.7 When to not use an index

Indexes are best for retrieving small data subsets. For large queries, they can be slower because they require two lookups: one for the index entry and one for the document. A collection scan needs only one lookup. If a query returns a large portion of the collection, using an index can be inefficient and slow. There's no exact rule about when an index helps or hinders; the decision to use one depends on data size and other factors. Typically, an index speeds queries if they return less than 30% of the collection, though this figure can range from 2% to 60%.

Suppose that you have a monitoring system that collects server logs. Your application queries the system for all logs from a specific server to analyze activity from the past week:

```
db.logs.find(
{ "server_id": "server123",
"timestamp": { "$gt": weekAgo } }
)
```

You index "`timestamp`" to speed this query. When you first launch, the result set is small, and the query returns instantly. But after a few weeks, the amount of data grows, and after a month, this query starts taking too long to run.

Summary

- The MongoDB query planner analyzes multiple execution plans to select the most efficient one, using indexes to minimize response times and resource use. If no suitable index is available, it performs a full collection scan, which is less efficient and can significantly burden the database, especially with large data sets.
- MongoDB uses two query engines—the classic query engine and the slot-based query engine—to find and return results. MongoDB chooses the engine automatically, and you can't select it manually. The slot-based engine usually offers better performance and lower CPU and memory use.
- To access query plan details in MongoDB, use `db.collection.explain()` or `cursor.explain()` with verboseness levels such as `"queryPlanner"`, `"executionStats"`, and `"allPlansExecution"` for varying detail. These tools help you understand performance characteristics and diagnose query efficiency problems.
- MongoDB supports various index types to enhance query performance, including single-field, compound, multikey, text, wildcard, geospatial, and hashed. Each index type caters to different query requirements, optimizing data retrieval based on the fields and operations involved.
- You can create an index using the `db.collection.createIndex()` mongosh helper method, the database `createIndexes` command, or the Compass or Atlas UI.
- MongoDB index attributes affect how the query planner uses indexes and stores documents. Partial indexes reduce storage and performance costs by indexing only documents that meet a filter expression. Sparse indexes include only documents with the indexed field, and TTL indexes delete documents automatically

after a set time. Hidden indexes let you test their absence without removal, remaining invisible to the planner but still enforcing constraints and TTL deletions.
- Index builds in MongoDB secure exclusive locks on collections at the beginning and end, allowing interleaved read and write operations during the process. You can monitor and terminate in-progress index builds using commands such as `db.currentOp()` and `dropIndexes`.
- To optimize sort operations, use compound indexes, ensuring that the sort keys match the order of the index fields. You can create an index on `{ field1: 1, field2: 1 }` and then sort documents by `field1` and `field2` in ascending order using `db.collection.find().sort({ field1: 1, field2: 1 })`.
- Managing indexes involves using tools such as the `$indexStats` aggregation stage to monitor index use and `hint()` to control which indexes are used for specific queries.
- Indexes that fit in RAM optimize performance, and covered queries improve efficiency by retrieving results directly from indexes without scanning documents.
- MongoDB uses indexes to evaluate a `$or` expression only if all clauses are supported by indexes; otherwise, it performs a collection scan.

Executing multidocument ACID transactions

This chapter covers

- Understanding the WiredTiger Storage Engine
- Examining the ACID principles
- Comparing the Core and Callback APIs
- Implementing transactions with the Node.js driver
- Performing transactions using the Python driver
- Managing transactions with the Ruby driver

Transactions are discrete units of operation within a database management system, comprising multiple related read and write actions. These operations are grouped together and must all succeed as a whole or fail together, ensuring that no partial updates are left in the database. Consider a transaction for booking a travel package that includes a flight and a hotel. If the booking process successfully reserves a flight but encounters a problem with the hotel reservation, the entire transaction must be aborted. This means the flight reservation would also be undone, maintaining the status quo in the database.

Although MongoDB is a nonrelational database and traditionally does not follow the relational model's approach to transactions, it has long ensured data integrity through its single-document operations. With the introduction of multidocument atomicity, consistency, isolation, and durability (ACID) transactions, however, MongoDB has significantly broadened its applicability and enhanced its capability to handle complex transaction scenarios.

8.1 WiredTiger storage engine

WiredTiger is a high-performance, scalable, open source NoSQL platform for data management, characterized by its extensibility and production-quality capabilities. MongoDB acquired WiredTiger, incorporating it as its default storage engine, which significantly enhances MongoDB's performance and scalability. WiredTiger uses multiversion concurrency control (MVCC) to allow multiple read and write operations to occur simultaneously without blocking, which minimizes contention. Its support for compression reduces the amount of storage needed and improves I/O efficiency. It also uses in-memory caching, which reduces the need for frequent disk access, further speeding read and write operations. Its free locking mechanism allows operations to target specific data, improving concurrency and reducing bottlenecks. It supports multiple storage architectures:

- *Row-oriented storage*—All columns of a row are stored together, which is efficient for accessing complete records.
- *Column-oriented storage*—Columns are stored separately, optimizing the storage and retrieval of subsets of columns.

WiredTiger also features ACID transactions, supporting standard isolation levels and providing durability at both checkpoint and fine-grained levels. It can function as a simple key-value store and offers a comprehensive schema layer that includes indices and projections.

8.1.1 Snapshots and checkpoints

WiredTiger uses MVCC to provide a consistent point-in-time snapshot of the data, ensuring consistent views of in-memory data. When writing to disk, all snapshot data is committed in a consistent manner across data files, creating a durable checkpoint. Checkpoints ensure data file consistency up to the last checkpoint and serve as recovery points.

MongoDB checkpoints are scheduled every 60 seconds. Even during checkpoint creation, the previous checkpoint remains valid, facilitating recovery from the last valid checkpoint in case of errors or shutdowns. A new checkpoint becomes permanent and replaces the old one when WiredTiger's metadata table is atomically updated.

Since MongoDB 5.0, you can use the `minSnapshotHistoryWindowInSeconds` parameter to specify how long WiredTiger retains snapshot history. Increasing this value results in greater disk use as more history is maintained—crucial in high-volume environments. The history is stored in the `WiredTigerHS.wt` file in the specified `dbPath`.

8.1.2 Journaling

WiredTiger uses a write-ahead logging journal in conjunction with checkpoints to ensure data durability. The journal records all modifications between checkpoints. If MongoDB exits unexpectedly between checkpoints, the journal is used to replay data modifications since the last checkpoint, ensuring no data loss. WiredTiger compresses journal entries using the snappy compression library by default, but you can customize it through the `storage.wiredTiger.engineConfig.journalCompressor` setting.

8.1.3 Compression

Compression in WiredTiger allows MongoDB to reduce storage for all collections and indexes; this incurs the cost of increased CPU use. WiredTiger defaults to block compression using the `Snappy` library for collections and prefix compression for indexes. Additional block compression options for collections include `zlib` and `zstd`. The WiredTiger journal is also compressed by default.

8.1.4 Memory use

In MongoDB, memory use is managed through both the WiredTiger internal cache and the filesystem cache. The default size for the WiredTiger internal cache is determined by whichever is greater:

- 50% of the remaining RAM after deducting 1 GB
- A minimum of 256 MB

On a system with 8 GB of RAM, the WiredTiger cache would be set to 3.5 GB of RAM, calculated as 50% of (8 GB–1 GB). Alternatively, on a system with only 1.28 GB of RAM, the WiredTiger cache would default to 256 MB because 50% of the remaining RAM after deducting 1 GB (which would be 128 MB) is below the 256 MB minimum threshold.

8.2 Single-document transaction

Let's start by discussing single-document transactions. In MongoDB, each operation on a single document is atomic. This means that any operation—whether it's updating, deleting, or inserting a document—is completed in full or not completed. This level of atomicity ensures data integrity without traditional locking mechanisms.

If an update operation on a document is initiated but fails midway due to a system crash or network problem, MongoDB ensures that no changes are applied, maintaining the pretransaction state of the document. This built-in atomicity is crucial for maintaining consistency and reliability in applications when they do not require the complexity of multidocument transactions.

MongoDB ensures atomicity at the single-document level by using an underlying storage WiredTiger mechanism. When an operation is performed on a document, the changes are first applied in-memory. Only when the operation is fully successful are the changes written to disk.

WiredTiger supports document-level concurrency control for write operations, allowing multiple clients to modify different documents in the same collection at the same time. This is achieved using optimistic concurrency control with intent locks at the global, database, and collection levels. If there is a conflict, WiredTiger detects it, and one operation might face a write conflict, causing MongoDB to retry the operation.

Optimistic concurrency control (OCC) handles data conflicts during transactions, which works well in MongoDB's WiredTiger, where conflicts are expected to be rare. Transactions use minimal up-front locking, reducing system overhead and improving performance. A transaction reads data and keeps a snapshot of the data at the beginning, using version numbers or timestamps to detect changes. If a change is detected during a write, it triggers a write conflict.

When a conflict occurs, the transaction might be aborted and restarted or forced to wait and retry, depending on the configuration. OCC's main benefit is preventing locks during the read phase, boosting performance when write conflicts are rare. If conflicts are frequent, however, the cost of restarting transactions can reduce this benefit.

8.3 Defining ACID

ACID is a set of principles that ensure reliable processing of database transactions:

- *Atomicity*—Guarantees that each transaction is treated as a single unit that either completes entirely or is completely undone; no intermediate states are allowed. If any part of a transaction fails, the entire transaction fails, and the database state is left unchanged.
- *Consistency*—Ensures that any transaction brings the database from one valid state to another. No transaction can violate the database rules.
- *Isolation*—Determines how transaction integrity is visibly affected by the interaction between concurrent transactions. The goal is to make transactions appear isolated from one another even though they may be executed concurrently.
- *Durability*—Ensures that when a transaction has been committed, it remains so, even in the event of a power loss, crash, or other system failures.

These properties are necessary for maintaining the integrity and reliability of a database, preventing data corruption and ensuring that the database accurately reflects confirmed transactions.

A database is said to be ACID-compliant when it consistently upholds the principles of atomicity, consistency, isolation, and durability across all its transactions. This compliance ensures that the database processes transactions in a reliable, error-resistant manner, safeguarding against data loss and ensuring data integrity even in adverse conditions such as system crashes or power failures. ACID compliance is crucial for applications that require strong data consistency, such as financial systems, in which the accuracy and reliability of transaction processing are paramount.

8.4 Multidocument transactions

In MongoDB, operations on single documents are atomic. Because MongoDB uses embedded documents and arrays to represent relationships within a single document rather than normalizing data across multiple documents and collections, its single-document atomicity often eliminates the need for distributed transactions in many common scenarios.

For use cases that require atomic operations across multiple documents or collections, MongoDB supports distributed transactions. These transactions can span multiple operations, collections, documents, databases, and shards.

8.4.1 Differentiating the Core and Callback APIs

MongoDB offers two distinct APIs for handling ACID transactions, detailed in table 8.1. The first, known as the *Core API*, employs syntax similar to that of relational databases, featuring commands such as `startTransaction` and `commitTransaction`. The second is the *callback API*, which is the preferred method for implementing transactions and the one we focus on in this chapter.

The core API, while straightforward, does not include automatic retry logic for most errors, leaving developers responsible for manually coding the transaction operations, the commit function, and any necessary retry and error-handling mechanisms.

Table 8.1 Core API vs. Callback API

Core API	Callback API
Requires an explicit call to initiate and commit the transaction	Initiates a transaction, performs the specified operations, and commits them or aborts if an error occurs
Does not automatically handle errors such as `TransientTransactionError` and `UnknownTransactionCommitResult`. Instead, it allows the integration of custom error-handling mechanisms.	Automatically includes error-handling logic for `TransientTransactionError` and `UnknownTransactionCommitResult`
Requires explicitly passing a logical session to the API for each transaction	Requires explicitly passing a logical session to the API for each transaction

The Callback API in MongoDB offers a comprehensive function that simplifies transaction management. It manages starting a transaction linked to a specific logical session, running a `callback` function, and committing or aborting the transaction based on the presence of errors. This function also integrates retry logic for handling commit errors. The Callback API aims to ease application development with transactions and facilitates the addition of retry logic for handling transaction errors.

In both the Core and Callback APIs, developers must initiate the logical session required for the transaction. Each operation within a transaction must be associated with this logical session. MongoDB uses logical sessions to track the timing and sequence of operations across the entire deployment. The logical or server sessions are fundamental for supporting retriable writes and causal consistency, which are essential for transaction capabilities. These sessions ensure that a sequence of related read and write operations maintains its causal relationships through their order, known as *causally consistent client sessions.* A client session started by an application engages with a server session for these purposes.

8.4.2 Using transactions with mongosh

Transactions are usually created and run through external applications using API methods via the appropriate MongoDB driver for the application's programming language. But let's start with the first example executed in MongoDB Shell (mongosh). Listing 8.1 demonstrates how to manually initiate a transaction in mongosh, perform specified operations, and commit or abort the transaction if an error occurs. Although this method requires explicit handling of each step and does not manage error-handling logic automatically, it is useful for understanding the fundamental steps involved in transaction management in MongoDB. Run this code in mongosh part by part.

Listing 8.1 Executing a multidocument transaction in mongosh

```
function executeTransaction(session) {
  const dbSampleAnalytics = session.getDatabase('sample_analytics')

  session.startTransaction({
    readConcern: { level: 'snapshot' },
    writeConcern: { w: 'majority' },
    readPreference: 'primary'
  })

  try {
    const account = dbSampleAnalytics.accounts.findOne
 ({ account_id: 371138 })
    if (!account) {
      throw new Error('Account not found')
    }

    const newTransactionCount = (account.transaction_count || 0) + 1

    dbSampleAnalytics.accounts.updateOne(
      { account_id: 371138 },
      { $set: { limit: 12000, last_transaction_date: new Date() },
        $inc: { transaction_count: 1 }
      }
    )
    dbSampleAnalytics.customers.updateMany(
      { accounts: { $in: [371138] } },
      { $inc: { transaction_count: 1 },
        $set: { last_transaction_date: new Date() }
      }
    )
    dbSampleAnalytics.transactions.insertOne({
```

```
        account_id: 371138,
        transaction_count: newTransactionCount,
        date: new Date(),
        amount: 1500,
        transaction_code: 'buy'
    })
    session.commitTransaction()
} catch (error) {
    session.abortTransaction()
    throw error;
  }
}
```

The first part of the code defines a function `executeTransaction(session)`, which initiates a transaction in MongoDB using `mongosh`. It starts a transaction with specified read and write concerns and read preferences. Within a `try` block, it performs several database operations: finding an account (ID 371138), updating the account and related customers, and inserting a new transaction document. If any operation fails, it aborts the transaction and throws an error. If all operations succeed, it commits the transaction:

```
function runTransactionWithRetry() {
  const maxRetries = 5
  let session
  for (let attempt = 0; attempt < maxRetries; attempt++) {
    session = db.getMongo().startSession()
    try {
      executeTransaction(session)
      return
    } catch (error) {
      console.error("Attempt " + attempt + ": an error occurred", error)
      if (error.hasOwnProperty('errorLabels') &&
         (error.errorLabels.includes('TransientTransactionError')
      || error.errorLabels.includes('UnknownTransactionCommitResult'))) {
          continue
      }
      throw error
    } finally {
      session.endSession()
    }
  }
  throw new Error('Max retries reached. Transaction failed.')
}
```

The second part of the code defines the `runTransactionWithRetry` function, which attempts to execute a transaction up to five times using the `executeTransaction` function. It starts a new session for each attempt. If an error labeled `TransientTransactionError` or `UnknownTransactionCommitResult` occurs, the function retries the transaction. If it encounters other errors or exceeds the retry limit, it throws an error. Each session ends in the `finally` block:

```
try {
  runTransactionWithRetry();
} catch (error) {
  throw new Error('Transaction failed after retries: ' + error.message)
}
```

The final code block attempts to run the `runTransactionWithRetry` function. If it fails after all retries, it catches the error and throws a new error with a message indicating the transaction failure.

8.4.3 Using transactions with the Callback API

It's important to use the Callback API instead of the Core API in any language, as the Core API can lead to potential problems with scalability and error handling. The Callback API provides a more robust and reliable approach to transaction management.

Each language has its own syntax and constructs for handling transactions, yet the underlying methodology for executing and managing transactions is similar.

> **TIP** You can also create collections and indexes in transactions.

> **NOTE** In most cases, distributed transactions come with higher performance costs compared with single-document writes, and their availability should not replace proper schema design. In many use cases, a denormalized data model using embedded documents and arrays remains the best choice. By modeling your data properly, you can often reduce the necessity for distributed transactions.

NODE.JS TRANSACTIONS

Now let's see how transaction handling works using Node.js. Listing 8.2 demonstrates a multidocument transaction in Node.js using the MongoDB Node.js. This script initiates a transaction using the `withTransaction` method from the MongoDB Driver's Callback API. The `withTransaction` method is part of the higher-level Callback API that simplifies transaction management by allowing you to define a `callback` function containing the operations to be performed within the transaction. It handles starting, committing, and retrying the transaction in case of transient errors, ensuring that all operations succeed or fail together, maintaining atomicity and consistency.

Listing 8.2 Executing a multidocument transaction with Node.js and Callback API

```
const { MongoClient } = require('mongodb')

// Replace with your actual connection string
const uri = "your_mongodb_connection_string"

async function run(accountId) {
  const client = new MongoClient(uri)

  try {
```

```
    await client.connect()
    const session = client.startSession()

    const transactionOptions = {
      readConcern: { level: 'snapshot' },
      writeConcern: { w: 'majority' },
      readPreference: 'primary'
    }

    await session.withTransaction(async () => {
      const accounts = client.db('sample_analytics').collection('accounts')
      const customers = client.db('sample_analytics').collection('customers')
      const transactions = client.db('sample_analytics').
collection('transactions')
      const currentDate = new Date()

      const account = await accounts.findOne(
        { account_id: parseInt(accountId) },
        { session }
      )
      if (!account) throw new Error('Account not found')

      const accountsUpdateResult = await accounts.updateOne(
        { account_id: parseInt(accountId) },
        {
          $set: { limit: 12000, last_transaction_date: currentDate },
          $inc: { transaction_count: 1 }
        },
        { session }
      )

      const customersUpdateResult = await customers.updateMany(
        { accounts: { $in: [parseInt(accountId)] } },
        {
          $inc: { transaction_count: 1 },
          $set: { last_transaction_date: currentDate }
        },
        { session }
      )

      const transactionsInsertResult = await transactions.insertOne(
        {
          account_id: parseInt(accountId),
          transaction_count: account.transaction_count + 1,
          bucket_start_date: currentDate,
          bucket_end_date: currentDate,
          transactions: [
            {
              date: currentDate,
              amount: 1500,
              transaction_code: 'buy',
              symbol: 'amzn',
              price: '125.00',
              total: '187500.00'
            }
```

```
            ]
          },
          { session }
        )

        console.log("Transaction committed.")
        console.log("Accounts updated:", accountsUpdateResult.modifiedCount)
        console.log("Customers updated:", customersUpdateResult.modifiedCount)
        console.log("New transaction inserted:", transactionsInsertResult.
insertedId)

      }, transactionOptions)

      session.endSession()
  } catch (error) {
      console.error("Transaction aborted due to error:", error)
  } finally {
      await client.close()
    }
}

// Get accountId from command line arguments
const accountId = process.argv[2]
if (!accountId) {
  console.error("Please provide an account ID as an argument.")
  process.exit(1)
}

run(accountId).catch(console.dir)
```

To run the script, first install Node.js from nodejs.org. Then install the MongoDB Node.js Driver by running `npm install mongodb` in your terminal. Create a file named `transaction.js`, and copy the script into this file. Update the `uri` variable in the script with your MongoDB connection string, and run the script with `node transaction.js 714727`. (714727 is one of the account IDs in the `accounts` collection.)

The script imports MongoClient from the MongoDB library and defines the connection URI. The `run` function creates a new MongoClient instance, connects to the MongoDB server, and defines collections for accounts, customers, and transactions. It fetches the current date and, inside a `try` block, retrieves an account document. If it finds an account document, the function calculates a new transaction count, updates the account's limit to 12000 using $set, increments the transaction count using $inc, updates the customers' transaction count and last transaction date using $inc, and inserts a new transaction document for $1,500. If all operations succeed, the transaction is committed; if any operation fails, the transaction is aborted, and the error is logged. The session ends in the `finally` block, and the client connection is closed.

As you can see, running transactions with the MongoDB Node.js Driver is more seamless than using `mongosh`. The script connects to MongoDB, starts a session, and uses the `withTransaction` method to streamline transaction management. This approach automatically handles starting, committing, and retrying transactions in case of errors, ensuring atomicity and consistency, which makes it ideal for production environments.

PYTHON TRANSACTIONS

In this section, you'll see how transactions are handled using Python. Listing 8.3 shows executing a transaction in MongoDB using Python, also with the Callback API. This example showcases a similar scenario to the Node.js driver: how to start a transaction, perform multiple operations across collections, and ensure atomicity by committing or aborting the transaction based on success or failure.

Listing 8.3 Executing a multidocument transaction with PyMongo and Callback API

```python
#!/usr/bin/env python3

from pymongo import MongoClient, WriteConcern, ReadPreference
from pymongo.read_concern import ReadConcern
from pymongo.errors import ConnectionFailure
from datetime import datetime
import sys

# Replace the uri string with your connection string
# Example: uri = "mongodb+srv://<username>:<password>@
mongodb-in-action.fpomkke.mongodb.net"
uri = "your_mongodb_connection_string"

# Callback function to be executed within the transaction
def callback(session, accountId):
    accounts = session.client.sample_analytics.accounts
    customers = session.client.sample_analytics.customers
    transactions = session.client.sample_analytics.transactions

    current_date = datetime.now()

    # Find the account document
    account = accounts.find_one({"account_id": int(accountId)},
session=session)
    if not account:
        raise Exception('Account not found')

    # Update the account document
    accountsUpdateResult = accounts.update_one(
        {"account_id": int(accountId)},
        {"$set": {"limit": 12000,
"last_transaction_date": current_date},
"$inc": {"transaction_count": 1}},
        session=session
    )

    # Update the customer documents
    customersUpdateResult = customers.update_many(
        {"accounts": {"$in": [int(accountId)]}},
```

```python
            {"$inc": {"transaction_count": 1},
     "$set": {"last_transaction_date": current_date}},
            session=session
        )

        # Insert a new transaction document
        transactionsInsertResult = transactions.insert_one({
            "account_id": int(accountId),
            "transaction_count": account.get('transaction_count', 0) + 1,
            "bucket_start_date": current_date,
            "bucket_end_date": current_date,
            "transactions": [{
                "date": current_date,
                "amount": 1500,
                "transaction_code": "buy",
                "symbol": "amzn",
                "price": "125.00",
                "total": "187500.00"
            }]
        }, session=session)

        # Log the results
        print("Transaction committed.")
        print("Accounts updated:", accountsUpdateResult.modified_count)
        print("Customers updated:", customersUpdateResult.modified_count)
        print("New transaction inserted:", transactionsInsertResult.inserted_id)

# Function to run the transaction
def run(accountId):
    client = None
    try:
        # Connect to the MongoDB client
        client = MongoClient(uri)

        # Start a session and execute the transaction
        with client.start_session() as session:
            session.with_transaction(
                lambda s: callback(s, accountId),
     # Pass accountId to the callback
                read_concern=ReadConcern("local"),
                write_concern=WriteConcern("majority"),
                read_preference=ReadPreference.PRIMARY,
            )
    except ConnectionFailure as err:
        print(f"Connection error: {err}")
    except Exception as e:
        print(f"Transaction aborted due to error: {e}")
    finally:
        if client:
            client.close()

# Entry point of the script
if __name__ == "__main__":
    if len(sys.argv) < 2:
        print("Please provide an account ID as an argument.")
```

```
        sys.exit(1)

    accountId = sys.argv[1]
    run(accountId)
```

To run the script, first install Python 3 from https://www.python.org and the `pymongo` library by running `pip install pymongo==4.7.3` in your terminal. Create a file named `transaction.py`, and copy the script into this file. Update the `uri` variable in the script with your MongoDB connection string. Finally, run the script with `python3 transaction.py 785786`. (785786 is one of the account IDs in the `accounts` collection.)

RUBY TRANSACTIONS

Let's also see how to use the Callback API and execute transactions with Ruby. The next listing shows an example of executing a transaction with Ruby, using the Callback API to manage the process.

Listing 8.4 Executing a multidocument transaction with Ruby and Callback API

```ruby
#!/usr/bin/env ruby

require 'mongo'
require 'date'

# Replace the uri string with your connection string
uri = "your_mongodb_connection_string"

# Function to be executed within the transaction
def transaction_callback(session, accountId)
  db = session.client.use('sample_analytics')
  accounts = db[:accounts]
  customers = db[:customers]
  transactions = db[:transactions]

  current_date = DateTime.now

  # Find the account document
  account = accounts.find({ "account_id" => accountId.to_i },
    session: session).first
  raise 'Account not found' if account.nil?

  # Ensure transaction_count is not nil
  account['transaction_count'] ||= 0

  # Update the account document
  accounts_update_result = accounts.update_one(
    { "account_id" => accountId.to_i },
    { "$set" => { "limit" => 12000, "last_transaction_date" =>
      current_date }, "$inc" => { "transaction_count" => 1 } },
    session: session
  )

  # Update the customer documents
```

```ruby
    customers_update_result = customers.update_many(
      { "accounts" => { "$in" => [accountId.to_i] } },
      { "$inc" => { "transaction_count" => 1 }, "$set" =>
    { "last_transaction_date" => current_date } },
      session: session
    )

    # Insert a new transaction document
    transactions_insert_result = transactions.insert_one({
      "account_id" => accountId.to_i,
      "transaction_count" => account['transaction_count'] + 1,
      "bucket_start_date" => current_date,
      "bucket_end_date" => current_date,
      "transactions" => [{
        "date" => current_date,
        "amount" => 1500,
        "transaction_code" => "buy",
        "symbol" => "amzn",
        "price" => "125.00",
        "total" => "187500.00"
      }]
    }, session: session)

    # Log the results
    puts "Transaction committed."
    puts "Accounts updated: #{accounts_update_result.modified_count}"
    puts "Customers updated: #{customers_update_result.modified_count}"
    puts "New transaction inserted: #{transactions_insert_result.inserted_id}"
end

# Function to run the transaction
def run(uri, accountId)
  client = Mongo::Client.new(uri, write_concern: { w: :majority })
  begin
    session = client.start_session

    # Start a session and execute the transaction
    session.with_transaction(
      read_concern: { level: :snapshot },
      write_concern: { w: :majority },
      read: { mode: :primary }
    ) do |s|
      transaction_callback(s, accountId)
    end

  rescue Mongo::Error::OperationFailure => e
    puts "Transaction aborted due to error: #{e.message}"
  ensure
    client.close
  end
end

# Entry point of the script
if ARGV.length < 1
  puts "Please provide an account ID as an argument."
```

```
    exit 1
end

accountId = ARGV[0]
run(uri, accountId)
```

To run the script, first install Ruby from https://www.ruby-lang.org and the `mongo` library by running `gem install mongo` in your terminal. Create a file named `transaction_script.rb`, and copy the script into this file. Update the `uri` variable in the script with your MongoDB connection string. Finally, run the script with `ruby transaction_script.rb 721914`. (721914 is one of the account IDs in the `accounts` collection.)

8.5 MongoDB transaction considerations

MongoDB supports multidocument distributed transactions on sharded clusters, enabling multidocument transactions across multiple shards. This ensures consistency across distributed data while preserving the ACID properties, even in complex sharded environments. Transactions allow rollback of changes if any operation within the transaction fails, providing a reliable mechanism for maintaining data integrity across different deployment topologies. Here are the best recommendations for transactions in MongoDB:

- Structure your data so that related data is stored together. This improves performance and often eliminates the need for transactions.
- Split long-running transactions into smaller parts to avoid exceeding the default 60-second timeout. This timeout can be extended if necessary.
- Ensure that all operations within a transaction use indexes for faster execution.
- Limit each transaction to modifying a maximum of 1,000 documents.
- Configure appropriate read and write concerns.
- Implement robust error-handling and retry mechanisms for transactions that fail due to transient errors.
- Be mindful that transactions involving multiple shards will have a performance overhead.

The following operations are not permitted within transactions:

- Creating new collections in cross-shard write transactions. If you write to an existing collection in one shard and implicitly create a collection in another shard, MongoDB cannot handle both operations in the same transaction.
- Explicitly creating collections (e.g., using the `db.createCollection()` method) and indexes (e.g., using the `db.collection.createIndexes()` and `db.collection.createIndex()` methods) when using a read concern level other than local. (Chapter 9 covers read concerns.)
- The `listCollections` and `listIndexes` commands and their corresponding helper methods.

- Other non-CRUD and noninformational operations, such as `createUser`, `getParameter`, and `count`, along with their helper methods.

Summary

- Transactions in database management systems ensure that sets of related read and write actions either fully succeed or fail as a unit, preventing partial updates.
- WiredTiger, MongoDB's default storage engine, enhances performance and scalability with row-oriented, column-oriented storage configurations.
- Write-ahead logging and checkpoints in WiredTiger ensure data durability, with changes logged in a journal to prevent data loss if MongoDB exits unexpectedly.
- Compression in WiredTiger reduces storage needs for collections and indexes, using `Snappy` for collections and prefix compression for indexes, though it increases CPU use.
- WiredTiger supports document-level concurrency for write operations, allowing multiple clients to modify documents simultaneously within the same collection.
- OCC in WiredTiger minimizes up-front locking and uses versioning to handle conflicts, enhancing performance when write conflicts are infrequent.
- MongoDB offers two APIs for managing ACID transactions: the Core API, similar to relational databases, and the Callback API, which automates processes.
- The Core API requires manual handling of transaction operations, commits, and error resolution, lacking automatic retry mechanisms.
- MongoDB allows multidocument transactions within sharded clusters, spanning multiple shards.
- Organize your data so that related information is kept together. This boosts performance and frequently makes transactions unnecessary.

Using replication and sharding

This chapter covers

- Learning the MongoDB replica set concept
- Identifying replica set members
- Understanding the MongoDB oplog
- Tracking change streams
- Creating sharded clusters in Atlas
- Horizontal scaling with sharding

People often mix up replication and sharding, though they're different systems used in database management for distinct purposes. What's the difference? *Replication* involves copying data and operations from a primary server to secondary ones to enhance data availability. It's particularly useful for recovering from disasters and distributing read queries among multiple nodes to improve read performance and reduce load on the primary. But all write operations still go through the primary server, which can become a bottleneck.

Conversely, *sharding* partitions a large database into smaller segments, known as *shards*, each housing a fraction of the complete data set on its own database server instance. Because the entire data set is distributed across multiple server instances, write operations affecting multiple shards can be handled by the corresponding primary server instances, reducing the write bottleneck. To preserve data integrity and availability, each shard must implement replication.

The integration of sharding and replication in MongoDB aims to bolster data durability and ensure consistent availability. Should a server instance of a shard fail, having solely one data copy on that shard could lead to temporary data inaccessibility until the server's functionality is recovered or substituted. When replication is adopted within each shard, however, the sharded architecture can sustain data accessibility and mitigate any service interruptions stemming from server downtimes. Moreover, this method facilitates seamless, downtime-free rolling updates across the sharded setup, promoting continuous and smooth operational maintenance.

MongoDB Atlas provides built-in replication by default to ensure high availability, whereas sharding is available as an option for horizontal scaling. That means when you're using Atlas, you don't have to set up and manage these configurations manually. Atlas automates the provisioning, setup, and scaling of your databases, taking the burden of manual administration off your shoulders. This allows developers to focus more on application development than on the operational challenges associated with database management.

9.1 Ensuring data high availability with replication

A *replica set* in MongoDB consists of a group of `mongod` processes that hold identical data sets. Replica sets ensure redundancy and high availability, serving as the foundation for all production environments. These members can exist in various states and fulfill different roles within the replica set.

9.1.1 Distinguishing replica set members

Listing 9.1 demonstrates the output of the `db.adminCommand("replSetGetStatus")` command within the Atlas cluster we created in chapter 2. This output details the status of each replica set member. This command is crucial for overseeing the health and configuration of the replica set within MongoDB cluster.

Listing 9.1 Output of the `replSetGetStatus` command

```
db.adminCommand("replSetGetStatus").members.map((m) =>
➥ ({ _id: m._id, name: m.name, state: m.state, stateStr: m.stateStr }))
[
  {
    _id: 0,
    name: 'ac-5dhjxpf-shard-00-00.fpomkke.mongodb.net:27017',
    state: 2,
    stateStr: 'SECONDARY'
  },
  {
    _id: 1,
```

```
      name: 'ac-5dhjxpf-shard-00-01.fpomkke.mongodb.net:27017'
      state: 1,
      stateStr: 'PRIMARY'
    },
    {
      _id: 2,
      name: 'ac-5dhjxpf-shard-00-02.fpomkke.mongodb.net:27017'
      state: 2,
      stateStr: 'SECONDARY'
    }
]
```

As you can see by checking the command output in listing 9.1 or using the helper method `rs.status()`, each member of a MongoDB replica set operates in a specific state. Table 9.1 outlines the 10 possible states that a replica set member can inhabit.

Table 9.1 Possible state of each member of a replica set

Number	Name	Description
0	STARTUP	Initial state. Parses config document.
1	PRIMARY	Accepts writes. Eligible to vote.
2	SECONDARY	Replicates data. Eligible to vote.
3	RECOVERING	In self-checks, rollback, or resync. No reads. Votes.
4	STARTUP2	Running initial sync. Can't vote.
5	UNKNOWN	State not known by others.
6	ARBITER	Only votes. Doesn't replicate data.
7	DOWN	Unreachable by others.
8	ROLLBACK	Performing a rollback. No reads. Votes.
9	REMOVED	Was part of a set, now removed.

Each state reflects the specific role and current condition of a member within the set. These states vary widely, from STARTUP, which denotes a member's initial setup phase, to PRIMARY and SECONDARY, which designate members that are handling write operations and data replication, respectively. STARTUP2 represents members in performing an initial sync with the replica set—a crucial step before they become fully functional members. ROLLBACK indicates that a member is reverting changes to align its data with the rest of the replica set, a process that temporarily prevents it from serving read queries or participating in the replica set as a data-bearing node.

In certain scenarios, such as when a replica set consists of a primary and a secondary, but additional costs deter the inclusion of another secondary, introducing an ARBITER into the set can be a strategic choice. An *arbiter* engages in electing a primary, yet it does not store a replica of the data set and is incapable of assuming the primary role.

Let's look at another helpful command. Listing 9.2 demonstrates the output of the command `db.adminCommand("replSetGetConfig")` command in MongoDB Shell (`mongosh`). This command retrieves the current configuration of a MongoDB replica set and is designed to gather detailed information about each member and its role within the set. Note that this operation works only on M10 clusters and larger, one of which you will create in section 9.3.2.

> **Listing 9.2 Output of the `replSetGetConfig` command**

```
db.adminCommand("replSetGetConfig").config.members.map((m) =>
 ({ host: m.host, arbiterOnly: m.arbiterOnly, hidden: m.hidden,
 priority: m.priority,
 secondaryDelaySecs: m.secondaryDelaySecs,votes: m.votes }))
[
  {
    host: ' ac-5dhjxpf-shard-00-00.fpomkke.mongodb.net:27017',
    arbiterOnly: false,
    hidden: false,
    priority: 1,
    secondaryDelaySecs: Long("0"),
    votes: 1
  },
  {
    host: 'ac-5dhjxpf-shard-00-01.fpomkke.mongodb.net:27017',
    arbiterOnly: false,
    hidden: false,
    priority: 1,
    secondaryDelaySecs: Long("0"),
    votes: 1
  },
  {
    host: 'ac-5dhjxpf-shard-00-02.fpomkke.mongodb.net:27017',
    arbiterOnly: false,
    hidden: false,
    priority: 1,
    secondaryDelaySecs: Long("0"),
    votes: 1
  }
]
```

The output of the `replSetGetConfig` command—alternatively, you can use the `rs.config()` mongosh helper—provides detailed information about each member of a MongoDB replica set, including its roles and behaviors within the set. Here's what the specific fields in the output tell you:

- `arbiterOnly`—This Boolean value indicates whether the member is an arbiter. Arbiters participate in elections but do not hold data.
- `hidden`—A *hidden* member is part of the replica set but is not visible to client applications. Hidden members can vote in elections but are not eligible to become primary. They do not accept read operations from clients. This setup is particularly useful for dedicated backup members or for members intended for reporting or analytics. These operations can run on hidden members without affecting the operational performance of the primary or secondary members

visible to clients. Hidden members ensure data redundancy and availability for specific tasks without influencing the primary selection process or serving client requests.
- `priority`—This setting determines the member's eligibility to become a primary during elections. A higher `priority` value increases the member's chances of being elected as the primary. A member with a priority of `0` cannot become primary, effectively making it a secondary member that can only replicate data.
- `secondaryDelaySecs`—This field indicates whether the replica set member is configured as a delayed member. *Delayed members*, which are required to be hidden, replicate and perform operations with a specified delay. This delay is intended to maintain a historical version of the replica set's data. If it is 09:15, and a member has a configured replication delay of one hour, the most up-to-date operation applied to this member would represent the state of the database at or before 08:15. These members provide a rolling backup and a historical account of the data, acting as a protective measure against human errors. They can assist in recovering from problems such as failed updates to applications or accidental deletions of databases and collections.
- `votes`—This field indicates how many votes a member has in replica set elections. In most configurations, each member has one vote, but certain configurations may change this to control the election process more finely.

Given that a replica set may comprise up to 50 members, with only 7 members eligible to vote, including nonvoting members enables a replica set to expand beyond 7 members. Members designated as nonvoting (their `votes` count is `0`) must have their `priority` set to `0`.

9.1.2 Electing primary replica-set member

MongoDB uses protocol version 1, which is based on the Raft consensus algorithm, to manage elections within a replica set, thereby ensuring data consistency across distributed systems. This protocol features a voting system that enables the replica set to determine which member will take on the primary role. Several scenarios can trigger an election, such as

- The addition of a node to or removal of a node from the replica set
- Initialization of the replica set
- A heartbeat failure between any of the secondary members and the primary lasting longer than the preset timeout period (default: 10 seconds)

Figure 9.1 shows the process of electing a new primary in a MongoDB replica set when the current primary becomes unavailable.

The replica that has the most up-to-date write timestamp has the highest probability of being elected. This approach reduces the likelihood of a rollback when a former primary is reintegrated into the set. The election also takes into account the *term*, a monotonically increasing number representing the number of election attempts. The term prevents double voting and enables faster detection of simultaneous primaries and multiple successful elections in a short period. After an election, a freeze period is implemented in which nodes are prevented from starting another election; this freeze aims to prevent frequent successive elections that could disrupt system stability. At present, MongoDB replica sets operate exclusively with a protocol referred to as `protocolVersion: 1` (PV1).

The replica set is prevented from performing write operations while the election is in progress.

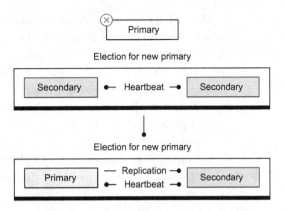

Figure 9.1 The election mechanism within a MongoDB replica set is activated when the primary node becomes nonoperational. The secondary replicas vote to elect a new primary. (Image © MongoDB 2024 CC BY-NC-SA 3.0)

Nonetheless, read queries can be processed during this time if they are configured to be served by the secondary nodes. Typically, with the standard configuration of a replica set, the cluster is expected to complete the election of a new primary in no more than 12 seconds. This period includes the necessary steps of recognizing the primary as unavailable, commencing the election, and concluding it with the selection of a new primary. You can adjust the election duration by modifying the `settings.electionTimeoutMillis` option in the replication configuration.

When an election concludes, MongoDB's algorithm prioritizes high-priority secondaries to initiate subsequent elections. Although these primaries are more likely to be chosen, occasionally a lower-priority member temporarily becomes primary. Elections persist until the highest-priority member assumes the primary role. Members with zero priority do not become primary and are ineligible to initiate elections.

It's crucial for your application's connection-handling strategy to accommodate automatic failovers and subsequent elections. MongoDB drivers are designed to detect the loss of the primary and can automatically retry certain read or write operations once, adding an extra layer of resilience to your application during elections.

> **TIP** You can find more details about the structure of a MongoDB replica set in the official documentation at https://www.mongodb.com/docs/manual/replication.

9.1.3 Understanding the oplog collection

The *oplog* (operations log) is a capped collection that stores an ordered history of logical writes to a MongoDB database. The oplog is the basic mechanism enabling replication in MongoDB. If write operations neither change data nor succeed, they won't generate oplog entries.

MongoDB executes database operations on the primary node and logs these operations in the primary's oplog. The primary streams these operations (push-based) to the secondaries as they occur. Secondary nodes asynchronously replicate and execute these operations. Every member of the replica set holds a copy of the oplog in the `local.oplog.rs` collection, enabling them to keep up with the database's current state. Every operation recorded in the oplog is *idempotent*, meaning that the outcome of applying an oplog operation to the target dataset remains consistent whether it is applied once or multiple times.

Following is an example of a single document from the oplog collection. This log entry captures a deletion event that occurred within the `sample_mflix.sessions` namespace.

Listing 9.3 A single document from the `oplog` collection

```
{
  op: 'd',
  ns: ' sample_mflix.sessions',
  ui: new UUID("99f8f10f-e144-4419-a543-da211dd1a2de"),
  o: { _id: ObjectId("65b1a0a4edf7e1f8d9ccc396") },
  ts: Timestamp({ t: 1710267182, i: 5 }),
  t: Long("38"),
  v: Long("2"),
  wall: ISODate("2024-03-12T18:13:02.838Z")
},
```

This listing presents an example of a single document from the `oplog` collection. The document details a delete operation (`op: 'd'`) on the `sessions` collection within the `sample_mflix` database. The operation has a unique identifier (`ui`) for the collection, and the deleted document is identified by its `_id`. The operation was timestamped (`ts`) at the moment of execution, with an increment (`i`) to ensure uniqueness. Additionally, the term (`t`) indicates the replica set election term during which the operation was logged, and the version (`v`) signifies the oplog entry format. Finally, the wall-clock time (`wall`) indicates the actual time when the operation occurred.

Let's see one more example. The following listing showcases an insert operation in the MongoDB oplog for the `sample_mflix.sessions` collection. This operation adds a new document containing user-specific data including `user_id` and `jwt` (JSON Web Token).

Listing 9.4 An insert operation visible in oplog

```
{
  op: 'i',
  ns: 'sample_mflix.sessions',
  ui: new UUID("b2d3f810-g234-5239-b543-da211dd1a3cd"),
  o: {
    _id: ObjectId("5fc8a1d3bcf1b3298b3fdb78"),
    user_id: "12345",
```

```
    jwt: "token123456"
  },
  ts: Timestamp({ "t": 1720567182, "i": 1 }),
  t: Long("39"),
  v: Long("2"),
  wall: ISODate("2024-03-15T10:20:30.123Z")
}
```

The document, uniquely identified by a MongoDB `ObjectId`, contains session-specific information such as the user's ID and JWT. Metadata including the timestamp (`ts`), operation sequence (`i`), transaction identifier (`t`), MongoDB oplog version (`v`), and exact time of the operation (`wall`) offer comprehensive details on how the transaction was processed within the MongoDB oplog, showcasing the database's capability for real-time logging and activity tracking.

Any secondary member can import oplog entries from any other member, facilitating a mechanism known as *chained replication*. This mode of replication manifests when a secondary member opts to replicate from another secondary rather than directly from the primary. Such a decision arises when a secondary member prioritizes replication targets by ping time, leading to situations in which the nearest available member is another secondary.

Chained replication can reduce load on the primary. But chained replication can also result in increased replication lag, depending on the topology of the network.

Listing 9.5 demonstrates the `db.getReplicationInfo()` command, which returns a document with the status of the replica set, using data polled from the oplog. Use this output to diagnose problems with replication. Note that this command works only on M10 clusters and larger, one of which you will create in section 9.3.2.

> **Listing 9.5 Output of the `db.getReplicationInfo()` command**

```
db.getReplicationInfo()
{
  configuredLogSizeMB: 4096,
  logSizeMB: 4096,
  usedMB: 4074.63,
  timeDiff: 635133,
  timeDiffHours: 176.43,
  tFirst: 'Wed Mar 20 2024 10:44:15 GMT+0000 (Coordinated Universal Time)',
  tLast: 'Wed Mar 27 2024 19:09:48 GMT+0000 (Coordinated Universal Time)',
  now: 'Wed Mar 27 2024 19:09:49 GMT+0000 (Coordinated Universal Time)'
}
```

The `db.getReplicationInfo()` method provides a snapshot of the replication status within a MongoDB replica set by analyzing the oplog data. It reveals that the replica set is configured with an oplog size of 4096 MB, which is fully matched by the actual oplog size, indicating that the total allocated disk space for oplog entries is configured to its capacity. The document shows that 4074.63 MB of the oplog space is currently in use, highlighting the volume of replication data stored. It covers a time span of 635,133 seconds, equivalent to 176.43 hours, reflecting the duration between the earliest and latest oplog entries. The timestamp of the first oplog entry is marked `'Wed Mar 20 2024 10:44:15 GMT+0000'`, establishing the beginning of the oplog window, whereas the last entry is timestamped `'Wed Mar 27 2024 19:09:48 GMT+0000'`, and the current time is `'Wed Mar 27 2024 19:09:49 GMT+0000'`, closely following the latest oplog entry. This information is important for understanding the operational and replication dynamics within the replica set.

> **TIP** For script-based automation in MongoDB, use `db.getReplication-Info()` because it outputs JSON, which is ideal for parsing. Conversely, `rs.printReplicationInfo()` is suited for manual checks within `mongosh` because it does not return JSON.

OPLOG SIZE

When you start a replica set member for the first time, MongoDB creates an oplog of a default size if you don't specify the size. On UNIX and Windows systems, the default oplog size depends on the storage engine:

- For the In-Memory Storage Engine, the oplog size is set to 5% of the physical memory, with a minimum of 50 MB and a maximum of 50 GB.
- The WiredTiger Storage Engine calculates the oplog size based on 5% of the available disk space, with a bottom limit of 990 MB and a top limit of 50 GB.

Typically, the default oplog size is adequate for most situations. When an oplog occupies 5% of the disk space and fills up after 24 hours of activity, for example, it allows secondary nodes to pause copying entries from the oplog for up to 24 hours without falling too far behind for replication.

Listing 9.6 shows the process of checking how behind the secondary nodes are in copying data from the primary node in MongoDB. This check is made via the `db.printSecondaryReplicationInfo()` command, which shows how current the secondary nodes are with the primary node's data, using the oplog for synchronization.

Listing 9.6 Output of the `db.printSecondaryReplicationInfo()` command

```
db.printSecondaryReplicationInfo()
source: ac-5dhjxpf-shard-00-00.fpomkke.mongodb.net:27017
{
  syncedTo: 'Wed Mar 27 2024 18:21:52 GMT+0000
  (Coordinated Universal Time)',
  replLag: '0 secs (0 hrs) behind the primary '
}
---
source: ac-5dhjxpf-shard-00-01.fpomkke.mongodb.net:27017
{
  syncedTo: 'Wed Mar 27 2024 18:21:53 GMT+0000
  (Coordinated Universal Time)',
  replLag: '10 secs (0 hrs) behind the primary '
}
```

The command reveals the synchronization status of two replica set members with the primary node. The first member, `ac-5dhjxpf-shard-00-00.fpomkke.mongodb.net:27017`, is synchronized to the primary with no delay, showing a replication lag of 0 seconds. The second member, `ac-5dhjxpf-shard-00-01.fpomkke.mongodb.net:27017`, has a replication lag of 10 seconds, indicating that it is 10 seconds behind the primary in receiving updates.

> **TIP** The `db.printSecondaryReplicationInfo()` method used in `mongosh` does not produce JSON output. To check things yourself, use `db.printSecondaryReplicationInfo()`; for automated scripts, use `rs.status()`.

If your application mainly performs read operations with few writes, a smaller oplog may suffice. But if your replica set's activity is expected to follow any of these patterns, consider using an oplog larger than the default size:

- *Batch document updates*—For maintaining idempotency, the oplog needs to break batch updates into separate actions, consuming substantial oplog space without necessarily increasing data or disk use.
- *Equal volumes of data deletions and insertions*—When data deletion volume matches data insertion, disk use remains stable, yet oplog size can expand significantly.
- *Frequent in-place updates*—When many updates alter existing documents without enlarging them, the database logs numerous operations, keeping the data volume on disk constant.

> **TIP** Before `mongod` initializes an oplog, you can define its size with the `oplogSizeMB` parameter. After initiating a replica set member for the initial time, employ the `replSetResizeOplog` admin command to modify the size of the oplog. The `replSetResizeOplog` command allows dynamic resizing of the oplog, eliminating the need to restart the `mongod` process.

OPLOG WINDOW

The oplog window needs to be sufficiently large to ensure that a secondary can retrieve all new oplog entries generated during the logical initial sync process (described in the next section). If the window is too short, there's a chance that entries will be purged from the oplog before the secondary has a chance to apply them.

By default, MongoDB doesn't enforce a minimum retention time for oplog entries; it automatically trims the oldest ones to keep within the maximum size limit. You can define a minimum time that an oplog entry must be kept, however. An entry will be deleted only if it satisfies two conditions:

- The oplog's size has hit its configured limit.
- The entry's age exceeds the set number of hours based on the system clock of the host.

> **TIP** To set the minimum oplog retention period when initiating `mongod`, you can include the `storage.oplogMinRetentionHours` setting in the `mongod` configuration file or use the command-line option `--oplogMinRetentionHours`.

MongoDB version 6.0 and later offers two different approaches to initial sync: logical initial sync and file-based initial sync (limited to MongoDB Enterprise). File-based initial sync is designed for large data sizes (1 TB+). If a failure occurs—either due to falling off the oplog or a transient network problem—MongoDB can resume a logical initial sync within a 24-hour window, or a file-based initial sync within a shorter 10-minute window. You can configure the time window of each approach with `mongod` parameters.

LOGICAL INITIAL SYNC PROCESS

During a logical initial sync, MongoDB does the following things:

- Clones all nonlocal databases by scanning and inserting data from each collection into its own versions
- Constructs indexes for each collection simultaneously with the document copying process
- Retrieves ongoing oplog entries while copying data, ensuring that the target member has adequate disk space to store these oplog records temporarily
- Applies all data modifications using the oplog records to update its data set to the current state of the replica set
- After completing the initial sync, changes the member status from `STARTUP2` to `SECONDARY`

MongoDB offers three methods for initial sync:

- Restart the mongod with an empty data directory, allowing MongoDB's standard initial sync process to restore the data. This method is simple, but replenishing the data may take longer.
- Reboot the machine using a recent data directory copy from another replica set member. This approach restores data faster but involves more manual effort.
- In MongoDB 6.0 and later, use the file-based initial sync approach by changing the `initialSyncMethod` parameter passed to the `mongod` to `fileCopyBased`.

9.2 Understanding change streams

Before the introduction of MongoDB change streams, tracking changes in a database required polling or tailing the oplog, which was both complex and inefficient. Developers had to query the database or oplog repeatedly to detect changes, often resulting in performance problems and increased latency in data processing. With the advent of MongoDB change streams, you can subscribe to real-time updates on changes (inserts, updates, deletes, and more) across a MongoDB collection, a database, or even the entire deployment. This feature provides a continuous, event-driven stream of data that reflects changes in the underlying data source. For applications that rely on real-time notifications of data changes, change streams are essential. The main benefits of using MongoDB change streams include

- *Access control*—Change streams respect MongoDB's role-based access control (RBAC, explained in chapter 20), allowing only authorized applications to access data changes based on their read permissions.
- *Reliable API*—Change streams offer a consistent, well-documented API across all MongoDB drivers, ensuring reliable change-event notifications.
- *Data durability*—Change events are guaranteed to be committed to a majority of the replica set, reducing the risk of data rollbacks during failovers.
- *Ordered changes*—MongoDB ensures a global order of changes across shards, making it safe to process events in the order in which they arrive.
- *Resumability*—Change streams can resume from the last known event after a network error or restart, using a resume token. A *resume token* is a unique identifier generated for each event in a MongoDB change stream, allowing the stream to resume exactly where it left off after an interruption, such as a network error or restart.
- *Aggregation pipeline integration*—Applications can filter or modify change events server-side using MongoDB's aggregation pipeline, enhancing data processing efficiency.

Change streams are available for replica sets and sharded clusters, and they require specific conditions to operate effectively:

- They require the WiredTiger storage engine.
- They must operate on replica set PV1.

9.2.1 Connections for a change stream

To establish connections for a change stream, you can use the +srv connection option with Domain Name System (DNS) seed lists or specify the servers directly in the connection string. When a driver loses its connection to a change stream or the connection fails, it tries to reconnect using another node in the cluster that meets the specified read preference. If it doesn't find a suitable node, it generates an exception.

You can initiate change streams on individual collections (except system, admin, local, and config collections), entire databases (excluding admin, local, and config databases), or across the entire deployment (replica sets or sharded clusters), excluding system collections and certain databases. This functionality has expanded over various MongoDB versions, allowing broader monitoring scopes.

Let's start with mongosh. The following operation in mongosh opens a change-stream cursor on the sample_mflix database. The returned cursor reports on data changes to all the nonsystem collections in that database:

```
> watchCursor = db.getSiblingDB("sample_mflix").watch()
ChangeStreamCursor on sample_mflix
>
```

To monitor these changes, iterate through the cursor to monitor new events. As in the following listing, combine the `cursor.isClosed()` method with `cursor.tryNext()` to ensure that the iteration stops only when the change-stream cursor is closed and no more documents are left in the current batch.

Listing 9.7 The `cursor.tryNext()` nonblocking method

```
// Iterate over the cursor to monitor for new events
while (!watchCursor.isClosed()) {
  let next = watchCursor.tryNext();
  // Continue retrieving the next document in the cursor as
  // long as there is a next document
  while (next !== null) {
    printjson(next); // Print the next document
    next = watchCursor.tryNext(); // Try to get the next document
  }
}
```

Now add a single document to the collection to observe how change streams work. To do this, use `mongosh` to open a new connection. Next, execute the following insertion operation to add a new document to the `sessions` collection in the `sample_mflix` database, containing fields for `user_id` and `jwt`:

```
db.getSiblingDB("sample_mflix").sessions.insertOne({
  user_id: "12345",
  jwt: "token123456"
});
```

The change-stream cursor captures and returns the operation's details, showing the insertion action, its timing, and the full document content. The following listing shows the returned document.

Listing 9.8 Change-stream cursor

```
{
  _id: {
    _data: '8266073FD1000000022B022C0100296E5A1004E43
C0CEEB6D74D84814318056E6EECDC46645F6964006466073FD1359139DD
FE70B1D70004'
  },
  operationType: 'insert',
  clusterTime: Timestamp({ t: 1711751121, i: 2 }),
  wallTime: ISODate("2024-03-29T22:25:21.073Z"),
  fullDocument: {
    _id: ObjectId("66073fd1359139ddfe70b1d7"),
    user_id: '12345',
    jwt: 'token123456'
  },
  ns: {
    db: 'sample_mflix',
```

```
    coll: 'sessions'
  },
  documentKey: {
    _id: ObjectId("66073fd1359139ddfe70b1d7")
  }
}
```

Every change event comes with an `_id` field, which holds a document. This document acts as a resume token for restarting a change stream. To resume a change stream, you specify this resume token using `resumeAfter` or `startAfter` when opening the cursor.

> **TIP** In change-stream event documents, the `_id` field is the resume token. Don't change or delete the `_id` field with the pipeline. From MongoDB 4.2 on, if the pipeline changes an event's `_id` field, change streams return an error.

9.2.2 Changing streams with Node.js

You can use Node.js to set up a change stream specifically for the `sessions` collection within the `sample_mflix` database. This setup allows you to monitor and log changes in that collection alone. Listing 9.9 demonstrates how to implement this change stream in JavaScript using the MongoDB Node.js driver. This code initializes a change stream on the `sessions` collection and iterates over it to process the change-stream documents.

Listing 9.9 Monitoring a change stream in Node.js

Replaces the uri string with your connection string. Example:
const uri = "mongodb+srv://<username>:<password>@mongodb-in-action.fpomkke.mongodb.net".

```javascript
const { MongoClient } = require('mongodb');

const uri = "<connection string uri>"
const client = new MongoClient(uri, { serverApi: '1' });

async function monitorChangeStream() {
  try {
    await client.connect();
    const database = client.db("sample_mflix");
    const sessionsCollection = database.collection('sessions');
    const changeStream = sessionsCollection.watch();

    console.log("Listening for changes in the sessions collection...");
    await changeStream.forEach(change => {
      console.log("Received a change in the sessions collection:", change);
    });
  } catch (error) {
    console.error("Error watching change stream for sessions collection:", error);
  } finally {
```

```
      await client.close();
  }
}

monitorChangeStream();
```

Replace `"<connection string uri>"` with the genuine MongoDB connection string specific to your database. This script establishes a connection to the `sample_mflix` database using MongoDB's Node.js driver and monitors the `sessions` collection for any changes in real time. When it detects a change (such as an insert, update, or delete operation), it outputs the details of that change to the console. It's useful for tracking and responding to data modifications in the `sessions` collection as they happen.

9.2.3 Modifying the output of a change stream

Tailoring the change stream to specific needs is straightforward. You can control the output of the change stream by providing an array of one or more pipeline stages during its setup. These stages could include `$addFields`, `$match`, `$project`, `$replaceRoot`, `$replaceWith`, `$redact`, `$set`, and `$unset`, allowing for extensive customization of the data received from the change stream. This allows you to filter the complete change stream down to only those changes you want to listen for. The following example shows how to modify the change stream's output with Node.js.

Listing 9.10 Modifying change-stream output with Node.js

Replaces the uri string with your connection string. Example:
const uri = "mongodb+srv://<username>:<password>@mongodb-in-action.fpomkke.mongodb.net".

```
const { MongoClient } = require('mongodb');

const uri = "<connection string uri>"

async function monitorChangeStream() {
  const client = new MongoClient(uri, { apiVersion: '1' });
  await client.connect();
  const sessionsCollection =
client.db("sample_mflix").collection('sessions');

  const pipeline = [
    { $match: { 'fullDocument.user_id': '12345' } },
    { $addFields: { newField: 'this is an added field!' } }
  ];
  const changeStream = sessionsCollection.watch(pipeline);

  changeStream.on('change', next => {
    console.log("Received a change in the sessions collection:", next);
  });
}

monitorChangeStream();
```

Replace "<connection string uri>" with the genuine MongoDB connection string specific to your database. This script connects to the `sample_mflix` database, targets the `sessions` collection, and sets up a change stream that filters for changes in documents in which `user_id` equals `12345`. Then it augments each detected change event with an additional field (`newField`) and outputs the modified event to the console. The script continuously monitors the collection for such changes, providing real-time updates when they occur.

9.3 Scaling data horizontally through sharding

When databases become sizable or encounter high processing loads, a single server may become insufficient. An influx of queries can exhaust the CPU resources of the server, for example. Likewise, if the data volume surpasses the server's RAM capacity, it can strain the disk's I/O capabilities. Also, as data volume increases, a problem with the capacity of the disks may occur.

To manage growth, systems can scale in two ways: vertically by enhancing the capabilities of a single server (such as increasing its CPU, RAM, or storage) or horizontally by integrating additional servers into the architecture.

Vertical scaling makes a single server more powerful, such as by upgrading its CPU, adding RAM, or expanding storage. There's a limit to how much a single server can be upgraded, however, due to technological constraints and the maximum configurations offered by cloud providers.

Horizontal scaling spreads the data and workload across many servers, enhancing capacity by adding more servers as needed. This approach doesn't rely on a single powerful machine but uses multiple units to handle parts of the workload, often more cost-effectively. The downside is added complexity in managing and maintaining a larger network of servers.

MongoDB uses sharding to partition data across multiple servers, enabling horizontal scaling and improved handling of large data volumes and high transaction rates. A MongoDB sharded cluster can consist of any number of shards (separate servers), each holding a fragment of data distributed across all machines. The total database size can easily exceed 100 TB; in fact, it's difficult to define an upper size limit.

Sharding occurs at the collection level within a database, which may contain both sharded and unsharded collections. Although sharded collections are split and dispersed among various shards within the cluster, unsharded collections reside on a primary shard. You can move these unsharded collections to other shards in MongoDB 8.0+ using the `moveCollection` command. Each database is assigned its own primary shard to manage these collections.

How can I be certain of the maturity and effectiveness of MongoDB's sharding capability for powering large-scale database clusters? This confidence comes from my experience working for a company in Munich, where I managed the operation of MongoDB sharded clusters. Each cluster was immense, exceeding 130 TB, with up to 135 shards per cluster. It was and perhaps still is the largest MongoDB farm in Europe. But for such a large cluster to function efficiently, both in operational terms and data-access logic, several requirements must be fulfilled, and I discuss them in this chapter.

The biggest challenge is managing this type of cluster, especially when the number of shards along with replica sets is large. I don't recommend running such clusters without the proper tools because it is difficult to meet challenges such as backups, restores, and upgrades.

You can employ Ops Manager, which is ideally suited for managing sharded clusters, by using agents installed on each server within the cluster. These agents automate tasks such as starting and stopping mongod processes, upgrading and downgrading database versions, performing backups and restores, and monitoring.

You can also run a MongoDB sharded cluster on Kubernetes with the MongoDB Enterprise Kubernetes Operator, using Kubernetes' native capabilities. Together with Ops Manager, this operator is a powerful tool for automating MongoDB sharded cluster operations.

Further, you have the option to create and operate a MongoDB sharded cluster using MongoDB Atlas. This book focuses on launching a sharded cluster with MongoDB Atlas.

9.3.1 Viewing sharded cluster architecture

A MongoDB sharded cluster architecture includes the following:

- *Shards*—Each shard contains a portion of the sharded data and functions as a replica set. The cluster can consist of 1 to *n* shards, with each shard holding a subset of the overall data. I recommend having shards no larger than 1 TB each. This limit facilitates faster index building, accelerates initial synchronization, and improves the efficiency of backup and restore processes.
- mongos—mongos functions as the gateway for client applications and enables tools such as mongosh to interact with the cluster, adeptly handling both read and write operations. It routes client requests to the suitable shards and amalgamates the outcomes from the shards into a unified client response. Connections to the cluster are made via mongos instances instead of directly to the shards. For high availability, I advise operating multiple mongos instances within production environments.
- *Config servers*—These servers operate as a replica set and serve as the specialized storage for sharding metadata, which is crucial for the cluster's operations. The metadata stored includes information about the composition of the sharded data, such as the list of sharded collections and the specifics of data routing. The role of config servers is vital for the efficient management and direction of queries within the sharded cluster. Starting with MongoDB version 8.0, configuration servers can be embedded in sharded clusters, simplifying the architecture and reducing infrastructure costs without affecting scale and performance.

MongoDB shards data at the collection level, distributing collection data across all the shards in the cluster. Some collections can be sharded; others may not be. There is no strict requirement that every collection be sharded. Figure 9.2 illustrates the interaction of components within a sharded cluster.

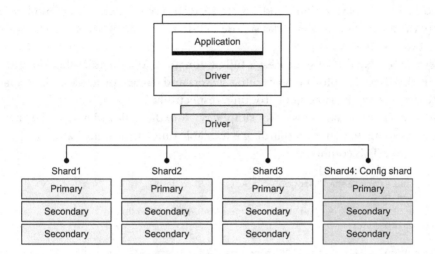

Figure 9.2 This MongoDB sharded cluster configuration includes multiple app servers connected to routers (mongos), which direct queries to the appropriate shard. Three shards, each of which is a replica set, hold segments of the data. Also, an embedded config shard contains the config servers (along with user data), which hold the cluster's metadata. Starting with MongoDB 8.0, config servers can be embedded in sharded clusters. (Image © MongoDB 2024 CC BY-NC-SA 3.0)

Sharding enables the scaling of your database to handle more extensive load capacity by enhancing read/write throughput and thereby expanding storage capability. Let's delve into these aspects more closely:

- *Enhanced read/write throughput*—Distributing the data set over several shards boosts capacity for read and write operations, especially when these operations are restricted to individual shards.
- *Expanded storage capability*—Adding more shards increases the total storage capacity of the database, facilitating near-limitless scalability.
- *Data locality*—Zone sharding permits you to allocate databases across varied geographical zones, which is optimal for distributed applications. Through policy enforcement, you can confine data to specific regions, each holding one or more shards, thus enhancing both efficiency and adaptability in data management. Zone sharding associates different shard-key value ranges with each zone, allowing swifter, more accurate data retrieval pertinent to geographical significance.

9.3.2 Creating sharded clusters via Atlas CLI

In this section, you create a MongoDB Atlas sharded cluster. These clusters are not free in Atlas, unlike the M0 cluster you set up in chapter 1, so you need to set up a payment method if you haven't already. To do this, see the official MongoDB documentation at https://mng.bz/AGVW.

After adding a payment method, you're ready to use the Atlas command-line interface (CLI) to set up your first Atlas sharded cluster. Use the `"MongoDB 8.0 in Action"` project you created in chapter 2.

Remember that the setup process is fully automated. Atlas handles the configuration of your shards and deployment of config servers and `mongos` processes, which manage your cluster's metadata and query routing, respectively.

Begin with a two-shard cluster for simplicity. Note that Atlas allows a variety of shard counts, from one to many, yet sharding is available only for clusters that are on the M30 tier or higher. This command

```
atlas clusters create "MongoDB-in-Action-Sharded"
--provider GCP
--region CENTRAL_US --tier M30 --type SHARDED --shards 2
--mdbVersion 8.0

Cluster 'MongoDB-in-Action-Sharded' is being created.
```

creates a new sharded cluster named `"MongoDB-in-Action-Sharded"` in MongoDB Atlas. It sets the cloud service provider to Google Cloud Platform (GCP) and selects the `CENTRAL_US` region for deployment. The cluster is created with the M30 tier, which supports sharding and is configured with two shards. The MongoDB version to be deployed on this cluster is 8.0.

After a few minutes, you can check the status of your new sharded cluster using the following Atlas CLI command:

```
atlas clusters list ID                  NAME                    MDB VER
6609c17a7396d94a17a9fb78  MongoDB-in-Action-Sharded        8.0.4
```

Figure 9.3 shows the MongoDB Atlas UI displaying the details of a new sharded cluster.

> **TIP** If you're not using your cluster for production purposes, you can pause it at any time to save costs. To use the Atlas CLI for this purpose, issue the command `atlas clusters pause "MongoDB-in-Action-Sharded"`, and to start the cluster, issue the command `atlas clusters start "MongoDB-in-Action-Sharded"`.

You also need to add a sample data set. Atlas creates databases and collections with test data, which are necessary for sharding the collections. Again, use the Atlas CLI:

```
atlas clusters sampleData load "MongoDB-in-Action-Sharded"
```

Scaling data horizontally through sharding

Figure 9.3 Each of the two shards—`atlas-up0q2r-config` (config shard) and `atlas-up0q2r-shard-0`—is a replica set with three nodes. In MongoDB 8.0+, a config server storing metadata and application data is called a *config shard*. Both shards are located in the Iowa (`us-central1`) region. Key statistics such as disk use, operations, and connections over the past six hours, are displayed. Each node is labeled PRIMARY or SECONDARY, indicating the node's replication status within the sharded cluster. (Image © MongoDB 2025)

In a few minutes, loading the sample data results in the creation of test databases and documents within their collections. Remember to display the connection string. You can interact with the cluster via `mongosh` or drivers:

```
atlas clusters connectionStrings describe "MongoDB-in-Action-Sharded"

STANDARD CONNECTION STRING
mongodb+srv://mongodb-in-action-shard.nu96v.mongodb.net
```

NOTE Your connection string will be different. Check it on your console.

Now connect `mongosh` to your Atlas sharded cluster, using the `'manning'` user you created in chapter 2 at the project level. This user is active in your new cluster, which is part of the project.

Note that this time, you are connected directly to `mongos`, not to the primary replica set member, as was the case in chapter 2 when you created a MongoDB replica set:

```
mongosh "mongodb+srv://mongodb-in-action-shard.nu96v.mongodb.net" \
--apiVersion 1 --username 'manning'

Atlas [mongos] test> show dbs
admin               296.00 KiB
config                2.26 MiB
sample_airbnb        52.21 MiB
```

```
sample_analytics       9.52 MiB
sample_geospatial      1.24 MiB
sample_guides         40.00 KiB
sample_mflix         111.07 MiB
sample_restaurants     6.19 MiB
sample_supplies        1.03 MiB
sample_training       47.62 MiB
sample_weatherdata     2.56 MiB
Atlas [mongos] test>
```

mongos is your interface for managing queries and distributing them across the various shards of a MongoDB sharded cluster. The show dbs command displays the list of databases created during loading of the sample data set.

9.3.3 Working with a shard key

MongoDB shards data at the collection level, distributing the collection data across the shards in the cluster using the shard key, which is made up of one or more fields within the documents. The choice of a shard key is pivotal in sharding clusters because an unsuitable selection may lead to inefficient distribution of data, create load imbalances across the shards, and result in subpar query performance. In certain scenarios, an overwhelmed shard, often referred to as a *hot shard*, may underperform and become a system bottleneck, adversely affecting the overall performance of the cluster. Therefore, it is crucial to choose an appropriate shard key to ensure optimal functionality within a sharded setup.

MongoDB uses the shard key, composed of one or more fields from the documents, to disperse the documents across the different shards. The data set is segmented into distinct, nonoverlapping chunks based on the range of shard-key values. The objective is to distribute these chunks as evenly as possible throughout the shards of a cluster, achieving an efficient distribution.

Recent updates to MongoDB have made significant enhancements in sharding:

- From version 4.4 on, sharded collection documents can lack shard-key fields, which are treated as null for distribution purposes.
- From MongoDB 4.4 on, you can augment a shard key by adding a suffix field or multiple fields to an existing shard key.
- Version 5.0 introduces the ability to reshard a collection by changing its shard key.
- Version 8.0 introduces embedded config servers in sharded clusters, allowing you to move unsharded collections to different shards without sharding the collections and selecting a shard key, improving the resharding process and making it four times faster.

9.3.4 Choosing a shard key

MongoDB offers two primary sharding strategies for distributing data across sharded clusters. The first strategy is *ranged sharding*, which involves partitioning data into continuous sequences according to the values of the shard key. Documents with similar shard-key values are initially stored in the same chunk, but MongoDB's balancer may redistribute chunks across shards as needed. An optimal shard key ensures even distribution of documents across the cluster (to prevent bottlenecks) and aligns well with common query patterns (to reduce scatter-gather queries). To choose an appropriate key for the ranged sharding strategy, consider the following:

- *Query pattern analysis*—Identify the most frequent read and write operations in your application. The optimal shard key ensures an even spread of data across the sharded cluster and supports frequent query patterns. When you choose a shard key, consider whether a given shard key covers your most common query patterns.
- *Cardinality*—Choose a shard key with high *cardinality* (a large number of unique values) to prevent clustering of data on a few shards.
- *Frequency*—Ensure that the shard-key values are evenly distributed. If certain values occur too frequently (using `status` as a shard key, for example, where `active` is a common value that can lead to an excessive concentration of data on one shard), data skew may result, causing bottlenecks.
- *Monotonically changing shard keys*—Using a consistently increasing or decreasing shard key, such as a datetime stamp, can lead to write bottlenecks. This happens because such keys concentrate new data into specific chunks (e.g., datetime stamp increases direct inserts to the `maxKey` chunk), causing an uneven load and affecting performance.

The second strategy is *hashed sharding*, which computes a hash value of the shard key field's value and then assigns each chunk a range based on these hashed values. Even if shard-key values in a set are close numerically, the corresponding hashed values are likely to be distributed across different chunks. It's crucial to understand that hashed sharding isn't suitable for range-based queries. Hashed keys help counteract problems caused by fields that change in a predictable, monotonic fashion, such as `ObjectId` values and timestamps. An example is the default `_id` field, provided that it contains `ObjectId` values.

A shard-key index could be a single ascending index on the shard key, a compound index beginning with the shard key in ascending order, or a hashed index.

> **NOTE** A shard-key index must not be a descending index on the shard key, a partial index, or any geospatial, multikey, text, or wildcard index type.

9.3.5 Using a shard-key analyzer

Beginning with version 7.0, MongoDB simplifies selecting a shard key. The `analyzeShardKey` command provides metrics to assess a potential shard key for unsharded or sharded collections. These metrics, derived from sampled queries, facilitate a data-driven decision on your shard key.

Let's see how this looks in practice and enable sharding on the `routes` collection, which is located in the `sample_training` database in the Atlas test data set. Following is an example document from the `routes` collection.

Listing 9.11 Single document from the `sample_training.routes` collection

```
Atlas [mongos] sample_training> db.routes.findOne()
{
  _id: ObjectId('56e9b39b732b6122f877fa36'),
  airline: { id: 410, name: 'Aerocondor', alias: '2B', iata: 'ARD' },
  src_airport: 'DME',
  dst_airport: 'NBC',
  codeshare: '',
  stops: 0,
  airplane: 'CR2'
}Atlas [mongos] sample_training >
```

The document contains flight route information, including airline details, source and destination airports, codeshare status, number of stops, and airplane type, illustrating the data structure for a flight route in the database. Let's assume that the most frequent query on this collection follows the pattern

```
{"src_airport": <value>, "dst_airport": <value>, "airline.name": <value>}
```

Using the shard-key analyzer, check whether a shard key composed of these fields is good enough to be the basis of the sharding logic for this collection.

ENABLING QUERY SAMPLING

Next, you must enable query sampling on the target `sample_training.routes` collection. The shard-key analyzer needs these statistics to determine whether the proposed key is good enough. Execute this command:

```
db.collection.configureQueryAnalyzer(
    {
      mode: <string>,
      samplesPerSecond: <double>
    }
)
```

The following code shows how to enable query sampling on the `routes` collection. This step is crucial for assessing the effectiveness of the shard key by analyzing the collection's query patterns.

Listing 9.12 Enabling query sampling

```
Atlas [mongos] sample_training>
↪db.routes.configureQueryAnalyzer({ mode: "full", samplesPerSecond: 1 })
{
  newConfiguration: { mode: 'full', samplesPerSecond: 1 },
```

```
  ok: 1,
  '$clusterTime': {
    clusterTime: Timestamp({ t: 1712592942, i: 1 }),
    signature: {
      hash: Binary.createFromBase64('cQVeIvFIgltUun2S4ycqZT+VEGw=', 0),
      keyId: Long('7352622473289924630')
    }
  },
  operationTime: Timestamp({ t: 1712592934, i: 1 })
}
Atlas [mongos] sample_training>
```

The `db.routes.configureQueryAnalyzer` command used in the `sample_training` database sets the query analyzer for the `routes` collection to `full` mode, with a rate of one sample per second. This setup enables detailed query tracking on the collection.

ANALYZING A SHARD KEY

Now you can move on to analyzing the proposed shard key, which is created on the fields `{"src_airport": 1, "dst_airport": 1, "airline.name": 1}` because the most frequent query on this collection follows the pattern: `{"src_airport": <value>, "dst_airport": <value>, "airline.name": <value>}`. The first step is creating a supporting compound index on these fields:

```
Atlas [mongos] sample_training>
 db.routes.createIndex({ src_airport: 1,
 dst_airport: 1, "airline.name": 1 })
src_airport_1_dst_airport_1_airline.name_1
```

Next, execute a few trial queries on real data to generate statistics:

```
db.routes.find({"src_airport": "YRB", "dst_airport": "YGZ",
 "airline.name": "Askari Aviation" })
```

This query searches the `routes` collection of the database for flights in which the source airport is `"YRB"`, the destination airport is `"YGZ"`, and the airline name is `"Askari Aviation"`. Substitute different values in this query pattern to try it out. Review the `routes` collection to see which `src_airport`, `dst_airport`, and airline names you can use to generate queries. Then check how effective the proposed shard key is by using the command `db.routes.analyzeShardKey(({ src_airport: 1, dst_airport: 1, "airline.name": 1 })`, as shown in the next listing.

> **Listing 9.13 Analyzing a proposed shard key**

```
Atlas [mongos] sample_training>
 db.routes.analyzeShardKey({ src_airport: 1,
 dst_airport: 1,"airline.name": 1 })
{
  keyCharacteristics: {
    numDocsTotal: Long('66985'),
```

```
          avgDocSizeBytes: Long('184'),
          numDocsSampled: Long('66985'),
          isUnique: false,
          numDistinctValues: Long('66984'),
          mostCommonValues: [
            {
              value: {
                src_airport: 'HAM',
                dst_airport: 'AMS',
                'airline.name': 'Eurowings'
              },
              frequency: Long('2')
            },
            {
              value: {
                src_airport: 'KTM',
                dst_airport: 'DXB',
                'airline.name': 'Fly Dubai'
              },
              frequency: Long('1')
            },
            {
              value: {
                src_airport: 'ADB',
                dst_airport: 'ARN',
                'airline.name': 'SunExpress'
              },
              frequency: Long('1')
            },
            {
              value: {
                src_airport: 'FOC',
                dst_airport: 'TNA',
                'airline.name': 'Air China'
              },
              frequency: Long('1')
            },
            {
              value: {
                src_airport: 'DTW',
                dst_airport: 'MEX',
                'airline.name': 'AeroMéxico'
              },
              frequency: Long('1')
            }
          ],
          monotonicity: {
            recordIdCorrelationCoefficient: 0.0163877874,
            type: 'not monotonic'
          }
        },
        readDistribution: {
          sampleSize: {
            total: Long('525'),
            find: Long('525'),
```

```
      aggregate: Long('0'),
      count: Long('0'),
      distinct: Long('0')
    },
    percentageOfSingleShardReads: 84.1904761905,
    percentageOfMultiShardReads: 12.1904761905,
    percentageOfScatterGatherReads: 3.6190476191,
  writeDistribution: {
    sampleSize: {
      total: Long('0'),
      update: Long('0'),
      delete: Long('0'),
      findAndModify: Long('0')
    }
  },
  ok: 1,
  '$clusterTime': {
    clusterTime: Timestamp({ t: 1712596218, i: 99 }),
    signature: {
      hash: Binary.createFromBase64('E31gLvizNd2gwwpFIx9AESXDg8A=', 0),
      keyId: Long('7352622473289924630')
    }
  },
  operationTime: Timestamp({ t: 1712596218, i: 99 })
}
Atlas [mongos] sample_training>
```

analyzeShardKey returns metrics about the key characteristics of a shard key and its read and write distribution. The metrics are based on sampled queries.

The shard-key analysis for { src_airport: 1, dst_airport: 1, "airline.name": 1 } on the routes collection yielded detailed metrics. The key is not unique, yet it distinguishes a high number of values (66,984 distinct values out of 66,985 total documents), facilitating effective data distribution across shards. The query distribution data shows that 84.19% of reads were single-shard, indicating the shard key's strong query-isolation capabilities and enhancing performance by directing queries efficiently to the relevant shard. The analysis also shows multishard (12.19%) and scatter-gather reads (3.62%), suggesting that some queries span multiple shards, which could affect performance and may require further optimization.

The monotonicity aspect is marked by a recordIdCorrelationCoefficient of 0.0163877874, denoting a not-monotonic sequence. This lack of strict sequencing in the shard-key values relative to document insertion means that there is less risk of creating write hotspots on specific shards, leading to more balanced shard use over time.

In this way, you can evaluate the adequacy of your proposed shard key before creating it. If you are satisfied with the analysis results for your key and are confident that it is sufficiently good (it's better to spend more time analyzing to create the best possible key at the outset rather than change the shard key later), you can initiate sharding on the routes collection by executing this command:

```
sh.shardCollection("sample_training.routes",
  { src_airport: 1, dst_airport:1,"airline.name": 1 } )
```

> **TIP** Use `sh.status()` to print a formatted report of the sharding configuration and information on existing chunks in a sharded cluster.

9.3.6 Detecting shard-data imbalance or uneven data distribution

There may be an existing imbalance or uneven distribution of your data across your shards, which you can identify by using various commands. The `sh.status()` command provides a summary overview of the sharded cluster, including the number of chunks per shard. If one or more shards have significantly more chunks than others, this may indicate an imbalance. The `db.collection.getShardDistribution()` command provides detail on the size of data and the number of documents on each shard for a specific collection. An uneven distribution of either metric may indicate an imbalance. `$shardedDataDistribution` is an aggregation stage that provides details on each sharded collection in the database. Starting with MongoDB 8.0, it provides details on the primary shard only when chunks or orphan documents are present.

To analyze the total size and number of chunks per shard, use the following aggregation pipeline stage:

```
db.getSiblingDB("config").chunks.aggregate([
  { $group: { _id: «$shard», totalSize: { $sum: «$size» },
➥ count: { $sum: 1 } } }
])
```

If a large difference exists in the sizes or the chunk counts across the shards, it is likely that you have an uneven distribution. These commands provide information to help you determine whether to take any additional steps.

9.3.7 Resharding a collection

The optimal shard key for MongoDB ensures uniform document distribution across the cluster and supports frequent query patterns. An inadequate shard key might cause uneven data distribution, leading to performance or scalability problems. From MongoDB 5.0 onward, it's possible to modify the shard key of a collection, allowing a redistribution of data throughout the cluster.

Resharding operates straightforwardly. Executing the `reshardCollection` command initiates the creation of a new, implicitly empty collection by MongoDB, using the specified new shard key; then data is transferred chunk by chunk from the current collection. The balancer needs a 2-second lock to ascertain the fresh data arrangement. Throughout the copying phase, however, the application can access and modify the collection without disturbances. As a result of this copying phase, the larger the collection is, the longer the resharding process takes.

Before beginning the resharding process, you must meet certain prerequisites, which can be costly in some instances:

- *Disk space*—Ensure that you have at least 1.2 times the size of the collection you plan to reshard. For a 1 TB collection, you should have at least 1.2 TB of available disk space.
- *I/O capacity*—This metric should remain below 50%.
- *CPU use*—This metric should stay below 80%.

It's crucial to assess available resources on each shard.

> **TIP** The database does not enforce these requirements, so not allocating enough resources can cause the database to run out of space and shut down, lead to decreased performance, and extend the duration of the resharding operation beyond expected time frames. I advise you to reshard your collection during times of lower traffic within your application, if possible.

Another crucial aspect is updating your application's queries. For optimal database performance during resharding, the queries should apply filters for both existing and new shard keys. You can remove the old shard-key filters from your queries only when the resharding process is complete.

You also need to be aware of other constraints:

- Resharding cannot occur while an index is being built.
- Certain queries—such as `deleteOne()`, `findAndModify()`, and `updateOne()`—produce errors unless the current and new shard keys are included.
- You can reshard only one collection at a time.
- Operations such as `addShard()`, `removeShard()`, `dropDatabase()`, and `db.createCollection()` are not possible during resharding.
- The new shard key must not have a uniqueness constraint, and resharding collections with a uniqueness constraint is unsupported.

If you meet these requirements and want to start the resharding process, execute the following command:

```
db.adminCommand({
  reshardCollection: "<database>.<collection>",
  key: <new shardkey>
})
```

To monitor the resharding operation, use the `$currentOp` pipeline stage:

```
db.getSiblingDB("admin").aggregate([
  { $currentOp: { allUsers: true, localOps: false } },
  {
    $match: {
      type: "op",
```

```
            "originatingCommand.reshardCollection": "<database>.<collection>"
      }
    }
])
```

NOTE Remember that the resharding operation requires proper preparation and can take a long time for large databases, so it's best to choose the optimal shard key from the beginning so you don't have to change it later.

WARNING If the resharded collection uses Atlas Search, the search index is unavailable upon completion of the resharding operation. You have to rebuild the search index manually when the resharding process is complete.

9.3.8 Understanding chunk balancing

MongoDB structures sharded data into units known as *chunks* or *ranges*. From version 5.2 on, each chunk defaults to 128 MB, an increase from the previous 64 MB. A *chunk* is defined by a lower bound (inclusive) and an upper bound (exclusive) set by the shard key, holding a continuous sequence of shard-key values within a shard. With the release of MongoDB 6.1, chunks ceased to autosplit; now they split only when transferred between shards. Before MongoDB 6.1, an autosplitter split chunks when they exceeded the maximum chunk size.

In MongoDB 6.0.3 and later, sharded clusters distribute data based on the size of the data, not merely the count of chunks. A background process known as the *balancer* ensures that each shard for every sharded collection has a uniform data distribution, moving chunks across shards to maintain balance. When a shard for a sharded collection reaches certain data limits, the balancer redistributes the data to maintain uniformity across shards, respecting any set zones.

This balancing act is managed by the primary node of the config server replica set (CSRS) and typically remains transparent to users and the Application layer, although you may notice slight performance effects during its operation. The balancer limits each shard to a single migration at a time, preventing concurrent data migrations on one shard. Although MongoDB allows for parallel migrations, a shard can only be involved in one migration at any time. In a cluster with n shards, MongoDB can handle up to $n/2$ migrations at the same time.

Balancing rounds are initiated when the data difference between the most- and least-loaded shards for a collection exceeds a set threshold. If the range size is 128 MB and the data variation exceeds 384 MB (three times the range size), a migration is triggered.

It's good practice to set a specific time frame for the balancer's operations, known as the *balancing window* or *balancer window*, to minimize disruption to peak production traffic. To schedule the balancing window, connect to `mongos` using `mongosh`, and switch to the config database:

```
use config
```

Ensure that the balancer is not stopped because it will not activate in a stopped state. Execute the following command:

```
sh.startBalancer()
```

Now you can set or modify the balancer window using the `updateOne()` command:

```
db.settings.updateOne(
  { _id: "balancer" },
  { $set: { activeWindow : { start : "<start-time>",
    stop : "<stop-time>" } } },
    { upsert: true }
)
```

For `<start-time>` and `<end-time>`, substitute time values formatted as two-digit hours and minutes (`HH:MM`) to define the start and finish times of the balancing window.

> **NOTE** The balancing window must be long enough to accommodate the migration of all data entered during the day. Given that the rate of data insertion can vary with different activity and use levels, it's crucial to select a balancing window that adequately meets the operational requirements of your system.

You can check the current state of the balancer by executing the following command in `mongosh` (while connected to `mongos`):

```
sh.getBalancerState()
```

This command retrieves the active status of the balancer process, showing whether it is enabled. You can also use the following command to determine whether the balancer is running:

```
sh.isBalancerRunning()
```

9.3.9 Administrating chunks

In most situations, it's best to allow the automatic balancer to transfer ranges between shards. In instances such as these, however, you may need to migrate ranges manually:

- To presplit an empty collection, move ranges manually to ensure even distribution across shards. Use presplitting in limited situations to support bulk data ingestion.
- If the balancer in an active cluster cannot distribute ranges within the balancing window, you have to migrate ranges manually.

In most cases, a sharded MongoDB cluster automatically creates, splits, and distributes chunks. Sometimes, however, it can't generate enough chunks or distribute data quickly enough to meet throughput needs. Presplitting chunks in a sharded collection can aid throughput, especially when large data volumes are ingested into an unbalanced cluster or when such ingestion would cause data imbalance, as with monotonically changing shard keys.

> **TIP** Presplit chunks only in an empty collection to avoid unpredictable chunk sizes and ineffective balancing. Manually splitting chunks in a populated collection can result in inefficient balancing and inconsistent chunk ranges.

To segment data within a sharded cluster manually, use the `split` command to divide a single chunk into multiple distinct chunks. This operation is performed within the admin database of the sharded cluster. Consider partitioning the `sample_training.routes` collection using the shard key:

```
{ "src_airport": 1, "dst_airport": 1, "airline.name": 1 }.
```

To presplit the collection into meaningful segments, you might target specific combinations of these fields that represent significant traffic routes. Here's how to set this up in `mongosh`:

```
// Split points to segment the collection into chunks
// based on common routes and airlines
var splitPoints = [
    { "src_airport": "JFK", "dst_airport": "LHR", "airline.name": "British Airways" },
    { "src_airport": "LAX", "dst_airport": "NRT", "airline.name": "Japan Airlines" },
    { "src_airport": "DXB", "dst_airport": "SYD", "airline.name": "Emirates" }
];

// Loop through the split points and apply the 'split' command
splitPoints.forEach(function(point) {
    db.adminCommand({
        split: "sample_training.routes",
        middle: point
    });
});
```

Executing the script organizes the `sample_training.routes` data in segments based on common air-travel routes:

- Flights between `"JFK"` and `"LHR"` operated by `"British Airways"`
- Flights between `"LAX"` and `"NRT"` operated by `"Japan Airlines"`
- Flights between `"DXB"` and `"SYD"` operated by `"Emirates"`
- Flights that do not fall into these categories, representing other combinations of source and destination airports with respective airlines

From MongoDB 6.0 on, the balancer is responsible for distributing data across shards according to the size of the data. Merely splitting ranges may not guarantee uniform distribution of data across shards. To ensure balanced distribution, you may need to relocate chunks manually:

```
// Define the shards for distributing the chunks
var shards = ["shard0000", "shard0001", "shard0002", "shard0003"];
var splitPoints = [ /* Route data split points */ ];

// Determine the bounds for each chunk
splitPoints.forEach(function(point, index) {
    var lowerBound = { "src_airport": MinKey,
 "dst_airport": MinKey, "airline.name": MinKey };
    var upperBound = { "src_airport": MaxKey,
 "dst_airport": MaxKey, "airline.name": MaxKey };
    if (index > 0) {
        lowerBound = splitPoints[index - 1];
    }
    if (index < splitPoints.length) {
        upperBound = point;
    }

    // Manually assign a chunk to a shard using the moveChunk command
    db.adminCommand({
        moveChunk: "sample_training.routes",
        find: lowerBound,
        to: shards[index % shards.length],
        bounds: [lowerBound, upperBound]
    });
});
```

This script manually assigns chunks of the `sample_training.routes` collection to specific shards by using the `moveChunk` command. It ensures even distribution of data across the shards based on predefined split points, which optimizes the sharding process and enhances query performance by aligning the data distribution with the access patterns.

JUMBO CHUNKS

In MongoDB, when a chunk surpasses the designated size range and can't be divided automatically, it is tagged as *jumbo*. MongoDB generally handles the division and distribution of chunks seamlessly, but occasionally, you need to manage a jumbo chunk manually. Split the chunk, and the jumbo tag is discarded. For this purpose, you can employ the `sh.splitAt()` or `sh.splitFind()` function to split the oversize chunk.

INVISIBLE CHUNKS

In certain cases, MongoDB is unable to split a no-longer-jumbo chunk, such as a chunk with a range of a single shard-key value, and you cannot split the chunk to clear the flag. In such cases, you can modify the shard key (reshard a collection) to make the chunk divisible or remove the flag manually.

To clear the flag manually, in the admin database, initiate the `clearJumboFlag` command, providing the namespace of the sharded collection and either of the following:

- The boundaries of the jumbo chunk:

```
db.adminCommand({
  clearJumboFlag: "sample_training.routes",
  bounds: [
    { "airline.id": 410 },
    { "airline.id": 411 }
  ]
})
```

- The find document with a shard key and value that falls within the jumbo chunk:

```
db.adminCommand({
  clearJumboFlag: "sample_training.routes",
  find: { "airline.id": 410 }
})
```

These commands clear the jumbo flag manually from chunks in the `sample_training.routes` sharded collection. The first command specifies chunk boundaries, targeting the chunk between `airline.id` 410 and `airline.id` 411. The second command targets a chunk containing a document in which `airline.id` is 410. Clearing the jumbo flag indicates that these chunks are no longer considered excessively large and can be split or migrated as needed.

9.3.10 Automerging chunks

In MongoDB 7.0, the introduction of AutoMerger as part of the balancer's functionality enhances the management of data shards. This feature automatically merges data chunks that meet predefined criteria, streamlining operations in the background.

The `mergeAllChunksOnShard` function in MongoDB combines all contiguous chunks within a collection on a single shard that qualify for merging. Chunks can be merged if they meet the following criteria:

- They reside on the same shard.
- They are not jumbo chunks. These larger chunks are ineligible for merging due to their inability to be moved during migrations.
- You must be able to remove their historical data safely, ensuring that transactions and snapshot reads remain intact. Specifically, enough time must have elapsed since the last migration of the chunk—at least the duration defined in `minSnapshotHistoryWindowInSeconds` and `transactionLifetimeLimitSeconds`.

Table 9.2 shows how `mergeAllChunksOnShard` works. The `routes` collection in the `sample_training` database is sharded and consists of chunks that are eligible for merging due to their nonjumbo size and lack of historical data. Each chunk has a minimum and a maximum shard-key value, indicating the range of data it contains. The Shard column specifies which shard hosts each chunk, indicating how the collection's data is partitioned across different shards in the cluster.

Table 9.2 Distribution of chunks in a sharded MongoDB collection

Chunk ID	Min	Max	Shard
A	x:0	x:15	Shard0
B	x:15	x:30	Shard0
C	x:30	x:45	Shard0
D	x:45	x:60	Shard1
E	x:60	x:75	Shard1
F	x:75	x:90	Shard1
G	x:90	x:105	Shard0
H	x:105	x:120	Shard0

If you want to merge contiguous chunks on Shard0, execute

```
db.adminCommand({ mergeAllChunksOnShard: "sample_training.routes",
 shard: "Shard0" })
```

Executing the `merge` command on Shard0 for the `sample_training.routes` collection merges the contiguous chunks A, B, and C into one chunk and G and H into another, reducing the total chunk count on Shard0.

On Shard1, execute

```
db.adminCommand({ mergeAllChunksOnShard: "sample_training.routes",
 shard: "Shard1" })
```

Executing the `merge` command on Shard1 for the `sample_training.routes` collection merges contiguous chunks D, E, and F into a single chunk, reducing the total chunk count on Shard1.

AutoMerger automates the merging of data chunks, enhancing shard management by intelligently combining eligible contiguous chunks based on predefined criteria:

```
sh.startAutoMerger()
sh.stopAutoMerger()
sh.enableAutoMerger()
sh.disableAutoMerger()
```

These methods control the AutoMerger behavior. This automation leads to improved query performance, optimized resource use, and reduced operational complexity, ultimately making database administration more efficient.

9.4 MongoDB 8.0 sharded cluster features

MongoDB 8.0 introduces new features in sharded clusters. The following sections describe the new features and improvements.

9.4.1 Embedding config servers in sharded clusters

In version 8.0, MongoDB introduces the capability to embed sharding configuration servers directly within sharded clusters. This enhancement simplifies the overall architecture and reduces infrastructure costs while maintaining scale and performance.

Separate replica sets dedicated to config servers are still supported and recommended for setups with more than three shards. Also, new commands have been introduced to facilitate transitions between embedded and dedicated config servers.

If you want to transition from a dedicated config server to an embedded config server, run the following command in `mongosh`:

```
db.adminCommand( { transitionFromDedicatedConfigServer: 1} )
```

If you want to transition from an embedded config server back to a dedicated config server, run the command

```
db.adminCommand( { transitionToDedicatedConfigServer: 1} )
```

You can switch configurations at any time for any reason. To switch to a dedicated CSRS, run the command

```
transitionToDedicatedConfigServer
```

This command executes `removeShard` in the background to convert the config shard to a config server and move your data from that shard to the other shards in the cluster.

To switch back to an embedded config server, run the command

```
transitionFromDedicatedConfigServer
```

> **TIP** Use dedicated config servers if you have more than three shards.

> **NOTE** Atlas uses embedded config servers for three or fewer shards. You can opt into or out of letting Atlas manage that configuration.

9.4.2 Moving unsharded collections seamlessly between shards

In MongoDB 8.0, you can relocate unsharded collections to different shards without extra configuration, such as sharding the collections or choosing a shard key. This simplifies horizontal scaling and allows geographic distribution of collections to meet compliance requirements.

The command `db.adminCommand({moveCollection:"database.collection", toShard: "shardName"})` is a new feature in MongoDB 8.0. Use it to move an unsharded collection to a different shard without sharding the collection or selecting a shard key.

MongoDB 8.0 sharded cluster features

Figure 9.4 illustrates the process of moving the unsharded collection `sample_training.zips` from `Shard0` to `Shard1`. Before the move, the `sample_training.zips` and `sample_training.routes` collections are located on `Shard0`. After you execute the command, the `sample_training.zips` collection is relocated to `Shard1`, and the `sample_training.routes` collection remains on `Shard0`:

```
db.adminCommand({moveCollection: "sample_training.zips", toShard:"shard1"})
```

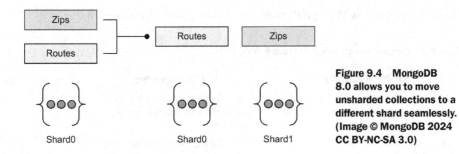

Figure 9.4 MongoDB 8.0 allows you to move unsharded collections to a different shard seamlessly. (Image © MongoDB 2024 CC BY-NC-SA 3.0)

In certain use cases, moving collections between shards could affect performance:

- Moving the collection that a view whose definition and collection are on different shards uses away from the primary shard
- Moving the collection that a view with `$lookup` between collections on different shards uses on a separate shard
- Moving the collection that an on-demand materialized view uses (with `$out`)
- Implicitly creating unsharded collections

9.4.3 Fragmentation

If your data has been sharded in versions of MongoDB before 6.0, it may suffer from a degree of fragmentation, with the data being spread across an unnecessarily large number of small chunks. In MongoDB 6.0 and later, functionality was added to allow defragmenting, which reduces the number of chunks merging smaller chunks into larger chunks. This improves create, read, update, and delete (CRUD) operation times. In MongoDB 6.0, you can perform this operation manually; in MongoDB 7.0 and later, it occurs automatically.

9.4.4 Faster resharding

Resharding data across shards is four times faster now and includes time-series collections, reducing the operational costs and complexity of managing the database architecture. In MongoDB version 8.0, the limitation has been removed. Now you can reshard to the same shard key using the `reshardCollection` command with forceRedistribution: true. This command allows the operation to run even if the new shard key is the same as the old one, and you can use it with the zones option to move data to specific zones:

```
db.adminCommand({
    reshardCollection: "database.collection",
    key: { fieldName: "hashed" },
    forceRedistribution: true
})
```

Table 9.3 shows how MongoDB made resharding faster in version 8.0.

Table 9.3 Comparison of resharding: pre-8.0 vs. 8.0+

Pre-8.0 resharding	8.0+ resharding
The resharding process performs an _id scan and fetch using random I/O reads on the source collection.	The resharding process performs a natural-order scan of the source collection.
Build indexes on the new collection at the beginning, and do incremental maintenance (random I/O writes).	Bulk-build the indexes on the new collection at the end.
_id scan and fetch reads sequentially across all shards.	Each recipient shard reads from all donor shards in parallel.

9.4.5 Unsharding collections

MongoDB 8.0 allows you to unshard existing sharded collections using the unshardCollection command, which facilitates consolidating all the documents from a sharded collection into a single shard. During the unsharding operation, MongoDB transfers the data to a specific shard chosen by the user or automatically to the shard with the smallest data footprint. This feature simplifies the management of sharded data by enabling the migration of collections back to a single shard environment, offering greater flexibility in how data is stored and managed.

You must execute the command on the admin database; you cannot run it on shared MongoDB instances. The command structure is

```
db.adminCommand({
    unshardCollection: "<database>.<collection>",
    toShard: "<shard-id>"
})
```

In this context, <database>.<collection> indicates the collection to be unsharded, and <shard-id> determines the shard where the collection's data will be consolidated. If <shard-id> is unspecified, the balancer selects the shard with the least data.

Before unsharding your collection, ensure that your application can tolerate a 2-second period during which writes to the affected collection are blocked, which may temporarily increase latency. Also, confirm that the target shard has sufficient storage space—at least twice the combined size of the collection and its indexes. It's also important to verify that the system's I/O capacity is below 50% and the CPU load is below 80%.

The `unshardCollection` operation can be performed on only one collection at a time and has a minimum duration of 5 minutes. After `unshardCollection` runs, Atlas Search indexes must be rebuilt. Further, you cannot make topology changes, such as adding or removing shards or transitioning between embedded and dedicated config servers, until the `unshardCollection` process is complete.

By implementing sharding, you can build highly scalable MongoDB clusters consisting of many nodes that are capable of storing hundreds of terabytes of data. Each shard contains a portion of the data and is a replica set for high availability. MongoDB efficiently distributes queries and writes across all shards. This gives MongoDB a significant advantage over traditional relational databases, which are constrained by vertical scaling. But it is crucial to focus on key considerations, such as selecting the right shard key to ensure even data distribution, prevent hotspots, and maintain optimal performance.

> **TIP** For detailed information on MongoDB sharding, I recommend reviewing the technical documentation at https://www.mongodb.com/docs/manual/sharding.

9.5 Managing data consistency and availability

In MongoDB, Read/Write Concern and Read Preference manage data consistency and fault tolerance, providing configurable tradeoffs among durability, performance, and availability based on application needs. You can configure these settings to ensure that writes are fully replicated for strong consistency or enable reads from secondary nodes to optimize performance and reduce the load on the primary.

Write Concern specifies how many replica set members must acknowledge a write for durability. Read Concern defines whether reads should reflect the latest writes or a more relaxed data view. Read Preference controls whether reads target the primary or secondary nodes to balance performance. My general advice is that is if you read your own writes on the primary, you should use the `"majority"` Read Concern and perform writes with the `{ w: "majority" }` Write Concern. The default Read Concern setting is `"local"`, and the default Write Concern setting is `"majority"`. The following sections discuss how these settings work.

9.5.1 Write Concern

Write Concern specifies how many members of a replica set must acknowledge a write operation before it's considered successful. This means that MongoDB waits for confirmation from a certain number of replica set members (nodes) before informing the client that the write operation (such as inserting, updating, or deleting a document) was successful. The more members that need to acknowledge the write, the more durable and reliable the data is, but this involves a tradeoff: higher durability can reduce performance because MongoDB waits for multiple nodes to confirm the operation.

The settings for Write Concern are controlled using { `w: <value>`, `j: <boolean>`, `wtimeout: <number>` } options. I discuss these components in the following sections.

W: <VALUE>

The `w` option specifies how many replica set members must acknowledge the write operation. The value can be

- `w: 1`—Only the primary node acknowledges the write. It's fast but less durable because the data may not have been replicated to secondaries. On a social media platform that handles temporary actions such as counting likes, this level allows faster response times to users but risks losing some likes if the primary node fails before replication occurs.
- `w: "majority"` *(default)*—A majority of voting members must acknowledge the write, which ensures stronger durability and data consistency. In an e-commerce system, this level ensures that an order placed by a customer is written safely across multiple nodes, so even if the primary node fails, the data is preserved and recoverable.
- `w: 0`—No acknowledgment is required, so MongoDB does not wait for any confirmation. This option provides maximum speed but no durability guarantee. You could use this option in scenarios such as logging systems in which losing some log entries is acceptable and the priority is on collecting data as quickly as possible.
- `w: "all"`—All members of the replica set must acknowledge the write. This option provides the highest level of durability but may slow the operation significantly. It is useful in critical applications such as banking systems in which every transaction must be written securely to all replica set members, ensuring that no data is lost even if several nodes fail.

J: <BOOLEAN>

The `j` option determines whether the write operation must be written to the on-disk journal before acknowledgment. Journaling provides added durability by ensuring that data is recoverable even if the server crashes after the write. The value can be

- `j: true`—The write is acknowledged only after being written to the on-disk journal. This option ensures that the data is durable and recoverable, making it suitable for systems in which data integrity is critical, such as health care systems, in which patient data must not be lost.
- `j: false`—MongoDB does not wait for the write to be committed to the on-disk journal before acknowledging it. This option can provide faster performance but less durability in the event of a crash

WTIMEOUT: <NUMBER>

The wtimeout option specifies (in milliseconds) how long MongoDB will wait for the required number of members to acknowledge the write. If the specified acknowledgment is not received within this time limit, the operation returns an error. The wtimeout option is useful for preventing indefinite blocking if some nodes are slow or unreachable. In a globally distributed system, if a replica in another region is slow to respond, the wtimeout option ensures that the write operation doesn't hang indefinitely.

You can define Write Concern in several places in MongoDB. You can set it per operation (e.g., during an insert, update, or delete operation), at the connection level in mongosh or the MongoDB driver, or globally for a replica set using setDefault-RWConcern. These options allow you to adjust the acknowledgment requirements based on the specific needs of the operation, client, or deployment. Here's an example of setting Write Concern for an insert operation in mongosh:

```
db.routes.insertOne(
  { src_airport: 'MUC'},
  { writeConcern: { w: "majority", j: true, wtimeout: 5000 } }
)
```

In this example, w: "majority" ensures that the write is acknowledged by the majority of replica set members, providing stronger durability. The option j: true ensures that the write is committed to the on-disk journal, adding durability in case of a system crash. The wtimeout: 5000 setting specifies a 5-second time limit for receiving the acknowledgment, preventing the operation from waiting indefinitely if the required nodes do not respond within that time.

9.5.2 Read Concern

Read Concern allows you to control the consistency and isolation properties of the data returned by queries in MongoDB, whether from replica sets or sharded clusters. It specifies how consistent the data should be, balancing performance and availability. Supported levels are

- local *(default)*—Reads data from the instance without guaranteeing that the data has been replicated to other replica set members. It is fast but may return data that could be rolled back later.
- available—Provides the lowest latency by reading data from the instance without waiting for confirmation that it has been replicated. This mode offers minimal consistency and is useful when availability is more important than accuracy, such as in a sharded cluster.
- majority—Ensures that the data returned has been acknowledged by most replica set members, guaranteeing that the data is durable and can withstand node failures. This level is typically used for applications that require strong consistency, such as e-commerce systems.

- `linearizable`—Provides the strictest consistency. Reads return only the latest version of the data after confirming that all previous majority-acknowledged writes have been applied. This level can be used in critical systems in which consistency is paramount, such as financial transactions, but it may introduce performance overhead.
- `snapshot`—Reads data from a point-in-time snapshot of majority-committed data across the entire cluster. This level is useful in multidocument transactions, ensuring that all data read within a transaction reflects a consistent state.

You can specify the Read Concern in MongoDB for queries by using the `.readConcern()` method on the cursor:

```
db.routes.find({ src_airport: 'MUC' }).readConcern('majority')
```

In this example, setting the Read Concern level to `'majority'` ensures that the query returns data that has been confirmed by a majority of the replica set members. This guarantees stronger consistency and durability, as the data has been acknowledged by most members of the replica set before being returned.

You can also set the Global Default Read and Write Concerns for all operations across a replica set using the `setDefaultRWConcern` command. This setting ensures consistent behavior for reads and writes without specifying concerns for each operation. Here's an example of setting the default Write Concern and Read Concern globally:

```
db.adminCommand({
  "setDefaultRWConcern": 1,
  "defaultWriteConcern": {
    "w": 2
  },
  "defaultReadConcern": {
    "level": "majority"
  }
})
```

The default Write Concern is set to `w: 2`, meaning that writes will be considered successful only when they are acknowledged by two replica set members. The default Read Concern is set to `level: "majority"`, ensuring that reads return data that has been confirmed by a majority of the replica set members. These global defaults, however, can be overridden by concerns set at the driver or operation level. If a Read Concern or Write Concern is explicitly specified in the application code or driver, for example, it takes precedence over the global default.

If you want to check the current global default Read and Write Concerns, use the following command:

```
db.adminCommand({
  "getDefaultRWConcern": 1
})
```

This command returns the configured global default Read Concern and Write Concern.

9.5.3 Read Preference

Read Preference determines which members of a replica set MongoDB should read data from. By default, MongoDB reads from the primary node to ensure the most up-to-date data. You can adjust Read Preference to allow reading from secondary nodes, however, which can help distribute read load and improve performance in certain situations.

You control the settings for Read Preference with the { mode: <value> } option. Let's take a closer look at the components:

- primary *(default)*—All reads are directed to the primary node, ensuring that the most up-to-date data is returned. This setting, however, can lead to performance bottlenecks if the primary node is handling both read and write operations. This setting is suitable for applications in which data consistency is critical, such as financial applications, in which every transaction must be based on the latest data.
- primaryPreferred—Reads are directed to the primary if it is available. If the primary is unavailable, MongoDB reads from a secondary node. This mode provides a balance between performance and availability, ensuring consistency while allowing for continued reads during primary downtime.
- secondary—Reads are directed exclusively to secondary nodes. This setting reduces the load on the primary node but may return slightly stale data because it has not yet been replicated. This mode is useful when availability and read performance are prioritized over strict consistency, such as in reporting systems or analytics. Analytical aggregation pipelines are good candidates to be run on secondary nodes to offload processing from the primary.
- secondaryPreferred—Reads are directed to secondary nodes if they are available. If no secondary is available, MongoDB reads from the primary. This setting provides flexibility by prioritizing secondary reads while still allowing reads from the primary in case of problems with the secondary nodes.
- nearest—MongoDB directs reads to the node with the lowest network latency, whether it's a primary or secondary. This setting is particularly useful in geographically distributed systems when you want to prioritize performance by reading from the closest available node, even though the data may not be the most up to date.

Here's an example of setting Read Preference for a specific query in mongosh:

```
db.routes.find({ src_airport: 'MUC' }).readPref('secondaryPreferred')
```

In this query, the .readPref('secondaryPreferred') method is appended to the cursor returned by find(). It directs the query to a secondary node if one is available but falls back to the primary if no secondaries are accessible. This approach helps distribute the load across replica set members while ensuring data availability.

By configuring Read Preference, you can optimize read performance across your application, distribute load efficiently, and adjust consistency guarantees based on the specific requirements of your deployment.

Summary

- A replica set in MongoDB is a group of mongod processes that store identical data sets, ensuring redundancy and high availability. Members can exist in various states and perform different roles within the replica set.
- MongoDB uses PV1, based on the Raft algorithm, for replica set elections, ensuring data consistency. It features a voting system to decide the primary member, including the term concept. The oplog is a capped collection that logs ordered write operations in MongoDB, enabling replication. Write operations that don't change data or fail don't generate oplog entries.
- MongoDB change streams offer reliable, ordered, resumable change-event notifications with RBAC, ensuring data durability across replica sets. They also integrate with the aggregation pipeline for efficient server-side data processing, unlike oplog tailing.
- MongoDB uses sharding to partition data across multiple servers, enabling horizontal scaling and improved handling of large data volumes and high transaction rates. A MongoDB sharded cluster can consist of any number of shards, each holding a fragment of data, allowing the total database size to exceed 100 TB without a clear upper limit.
- MongoDB shards data at the collection level, distributing the collection data across the shards in the cluster using the shard key, which consists of one or more fields within the documents.
- You can create a sharded cluster in MongoDB Atlas. Unlike the M0 cluster you set up in chapter 1, these clusters are not free in Atlas, so you must set up a payment method. Sharded clusters are supported starting from the M30 tier.
- Starting with MongoDB 8.0, config servers can be embedded in sharded clusters, simplifying the architecture and reducing overall infrastructure costs.
- Choosing the right shard key is crucial in sharding clusters. A poor choice can lead to inefficient data distribution, load imbalances, and poor query performance. In some cases, an overloaded shard, known as a *hot shard*, can become a bottleneck, negatively affecting the cluster's overall performance.
- MongoDB simplifies shard-key selection with the analyzeShardKey command, which provides metrics based on sampled queries for informed decision-making in both unsharded and sharded collections.
- MongoDB organizes sharded data in chunks or ranges, each defaulting to 128 MB. A chunk is defined by a shard key's lower bound (inclusive) and upper

bound (exclusive), containing a continuous sequence of shard-key values within a shard.
- Presplitting chunks in a sharded collection can improve throughput, particularly when you're dealing with large data volumes in an unbalanced cluster or ingesting data that could lead to imbalance, such as with monotonically changing shard keys.
- AutoMerger, integrated into the balancer's functionality, improves data shard management by automatically merging eligible data chunks based on predefined criteria, optimizing operations seamlessly in the background.
- In MongoDB 8.0, you can move unsharded collections between shards without additional configuration such as sharding or selecting a shard key. This simplifies scaling horizontally and supports geographical distribution for compliance needs.
- In MongoDB 8.0, data resharding across shards is four times faster and includes support for time-series collections, which reduces operational costs and simplifies database architecture management.
- In MongoDB 8.0, you can use the `unshardCollection` command to move all documents from a sharded collection to a single shard—a specified one or the shard with the least data.
- Write Concern defines how many replica set members must acknowledge a write operation for it to be successful. The levels include `w: 1` (only the primary acknowledges), `w: "majority"` (a majority of members acknowledge), `w: 0` (no acknowledgment is required), and `w: "all"` (all members must acknowledge).
- Read Concern defines the consistency level for read operations. The levels include `local` (reads from the current node), `majority` (data confirmed by the majority), `linearizable` (strict consistency), and `snapshot` (consistent view at a specific point in time).
- Read Preference determines which replica set members handle read operations. The options include `primary` (reads from the primary), `primaryPreferred` (primary if available; otherwise, secondary), `secondary` (reads from secondaries), `secondaryPreferred` (secondary if available; otherwise, primary), and `nearest` (reads from the node with the lowest latency).

Part 2

MongoDB Atlas data platform

Imagine being able to build a production-ready backend in minutes, not days—without configuring servers, setting up backups, worrying about patching, or managing replica sets. You write the code, define your data, and deploy. The rest? Handled automatically by the cloud.

That's the idea behind MongoDB Atlas. It's not just a managed MongoDB cluster running in the cloud; it's a full-featured data platform, designed to simplify application development while giving you access to enterprise-grade performance, availability, and security out of the box. Built on top of the core MongoDB database, Atlas extends your capabilities with tools for search, AI integration, real-time data processing, analytics, and event-driven architectures, all deeply integrated and fully managed.

The days of stitching together ten tools to build a modern application stack are fading. With Atlas, you can store your data, search it, analyze it, process it as it streams in, and even build AI-powered applications, and do it all within a single platform.

This part of the book walks you through the many services offered by Atlas and shows how to use them in real-world applications. You'll start in chapter 10 by learning what it means to run MongoDB as a fully managed service and how Atlas automates key operations such as scaling, backups, and high availability.

Chapter 11 introduces Atlas Search, which brings powerful full-text search capabilities to your data using Apache Lucene under the hood. You'll learn how to build custom search indexes and integrate search directly into your application workflows using familiar MongoDB aggregation pipelines.

Chapter 12 takes things further with Atlas Vector Search, a next-generation technique for building applications that understand context and meaning—not just keywords. You'll see how to use embeddings to perform semantic search, power recommendation engines, and even build AI chatbots that retrieve facts from your data.

Speaking of AI, chapter 13 guides you through creating local AI-powered applications with the Atlas command-line interface (CLI), showing you how to spin up local clusters and prototype features quickly. Then, in chapter 14, you'll learn how to build a retrieval-augmented generation (RAG) chatbot using MongoDB, LangChain, and vector search—an architecture that's quickly becoming the standard in generative AI systems.

In chapter 15, you'll explore event-driven development with Atlas Stream Processing, which allows your applications to react to data changes in real time. Whether MongoDB is syncing updates to a dashboard, sending notifications, or triggering downstream processes, you'll see how it can power real-time pipelines from source to action.

Chapter 16 introduces Atlas Data Federation, which lets you run queries across multiple data sources, including Azure Blob Storage, Amazon S3 buckets, and MongoDB collections without moving or duplicating data.

In chapter 17, you'll learn how to optimize storage costs with Atlas Online Archive, automatically tiering infrequently accessed data while keeping it queryable.

Chapter 18 explores SQL access to MongoDB, showing how you can connect business intelligence (BI) tools, write SQL queries, and integrate MongoDB with analytics platforms. Finally, in chapter 19, you'll dive into charts, functions, and triggers—tools that let you build visualizations, automate server-side logic, and react to data changes in powerful ways.

Atlas gives developers a unified toolbox for building intelligent, scalable, real-time apps without gluing together separate systems. By the end of this part, you'll know how to turn MongoDB Atlas into the heart of your modern application stack.

Delving into Database as a Service

This chapter covers
- Mastering MongoDB Atlas's Database as a Service
- Differentiating M0 and Flex Atlas clusters
- Comprehending dedicated M10+ Atlas clusters
- Scaling Atlas cluster and storage with autoscaling
- Going multicloud with Atlas multicloud and region clusters

In part 1 of this book, I intentionally avoided MongoDB server administration problems to focus on Atlas, a managed Database as a Service (DBaaS). Atlas handles most MongoDB administrative tasks, simplifying database operations and allowing developers to concentrate on application development. It automates critical functions such as deployment, scaling, upgrades, and backups to ensure optimal performance and security. Its features include real-time analytics, comprehensive monitoring, and performance optimization.

Atlas offers various cluster options: M0 for beginners, Flex for development and testing, M10 and M20 for development, and M30+ for production, all with support for replica sets and sharded deployments. It allows automatic adjustments of cluster tiers and storage.

In Atlas, you can select your desired cluster tier, which determines the memory, storage, virtual CPUs (vCPUs), and input/output operations per second (IOPS) specifications for each data-bearing server in the cluster. You can also automatically scale your cluster tier, storage capacity, or both in response to cluster use.

Atlas offers several types of clusters to cater to different needs and use cases. The types of clusters vary depending on the tier. The beginner-tier clusters have limited functionalities, whereas the developer and higher-tier clusters offer a full range of features that are necessary for production use cases.

Also, Atlas extends the functionalities of the core MongoDB server by adding Atlas Search, Atlas Vector Search, Atlas SQL Interface, Atlas Stream Processing, Atlas Data Federation, Atlas Online Archive, and more, making it a comprehensive developer data platform.

10.1 Shared M0 and Flex clusters

Atlas M0 (free tier) and Flex clusters are ideal for getting started with MongoDB and for low-throughput applications:

- *M0 (free tier)*— Ideal for learning MongoDB and building small development projects. It provides limited resources and storage.
  - *Deployment type*—Replica set
- *Flex*—The base monthly plan includes 5 GB of storage, 100 operations per second, and unlimited data transfer. Clusters scale with your use, and additional operations may incur charges, though your monthly bill stays under control. This cluster type is suitable for small applications and development environments.
  - *Deployment type*—Replica set

These clusters run in a shared environment and provide limited access to Atlas features. You can deploy one M0 cluster (a free sandbox replica set) per Atlas project, and you have the option to upgrade an M0 free cluster to Flex or M10 at any time. To change your cluster tier, select Edit Configuration from the drop-down menu in the Atlas UI (figure 10.1).

In the Cluster Tier section, shown in figure 10.2, choose the tier you want to migrate to.

TIP Scaling up or down a M0, Flex, or M10 cluster requires 7 to 10 minutes of downtime.

In a shared environment, multiple clusters use the same underlying hardware resources. This setup reduces costs but may limit performance and the range of available features compared with those of dedicated clusters. Table 10.1 shows the limits for these clusters.

Shared M0 and Flex clusters

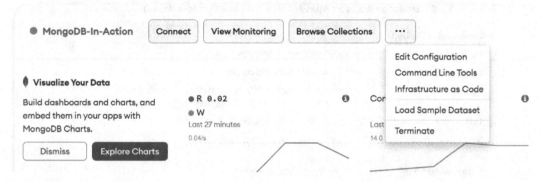

Figure 10.1 Edit the configuration in the Atlas UI. (Image © MongoDB 2025)

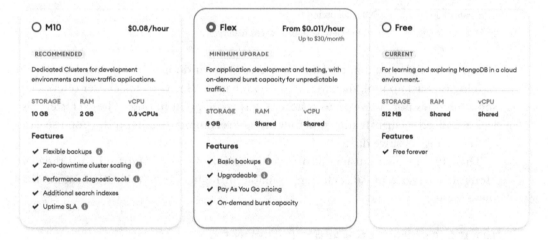

Figure 10.2 Cluster Tier section of the Atlas UI with available M0, Flex, and M10 clusters (Image © MongoDB 2025)

Table 10.1 Configuration limits for Atlas M0 (free tier) and Flex

Configuration option	Limit
Cloud service provider and region	Deploy only in a subset of regions in Amazon Web Services (AWS), Google Cloud Provider (GCP), and Microsoft Azure
MongoDB version upgrade	Can't upgrade manually. Atlas automatically upgrades after several patch versions become available.
Cluster tier	Only one M0 cluster per project
Cluster memory	Can't configure memory
Cluster storage	Can't configure storage size
Replication factor	Set to three nodes and can't be modified

Table 10.1 Configuration limits for Atlas M0 (free tier) and Flex (*continued*)

Configuration option	Limit
Replica set tags	No predefined replica set tags
Sharded cluster	Can't deploy as a sharded cluster
Backup	Can't enable backups in M0. You can use `mongodump` for backup and `mongorestore` for restore.
Test primary failovers	Can't perform primary failover testing
Simulate regional outage	Can't perform regional outage testing
Database auditing	Can't configure database auditing
Encryption at rest using customer key management	Can't configure
Network peering connections	Can't configure
Private endpoints	Not supported
Access tracking	Can't view database access history

It's important to note that backups for the M0 cluster do not exist; you must use your own logical backup tool, such as `mongodump` (chapter 21). The Flex cluster offers snapshots but does not allow you to restore to a specific point in time. These clusters also lack advanced security features, so they are not recommended in production use cases or for storing sensitive data.

The M0 and Flex clusters also have operational limits compared with the core MongoDB server and Atlas clusters available in higher tiers. Table 10.2 summarizes these limits.

Table 10.2 Operational limits for Atlas M0 (free tier) and Flex

Operation	Limit
Aggregation and queries	No `allowDiskUse` option; no `$currentOp`, `$listLocalSessions`, `$listSessions`, or `$planCacheStats` stages; maximum 50 stages
API access	Create M0 free cluster using the Clusters API resource, but can't modify; subset of API endpoints supports Flex clusters
Atlas alerts	Can trigger alerts only for connections, logical size, network, and opscounter
Atlas monitoring	Metrics view displays only connections, logical size, network, and opscounter
Authentication	Supports password (SCRAM-SHA1), X.509 certificates, and AWS identity and access management (IAM)
Autoexpand storage	Not provided
BSON nested object depth	Maximum 50 nested levels

Table 10.2 Operational limits for Atlas M0 (free tier) and Flex (*continued*)

Operation	Limit
Build index with rolling build	Not supported
Change-stream filtering	Only strings and regular expressions for database names; no commands such as `$in` for database namespace filters
Cluster persistence	Atlas may deactivate idle M0 free clusters
Command-line tools	`mongorestore` options `--restoreDbUsersAndRoles`, `--oplogReplay`, and `--preserveUUID` are not supported.
	`mongodump` options `--dumpDbUsersAndRoles` and `--oplog` are not supported.
Connections	Maximum 500 connections
Cursors	No `noTimeout` cursor option
Custom roles	Changes might take up to 30 seconds to deploy
Database and collections	Maximum 100 databases and 500 collections
Access to collections in local, admin, and config databases	No read access to local except oplog; no write access to local and config; no read/write access to admin
Database logs	Can't download logs
DatarRecovery	No custom policies; single daily snapshot; can't restore to sharded cluster
Data storage	M0, 0.5 GB; Flex, 5 GB
JavaScript	Server-side JavaScript not supported (e.g., `$where`)
Namespaces and database names	Namespaces are limited to 95 bytes; database names are limited to 38 bytes.
Number of free clusters	One M0 free cluster per Atlas project
Performance advisor	Not provided
Query use	Must remain below 100% use over any 5-minute period
Real-time performance panel	Not provided
Sort in memory	Limit is 32 MB
Throughput	M0:,100 operations/second; Flex, 500 operations/second. Throttling and cooldown period apply if these limits are exceeded.
Automatic pause of idle clusters	Paused after 60 days of inactivity; can resume unless version can't be restored

10.2 Dedicated clusters

Atlas offers additional tiers:

- *M10 to M40*—Suitable for medium-size applications, providing more resources, better performance, and additional features such as virtual private cloud (VPC) peering
  - *Deployment type*—Replica set or sharded cluster (from M30)
- *M50 to M200*—Designed for large-scale applications requiring high performance, increased storage, and advanced configurations

- *Deployment type*—Replica set or sharded cluster
- *M300 and higher*—Tailored for enterprise-level deployments with very high performance, large storage capacities, and extensive scalability options
  - *Deployment type*—Replica set or sharded cluster

Table 10.3 compares the most important features of MongoDB Atlas across tiers. You can find more information about dedicated cluster features in part 3 of this book.

Table 10.3 Key differences among M0 (free), Flex, and M10+ (dedicated) clusters

Feature	M0 (free)	Flex	M10+ (dedicated)
Storage (data storage size+index size)	512 MB	5 GB	10 GB to 4 TB
Metric and alerts	Limited	Limited	Full metrics, the Real Time Performance tab, and full alert configuration
VPC peering	No	No	Yes
Global region selection	M0 clusters in subset of AWS, GCP, and Azure regions	Flex clusters in subset of AWS, GCP, and Azure regions	Available in AWS, GCP, and Azure
Cross-region deployments	No	No	Yes
Backups	No	Yes; daily backup snapshots	Yes, including queryable backups
Sharding	No	No	Yes, for M30+ tier
Dedicated cluster	No	No	Yes. M10+ clusters deploy each mongod process to its own instance.
Performance advisor	No	No	Yes

10.2.1 Atlas clusters for low-traffic applications

The M10 and M20 cluster tiers are ideal for development environments and low-traffic applications. These tiers support only replica set deployments but offer full access to Atlas features. M10 and M20 clusters operate on a burstable performance infrastructure, meaning that they can handle occasional increases in traffic but are optimized for lower, steady workloads.

In addition, M10 and M20 clusters provide robust security, automated backups, and monitoring (chapter 21), ensuring a reliable, secure environment for your applications. They also allow seamless upgrades to higher tiers as your application's demands grow.

> **TIP** For any M10+ cluster, you can use the Atlas command-line interface (CLI) and the command `atlas cluster update <your cluster> --tier <any tier larger than M10>` to change the cluster size.

10.2.2 Atlas clusters for high-traffic applications

Clusters in the M30 tier and higher are ideal for production environments. These clusters support replica set and sharded cluster deployments, providing full access to all Atlas features.

Certain clusters have variants, marked by the > character. When you choose one of these clusters, Atlas displays the variants and tags each cluster to highlight their key characteristics.

10.2.3 Autoscaling clusters and storage

You can set the cluster tier ranges that Atlas uses to automatically adjust your cluster tier, storage capacity, or both based on use. Cluster autoscaling handles most scaling needs, but advanced use cases may require custom scripts or consulting services. To manage costs, you can define a maximum and minimum range for cluster sizes and adjust those ranges automatically. Autoscaling operates on a rolling basis, ensuring no downtime during the process.

AUTOSCALING CLUSTERS

Atlas evaluates the following cluster metrics to decide when and how to scale a cluster up or down:

- CPU use
- Memory use

Atlas calculates memory use with this formula:

```
(memoryTotal - (memoryFree + memoryBuffers +
memoryCached))/(memoryTotal) * 100
```

Here, `memoryFree`, `memoryBuffers`, and `memoryCached` represent the memory that can be reclaimed for other uses. Atlas will not scale your cluster tier if

- The new cluster tier is outside your specified minimum and maximum cluster size range (figure 10.3).
- Memory use would exceed available memory for the new cluster tier.
- Atlas scales only within the same cluster class. That is, General clusters scale to other General cluster tiers but not to Low-CPU tiers.
- For replica sets, Atlas does not autoscale by adding more nodes or converting to a sharded cluster.
- For sharded clusters, Atlas does not autoscale horizontally by adding shards.

In the Cluster Tier section of the Auto-Scale options section, you can specify the Maximum Cluster Size and Minimum Cluster Size values for automatic scaling. Atlas sets these values as follows:

- Maximum Cluster Size is set to one tier above your current cluster tier.
- Minimum Cluster Size is set to the current cluster tier.

Figure 10.3 shows the configuration options for autoscaling in Atlas. If the Cluster Tier Scaling option is enabled, you can set the Minimum and Maximum Cluster Size values. For this configuration, Minimum Cluster Size is set to M30, and the Cluster Size is set to M50. You also have an option to allow the cluster to scale down.

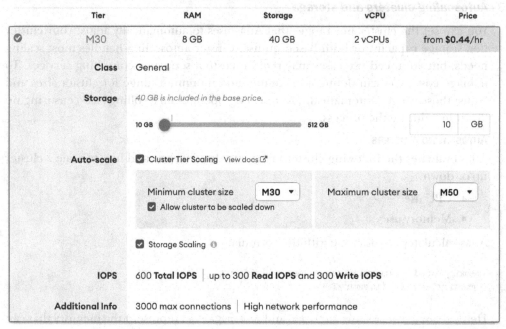

Figure 10.3 The Atlas UI's Cluster Tier section, where you can configure cluster and storage autoscaling (Image © MongoDB 2025)

> **TIP** When you create clusters using the Atlas UI, autoscaling for cluster tiers is enabled by default. If you create clusters via the API or Atlas CLI, however, autoscaling for cluster tiers is disabled by default.

> **NOTE** Atlas activates Cluster Auto-Scaling for all cluster tiers within the General and Low-CPU tiers, excluding only the highest cluster tier.

AUTOSCALING STORAGE

Atlas enables cluster storage autoscaling by default. When any node in the cluster reaches 90% disk space usage, Atlas automatically increases the storage. This process requires time to prepare and copy data to new disks. Automatic scaling may not occur during a sudden surge of high-speed write activity, such as a bulk insert. To avoid running out of disk storage, cluster managers should plan to scale up clusters before bulk inserts and other high-speed write activity.

Autoscaling behavior differs by cloud provider:

- *AWS and GCP clusters*—Atlas increases cluster storage capacity to achieve 70% disk space use. For more information on AWS storage change limitations and how Atlas handles them, see the documentation on changing storage capacity or IOPS in AWS at https://mng.bz/5vm1.
- *Azure clusters*—Atlas doubles the current amount of cluster storage.

NOTE Atlas automatically scales cluster storage up but never down. You can reduce your cluster storage manually if necessary.

SCALING CLUSTER TIER AND CLUSTER STORAGE IN PARALLEL

When Atlas attempts to scale your cluster storage capacity automatically, it might exceed the limits supported by your current cluster tier. To prevent downtime, Atlas also scales your cluster tier to match the new storage capacity. If your maximum specified tier can't support the new capacity, Atlas does the following:

- Raises your maximum cluster tier to the next suitable tier
- Scales your cluster to this new maximum tier

If Atlas tries to scale down, and the target tier can't support the current disk capacity or IOPS, it won't scale down. Instead, it will adjust the autoscaling settings as follows:

- If the cluster is at the maximum tier, Atlas disables downward scaling.
- If not, it raises the minimum tier to the current tier.

This logic ensures minimal downtime due to mismatched storage settings. Atlas notifies all project owners via email about any changes to the cluster tier and the adjusted minimum or maximum tiers.

10.2.4 *Customizing Atlas cluster storage*

Atlas offers flexible storage configuration options tailored to your needs, varying by cloud provider and cluster tier. Each cluster tier has a predefined set of resources, and M10+ clusters allow you to customize your storage capacity. For M40+ clusters, Atlas provides three distinct cluster classes:

- *Low CPU*—This cost-effective option is ideal for applications that need more memory but fewer CPUs. It includes half the vCPUs of the General class of the same tier. A General M40 instance has four vCPUs, for example, whereas a Low CPU M40 instance has two vCPUs. Depending on the tier, this option may also offer fewer maximum connections.
- *General*—Suitable for all production environments, this balanced option provides a standard allocation of resources, ensuring robust performance.

- *Local NVMe solid-state drive (SSD)*—This option offers high-speed, low-latency storage and is ideal for demanding applications. Atlas offers NVMe SSD storage for dedicated clusters on AWS and Azure, ensuring low-latency and high-throughput I/O. Currently, NVMe clusters are not supported in GCP.

TIP Choosing a different cluster class affects overall cost, allowing you to select the configuration that best fits your performance and budget requirements.

OPLOG COLLECTION SIZE IN ATLAS

Atlas handles the cluster's oplog size and entries differently depending on whether storage autoscaling is enabled. By default, Atlas enables storage autoscaling for clusters. When storage autoscaling is active, the oplog entries are managed based on the minimum oplog retention window (`oplogMinRetentionHours`) setting. The oplog window represents the time difference between the newest and oldest timestamps in the oplog.

The minimum oplog retention window is set to 24 hours by default, ensuring that oplog entries are retained for at least 24 hours or until the oplog reaches the maximum size allowed by MongoDB best practices. You can customize this retention window via the Atlas UI. For successful autoscaling, the minimum oplog retention window should be (60 seconds) * (GB of disk space configured).

Opt out of storage autoscaling by clearing the Storage Scaling check box in the Auto-Scale section. Then Atlas manages the oplog size as follows:

- *General and Low-CPU clusters*—5% of disk size at cluster creation
- *Clusters with NVMe storage*—10% of disk size

If the storage size changes, Atlas does not adjust the oplog size automatically. You can set the oplog size manually when creating a cluster, however, ensuring that it scales proportionally with storage increases:

- *General and Low-CPU clusters*—The oplog size scales remain at 5% of storage capacity, adhering to a maximum size determined by MongoDB best practices.
- *NVMe storage clusters*—The oplog size scales remain at 10% of storage capacity, following the same best practice limits. Decreasing storage capacity does not result in a change to the oplog size.

CHANGING STORAGE CAPACITY

Atlas handles changes in storage capacity and IOPS differently depending on the cloud provider:

- *AWS*—In AWS, when storage or throughput increases, Atlas modifies data volumes in place without downtime for the first change. For later changes, if the volume is less than 1 TB and the last change occurred less than 5 hours and 30 minutes ago, Atlas provisions new volumes and syncs data. For volumes over 1 TB, Atlas makes changes in place. Decreasing storage capacity involves provisioning

new volumes and syncing data because AWS doesn't allow in-place reductions. But AWS does allow in-place reduction of IOPS.
- *Azure*—You can change storage capacity in preset amounts. Increases are made in place without downtime, but decreases require replacing nodes and performing initial syncs, causing temporary unavailability for modified nodes.
- *GCP*—Increasing storage capacity is done in place with zero downtime. For decreases, new volumes are provisioned and data is synced, similar to Azure.
- *Multicloud deployments*—Atlas uses the lowest common denominator across providers to ensure consistency.

AWS IOPS

For AWS-backed M30+ clusters, Atlas allows you to provision IOPS. Provisioned IOPS let you customize the maximum IOPS rate for your cluster; they deliver a more consistent IOPS rate and lower the cluster's p90 latency (the time within which 90% of requests are completed), resulting in faster response times.

General-purpose SSD volumes are designed to deliver baseline performance 99% of the time, whereas provisioned IOPS SSD volumes are designed to deliver their performance 99.9% of the time. When you select the Provision IOPS option, the storage type changes from general-purpose SSD volumes to provisioned IOPS SSD volumes, affecting characteristics, performance, and cost.

If you do not select the Provision IOPS option when creating your M30+ tier cluster, it defaults to standard IOPS:

- Minimum standard IOPS is 3,000 and stays at 3,000 unless storage reaches 1 TB or more.
- For 1 TB+ storage, Atlas uses a 3:1 IOPS-to-storage ratio, up to 16,000 IOPS for AWS network storage.

Local NVMe SSD clusters must use standard IOPS.

10.3 Atlas Global Clusters

Atlas Global Clusters are sharded clusters designed to distribute data across multiple geographic regions, optimizing for low latency and high availability. They are designed for applications that require low latency and data locality. These clusters enable you to deploy your MongoDB database across various regions worldwide, ensuring that your application remains responsive and reliable regardless of user location.

Atlas Global Clusters, supported in M30 and higher tiers, offer several key features that enhance performance and compliance:

- *Global data distribution*—You can distribute your data across various regions to give users low-latency access by keeping data closer to them.
- *Geopartitioning*—You can control data residency at a detailed level to meet regulatory requirements, ensuring that specific data stays within designated geographic areas.

- *Read and write anywhere*—You can configure your global cluster to support read and write operations in any region, enhancing application resilience and user experience with faster access times.

Fundamentally, you can establish zones globally, each containing at least one shard—essentially, a replica set. This configuration enables you to read and write data specific to each region from its local shard(s).

Atlas Global Clusters require defining single or multiregion zones that support write and read operations from geographically local shards and can be configured for low-latency global secondary reads. Each cluster supports up to nine distinct zones, each including one Highest Priority region and one or more Electable, Read-only, or Analytics regions. The available regions vary based on the selected cloud service provider. Table 10.4 describes the available regions in Atlas.

Table 10.4 MongoDB Atlas region types

Region type	Description
Highest Priority	Region where Atlas deploys the primary replica set member. Clients can issue only write operations to the primary. This region's location helps you construct a map for directing write operations to the correct zone.
Electable	Region where Atlas deploys electable secondary replica set members, providing additional fault tolerance in case of a regional outage in the Highest Priority region.
Read-only	Region where Atlas deploys nonelectable secondary replica set members to support secondary read.

TIP Add a Read-only node in the Highest Priority region of each zone for low-latency local reads.

You can configure Atlas Global Cluster as a multicloud cluster, spanning major cloud providers such as AWS, GCP, and Azure.

10.4 Going multiregion with workload isolation

You can set up multiregion and multicloud MongoDB deployments in Atlas using any combination of AWS, Azure, and GCP. You can configure the nodes in your MongoDB deployment to use different cloud providers, geographic regions, workload priorities, and replication configurations, enhancing the availability and workload balancing of your cluster.

Figure 10.4 shows the configuration of a multicloud, multiregion MongoDB deployment in Atlas. The interface shows the selection of three major cloud providers: GCP, AWS, and Azure. The cluster is configured to ensure high availability and resilience to partial region outages, full region outages, and cloud provider outages.

In the Electable Nodes for High Availability section, set up the deployment with nodes distributed across regions and cloud providers. The regions selected in figure 10.4 are USA (Iowa) for Google Cloud, Ireland for AWS, and Germany (Frankfurt) for

Going multiregion with workload isolation

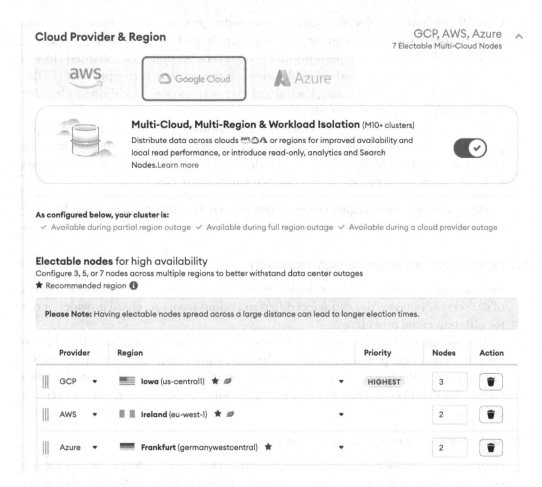

Figure 10.4 The Atlas UI's Cloud Provider & Region section, where you can configure multicloud clusters (Image © MongoDB 2025)

Azure. Each region is assigned a priority level, with GCP in Iowa having the highest priority and three nodes, whereas AWS in Ireland and Azure in Frankfurt have two nodes each.

Spreading electable nodes across large distances can lead to longer election times, indicating a tradeoff between geographic distribution and election latency. This setup aims to enhance the overall availability and workload balancing of the cluster by using different cloud providers, geographic regions, and prioritization settings.

> **TIP** A large number of regions or nodes spread across long distances can cause long election times or replication lag.

In sharded clusters, Atlas distributes the three config server nodes based on the number of electable regions. If you have one electable region, all three nodes are deployed there. If you have two electable regions, two nodes go to the highest-priority region, and one goes to the second-highest-priority region. If you have three or more electable regions, each of the three highest-priority regions receives one node. Sharded clusters include additional nodes, and electable nodes on the config server replica set (CSRS) count toward the total node limit. Each sharded cluster also has an additional electable node per region as part of the CSRS.

Clusters can span regions and cloud service providers, with a node limit of 40 per project. The number of availability zones or fault domains in a region has no effect on the number of MongoDB nodes Atlas can deploy. MongoDB Atlas clusters are always made of replica sets with a minimum of three MongoDB nodes.

TIP Creating a multiregion cluster is not allowed in a project that already has clusters with 40 or more nodes in other regions.

10.4.1 Adding electable nodes for high availability

Adding regions with electable nodes increases data availability and reduces the effect of data center outages. You can select different regions from one cloud provider or opt for different cloud providers.

Atlas designates the node in the first row of the electable-nodes table as the highest-priority region and prioritizes these nodes for primary eligibility. Other nodes are ranked in the order in which they appear. Each electable node can participate in replica set elections and become the primary as long as most nodes in the replica set remain available.

10.4.2 Adding read-only nodes for local reads

Deploy read-only nodes to enhance local read performance within their specific service areas. Read-only nodes do not contribute to high availability because they don't participate in elections and cannot become the primary for their cluster; they are used mainly to offload read traffic and optimize performance for read-heavy workloads.

10.4.3 Using analytics nodes for workload isolation

Available for M10+ clusters, analytics nodes are specialized read-only nodes designed to isolate queries that shouldn't interfere with your operational workload. They are particularly useful for handling analytic data, such as reporting queries executed by business-intelligence tools.

Both analytics nodes and read-only nodes have distinct replica set tags (section 10.5), enabling you to direct queries to specific node types and regions. For more information on the predefined replica set tags used by Atlas, see section 10.5.

A multiregion cluster can have up to 50 nodes, with no limit on the number of analytics nodes within that total. Analytics nodes do not enhance a cluster's availability because they do not participate in elections and cannot become the primary node for their cluster.

10.5 Using predefined replica set tags for querying

Atlas clusters come with built-in replica set tags for various member types within the cluster. These tags route queries from specific applications to designated node types, regions, or availability zones. By using these predefined tags, you can tailor read preferences for a replica set, enhancing the overall performance and reliability of your cluster. Table 10.5 describes the predefined replica set tags available in Atlas.

Table 10.5 Predefined replica set tags in Atlas

Tag name	Description	Example
Availability Zone	Identifies the AWS availability zone ID, GCP fully qualified name for a zone, or Azure zone number	AWS—{"availabilityZone": "use1-az3"}, GCP—{"availabilityZone": "us-east1-c"} Azure—{"availabilityZone": "2"}
Node Type	Specifies the type of node. Possible values are ELECTABLE, READ_ONLY, and ANALYTICS.	{"nodeType": "ANALYTICS"}
Provider	Indicates the cloud provider where the node is provisioned. Possible values are AWS, GCP, and AZURE.	{"provider": "GCP"}
Region	Specifies the cloud region of the node	{"region": "US_EAST_2"}
Workload Type	Distributes your workload evenly among nonanalytics (electable or read-only) nodes. Possible value is OPERATIONAL.	{"workloadType": "OPERATIONAL"}
Disk State	Indicates the state of your disk. Possible value is READY.	{"diskState": "READY"}

NOTE This feature is unavailable for M0 and Flex clusters.

Table 10.6 describes possible nodeType values in your predefined replica set tags.

Table 10.6 Possible nodeType values in MongoDB Atlas

Node type	Description
ELECTABLE	Read from nodes eligible to be elected primary. ELECTABLE nodes correspond to electable nodes for high availability in the cluster-creation UI.
READ_ONLY	Read from read-only nodes. READ_ONLY nodes correspond to read-only nodes for optimal local reads in the cluster-creation UI.
ANALYTICS	Read from read-only analytics nodes. ANALYTICS nodes correspond to analytics nodes for workload isolation in the cluster-creation UI.

To use predefined replica set tags in your connection string and direct queries to specific nodes, include the following options in your connection string: `readPreference`, `readPreferenceTags`, and `readConcernLevel`.

> **TIP** These connection string options are unavailable for `mongosh`. Instead, use `cursor.readPref()` and `Mongo.setReadPref()`.

10.5.1 Routing queries to analytics nodes

If your application performs complex or long-running tasks such as extract, transform, load (ETL) or reporting, you can isolate these queries from your operational workload by connecting exclusively to analytics nodes. This connection string shows how it works:

```
mongodb+srv://<USERNAME>:<PASSWORD>@mongodb-in-
action.mongodb.net/test?readPreference=secondary&
readPreferenceTags=nodeType:ANALYTICS&
readConcernLevel=local
```

The connection string options are as follows:

```
readPreference=secondary,
readPreferenceTags=nodeType:ANALYTICS,
readConcernLevel=local.
```

The `readPreference` set to `secondary` and the `readPreferenceTags` set to `{ nodeType: ANALYTICS }` restrict application connections to analytics nodes.

10.5.2 Isolating normal application secondary reads from analytics nodes

If your application needs to isolate regular reads from the workload on analytics nodes, you may want to separate these reads accordingly. This connection string shows how it works:

```
mongodb+srv://<USERNAME>:<PASSWORD>@mongodb-in-
action.mongodb.net/test?readPreference=secondary&
readPreferenceTags=workloadType:OPERATIONAL&
readConcernLevel=local
```

The connection string options are as follows:

```
readPreference=secondary, readPreferenceTags=nodeType:OPERATIONAL,
readConcernLevel=local.
```

The `readPreference` set to `secondary` and the `readPreferenceTags` set to `{ nodeType: OPERATIONAL }` restrict application connections to operational, nonanalytics nodes.

10.5.3 Routing local reads for geographically distributed applications

If your application requires local reads in specific regions for globally distributed data, use predefined replica set tags. Previously, local reads depended on accurately calculating the nearest read preference. Now, with predefined replica set tags, you can achieve more consistent behavior by using geographic tags combined with the nearest read preference mode. This connection string shows how it works:

```
mongodb+srv://<USERNAME>:<PASSWORD>@mongodb-in-action.mongodb.net
/test?readPreference=nearest&readPreferenceTags=provider:GCP,
region:us-east1&readPreferenceTags=provider:GCP,
region:us-east4&readPreferenceTags=&readConcernLevel=local
```

The connection string options appear in the following order:

```
readPreference=nearest
readPreferenceTags=provider:GCP,region:us-east1
readPreferenceTags=provider:GCP,region:us-east4
readPreferenceTags=
readConcernLevel=local
```

Atlas evaluates read preference tags in the order in which you list them. When Atlas matches a node to a tag, it identifies all eligible nodes with that tag and disregards any subsequent `readPreferenceTags`. In this example, the application first attempts to connect to a node in the GCP region `us-east1`. If nodes in that region are unavailable, it tries to connect to a node in the GCP region `us-east4`. The final, empty `readPreferenceTags=` acts as a fallback. This empty option allows the application to connect to any available node, regardless of the provider or region. These settings ensure that the application connects to the nearest geographic region, reducing latency and improving performance.

10.6 Understanding the Atlas custom Write Concerns

Atlas offers built-in custom Write Concerns designed for multiregion clusters. *Write Concern* refers to the level of acknowledgment MongoDB requires for write operations to a cluster (chapter 3).

These custom Write Concerns enhance data consistency by guaranteeing that your operations are propagated to a specific number of regions before they are considered successful. To use a custom Write Concern, include it in the write-concern document of your operation. Table 10.7 describes the custom Write Concerns that Atlas provides for multiregion clusters.

Table 10.7 Atlas custom Write Concerns for multiregion clusters

Write concern	Tags	Description
`twoRegions`	`{ region: 2 }`	Write operations must receive acknowledgment from at least two regions in your cluster.
`threeRegions`	`{ region: 3 }`	Write operations must receive acknowledgment from at least three regions in your cluster.
`twoProviders`	`{ provider: 2 }`	Write operations must be acknowledged by at least two different regions in your cluster, each hosted by a distinct cloud provider.

If your application uses a multiregion cluster across the three regions (us-east-1, us-east-2, and us-west-1), you want write operations to propagate to all three regions in your cluster before Atlas accepts them.

The following operation inserts a document into the routes collection and requires propagation to all three regions due to the { w: "threeRegions" } write-concern object:

```
db.routes.insertOne(
  {
    airline: { id: 410, name: 'Lufthansa', alias: 'LH', iata: 'DLH' },
    src_airport: 'MUC',
    dst_airport: 'JFK'
  },
  { writeConcern: { w: "threeRegions" } }
)
```

Summary

- Atlas automates deployment, backups, and scaling, simplifying database administration and ensuring optimal performance and security. It includes features such as real-time analytics, comprehensive monitoring, automated performance optimization, Atlas SQL Interface, Atlas Stream Processing, Atlas Data Federation, and Atlas Online Archive.
- Atlas M0 (free tier) and Flex clusters are affordable options for beginners and low-throughput applications, running in a shared environment with limited Atlas features. Each project can have one M0 cluster, which can be upgraded to Flex and an M10+ cluster at any time.
- Dedicated M10 and M20 clusters are ideal for development and low-traffic applications, supporting replica set deployments with full Atlas features. They operate on burstable performance infrastructure, handling occasional traffic spikes but optimized for steady workloads.
- Dedicated M30 and higher clusters are ideal for production, supporting replica set and sharded deployments with full Atlas features. Variants, marked by >, display key characteristics when selected.
- Atlas allows automatic adjustment of cluster tier and storage capacity based on use, eliminating the need for custom scripts. Autoscaling operates without downtime and lets you set maximum and minimum ranges to control costs.
- Atlas Global Clusters distribute data across multiple geographic regions, optimizing for low latency and high availability. This feature is supported in M30 and higher tiers.
- In Atlas, you can deploy multicloud MongoDB clusters using any combination of AWS, Azure, and GCP. This setup allows you to configure nodes across providers and regions, optimizing availability and workload balancing.

- Available for M10+ clusters, analytics nodes are specialized read-only nodes that isolate queries from your operational workload. They are especially useful for handling analytic data, such as reporting queries executed by business-intelligence tools.
- Atlas clusters include built-in replica set tags for different member types. These tags route queries to specific node types, regions, or availability zones, optimizing read preferences and enhancing cluster performance and reliability.
- Atlas includes built-in custom Write Concerns tailored to multiregion clusters. Write concern specifies the level of acknowledgment MongoDB requires for write operations in a cluster.

Carrying out full-text search using Atlas Search

This chapter covers
- Enabling full-text search capabilities
- Understanding Apache Lucene's inverted index
- Discovering the Atlas Search environment
- Creating an Atlas Search Index with the Atlas CLI
- Using $search and $searchMeta aggregation stages
- Playing with Atlas Search Playground

Full-text search is invaluable across a variety of fields, including e-commerce platforms, digital libraries, customer support systems, content management systems, legal document analysis, academic research, human resources platforms, logs searches, social media platforms, email search tools, and medical record management. This sophisticated technique surpasses traditional exact-word matching by analyzing document content to identify matches based on relevance, specific phrases, and text attributes. Its versatility makes it well suited to a wide range of needs and formats.

The method enhances simple keyword searches, allowing you to find relevant documents quickly, narrowing search results, and providing rapid access to necessary information. Boolean searches use operators such as AND, OR, and NOT to refine query precision, effectively filtering results to precise criteria. Fuzzy and wildcard searches address misspellings and different word forms, increasing search flexibility and accuracy by anticipating user input variations.

Also, phrase and proximity searches target exact word sequences and terms close in text, which is ideal for detailed analysis. These approaches excel at uncovering specific phrases and contextual relationships. Range and faceted searches identify items within set parameters and categorize results by attributes, streamlining searches in areas like online shopping, where users can sort data based on characteristics such as dates or product features.

These methods boost the precision and efficiency of searches, making full-text search essential in data-rich environments. Its capabilities are crucial for managing and retrieving large data sets across various platforms, significantly improving user experience and operational effectiveness.

11.1 Implementing full-text search

MongoDB provides basic support for full-text search through the $text index, but it may not be sufficient for more complex queries, especially those involving multiple nested fields. Consequently, to accommodate more sophisticated search requirements, you often have to replicate data from MongoDB collections to a dedicated search engine to give applications full-text search capabilities. Various search engines are available, each designed to cater to different data handling needs and levels of query complexity, and each offering unique advantages and constraints:

- *Algolia*—Known for its robustness and flexibility, Algolia is a search and discovery platform that, although effective for many use cases, can become expensive. The cost escalates with the increase in data volume and the number of API interactions, making it less suitable for very large data sets.
- *Elasticsearch*—Operating as a distributed and RESTful search and analytics engine, Elasticsearch supports a broad range of use cases. It is built on Apache Lucene, similar to Atlas Search, and provides comprehensive search capabilities.
- *Solr*—Also based on Apache Lucene, Solr is a powerful search platform celebrated for its reliability and scalability. It excels in managing distributed indexing, replication, and load-balanced querying, making it a strong candidate for complex search environments.

Using separate solutions for database management and full-text search, however, can present several challenges. I encountered these challenges while working at a company that replicated certain collections from MongoDB to Elasticsearch by using a tool called Monstache, a Go daemon that syncs MongoDB to Elasticsearch by using change streams to monitor real-time changes and sending updates to Elasticsearch. Here are some of the problems I faced:

- *Integration complexity*—Integrating a standalone full-text search engine with a database system is complex and time-consuming, requiring additional setup, configuration, and ongoing maintenance. Imagine having to copy all the data for a multiterabyte database into Elasticsearch. It is also important to set up a monitoring and alerting system that will detect anomalies in replication.
- *Data synchronization*—Ensuring that data remains synchronized between the database and the search engine is hard. Any changes in the database need to be reflected in the search engine, often requiring complex mechanisms to keep both systems in sync. Figure 11.1 illustrates the relevant aspects. Also, you must have a mechanism in place to enforce the replication of documents that for some reason were not replicated initially.
- *Query challenge*—Maintaining and querying two separate systems means that the application must use a different query language for each system.
- *Operational overhead*—Managing two separate systems enhances the sophistication of the overall architecture. This leads to difficulties in troubleshooting, monitoring, and scaling both systems independently, adding to the operational burden on the DevOps teams.
- *Cost*—Running and maintaining separate systems is more expensive. It involves additional infrastructure costs, more complex licensing arrangements, and potentially higher operational expenses due to the need for specialized knowledge and tools to manage both systems effectively.

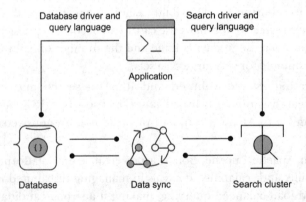

Figure 11.1 High-level data synchronization architecture. The application uses separate drivers and query languages to interact with the database and search clusters. Data is replicated from the database cluster to the search cluster to keep the index updated. This setup adds complexity, increases resource usage, and can lead to consistency issues. (Image © MongoDB 2024 CC BY-NC-SA 3.0)

Overall, although using separate solutions for database management and full-text search can provide powerful capabilities for applications, it also introduces significant drawbacks that can affect development speed, system performance, and operational efficiency.

11.2 Understanding Apache Lucene

Apache Lucene is an open source library developed by the Apache Software Foundation, initially coded entirely in Java but now available in other programming languages as well. It's widely used as a base for more complex search platforms such as Solr and Elasticsearch. Lucene specializes in full-text searching and is capable of indexing various document types (such as HTML, emails, and PDFs) across platforms, including web applications, libraries, and personal desktops.

The key to Lucene's search efficiency is its use of an inverted index, which is akin to a book's glossary but maps keywords to their document locations instead of pages to keywords. This allows for fast, accurate data retrieval. Consider the following documents from the `sample_training.inspections` namespace:

- Document 1:

```
{ _id: ObjectId('56d61033a378eccde8a8355f'),
  id: '10423-2015-CMPL',
  certificate_number: 9304139,
  business_name: 'LISANDRO CABRERA',
  date: 'Jul 17 2015',
  result: 'No Violation Issued',
  sector: 'Mobile Food Vendor - 881',
  address: { city: 'BRONX', zip: 10475,
  street: 'PALMER AVE', number: 2234 } }
```

- Document 2:

```
{ _id: ObjectId('56d61033a378eccde8a83560'),
  id: '1044-2016-ENFO',
  certificate_number: 9318079,
  business_name: 'AZMY KIROLES',
  date: 'Dec 23 2015',
  result: 'No Violation Issued',
  sector: 'Mobile Food Vendor - 881',
  address: { city: 'JERSEY CITY', zip: 7306,
  street: 'VROOM ST', number: 160 } }
```

An inverted index for these documents would be represented as shown in table 11.1 in a simplified form.

Table 11.1 Apache Lucene inverted index

Token	Document 1	Document 2
LISANDRO CABRERA	+	
AZMY KIROLES		+
BRONX	+	
JERSEY CITY		+
PALMER AVE	+	

Table 11.1 Apache Lucene inverted index (*continued*)

Token	Document 1	Document 2
VROOM ST		+
10475	+	+
7306		
2234	+	
160		+
NO VIOLATION ISSUED	+	+
MOBILE FOOD VENDOR - 881	+	+
JUL 17 2015	+	
DEC 23 2015		+

Lucene processes documents through tokenization, which involves breaking the text into smaller searchable units known as *tokens* (see the "Handling data using analyzers" section). This is typically done using simple delimiters such as spaces. Also, Lucene can handle multiword terms by using extra dictionaries, expanding its capability to index phrases and specific terminology. Normalization is another crucial step during tokenization; Lucene converts all characters to lowercase to ensure uniform search results.

Furthermore, each document within Lucene receives a relevance score, ranking the query results from most to least relevant. The basic scoring mechanism enhances the scores of documents in which the query term appears frequently while reducing the scores for terms that are common across the entire collection, distinguishing the relevance of documents more effectively. Lucene allows you to customize scoring to suit specific search domains, employing techniques such as boosting or decaying scores, which enables you to tailor search results to meet your needs. Here are a few examples of search queries:

- The search query `"No Violation Issued Mobile Food Vendor - 881"` is divided into two tokens: `"No Violation Issued"` and `"Mobile Food Vendor - 881"`. Then these tokens are matched with the inverted index, and both Document 1 and Document 2 are returned because both documents contain these tokens. The score for each document may vary depending on factors such as token frequency, token proximity, and other indexing parameters defined in Lucene. Typically, both documents have similar scores if no other content in the documents influences the scoring algorithm differently.

- The search query `"No Violation Issued BRONX"` is divided into two tokens: `"No Violation Issued"` and `"BRONX"`. Then these tokens are matched with the inverted index, and only Document 1 is returned because it is the only document containing both tokens. The score for Document 1 may be higher due to the complete matching of both tokens.

- The search query "Mobile Food Vendor - 881 PALMER AVE" is divided into two tokens: "Mobile Food Vendor - 881" and "PALMER AVE". Then these tokens are matched with the inverted index, and only Document 1 is returned because it is the only document containing both tokens. The score for Document 1 will likely be high due to the precise match of both specified tokens.

You can interact with Lucene by submitting search queries that can incorporate logical operators such as AND, OR, and NOT. Lucene's QueryParser, a component that interprets these queries and transforms them into executable search commands, facilitates a range of search capabilities tailored to diverse needs:

- `term`—Searches for a specific word within a document, using Lucene's inverted index to quickly locate documents containing the term.
- `phrase`—Looks for an exact sequence of words or a specific phrase, using Lucene's ability to track term positions within the index to ensure that the words not only exist but also appear in the specified sequence.
- `wildcard`—Allows searches with placeholders, such as * for multiple characters and ? for a single character, which is particularly useful for matching partial words. Lucene scans these patterns against the indexed terms to find matches.
- `fuzzy`—Finds words that are spelled similarly to the query term. It typically uses the Levenshtein distance algorithm to identify terms within a specified edit distance from the search term. This search type is useful for catching typos.
- `proximity`—Identifies terms that occur near each other within a specified distance in a document. Lucene calculates the proximity of terms based on their positions to satisfy this criterion.
- `range`—Filters documents containing terms that fall within a specified range. This search type is useful for searching numbers, dates, and any ordered data. Lucene handles these queries efficiently through range filtering.
- `autocomplete`—Enhances user interaction by providing real-time suggestions as the user types their query. This feature is implemented using techniques such as edge n-gram indexing; Lucene generates edge n-grams from the start of words to suggest completions or prefix queries that match terms starting with the user's input.

Each search type is meticulously designed to enhance the flexibility and precision of retrieving information, making Lucene an effective tool for full-text searching across various applications and large data sets.

11.3 Getting to know Atlas Search

Atlas Search, built on Apache Lucene, eliminates the need to run a separate search system alongside your MongoDB database. As shown in figure 11.2, Atlas Search integrates a Lucene search index with the database, ensuring automatic synchronization of data between the two systems. Management is streamlined through a single API, reducing the need for separate systems and lowering operational complexity. Full-text search is accessible through a single MongoDB Query API, eliminating the need for different query languages—one for MongoDB and another for the search engine. This unified system architecture improves data indexing and retrieval speeds while simplifying the maintenance of database and search engine components.

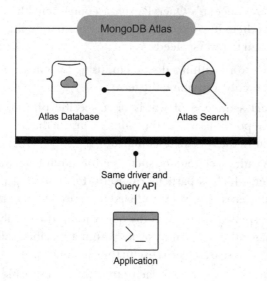

Figure 11.2 High-level overview of Atlas Search. The application uses MongoDB Atlas with a unified driver and query API to access both database and search functionality. Within the Atlas environment, data storage and search are integrated, eliminating the need for separate systems or synchronization. This unified approach simplifies the architecture and reduces operational overhead. (Image © MongoDB 2024 CC BY-NC-SA 3.0)

11.3.1 Learning Atlas Search architecture

The Atlas Search architecture incorporates components that integrate Apache Lucene with a MongoDB Atlas database, facilitated by a process commonly known as the `mongot`, as illustrated in figure 11.3. The `mongot` process operates in parallel with the MongoDB server process (`mongod`) on each node of the Atlas cluster.

The `mongot` process is responsible for the following tasks:

- Establishing Atlas Search indexes according to the specified rules in the index definitions for each collection
- Tracking MongoDB database change streams to monitor the current status of documents and updating the Atlas Search indexes for collections in which those indexes are defined
- Handling Atlas Search queries and delivering documents that match the search criteria

Atlas Search offers a variety of text analyzers, a robust query language that incorporates Atlas Search aggregation pipeline stages such as `$search` and `$searchMeta` alongside other MongoDB aggregation stages, and score-based results ranking.

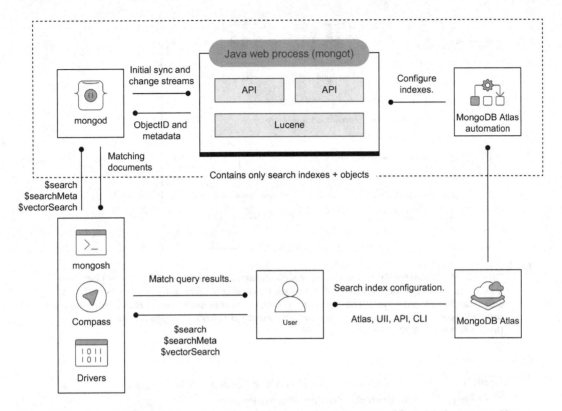

Figure 11.3 The Atlas Search architecture integrates MongoDB with the Lucene Search Index managed by the mongot process. MongoDB (mongod) serves as the primary database, sending object IDs and metadata to mongot via change streams for synchronization and monitoring. mongot uses APIs for index configuration and search operations. The Lucene component handles search indexes and ObjectIDs, enabling efficient query processing. Index configuration is managed through MongoDB Atlas Automation, interfacing with the Atlas UI, API, and CLI. Search queries initiated via mongosh, Compass, or drivers are processed by the Atlas Search cluster. (Image © MongoDB 2024 CC BY-NC-SA 3.0)

11.3.2 Using Atlas Search Nodes

Atlas Search Nodes are specialized nodes within MongoDB Atlas dedicated to handling the search functionality by running the mongot process. Figure 11.4 shows the Search Nodes architecture. Search nodes provide workload isolation, ensuring that search operations do not interfere with other database operations. In dedicated (M10 or higher) sharded and unsharded Atlas clusters on any cloud provider, you can deploy these Search Nodes with each cluster or with each shard in the cluster. Deploying two Search Nodes for a cluster with three shards means that Atlas will deploy six Search Nodes, with two dedicated to each shard.

When you deploy separate Search Nodes, Atlas automatically assigns a mongod for each mongot. The mongot communicates with the mongod to listen for and sync index changes for the indexes it stores.

270 CHAPTER 11 *Carrying out full-text search using Atlas Search*

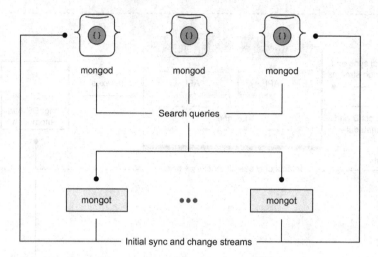

Figure 11.4 Within the Atlas Search Nodes architecture, multiple MongoDB (mongod) instances manage data storage and execute search queries, forwarding them to mongot processes. These processes handle initial synchronization and continuous updates via change streams, ensuring that search indexes are consistently updated with the latest data changes across all nodes. (Image © MongoDB 2024 CC BY-NC-SA 3.0)

NOTE Local solid-state drives (SSDs) for Search Nodes need a 20% storage overhead to accommodate index operations.

11.3.3 Atlas Search indexes

An Atlas Search index, powered by Apache Lucene, is a data structure that organizes data in a format optimized for search. It maps terms to the documents containing those terms, enabling faster document retrieval using specific identifiers. Similar to an index in the back of a book that links terms to their locations, a search index creates associations between terms and the documents where those terms appear. Search indexes also include important metadata, such as the positions of terms within the documents.

To query data in your Atlas cluster with Atlas Search, first configure an Atlas Search index. You can create a search index on a single field or multiple fields. To improve query performance, create indexes on fields that are frequently used for sorting or filtering. This allows Atlas Search to retrieve relevant documents more efficiently. You can use the following methods to index fields:

- *Dynamic mappings*—This method automatically indexes all fields of supported types in each document. Although this method is convenient, it consumes disk space and can negatively affect cluster performance.
- *Static mappings*—This method allows you to selectively identify the fields to index. For fields containing polymorphic data, Atlas Search indexes only documents that match the index definition, ignoring those with mismatched data types.

NOTE Static mappings are preferred for better performance and efficient use of disk space. They are recommended for production use cases.

Listing 11.1 shows Atlas Search index definition syntax. In the config file, you can tell Atlas to index specific fields while excluding others or dynamically index every field in a collection. You can also use a specific analyzer (described in the next section) or multiple analyzers to index particular fields.

Listing 11.1 Atlas Search index syntax

```
{
  "analyzer": "<analyzer-for-index>",
  "searchAnalyzer": "<analyzer-for-query>",
  "mappings": {
    "dynamic": <boolean>,
    "fields": { <field-definition> }
  },
  "analyzers": [ <custom-analyzer> ],
  "storedSource": <boolean> | {
    <stored-source-definition>
  },
  "synonyms": [
    {
      "name": "<synonym-mapping-name>",
      "source": {
        "collection": "<source-collection-name>"
      },
      "analyzer": "<synonym-mapping-analyzer>"
    }
  ]
}
```

Table 11.2 details the various options for configuring an Atlas Search index from the template showed earlier in listing 11.1.

Table 11.2 Template options for configuring Atlas Search index

Field	Type	Necessity	Description
analyzer	String	Optional	Specifies the analyzer to apply to string fields when indexing
analyzers	Array of custom analyzers	Optional	Specifies the custom analyzers to use in this index
mappings	Document field definition	Required	Specifies how to index fields at different paths for this index
mappings.dynamic	Boolean	Optional	Enables or disables dynamic mapping of fields. `true` means all dynamically indexable fields are indexed; `false` means you must specify individual fields to index. If the `mappings.dynamic` option is omitted, it defaults to `false`.

Table 11.2 Template options for configuring Atlas Search index (*continued*)

Field	Type	Necessity	Description
`mappings.fields`	Document	Conditional	Required only if dynamic mapping is disabled; specifies the fields you want to index
`searchAnalyzer`	String	Optional	Specifies the analyzer to apply to query text before searching. It defaults to the analyzer setting if omitted or to the standard analyzer if both are omitted.
`storedSource`	Boolean or stored source definition	Optional	Specifies fields to store for query-time lookups. It can be `true` to store all fields, `false` to store none, or an object to specify fields to include or exclude. If the `storedSource` option is omitted, it defaults to `false`.
`synonyms`	Array of synonym mapping definition	Optional	Specifies synonym mappings to use in your index. Only one synonym mapping can be defined per index.

Although Atlas Search doesn't create an exact copy of the data from your MongoDB cluster collections, it builds search indexes directly on your data, which requires some disk space and memory. These indexes enable fast, efficient searching without duplicating your entire data set.

When you perform a search query, the search index quickly identifies relevant document IDs. Then the actual documents are fetched directly from your original MongoDB collection based on the information from the search index. This ensures that you're always working with the most up-to-date data and that the search process remains optimized for performance.

HANDLING DATA USING ANALYZERS

To get your data ready for indexing, you must process it through tokenization. Tokenization involves dividing a stream of text into smaller elements known as tokens, such as words, phrases, and symbols. This task is performed by components called analyzers, which are integral to the search engine's functionality. These analyzers not only generate tokens from the text but also apply parsing and language rules to ensure that the text is searchable. Furthermore, when creating an index or executing a query, you can specify which analyzer to use, giving you control of how text is converted from a string field to searchable terms. These tokens are stored in the index for future search queries. Table 11.3 summarizes the built-in analyzers provided by Atlas Search.

Table 11.3 Atlas Search built-in analyzers

Analyzer	Description
Standard	Uses the default analyzer for all Atlas Search indexes and queries
Simple	Divides text into searchable terms wherever it finds a nonletter character

Table 11.3 Atlas Search built-in analyzers (*continued*)

Analyzer	Description
Whitespace	Divides text into searchable terms wherever it finds a whitespace character
Language	Provides a set of language-specific text analyzers
Keyword	Indexes text fields as single terms

Analyzers are made up of a tokenizer, which segments the text into tokens, and the filters that you set. Atlas Search applies filters to the tokens to form terms that can be indexed, helping you adjust for variations in things like punctuation, capitalization, and unnecessary words.

> **NOTE** If you don't specify an analyzer, MongoDB Atlas uses the default standard analyzer.

> **TIP** In Atlas, you have the option to create a custom analyzer using the built-in character filters, tokenizers, and token filters. Check the MongoDB official documentation at https://mng.bz/Z9pZ.

REINDEXING IN ATLAS SEARCH

If you want to modify the mapping of an existing index, reindexing is required. In this process, Atlas Search initiates the construction of a new index based on the updated mapping. It reads all the data relevant to the index and reorganizes it according to the new mapping specifications. This reindexing occurs in the background, allowing the old index to continue handling existing and new queries without downtime. When the rebuild is complete, the system seamlessly transitions to the new index, and the old one is removed.

> **TIP** Updating the Atlas Search index requires time and resources. Ensure that you have free disk space equal to 125% of your current index's size for a successful update.

If you have deployed separate Search Nodes, Atlas Search rebuilds indexes during the following events:

- Adding search nodes.
- Scaling search nodes.
- Internal `mongot` changes that require an index resync (such as updates needed for some Atlas Search features). See the official MongoDB documentation to check details at https://mng.bz/649D.

During an index rebuild, Atlas automatically deploys additional Search Nodes to ensure that the old index remains up to date and available for queries while the new index is being built.

When changes are made to the collection with defined Atlas Search indexes, the latest data may not be available for queries immediately. But mongot monitors change streams, allowing it to update stored data copies and ensure that Atlas Search indexes are eventually consistent.

> **NOTE** Atlas Search automatically rebuilds the index only when the index definition changes, an Atlas Search update includes breaking changes, or hardware-related problems such as index corruption occur.

> **TIP** When you use the $out aggregation stage to alter a collection that includes an Atlas Search index, you must delete and then re-create the search index. If feasible, you should use $merge instead of $out.

11.4 Building an Atlas Search index

To understand how Atlas Search indexes work, create one by using the MongoDB M0 cluster (dedicated search nodes are not supported in this cluster tier), which is named "MongoDB-in-Action" and which you built in part 1 of this book. The sample data is already in the cluster.

> **WARNING** Creating an Atlas Search index is resource-intensive. The performance of your Atlas cluster may be affected while the index builds.

It's important to be aware of the specific limitations that apply to Atlas search on M0 (three indexes). Conversely, if you're operating on M10 or higher clusters, there are no restrictions on the number of indexes you can create. When the maximum number of indexes for your cluster tier is reached, you can upgrade your cluster tier to create more indexes.

> **NOTE** When you enable Atlas Search on your Atlas cluster, no extra fees or charges apply. But you may notice increased resource use on the cluster, which can vary based on factors such the size of the collections being indexed and the complexity of the index definitions.

To refresh your knowledge of the `"MongoDB-in-Action"` cluster, use this Atlas command-line interface (CLI) command:

```
atlas cluster list
```

The command displays the cluster created in chapter 2:

```
ID                         NAME                  MDB VER    STATE
6658a85ba9e6a9047d15cf98   MongoDB-in-Action     8.0.4      IDLE
```

Using the command `atlas clusters search indexes create`, build a new Atlas Search index using the `sample_training` database and the `inspections` collection as an index source. As a prerequisite, you need to define static mapping in the file, setting a predefined schema for the data. This method enhances search performance, prevents schema conflicts, and ensures consistent handling of the indexed data. Following is an example mapping file.

Listing 11.2 Atlas Search index config

```
{
  "name": "MongoDB-in-Action",
  "database": "sample_training",
  "collectionName": "inspections",
  "mappings": {
    "dynamic": false,
    "fields": {
      "business_name": {
        "type": "string",
        "analyzer": "lucene.standard"
      },
      "date": {
        "type": "date"
      },
      "result": {
        "type": "string",
        "analyzer": "lucene.standard"
      },
      "sector": {
        "type": "string",
        "analyzer": "lucene.standard"
      },
      "address": {
        "type": "document",
        "fields": {
          "city": {
            "type": "string",
            "analyzer": "lucene.standard"
          },
          "zip": {
            "type": "string",
            "analyzer": "lucene.standard"
          },
          "street": {
            "type": "string",
            "analyzer": "lucene.standard"
          },
          "number": {
            "type": "string",
            "analyzer": "lucene.standard"
          }
        }
      }
    }
  }
}
```

In the mapping file, the Atlas cluster is defined and named `"MongoDB-in-Action"`. This cluster hosts the MongoDB database `sample_training` and the `inspections` collection for constructing the search index. The index uses a static mapping (`"dynamic"` is set to `false`) to enhance search functionalities, meaning that only predefined fields—`business_name`, `date`, `result`, `sector`, and `address`—are indexed. Within the `address` field, subfields such as `city`, `zip`, `street`, and `number` are also indexed. Each field employs the Lucene standard analyzer.

The standard analyzer is the default for all Atlas Search indexes and queries. It splits text into terms using word boundaries, making it suitable for various languages. It converts all terms to lowercase and eliminates punctuation. This analyzer supports grammar-based tokenization, recognizing elements such as email addresses; acronyms; Chinese, Japanese, and Korean characters; and alphanumerics.

Next, insert the contents of this configuration into the `index-definition.json` file, and execute the following command.

Listing 11.3 Creating an Atlas Search Index

```
atlas clusters search indexes create \
--clusterName MongoDB-in-Action \
--file index-definition.json --output json
```

After executing this command, you see a summary of your index, which is currently being created. In my example, it looks like this:

```
{
  "collectionName": "inspections",
  "database": "sample_training",
  "indexID": "6689a58d744a7d5ef40a37b5",
  "name": "MongoDB-in-Action",
  "status": "IN_PROGRESS",
  "type": "search",
  "mappings": {
    "dynamic": false,
    "fields": {
      "address": {
        "fields": {
          "city": {
            "analyzer": "lucene.standard",
            "type": "string"
          },
          "number": {
            "analyzer": "lucene.standard",
            "type": "string"
          },
          "street": {
            "analyzer": "lucene.standard",
            "type": "string"
          },
          "zip": {
            "analyzer": "lucene.standard",
```

```
          "type": "string"
        }
      },
      "type": "document"
    },
    "business_name": {
      "analyzer": "lucene.standard",
      "type": "string"
    },
    "date": {
      "type": "date"
    },
    "result": {
      "analyzer": "lucene.standard",
      "type": "string"
    },
    "sector": {
      "analyzer": "lucene.standard",
      "type": "string"
    }
  }
 },
 "synonyms": []
}
```

The command `atlas clusters search indexes create` triggers creation of the search index and initiates initial synchronization of data from the `inspections` collection. The process of indexing involves replicating the data in a Lucene-based index. *Indexing* in this context means transforming the data into a format optimized for efficient search by Lucene, facilitating faster, more effective query execution.

After a few minutes, the initial synchronization process is complete, and the search index is ready to use. You can verify this by using the following command:

```
atlas clusters search indexes list \
--clusterName MongoDB-in-Action \
--collection inspections \
--db sample_training
```

You can also view your Atlas Search index in the Atlas UI. To do this, navigate to the Atlas Search section in the middle of the top menu below the Data Services tab within your `MongoDB-in-Action` cluster. Figure 11.5 shows the Atlas UI displaying the details of the current Atlas Search index configuration.

The namespace `sample_training.inspections` has one active search index, named `MongoDB-in-Action`. The interface displays the status of the index (active), the indexed fields, the size of the index, and the number of documents indexed. It also provides options to query the index and view detailed status information.

> **TIP** You can create an Atlas Search index on M10 and higher clusters using MongoDB Compass or `mongosh`. In `mongosh`, use the `db.collection.createSearchIndex()` helper method.

278   CHAPTER 11   *Carrying out full-text search using Atlas Search*

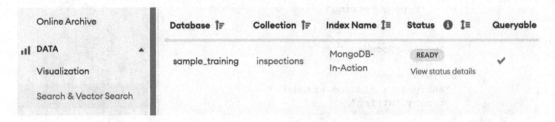

Figure 11.5   Atlas Search index. On the left side of the screen is a collapsible navigation menu. To access Search Index view, click the Search & Vector Search option in the Data section. When you do, the main panel displays details on the search indexes. In this example, the `sample_training` database and its `inspections` collection are shown, with an active search index named `MongoDB-In-Action`. The index is marked as Ready and is fully queryable, indicated by the green check. (Image © MongoDB 2025)

> **NOTE**   An index definition JSON object cannot exceed 3 KB.

11.5   *Running Atlas Search queries*

Atlas Search queries are structured as aggregation pipeline stages. They include the `$search` and `$searchMeta` stages, which must be positioned as the initial stage in the query pipeline. These stages can be combined with additional stages of the aggregation pipeline within your query pipeline. Atlas Search offers query operators that you can use within the `$search` aggregation pipeline stages, described in table 11.4. The operators enable you to find and retrieve relevant data from your collection in the Atlas cluster.

Table 11.4   The aggregation pipeline `$search` stage supported operators

Operator	Description	Supported Atlas search types
`autocomplete`	Performs a search-as-you-type query from an incomplete input string	autocomplete
`compound`	Combines other operators into a single query	Field types supported by the operators used inside the compound operator
`embeddedDocument`	Queries fields in embedded documents, which are documents that are elements of an array	Embedded documents and field types supported by the operators used inside the `embeddedDocument` operator
`equals`	Checks whether the field contains the specified value	boolean, date, objectId, number, token, uuid
`exists`	Tests for the presence of a specified field, regardless of field type	Field type isn't used by the `exists` operator
`geoShape`	Queries for values with specified geographical shapes	geo
`geoWithin`	Queries for points within specified geographical shapes	geo
`in`	Queries single values and arrays of values	boolean, date, objectId, number, token, uuid

Table 11.4 The aggregation pipeline `$search` stage supported operators (*continued*)

Operator	Description	Supported Atlas search types
`moreLikeThis`	Queries for similar document	string
`near`	Queries for values near a specified number, date, or geographical point	date, geo point, number
`phrase`	Searches documents for terms in an order similar to the query	string
`queryString`	Supports querying a combination of indexed fields and values	string
`range`	Queries for values within a specific numeric or date range	date, number
`regex`	Interprets the query field as a regular expression	string
`text`	Performs textual analyzed search	string
`wildcard`	Supports special characters in the query string that can match any character	string

Search operators allow you to conduct queries for terms, phrases, geographical shapes and points, numeric values, and similar documents, among others. Also, you can perform searches using regex and wildcard expressions.

Atlas Search also provides query collectors you can use inside the `$search` and `$searchMeta` aggregation pipeline stages. Collectors return a document representing the metadata results, typically an aggregation over the matching search results. The `facet` operator groups query results by values or ranges in specified, faceted fields and returns the count for each of those groups. It supports `dateFacet`, `numberFacet`, and `stringFacet` field types.

11.5.1 Using the $search aggregation pipeline stage

The `$search` stage conducts full-text searches by querying the Atlas Search index, which uses Lucene technology. The field or fields involved in the query must be included in this index. The process of indexing preprocesses and organizes your data into a Lucene index to optimize and accelerate search queries, ensuring precise, efficient search results across the indexed fields. The following listing shows the `$search` pipeline stage structure.

Listing 11.4 The `$search` prototype form

```
{
  $search: {
    "index": "<index-name>",
    "<operator-name>"|"<collector-name>": {
      <operator-specification>|<collector-specification>
    },
    "highlight": {
```

```
      <highlight-options>
    },
    "concurrent": true | false,
    "count": {
      <count-options>
    },
    "searchAfter"|"searchBefore": "<encoded-token>",
    "scoreDetails": true| false,
    "sort": {
      <fields-to-sort>: 1 | -1
    },
    "returnStoredSource": true | false,
    "tracking": {
      <tracking-option>
    }
  }
}
```

Let's look at the options:

- `index`—Specifies the name of the Atlas Search index to be used for the query. If omitted, the system defaults to an index named `default`.
- `operator/collector`—Essential for defining the search behavior. This can be a search operator that specifies how data should be queried or a collector that aggregates and processes data. Each comes with its own set of specifications.
- `highlight`—Provides options for highlighting search terms within the results, enhancing the visibility of query matches.
- `concurrent`—A Boolean setting that, when enabled, allows the search process to be parallelized across multiple segments on dedicated search nodes, improving performance.
- `count`—Offers a way to include a count of the results within the search output; useful for understanding the scope of the data returned.
- `SearchAfter/SearchBefore`—Facilitate pagination by specifying a reference point (encoded token) from which to continue returning results after or before the token.
- `ScoreDetails`—When set to `true`, returns a detailed breakdown of how each result was scored during the search; can be useful for debugging and refining search parameters.
- `sort`—Allows specifying which fields should be sorted and in what order (ascending or descending), helping you organize the output according to specific criteria.
- `ReturnStoredSource`—Determines whether to fetch the full document from the backend database or only the fields that are stored directly in the Atlas Search index.
- `tracking`—Enables tracking of search operations, which helps in collecting analytics and insights into how searches are being performed.

To test the aggregation pipeline `$search` stage, log in to your Atlas cluster, using `mongosh` and the connection string. As a reminder, you can obtain the connection string by running the command `atlas clusters connectionStrings describe`:

```
atlas clusters connectionStrings describe "MongoDB-in-Action"
```

This command returned my connection string, which looks like this:

```
STANDARD CONNECTION STRING
mongodb+srv://mongodb-in-action.a7niyd4.mongodb.net
```

Now connect to the MongoDB cluster using `mongosh` by executing the following command:

```
mongosh "mongodb+srv://mongodb-in-action.a7niyd4.mongodb.net/" \
--apiVersion 1 --username  manning
```

Next, use the `use` command to select the `sample_training` database:

```
use sample_training
```

You are redirected to the target database:

```
switched to db sample_training
```

Now you can start using Atlas Search with the `$search` stage.

ATLAS TEXT OPERATOR

The Atlas `text` operator conducts a full-text search using the analyzer designated in the index settings. For reference, we are using `lucene.standard`.

Perform the first aggregation pipeline using the `$search` stage and `text` operator, together with the `compound` and `score` operators. The `compound` operator combines other operators into a single query. The `score` represents the relevance of each document based on the search criteria. Here is the query:

```
db.inspections.aggregate([
  {
    $search: {
      index: "MongoDB-in-Action", // Specifying the search index
      compound: {
        // The must array specifies conditions that must be met
        must: [
          {
            text: {
              query: "food", // Searching for the word "food"
              path: "business_name" // in the business_name field
            }
          },
          {
```

```
            text: {
              query: "PASS", // Searching for the word "PASS"
              path: "result" // in the result field
            }
          },
          {
            text: {
              query: "127", // Searching for the number "127"
              path: "sector" // in the sector field
            }
          }
        ]
      }
    }
  },
  {
    $set: {
      score: {
        $meta: "searchScore" // Adding the search score,
                 // indicating the relevance of each
                 // document based on the search criteria
      }
    }
  }
])
```

This Atlas Search full-text search aggregation pipeline returns the following result:

```
[
  {
    _id: ObjectId('56d61034a378eccde8a910f4'),
    id: '20958-2015-ENFO',
    certificate_number: 9284194,
    business_name: 'MARTES FOOD CENTER CORP',
    date: 'Apr 16 2015',
    result: 'Pass',
    sector: 'Cigarette Retail Dealer - 127',
    address: { city: 'BRONX', zip: 10452,
    street: 'WALTON AVE', number: 1055 },
    score: 2.944375991821289
  }
]
```

The query performs a full-text search. It applies a `compound` condition that combines multiple criteria and requires all three `must` clauses to be met:

- The `business_name` must contain `"food"` (using the `text` search operator with `"food"` as the query and `business_name` as the path).
- The `result` field must contain `"PASS"`.
- The `sector` field must contain `"127"`. The score is calculated by the `$meta: "searchScore"` operator. This score is a numerical value that indicates how well each document matches the search criteria.

In systems like Apache Lucene, scores are calculated dynamically to reflect how well documents match a search query, with no fixed upper limit. A higher score indicates a stronger alignment with the search criteria. The score of 2.944375991821289 for 'MARTES FOOD CENTER CORP' suggests a moderate relevance to the specified search terms. Such scores are crucial for ranking documents in search results, as they help order the documents by relevance. A higher score signifies a document that is more closely related to your query, thereby guiding you more efficiently to the most relevant information.

> **NOTE** We are discussing full-text search in Atlas using the $text operator, not the $text operator available in the self-hosted MongoDB. Despite having the same name, the two operators have significant differences.

FUZZY PROPERTY

Perform another query using the text operator with the fuzzy property. The fuzzy property allows searches that can match similar terms, accounting for possible typographical errors or variations in spelling:

```
db.inspections.aggregate([
  {
    $search: {
      index: "MongoDB-in-Action",
      text: {
        query: "BUILNG TO SERV INC", // Intentionally introduced
                // errors: "BUILDING" missing an "I",
                // "SERVE" missing an "E"
        path: "business_name",
        fuzzy: {
          maxEdits: 2, // Allows for up to two typographical errors
          prefixLength: 1 // The first letter must be exactly the same
        }
      }
    }
  },
  {
    $limit: 2 // Limits the number of results to 2 for easier verification
  },
  {
    $set: {
      // Dynamically copies the fields to be retained in the output
      business_name: "$business_name",
      date: "$date",
      result: "$result",
      sector: "$sector",
      address: "$address",
      score: { $meta: "searchScore" } // Adds the search score
    }
  },
  {
    $unset: ["_id"] // Removes the '_id' field from the output documents
  }
])
```

This aggregation pipeline returns the following result:

```
[
  {
    id: '1044-2015-CMPL',
    certificate_number: 5382334,
    business_name: 'BUILDING TO SERVE INC.',
    date: 'Jul 22 2015',
    result: 'Violation Issued',
    sector: 'Home Improvement Contractor - 100',
    address: {
      city: 'JAMAICA',
      zip: 11432,
      street: 'HILLSIDE AVE',
      number: 17939
    },
    score: 7.316098690032959
  },
  {
    id: '4290-2016-ENFO',
    certificate_number: 9324927,
    business_name: 'SEND TO PRINT LLC',
    date: 'Jan 12 2016',
    result: 'Out of Business',
    sector: 'Misc Non-Food Retail - 817',
    address: {
      city: 'JACKSON HEIGHTS',
      zip: 11372,
      street: '37TH AVE',
      number: 8821
    },
    score: 3.824653387069702
  }
]
```

This aggregation pipeline uses the `text` operator with a query for `"BUILNG TO SERV INC"`, incorporating intentional misspellings to demonstrate the `fuzzy` property capability. The `fuzzy` property is configured to allow up to two typographical errors (`maxEdits: 2`) and requires the first letter to match exactly (`prefixLength: 1`). The search results are limited to two documents for simplicity, using the `$limit` operator.

The `fuzzy` property is ideal for searches in which data may have typographical errors, enhancing the robustness of search functions and accommodating slight spelling mistakes in queries. This feature allows users to search effectively within applications or databases directly from the search interface, even if their input is not perfectly accurate.

PROXIMITY SEARCH

Next, perform a query using the `phrase` operator to execute a proximity search:

```
db.inspections.aggregate([
  {
    $search: {
```

```
        index: "MongoDB-in-Action",
        phrase: {
          query: ["food", "license"], // Words to search for
          path: "business_name", // Field to search in
          slop: 3 // Allows up to 3 intervening words
                 ⇥ // between "food" and "license"
        }
      }
    },
    {
      $limit: 1 // Limits the number of results to 1
    },
    {
      $set: {
        // Adds necessary fields to the output documents
        business_name: "$business_name",
        result: "$result",
        sector: "$sector"
      }
    },
    {
      $unset: ["_id", "address", "date"] // Removes the '_id',
               ⇥ // 'address', and 'date' fields from
               ⇥ // the output documents
    }
])
```

This aggregation pipeline returns the following result:

```
[
  {
    id: '9118-2015-CMPL',
    certificate_number: 9305560,
    business_name: 'FOOD CART VENDOR LICENSE# C4029',
    result: 'Unable to Locate',
    sector: 'Mobile Food Vendor - 881'
  }
]
```

Proximity search is useful when the exact order of words is not known but their relative positioning is important. The `slop` property in such queries specifies how many words can appear between the searched terms, allowing flexibility in how closely the terms need to be positioned. In a legal document search, for example, it helps to find legal clauses or terms that are near each other within a specified distance. In customer-review analysis, it identifies phrases in which certain keywords are close together, aiding in sentiment analysis. It enhances search capabilities in content management systems by finding relevant documents or articles based on the proximity of keywords. In academic research, it locates references or quotes in which specific terms are used near each other, which is useful for literature reviews and research papers. Finally, it improves user search experience on websites by accommodating queries that may not have the exact keyword order, allowing a more natural input of search terms while delivering relevant results.

WILDCARD SEARCH

Special characters can stand in for unknown characters in a text value and are handy for locating multiple items with similar but not identical data using the `wildcard` operator:

```
db.inspections.aggregate([
  {
    $search: {
      index: "MongoDB-in-Action",
      wildcard: {
        path: "business_name",
        query: "*L?CE*", // Searches for phrases containing
        // "L?CE", where "?" represents any single
        // character and "*" represents zero
        // or more characters
        allowAnalyzedField: true // Allows searching on an analyzed field
      }
    }
  },
  {
    $set: {
      score: { $meta: "searchScore" } // Adds the search
              // score to each document
    }
  },
  {
    $sort: {
      score: -1 // Sorts by search score in descending order
    }
  },
  {
    $limit: 2 // Limits the number of results to 2
  },
  {
    $unset: ["_id", "address", "date"] // Removes the '_id',
    // 'address', and 'date' fields
    // from the output documents
  }
])
```

This Atlas Search aggregation pipeline returns the following result:

```
[
  {
    id: '10172-2015-CMPL',
    certificate_number: 9304489,
    business_name: 'UNNAMED HOT DOG VENDOR LICENSE NUMBER TA01158',
    result: 'No Violation Issued',
    sector: 'Mobile Food Vendor - 881',
    score: 1
```

```
    },
    {
      id: '10268-2015-CMPL',
      certificate_number: 9304816,
      business_name: 'UNNAMED HOT DOG VENDOR NO LICENSE NUMBER PROVIDED',
      result: 'No Violation Issued',
      sector: 'Mobile Food Vendor - 881',
      score: 1
    }
]
```

The query searches for businesses with names matching a specific pattern using the `wildcard` operator. It looks for names containing any variant of `"L?CE"`, where `"?"` can be any single character and `"*"` any sequence of characters. After identifying matches, the pipeline uses the `$set` stage to append a search relevance score to each document. Then this score is used in the `$sort` stage to order the documents by relevance in descending order. The pipeline limits the results to the top two entries by using the `$limit` stage. Finally, certain fields such as `_id`, `address`, and `date` are removed from the output with the `$unset` stage, streamlining the data for presentation or further processing.

Use this type of query when you need to find records with field values that match a specific pattern, which is useful for filtering data with partial or uncertain information.

THE FACET OPERATOR

The `facet` operator in Atlas Search creates faceted search results. *Faceted search* allows you to categorize search results in multiple groups (*facets*) based on specified fields, such as price ranges, categories, and tags. This enables you to filter and refine search results by selecting specific facets, improving the search experience by making it easier to navigate large sets of results. The `facet` operator aggregates data based on the specified fields and provides counts of documents in each category, allowing quick, efficient filtering.

The following query employs faceted search in a practical context. It initiates with a `fuzzy` text search for businesses with `"HOT DOG"` in their names, allowing for minor spelling discrepancies. Following the search, the data is processed through three facets. `ResultsByStatus` groups inspection outcomes, `ResultsByYear` organizes the data by the year of inspection, and `SectorSummary` categorizes businesses by their sector, providing a count for each:

```
db.inspections.aggregate([
  {
    $search: {
      index: "MongoDB-in-Action",
      text: {
        query: "HOT DOG",
        path: "business_name",
        fuzzy: {
          maxEdits: 1, // Allows for one typo
          prefixLength: 3 // The first 3 letters must be exactly the same
```

```
          }
        }
      }
    },
    {
      $facet: {
        "ResultsByStatus": [
          { $group: { _id: "$result", count: { $sum: 1 } } }
        ],
        "ResultsByYear": [
          {
            $group: {
              _id: { $year: { $dateFromString: { dateString: "$date" } } },
              count: { $sum: 1 }
            }
          }
        ],
        "SectorSummary": [
          { $sortByCount: "$sector" }
        ]
      }
    },
    { $limit: 1 } // This is only for illustration;
                  // typically, limit wouldn't be
                  // used after a facet.
])
```

Here's example output of the query:

```
[
  {
    ResultsByStatus: [
      { _id: 'No Violation Issued', count: 30 },
      { _id: 'No Evidence of Activity', count: 5 },
      { _id: 'Unable to Locate', count: 3 },
      { _id: 'Out of Business', count: 5 },
      { _id: 'Posting Order Served', count: 1 },
      { _id: 'Violation Issued', count: 19 },
      { _id: 'Pass', count: 19 }
    ],
    ResultsByYear: [ { _id: 2015, count: 74 }, { _id: 2016, count: 8 } ],
    SectorSummary: [
      { _id: 'Cigarette Retail Dealer - 127', count: 32 },
      { _id: 'Grocery-Retail - 808', count: 20 },
      { _id: 'Misc Non-Food Retail - 817', count: 12 },
      { _id: 'Mobile Food Vendor - 881', count: 6 },
      { _id: 'Wearing Apparel - 450', count: 5 },
      { _id: 'Salons And Barbershop - 841', count: 3 },
      { _id: 'Tow Truck Company - 124', count: 2 },
      { _id: 'Restaurant - 818', count: 1 },
      { _id: 'Tax Preparers - 891', count: 1 }
    ]
  }
]
```

This output exemplifies how faceted search can reveal insights into data distribution across various categories, helping businesses and analysts make informed decisions based on specific aspects of the data.

Let's look at another example. In the next Atlas Search query, the `facet` operator analyzes the results after searching for business names containing `"BUILDING"`. The query organizes the data in different groups to make it easier to understand. First, it counts how many businesses match the search. Then it groups the results by the outcome of their inspections (such as whether they passed or had violations) and by the zip codes of their addresses:

```
db.inspections.aggregate([
  {
    // Searches documents using the specified
    // index and text search on
    // the business_name field
    $search: {
      index: "MongoDB-in-Action", // Uses the "MongoDB-in-Action"
                  // index for search
      text: {
        query: "BUILDING", // The search query,
                  // looking for "BUILDING" in the business names
        path: "business_name" // Specifies that the search
                  // should focus on the 'business_name' field
      }
    }
  },
  {
    // Facets the results into multiple categories for detailed analysis
    $facet: {
      "TotalResults": [
        { $count: "totalCount" }   // Counts the total
                  // number of matching documents
      ],
      "ResultsByStatus": [
        // Groups documents by the 'result' field and counts the occurrences
        { $group: { _id: "$result", count: { $sum: 1 } } },
        // Sorts the grouped results by count in descending order
        { $sort: { count: -1 } }
      ],
      "ResultsByZip": [
        // Groups documents by the zip code field
        // in the address and counts the occurrences
        { $group: { _id: "$address.zip", count: { $sum: 1 } } },
        // Sorts the results by count in descending order
        { $sort: { count: -1 } }
      ]
    }
  }
])
```

This aggregation pipeline with `facet` returned the following result:

```
[
  {
    TotalResults: [ { totalCount: 29 } ],
    ResultsByStatus: [
      { _id: 'No Violation Issued', count: 14 },
      { _id: 'Violation Issued', count: 5 },
      { _id: 'Out of Business', count: 5 },
      { _id: 'Pass', count: 5 }
    ],
    ResultsByZip: [
      { _id: 11214, count: 3 },
      { _id: 11101, count: 2 },
      { _id: 11216, count: 2 },
      { _id: 11220, count: 2 },
      { _id: 11232, count: 1 },
      { _id: 10469, count: 1 },
      { _id: 11436, count: 1 },
      { _id: 10457, count: 1 },
      { _id: 11205, count: 1 },
      { _id: 10312, count: 1 },
      { _id: 11236, count: 1 },
      { _id: 11411, count: 1 },
      { _id: 11357, count: 1 },
      { _id: 10459, count: 1 },
      { _id: 11418, count: 1 },
      { _id: 10002, count: 1 },
      { _id: 11235, count: 1 },
      { _id: 11249, count: 1 },
      { _id: 11432, count: 1 },
      { _id: 11361, count: 1 },
      { _id: 10455, count: 1 },
      { _id: 11416, count: 1 },
      { _id: 11417, count: 1 },
      { _id: 11354, count: 1 }
    ]
  }
]
```

The result reveals that 29 businesses were involved in this query. When the result was broken down by inspection results, 14 businesses had no violations, 5 had violations issued, 5 were out of business, and the remaining 5 passed their inspections. Also, the data is organized by zip code to show geographical trends, with the highest occurrences in the 11214 area. This structured output is essential for understanding the distribution and common problems of building-related businesses, aiding in targeted regulatory and business planning strategies.

THE FACET OPERATOR WITH $$SEARCH META

You can employ the SEARCH_META variable to access the metadata results of your $search query. The SEARCH_META aggregation variable is applicable in any pipeline following a $search stage.

In the following aggregation pipeline, a `fuzzy` search is conducted on the `business_name` field using the query `"smok skop"`, intended to capture variations like `"smoke shop"`. This approach allows one typographical error and requires the first three letters to be exactly the same, enhancing the search's tolerance for input discrepancies. Next, the pipeline employs a `facet` stage to organize the results, which includes limiting the display to the first five relevant documents while maintaining essential information such as business name, date, result, and sector. Simultaneously, it categorizes results in automatically generated buckets based on the `result` field and gathers metadata such as total document counts through the `$$SEARCH_META` variable, providing valuable insights into the search's effectiveness and reach:

```
db.inspections.aggregate([
  {
    $search: {
      index: "MongoDB-in-Action",
      text: {
        query: "smok skop", // Intentionally misspelled,
                            // likely meant to be "smoke shop"
        path: "business_name",
        fuzzy: {
          maxEdits: 1, // Allows for one typo in the search query
          prefixLength: 3 // The first 3 letters must match exactly
        }
      }
    }
  },
  {
    $facet: {
      docs: [
        { $limit: 5 }, // Limits the number of documents to 5
        {
          $set: {
            // Dynamically retains the necessary fields
            // in the output documents
            business_name: "$business_name",
            date: "$date",
            result: "$result",
            sector: "$sector",
            address: "$address"
          }
        },
        { $unset: ["_id"] } // Removes the '_id' field
                            // from the output documents
      ],
      resultFacets: [
        {
          $bucketAuto: {
            groupBy: "$result", // Groups documents by the 'result' field
            buckets: 5 // Automatically determines range
                       // and creates 5 buckets based
                       // on result distribution
          }
```

```
        }
      ],
      meta: [
        { $replaceWith: "$$SEARCH_META" }, // Replaces the
                              ⇨      // document with search metadata
        { $limit: 1 } // Limits the metadata results to 1
      ]
    }
  }
])
```

This aggregation pipeline with the $$SEARCH_META variable returned the following result:

```
[
  {
    docs: [
      {
        id: '70695-2015-ENFO',
        certificate_number: 50065977,
        business_name: 'SMOKE SHOP',
        date: 'Dec 31 2015',
        result: 'No Evidence of Activity',
        sector: 'Cigarette Retail Dealer - 127',
        address: {
          city: 'NEW YORK',
          zip: 10075,
          street: 'YORK AVE',
          number: 1485
        }
      },
      {
        id: '13076-2015-ENFO',
        certificate_number: 50057527,
        business_name: 'SMOKE SHOPE',
        date: 'Mar 28 2015',
        result: 'No Evidence of Activity',
        sector: 'Cigarette Retail Dealer - 127',
        address: {
          city: 'OZONE PARK',
          zip: 11416,
          street: '101ST AVE',
          number: 10506
        }
      },
      {
        id: '30922-2015-ENFO',
        certificate_number: 9259353,
        business_name: 'SMOKE SCENE, INC.',
        date: 'May 18 2015',
        result: 'No Violation Issued',
        sector: 'Cigarette Retail Dealer - 127',
        address: {
          city: 'NEW YORK',
```

```
        zip: 10022,
        street: '1ST AVE',
        number: 901
      }
    },
    {
      id: '43869-2015-ENFO',
      certificate_number: 50061178,
      business_name: 'DELI SMOKE SHOP',
      date: 'Aug 12 2015',
      result: 'Out of Business',
      sector: 'Cigarette Retail Dealer - 127',
      address: {
        city: 'BROOKLYN',
        zip: 11207,
        street: 'FULTON ST',
        number: 2859
      }
    },
    {
      id: '35088-2015-ENFO',
      certificate_number: 50060202,
      business_name: 'SMOKE SCENE, INC.',
      date: 'Jun 19 2015',
      result: 'No Violation Issued',
      sector: 'Cigarette Retail Dealer - 127',
      address: {
        city: 'NEW YORK',
        zip: 10022,
        street: '1ST AVE',
        number: 901
      }
    }
  ],
  resultFacets: [
    { _id: { min: 'Closed', max: 'Out of Business' }, count: 145 },
    {
      _id: { min: 'Out of Business', max: 'Violation Issued' },
      count: 118
    }
  ],
  meta: [ { count: { lowerBound: Long('263') } } ]
  }
]
```

When you run a query using the $search stage in Atlas Search, the system stores metadata results in the $$SEARCH_META variable while returning the actual search results to you. You can use the $$SEARCH_META variable in any supported aggregation pipeline stage to view and analyze the metadata associated with your $search query.

The $$SEARCH_META variable is useful when you need to analyze additional information about the search operation itself, such as search scores and other diagnostics that help you understand the relevance and performance of your search results. It can be useful for optimizing your search queries based on performance metrics or for debugging to ensure that the search results align accurately with the expected criteria.

11.5.2 Executing the $searchMeta aggregation pipeline stage

The `$searchMeta` aggregation pipeline stage accesses metadata about the search operation itself. This stage allows you to retrieve and use search-related metadata such as total number of hits or pagination data, which can be critical for understanding the context and scale of the search results. You can use this information for logging, debugging, or enhancing user interfaces with details on the number of results returned and the relevance of the search performed. The following listing shows the `$searchMeta` pipeline stage structure.

Listing 11.5 The `$searchMeta` prototype form

```
{
  $searchMeta: {
    "index": "<index-name>",
    "<collector-name>"|"<operator-name>": {
      <collector-specification>|<operator-specification>
    },
    "count": {
      <count-options>
    }
  }
}
```

Let's look at the available options:

- `<collector-name>` *(conditional)*—Selects a collector for the query, such as `"facet"` for grouping results. You must specify either this option or `<operator-name>`
- `count` *(optional)*—Provides options for counting the number of search results and is useful for understanding the scale of results without retrieving all data.
- `index`—Specifies the name of the Atlas Search index to be used for the query. If this option is omitted, the system defaults to an index named `"default"`.
- `<operator-name>` *(conditional)*—Determines the search operator to use. If `<collector-name>` is not used, this option must be specified and will return only default count metadata.

The following query employs the `$searchMeta` stage to search for businesses named `"Deli"`. It focuses on `"business_name"`. `$searchMeta` returns only metadata about the search results, such as the count of matching documents:

```
db.inspections.aggregate([
  {
    $searchMeta: {
      index: "MongoDB-in-Action",
```

```
      text: {
        query: "Deli", // Searches for the term "Deli"
                      // within the business names.
        path: "business_name" // Specifies that the search
                              // should be conducted on
                              //the 'business_name' field.
      }
    }
  }
])
```

The pipeline returns the following result:

```
[ { count: { lowerBound: Long('2447') } } ]
```

The output from this search operation is expressed as metadata, specifically showing a count with a lower bound. This indicates the minimum number of records that match the query criteria, providing a lower estimate of 2,447 businesses named `"Deli"`.

In the next example, the `$searchMeta` operation within the aggregation pipeline gathers metadata about businesses with `"Hot Dog"` in their names and `"No Violation Issued"` in the inspection results. The query is designed to favor documents related to the "`Grocery-Retail`" sector, although these are preferred but not essential for a match. It strictly includes only businesses located in `"Brooklyn"`, as indicated by the `city` field in their addresses. The pipeline uses a compound query that combines conditions to match and prioritize results based on business name, inspection outcome, and sector while specifically filtering for locations in Brooklyn:

```
db.inspections.aggregate([
  {
    $search: {
      index: "MongoDB-in-Action", // Utilizes the MongoDB Atlas
                    // Search index for optimized
                    // text search.
      compound: {
        // Requires matching both business
        // name and inspection result,
        // prefers matching the sector,
        // and filters by city.
        must: [
          {
            text: { // Must match 'Hot Dog' in the business name.
              query: "Hot Dog",
              path: "business_name"
            }
          },
          {
            text: { // Must match 'No Violation Issued'
                    // in the inspection results.
              query: "No Violation Issued",
              path: "result"
            }
```

```
        }
      ],
      should: [
        {
          text: { // Prefers businesses in the
                  // 'Grocery-Retail' sector but it's
                  // not mandatory.
            query: "Grocery-Retail",
            path: "sector"
          }
        }
      ],
      filter: [
        {
          text: { // Strictly includes only businesses
                  // located in Brooklyn.
            query: "BROOKLYN",
            path: "address.city"
          }
        }
      ]
    }
  }
},
{
  $addFields: {
    score: { $meta: "searchScore" } // Adds a search relevance
                                    // score to each matched document.
  }
},
{
  $facet: { // Summarizes the total documents and score statistics.
    totalDocuments: [{ $count: "totalCount" }], // Counts
                                    // total matching documents.
    scoreStats: [
      {
        $group: { // Aggregates maximum, minimum, and average scores.
          _id: null,
          maxScore: { $max: "$score" },
          minScore: { $min: "$score" },
          averageScore: { $avg: "$score" }
        }
      }
    ]
  }
}
])
```

The metadata provided in the output of the pipeline offers insights into the search results for businesses related to the query:

```
[
  {
    totalDocuments: [ { totalCount: 13 } ],
    scoreStats: [
```

```
            {
                _id: null,
                maxScore: 7.446932792663574,
                minScore: 3.273611068725586,
                averageScore: 4.741124574954693
            }
        ]
    }
]
```

The metadata shows that the query returned 13 documents matching the criteria with businesses named "Hot Dog" and inspection results of "No Violation Issued" in Brooklyn. The score statistics reveal the search relevance scores; the highest is 7.446932792663574, indicating a close match to the search criteria, and the lowest is 3.273611068725586, suggesting a document that barely meets the threshold. The average relevance score across all documents is 4.741124574954693, reflecting the general relevance of the results to the specified parameters.

This approach is useful for obtaining quick statistics about the data without retrieving the actual documents. It can be efficient for large data sets or preliminary data analysis.

11.6 Learning Atlas Search commands

MongoDB includes four commands that enhance search index management. These commands can be run only on a deployment hosted on MongoDB Atlas and require an Atlas cluster tier of at least M10:

- db.collection.createSearchIndex()—Use this command to create a new Atlas Search index. It requires the index name and a document specifying the index configuration as arguments. Executing db.collection.createSearch-Index("mySearchIndex", {"mappings": {"dynamic": true}}) will create an index named "mySearchIndex" with dynamic mappings.

- db.collection.updateSearchIndex()—This command updates an existing Atlas Search index. It takes the index name and a new configuration document as arguments. db.collection.updateSearchIndex("mySearchIndex", {"mappings": {"dynamic": false, "fields": {"description": {"type": "string"}}}}) modifies the "mySearchIndex" to use static mappings and adds a string field named "description".

- db.collection.dropSearchIndex()—Use this command to delete an Atlas Search index. You need to provide the index name as the argument. db.collection.dropSearchIndex("mySearchIndex") deletes the "mySearch-Index" index.

- db.collection.getSearchIndex()—This command retrieves the configuration of an existing Atlas Search index. When called with an index name, it returns that specific index's configuration; without an argument, it returns configurations for all indexes in the collection.

11.7 Using Atlas Search Playground

You can also try Atlas Search on the Playground. The MongoDB Atlas Search Playground is an intuitive, interactive platform designed to showcase the robust capabilities of Atlas Search. Without the need for a MongoDB Atlas account, cluster, or data collection, it allows you to engage directly with the technology by creating search indexes and executing queries in a controlled environment. Figure 11.6 shows the interface of the Atlas Search Playground, which you can find at https://mng.bz/RwvP without logging in.

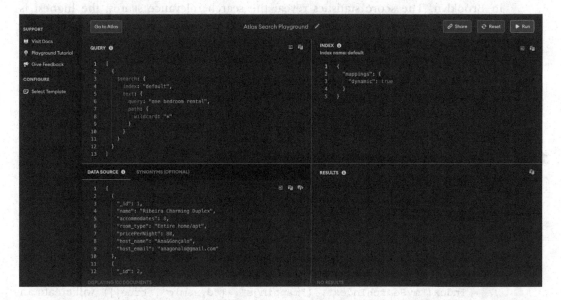

Figure 11.6 The Atlas Search Playground, where users can configure and test search queries in MongoDB Atlas. It includes sections for writing queries, configuring the search index, viewing the data source, and displaying results. This interface allows users to experiment with search features and see how their queries perform on sample data before applying them in a live environment. (Image © MongoDB 2025)

You can choose among three distinct preconfigured environments to explore specific functionalities of Atlas Search, as shown in figure 11.7.

The Basic environment enables searching all document fields and is ideal for broad queries. The Catalog Search environment is designed for detailed searches within Airbnb listings, using tools such as EQUALS, RANGE, SORT, SYNONYMS, and TEXT to refine results. If you're interested in identifying individual accounts, the Customer Lookup environment offers features such as AUTOCOMPLETE, COMPOUND, CUSTOM ANALYZER, SORT, and TEXT, enhancing the precision and efficiency of searches by name or email.

This setup is beneficial for quick testing, experimentation, and educational purposes, providing a risk-free way to learn and understand the various search functionalities

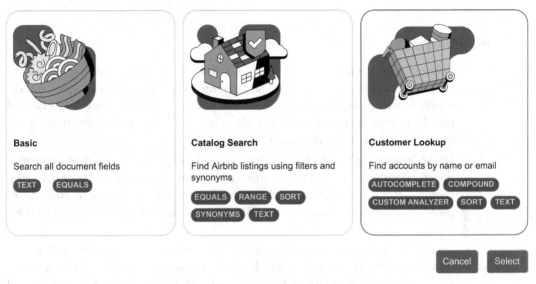

Figure 11.7 Atlas Search Playground preconfigured environments (Image © MongoDB 2024 CC BY-NC-SA 3.0)

and their applications. Whether you're a developer looking to integrate search capabilities into your applications or are simply curious about the potential of MongoDB Atlas Search, the Playground offers a convenient, accessible way to explore these features in depth. Also, it gives you the option to share snapshots of your Playground sessions, making it easy to collaborate with colleagues or demonstrate your work.

The Atlas Search Playground is a useful tool for experimenting with MongoDB's search capabilities, but it has several limitations:

- It does not support Atlas Vector Search (described in chapter 12), restricting the range of functionalities you can explore. The environment is designed to work with only a single collection; hence, you cannot use operations such as `$lookup` and `$unionWith` to search across multiple collections.
- Another significant limitation is that the Atlas Search Playground environment does not persist. If you want to save your setup, you must click the Share button to create a snapshot URL, which remains valid for 30 days.
- The Playground imposes data restrictions as well. You cannot add more than 500 documents or import files larger than 100 KB, and the total data in your Playground environment (which includes the collection, search index, synonyms, and queries) cannot exceed 300 KB. These constraints may affect the extent to which you can realistically test and demonstrate larger or more complex search functionalities.

TIP To stay up to date with the Atlas Search architecture, visit the official MongoDB documentation at https://www.mongodb.com/docs/atlas/atlas-search.

Summary

- Full-text search surpasses traditional methods by analyzing document content for relevance, phrases, citations, and attributes. It supports various types, such as simple keyword, Boolean, fuzzy, wildcard, phrase, proximity, range, and faceted searches. This versatility makes it ideal for applications ranging from quick queries to complex filtering tasks.
- Using separate solutions for database management and full-text search introduces complexity in data synchronization and query handling. This setup requires extra maintenance and monitoring, leading to potential consistency problems, increased costs, and additional operational overhead for DevOps teams.
- Apache Lucene is a high-performance Java library that offers advanced search features including indexing, spell-checking, and text analysis. It's part of an open source project that includes PyLucene, providing Python bindings to extend Lucene Core's capabilities.
- Lucene uses inverted indexing to map terms to document locations, significantly speeding search queries and enhancing performance.
- Atlas Search, embedded in MongoDB Atlas, delivers a scalable full-text search feature using Apache Lucene, allowing seamless integration of search capabilities without an additional system.
- The `mongot` process is crucial for creating, managing, and updating Atlas Search indexes using Apache Lucene technology, ensuring that they stay synchronized with MongoDB's current state by monitoring change streams and applying updates promptly. It also handles Atlas Search queries directly, providing accurate real-time search results.
- Atlas Search Nodes in MongoDB Atlas are specialized, separated nodes focused solely on search functions via the `mongot` process. They provide workload isolation in dedicated (M10 or higher) sharded and unsharded clusters across various cloud providers.
- An Atlas Search index can be on a single field or multiple fields, preferably those used for sorting or filtering to speed queries. Use dynamic mappings to index all supported fields automatically, though this approach may affect performance, or use static mappings to index specified fields selectively, ignoring mismatched data types.
- Atlas Search index limits vary by cluster tier. M0 clusters allow up to three indexes. M10 and higher clusters place no restrictions on the number of indexes you can create.

- There are no additional fees or charges when you enable Atlas Search on your Atlas cluster. But you may observe an increase in resource use on the cluster, depending on factors such as the size of the indexed collections and index definitions.
- Atlas Search queries are formatted as stages within an aggregation pipeline. They incorporate the $search and $searchMeta stages, which are required to be the first stage in any query pipeline. These stages can be integrated with other aggregation pipeline stages to enhance your query pipeline.
- You can use the text operator with the fuzzy operator. The fuzzy operator allows for searches that can match similar terms, accounting for possible typographical errors or variations in spelling. This enhances search functionality by accommodating minor mistakes in the search query.
- In systems such as Apache Lucene, which supports Atlas Search, scores are calculated dynamically based on document relevance, with no upper limit. Higher scores indicate a closer match to the search criteria, effectively helping users find the most relevant information quickly.
- The facet operator in Atlas Search structures search results in distinct categories based on criteria such as price ranges, categories, and tags, facilitating easier navigation and organization of data.
- You can explore Atlas Search using the MongoDB Atlas Search Playground. This user-friendly platform demonstrates the powerful features of Atlas Search without requiring a MongoDB Atlas account, cluster, or data collection. It lets you create search indexes and run queries in a simplified environment.

Learning semantic techniques and Atlas Vector Search

This chapter covers
- Working with embeddings and vector databases
- Creating an Atlas Vector Search
- Exploring the $vectorSearch aggregation pipeline stage
- Using Atlas Triggers to generate embeddings

Chapter 11 introduced Atlas Search, which is built with Apache Lucene. This powerful open source search engine enhances database functionality by providing full-text search capabilities integrated directly into MongoDB.

In this chapter, we explore Atlas Vector Search. This feature, also built on the foundation of Apache Lucene, extends MongoDB's core server capabilities further by enabling vector-based search functionalities.

Unlike traditional full-text search that primarily matches exact text, vector search identifies vectors that are near your query within a multidimensional space. The closer these vectors are to your query, the greater their semantic similarity is. By incorporating vector search, Atlas uses Lucene's capabilities to index and navigate high-dimensional vectors, yielding more nuanced, contextually appropriate search results. If you search "renewable energy" using vector search, for example, you might get results related to solar power, wind energy, and sustainable resources, capturing the broader concept of renewable energy rather than exact matches of the phrase *renewable energy*. This approach is particularly beneficial in applications involving image, video, and audio searches, as well as scenarios requiring semantic text search.

Vector search also helps applications like chatbots find and use the most relevant data from large data sets, searching this data based on the theme of the request and using it to provide context for queries sent to advanced language models. This approach is called the *retriever-augmented generation* (RAG) model. One of the major challenges in advanced language models is hallucinations, in which the AI generates plausible-sounding but incorrect or nonsensical information. RAG was developed to address this problem. RAG uses vector search to quickly identify and retrieve important information from these data sets based on the user's input. Then this real data is sent to advanced language models like Generative Pretrained Transformer (GPT), which process it to generate accurate, contextually relevant responses. By grounding responses in factual information, RAG enhances the performance of chatbots and other AI applications, allowing them to provide more precise and detailed answers to user queries.

12.1 Starting with embeddings

Vector search relies on embeddings. Vector embeddings convert various data types—such as text, voice, and sentences—to numerical values that reflect their meaning and relationships. These data types are represented as points in a multidimensional space, with similar data points located closer together. This numerical approach helps machines understand and process the data more efficiently.

Word and sentence embeddings are common types of vector embeddings, but this category also includes document embeddings, image vectors, user profile vectors, and product vectors, among others. These embeddings help machine learning algorithms identify patterns in data and perform tasks such as sentiment analysis, language translation, and recommendation systems. Figure 12.1 shows how different data types are represented as points in a 3D space, clustered based on similarities.

The categories Renewable Energy, Wind Energy, and Solar Power are grouped, with the query Renewable Energy falling within this cluster, illustrating how closely related terms are positioned near one another. The MongoDB and Apache Lucene symbols are distinctly represented, indicating their separate vector embeddings, which are used for different types of data storage and search functionalities. Similarly, unique clusters such as Apache Lucene and MongoDB are distinctly grouped away from the Renewable Energy categories. This spatial arrangement helps illustrate how embeddings allow machines to understand and process related data efficiently, supporting tasks like pattern recognition in sentiment analysis, language translation, and recommendation systems.

304   CHAPTER 12 *Learning semantic techniques and Atlas Vector Search*

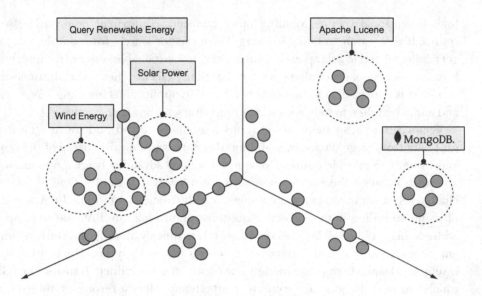

Figure 12.1 A visual representation of vector embeddings shows how the query Renewable Energy is mapped in semantic space. Clusters such as Wind Energy and Solar Power appear close to the query, indicating high semantic similarity. By contrast, unrelated clusters like MongoDB and Apache Lucene are positioned farther away. (Image © MongoDB 2024 CC BY-NC-SA 3.0)

Various vector embeddings serve different purposes across multiple applications. Here are some common types:

- *Text embeddings*—Transform text strings into vectors, capturing semantic relationships and contextual nuances from large text data sets. They are used for tasks such as search, clustering, recommendations, anomaly detection, diversity measurement, and classification.
- *Sentence embeddings*—Convert entire sentences to vector form. Specific models are designed to encapsulate the overall meaning and contextual essence of sentences.
- *Document embeddings*—Turn entire documents, ranging from newspaper articles to books, into vectors. These embeddings aim to grasp the semantic depth and contextual breadth of the documents through specialized techniques.
- *Image embeddings*—Translate visual content into vector representations by identifying various visual attributes. Methods employing convolutional neural networks and certain pretrained models are commonly used for tasks such as image classification and similarity assessments.
- *Audio embeddings*—Convert audio signals to vector representations by capturing features such as pitch, tone, and rhythm. They are used for tasks like speech recognition and music classification by analyzing various acoustic properties of the audio.

- *User embeddings*—Create vector representations of users within a system, capturing preferences, behaviors, and traits. These embeddings are useful in applications such as recommendation systems and personalized marketing.
- *Product embeddings*—Encode the characteristics and attributes of products in vectors, which can be used to analyze, compare, and recommend products in systems such as e-commerce platforms.

Embeddings and vectors are essentially the same, representing data as numerical points in high-dimensional space, but embeddings specifically apply techniques to capture meaningful information and relationships. The term *vector* describes an array of numbers that indicates a specific dimensionality, whereas *embeddings* refers to representing data as vectors to encapsulate semantic relationships or contextual details. Although you can use these terms interchangeably when discussing vector embeddings, embeddings emphasize a structured and meaningful representation of data, whereas vectors are more about the numerical format itself.

12.1.1 Converting text to embeddings

Let's explore various methods for converting text to embeddings. MongoDB Atlas does not support embedding creation; you need to use an external system. One option is the OpenAI Embeddings API, available at https://mng.bz/YZ1B, which provides high-quality text embeddings.

Another alternative is Google's Universal Sentence Encoder, which offers embeddings for sentences and paragraphs and is available via TensorFlow Hub at https://www.tensorflow.org/hub. BERT, also developed by Google, provides context-aware embeddings, with Sentence-BERT (https://www.sbert.net) being a variant designed for more effective sentence embeddings.

Hugging Face offers a wide range of pretrained models and embeddings for various NLP tasks, accessible at https://mng.bz/Gwyv.

Additionally, Large Language Model Meta AI (LLaMA), developed by Meta, is designed for scalable text embeddings and various natural language processing (NLP) applications. LLaMA is an open source large language model (LLM) that can be run locally, offering flexibility for those who prefer or require on-premises solutions. To run LLaMA locally, you need a machine with sufficient computational power. For details, check the LLaMA GitHub repository (https://github.com/meta-llama/llama).

I decided to use the OpenAI Embeddings API in this book because it provides highly accurate, context-aware text embeddings based on state-of-the-art machine learning models. I believe it is the most mature and reliable solution available. When I wrote this chapter, `text-embedding-3-small` and `text-embedding-3-large` were the newest, most performant embedding models available.

`text-embedding-3-small` and `text-embedding-3-large` are advanced models that generate dense vector representations of text, capturing semantic meanings and relationships. The large model has more parameters and provides higher accuracy than the small model. Both models perform well in multilingual contexts and are cost-effective. The model size balances efficiency and accuracy for specific needs. These embeddings enhance tasks such as text classification, clustering, and search by providing precise, context-aware text analysis. The small model is faster and more resource-efficient, whereas the large model offers more detailed and nuanced text analysis. Both models support multiple languages and are optimized for applications requiring deep understanding and manipulation of text data.

To communicate with the OpenAI Embeddings API, start by obtaining your API key from the OpenAI platform. Store this key securely. Set up your environment to include the API key, typically through environment variables or secure secret management. After you create an account, you can also generate an OpenAI API key at https://platform.openai.com/api-keys.

Using `curl` (a command-line tool for transferring data with URLs), you can send a request to the OpenAI Embeddings API to transform the text `"MongoDB in Action 8.0"` into an embedding, as shown in the following listing. First, ensure that you have `curl` installed on your system. Next, set your OpenAI API key as an environment variable.

Listing 12.1 Creating text embeddings with the OpenAI Embeddings API

```
export OPENAI_API_KEY=your-api-key
curl https://api.openai.com/v1/embeddings \
  -H "Content-Type: application/json" \
  -H "Authorization: Bearer $OPENAI_API_KEY" \
  -d '{
    "input": "MongoDB in Action 8.0",
    "model": "text-embedding-3-small"
  }'
```

This command returns a response including the embedding vector in JSON format. The shortened response looks something like this:

```
{
  "object": "list",
  "data": [
    {
      "object": "embedding", // Embedding object
      "index": 0, // Index of the embedding
      "embedding": [
        // Example embedding values
        0.0022989365, -0.06971052, 0.012823246, 0.05579968,
        -0.013507065, -0.049443416, 0.005815723, 0.010315907,
        -0.006538618, 0.023809947, 0.022989364, 0.009593013,
        0.0030478816, 0.035089716, 0.005172153, 0.017217182,
        -0.01868694, -0.02883528, -0.0021947355, -0.01346799,
        -0.0057636225, 0.015096132, 0.008896167, -0.02650615,
        0.0017714185, -0.016711248, -0.017154103,
        0.014470926, -0.025060361, -0.0010965536, -0.019576779,
        0.005216567, -0.008088609, 0.010875988, -0.012849296,
        -0.0005344376, 0.020514589, -0.005760366, 0.040924978,
```

Starting with embeddings

```
            -0.03386535, 0.024383053, -0.016567972, -0.0072224378,
            -0.030478816, 0.015044032, -0.0011852874, -0.007339664,
            0.020918367, 0.019615855,-0.04470868, 0.015103527,
            0.013199839, 0.0069814725, -0.0049756016, 0.021869203,
            -0.036965333, 0.03076537, 0.022507435, 0.0014889358,
            0.034099806, -0.02985361, 0.024343979, 0.053246755,
            0.0054086875, 0.0065223365, 0.012360854, 0.01742763,
            0.005092828, 0.011664009, 0.040951025, 0.02614772,
            -0.019582793, -0.009371466, -0.019904742, 0.0034031929,
            0.019246848, 0.012331981, -0.06114199, -0.05027977,
            -0.04470868, 0.035089716,-0.0028573892, -0.025255738,
            0.038137596, 0.09221796, -0.02257256,0.014470926,
            -0.025060361, -0.0010965536, -0.019576779, 0.005216567,
            -0.008088609, 0.010875988, -0.012849296, -0.0005344376,
            0.020514589, -0.049391314, 0.016346546, -0.01772721,
            -0.0018902728, 0.0048714005, 0.014796554, 0.0014954484,
            -0.021361222, 0.023067515, 0.04126363, -0.02690993,
            0.02602422, -0.015734363, -0.0052002855, -0.03563677,
            0.024409104, -0.026532201, -0.029228404, 0.003360485,
            0.018469643, 0.016620073, -0.020123834, -0.003936847,
            0.0033230376, 0.007489453, 0.0032041834, 0.0016672174,
            0.0069814725, 0.0049756016, 0.021869203, 0.036965333,
            0.03076537, 0.022507435, 0.0014889358, 0.034099806,
            0.02985361, 0.024343979, 0.053246755, 0.0054086875,
            0.0065223365, 0.012360854, 0.01742763, 0.005092828,
            0.011664009, 0.040951025, 0.00892873, 0.051266935,
            0.005219823, 0.038137596, 0.0028997208, -0.03266704,
            0.09221796, 0.0026896906,-0.0030918415, 0.01542176,
            0.01978518, -0.06220805, 0.022767937, 0.009488812,
            -0.0028573892, -0.005760366, 0.040924978, 0.03386535,
            0.024383053, -0.016567972, -0.0072224378, 0.030478816
            // List continues...
        ]
    }
  ],
  "model": "text-embedding-3-small", // Model used for embedding
  "usage": {
    "prompt_tokens": 5, // Number of prompt tokens used
    "total_tokens": 5  // Total tokens used
  }
}
```

The `curl` command retrieves a JSON response containing the embedding vector for the text `"MongoDB in Action 8.0"`. The response shows the embedding as a list of numerical values that represent the input text in a high-dimensional space. It also includes details about the model used (`"text-embedding-3-small"`) and token use. For `text-embedding-3-small`, the embedding vector has 1,536 dimensions, whereas `text-embedding-3-large` has 3,072 dimensions. Having 1,536 dimensions means that each text is represented as a vector in a 1,536-dimensional space; having 3,072 dimensions means that each text is represented in a 3,072-dimensional space. More dimensions provide a more detailed text representation, improving model performance.

To create embeddings, you can use programming languages such as Python or JavaScript instead of `curl`. In Python and in JavaScript (Node.js), you can use the `openai` library.

12.1.2 Understanding vector databases

A vector embedding is generally depicted as a series of numerical values. Each value in this sequence correlates to a distinct feature or dimension, collectively forming the data point's representation. The individual numbers in the vector do not have intrinsic meaning; instead, the comparative values and their interrelationships encapsulate the semantic information, enabling algorithms to process and analyze the data efficiently.

A *vector database* (also known as a *vector search database* or *vector similarity search engine*) manages the storage, retrieval, and search of these vectors. Unlike traditional relational databases that store data in rows and columns, vector databases organize data as points within a multidimensional space, each point represented by vectors like [0.3, 0.8, -0.8, 0.6, 0.4, 0.1, -0.5, 0.2, ...]. This method of organization is particularly advantageous for applications that require fast, accurate data matching based on similarity rather than exact matches, making them ideal for semantic searches and recommendation systems.

Figure 12.2 provides an overview of the workflow within a vector database. Content is initially processed through an embedding model. These models generate embeddings by transforming text or other data types into numerical vectors.

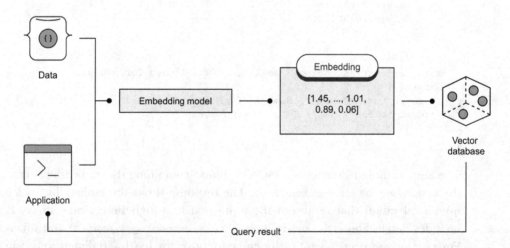

Figure 12.2 Vector database operations. Data is processed by an embedding model, transforming it into vector embeddings such as [1.45, ..., 1.01, 0.89, 0.06]. These embeddings are stored in a vector database. Queries from the application are also transformed into embeddings before the database is searched. The most relevant results based on these query embeddings are then retrieved and returned as query results. (Image © MongoDB 2024 CC BY-NC-SA 3.0)

After the data is converted to vectors, it is stored in the vector database. The database organizes these vectors within a high-dimensional space in which each vector represents a point. When a query is made, it is also transformed into a vector using the same or a similar embedding model. Then the vector database performs a similarity search to find vectors that are closest to the query vector. This search is typically done using algorithms such as cosine similarity, which measures the cosine of the angle between two vectors, or Euclidean distance, which calculates the straight-line distance between vectors in the space.

These algorithms help determine the degree of similarity between the query vector and the stored vectors. The closest vectors are retrieved and returned as the query results. This process ensures that the data retrieved is semantically similar to the query, enabling applications to provide relevant, precise results. The efficiency and accuracy of vector databases make them essential for various applications, including context-aware search, fraud detection, and question answering systems.

12.2 Using embeddings with Atlas Vector Search

Atlas Vector Search, similar to Atlas Search, uses the `mongot` process, a Java wrapper for Apache Lucene. It monitors the MongoDB operation log (oplog) using change streams to keep a set of Lucene indexes up to date. Also, it provides an API for MongoDB to perform queries on these indexes. Recent versions of Apache Lucene have been enhanced to support vector search capabilities by using algorithms such as Hierarchical Navigable Small Worlds (HNSW) for approximate nearest neighbor (ANN) searches and exact nearest neighbor (ENN) search.

The HNSW algorithm constructs a hierarchical graph in which nodes represent data points and edges connect nodes that are similar based on a distance metric like Euclidean distance. This graph is organized in multiple layers, with the upper layers containing fewer data points and providing a broad overview of the data set, acting as entry points for the search. These upper layers are faster but less precise. As the search descends to the lower layers, it encounters more nodes, offering finer granularity and increased precision. Each lower layer refines the search results from the upper layers, enhancing accuracy.

The search process in HNSW begins at an entry point in the topmost layer, performing a greedy search by navigating the graph and moving to the nearest neighbor nodes based on the distance metric. The search continues to move down to lower layers, progressively refining the results until it reaches the bottom layer, providing a highly accurate result. This layered approach significantly reduces search time compared with brute-force methods, making HNSW suitable for large-scale, real-time applications.

By contrast, ENN search involves comparing the query vector with every vector in the data set to find the exact closest match. This method guarantees precise results but is computationally expensive (especially for large data sets) due to its linear complexity. The key differences between HNSW (ANN) and ENN lie in computational complexity, speed versus precision, and scalability. HNSW offers logarithmic to sublinear complexity, balancing speed and accuracy for real-time applications. ENN provides exact matches but at higher computational costs and is less scalable for large data sets.

Overall, HNSW is favored for applications requiring fast, approximate results with high accuracy, such as recommendation systems, image retrieval, and NLP, whereas ENN is used when exact precision is crucial, albeit with greater computational demands.

Atlas Vector Search supports both ANN search, which avoids scanning every vector embedding, and ENN search, which exhaustively examines all indexed vector embeddings to find the most similar vectors.

12.2.1 Building an Atlas Vector Search index

To use vector search on your data in Atlas, you need to create an Atlas Vector Search index. This index, which is separate from your MongoDB database, helps you quickly find documents with vector embeddings during queries. In your index definition, specify the fields with embeddings in your collection to enable vector searches on those fields. Atlas Vector Search supports embeddings up to 4,096 dimensions—with *4,096 dimensions* referring to the size or length of a vector, which can have up to 4,096 elements or components. Each element of the vector represents a feature or characteristic of the data.

In NLP, for example, a word embedding with 4,096 dimensions represents a word with a vector containing 4,096 numerical values, each capturing different aspects of the word's meaning.

Recommended dimensions typically depend on the specific use case and the complexity of the data. Commonly used dimensions are 128, 256, 512, and 1,024 because they balance performance and accuracy. Higher dimensions, such as 4,096, may provide more detailed representations but can be computationally expensive.

12.2.2 Selecting a Vector Search source

To build an Atlas Vector Search index, first you need a MongoDB collection with documents containing embeddings. You can create this collection yourself by using an external embedding model and inserting the documents with their corresponding embeddings into a MongoDB collection. (Details on how to do this are in chapter 14.) Alternatively, for learning purposes, you can employ a ready-to-use collection with embeddings created during the loading of the sample data set in chapter 2. The ready-to-use documents, along with their embeddings, are located in the `sample_mflix` database within the `embedded_movies` collection, shown in the next listing. After logging into Atlas, use MongoDB Shell (`mongosh`) to switch to the `sample_mflix` database with the use command; then display a sample document using `findOne`.

Listing 12.2 Using `findOne` to find one document

```
use sample_mflix //
switched to db sample_mflix //
Atlas shard-0 [primary] sample_mflix> //
```
Command switches to the sample_mflix database.

Using embeddings with Atlas Vector Search 311

```
db.embedded_movies.findOne() //          ◄─────┐ Command finds one document.
{
  _id: ObjectId('573a1390f29313caabcd5293'), //  ◄──┐ Start of movie
  plot: "Young Pauline is left a lot of money when her    record found
⇒ wealthy uncle dies. However, her uncle's secretary has
⇒ been named as her guardian until she marries,
⇒ at which time she will officially take ...",
  genres: [ 'Action' ],
  runtime: 199,
  cast: [ 'Pearl White', 'Crane Wilbur', 'Paul Panzer', 'Edward Josè' ],
  num_mflix_comments: 0,
  poster: 'https://m.media-amazon.com/images/M/
⇒ MV5BMzgxODk1Mzk2Ml5BMl5BanBnXkFtZTgwMDg0NzkwMjE@
⇒ ._V1_SY1000_SX677_AL_.jpg',
  title: 'The Perils of Pauline',
  fullplot: `Young Pauline is left a lot of money when her
⇒   wealthy uncle dies. However, her uncle's secretary has
⇒   been named as her guardian until she marries, at which
⇒   time she will officially take possession of her inheritance.
⇒   Meanwhile, her "guardian" and his confederates constantly
⇒   come up with schemes to get rid of
⇒ Pauline so that he can get
⇒ his hands on the money himself.`,
  languages: [ 'English' ],
  released: ISODate('1914-03-23T00:00:00.000Z'),
  directors: [ 'Louis J. Gasnier', 'Donald MacKenzie' ],
  writers: [
    'Charles W. Goddard (screenplay)',
    'Basil Dickey (screenplay)',
    'Charles W. Goddard (novel)',
    'George B. Seitz',
    'Bertram Millhauser'
  ],
  awards: { wins: 1, nominations: 0, text: '1 win.' },
  lastupdated: '2015-09-12 00:01:18.647000000',
  year: 1914,
  imdb: { rating: 7.6, votes: 744, id: 4465 },
  countries: [ 'USA' ],
  type: 'movie',
  tomatoes: {
    viewer: { rating: 2.8, numReviews: 9 },                ┌ Dense vector
    production: 'Pathè Frères',                            │ representation of the
    lastUpdated: ISODate('2015-09-11T17:46:19.000Z')       │ movie plot; the data
  },                                                       │ and embedding are
  plot_embedding: [ //          ◄────────────────────────  │ stored together
    0.00072939653,   -0.026834568,    0.013515796,  -0.033257525,
   -0.001295428,      0.022092875,   -0.015958885,   0.018283758,
   -0.030315313,     -0.019479034,    0.019400224,   0.0106917955,
   -0.005001107,      0.017981656,    0.0036416466, -0.012918158,
    0.029816188,     -0.00018706948,  0.013193991,  -0.024483424,
   -0.016011424,      0.0019275442,  -0.007467182,  -0.011768856,
    0.012859052,     -0.011722884,   -0.002154121,  -0.022539461,
    0.0010910163,    -0.017351182,   -0.005122605,  -0.010035052,
    0.0073161307,    -0.04103338,    -0.021068355,   0.009877433,
    0.023918625,     -0.0037828467,   0.0067776004,  0.02159375,
    0.018993042,      0.0034905956,   0.0053557493,  0.001825749,
```

```
         -0.026493061,    0.021580614,    0.0004851698,    -0.02837135,
          -0.00970668,    0.009279796,    0.021751368,     0.007834959,
        -0.0130495075,   -0.02049042,    -0.0009054861,   -0.0011345256,
        0.00089563493,    0.02842389,    -0.012957564,     0.014133136,
          0.035831966,   -0.015538569,   -0.0022296465,   -0.0038419536,
          0.005523219,   -0.009240391,   -0.012215442,     0.011447052,
         -0.032574512,    0.017232968,    0.03985124,      0.009719814,
           0.01255695,    0.0013964024,   0.014592856,    -0.020319667,
         -0.022119146,    0.013922977,   -0.021948392,     0.0051423074,
          0.024930011,   -0.037014104,    0.0042688376,    0.0041407724,
          0.009752652,    0.0025235396,   -0.02721548,     0.004038977,
          -0.02274962,   -0.0015835745,   0.035884503,     0.029317062,
         -0.012727703,    0.0074080746,  -0.0012510978,    0.009844596,
         -0.003332977,    0.023432633,    0.00880694,     -0.0066364002,
    ... 1436 more items
  ]
}
```

The document is a movie record from the `embedded_movies` collection in the `sample_mflix` database. It includes fields such as `_id`, which is a unique identifier for the document, and `plot`, which provides a summary of the movie's storyline. The document includes other fields, such as `genres`, `runtime`, `cast`, `num_mflix_comments`, `poster`, `title`, `fullplot`, `languages`, `released`, `directors`, `writers`, `awards`, `lastupdated`, `year`, `imdb`, `countries`, `type`, and `tomatoes`. It's important to notice that it includes a `plot_embedding` field, which is a dense vector representation of the plot. The data and embedding are stored together in the document, designed for use in vector search operations to efficiently retrieve similar documents based on their plot content.

12.2.3 Defining your Vector Search index

Next, you define your Atlas Vector Search index. You can use the Atlas UI for this purpose, but this book focuses on the Atlas command-line interface (CLI). Therefore, use the Atlas CLI to create the index, and place the index configuration in a file for use with the Atlas CLI.

Create the Vector Search index definition. In the definition, specify the name of the database and collection that are the sources for the index, the path in the document where the embedding is located, and `numDimensions` and `similarity`.

Similarity refers to the metric used to measure how close or similar two vectors are. This metric determines how the system calculates the similarity between the vector embeddings of different documents. Common similarity metrics include cosine similarity, Euclidean distance, and dot product, which help efficiently retrieve documents that are most similar to the query vector based on their embeddings:

- *Cosine similarity*—Calculates the cosine of the angle between two vectors, indicating how aligned they are. This metric is ideal for text analysis and NLP tasks, such as identifying similar sentences or documents.
- *Euclidean distance*—Measures the straight-line distance between two points in the vector space. This metric is commonly used in image recognition and clustering tasks in which the spatial distance between data points is significant.

- *Dot product*—Calculates the sum of the products of corresponding elements of the two vectors. This metric is often used in recommendation systems to find items that have a high degree of similarity based on user preferences or behavior.

Create a file named `vector-definition.json`, and place the following content inside it:

```
{
  "name": "MongoDB-in-Action-VectorSearchIndex",
  "type": "vectorSearch",
  "collectionName": "embedded_movies",
  "database": "sample_mflix",
  "fields": [
    {
      "type": "vector",
      "path": "plot_embedding",
      "numDimensions": 1536,
      "similarity": "cosine"
    },
    {
      "type": "filter",
      "path": "genres"
    },
    {
      "type": "filter",
      "path": "languages"
    },
    {
      "type": "filter",
      "path": "year"
    }
  ]
}
```

The `vector-definition.json` file defines a vector search index for MongoDB Atlas. It specifies the index name as `"MongoDB-in-Action-VectorSearchIndex"` and sets the index type to `vectorSearch`. The index targets the `embedded_movies` collection within the `sample_mflix` database. The index configuration includes a field of type `"vector"` located at the `plot_embedding` path (a path to the embedding in the MongoDB document from the `embedded_movies` collection), with 1,536 dimensions. This means that each plot embedding is represented by a vector with 1,536 numerical values, capturing various aspects of the plot's content. The index uses cosine similarity to measure the similarity between vectors. The index definition includes several filter fields:

- `genres`—Filters the results based on movie genres
- `languages`—Filters the results based on the languages of the movies
- `year`—Filters the results based on the release year of the movies

These filters refine the search results by applying criteria beyond the vector similarity.

12.2.4 Creating an Atlas Vector Search index

For this task, you'll use an M0 cluster, which supports vector search and which you created in chapter 11. Use the `atlas cluster list` command to display its details:

```
atlas cluster list
ID                          NAME                MDB VER    STATE
6658a85ba9e6a9047d15cf98    MongoDB-in-Action   8.0.4      IDLE
```

Next, as you did when creating a full-text search index, use the Atlas CLI command `atlas cluster search index` to build the Atlas Vector Search index:

```
atlas cluster search index create \
--clusterName MongoDB-in-Action \
--file vector-definition.json
```

This command initiates the creation of the vector search index. You can check the status using the `atlas clusters search indexes list` command:

```
atlas clusters search indexes list \
--clusterName MongoDB-in-Action \
--db sample_mflix --collection embedded_movies
```

The vector search index has been created and is ready to use:

```
ID                       NAME                 DATABASE       COLLECTION       TYPE
66ade3f42fbc060637eb60f4 MongoDB-in-ActionVectorSearchIndex
  sample_mflix           embedded_movies      vectorSearch
```

The vector search index is also visible in the Atlas Search section of the Atlas UI, as shown in figure 12.3.

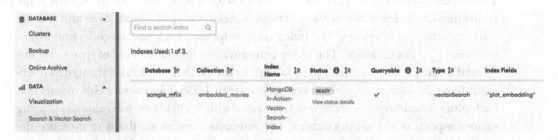

Figure 12.3 Atlas Vector Search index panel. On the left side of the screen is a collapsible navigation menu. To view vector search indexes, click the Search & Vector Search option in the Data section. The main panel displays existing search index configurations. In this case, the `sample_mflix` database and the `embedded_movies` collection are shown with an active vector search index named `"MongoDB-In-Action-Vector-Search-Index"`. The index is marked as Ready and is fully queryable, as indicated by the check. The Type is listed as vectorSearch, and Index Fields includes `"plot_embedding"`, which indicates the field being used for vector similarity searches. (Image © MongoDB 2025)

12.3 Running Atlas Vector Search queries

The $vectorSearch stage of MongoDB's aggregation pipeline is designed to perform vector-based search operations on your data. It uses vector embeddings to find and retrieve documents that are semantically similar to a given query vector.

To use the $vectorSearch stage, you need a vector search index created on the relevant fields in your collection. The pipeline stage typically includes parameters such as the index name, the query vector, the path to the vector field in the documents, and the similarity metric to use. The following listing shows the $vectorSearch aggregation pipeline stage prototype.

> Listing 12.3 The $vectorSearch aggregation pipeline stage

```
{
  "$vectorSearch": {
    "exact": true | false,
    "filter": {<filter-specification>},
    "index": "<index-name>",
    "limit": <number-of-results>,
    "numCandidates": <number-of-candidates>,
    "path": "<field-to-search>",
    "queryVector": [<array-of-numbers>]
  }
}
```

This prototype includes several key parameters:

- exact—A Boolean value (true or false) that specifies whether to perform an exact search (ENN) or an approximate one (ANN). Exact searches are more precise but can be slower, whereas approximate searches are faster but may return less precise results. The default is ANN.
- filter—An optional filter specification that allows you to restrict the search to documents that match certain criteria. This parameter is useful for narrowing the search results to a more relevant subset of documents.
- index—The name of the vector search index to use. This index must be created beforehand on the field containing the vector embeddings.
- limit—The maximum number of search results to return. This parameter controls the number of documents retrieved, which can be useful for paginating or limiting the scope of the results.
- numCandidates—The number of candidate vectors to consider during the search. This parameter can affect the performance and accuracy of the search because a higher number may increase processing time as well as precision.
- path—The field in the documents where the vector embeddings are stored. This parameter specifies which field the search should be conducted on.

- `queryVector`—An array of numbers representing the query vector. This vector finds similar documents based on the similarity metric defined in the vector search index.

12.3.1 Querying with embeddings

To execute a query using the `$vectorSearch` aggregation pipeline stage, you must have the embedding of your query ready because Vector Search relies on the mathematical representation of the query to find semantically similar documents. It cannot use text alone because text needs to be transformed into a numerical format that captures its meaning. Atlas Vector Search operates as a vector database, which stores these embeddings, and queries must compare the embeddings from the query with those stored in the database.

> **NOTE** When I wrote this book, MongoDB Atlas did not offer models that enabled text-to-embedding conversion. You may need to use external systems for this purpose, such as OpenAI, Hugging Face, Google's TensorFlow, and LLaMA.

> **TIP** You need to embed your query using the same model that you used to embed your data. If you used OpenAI's GPT-4o model to embed your data set, for example, you must use the same GPT-4o model to embed your query. This ensures that the embeddings are compatible and the vector search can accurately retrieve similar documents.

In chapter 14, I demonstrate a quick, efficient way to generate embeddings for queries using an external framework called LangChain. In this chapter, I don't include a working example of a query with embeddings because it would span several pages of the book. For now, it is important to understand that an embedding is required for the query to function properly. The general outline of a query designed to search the `"MongoDB-in-Action-VectorSearchIndex"` index looks like this example:

```
db.embedded_movies.aggregate([
  {
    "$vectorSearch": {
      "index": "MongoDB-in-Action-VectorSearchIndex", // The name of the vector search index
      "path": "plot_embedding", // The field in the documents where the embeddings are stored
      "queryVector": [<array-of-numbers>], // The embedding array representing your query; must be created outside Atlas
      "numCandidates": <number-of-candidates>, // The number of candidate vectors to consider
      "exact": false, // ANN
      "limit": <number-of-results> // Maximum number of results to return
    }
  }
])
```

Pay attention to the following:

- Ensure that the correct name of the vector search index is used (`index`).

- Specify the correct field in the documents where the embeddings are stored (path).
- Provide the embedding array representing your query (queryVector).
- Set the number of candidate vectors to consider for the search (numCandidates).
- Define the maximum number of results to return (limit).

Listing 12.4 shows an example of the aggregation pipeline with the $vectorSearch stage, along with a portion of the embedding for the search phrase "village life," which will be searched for in the plot_embedding field. The full embedding definition for "village life" has already been created but has been shortened here due to its length, which could span several pages. This embedding replaces the text phrase "village life," is placed in queryVector, and is used to search for documents with similar vector embeddings within the plot_embedding field. If you run the query without the complete embedding definition, it will not work.

Listing 12.4 Atlas Vector Search $vectorSearch stage with embedding

```
db.embedded_movies.aggregate([
  {
    // The $vectorSearch stage performs a search based on vector similarity
    "$vectorSearch": {
      "index": " MongoDB-in-ActionVectorSearchIndex",   // Name of the vector search index
      "path": "plot_embedding",   // Field in the documents where the embeddings are stored
      "queryVector": [-0.0016261312,-0.028070757,
       0.012775794,-0.0027440966,0.008683807,-0.02575152,
0.010283281,-0.0041719596,0.021392956,0.028657231,
0.006634482,0.007490867,0.01859878,0.0038187427,
0.01451522,0.01661379,0.000528442,0.00843722,0.01627464,
0.024311995,-0.025911469, 0.008863748,0.008823762,
-0.034921836,0.007910728,-0.01515501,0.035801545,
-0.0035688248,-0.020299982,0.032256044,-0.028763862,-0.0071576433,
-0.012769129,0.012322609,-0.006621153,0.010583182,0.024085402,
-0.001623632,0.007864078,-0.021406285,0.002554159,
0.012229307,0.011762793,0.0051682983,0.0048484034,0.01808737,
0.024325324,-0.037694257,0.026537929,0.008803768,0.017767,
0.012642504,0.005218282,0.00584807,0.020153364,0.0032805866,
0.004248601,0.0051449724,0.006791097,0.007650814,
0.003458861,-0.0031223053,-0.01932697, 0.012769129,
-0.033615597,0.00745088,0.006321252,0.0038154104,
0.014555207,0.027697546,0.02828402,0.0066711367,0.0077,
0.01794076,0.011349596,-0.0052715978,0.014755142,-0.01975,
-0.011156326,0.011202978,0.0222,0.00846388,0.030549942,
0.0041386373,0.018847128,0.00033655585,0.024925126,
0.003555496,0.019300312,0.010749794,0.0075308536,
0.016567878,-0.012869096,-0.015528221,0.0078107617,
0.011156326,0.013522214,0.020646535,0.01211601,0.055928253,
0.011596181,-0.017247654,0.0005939711,-0.026977783,
0.003942035,0.009583511,0.0055248477,0.028737204,0.023179034,
0.003995351,0.0219661,0.008470545,0.023392297,0.010469886,
0.015874773,0.007890735,0.009690142,0.00024970944,0.012775794,
```

```
            0.03686786,0.00671778,0.027484283,0.011556195,0.036068123,
            0.013915418,0.0016327957,0.0151016945,7438237429348,
            0.004671795,0.012555866,0.0209531,0.01982014,0.02448,
            0.0105431955,0.005178295,0.033162415,0.013795458,0.007150979,
            0.010243294,0.0045618312,0.0024725192,0.004305249,0.008197301,
            0.0014203656,0.0018460588,0.005015015,0.011142998,0.01439526,
            0.022965772,0.02552493,0.007757446,0.0019726837,0.009503538,
            0.032042783,0.008403899,0.04609149,0.013808787,0.011749465,
            0.036388017,0.016314628,0.021939443,-0.0250051,-0.017354285,
            -0.012962398,0.00006107364,0.019113706,0.03081652,-0.018114036,
            0.0084572155,0.009643491,0.0034721901,0.0072642746,0.0090636825,
            0.01642126,0.013428912,0.027724205,0.0071243206,
            0.6858542,0.031029783,0.014595194,0.011449563,0.017514233,
            0.01743426,0.009950057,0.0029706885,-0.015714826,
            -0.001806072,0.011856096,0.026444625,-0.0010663156,
            -0.006474535,0.0016161345,-0.020313311,0.0148351155,
            0.001839943,0.005737785,0.01830641,0.018647194,0.03345565,
            0.008070676,0.007143142,0.01430958,0.0044818576,0.003838736,
            0.007350913,0.018620536,0.017247654,0.007037683,0.010236629,
            0.012122675,0.037694257,0.0055081863,0.042492677,0.00021784494,
            010276617,0.022325981,0.005984696,0.009496873,0.013382261,
            0.0010563189,0.0026507939,0.041639622,0.008637156,0.026471283,
            0.00803899,0.024858482,0.006686375,0.0016252982,0.027590916,
            0.015381602,0.0043718936,0.002159289,0.0359077,0.008243952,
            0.0119360695,0.027590916,0.046971202,0.0015194997,0.022405956,
            0.0016677842,0.00018535563,0.015421589,0.031802863,
            0.03814744,0.0065411795,0.016567878,-0.015621523,         ◀── Query embedding
            0.022899127,-0.002679118,, ...],                              (extremely long)
          "numCandidates": 150,         ◀──────────────┐
          "exact": false,        ◀──┐                  │ Number of candidate
          "limit": 5                 │ ANN             │ vectors to consider
        }                            │
      },                             │ Maximum number
      {                              │ of results to return
        // The $project stage specifies which fields to include in the output
        "$project": {
          "_id": 0,          ◀───┐ Excludes the _id field   │ Includes the
          "plot": 1,         ◀───────────────────────────── │ plot field
          "title": 1,        ◀──────────────────────────────────── Includes the title field
          "score": { $meta: "vectorSearchScore" }  ◀──┐
        }                                             │ Includes the
      }                                               │ vector search score
    ])
```

The `$vectorSearch` stage finds the top five documents based on similarity to the given query vector. The `queryVector` is a very long array of numbers representing the embedding, and only part of it is shown here for brevity. The `numCandidates` parameter specifies how many candidate vectors to consider during the search.

The `exact` parameter is set to `false`, indicating the use of ANN for faster search results. This means that instead of finding the precise nearest neighbors, the search finds approximate neighbors that are close enough, which significantly speeds the search process while maintaining a high level of accuracy.

The `$project` stage includes the plot, title, and search score in the output while excluding the `_id` field. To obtain the score of your Atlas Vector Search query results, use `vectorSearchScore` within the `$meta` expression. The score field uses the `$meta` expression with the `vectorSearchScore` value. This setup ensures that the score of the documents returned from the vector search is included in the results. The score indicates the similarity between the query vector and the document's vector embedding.

A document returned by the `$vectorSearch` aggregation pipeline might look like this:

```
[
  {
    plot: 'A young woman moves to a small village
      and discovers the simple joys and hidden
      secrets of rural life.',
    title: 'Village Secrets',
    score: 0.9523144960403442
  },
  {
    plot: 'A documentary exploring the daily lives
      and traditions of villagers in a remote
      mountain community.',
    title: 'Mountain Village',
    score: 0.9487524032592773
  },
  {
    plot: 'An architect travels to a rural village
      to design a community center and finds
      himself enchanted by the local way of life.',
    title: 'Building Dreams',
    score: 0.9468201398849487
  },
  {
    plot: 'A retired couple moves to the countryside
      and becomes involved in village affairs,
      rediscovering their passion for life.',
    title: 'New Beginnings',
    score: 0.9453170895576477
  },
  {
    plot: 'A city boy spends a summer with his
      grandparents in their village, learning valuable
      lessons about family and nature.',
    title: 'Summer in the Village',
    score: 0.9438151121139526
  }
]
```

In this example, the `plot` provides a summary of the movie's storyline, which is closely related to village life. The `title` gives the name of the movie. The `score` indicates the similarity between the query vector for "village life" and the document's vector embedding. Higher scores reflect a closer match to the query, showcasing how vector search captures the semantic meaning and context of the query. (0 indicates low similarity, and 1 indicates high similarity.) The score assigned to a returned document is part of the document's metadata.

> **TIP** If you want to use ENN, change the value of "exact": false to "exact": true in the $vectorSearch stage definition. ENN ensures that the search retrieves the most precise matches for the query vector by exhaustively comparing the query vector against all stored vectors. This method guarantees highest accuracy in finding similar documents, but it can be more computationally intensive and slower than ANN, which uses heuristics to speed the search at the cost of some accuracy.

12.3.2 Using prefiltering with Atlas Vector Search

Prefiltering allows you to apply additional criteria to your search, narrowing the data set before the vector similarity search is performed. This can significantly reduce the search space and improve the performance of your queries.

The $vectorSearch filter option can match only Binary JSON (BSON) boolean, date, objectId, string, and numeric values. To filter your data, you must index the desired fields by specifying them as the filter type in your vectorSearch index definition.

Atlas Vector Search supports the $vectorSearch filter option for the following MongoDB Query API match expressions, though certain limitations apply:

- $gt (greater than)
- $lt (less than)
- $gte (greater than or equal to)
- $lte (less than or equal to)
- $eq (equal to)
- $ne (not equal to)
- $in (in a set)
- $nin (not in a set)
- $nor (none of the conditions is met)
- $and (all conditions must be met)
- $or (any of the conditions must be met)

The $vectorSearch filter option supports only the following operators in aggregation pipelines:

- $and (all conditions must be met)
- or (any of the conditions must be met)

Also, the $vectorSearch filter option on fields with the objectId type does not support the following MQL match expressions:

- $gt (greater than)

- `$lt` (less than)
- `$gte` (greater than or equal to)
- `$lte` (less than or equal to)

`$vectorSearch` can't be used in view definitions and the following pipeline stages:

- `$lookup` subpipeline
- `$unionWith` subpipeline
- `$facet` pipeline stage

For more information, see the MongoDB documentation at https://mng.bz/26rX.

Listing 12.5 demonstrates prefiltering using `$vectorSearch` stage with filters, which are the classic filters known from the MongoDB query language. Note that `queryVector` has been shortened due to its length, which would otherwise span several pages. If you run the query without the complete embedding definition, it will not work.

Listing 12.5 Prefiltering data with the `$vectorSearch` pipeline stage

Name of the vector search index

```
db.embedded_movies.aggregate([
  {
    // The $vectorSearch stage performs a search based on vector similarity
    "$vectorSearch": {
      "index": "MongoDB-in-ActionVectorSearchIndex",
      //
      "path": "plot_embedding", //
      "queryVector": [
      -0.0016261312, -0.028070757, -0.011342932, -0.012775794,
      -0.0027440966,0.008683807, -0.02575152, -0.02020668, 0.010283281,
      -0.0041719596,0.021392956, 0.028657231, -0.006634482,
      0.01853878, 0.0038187427,0.02959257, 0.01451522, 0.016061379,
      0.000028442, 0.008943722, 0.01627464, 0.024311995,
      -0.025911469, 0.00022596726,-0.008863748, 0.008823762,
      -0.034921836, 0.007910728,0.01515501,0.019300312,0.010749794,
      0.0075308536,0.018287312,0.016567878,0.012869096,0.015528221,
      0.0078107617,0.003415542,0.025911469,0.00022596726,
      0.0088637480.011156326,0.013522214,0.020646530.0121601,
      0.011596181,0.017247654,0.0005939711,-0.026977783,-0.003942035,
      0.007890735,0.009690142,0.02020668,0.0012962399,0.025911469,
      0.00022596726,0.0088637480.003415542,0.00024970944,0.012775794,
      0.0114762215,0.013422247,0.010429899,0.03686786,0.006717788,
      0.027484283,0.011556195,0.036068123,0.013915418,0.02020668,
      0.001292399,0.02020668,0.001292399,0.003415542,0.003415542,
      0.0016327957,0.0151016945,0.020473259,0.004671795,0.012555866,
      0.0209531,0.01982014,0.024485271,0.0105431955,0.005178295,
      0.033162415,0.013795458,0.007150979,0.010243294,0.005644808,
      0.0045618312,0.0024725192,0.004305249,0.008197301,0.0014203656,
      0.0018460588,0.005015015, 0.02020668,-0.0012962399,-0.003415542
      ], // The shortened query embedding
      "filter": {
        "$or": [
```

Field in the documents where the embeddings are stored

```
            { genres: "Action" },//          ◄──┐  Matches documents with
            { runtime: { "$lt": 120 } } //   ◄─┐ └─ the genre "Action"
          ]                                    │
        },                                     └── Matches documents with
        "numCandidates": 150,//                    runtime less than 120 minutes
        "exact": false, //    ◄────┐ ANN ┌── Number of candidate
        "limit": 5 //         ◄────┘     │   vectors to consider
      }                                  └── 
    },                               Maximum number
    {                                of results to return
      // The $project stage specifies which fields to include in the output
      "$project": {
        "_id": 0, //       ◄────── Excludes the _id field
        "plot": 1, //      ◄────── Includes the plot field
        "title": 1, //                                      ◄──┐ Includes the
        "score": { $meta: "vectorSearchScore" } //  ◄──┐       └─ title field
      }                                                │
    }                                                  └── Includes the
])                                                        vector search score
```

In this query, the filter option in the `$vectorSearch` stage uses `$or` to match documents that have the genre `"Action"` or a `runtime` of less than 120 minutes. The `queryVector` contains a shortened version of the query embedding.

The `numCandidates` and `limit` parameters control the number of candidates considered and the number of results returned, respectively. The `$project` stage specifies the fields to include in the output: `plot`, `title`, and `score`.

12.4 Executing vector search with programming languages

`mongosh` is not the only way to perform vector searches on your data, of course. You can also execute vector search queries using various programming languages. Many MongoDB drivers for languages such as Python, JavaScript, Ruby, and others support the `$vectorSearch` filter option, enabling you to integrate vector search capabilities directly into your applications.

12.4.1 Using vector search with JavaScript

To use vector search in JavaScript, you need a MongoDB library such as `mongodb` for Node.js. Here's an example:

```
const { MongoClient } = require('mongodb');

async function vectorSearch() {
  // MongoDB connection string
  const uri = 'your_mongodb_connection_string';
  // Create a new MongoClient
  const client = new MongoClient(uri,
   { useNewUrlParser: true, useUnifiedTopology: true });

  try {
```

Executing vector search with programming languages

```
    // Connect to the MongoDB server
    await client.connect();
    // Select the database and collection
    const database = client.db('your_database_name');
    const collection = database.collection('your_collection_name');

    // Define the vector search query
    const query = {
      $vectorSearch: {
        queryVector: [/* your query vector here */],
        numResults: 10,
        path: 'your_vector_field_name'
      }
    };

    try {
      // Execute the vector search query        const results = await
collection.find(query).toArray();
      // Log the results to the console
      console.log(results);
    } catch (queryError) {
      // Handle errors that occur during the query execution
      console.error('Error executing vector search query:', queryError);
    }
  } catch (connectionError) {
    // Handle errors that occur while connecting to MongoDB
    console.error('Error connecting to MongoDB:', connectionError);
  } finally {
    try {
      // Ensure the MongoDB client is closed
      await client.close();
    } catch (closeError) {
      // Handle errors that occur while closing the MongoDB connection
      console.error('Error closing MongoDB connection:', closeError);
    }
  }
}

// Call the vectorSearch function and handle any unhandled errors
vectorSearch().catch(console.error);
```

In this example, the `$vectorSearch` operator is part of the MongoDB library for Node.js. It allows you to perform vector-based similarity searches within your database by specifying a query vector, the number of desired results, and the path to the vector field in your documents. This operator is essential for tasks that involve finding similar items based on their vector representations, such as in machine learning and recommendation systems.

12.4.2 Using vector search and prefiltering with Python

To use vector search in Python, you can use the `pymongo` library. Here's an example that performs a vector search with prefilters:

```python
from pymongo import MongoClient

def vector_search():
    # MongoDB connection string
    uri = 'your_mongodb_connection_string'
    # Create a new MongoClient
    client = MongoClient(uri)

    try:
        # Connect to the MongoDB server
        client = MongoClient(uri)
        # Select the database and collection
        database = client['your_database_name']
        collection = database['your_collection_name']

        # Define the pre-filters and vector search query
        query = {
            "$and": [
                {"category": "electronics"},  # Example pre-filter
                {"price": {"$lt": 500}},  # Another example pre-filter
                {
                    "$vectorSearch": {
                        "queryVector": [/* your query vector here */],
                        "numResults": 10,
                        "path": "your_vector_field_name"
                    }
                }
            ]
        }

        try:
            # Execute the vector search query
            # and convert the results to a list
            results = list(collection.find(query))
            # Print the results
            for result in results:
                print(result)
        except Exception as query_error:
            # Handle errors that occur during the query execution
            print('Error executing vector search query:', query_error)
    except Exception as connection_error:
        # Handle errors that occur while connecting to MongoDB
        print('Error connecting to MongoDB:', connection_error)
    finally:
        try:
            # Ensure the MongoDB client is closed
            client.close()
        except Exception as close_error:
            # Handle errors that occur while closing the MongoDB connection
            print('Error closing MongoDB connection:', close_error)

# Call the vector_search function
vector_search()
```

The code connects to a MongoDB instance and selects the appropriate database and collection. The query is constructed with a combination of prefilters and the $vectorSearch operator. Prefilters are applied to narrow the search to specific categories and price ranges before performing the vector search. The $vectorSearch operator specifies the query vector, the number of desired results, and the path to the vector field in the documents. Then the query is executed, and the results are converted to a list and printed. Error handling is included to manage any problems that arise during the connection, query execution, and connection closure processes. This approach allows for efficient similarity searches in MongoDB with additional filtering criteria applied before the vector search.

12.4.3 Using vector search with prefilters in Ruby

To perform a vector search in Ruby, you can use the mongo gem. Here's an example that performs a vector search with prefilters:

```ruby
require 'mongo'

def vector_search
  # MongoDB connection string
  uri = 'your_mongodb_connection_string'
  # Create a new MongoClient
  client = Mongo::Client.new(uri)

  begin
    # Select the database and collection
    database = client.database
    collection = database['your_collection_name']

    # Define the pre-filters and vector search query
    query = {
      "$and" => [
        {"category" => "electronics"},  # Example pre-filter
        {"price" => {"$lt" => 500}},  # Another example pre-filter
        {
          "$vectorSearch" => {
            "queryVector" => [/* your query vector here */],
              # Replace with your query vector
            "numResults" => 10,  # Number of results to retrieve
            "path" => 'your_vector_field_name'
              # Field containing the vectors in your documents
          }
        }
      ]
    }

    begin
      # Execute the vector search query and convert the results to an array
      results = collection.find(query).to_a
      # Print the results
      results.each { |result| puts result }
    rescue => query_error
```

```
      # Handle errors that occur during the query execution
      puts "Error executing vector search query: #{query_error}"
    end
  rescue => connection_error
    # Handle errors that occur while connecting to MongoDB
    puts "Error connecting to MongoDB: #{connection_error}"
  ensure
    # Ensure the MongoDB client is closed
    client.close
  end
end

# Call the vector_search function
vector_search
```

The code connects to the MongoDB server using the provided connection string and selects the appropriate database and collection. The query is constructed with a combination of prefilters and the $vectorSearch operator. Prefilters are applied to narrow the search to specific categories and price ranges before performing the vector search. The $vectorSearch operator specifies the query vector, the number of desired results, and the path to the vector field in the documents. Then the query is executed, and the results are converted to an array and printed. Error handling is included to manage any problems that arise during the connection, query execution, and connection closure processes.

12.5 Using Atlas Triggers for automated embeddings creation

Atlas Triggers is a feature in MongoDB Atlas that allows you to execute server-side logic in response to database events or on a scheduled basis. These triggers enable you to automate workflows, enforce business logic, and respond to changes in your data in real time without managing a separate application server.

You can find more information about Atlas Triggers in chapter 19. For now, it is important to know that you can use this feature to create embeddings automatically by using an external model, such as the OpenAI embeddings API, for documents newly added to a MongoDB collection. It is also important to understand that Atlas Triggers are not available in the core MongoDB server; they are available exclusively in the Atlas developer data platform. To create your first Atlas Trigger, use the Atlas UI as shown in figure 12.4.

The following steps guide you through the process of creating a trigger in your MongoDB Atlas cluster. Triggers allow you to run functions automatically in response to specific database events:

1 In your "MongoDB-in-Action" cluster, go to the Triggers tab located in the Services section in the left panel.
2 Click the Get Started button.
3 Enter a name for your new Atlas Trigger. I used the name "MongoDB-in-Action-Trigger".

Using Atlas Triggers for automated embeddings creation 327

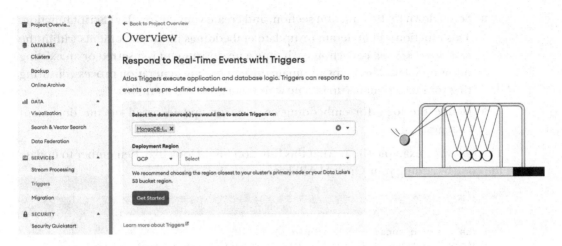

Figure 12.4 Creating an Atlas Trigger within a data platform (Image © MongoDB 2025)

4 Provide the cluster name. I used the cluster name M0, as shown in figure 12.5, where I previously configured the vector search index `"MongoDB-in-Action"`.

5 For the Database Name, enter `sample_mflix`, and for the collection, enter `embedded_movies`.

6 Select the operations that will activate the trigger: Insert Document, Update Document, and Replace Document.

7 Check the Full Document option.

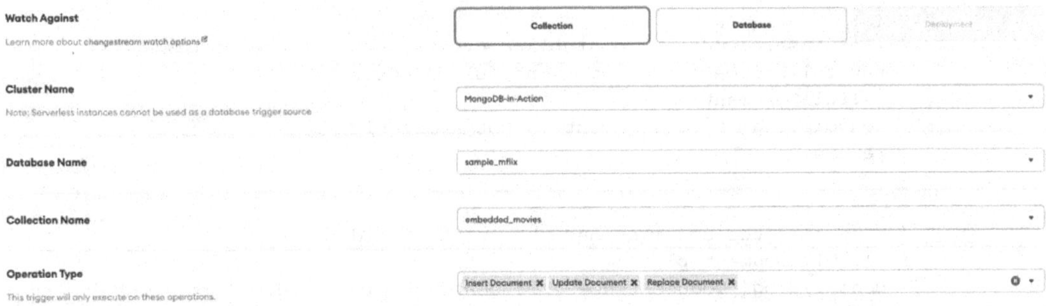

Figure 12.5 The configuration screen for setting up an Atlas Trigger in the MongoDB Atlas UI. The Watch Against section allows you to specify whether the trigger will monitor collections, databases, or deployments, with Collection selected in this example. The Cluster Name field is set to `"MongoDB-in-Action"`, indicating the cluster where the trigger will be applied. The Database Name field is set to `"sample_mflix"`, specifying the database that the trigger will monitor. The Collection Name field is set to `"embedded_movies"`, indicating the collection within the database to watch for changes. In the Operation Type section, the trigger is configured to activate on Insert, Update, and Replace Document operations. The Full Document option is enabled, meaning that the entire document will be retrieved when a change event occurs. (Image © MongoDB 2025)

328   CHAPTER 12   *Learning semantic techniques and Atlas Vector Search*

8   Scroll down to the Function section, and create your custom JavaScript function. This function will generate or update embeddings in the documents within the `embedded_movies` collection each time a new document is inserted or an existing one is updated. This helps automate the embedding generation process, ensuring that your data remains up to date without manual intervention.

9   Define the logic for embedding creation or update based on the document changes.

The following example shows what this function might look like. Remember to update the code by adding your OpenAI API key.

Listing 12.6   Atlas Trigger function for generating automated embeddings

```
exports = async function(changeEvent) {
  console.log("Change Event: ", JSON.stringify(changeEvent));

  // Check if documentKey is available
  if (!changeEvent.documentKey || !changeEvent.documentKey._id) {
    console.log("documentKey or _id is not available.");
    return;
  }

  // Access the _id of the changed document:
  const docId = changeEvent.documentKey._id;

  // Get the MongoDB service you want to use
  const serviceName = "MongoDB-in-Action";
  const database = "sample_mflix";
  const collection = context.services.get(serviceName)
    .db(database).collection(changeEvent.ns.coll);

  try {
    // For insert, update, or replace events, process the document
    const fullDocument = changeEvent.fullDocument;
    if (!fullDocument) {
      console.log("Full document is not available.");
      return;
    }

    // Check if the document has the 'plot' field
    if (!fullDocument.plot) {
      console.log("Document does not contain 'plot' field.");
      return;
    }

    const url = 'https://api.openai.com/v1/embeddings';

    // Add your OpenAI API key here
    const openai_key = "<Your OpenAI API key>";

    // HTTP call to OpenAI API to get embedding for the plot
    let response = await context.http.post({
```

```
        url: url,
        headers: {
          'Authorization': [`Bearer ${openai_key}`],
          'Content-Type': ['application/json']
        },
        body: JSON.stringify({
          input: fullDocument.plot,
          model: "text-embedding-3-small"
        })
      });

      // Parse the JSON response from the API
      let responseData = EJSON.parse(response.body.text());

      if (response.statusCode === 200) {
        console.log("Successfully received embedding.");
        const responseEmbedding = responseData.data[0].embedding;

        // Update the document in MongoDB with the new embedding
        const result = await collection.updateOne(
          { _id: docId },
          { $set: { plot_embedding: responseEmbedding }}
        );

        if (result.modifiedCount === 1) {
          console.log("Document successfully updated.");
        } else {
          console.log("Failed to modify document.");
        }
      } else {
        console.log(`Failed embedding with code:
 ➥${response.statusCode}, response: ${response.body.text()}`);
      }

    } catch (err) {
      console.log("Error performing MongoDB write
 ➥or API call: ", err.message);
    }
};
```

This function handles change events in a MongoDB collection. It logs the change event and checks whether the `documentKey` and `_id` are present. It accesses the `_id` of the changed document and retrieves the relevant MongoDB service, database, and collection.

For insert, update, or replace operations, the function processes the full document and ensures that the document contains a `plot` field. If the `plot` field is present, the function makes an HTTP POST request to the OpenAI API to generate an embedding for the plot, using the specified model.

Upon successfully receiving the embedding from the API, the function updates the document in MongoDB with the new embedding. The function includes comprehensive error handling for both the API call and MongoDB operations, logging any problems that occur.

After copying this function and pasting it into the Atlas UI Triggers section below Function, click the Save button. Your trigger is ready to use. You can log in to `mongosh` to test its functionality:

```
use sample_mflix
db.embedded_movies.insertOne({plot:"The text will be
 converted into an embedding using Atlas Triggers
 and the OpenAI Embedding API"})
{
  acknowledged: true,
  insertedId: ObjectId('66af497f4873bfed1b091550')
}
```

This command inserts a document into the `embedded_movies` collection. The document contains the `plot` field with the text "The text will be converted into an embedding using Atlas Triggers and the OpenAI Embedding API". Via Atlas Triggers, this document is sent to the OpenAI Embedding API, which generates an embedding from the `plot` field. Then the embedding is added to this document in the `plot_embedding` field, using the `$set` operator as declared in the function. Using `find`, display this document now:

```
use sample_mflix
db.embedded_movies.find({ _id: ObjectId('66af497f4873bfed1b091550') })
[
  {
    _id: ObjectId('66af497f4873bfed1b091550'),
    plot: 'The text will be converted into an
      embedding using Atlas Triggers and
      the OpenAI Embedding API',
    plot_embedding: [
      -0.026205065,  0.012598104,  0.022182247, -0.04040473,  -0.026734715,
       0.0091301575, 0.018272925,  0.029786507, -0.031879887,  0.022875836,
      -0.010574084, -0.013102532, -0.0019262866,-0.000014433357,
      -0.024414344,  0.048299037, -0.0062423036, 0.010593,     0.009754388,
      -0.029408187, -0.033115737,  0.001923134, -0.011255062, 0.00028216472,
       0.019748379,  0.003698092,  0.068753615,  0.005387928,  0.029130751,
       0.017453229, -0.011368559,  0.0045524677, 0.008770752,  0.014161833,
      -0.026205065,  0.012598104,  0.022182247, -0.04040473,  -0.026734715,
      -0.021602154,  0.0091301575, 0.018272925,  0.029786507, -0.031879887,
       0.022875836, -0.00068452535,-0.010574084,-0.013102532, 0.0019262866,
      -0.000014433357,0.023052385, 0.0063211205,-0.034275923,
      -0.023518983, -0.018474696,  0.03215732,   0.020164533, -0.013165586,
      -0.008587897, -0.012081064,  0.025486253,  0.029811729,  0.0029051933,
       0.015687728, -0.03641974,  -0.0031873581,-0.008291544,  0.00013743708,
       0.07561384,   0.04171464,   0.025183598,  0.017390175,  0.027340028,
       0.020063646,  0.005096065,  0.0018269772, 0.0036823286, 0.02582711,
       0.02102206,  -0.012320668,  0.033872377,  0.004316017,  0.04746673,
       0.0229515,    0.063709326,  0.028727207, 0.024830496,  0.036495406,
       0.0048898044, 0.016204769,  0.018260315,  0.008140217,  0.027062593,
       0.017743275,  0.066483684,  0.040757827,  0.008014109, -0.008133911,
       0.024061244,  0.0367224,    0.0144771,    0.0117279645, 0.007534902,
       0.0011042256, 0.019042179,  0.06537394,   0.019748379,  0.030618815,
```

```
            0.0005710289, 0.0043317806, 0.017137961, 0.031274572, 0.046407428,
            0.03266175, 0.00415502, 0.006513434, 0.0133295255, 0.030755,
            0.021665208, 0.00158621, 0.02082029, 0.012062148, 0.03515867,
            0.014174443, 0.054074742, 0.02272507, 0.054579172, 0.04232156,
            0.0035499162, 0.01230057, 0.0013595927, 0.06476863, 0.0724037,
            0.05996115, 0.042119786, 0.017881993, 0.005952257, 0.00128956,
            0.0020397832,0.020971619,0.045121137,0.058009285,
        -0.04711363, 0.028903758, 0.01675964, -0.051249944,
            "The array plot_embedding has been shortened due to its length."
        ]
    }
]
```

Using Atlas Triggers, you can automate the process of generating embeddings for newly added documents in your MongoDB collection. When a document is inserted or updated, Atlas Triggers can send the relevant data to an external API, such as the OpenAI Embedding API, to generate embeddings. Then these embeddings are added back to the document in the specified field, streamlining the workflow and ensuring that your data is enriched with embeddings without manual intervention.

12.6 Workload isolation with vector search dedicated nodes

As in Atlas full-text search, you can enhance query performance by using dedicated search nodes for Atlas Vector Search. The `mongod` process and `mongot` will run on separate machines, so the MongoDB database will be separated from Apache Lucene. When Atlas Vector Search operates on these nodes, it parallelizes query execution across different segments of data, which improves response times, especially for large data sets. This intraquery parallelism uses more resources but significantly reduces latency for individual queries.

Search nodes offer workload isolation, ensuring that search operations do not affect other database activities. In dedicated (M10 or higher) sharded and unsharded Atlas clusters on any cloud provider, you can deploy these search nodes with each cluster or with each shard within the cluster.

Parallelizing query processing is particularly effective for large data sets, as it can dramatically improve response times. By employing intraquery parallelism in Atlas Vector Search, you use more system resources, but the result is a notable reduction in the latency of each query. This approach ensures that even complex searches are handled more efficiently, providing quicker results. Chapter 11 describes more search nodes.

12.7 Improving Atlas Vector Search performance

Several proven recommendations improve the performance of Atlas Vector Search. Implementing these strategies can lead to faster and more efficient query processing.

Primarily, aim to perform ANN queries that search for results similar to a selected product, images, and so on. Use ENN only when necessary because it is more computationally intensive and slower than ANN. ANN provides a good balance between speed and accuracy in most use cases, but other best practices can ensure optimal performance for your queries. Here are some of them:

- *Reduce vector dimensions.* Atlas Vector Search supports up to 4,096 vector dimensions. Larger vectors, however, require more computational resources due to the increased number of floating-point comparisons. To optimize performance, reduce the number of dimensions whenever possible, but first ensure that changing the embedding models does not significantly affect the accuracy of your vector queries.
- *Avoid indexing vectors during queries.* Indexing vector embeddings consumes significant computational resources. To maintain optimal query performance, avoid indexing and reindexing vectors while running vector searches. If you need to update the embedding model, create a new index for the new vectors instead of updating the existing index.
- *Exclude vector fields from results.* In the $project stage, request only the necessary fields from the documents in the results. Exclude the vector fields; they can be large and increase query latency. This selective approach improves query performance by reducing the amount of data returned.
- *Ensure sufficient memory.* Efficient vector search relies on having vector data and indexes held in memory. Ensure that data nodes have enough RAM to accommodate this. Deploy separate search nodes for workload isolation to maximize memory efficiency for vector search operations.
- *Warm up the filesystem cache.* Without dedicated search modes, initial vector search queries may experience high latency due to random disk seeks during HNSW graph traversal. Performance improves as the indexed vectors are read into memory. Warm up the filesystem cache to reduce latency for subsequent queries, allowing faster access to vector data. To warm up the filesystem cache, perform a full index scan or run targeted queries that load frequently accessed data into memory. This process ensures that the necessary data is readily available for faster query responses.

Summary

- Vector embeddings transform different data types, such as words and sentences, into numerical values, representing them as points in a multidimensional space. Similar items are positioned closer together, helping machines understand and process the data more effectively.
- A vector database (or vector similarity search engine) stores, retrieves, and searches data organized as points in a multidimensional space, each represented by vectors such as [0.3, 0.8, -0.8, 0.6, 0.4, 0.1, -0.5, 0.2, ...], unlike traditional databases, which use rows and columns.

- In a vector database, content is first processed by an embedding model (such as OpenAI's GPT-4 or Hugging Face's Transformers), which converts the data to numbers. Then these vectors are stored in the database for efficient similarity-based retrieval.
- A vector index is a specialized data structure designed to store and manage vector embeddings from large data sets. It enables efficient similarity searches by organizing vectors for quick retrieval, using algorithms such as ANN. ANN algorithms, such as HNSW, ensure fast, scalable searches. This structure is essential for applications such as recommendation systems, semantic search, and machine learning.
- Atlas Vector Search, similar to Atlas Search, uses the `mongot` process to replicate and sync data from the target MongoDB collection to an Apache Lucene index optimized for vector search. Recent versions of Apache Lucene support vector search using algorithms such as HNSW for ANN searches and ENN search.
- To perform vector search in Atlas, create an Atlas Vector Search index. These indexes, separate from other database indexes, efficiently retrieve documents with vector embeddings. Atlas Vector Search supports embeddings up to 4,096 dimensions.
- The `$vectorSearch` stage in MongoDB's aggregation pipeline is designed to perform vector-based search operations on your data. It uses vector embeddings to find and retrieve documents that are semantically similar to a given query vector. To use the `$vectorSearch` stage, you need a vector search index created on the relevant fields in your collection.
- You must embed your query with the same model used for your data. This ensures compatibility and accurate vector search results.
- When I wrote this chapter, MongoDB Atlas did not provide models for converting text to embeddings, so you may need to use an external system such as OpenAI, Hugging Face, TensorFlow, or LLaMA.
- To use ENN, change `"exact": false` to `"exact": true` in the `$vectorSearch` stage definition. ENN ensures the most precise matches for the query vector by exhaustively comparing it against all stored vectors. Although this method guarantees the highest accuracy, it is more computationally intensive and slower than ANN, which speeds the search using heuristics but sacrifices some accuracy.
- Prefiltering enables you to add specific criteria to your search, which narrows the data set before the vector similarity search. This approach can greatly reduce the search space and enhance the performance of your queries.
- You can enhance query performance by using dedicated search nodes for vector search processing. High-CPU systems may offer even greater performance benefits. When Atlas Vector Search operates on these nodes, it parallelizes query execution across different data segments, resulting in more efficient processing.

- `mongosh` is not the only way to perform vector searches. You can also use programming languages like Python, JavaScript, and Java; their MongoDB drivers support the `$vectorSearch` filter option.
- Atlas Triggers is a MongoDB Atlas feature that enables you to execute server-side logic in response to database events or on a schedule. These triggers help automate workflows, enforce business logic, and respond to data changes in real time without a separate application server.

Developing AI applications locally with the Atlas CLI

This chapter covers
- Deploying locally with the Atlas CLI
- Creating an Atlas cluster on your local host
- Using `mongorestore` to load data into a local cluster
- Diving into a local Atlas cluster
- Using the `createSearchIndex()` wrapper

The Atlas command-line interface (CLI) simplifies working with MongoDB Atlas in the cloud and locally by managing setup, connections, and tasks across environments. It allows you to handle deployments efficiently, ensuring a seamless workflow from development to production.

You can use the Atlas CLI to develop locally with MongoDB Atlas deployments, including Atlas Search and Atlas Vector Search. This interface allows you to create full-text search or AI-powered applications in your preferred development environment. You can use the Atlas CLI to handle setup, connections, and management tasks from development to production. For full-text search, the Atlas CLI allows you to create and manage Atlas Search indexes, whether you're working locally or in the cloud. For applications using semantic search and AI, the Atlas CLI supports creating and managing local instances with Atlas Vector Search indexes.

13.1 Introducing local Atlas clusters

To create a local Atlas deployment with default settings in interactive mode, you can use the command `atlas deployments`. The following listing shows what this command offers.

Listing 13.1 Atlas CLI local deployment option

```
atlas deployments --help
Manage cloud and local deployments.

Usage:
  atlas deployments [command]

Aliases:
  deployments, deployment

Cloud and local deployments commands:
  setup       Create a local deployment.
  delete      Delete a deployment.
  list        Return all deployments.
  connect     Connect to a deployment that is running
 locally or in Atlas. If the deployment is paused,
 make sure to run atlas deployments start first.
  logs        Get deployment logs.
  start       Start a deployment.
  pause       Pause a deployment.
  search      Manage search for cloud and local deployments.

Flags:
  -h, --help   help for deployments

Global Flags:
  -P, --profile string   Name of the profile to use from
 your configuration file. To learn about profiles f
 or the Atlas CLI, see https://dochub.mongodb.org/core/
 atlas-cli-save-connection-settings.

Use "atlas deployments [command] --help" for more
 information about a command.
```

The `atlas deployments` command in the Atlas CLI allows you to manage cloud and local deployments. You can use it to create a local deployment with the `setup` command, delete a deployment with the `delete` command, and `list` all deployments with the `list` command. The `connect` command lets you connect to a deployment that is running locally or in Atlas, and if the deployment is paused, you can start it with the `start` command. You can also retrieve deployment logs using the `logs` command, pause a deployment with the `pause` command, and manage search for both cloud and local deployments using the `search` command. The `--help` flag provides additional information for the `deployments` command and its subcommands.

An Atlas local cluster creates a local environment that mimics a cloud-based MongoDB Atlas cluster. The process starts in the Atlas CLI, where you download and configure the necessary Docker images that contain MongoDB binaries and dependencies on your local machine. You deploy the local cluster using Docker or deploy it directly on the host machine, which includes `mongod`, a single-node replica set instance of MongoDB and configuration files used to simulate an environment. MongoDB configures a `mongod` instances running locally on port `27017`. The local cluster uses the local network for connectivity, enabling applications to connect and interact with the cluster as though it were deployed in the cloud.

Also, the `mongot` process runs as a separate component alongside `mongod`, handling indexing and search operations. It provides full-text search and vector search capabilities within your local cluster as it does in a cloud-based deployment (figure 13.1).

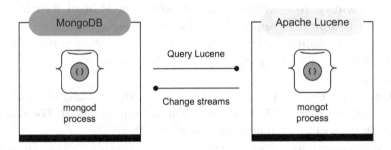

Figure 13.1 The `mongod` process alongside `mongot` for local deployments running in Docker (Image © MongoDB 2025)

The `mongot` process is a Java wrapper for Apache Lucene. It uses MongoDB change streams to monitor changes in MongoDB collections and automatically update the corresponding Lucene indexes in real time, ensuring that the indexes are always in sync with the data. Also, it provides an API for querying these indexes directly from MongoDB.

13.2 Creating an Atlas cluster locally with Atlas CLI

You should use local deployments only for testing and development. The supported operating systems for local Atlas deployments include the following:

- *macOS*—The supported versions are 13.2 and later, with architectures x86-64 and ARM. The minimum requirements are two CPU cores and 2 GB of free RAM.
- *Red Hat Enterprise Linux/CentOS*—The supported versions are 8 and 9, also with architectures x86-64 and ARM. The minimum requirements are the same, with two CPU cores and 2 GB of free RAM.

- *Ubuntu*—The supported versions are 22.04 and 24.04, with architectures x86-64 and ARM. The minimum requirements are two CPU cores and 2 GB of free RAM.
- *Debian*—The supported versions are 11 and 12, with architectures x86-64 and ARM. The minimum requirements are two CPU cores and 2 GB of free RAM.
- *Amazon Linux*—The supported version is 2023, with architectures x86-64 and ARM. The minimum requirements are two CPU cores and 2 GB of free RAM.
- *Windows*—The supported versions are 10 and 11, with architecture x86. The minimum requirements are two CPU cores and 2 GB of free RAM.

13.2.1 Configuring Docker

Running a local Atlas cluster requires Docker to be installed. Docker is an open source platform that automates the deployment, scaling, and management of applications using containerization. Containers package an application and its dependencies into a single lightweight unit that can run consistently across environments.

Using Docker with Atlas locally provides several benefits. It ensures that the application runs consistently across environments and isolates the MongoDB environment, preventing conflicts with other applications. Docker also makes it easy to scale your local Atlas cluster for testing and development, simplifies the setup process with pre-configured containers, and allows you to move and replicate the local setup easily across systems.

For macOS, install Docker Desktop v4.31 or later (https://mng.bz/z2XB). For Linux, install Docker Engine v27.0+ or later (https://mng.bz/0zKN). For Windows, install Docker Desktop v4.31 or later (https://mng.bz/z2XB).

Docker requires a network connection for pulling and caching MongoDB images. Additionally, Podman is supported only for Linux RHEL versions (https://podman.io/getting-started/installation). I focus on Docker in this book.

After installing Docker successfully, ensure that it is running by executing the `docker info` command:

```
docker info
Client:
 Version:    27.0.3
 Context:    desktop-linux
 Debug Mode: false
 Plugins:
  buildx: Docker Buildx (Docker Inc.)
    Version:  v0.15.1-desktop.1
  compose: Docker Compose (Docker Inc.)
    Version:  v2.28.1-desktop.1
  debug: Get a shell into any image or container (Docker Inc.)
    Version:  0.0.32
  desktop: Docker Desktop commands (Alpha) (Docker Inc.)
    Version:  v0.0.14
  dev: Docker Dev Environments (Docker Inc.)
    Version:  v0.1.2
  extension: Manages Docker extensions (Docker Inc.)
```

```
      Version:  v0.2.25
    feedback: Provide feedback, right in your terminal! (Docker Inc.)
      Version:  v1.0.5
    init: Creates Docker-related starter files for your project (Docker Inc.)
      Version:  v1.3.0
    sbom: View the packaged-based Software Bill Of
          Materials (SBOM) for an image (Anchore Inc.)
      Version:  0.6.0
    scout: Docker Scout (Docker Inc.)
      Version:  v1.10.0
Server:
 Containers: 1
  Running: 1
  Paused: 0
  Stopped: 0
 Images: 1
 Server Version: 27.0.3
 Storage Driver: overlay2
  Backing Filesystem: extfs
  Supports d_type: true
  Using metacopy: false
  Native Overlay Diff: true
  userxattr: false
 Logging Driver: json-file
 Cgroup Driver: cgroupfs
 Cgroup Version: 2
 Plugins:
  Volume: local
  Network: bridge host ipvlan macvlan null overlay
  Log: awslogs fluentd gcplogs gelf journald json-file local splunk syslog
 Swarm: inactive
 Runtimes: io.containerd.runc.v2 runc
 Default Runtime: runc
 Init Binary: docker-init
 containerd version: ae71819c4f5e67bb4d5ae76a6b735f29cc25774e
 runc version: v1.1.13-0-g58aa920
 init version: de40ad0
 Security Options:
  seccomp
   Profile: unconfined
  cgroupns
 Kernel Version: 6.6.32-linuxkit
 Operating System: Docker Desktop
 OSType: linux
 Architecture: aarch64
 CPUs: 10
 Total Memory: 7.657GiB
 Name: docker-desktop
 ID: cd9721bf-e6af-40df-9033-7ae08eb21b7a
 Docker Root Dir: /var/lib/docker
 Debug Mode: false
 HTTP Proxy: http.docker.internal:3128
 HTTPS Proxy: http.docker.internal:3128
 No Proxy: hubproxy.docker.internal
 Labels:
```

13.2.2 Building your first local Atlas cluster

After installing Docker and ensuring that it's working, you can create your local Atlas cluster:

1. Run the `atlas deployments setup --type local` command. You see default settings such as `Deployment Name`, `MongoDB Version`, and `Port`:

    ```
    atlas deployments setup --type local

    Please note that your session expires periodically.
    If you use Atlas CLI for automation,
    see https://www.mongodb.com/docs/atlas/cli/stable/
    atlas-cli-automate/ for best practices.
    To login, run: atlas auth login

    [Default Settings]
    Deployment Name    local9619
    MongoDB Version    8.0
    Port               27017
    ```

2. When asked how you want to set up your local Atlas deployment, choose the default option. The process of creating the cluster begins; it might take several minutes. The steps include starting the local environment, downloading the latest MongoDB image, and creating the deployment. When the deployment is created, a connection string is provided:

    ```
    ? How do you want to set up your local Atlas deployment? default
    Creating your cluster local9619 [this might take several minutes]
    1/3: Starting your local environment...
    2/3: Downloading the latest MongoDB image to your local environment...
    \
    3/3: Creating your deployment local9619...
    Deployment created!
    Connection string: mongodb://localhost:27017/?directConnection=true
    ```

3. When asked how you want to connect to the deployment, choose `mongosh`. After connecting, you see confirmation messages, information about the MongoDB and `mongosh` versions, and any server startup warnings. Your local Atlas cluster is ready for use:

    ```
    ? How would you like to connect to local9619? mongosh
    Current Mongosh Log ID:    66af77b202b82525cbf9e5bd
    Connecting to:
    mongodb://localhost:27017/?directConnection=true&
    serverSelectionTimeoutMS=2000&appName=mongosh+2.2.15
    Using MongoDB:       8.0.4
    Using Mongosh:       2.2.15

    For mongosh info see: https://docs.mongodb.com/mongodb-shell/
    ```

```
------
    The server generated these startup warnings when booting
    2024-08-04T12:44:27.729+00:00: Using the XFS
    ➥filesystem is strongly recommended with the WiredTiger
    ➥storage engine. See http://dochub.mongodb.org/core
    ➥/prodnotes-filesystem
    2024-08-04T12:44:28.520+00:00:
/sys/kernel/mm/transparent_hugepage/enabled
➥is 'always'.
➥We suggest setting it to 'never' in this binary version
------

AtlasLocalDev rs-localdev [direct: primary] test>
```

4 Use the `use dbs` command to display the available databases in your local Atlas cluster:

```
test> show dbs
admin   120.00 KiB
config  228.00 KiB
local   436.00 KiB
AtlasLocalDev rs-localdev [direct: primary] test>
```

5 Use `docker ps` to display the running Docker containers associated with your local Atlas cluster:

```
docker ps

CONTAINER ID IMAGE COMMAND CREATED STATUS PORTS NAMES
b32351f3a7c7 mongodb/mongodb-atlas-local:8.0
➥"/usr/local/bin/runn…" 20 minutes ago
➥Up 20 minutes (healthy) 127.0.0.1:27017->27017/tcp
➥local9619
```

When you run `docker ps`, you see details such as the container ID, image, command, creation time, status, ports, and names of the running containers. The output shows a container with ID `b32351f3a7c7` running the image `mongodb/mongodb-atlas-local:8.0`. This container was created 20 minutes ago and has been up for 20 minutes with a status of `healthy`. The ports show that the container is mapping port `27017` to `127.0.0.1:27017`, and the container name is `local9619`.

13.3 Managing your local Atlas cluster

You can manage your local Atlas cluster using the Atlas CLI—specifically, `atlas deployments`. You can stop, start, connect to the database, delete, and view logs of your cluster, as well as monitor cluster health by reviewing the logs.

13.3.1 Stopping, starting, checking, and deleting your local cluster

Let's break down how this works in practice. The following sequence of commands gives you an idea of how to manage your local cluster:

1   *Check the cluster.* If you want to display and ensure that the cluster is still available on your machine, run `atlas deployments list --type LOCAL`:

```
atlas deployments list --type LOCAL
```

You see a console message similar to this one:

```
NAME        TYPE    MDB VER   STATE
local9619   LOCAL   8.0.4     IDLE
```

The output of the command shows that one local Atlas cluster is running, `local9619`, and currently has the status `IDLE`.

2   *Temporarily stop the cluster.* Using `atlas deployments`, you can temporarily stop your cluster by using the command `atlas deployments pause <cluster name> --type LOCAL`, where `<cluster name>` (in this case) is `local9619`. Your cluster will have a different name:

```
atlas deployments pause local9619 --type LOCAL
```

You see a console message similar to this one:

```
To login, run: atlas auth login
Pausing deployment 'local9619'.
```

Now you can validate the status of your cluster by running `atlas deployments` again:

```
atlas deployments list --type LOCAL
```

The cluster is stopped, as indicated by the state `STOPPED`:

```
NAME        TYPE    MDB VER   STATE
local9619   LOCAL   8.0.4     STOPPED
```

3   *Restart the cluster.* Using the command `atlas deployments start`, you can restart your local cluster:

```
atlas deployments start local9619 --type LOCAL
```

Based on this message, you see that the cluster is starting:

```
Starting deployment 'local9619'.
```

Now, using the command `atlas deployments connect`, connect to your started local Atlas cluster.

```
atlas deployments connect --type LOCAL
```

You will be prompted to choose between `mongosh` and MongoDB Compass. I chose `mongosh` and then connected to the database:

```
Please note that your session expires periodically.
If you use Atlas CLI for automation,
 see https://www.mongodb.com/docs/atlas/cli/stable/
 atlas-cli-automate/
 for best practices.
To login, run: atlas auth login
? How would you like to connect to local9619? mongosh
Current Mongosh Log ID:    66af86eb95acd9c6bd663f89
Connecting to:
mongodb://localhost:27017/?directConnection=true&
 serverSelectionTimeoutMS=2000&appName=mongosh+2.2.15
Using MongoDB:          8.0.4
Using Mongosh:          2.2.15

For mongosh info see: https://docs.mongodb.com/mongodb-shell/
AtlasLocalDev rs-localdev [direct: primary] test>
```

4 *Monitor the cluster.* The Atlas CLI also enables you to monitor the logs of your local Atlas cluster. This provides the benefit of real-time insights into cluster operations, helping you diagnose problems, monitor performance, and ensure the smooth functioning of your cluster.

You can view the logs of your local cluster using the command `atlas deployments logs`:

```
atlas deployments logs --deploymentName local9619  --type LOCAL
```

The logs are displayed in your console:

```
{"t":{"$date":"2024-08-04T13:54:35.299+00:00"},"s":"I",  "c":"NETWORK",
"id":2944,"ctx":"conn117","msg":"Connection
 ended","attr":{"remote":"127.0.0.1:45150",
 "uuid":{"uuid":
{"$uuid":"4fa06363-affa-47e7-960c-a331e8d1f95"}},
 "connectionId":117,"connectionCount":24}}
{"t":{"$date":"2024-08-04T13:54:35.299+00:00"},"s":"I",
"c":"NETWORK","id":22944,"ctx":"conn116","msg":"Connection
  ended","attr":{"remote":"127.0.0.1:45142",
 "uuid":{"uuid":{"$uuid":"bfdbe0-c191-42d-9c51-
  af9a9f2d0bd5"}},"connectionId":116,
 "connectionCount":23}}
{"t":{"$date":"2024-08-04T13:54:35.300+00:00"},"s":"I",
"c":"NETWORK","id":22944,"ctx":"conn115",
 "msg":"Connectionended","attr":{"remote":
 "127.0.0.1:45134","uuid":{"uuid":
{"$uuid":"61e66ddb-b2ea-44df-b281-a6f4b62d3ef3"}},
"connectionId":115,"connectionCount":22}}
```

5   *Delete the cluster.* If you want to delete your local Atlas cluster, run the command `atlas deployment delete`:

```
atlas deployments delete local9619  --type LOCAL
```

The command prompts you for confirmation and then deletes the cluster.

13.3.2 Loading a sample data set

You may want to load a sample data set that can be used for exercises, as in previous examples. Currently, the Atlas CLI does not support this option for local clusters, but you can download the sample data set and import it into the cluster using `mongorestore` (chapter 21). For now, it's important to know that `mongorestore` restores data from a Binary JSON (BSON) dump to a MongoDB database. Here's how:

1   Run the following `curl` command to download the sample data file to your local machine. This can take a few minutes. When the sample data set download is complete, you see the file `sampledata.archive` on your local machine:

```
curl https://atlas-education.s3.amazonaws.com/
↪sampledata.archive -o sampledata.archive
```

2   To use `mongorestore`, install MongoDB Database Tools. The official MongoDB documentation provides instructions based on your operating system. You can find it at https://mng.bz/Qwnw.

3   Find the connection string for the local Atlas cluster. You can display it using the command `atlas deployments connect --connectWith connectionString <name>`, where `<name>` is the name of the local cluster:

```
atlas deployments connect --connectWith connectionString local9619
```

The connection string for my local Atlas cluster looks like this:

```
mongodb://localhost:32769/?directConnection=true
```

Now you can use this connection string with the `mongorestore` command.

4   Start loading the sample data set to your local MongoDB cluster:

```
mongorestore --archive=sampledata.archive \
--uri mongodb://localhost:32769/?directConnection=true
```

During data import, you may see messages like these:

```
2024-08-04T16:41:25.573+0200    preparing collections to restore from
2024-08-04T16:41:25.577+0200    reading metadata for sample_
training.routes from archive
```

```
'sampledata.archive'
2024-08-04T16:41:25.577+0200 reading metadata for
 sample_training.trips from archive 'sampledata.archive'
2024-08-04T16:41:25.577+0200 reading metadata for
 sample_analytics.accounts from archive
'sampledata.archive'
….
2024-08-04T16:41:34.746+0200    restoring indexes for
collection sample_geospatial.shipwrecks from
metadata 2024-08-04T16:41:34.746+0200
index: &idx.IndexDocument
{Options:primitive.M{"2dsphereIndexVersion":3,
"background":true,
➥ "name":"coordinates_2dsphere",
➥ "ns":"sample_geospatial.shipwrecks","v":2},
➥ Key:primitive.D{primitive.E
➥ {Key:"coordinates",Value:"2dsphere"}},
➥ PartialFilterExpression:primitive.D(nil)}
2024-08-04T16:41:34.781+0200
no indexes to restore for collection sample_weatherdata.data
2024-08-04T16:41:34.781+0200
no indexes to restore for collection sample_restaurants.restaurants
2024-08-04T16:41:34.781+0200
no indexes to restore for collection sample_restaurants.neighborhoods
2024-08-04T16:41:34.781+0200
no indexes to restore for collection sample_supplies.sales
2024-08-04T16:41:36.173+0200    425367 document(s) restored
successfully. 0 document(s) failed to restore.
```

5 Log in to the local Atlas cluster again, using the command `atlas deployments connect`:

```
atlas deployments connect --type LOCAL
```

After logging back in to the local Atlas cluster, you see the databases created with the sample data set for the exercises in previous sections:

```
AtlasLocalDev rs-localdev [direct: primary] test> show dbs
admin                120.00 KiB
config               296.00 KiB
local                220.30 MiB
sample_airbnb         52.69 MiB
sample_analytics       9.54 MiB
sample_geospatial      1.21 MiB
sample_guides         40.00 KiB
sample_mflix         110.28 MiB
sample_restaurants     6.20 MiB
sample_supplies        1.03 MiB
sample_training       47.62 MiB
sample_weatherdata     2.55 MiB
AtlasLocalDev rs-localdev [direct: primary] test>
```

13.4 Diving into a local Atlas cluster

The `docker inspect` command obtains detailed information about Docker objects such as containers, images, volumes, and networks. You can find the name of the image by running `docker ps`. Docker `inspect` provides JSON-formatted output containing a wide range of configuration and state data about the specified object. You can use this information for troubleshooting, monitoring, and understanding the specific details of the Docker environment. Here's the output of the `docker inspect` command:

```
docker inspect  mongodb/mongodb-atlas-local:8.0
[
    {
        "Id": "sha256:9acf037d83ece5c2bf8ef2818a72a026e7df9ef83
7096c1b898f4b792fbe3bad",
        "RepoTags": [
            "mongodb/mongodb-atlas-local:8.0"
        ],
        "RepoDigests": [
            "mongodb/mongodb-atlas-
local@sha256:c40e17fc675c294fe8464fca2654640e60cc
10f375bb90b98f47674737"
        ],
        "Parent": "",
        "Comment": "buildkit.dockerfile.v0",
        "Created": "2024-07-22T09:54:50.165656127Z",
        "DockerVersion": "",
        "Author": "",
        "Config": {
            "Hostname": "",
            "Domainname": "",
            "User": "mongod",
            "AttachStdin": false,
            "AttachStdout": false,
            "AttachStderr": false,
            "ExposedPorts": {
                "27017/tcp": {}
            },
            "Tty": false,
            "OpenStdin": false,
            "StdinOnce": false,
            "Env": [
                "PATH=/usr/local/sbin:/usr/local/bin:/usr/sbin:/usr/bin:
/sbin:/bin:/opt/mongot",
                "container=oci",
                "TOOL=CONTAINER"
            ],
            "Cmd": [
                "/usr/local/bin/runner",
                "server"
            ],
            "Healthcheck": {
                "Test": [
                    "CMD",
```

```
                    "/usr/local/bin/runner",
                    "healthcheck"
                ],
                "Interval": 30000000000,
                "Timeout": 60000000000,
                "StartPeriod": 60000000000,
                "Retries": 3
            },
            "ArgsEscaped": true,
            "Image": "",
            "Volumes": {
                "/data/configdb": {},          | Volumes for data/
                "/data/db": {}                 | configdb and /data/db
            },
            "WorkingDir": "",
            "Entrypoint": null,
            "OnBuild": null,
            "Labels": {
                "architecture": "aarch64",
                "build-date": "2024-06-28T07:36:05",
                "com.redhat.component": "ubi9-container",
                "com.redhat.license_terms":
"https://www.redhat.com/en/about/
red-hat-end-user-license-agreements#UBI",
                "description": "Container configured
with a single node replicaset instance of
MongoDB and Atlas Search",
                "distribution-scope": "public",
                "io.buildah.version": "1.29.0",
                "io.k8s.description": "The Universal Base Image
is designed and engineered to be the base layer for
all of your containerized applications, middleware and utilities.
This base image is freely redistributable, but Red Hat
only supports Red Hat technologies through subscriptions for
Red Hat products. This image is maintained by
Red Hat and updated regularly.",
                "io.k8s.display-name": "Red Hat Universal Base Image 9",
                "io.openshift.expose-services": "",
                "io.openshift.tags": "base rhel9",
                "maintainer": "support@mongodb.com",
                "mongodb-atlas-local": "container",
                "name": "MongoDB Atlas Local",
                "release": "1123.1719560047",
                "summary": "MongoDB Atlas Local Container",
                "url": "https://access.redhat.com/containers/
#/registry.access.redhat.com/
ubi9/images/9.4-1123.1719560047",
                "vcs-ref": "92a4a475241865d0d11bd861fb2b29fbd9b17df0",
                "vcs-type": "git",
                "vendor": "MongoDB",
                "version": "8.0.4"
            }
        },
        "Architecture": "arm64",
        "Os": "linux",
```

```
            "Size": 896833968,
            "GraphDriver": {
                "Data": {
                    "LowerDir": "/var/lib/docker/overlay2/afc6c2468758a5e3b60a51
ca07f3f3576fe9bc2cf57211bfa230feac325/diff:/var/lib/docker/
overlay2/4bef8399c049c97cd7ee9ab851ef4ddc8831a1b47eb41fffc
b26d1b9e946a95a/diff:/var/lib/docker/overlay2/
ac46bcbe95082dcf80258fdf4e300c89047b3abbafa73a1ecf45692f1d180c3b/
diff:/var/lib/docker/overlay2/
2a153597089c5c23afb712540d735da81dd5bd1ba9e388aafc571ed1fa54bbc2
/diff:/var/lib/docker/overlay2/
90a2c43b668796a2ae4d2f377772551f4ef104a1216c9243e6caaa8f0f5f77aa/
diff:/var/lib/docker/overlay2/
d85cc2c9485c25bf1b5f487b7eb0cb7a52e414614ec4e4b8cd1ebf4cf0919f0d
/diff:/var/lib/docker/overlay2/e9bb493bd34fcd7fcf
0d76ffe8ef55ac14ef215c01788d2e02de02183f3ad/diff:
/var/lib/docker/overlay2/
8a0e3e2e2d7098171fcc15a9040433298030d9095924c08f863377b8f3085291/diff",
                    "MergedDir": "/var/lib/docker/overlay2/
cac61befd10c97387d66427f882d1ac377e40532541f166d02e808c25/merged",
                    "UpperDir": "/var/lib/docker/overlay2/
cac61befd10c997387d66427f882d1ac377e40532541fd50bcf166d02e808c25/
diff",
                    "WorkDir": "/var/lib/docker/overlay2/
cac61befd10c997387d66427f882d1ac377e40532541fd50bcf166d02e808c25/
work"
                },
                "Name": "overlay2"
            },
            "RootFS": {
                "Type": "layers",
                "Layers": [
"sha256:deb67401b5c584abadd5d179bdd276cfdd8aa144215f3a84080c597a9",
"sha256:5f76de7bb454d1aa238cd62251c0df8267b8e9216ee738db710aedefe",
"sha256:02346a59a9633b362209feffea349f8fe55dc27f750ea061667907e29",
"sha256:6c6cc35f5a5fe86ed0da435332830b88330b95773c4358c0d35349569",
"sha256:786fcd51af4c88de964798d72d416d580db9cb8fa5fab980b2a89fc15",
"sha256:701d5f46dcfadd41c360b24ffc08bc95886481a5df993405c510f2355",
"sha256:d8103d3d8cc12ce82eee6f21f4a67400f3c913f63e1b0493aeef757ad",
"sha256:866468f4505fccacbab3b341219a9eb036040c64f5dcc5dc2d21274f6",
    "sha256:ad94e6ecc9774f1d74fa0749e97207aca23a141b3d53ebe2552eb6f210e14251"
                ]
            },
            "Metadata": {
                "LastTagTime": "0001-01-01T00:00:00Z"
            }
        }
    ]
```

Here's how the `docker inspect` command works:

- The `docker inspect` command for `mongodb/mongodb-atlas-local:8.0` provides detailed information about the Docker image. The image runs the `mongod` user and exposes port `27017/tcp`.

Diving into a local Atlas cluster 349

- The `PATH` environment variable includes `/opt/mongot`, indicating that this directory is part of the image's executable path.
- The container command is `/usr/local/bin/runner server`. It includes a health check that runs the command `/usr/local/bin/runner healthcheck` every 30 seconds with a timeout of 60 seconds, starting after a 60-second initial delay, and retries up to three times.
- The image supports volumes for `/data/configdb` and `/data/db`, indicating where MongoDB stores its data. The image labels provide metadata such as architecture (`aarch64`) and build date (`2024-06-28T07:36:05`) and confirm that it is based on Red Hat Universal Base Image 9. The image architecture is `arm64`, operating on the Linux system, and its size is approximately 896 MB. The image uses the `overlay2` storage driver, and the `RootFS` section lists multiple layers that make up the filesystem of the Docker image.

13.4.1 Displaying processes

Use the `docker top` command to understand the processes running in the container. The `docker top` command is helpful because it allows you to see the list of processes running inside a specific container without installing additional tools within the container. This command provides information similar to that of the `ps` command but can be executed directly from the Docker host.

Execute `docker top <container name>`. In the case of my deployment, the container name is `local9619`:

```
docker top local9619
```

The command displays the following information about the processes running inside the container:

```
UID    PID    PPID   C STIME TTY TIME     CMD
997    4395   4375   0 15:19 ?   00:00:00 /usr/local/bin/runner server

997    4426   4395   2 15:19 ?   00:03:45 mongod --replSet
rs-localdev --dbpath /data/db --keyFile /data/configdb/keyfile
--maxConns 32200 --bind_ip_all
--setParameter mongotHost=localhost:27027
--setParameter
searchIndexManagementHostAndPort=localhost:27027 -transitionToAuth

997    4520   4395   0 15:20 ?   00:01:09 /opt/mongot/bin/jdk/bin/java
-XX:+ExitOnOutOfMemoryError
-Djava.security.egd=file:/dev/urandom
-cp /opt/mongot/lib/*:
/opt/mongot/bin/mongot_deploy.jar com.xgen.mongot.MongotCli
--keyFile /data/configdb/keyfile
--data-dir /data/mongot
--mongodHostAndPort localhost:27017
```

Here's how the `docker top` command works:

- The `/usr/local/bin/runner server` process is the main command responsible for starting the container. It operates under the user with UID 997 and has been running since 15:19, but it hasn't consumed much CPU time.
- The `mongod` process is the MongoDB server instance configured with various parameters. It is set up as part of a local development replica set (`rs-localdev`) with its database files stored in `/data/db`. The server uses a key file for authentication, limits maximum connections to 32,200, and binds to all network interfaces. Also, it is configured to interact with mongot on `localhost:27027` for search and indexing operations. This process is also owned by UID 997.
- The Java process `/opt/mongot/bin/jdk/bin/java` runs the mongot component, which handles search and indexing tasks. It is configured to exit on out-of-memory errors and uses `/dev/urandom` for secure random-number generation. The `classpath` includes necessary libraries and the `mongot_deploy.jar` file, and it runs the `MongotCli` main class. This process also uses the key file for authentication and stores its data in `/data/mongot`. It connects to the MongoDB server on `localhost:27017`. This process is owned by UID 997.

13.4.2 Executing into the container

The final test is logging into the MongoDB Atlas container using `docker exec`. The command is `docker exec -it <container_id> /bin/bash`. The command `docker ps` provides the container ID:

```
docker exec -it b32351f3a7c7 /bin/bash
```

After executing the command, I successfully logged in to the container with ID b32351f3a7c7, which is running on my local machine as the default user. The prompt `bash-5.1$` indicates that I'm inside the container's bash shell but without root privileges:

```
bash-5.1$
```

After executing into the container, navigate to the `/opt/mongot/` directory using the command `cd /opt/mongot/`:

```
bash-5.1$ cd /opt/mongot/
bash-5.1$ ls
LICENSE.txt  README.md
THIRD_PARTY_NOTICES.txt
 bin  exampleIndexDefinition.json
indexManager  lib  mongot
bash-5.1$
```

The directory contains important files and directories, including license information, instructions, third-party-component listings, executables, an example index definition file, index management files, libraries, and components related to mongot.

Display the README.md file using the cat command to thoroughly understand the concept of the local Atlas cluster and mongot process:

```
cat README.md
`mongot` runs as a separate process alongside `mongod`.
When configured, `mongot` handles requests related to search
and index management for `mongod`.

The mongot binary for local development is in Private Preview.
It is available for testing in order to gather feedback.
Do not use the mongot binary for production deployments.

## Setup

1. Create a keyfile for the connection between mongod and mongot.
    * `mkdir data && echo keyfile > data/keyfile && chmod 600 data/keyfile`
    * If you already have replication enabled you don't
need to create another keyfile, and you
      can keep your existing `replSetName` and `keyFile`
configurations in the following step.

2. Configure mongod
    * If you're using a configuration file, add these lines:
      ```yaml
      replication:
        replSetName: rs0
      security:
        keyFile: data/keyfile
      setParameter:
        mongotHost: localhost:27027
        searchIndexManagementHostAndPort: localhost:27027
      ```

    * If you're using command line flags, add these:
      ```shell
      --replSet rs0
      --keyFile data/keyfile
      --setParameter "mongotHost=localhost:27027"
      --setParameter "searchIndexManagementHostAndPort=localhost:27027"
      ```
3. Restart mongod. If a new replica set was created,
connect and run `rs.initiate()`
4. Start mongot: `./mongot --mongodHostAndPort=localhost:27017
--keyfile=data/keyfile`
    * Other optional arguments include:
        * `--data-dir`: where mongot should persist data.
The default value is to data/mongot.
        * `--log-path`: location where mongot should write logs.
The default is to print to stdout.
5. Test the local Atlas Search server.
    ```js
    db.coll.createSearchIndex({"mappings": {"dynamic": true}})
    db.coll.aggregate([{"$listSearchIndexes": {}}])
    db.coll.dropSearchIndex("default")
```
```

mongot operates as a separate process alongside mongod, handling search and index management requests. It's designed for local development and currently in private preview, which means that it's available for testing and feedback but is not recommended for production use.

The secure communication between mongod and mongot is established with a keyfile, which ensures that only authorized processes can join the replica set and interact with one another.

The mongod configuration includes replication settings, the location of the security key file, and parameters for mongotHost and searchIndexManagementHostAndPort. These configurations direct mongod on how to connect to mongot and manage search indexes.

After you configure mongod, you must restart. If a new replica set is created, the initialization command rs.initiate() is executed to set up the replica set.

When mongod is set up, mongot starts with the necessary parameters, including mongodHostAndPort and the keyfile location. Optional parameters for mongot specify the directory for data persistence and the log path for logging activities.

To test the local Atlas Search server, you can use mongosh commands to create a search index, list existing search indexes, and drop a search index. This testing verifies that the search and index management functionalities of mongod and mongot are operating correctly.

13.5 Creating search indexes

You can run queries in your local MongoDB Atlas cluster by using not only the MongoDB database but also features such as full-text search and vector search, which are provided through the integration of mongod with Apache Lucene via the mongot process. The mongosh method db.collection.createSearchIndex() provides a wrapper around the createSearchIndexes database command.

13.5.1 Executing full-text search locally

After logging in to the local cluster, you can create a full-text search index using the db.collection.createSearchIndex() wrapper. (Chapter 11 discusses full-text search.) Because this environment is a test environment, use dynamic mapping:

```
use sample_training
db.inspections.createSearchIndex(
    "LocalSearchIndex",
    { mappings: { dynamic: true } }
)
```

This command creates a search index in the local Atlas cluster. You can verify it by running the getSearchIndexes() method:

```
db.inspections.getSearchIndexes()
[
  {
```

```
    id: '66afda78a85a4d1064106881',
    name: 'LocalSearchIndex',
    type: 'search',
    status: 'READY',
    queryable: true,
    latestVersion: 0,
    latestDefinition: { mappings: { dynamic: true, fields: {} } }
  }
]
```

Now you can perform full-text queries with the search index named `LocalSearchIndex`. The following listing shows how to perform an advanced full-text search query in a MongoDB collection using the Atlas Search functionality locally.

Listing 13.2 Executing a full-text search locally

```
db.inspections.aggregate([                    Performs a full-text search
  {                                           with fuzzy matching
    $search: {
      index: 'LocalSearchIndex',              Specifies the name of
      text: {                                 the search index
        query: 'No Violation Issued',         The text you want
        path: ['result', 'business_name'],    to search for
        fuzzy: {
          maxEdits: 2                         The fields you
        }                    Allows up to two want to search in
      }                      typographical errors
    }
  },
  {                                           Additional filter criteria
    $match: {
      sector: 'Cigarette Retail Dealer - 127',   Filters by sector
      'address.city': 'RIDGEWOOD'
    }                                            Filters by city
  },
  {
    $addFields: {
      score: { $meta: "searchScore" }         Includes the search
    }                                         score in the results
  },
  {                        Sorts the results by search
    $sort: {               score in descending order
      score: -1
    }
  },
  {                        Limits the results
    $limit: 3              to the top three
  },
  {                        Specifies the fields
    $project: {            to include in the output
      _id: 0,
      business_name: 1,            Excludes _id from
      certificate_number: 1,       the result
```

```
            date: 1,
            result: 1,
            'address.street': 1,
            'address.number': 1,
            'address.zip': 1,
            score: 1            ◀────┐ Includes the search score
        }
    }
])
```

The query uses fuzzy search to handle typographical errors, filters results based on specific criteria, sorts the results by relevance score, and limits the output to the top three entries. It also demonstrates how to include the search score in the final output for better understanding of the relevance of each result:

```
[
    {
        certificate_number: 50063474,
        business_name: 'GRACE NY INC',
        date: 'Nov 22 2015',
        result: 'No Violation Issued',
        address: { zip: 11385, street: 'WOODWARD AVE', number: 466 },
        score: 1.7540767192840576
    },
    {
        certificate_number: 50065725,
        business_name: 'GRACE NY INC',
        date: 'Dec 19 2015',
        result: 'No Violation Issued',
        address: { zip: 11385, street: 'WOODWARD AVE', number: 466 },
        score: 1.7540767192840576
    },
    {
        certificate_number: 50063482,
        business_name: 'WALGREEN EASTERN CO., INC.',
        date: 'Nov 22 2015',
        result: 'No Violation Issued',
        address: { zip: 11385, street: 'METROPOLITAN AVE', number: 5802 },
        score: 1.637845516204834
    }
]
```

The query performed a full-text search with fuzzy matching using the specified index `LocalSearchIndex`. It searched for the text `"No Violation Issued"` within the fields result and `business_name`, allowing up to two typographical errors. Additional filters were applied to limit the results to the sector `"Cigarette Retail Dealer - 127"` and the city `"RIDGEWOOD"`. The search score was included in the results and used to sort them in descending order. The results were limited to the top three matches and included specific fields in the output. The query returned three results with the highest score. You can find more examples of full-text search in chapter 11.

Creating search indexes

If you want to delete this index, use the command `db.collection`
`.dropSearchIndex(<name>)`:

```
db.inspections.dropSearchIndex("LocalSearchIndex")
```

After you run the command, the index `LocalSearchIndex` will be dropped.

13.5.2 Executing vector search locally

Switch to the `sample_mflix` database, and create a vector search index on the `plot_embedding` field of the `embedded_movies` collection. (This collection already has embeddings in the `plot_embedding` field, as explained in chapter 12.) This field is configured as a `knnVector` with 1,536 dimensions and Euclidean similarity:

```
use sample_mflix
db.embedded_movies.createSearchIndex({
  "name": "vectorSearchIndex",
  "mappings": {
    "dynamic": true,
    "fields": {
      "plot_embedding": {
        "type": "knnVector",
        "dimensions": 1536,
        "similarity": "euclidean"
      }
    }
  }
})
```

A `knnVector` with 1,536 dimensions and Euclidean similarity means that the field is used for k-nearest neighbors (k-NN) searches, specifically for approximate nearest neighbor (ANN) searches, which identify the closest points in a multidimensional space based on a similarity measure. The vector has 1,536 numerical values, representing its position in a 1,536-dimensional space, with each dimension corresponding to a specific feature or attribute of the data. The similarity between vectors is measured using Euclidean distance, which calculates the straight-line distance between two points in this high-dimensional space. Run `getSearchIndexes()` to display the vector search index:

```
db.embedded_movies.getSearchIndexes()
[
  {
    id: '66afe77ea85a4d1064106885',
    name: 'default',
    type: 'search',
    status: 'READY',
    queryable: true,
    latestVersion: 0,
    latestDefinition: {
      mappings: {
```

```
            dynamic: true,
            fields: {
              plot_embedding: {
                type: 'knnVector',
                dimensions: 1536,
                similarity: 'euclidean'
              }
            }
          }
        }
      }
    }
]
```

Chapter 14 delves deeper into Atlas Vector Search and methods for creating embeddings automatically, executing queries using semantic search, and creating AI chatbots using a local Atlas cluster.

Summary

- You can use the Atlas CLI to develop locally with MongoDB Atlas deployments, including Atlas Search and Atlas Vector Search. This enables the creation of full-text search or AI-powered applications in your preferred development environment. The Atlas CLI handles setup, connections, and management tasks from development to production. For full-text search, the Atlas CLI allows you to create and manage Atlas Search indexes locally and in the cloud.
- Running a local Atlas cluster requires Docker to be installed. Docker is a lightweight containerization platform that simplifies how applications are deployed and managed. It enables consistent operation across various environments by bundling applications with their dependencies.
- Using Docker with Atlas locally ensures consistent application performance across environments and isolates the MongoDB environment, preventing conflicts with other applications. Docker also simplifies scaling the local Atlas cluster for testing and development, streamlines the setup process with preconfigured containers, and enables easy movement and replication of the local setup across systems.
- To create your local Atlas cluster, you can use the command `atlas deployments setup --type local`. This command guides you through the setup process, prompting you for deployment settings and providing default values.
- You can use `atlas deployments` to manage your local cluster. This command lets you stop, start, and connect to the database, view logs, and delete your cluster.
- The Atlas CLI currently does not support loading a sample data set for local clusters. Instead, you can download the sample data set and import it into the cluster using `mongorestore`.
- `mongot` runs as a distinct process alongside `mongod`, focusing on search functionality. When configured, `mongot` processes search queries and manages indexes,

allowing `mongod` to handle the core database operations efficiently. This separation of concerns optimizes performance and scalability for applications using MongoDB with advanced search capabilities.

- You can use the `db.collection.createSearchIndex()` wrapper around the `createSearchIndex` database command to create a full-text search index in the local Atlas cluster. To verify the existence of the index, you can use the `getSearchIndexes()` method.
- To drop an index, use the `db.collection.dropSearchIndex(<name>)` monogsh wrapper around the `dropSearchIndex` database command.
- You can manage Atlas Search and Vector Search indexes using the `atlas deployments search indexes create` command locally and in the cloud.

Building retrieval-augmented generation AI chatbots

This chapter covers

- Experiencing large language model hallucinations
- Gaining insight into retrieval-augmented generation and MongoDB
- Localizing Atlas Vector Search within RAG
- Orchestrating the RAG pattern with LangChain
- Building a generative AI chatbot
- Playing with the LangServe playground

Large language model (LMM) hallucinations occur when the model generates information that isn't based on facts or given inputs. These errors can be made-up details, wrong facts, or believable but incorrect responses. They happen because LMMs like GPT-4 generate text from patterns they learned during training, not by checking facts. As a result, they may produce content that looks right but isn't accurate. Reducing these mistakes is important for the reliability of LMMs. Methods include improving training data quality, using real-time fact-checking, adding better verification systems, and using retrieval-augmented generation (RAG), which combines generating text with real-time information retrieval to improve accuracy. MongoDB Atlas Vector Search can serve as a key component for storing and retrieving data that RAG systems rely on, ensuring that LLMs have access to accurate, up-to-date information during the generation process.

RAG is a pattern that enhances the accuracy of language models by integrating text generation with information retrieval techniques. This approach allows the model to access relevant data from external sources during the generation process, reducing the likelihood of producing incorrect or fabricated information. RAG uses a vector database like Atlas Search to store and retrieve high-dimensional data such as text embeddings, enabling the model to efficiently find and use the most relevant information during the text generation process, significantly reducing the chances of hallucinations.

RAG is employed across various applications to enhance the accuracy and reliability of language models. In chatbots, RAG ensures that responses are precise and grounded in relevant, real-time information. In customer support, it helps deliver up-to-date assistance by retrieving the latest data. In technical assistance, RAG enables accurate answers by accessing verified technical resources. For academic research, it aids in producing comprehensive reviews by sourcing data from multiple scholarly articles. In content creation, RAG integrates relevant and verified information, ensuring that the generated content is accurate and credible.

14.1 Gaining insight into retrieval-augmented generation

From a high-level perspective, the RAG pattern operates as illustrated in figure 14.1.

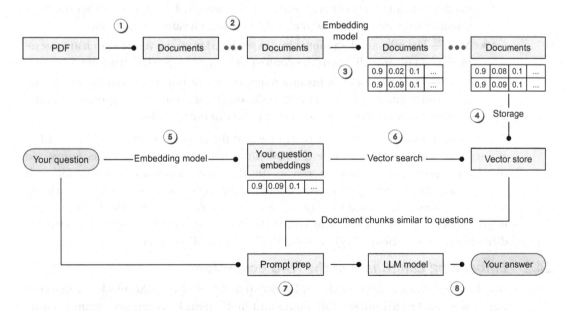

Figure 14.1 RAG paradigm step by step (Image © MongoDB 2024 CC BY-NC-SA 3.0)

The RAG process breaks down into several key steps:

- *Steps 1 and 2*—The process starts with documents, such as PDFs, Microsoft Word documents, and other text-based files, that are broken into small, manageable chunks of text. Typically, these documents are rich in information and may contain detailed content on a specific topic.

    The first technical step involves parsing these documents to extract the raw text, which is then segmented into smaller coherent chunks. Each chunk usually represents a complete piece of information, such as a paragraph or section, making it easier for the system to process and retrieve relevant data later. When processed, these documents become the *source of truth* for the system, meaning that the responses generated by the model are grounded in and derived directly from the information contained within these documents.

- *Step 3*—The process passes the text chunks through an embedding model. This model converts each chunk to a high-dimensional vector representation, capturing the semantic meaning of the text in a format that is easy to compare and search against other vectors.

- *Step 4*—The vector representations are stored in a vector database. This database is optimized for storing and quickly retrieving high-dimensional data, making it easier to find and access relevant information.

- *Step 5*—When a user submits a query, it is similarly processed by the embedding model, converting the query to a vector representation that encapsulates the semantic content of the user's question.

- *Step 6*—The query vector is compared against the stored vectors in the vector database through a process known as vector search. This step identifies the most semantically similar document chunks that are relevant to the query.

- *Step 7*—The relevant document chunks retrieved from the vector search are assembled into a prompt that provides context-rich input for the language model.

- *Step 8*—The LLM uses this prompt to generate a response that is informed by the retrieved information, ensuring that the output is accurate and grounded in the source-of-truth documents processed earlier in the workflow.

The process uses a vector database to ensure that the responses generated by the LLM are accurate and contextually relevant. Documents are parsed into chunks, converted to vector representations, and stored in the database. When a query is made, it is transformed into a vector and matched against the stored vectors. Then the retrieved relevant information is used to generate a response, ensuring that the LLM's output is grounded in verified data. The vector database is essential for efficient retrieval, directly enhancing the quality and reliability of the LLM's responses.

14.2 Embedding LangChain in the RAG ecosystem

Building a generative AI (GenAI) application that relies on the RAG model without the right tools can be extremely challenging and inefficient. RAG requires seamless integration among multiple components: LLMs, embedding models, and vector databases like MongoDB Atlas Vector Search, all of which must work together to retrieve and use relevant information in real time. Without the right tools, you would have to manage the complex interactions between these systems manually, such as by generating embeddings, storing them in a vector database, and ensuring that the LLM can query this database effectively to retrieve contextually appropriate information. This process requires a deep understanding of both machine learning and system architecture, as well as the technical expertise to integrate these diverse components in a way that maintains efficiency and accuracy.

Two of the best frameworks that address these challenges are LangChain and LlamaIndex. Although LlamaIndex is a powerful tool for building datacentric applications, in this book, I focus on using LangChain due to its versatility and robust integration capabilities. LangChain offers a broad range of tools and features that are essential for the topics we will explore. It is a sophisticated framework that facilitates the development of AI applications by seamlessly integrating LLMs with various external data sources and computational tools. This framework is designed to manage complex workflows that require not only text generation but also advanced data retrieval and processing. Figure 14.2 illustrates how LangChain and LlamaIndex are embedded in the ecosystem for developing GenAI applications based on the RAG pattern.

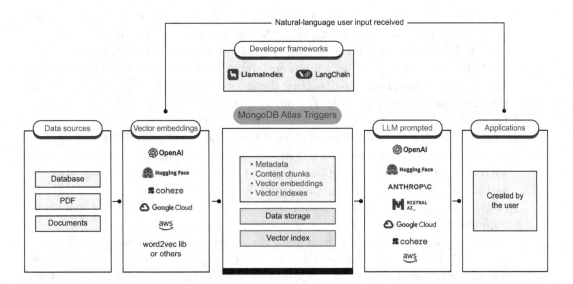

Figure 14.2 Embedding LangChain in the RAG pattern. Data from sources like databases, PDFs, and JSON files is converted to vector embeddings using tools like OpenAI, Cohere, and Hugging Face. These embeddings are stored and indexed in a database. Developer frameworks like LlamaIndex and LangChain manage the processing, storing, and indexing of these embeddings in databases, like MongoDB Atlas, along with metadata and context chunks. When a natural-language input is received, the system retrieves relevant data from the vector index and prompts the LLMs; then the generated output is delivered to the application. Also visible are Atlas Triggers, which react to new documents in the database by automatically using tools like OpenAI to convert them to embeddings and store them in the vector database. (Image © MongoDB 2024 CC BY-NC-SA 3.0)

LangChain serves as a bridge that connects LLMs with external data sources and computational tools. It orchestrates the entire process, starting with receiving natural-language input from various sources, such as user queries in chatbots, databases, transcribed speech, and text extracted from documents, emails, PDFs, and other written formats. Then it manages the generation of vector embeddings using providers like OpenAI, Cohere, and Hugging Face; it also oversees the storage and indexing of these embeddings within a vector search index. This setup enables efficient retrieval and contextual processing of data across formats, ensuring that LLMs can access and use relevant information effectively in AI-driven applications.

One of LangChain's key technical features is its ability to interact with vector databases. These databases store high-dimensional vector representations of text, which are generated by pretrained models. LangChain doesn't generate these embeddings directly; instead, it coordinates the process by which text data is passed through an embedding model, converted to vectors, and stored in a database. Using the `langchain-mongodb` package, LangChain can integrate with Atlas Vector Search, a capability provided by MongoDB Atlas. This integration allows LangChain to store and retrieve embeddings in MongoDB Atlas, using its vector search functionality to find data efficiently based on semantic similarity.

14.3 Introducing the MongoDB Atlas Vector Search RAG template

MongoDB, in collaboration with LangChain, has developed a RAG template called `mongo-ra` that uses MongoDB Atlas Vector Search and OpenAI. This template makes it easy for developers to build and deploy chatbot applications on their proprietary data. LangChain Template provides a reference architecture that can be readily deployed as a REST API using LangServe, making the integration straightforward and efficient. You can check the project in the GitHub `langchain-ai` repo at https://github.com/langchain-ai/langchain.

LangServe is a framework for deploying LangChain models as REST APIs. It integrates with `FastAPI` and uses `pydantic` for data validation, automatically inferring input and output schemas from LangChain objects. LangServe supports invoking, batching, and streaming endpoints, making it suitable for real-time AI applications. It includes built-in tracing and uses Python libraries like `uvloop` and `asyncio` to handle concurrent requests.

Also, when you deploy your chain using LangServe, you gain access to a built-in playground. This playground allows you to modify configurable parameters, experiment with different inputs, and see the responses streamed in real time, enhancing the development and testing experience.

14.4 Getting started with AI chatbots

In this section, you use OpenAI's GPT-4 model to build a chatbot that answers questions about MongoDB Atlas best practices. To minimize the risk of *hallucinations*, which occur when the model generates inaccurate or misleading information by relying solely on learned patterns, you will implement RAG.

In this setup, the chatbot not only generates answers but also retrieves relevant, verified information from an Atlas Vector Search database. This vector database stores embeddings generated from prevalidated data extracted from a PDF file of MongoDB documentation (from https://mng.bz/PwxP), specifically about Atlas. By using this data as context for queries sent to the LLM, the chatbot can provide more reliable, precise answers. The entire setup will be orchestrated by LangChain, ensuring seamless integration and management of all components.

Technically, this process involves embedding the user's query in a vector space and then using this vector to search the database for the most relevant documents. The retrieved documents are used as additional context for the GPT-4 model to generate the final response. This approach significantly reduces the likelihood of errors and improves the reliability of the chatbot by ensuring that it references accurate, up-to-date information when generating responses.

14.4.1 Describing LangChain capabilities

LangChain is a framework for building applications that use LLMs, with one use case being the development of AI-powered chatbots. It is available through the Python LangChain library as well as the JavaScript LangChain. This chapter focuses on the Python version.

LangChain consists of several open source libraries, each serving a distinct purpose in the overall architecture. These libraries work together to provide a toolset for building, integrating, and deploying LLM-powered applications. The LangChain framework includes these key components:

- `langchain-core`—Provides base abstractions and the LangChain Expression Language. It serves as the foundational layer for language model-powered applications.
- `langchain-community`—Facilitates third-party integrations. This library makes it easy for developers to connect LangChain with a variety of external tools and services.
- *Partner packages (e.g.,* `langchain-openai` *and* `langchain-mongodb`*)*—Split certain integrations into their own lightweight packages that depend only on `langchain-core`. These packages simplify the integration process by focusing on specific APIs and services.
- `langchain`—Contains the chains, agents, and retrieval strategies that form an application's cognitive architecture. It provides the essential components to build intelligent and responsive applications.
- `LangGraph`—Enables the construction of robust, stateful multifactor applications with LLMs by modeling steps as edges and nodes in a graph. This approach ensures a clear, scalable structure for managing complex workflows.
- `LangServe`—Allows deployment of LangChain chains as REST APIs. It makes it easy to turn your LangChain models into accessible, scalable web services.

- `LangSmith`—Provide a developer platform designed for debugging, testing, evaluating, and monitoring LLM applications. It offers comprehensive tools to ensure that your models are performing optimally throughout the development life cycle.

> **TIP** If you want to discover more LangChain features, see the official LangChain website (https://mng.bz/Mw07).

14.4.2 Starting with the LangChain CLI

The LangChain command-line interface (CLI) allows you to interact with the LangChain framework directly from the command line. It provides a range of commands for managing and deploying applications built with LangChain, such as creating new projects, running and testing chains, and managing configurations. The CLI simplifies the development process by enabling quick, efficient operations that don't rely on a graphical user interface. This makes it easier to automate tasks, integrate with other tools, and streamline the workflow for building and deploying LLM-powered applications.

To use the LangChain CLI, make sure you have the latest version installed. You can achieve this by using `pip3`, the package manager for Python 3. Run the following command:

```
pip3 install -U langchain-cli
```

After completing the installation, you can launch the LangChain CLI to view the user interface by typing `langchain-cli`. You've successfully launched the CLI when you see this message:

```
langchain-cli
 Usage: langchain-cli [OPTIONS] COMMAND [ARGS]...
┌─Options─────────────────────────────────────────────────┐
│ --version   -v        Print the current CLI version.    │
│ --help                Show this message and exit.       │
└─────────────────────────────────────────────────────────┘
┌─Commands────────────────────────────────────────────────┐
│ app           Manage LangChain apps                     │
│ integration   Develop integration packages for LangChain.│
│ migrate       Migrate LangChain to the most recent version.│
│ serve         Start the LangServe app, whether it's a template or an app.│
│ template      Develop installable templates.            │
└─────────────────────────────────────────────────────────┘
```

> **TIP** You can use the LangChain CLI to interact with LangChain templates such as `mongo-rag`, which allow you to build AI applications quickly.

14.5 Creating an AI-powered MongoDB chatbot

Use the LangChain CLI to set up a LangServe project quickly. In this example, the project is named `mongodb-in-action` and specifies the template to use: `rag-mongo`.

This approach allows you to bootstrap the project with all the necessary components in place.

14.5.1 Setting up a new application

Follow these steps to create a new LangChain project:

1. Run the following command:

```
langchain app new mongodb-in-action --package rag-mongo
```

2. Confirm that you want to install LangChain by typing Y at the following prompt:

```
Would you like to install these templates into
➥your environment with pip? [y/N]:
```

This command creates a new LangChain project and adds the `mongo-rag` template for building applications based on MongoDB Atlas. When successful, you see the following message:

```
Success! Created a new LangChain app under "./mongodb-in-action"!
```

The command creates a new LangChain application named `mongodb-in-action` using the `rag-mongo` template. You can also use the `--non-interactive` flag to ensure that the process runs automatically without prompting you for additional input.

The command creates a new directory called `mongodb-in-action`. The following listing shows the structure of the files and directories in the new directory.

> **Listing 14.1 Files and directories in the LangChain project**

```
├── Dockerfile
├── README.md
├── app
│   ├── __init__.py
│   ├── __pycache__
│   │   ├── __init__.cpython-312.pyc
│   │   └── server.cpython-312.pyc
│   └── server.py
├── packages
│   ├── README.md
│   └── rag-mongo
│       ├── LICENSE
│       ├── README.md
│       ├── _images
│       │   ├── cluster.png
│       │   ├── collections.png
│       │   ├── connect.png
│       │   ├── create.png
│       │   ├── driver.png
│       │   ├── json.png
│       │   ├── json_editor.png
```

```
|   |       ├── search-indexes.png
|   |       └── uri.png
|   ├── ingest.py
|   ├── pyproject.toml
|   ├── rag_mongo
|   |   ├── __init__.py
|   |   └── chain.py
|   ├── rag_mongo.ipynb
|   └── tests
|       └── __init__.py
└── pyproject.toml
```

The structure shows a Python-based `LangChain` application organized under a root directory called `mongodb-in-action` with the `rag-mongo` template:

- `__init__.py` *file in the* `app` *directory*—Designates this folder as a Python package, enabling its modules to be imported throughout the application
- `__pycache__` *directory*—Contains compiled Python files (`.pyc`), speeding the execution of Python code
- `server.py` *file*—Handles the server-side logic of the application, managing API requests and database interactions
- `rag-mongo` *subdirectory within packages*—Manages MongoDB-related tasks within the LangChain application
- `ingest.py` *file*—Ingests data into MongoDB and interacts with Atlas Vector Search
- `rag_mongo` *folder* (subpackage within `rag-mongo`)—Contains code specific to MongoDB Atlas operations
- `chain.py` *file*—Sets up a process to answer questions by combining data from a MongoDB Atlas database with a language model, following the RAG pattern

You also need to install the `langchain_openai` module, which you can do via this command:

```
pip3 install langchain_openai
```

Next, you must make some minor adjustments to the default settings of the new project. Modify the `mongodb-in-action/app/server.py` file by adding the following code:

```
from rag_mongo import chain as rag_mongo_chain
add_routes(app, rag_mongo_chain, path="/rag-mongo")
```

After the modification, the `mongodb-in-action/app/server.py` file looks like this:

```
from fastapi import FastAPI
from langserve import add_routes
from rag_mongo import chain as rag_mongo_chain

app = FastAPI()
```

Creating an AI-powered MongoDB chatbot

```
# Edit this to add the chain you want to add
add_routes(app, rag_mongo_chain, path="/rag-mongo")

if __name__ == "__main__":
    import uvicorn

    uvicorn.run(app, host="0.0.0.0", port=8000)
```

Each of the following lines plays a specific role. Here's what they do:

- `#from rag_mongo`—Imports the chain module from the `rag_mongo` package and assigns it to `rag_mongo_chain` for clarity in the code. You must add this line to the `mongodb-in-action/app/server.py` file.
- `add_routes`—Adds the routes defined in `rag_mongo_chain` to the FastAPI application, making them accessible under the path `/rag-mongo`. You must add this line to the `mongodb-in-action/app/server.py` file.
- `if __name__ == "__main__"`—Ensures that the FastAPI app runs when the script is executed directly, using `uvicorn.run()` on host `0.0.0.0` and port `8000`.

14.5.2 Inserting embeddings into MongoDB Atlas

As I mentioned earlier, LangChain automates the process of creating embeddings from our data and storing them in a MongoDB collection. These embeddings serve as verified data and become the source of truth, which is sent as context to the LLM module in response to queries, following the principles of RAG.

The chatbot will answer questions about MongoDB Atlas best practices, so you'll use the official MongoDB documentation in PDF format as the data. This data will be stored in a MongoDB collection as embeddings.

To do this, navigate to the directory `mongodb-in-action/packages/rag-mongo`, and open the `ingest.py` file. In this file, change the default names of the MongoDB database, collection, and vector search index. Also update the URL of the document you want to use to generate embeddings. In this case, the database name will be `langchain`, the collection name will be `mongodb`, the index name (which you'll create in MongoDB Atlas) will be `default`, and the link to the MongoDB documentation in PDF format will be https://mng.bz/PwxP. After modification, the `ingest.py` file looks like this:

```
import os
from langchain_community.document_loaders import PyPDFLoader
from langchain_openai import OpenAIEmbeddings
from langchain.text_splitter import RecursiveCharacterTextSplitter
from langchain_community.vectorstores import MongoDBAtlasVectorSearch
from pymongo import MongoClient

MONGO_URI = os.environ["MONGO_URI"]

# Note that if you change this, you also
 need to change it in `rag_mongo/chain.py`
DB_NAME = "langchain"                              ◀──── Database name
```

```
COLLECTION_NAME = "mongodb"                          ◄─── Collection name
ATLAS_VECTOR_SEARCH_INDEX_NAME = "default"           ◄───
EMBEDDING_FIELD_NAME = "embedding"                        Index name
client = MongoClient(MONGO_URI)
db = client[DB_NAME]
MONGODB_COLLECTION = db[COLLECTION_NAME]

if __name__ == "__main__":
    # Load docs
    loader = PyPDFLoader("https://mng.bz/PwxP")   ◄───  Link to the MongoDB
    data = loader.load()                                documentation

    # Split docs
    text_splitter = RecursiveCharacterTextSplitter
 ⇨ (chunk_size=500, chunk_overlap=0)
    docs = text_splitter.split_documents(data)

    # Insert the documents in MongoDB Atlas Vector Search
    _ = MongoDBAtlasVectorSearch.from_documents(
        documents=docs,
        embedding=OpenAIEmbeddings(disallowed_special=()),
        collection=MONGODB_COLLECTION,
        index_name=ATLAS_VECTOR_SEARCH_INDEX_NAME,
    )
```

The following list explains the main components of the preceding code:

- `PyPDFLoader`—Loads and processes PDF documents
- `OpenAIEmbeddings`—Generates vector embeddings for the text chunks
- `RecursiveCharacterTextSplitter`—Splits the document text into smaller chunks
- `MongoDBAtlasVectorSearch`—Handles inserting and searching documents in MongoDB Atlas using vector embeddings
- `MongoClient`—Establishes a connection with MongoDB
- `MongoDB URI`—Connects to the database
- `DB_NAME`—Specifies the name of the database used in MongoDB
- `COLLECTION_NAME`—Specifies the collection name where vector embeddings will be stored
- `ATLAS_VECTOR_SEARCH_INDEX_NAME`—Defines the name of the vector search index in MongoDB Atlas
- `EMBEDDING_FIELD_NAME`—Specifies the field name where the embeddings will be stored
- `client`—Initializes the MongoDB client with the specified URI
- `MONGODB_COLLECTION`—Establishes a reference to the MongoDB collection where documents will be stored
- `PyPDFLoader`—Loads the PDF document from a specified URL for processing

- `text_splitter`—Splits the document into chunks of 500 characters each, with no overlap
- `embedding`—Generates vector embeddings for each chunk using `OpenAIEmbeddings`
- `index_name`—Inserts the processed documents with their embeddings into MongoDB Atlas, making them searchable via vector search

You also need to update the `chain.py` file, located at `mongodb-in-action/packages/rag-mongo/rag_mongo/chain.py`, by setting `DB_NAME = "langchain"`, `COLLECTION_NAME = "mongodb"`, and `ATLAS_VECTOR_SEARCH_INDEX_NAME = "default"`. Here's the modified `chain.py` file:

```
import os
from langchain_openai import ChatOpenAI
from langchain_community.document_loaders import PyPDFLoader
from langchain_openai import OpenAIEmbeddings
from langchain_community.vectorstores import MongoDBAtlasVectorSearch
from langchain_core.output_parsers import StrOutputParser
from langchain_core.prompts import ChatPromptTemplate
from langchain_core.pydantic_v1 import BaseModel
from langchain_core.runnables import (
    RunnableLambda,
    RunnableParallel,
    RunnablePassthrough,
)
from langchain_text_splitters import RecursiveCharacterTextSplitter
from pymongo import MongoClient

# Set DB
if os.environ.get("MONGO_URI", None) is None:
    raise Exception("Missing `MONGO_URI` environment variable.")
MONGO_URI = os.environ["MONGO_URI"]

DB_NAME = "langchain"
COLLECTION_NAME = "mongodb"
ATLAS_VECTOR_SEARCH_INDEX_NAME = "default"

client = MongoClient(MONGO_URI)
db = client[DB_NAME]
MONGODB_COLLECTION = db[COLLECTION_NAME]

# Read from MongoDB Atlas Vector Search
vectorstore = MongoDBAtlasVectorSearch.from_connection_string(
    MONGO_URI,
    DB_NAME + "." + COLLECTION_NAME,
    OpenAIEmbeddings(disallowed_special=()),
    index_name=ATLAS_VECTOR_SEARCH_INDEX_NAME,
)
retriever = vectorstore.as_retriever(search_kwargs={"k": 1})

# RAG prompt
template = """Answer the question based only on the following context:
```

```
{context}
Question: {question}
"""
prompt = ChatPromptTemplate.from_template(template)

# RAG
model = ChatOpenAI()
chain = (
   RunnableParallel({"context": retriever,
"question": RunnablePassthrough()})
   | prompt
   | model
   | StrOutputParser()
)


# Add typing for input
class Question(BaseModel):
    __root__: str


chain = chain.with_types(input_type=Question)


def _ingest(url: str) -> dict:
    loader = PyPDFLoader(url)
    data = loader.load()

    # Split docs
    text_splitter = RecursiveCharacterTextSplitter
(chunk_size=500, chunk_overlap=0)
    docs = text_splitter.split_documents(data)

    # Insert the documents in MongoDB Atlas Vector Search
    _ = MongoDBAtlasVectorSearch.from_documents(
        documents=docs,
        embedding=OpenAIEmbeddings(disallowed_special=()),
        collection=MONGODB_COLLECTION,
        index_name=ATLAS_VECTOR_SEARCH_INDEX_NAME,
    )
    return {}

ingest = RunnableLambda(_ingest)
```

Here's how it works:

- `ChatOpenAI`—Uses this language model to generate answers
- `PyPDFLoader`—Loads and processes PDF documents from a given URL
- `OpenAIEmbeddings`—Generates vector embeddings from text chunks
- `MongoDBAtlasVectorSearch`—Interacts with MongoDB Atlas for storing and retrieving vector embeddings
- `StrOutputParser`—Parses the model's output into a string format

- `ChatPromptTemplate`—Formats the prompts sent to the language model
- `BaseModel` *from* `pydantic`—Handles data validation and typing
- `RunnableLambda` *(runnable task)*—Executes a lambda function
- `RunnableParallel` *(runnable task)*—Runs multiple tasks in parallel
- `RunnablePassthrough` *(simple runnable task)*—Passes its input to the next stage
- `RecursiveCharacterTextSplitter`—Splits the text into smaller chunks for processing
- `MongoClient`—Connects to MongoDB
- `Set DB`—Checks whether the `MONGO_URI` environment variable is set and raises an exception if it's missing
- `DB_NAME`—Specifies the name of the MongoDB database
- `COLLECTION_NAME`—Specifies the collection where the vector embeddings are stored
- `ATLAS_VECTOR_SEARCH_INDEX_NAME`—Defines the name of the vector search index in MongoDB Atlas
- `client`—Initializes the MongoDB client with the specified URI
- `MONGODB_COLLECTION`—References the MongoDB collection where the documents are stored
- `index_name`—Sets up the vector store for reading from MongoDB Atlas Vector Search
- `prompt`—Creates a prompt template for the RAG process, specifying the format of the question and context
- `mode`—Initializes the ChatOpenAI model to handle the RAG process
- `RunnablePassthrough`—Configures a parallel runnable to retrieve context and pass the question through the chain
- `StrOutputParser`—Converts the model's output to a string format
- `class`—Defines a `Question` class for typing the input question
- `chain`—Associates the `Question` class with the input type for the chain
- `def`—Defines the `_ingest` function, which loads a PDF, splits it into chunks, and stores these chunks in MongoDB Atlas as vector embeddings

NOTE You might get this error message: `openai.BadRequestError: Error code: 400 - {'error': {'message': "This model's maximum context length is 16385 tokens. However, your messages resulted in 47259 tokens}`. To avoid this message, set the limit to one embedding by adjusting the retriever configuration. This ensures that only one result is returned, minimizing context passed to the model.

Next, export your OpenAI API key and MongoDB Atlas URI:

```
export OPENAI_API_KEY="<your OpenAI API key>"
```

Replace `<your OpenAI API key>` with your actual OpenAI API key. For this example, I use a local Atlas cluster that I created using the Atlas CLI in chapter 13. You can do the same or use your own Atlas cluster available in the cloud. LangChain works the same way with either cluster. As a reminder, you can display the local Atlas cluster by using the command `atlas deployments connect -connectWith` as in this example:

```
atlas deployments connect --connectWith local9619
```

The local Atlas cluster named `local9619` connection string URI is displayed:

```
mongodb://localhost:27017/?directConnection=true
```

Note that it does not include a username or password; this local test cluster should not be used to store sensitive data. The cluster is only for tests and development proposes. Export the MongoDB Atlas local cluster URI as follows:

```
export MONGO_URI="mongodb://localhost:27017/?directConnection=true"
```

Now you can begin creating embeddings from a PDF document containing best practices. You'll use MongoDB Atlas and insert those embeddings into MongoDB Atlas using LangChain. The directory `mongodb-in-action/packages/rag-mongo` contains a file named `ingest.py`. Run this file with the following command:

```
python3 ingest.py
```

Creating and inserting embeddings into the MongoDB Atlas collection takes a few minutes. When the process is complete, log in to the local Atlas cluster using MongoDB Shell (`mongosh`):

```
mongosh "mongodb://localhost:27017/?directConnection=true"
```

Now, using the command `show dbs`, display the available databases. Notice that along with the databases created during the sample data load in chapter 13, there is a new database named `langchain`:

```
admin                 120.00 KiB
config                332.00 KiB
langchain               2.26 MiB
local                 250.84 MiB
sample_airbnb          52.75 MiB
sample_analytics        9.54 MiB
sample_geospatial       1.21 MiB
sample_guides          40.00 KiB
sample_mflix          110.28 MiB
sample_restaurants      6.20 MiB
sample_supplies         1.03 MiB
sample_training        47.62 MiB
sample_weatherdata      2.55 MiB
```

Creating an AI-powered MongoDB chatbot

With the command `use langchain`, set the `langchain` database as your current database, and display the collections using the `show collections` command:

```
use langchain
show collections
    mongodb
```

Use the `find()` command to display a single arbitrary document from the new `mongodb` collection: `db.mongodb.find({})`. The arbitrary document returned looks like this:

```
[
  {
    _id: ObjectId('66b7c4cd9f3322f67d485f1f'),
    text: 'Indexes\n' +
      'MongoDB uses B-tree indexes to optimize queries. Indexes\n' +
      'are defined on a collection\'s document fields. MongoDB\n' +
      'includes support for many indexes, including compound,\n' +
      'geospatial, TTL, text search, sparse, partial, unique, and\n' +
      'others. For more information see the section on indexing\n' +
      'below.\n' +
      'Transactions\n' +
      'Multi-document ACID transactions are available for users\n' +
      'of MongoDB 4.0 and later. With snapshot isolation and\n' +
      'all-or-nothing execution, transactions extend MongoDB',
    embedding: [
      -0.01761315017938614,  0.03746514022350311,  0.003932139370590448,
      -0.013999832794070244, -0.042311232537031174, 0.017117204144597054,
      -0.002088284818455577, -0.024598896503448486, -0.0032502140384167433,
      -0.01795322634279728,  0.025094840675592422, 0.026355959475040436,
       0.007311653345823288, 0.017698168754577637, 0.0034751608036458492,
       0.023592835292220116, 0.00828937441110611, -0.008346053771674633,
       0.021934960037469864, -0.008353139273822308, -0.011087924242019653,
      -0.0037443884648382664, -0.00025882155750878155,
      -0.013000856153666973, 0.016748787835240364,  0.02961502969264984,
      -0.016791297122836113, -0.0041694846004247665, 0.01585608534514904,
       0.021779092028737068, -0.001471895375289023, -0.038060273975133896,
      -0.040185753256082535, -0.024924803525209427, -0.011683058924973011,
       0.0006960948812775314, -0.014219465665519238, 0.0007306339684873819,
       0.008473582565784454, 0.022912681102752686, -0.015601027756929398,
      -0.009352114982903004, -0.001107906806282699, 0.01379436906427145,
       0.014793344773352146, -0.0029933853074908257, -0.01463747776461935,
      -0.005756509955972433, -0.03650158643722534,  0.008579856716096401,
       0.04593872278928757, -0.042197875678539276,  0.013851048424839973,
       0.008721555583178997, -0.03199556842446327,  0.027687927708029747,
      -0.0014267289079725742, 0.00809808075428009, -0.01104541402310133,
      -0.01019522175192833, 0.019129326567053795,  0.01867588981986046,
      -0.04163108002102 0889, 0.020971408113837242, -0.02659684792160988,
       0.016720447689294815, 0.01928519457578659,  0.025264879688620567,
      -0.014488693326711655, -0.01142800040543 0794, 0.012568674981594086,
       0.010400685481727123, 0.012143579311668873, 0.03550969809293747,
      -0.02451387606561184, -0.010365260764956474, 0.014460353180766106,
       0.00586278410628438, -0.00844524335116148, -0.007014086004346609,
       0.030578581616282463, -0.008331883698701859, 0.019568592309951782,
      -0.0006650983123108745, -0.6098712682723999, -0.016040293499827385,
```

```
        -0.0033529456704854965, -0.041546061635017395, 0.02206248976290226,
        0.007417927496135235, 0.01379436906427145, 0.028523949906229973,
        -0.006496885791420937, 0.004998421762138605, -0.002538178116083145,
        -0.006082416977733374, -0.00103262928314507, -0.02481144294142723,
        -0.010471534915268421, -0.017414771020412445, 0.0028392879758030176,
        -0.02516569010913372, -0.010747847147285938, 0.003857747418805957,
        -0.012915837578475475, 0.016621258109807968, -0.01278122328221798,
        0.005774222314357758, -0.013418867252767086, -0.0010414854623377323,
        0.025307388976216316, -0.0017641489394009113, 0.0011318183969706297,
        0.02381955273449421, -0.005830901674926281, 0.006202860735356808,
        0.01650789938867092, -0.02930329367518425, -0.049537867307662964,
        -0.0047398218885064125, -0.004792958963662386, 0.013681010343134403,
        -0.0012141808401793242, 0.020475463941693306, -0.00981972087174654,
        -0.010790356434881687, -0.012462401762604713, 0.0011132204672321677,
        -0.022558433935046196, -0.007382502779364586, -0.025080671533942223,
        -0.009040378034114838, 0.018746739253401756, 0.015955274924635887,
        0.0034096252638846636, ... 1436 more items   ],
    source: 'https://query.prod.cms.rt.microsoft.com/
  cms/api/am/binary/RE4HkJP',
    page: 4
  }
]
```

In the document, you can see that LangChain split the PDF into chunks and sent these chunks to the OpenAI Embedding API, where they were converted to embeddings; then the embeddings were stored in the `MongoDB` collection along with the original text. The `text` field containing the human-readable content has been converted to a corresponding embedding:

```
'MongoDB uses B-tree indexes to optimize queries.
Indexes are defined on a collection's document fields.
MongoDB includes support for many indexes, including
compound, geospatial, TTL, text search, sparse, partial,
unique, and others. For more information see the section
on indexing below. Transactions Multi-document ACID
transactions are available for users of MongoDB 4.0 and later.
With snapshot isolation and all-or-nothing execution,
transactions extend MongoDB'
```

This embedding, along with the original text, is stored in the same document under the embedding key. The text originates from page 4 of the document at the source URL: https://mng.bz/PwxP.

By running the command `db.vectorSearch.countDocuments()`, you see that 158 documents were created, containing chunks from the PDF document along with the corresponding embeddings.

14.5.3 Creating an Atlas Vector Search index

The next step in building the AI chatbot is creating an Atlas Vector Search index. You can do this because you generated embeddings in the `langchain` database within the vectorSearch collection. Using the Atlas CLI, create a file named vector-search.json with the following content:

```
{
  "name": "default",
  "type": "vectorSearch",
  "collectionName": "mongodb",
  "database": "langchain",
  "fields": [
    {
      "type": "vector",
      "path": "embedding",
      "numDimensions": 1536,
      "similarity": "cosine"
    }
  ]
}
```

This JSON configuration defines an index named `default` of type `vectorSearch`. The index is applied to the `mongodb` collection within the `langchain` database. It is designed to handle vector data stored in the `embedding` field, which contains 1,536-dimensional vectors. The index uses cosine similarity to compare these vectors—a common method for measuring similarity between vectors.

Next, using the Atlas CLI and the command `atlas deployments search indexes create`, create the vector search index in the local Atlas cluster. Use `vector-search.json` file with an index definition as an input parameter to the command:

```
atlas deployments search indexes create \
--file vector-search.json --type LOCAL
```

In about a minute, the vector search index is created:

```
Search index created with ID: 66b7d2aea85a4d1064106886
```

Log in to the local Atlas cluster again using `mongosh`, switch to the `langchain` database, and use the command `getSearchIndexes()` to ensure that the index was created correctly:

```
use langchain
db.mongodb.getSearchIndexes()
[
  {
    id: '66b88766a85a4d1064106890',
    name: 'default',
    type: 'vectorSearch',
    status: 'READY',
    queryable: true,
    latestVersion: 0,
    latestDefinition: {
      fields: [
```

```
              {
                type: 'vector',
                path: 'embedding',
                numDimensions: 1536,
                similarity: 'cosine'
              }
            ]
          }
        }
      ]
```

The output confirms that the vector search index named `default` was successfully created in the `monogdb` collection of the `langchain` database. The index is of type `vectorSearch`, uses cosine similarity, and is marked as READY, indicating that it is fully operational and queryable. The index targets the `embedding` field, which has 1,536 dimensions.

14.5.4 Testing a chatbot with LangServe

Now you can start testing whether the chatbot, which answers questions about best practices for using Atlas, is working. To do this, launch the LangServe playground by running the following command from the main directory of LangChain, `mongodb-in-action`:

```
langchain serve
```

After starting the server, you see the message shown in figure 14.3.

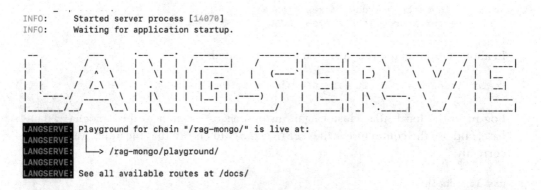

Figure 14.3 The server LangServe process has started, and the application is waiting for further commands. The message indicates that the playground for the chain `/rag-mongo/` is live and accessible at `/rag-mongo/playground`. It also provides a link to all available routes at `/docs/`, where you can explore the API documentation and test the chatbot's functionality. (Image © MongoDB 2025)

The server is running on port 8000 on the local host. In your web browser, enter the following URL: `http://127.0.0.1:8000/rag-mongo/playground/`. You see an interface for interacting with the chatbot.

Creating an AI-powered MongoDB chatbot 377

To start testing the chatbot, type "What indexes does MongoDB support?" in the Inputs field; then click Start. In a few seconds, you see the response in the Output field (figure 14.4).

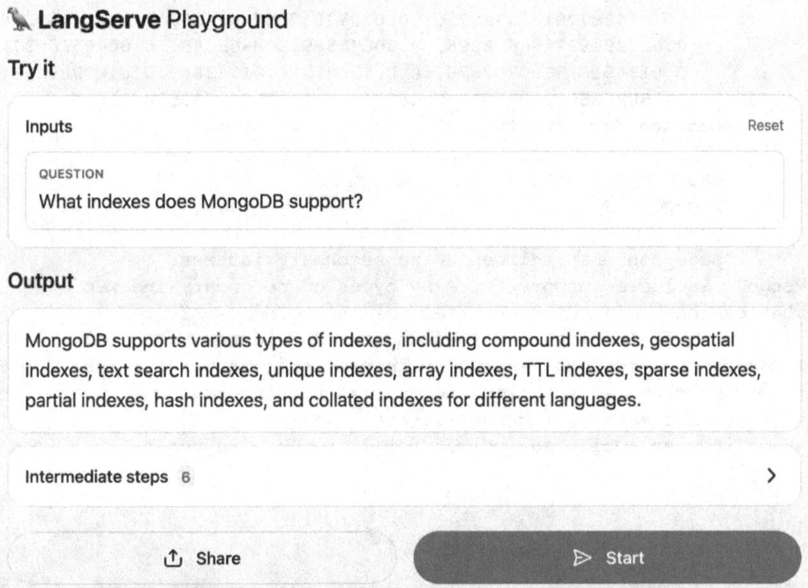

LangServe Playground

Try it

Inputs   Reset

QUESTION
What indexes does MongoDB support?

Output

MongoDB supports various types of indexes, including compound indexes, geospatial indexes, text search indexes, unique indexes, array indexes, TTL indexes, sparse indexes, partial indexes, hash indexes, and collated indexes for different languages.

Intermediate steps 6   >

                 Share   ▷ Start

Figure 14.4 The LangServe Playground interface when a user asks "What indexes does MongoDB support?" The output lists various types of indexes supported by MongoDB, including compound, geospatial, text search, and unique. Below the output, the interface shows that six intermediate steps are visible, highlighting the process taken to generate the response. The interface also includes a Start button to initiate the process and a Share button for sharing results. (Image © MongoDB 2025)

Click the Intermediate Steps menu in the LangServe Playground interface, and you'll see how the LangChain `mongo-rag` template works under the hood:

1 `RunnableParallel<context,question>` stakes the user's question and the provided context as input and converts the question to an embedding, a numerical representation of the text.

This embedding is used to match the question with the most relevant context or documents. The prepared data is set up for parallel processing in subsequent steps:

```
{
  "question": "What indexes does MongoDB support?",
  "context": [
    {
      "id": null,
```

```
        "metadata": {
            "_id": "66b88ee93df2356d3d74556a",
            "embedding": [
                0.009976638481020927, 0.03502347320318222, 0.0018557107541710138,
                -0.020332135260105133, -0.04843791201710701, 0.0358373187482357,
                -0.0036973897367715836, 0.02977556362748146,0.012319955043494701,
                -0.009632858447730541, -0.006668631918728352, 0.00555660855025053,
                -0.0148877818137407, -0.03277837857604027, 0.03014039248228073,
                0.027291927486658096, 0.006345899309962988, 0.004051693715155125,
                0.013491613790392876, 0.021188078448176384, 0.018928952515275,
        0.049813032150268555, 0.00909964833441, 0.001960949506610632
➡ // shortened for clarity
            ],
            "source": "https://mng.bz/PwxP",
            "page": 7
        },
        "page_content": "indexes are secondary indexes.
MongoDB includes support for many types of secondary indexes
that can be declared on any field(s) in the document,
 including fields within arrays and sub-documents.
Index options include: •Compound indexes •Geospatial indexes
•Text search indexes •Unique indexes •Array indexes
•TTL indexes •Sparse indexes •Partial Indexes
•Hash indexes •Collated indexes for different languages."
        }
    ]
}
```

2 **Retriever** fetches relevant documents from the Atlas Vector Search index based on the question.

It uses the embeddings (numerical representations) in the context to find the most relevant documents. The embeddings allow the retriever to identify and rank documents that are semantically similar to the query, ensuring that the most relevant information is retrieved for the next steps in the process:

```
{
    "documents": [
        {
            "id": null,
            "metadata": {
                "_id": "66b88ee93df2356d3d74556a",
                "embedding": [
0.009976638481020927, 0.03502347320318222, 0.0018557107541710138,
-0.020332135260105133, 0.04843791121710701,0.02515908894724846,
0.0015636731404811144, 0.0405800785946503, 0.00609332640372419,
0.010439688339829445, 0.001372489377188997, 0.002436781550735235,
0.020247945562005043, 0.013246056623756886, 0.021398555487394333,
0.019490225240588188, 0.025972936302423477, 0.0024818817619234324,
0.03564087301492691, 0.026337763945776, 0.03909270465373993,
0.005093557760119438, 0.014957941137254238, 0.03900851309299469,
0.00571095896884799, 0.0010339712025597692, 0.008026212453842163,
0.0075349858850241, 0.0289897064246292, 0.02027008173823357,
        ... // shortened for clarity
```

```
              ],
              "source": "https://mng.bz/PwxP",
              "page": 7
          },
          "page_content": "indexes are secondary indexes.
MongoDB includes support for many types of secondary indexes
 that can be declared on any field(s) in the document,
including fields within arrays and sub-documents.
Index options include: •Compound indexes
•Geospatial indexes •Text search indexes •Unique indexes
•Array indexes •TTL indexes •Sparse indexes •Partial Indexes
•Hash indexes •Collated indexes for different languages."
      }
   ]
}
```

3 `RunnablePassthrough` passes the output from step 2 (likely the retrieved documents or context) directly to step 4 without any changes:

```
{
    "output": "What indexes does MongoDB support?"
}
```

4 `ChatPromptTemplate` takes the retrieved document content and the relevant metadata, which is the context information obtained from the vector search.

This metadata includes details such as the document's source, page number, and embedding vectors that represent the content of the document. The step combines this context with the user's question to create a structured prompt. This clear, organized prompt allows the AI to fully understand the question in relation to the provided context, enabling it to generate a precise, relevant answer:

```
{
  "messages": [
    {
      "content": "Answer the question based only
➥ on the following context:\n[Document(
➥ metadata={'_id': ObjectId('66b88ee93df2356d3d74556a'),
➥ 'embedding': [
         0.00997638481020927, 0.035347320318222, 0.00185571075417138,
0.020332135260105133,0.04843791201710701,0.0251590888724846,
0.0015636731404811144,0.04058007895946503,0.006093326490372419,
0.01894298382103443,0.011050073429942131,0.015336801297962666,
0.015266641974449158,0.0098228759676218,0.009646889753639698,
0.02243691124022007,0.0010778206633403897,0.013709107413887978,
0.027923360466957092,0.013309200294315815,0.00028173302416689694,
0.010888707782405138,0.007408811245113611,0.0102502590797806,
-0.014080950990319252,0.016908366233110428,0.018522027879953384,
0.019714735448360443,0.00040188065031543374,0.0038306922651827335,
0.019209587946534157,0.013442502357065678,0.014452794566750526,
0.026562273502349854,0.016304997727274895,0.04108522832393646,
0.0018241391517221928, 0.0030817429069429636, -0.009338188916444778,
```

```
            -0.020570676773786545, -0.01960247941315174
    ... // shortened for clarity
            ], 'source': 'https://query.prod.cms.rt.microsoft.com/cms/api
    /am/binary/RE4HkJP', 'page': 7},
    page_content='indexes are secondary indexes.
MongoDB includes support for many types of secondary
indexes that can be declared on any field(s) in the document,
including fields within arrays and sub-documents.
Index options include: •Compound indexes •Geospatial indexes
•Text search indexes •Unique indexes •Array indexes
•TTL indexes •Sparse indexes •Partial Indexes •Hash indexes
•Collated indexes for different languages.
You can learn more about each of these
    indexes from the')]\nQuestion:
What indexes does MongoDB support?\n",
        "additional_kwargs": {},
        "response_metadata": {},
        "type": "human",
        "name": null,
        "id": null,
        "example": false
      }
    ]
}
```

5 The `ChatOpenAI` model processes the prompt generated in step 4 and generates a response.

The response contains the answer to the user's question based on the context provided. The output includes details such as the reason why the generation stopped and which AI model was used:

```
{
  "generations": [
    [
      {
        "text": "MongoDB supports various types of indexes,
including compound indexes, geospatial indexes,
text search indexes, unique indexes, array indexes,
TTL indexes, sparse indexes, partial indexes, hash indexes,
and collated indexes for different languages.",
        "generation_info": {
          "finish_reason": "stop",
          "model_name": "gpt-3.5-turbo-0125"
        },
        "type": "ChatGenerationChunk",
        "message": {
          "content": "MongoDB supports various types of indexes,
including compound indexes, geospatial indexes,
text search indexes, unique indexes, array indexes,
TTL indexes, sparse indexes,
partial indexes, hash indexes,
and collated indexes for different languages.",
          "additional_kwargs": {},
```

```
                    "response_metadata": {
                      "finish_reason": "stop",
                      "model_name": "gpt-3.5-turbo-0125"
                    },
                    "type": "AIMessageChunk",
                    "name": null,
                    "id": "run-aea0b101-c006-4ec9-b4de-4e98d021e35d",
                    "example": false,
                    "tool_calls": [],
                    "invalid_tool_calls": [],
                    "usage_metadata": null,
                    "tool_call_chunks": []
                  }
                }
              ]
           ],
           "llm_output": null,
           "run": null
         }
```

6 `StrOutputParser` extracts the relevant text from the AI's response, which is presented to the user as the final output:

```
{
  "output": "MongoDB supports various types of indexes,
including compound indexes, geospatial indexes, text search indexes,
unique indexes, array indexes, TTL indexes, sparse indexes,
partial indexes, hash indexes, and collated indexes
for different languages."
}
```

The process begins with the `RunnableParallel` step, in which the user's question and context are converted to embeddings for parallel processing. The `Retriever` uses these embeddings to fetch relevant documents from the Atlas Vector Search index. The `RunnablePassthrough` step forwards the retrieved documents to the next step. In the `ChatPromptTemplate` step, the document content and metadata from the vector search are combined with the user's question to create a structured prompt. The `ChatOpenAI` step processes this prompt, generating a response based on the context. Finally, the `StrOutputParser` extracts the key text from the AI's response to be presented as the final output.

14.5.5 Communicating programmatically with a chatbot

You can communicate with the server without using the GUI by using tools such as `curl`. This method enables programmatic communication via the command line, allowing you to send HTTP requests directly to the server. This approach is particularly useful for automation, scripting, and testing, as it allows you to interact with the server programmatically and efficiently manage requests and responses without relying on a graphical interface. You can achieve similar communication by using various programming languages.

Use `curl` to send a POST request to the chatbot with a question:

```
curl -X POST "http://127.0.0.1:8000/rag-mongo/invoke" \
    -H "Content-Type: application/json" \
    -d '{"input": "Explain how MongoDB Atlas uses encryption."}'
```

The response from the chatbot explains that MongoDB Atlas uses encryption in two ways:

```
{"output":"MongoDB Atlas uses encryption in two ways:
it provides encryption of data at rest with encrypted storage
volumes by default, and users can configure an additional
layer of encryption on their data at rest using the
MongoDB Encrypted Storage Engine and their Atlas-compatible key.
This ensures that data stored in MongoDB Atlas is secure and
protected from unauthorized access.",
"metadata":{"run_id":"53a7e3d5-88fd-4943-
9c9d-09ed68ffe5b1","feedback_tokens":[]}}
```

Using methods like `curl` to interact with a LangChain chatbot enables direct command-line communication, which is ideal for automation, scripting, and testing. This approach efficiently handles server requests without a GUI, making it suitable for technical workflows that require programmatic interaction.

Summary

- LLM hallucinations occur when the model generates information that is not based on facts or input data, leading to fabricated or incorrect details. This happens because models like GPT-4 rely on patterns learned during training rather than fact-checking. To reduce these errors, strategies include improving training data, adding real-time fact-checking, enhancing verification systems, and using RAG to combine text generation with real-time data retrieval.
- RAG enhances language model accuracy by combining text generation with information retrieval. This approach allows the model to access external data in real time, reducing the risk of generating incorrect or fabricated content. RAG uses a vector database to store and retrieve text embeddings, enabling the model to efficiently find and use relevant information during generation, thereby minimizing hallucinations.
- Building a GenAI application using the RAG paradigm is challenging without the right tools because it requires seamless integration among LLMs, embedding models, and vector databases. Without proper tools, you'd have to manage complex interactions manually, including embedding generation, storage, and real-time querying, which demands deep technical expertise and understanding of system architecture.

- LangChain is one of the top frameworks for addressing RAG challenges. It streamlines AI application development by seamlessly integrating LLMs with external data sources and computational tools.
- LangChain connects LLMs with external data sources and tools, managing the process from receiving natural-language input to generating and indexing vector embeddings. It handles data from various sources, such as chatbots, databases, and documents, enabling efficient retrieval and processing, so that LLMs can use relevant information effectively in AI applications.
- MongoDB and LangChain created a RAG template using MongoDB Atlas Vector Search and OpenAI. This template streamlines the development and deployment of chatbot applications on proprietary data. LangChain Templates offer a reference architecture that can be easily deployed as a REST API with LangServe, simplifying integration.
- LangServe deploys LangChain models as REST APIs with FastAPI and `pydantic` for data validation. It supports invoking, batching, and streaming endpoints for real-time AI apps and uses `uvloop` and `asyncio` for concurrency. It also includes a playground for testing and tweaking parameters in real time.
- The LangChain CLI is a tool that lets you interact with the LangChain framework directly from the command line. It offers commands for tasks such as creating projects, running tests, and managing configurations. The CLI simplifies development by enabling quick, efficient operations, making it easier to automate tasks and streamline the workflow for building and deploying LLM-powered applications.
- The `mongo-rag` template orchestrates the chatbot process, starting with `RunnableParallel` to convert the question and context to embeddings. The `Retriever` fetches relevant documents, which `RunnablePassthrough` forwards to `ChatPromptTemplate` to create a structured prompt. `ChatOpenAI` generates a response, and `StrOutputParser` extracts the final output.
- You can communicate with the chatbot without a GUI by using tools like `curl`, enabling direct command-line HTTP requests. This method is ideal for automation, scripting, and testing, allowing efficient, programmatic interaction with the server. You can also use various programming languages to achieve this type of communication.

Building event-driven applications

This chapter covers

- Understanding event-driven architecture
- Gaining insight into the streaming platform concept
- Learning about stream processor integration challenges
- Starting with Atlas Stream Processing
- Exploring the Atlas Stream Processing architecture
- Mastering the `$source` aggregation pipeline stage

Event-driven applications represent a fundamental shift from the traditional request/response model. In the conventional approach, services are tightly coupled and must request data directly from one another, creating a web of dependencies and introducing latency, as each service must frequently poll the others for updates, often processing data in batches. This method not only slows the system but also makes it difficult to scale or adapt to new business requirements due to the rigid interconnections between services.

By contrast, event-driven architecture decouples these services by enabling them to communicate through events. Instead of polling for data, upstream services immediately notify downstream services whenever new data or events are generated. This real-time event notification system is typically managed through centralized platforms like Apache Kafka and RabbitMQ, which ensure that events are processed in the order in which they occur.

The benefits of this approach are substantial. Event-driven systems are highly responsive and reactive, processing data in real time rather than waiting for periodic updates. This leads to lower system overhead, reduced latency, and more efficient performance overall.

In such a system, when an event occurs, the event producer sends a message to a central platform. The event is picked up and processed by event consumers, ensuring that events are handled immediately even if different components operate independently or asynchronously. Where does MongoDB fit into this picture, and how can it enhance the architecture described previously? You'll find the answers in this chapter.

15.1 Understanding event-driven technology

Events are the backbone of event-driven applications, capturing key moments or changes within a system. When a user logs in to an online platform, that's an event. Similarly, when a thermostat adjusts the temperature in response to a change in the environment or when an e-commerce site updates inventory levels after a purchase, these are events. These events can be simple, containing basic information, or complex, involving detailed data that must be securely transmitted, processed, and stored to ensure precision and consistency. In traditional request/response systems, applications often communicate by directly querying one another to retrieve the latest data or trigger specific actions. This point-to-point communication pattern leads to tightly coupled architectures in which each application depends on the specific implementation details of the others. As a result, the system becomes complex, difficult to maintain, and challenging to adapt when new business requirements arise. Figure 15.1 shows an example of such a tightly coupled system.

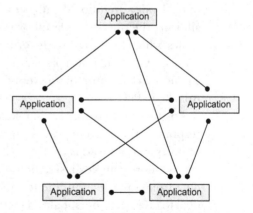

Figure 15.1 Point-to-point communication pattern, in which multiple applications are interconnected through direct communication links. Each application relies on others to send or request data, creating a web of dependencies that can make the entire system fragile and resistant to change. (Image © MongoDB 2024 CC BY-NC-SA 3.0)

Traditionally, applications have approached event processing in two main ways:

- *In-app event processing*—In this approach, the logic for processing events is embedded directly within the application code. This includes managing the necessary state between events. As the complexity of event processing increases, the code becomes more challenging to write, debug, optimize, and maintain.
- *In-database event processing*—Events are not processed within the application but sent directly to a database, using its query capabilities to process the data. Although this approach reduces the complexity of the application code, it introduces additional latency, as each event must be ingested, indexed, and stored before processing. Furthermore, traditional databases are typically designed to process fixed batches of data at rest rather than the continuous data streams characteristic of modern event-driven systems.

To address the problems of tightly coupled architectures and the challenges they pose in maintaining and adapting systems, new approaches have been introduced. With the rise of microservices and cloud computing, events were often packaged as messages and exchanged using *pub/sub* (publish/subscribe) queues. In this model, a publisher sends messages (events) to a central system called a *message broker*. The broker distributes these messages to *subscribers*: components that have expressed interest in specific types of messages. This setup allows different parts of an application to communicate without being directly connected, meaning that they can work independently and handle events as they receive them.

In recent years, event streaming platforms like Apache Kafka have gained prominence. Kafka is a distributed system designed to handle large volumes of data in real time. Unlike traditional pub/sub systems, Kafka stores events persistently on disk, allowing them to be replayed or processed later. It operates by streaming events into topics, which are stored in the order in which they were received. Consumers can read these events at their own pace, ensuring reliable, ordered processing. Figure 15.2 shows a typical architecture for an event-driven system using an event streaming platform like Apache Kafka.

For these events to be valuable, the systems that consume them must process and respond to them. Event processing can be straightforward, such as tracking the number of times an online ad is viewed or transforming data types within a message. But it can involve more complex tasks, such as detecting fraudulent transactions, analyzing sensor data from a production line to predict equipment failures, or processing clickstream data to offer users personalized content.

Today, several mature event streaming platforms and databases are available to handle the transport and persistence of events. But processing high-volume streams of events in real time presents a different problem—one that many developers struggle with. This difficulty arises because processing data in motion is fundamentally different from working with it within an application or in a database. The experience becomes fragmented due to differences in programming languages, APIs, drivers, and tools.

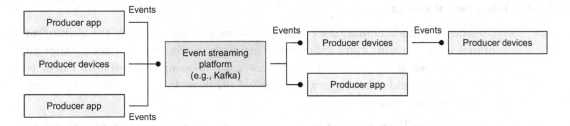

Figure 15.2 An event-driven system using an event streaming platform. Multiple producer applications and devices generate events, which are sent to the event streaming platform. The platform manages these events, ensuring that they are efficiently processed and delivered to the appropriate consumers. On the other side, various consumer applications subscribe to the events in which they are interested, consuming the data at their own pace. This architecture allows parallel processing and ensures that if one part of the system fails, the rest can continue functioning smoothly, maintaining the overall system's reliability and scalability. An event streaming platform acts like the backbone that facilitates communication and event transfer between applications and microservices. Events are stored in a message log, and message brokers work with producer and consumer APIs to ensure reliable delivery of events between independent services. (Image © MongoDB 2024 CC BY-NC-SA 3.0)

These inconsistencies slow development, increasing the time, cost, and complexity of building and evolving applications. The stream processor is an independent technology that must be integrated into the application stack, so you have to manage an additional set of challenges.

15.2 Examining the concepts of stream processing

To fully grasp the true potential of stream processing, it's important to dive deeply into its underlying concepts. By breaking down these key elements, you can better appreciate how they work together to enable real-time data analysis and processing.

15.2.1 Differentiating event time and processing time

Event time refers to the actual time when an event occurred, whereas *processing time* is the time when the system processes that event. In streaming systems, event time is more precise because it captures the real occurrence of events, allowing accurate analytics and event ordering. But event time may require synchronization because events might arrive late or out of order due to network delays, system lag, or varying event sources. In distributed systems, for example, events might be generated at different times across multiple machines, so timestamps (such as event timestamps) are used to synchronize them and ensure correct ordering.

On the other hand, processing time is based on the time when the system processes the event, which depends on the system's current performance and state. Although processing time is easier to implement because it doesn't require additional synchronization mechanisms, it is less accurate if system delays or network problems cause events to be processed later than when they occurred, which can lead to inaccuracies in time-sensitive analytics.

15.2.2 Using time windows

Windowing is a fundamental concept in stream processing, enabling the division of continuous data streams into smaller, more manageable windows over time. Different types of windows group events in specific intervals, allowing the system to calculate trends, averages, and other aggregations based on those intervals. The two primary types of time windows are

- *Tumbling*—These windows are fixed and nonoverlapping. Each event belongs to only one window. When you are calculating daily sales totals, for example, each 24-hour period is treated independently; data from one day doesn't mix with the next. Tumbling windows are best suited to tasks that require distinct intervals and no data overlap, such as generating daily reports, hourly summaries, or end-of-period accounting.
- *Hopping*—These windows can overlap, meaning that an event may belong to multiple windows. With a 5-minute window that hops every minute, data from a single event could appear in multiple overlapping windows. That is, an event at 12:03 will be counted in windows 12:00–12:05, 12:01–12:06, and so on. Hopping windows are useful for continuous, rolling analysis that requires the system to update results over time, such as by calculating moving averages.

The choice of time windows depends on the needs of the stream processing application, and selecting the right window type can have a significant effect on performance and accuracy:

- *Aggregations*—Time windows are important for calculating things like averages, sums, and counts over specific time intervals. A tumbling window is ideal for computing total sales per hour because each hour is treated separately. A hopping window is better for rolling averages, such as a 5-minute moving average of stock prices; data from previous minutes overlaps with the current window.
- *Anomaly detection*—Time windows help you spot anomalies or outliers within certain time frames. Tumbling windows are suitable when you want to detect anomalies within fixed, nonoverlapping periods, such as checking for unusual spikes in traffic every 10 minutes. Hopping windows are better for real-time monitoring, in which continuous, overlapping analysis helps you catch spikes or anomalies more quickly, such as monitoring rolling 5-minute windows for sudden surges in network traffic.

15.3 Starting with Atlas Stream Processing

Integrating a stream processing platform into an application stack introduces additional complexity, requiring extra drivers, tools, and security measures. Technologies like Apache Kafka Streams, ksqlDB, Apache Flink, Apache Storm, and Amazon Web Services (AWS) Kinesis offer powerful solutions for processing real-time data streams, but they also come with challenges such as API fragmentation and schema rigidity. Maintaining consistent application state between the stream processor and the database can become especially difficult in the event of failures. Modern stream processors typically rely on Java-based APIs, which can be problematic if the application is developed in a different language. Also, the APIs for persisting and processing data in databases often differ significantly from those used by stream processors, adding further intricacies.

Some stream processors offer a SQL interface to address API fragmentation, but this approach often forces users to adapt complex event data into rigid, tabular structures that may not align with the original event objects in the application, leading to inefficiencies and confusion. Rigid schemas also make it difficult to manage sparse data or implement necessary schema changes. These changes must be coordinated across the application, object-relational mapping (ORM) layer, stream processor, and database, which increases the time and risk involved in deploying new features.

Atlas offers a more integrated solution. Events naturally map to flexible, JSON-like document structures and can be processed using a powerful Query API, both of which are central to MongoDB's design. This provides a more efficient and cohesive approach to handling event-driven applications. MongoDB's adaptable document-based data model combined with its Query API provide a unified approach to interacting with data, whether it's being processed in a stream or stored in the database. Figure 15.3 illustrates the key benefits.

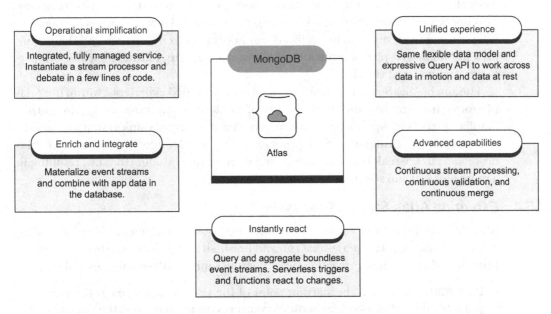

Figure 15.3 Atlas streamlines operations with its fully managed service, allowing easy instantiation of a stream processor and database with minimal code. The platform offers a unified experience by using the same flexible data model and Query API for data in motion and at rest. Atlas enhances applications by integrating event streams with database data and supports advanced stream processing, including continuous processing and validation. It also enables immediate reactions to events through serverless triggers and functions, with support for Kafka and other streaming platforms. This all-in-one approach simplifies the development and management of event-driven applications. (Image © MongoDB 2024 CC BY-NC-SA 3.0)

It is worthwhile to mention that the document data model is good for building event-driven applications due to its natural alignment with event structures in motion and at rest. Unlike traditional tabular data, documents map directly to event objects in code, making it easier for you to represent and manage complex data without additional mapping layers. The model's flexibility allows you to handle sparse data and adapt document structures as application needs change; MongoDB's schema validation (chapter 5) ensures data integrity before processing or storage. Furthermore, documents support a wide range of data models, from hierarchical objects to graphs, and their ability to consolidate related data reduces the need for complex joins, enabling faster, more efficient real-time processing.

> **NOTE** An Atlas Stream Processor is essentially a MongoDB aggregation pipeline that continuously processes incoming data streams from a designated source and outputs the results to a specified destination. Atlas Stream Processing allows you to handle high-velocity streams of complex data using the same data model and Query API as in Atlas databases.

By using Atlas, you gain all the necessary tools to develop applications that respond instantly to live events. These applications can analyze vast streams of data in real time, enabling quick responses to opportunities and early detection of potential threats. They also allow the integration of live events with existing stored data, enhancing business operations by enriching and searching this combined data. As events become less relevant over time, they can be archived seamlessly from active systems. All this is built on a fully managed platform that offers robust data security, redundancy, and comprehensive operational visibility.

The aim of Atlas Stream Processing is to provide a unified experience within the Atlas platform. It centralizes the development of modern applications using MongoDB's familiar query language and aggregation pipeline, allowing a seamless shift to real-time data processing. Bridging stream processing with the MongoDB ecosystem enables developers to use real-time data while using their existing MongoDB skills, resulting in a more efficient and streamlined development process.

15.4 Exploring Atlas Stream Processing

Atlas Stream Processing introduces several new stages and methods for handling streams. Unlike regular queries that run and finish, stream processors run continuously. Data flows through the aggregation pipeline from source to destination in real time.

> **DEFINITION** A *source* is the starting point of the stream, and a *sink* is the endpoint to which data flows. In between, various stages can process the data as it moves through the pipeline.

15.4.1 Discovering Atlas Stream Processing components

Atlas Stream Processing scales your stream processing instance dynamically by allocating workers as you launch new stream processors. When all stream processors on a worker are stopped, the worker can be deprovisioned. The system prioritizes assigning new stream processors to available workers before creating additional ones. It is built around a few key components.

CONNECTION REGISTRY

The Atlas Stream Processing Connection Registry (key store) holds the configuration details for all connections between the stream processing instance and external data sources or sinks. It includes information such as connection endpoints and authentication credentials that enable secure, reliable communication between the stream processor and external systems. Each registry contains one or more connections, allowing a stream processor to interact with external services. The following list summarizes how connections operate within this framework:

- Connections defined in the registry of a specific stream processing instance are exclusively available to stream processors running within that instance.
- A single connection can support multiple stream processors simultaneously.
- A stream processor can have only one connection designated as its data source.
- A stream processor can have only one connection designated as its data sink.
- Connections are flexible and can function as either a source or a sink, depending on how they are used by the stream processor.

STREAM PROCESSOR

A *stream processor* in Atlas Stream Processing is a MongoDB aggregation pipeline query that runs continuously against your data stream. Stream processors are instances in which data processing pipelines are created and managed. You can think of them as being like modular units that process data streams in real time. These processors consist of specialized aggregation stages that control how events flow from the source to the destination. Within the pipeline, you can incorporate filters, validations, time-based windowing, and other operations to handle complex data transformations.

STREAM PROCESSOR INSTANCE

A *stream processor instance* in Atlas is a designated namespace linked to a specific connection string, cloud provider, region, and (optionally) security context for added protection. When you create a stream processor, it is available only within the stream processing instance in which it was defined (figure 15.4).

Each instance can manage up to four active stream processors. As you initiate more stream processors, Atlas Stream Processing automatically scales the instance by adding workers. A *worker* in this context is a virtual resource that provides the necessary computational power, such as CPU and RAM, to execute these tasks. Conversely, a worker can be deprovisioned by stopping all stream processors running on it. The system prioritizes assigning stream processors to existing workers before provisioning new ones, optimizing resource use.

When scaling, Atlas Stream Processing takes into account only the number of stream processors that are actively running, excluding any that are defined but not active. The

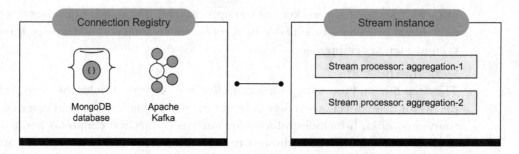

Figure 15.4 A stream processing instance is composed of multiple stream processors, such as `aggregation-1` and `aggregation-2`, each dedicated to a specific task within the stream processing environment. These processors reside within the stream instance and are closely tied to the Connection Registry, which serves as a key store for managing secure connections to external resources. The bidirectional arrow between the Connection Registry and the stream instance signifies a dynamic interaction in which the stream instance relies on the registry for credentials or configuration settings to execute processing tasks effectively. (Image © MongoDB 2024 CC BY-NC-SA 3.0)

amount of RAM and CPU allocated to its workers is determined by the tier of the stream processing instance. These instances are configured with several key components:

- One or more workers that supply the necessary RAM and CPU resources to run the stream processors
- A cloud provider and region where the processing takes place
- A Connection Registry that manages the available data sources and destinations
- A security framework that governs user permissions and access
- A connection string that links to the stream processing instance itself

The Atlas Streaming Processor operates within dedicated customer containers on a shared, multitenant infrastructure. It functions as an independent aggregation pipeline separate from your Atlas cluster, capable of consuming events from Kafka topics or MongoDB change streams, processing the data, and storing the output in a MongoDB database or emitting a new event to Kafka.

15.4.2 Understanding Atlas Stream Processing capabilities

In Atlas, *stream processing components* are embedded in projects but function independently from the underlying clusters. This decoupling provides significant flexibility by allowing you to manage, scale, and optimize stream processing workloads without affecting cluster performance. It ensures that stream processing tasks can be scaled independently based on demand, offering a more efficient use of resources and greater control of processing workloads without cluster constraints. This architecture enables seamless scaling, better fault isolation, and more efficient resource management across workloads. Figure 15.5 shows how Atlas Stream Processing interacts with various components to handle data flows.

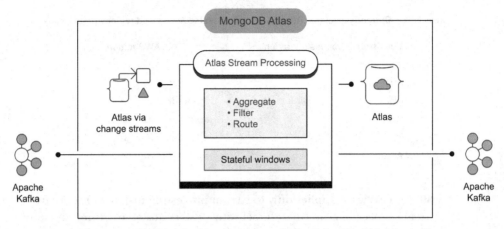

Figure 15.5   The process flow in Atlas Stream Processing. On the left, data from Apache Kafka is ingested into Atlas through Kafka or via Atlas change streams, which capture real-time data changes. This data is passed to Atlas Stream Processing, where it is processed continuously via operations such as aggregation, filtering, and routing. The figure highlights the stateful windows used within the processing to manage and analyze data over specific time intervals. After processing, the results are materialized into an Atlas database for storage, or the data can be sent back to external systems like Apache Kafka for further use. (Image © MongoDB 2024 CC BY-NC-SA 3.0)

With Atlas Stream Processing, you can

- Create aggregation pipelines that process data streams in real time, eliminating the delays in batch processing
- Perform ongoing schema validation to ensure that messages are correctly formatted, detect corruption, and identify late-arriving data
- Continuously push results to Atlas collections or Apache Kafka clusters, maintaining up-to-date data views and analysis

Atlas Stream Processing allows you to deploy stream processing instances in various AWS regions. Currently, Atlas Stream Processing is not supported by other cloud providers. Table 15.1 lists the supported AWS regions in which you can set up your instances.

Table 15.1   Currently available Atlas Stream Processing AWS cloud regions

Atlas Stream Processing region	AWS region
Virginia, USA	`us-east-1`
Oregon, USA	`us-west-2`
Canada (central)	`ca-central-1`
Sao Paulo, Brazil	`sa-east-1`
Ireland	`eu-west-1`

Table 15.1 Currently available Atlas Stream Processing AWS cloud regions (*continued*)

Atlas Stream Processing region	AWS region
London, England	`eu-west-2`
Frankfurt, Germany	`eu-central-1`
Mumbai, India	`ap-south-1`
Tokyo, Japan	`ap-northeast-1`
Singapore	`ap-southeast-1`
Sydney, Australia	`ap-southeast-2`

NOTE This table applies only to stream processing instances themselves. Your stream processors can still interact with clusters hosted on different cloud providers or in different regions as long as they are within the same project as the stream processing instance.

15.5 Structuring a stream processor aggregation pipeline

Atlas Stream Processing extends the core MongoDB aggregation pipeline by adding features tailored to the specific needs of stream processing, allowing continuous real-time data handling and transformation. Each processor pipeline must start with a `$source` stage, which connects to a data source and begins receiving a continuous stream of data in the form of documents. The `$source` stage is the first step in every stream processing pipeline. After the `$source`, each subsequent aggregation stage processes records from the stream sequentially. These stages can generally be categorized as follows:

- *Validation*—The `$validate` stage enables schema validation for ingested documents, ensuring that only properly formatted documents proceed to the next steps in the pipeline. It also allows you to define the handling of documents that fail validation. This stage is optional.
- *Stateless operations*—These aggregation stages or operators work directly on the incoming data stream. They process, transform, and forward documents individually as they pass through the pipeline. Stateless operations can be placed anywhere between the `$source` stage and the final stages, such as `$emit` and `$merge`.
- *Stateful operations*—These stages or operators handle sets of documents as a whole rather than processing them one by one. They require bounded sets of documents, which means that they operate within defined windows of data. Stateful operations can be used only within these windows.

Time windows are pipeline stages that consume streaming data and partition it into time-delimited sets, enabling the use of stages and operators that wouldn't work with infinite data, such as `$group` and `$avg`. Each stream processor can have only one window stage, which defines how the data is divided for stateful processing. Atlas Stream Processing supports two key window stages (also described earlier in this chapter):

- $tumblingWindow—This stage divides the data stream into nonoverlapping, continuous windows based on a user-defined duration. Each window collects a set of documents, and when the window closes, a new window begins with no overlap, ensuring that each document is processed in only one window.
- $hoppingWindow—This stage creates overlapping windows, with each window defined by a specific duration and a hop interval. The windows overlap according to the hop interval, meaning that a document can belong to more than one window. This approach is useful for generating a sliding window view of the data stream.

When the data has been processed through the defined stages, it is output via the $emit stage, which sends the data to a streaming platform, or the $merge stage, which writes the processed data to an Atlas database. These output stages are mutually exclusive; a stream processor can use only one of them.

15.5.1 Taking a deep dive into the $source aggregation stage

Each processor starts with a $source aggregation pipeline stage that connects to a data source, initiating the reception of a continuous stream of documents. These documents must be in valid JSON or Extended JSON (EJSON) format, which extends the standard JSON to include data types that are not natively supported by JSON. These additional types are necessary for representing richer data structures commonly used in databases like MongoDB. Although standard JSON can represent basic data types such as strings, numbers, arrays, and objects, it does not natively support types like dates, binary data, and ObjectIds (which are often used as unique identifiers in MongoDB). EJSON extends JSON by adding these types, allowing a more complete representation of the data as it exists in a MongoDB database. EJSON is designed to be human-readable and machine-parsable, like regular JSON, but with the ability to represent MongoDB's more complex data types accurately.

The $source aggregation pipeline stage defines a connection from the Connection Registry to stream data. The Connection Registry is a centralized repository where connections to various data sources are defined and managed. It allows you to specify and store the details needed to connect to different data sources, such as an Apache Kafka broker or a MongoDB collection. When you set up a stream processor, the Connection Registry provides the necessary connection information for the $source stage to begin streaming data from the specified source. The following sections describe the connections that are currently supported.

APACHE KAFKA BROKER

The $source stage can be configured to operate on streaming data from an Apache Kafka broker. The configuration involves specifying the connection name, Kafka topic, and optional settings, such as timestamp fields and partition idle timeouts:

```
{
    "$source": {
        "connectionName": "<registered-connection>",     ◄─┤ Connection name
        "topic": "<source-topic>",                        ◄─┤ Kafka topic
        "timeField": {
            "$toDate": "<expression>" |
            "$dateFromString": "<expression>"            ─┤ Timestamp, format,
        },                                                │ and override
        "tsFieldName": "<timestamp>",
        "partitionIdleTimeout": {
            "size": <duration-number>,                   ─┤ Idle duration before a partition is
            "unit": "<duration-unit>"                     │ ignored in watermarking
        },
        "config": {
            "auto_offset_reset": "<start-event>",
            "group_id": "<group-id>",                    ─┤ Additional
            "keyFormat": "<deserialization-type>",        │ configuration settings
            "keyFormatError": "<error-handling>"
        }
    }
}
```

This configuration streams messages from a specified Kafka topic, allowing detailed control of how data is ingested and processed. Here are the key points of the prototype:

- registered-connection—Defines the connection name in the Connection Registry; used to ingest data from a specific Kafka broker
- source-topic—Defines the name of the Kafka topic from which messages will be streamed
- timeField—Specifies an authoritative timestamp field for incoming messages
- expression—Defines the format for the timestamp by converting to a date or parsing a date string
- timestamp—Overrides the default timestamp field name if necessary
- partitionIdleTimeout—Configures how long a partition can remain idle before it is ignored in watermark calculations
- duration-number—Specifies the duration of the partition idle timeout
- duration-unit—Sets the unit of time for the idle timeout duration, such as milliseconds or seconds
- config—Contains additional configuration settings for the Kafka source
- start-event—Specifies the event from which to start ingesting data, such as the earliest or latest event in the topic
- group-id—Sets the consumer group ID to associate with the stream processor
- deserialization-type—Specifies the data type used to deserialize the Kafka key data, such as binary data or JSON
- error-handling—Defines how to handle errors encountered during deserialization, such as writing to a dead-letter queue (DLQ)

MongoDB COLLECTION CHANGE STREAM

The `$source` stage can also stream data from a MongoDB collection change stream. This involves connecting to a MongoDB database and specifying the collections to monitor for changes:

```
{
  "$source": {
    "connectionName": "<registered-connection>",          ◀── Connection name
    "timeField": {
      "$toDate": "<expression>" |
      "$dateFromString": "<expression>"                    Timestamp, format,
    },                                                     and override
    "tsFieldName": "<timestamp>",
    "db": "<source-db>",                                  ◀── MongoDB database
    "coll": ["<source-coll>"],                            ◀── MongoDB collection
    "config": {
      "startAfter": "<start-token>" |
      "startAtOperationTime": "<timestamp>",
      "fullDocument": "<full-doc-condition>",              Configuration settings
      "fullDocumentOnly": <boolean>,
      "fullDocumentBeforeChange":
        "<before-change-condition>",
      "pipeline": [{
        "<aggregation-stage>": {
          "<stage-input>": ". . ."
        }
      }]
    }
  }
}
```

This configuration allows the stream processor to monitor specified collections continuously for any updates and process them in real time. Here are the key points of the prototype:

- `registered-connection`—Defines the connection name in the Connection Registry; used to ingest data from a MongoDB collection
- `timeField`—Specifies an authoritative timestamp field for incoming messages
- `expression`—Defines the format for the timestamp by converting to a date or parsing a date string
- `timestamp`—Overrides the default timestamp field name if necessary
- `source-db`—Sets the name of the MongoDB database hosting the collection change stream
- `source-coll`—Sets the name(s) of the MongoDB collections to stream changes from
- `config`—Contains additional configuration settings for the MongoDB collection change stream

398 CHAPTER 15 *Building event-driven applications*

- `start-token`—Specifies the point in time or event from which to start streaming changes
- `full-doc-condition`—Controls whether a full document should be returned on update
- `boolean`—Specifies whether to return the full document or the entire change event document
- `before-change-condition`—Determines whether to include the full document in its original state before changes in the output
- `pipeline`—Specifies an aggregation pipeline to filter the change stream output at the source

MONGODB DATABASE CHANGE STREAM

To stream data from an entire MongoDB database, you can configure the `$source` stage to track changes across all collections within a specified database:

```
{
  "$source": {
    "connectionName": "<registered-connection>",        ← Connection name
    "timeField": {                                       ← Timestamp, format, and override
      "$toDate": "<expression>" |
      "$dateFromString": "<expression>"                  ← Format expression
    },
    "tsFieldName": "<timestamp>",                        ← Custom timestamp field
    "db": "<source-db>",                                 ← MongoDB database
    "config": {                                          ← Configuration settings
      "startAfter": "<start-token>" |
      "startAtOperationTime": "<timestamp>",             ← Start token or time
    },
    "fullDocument": "<full-doc-condition>",              ← Full document on update
    "fullDocumentOnly": <boolean>,                       ← Boolean for document return type
    "fullDocumentBeforeChange":
      "<before-change-condition>",                       ← Document state before change
    "pipeline": [{
      "<aggregation-stage>": {
        "<stage-input>": ". . ."
      }
    }]                                                   ← Aggregation pipeline
  }
}
```

This setup is ideal for applications that need to track changes across an entire database rather than specific collections. Here are the key points of the prototype:

- `registered-connection`—Specifies the connection name in the Connection Registry; used to ingest data from a MongoDB database
- `timeField`—Specifies an authoritative timestamp field for incoming messages
- `expression`—Defines the format for the timestamp by converting to a date or parsing a date string

- `timestamp`—Overrides the default timestamp field name if necessary
- `source-db`—Sets the name of the MongoDB database hosting the change stream
- `config`—Contains additional configuration settings for the MongoDB database change stream
- `start-token`—Specifies the point in time or event from which to start streaming changes
- `full-doc-condition`—Controls whether a full document should be returned on update
- `boolean`—Specifies whether to return the full document or the entire change event document
- `before-change-condition`—Determines whether to include the full document in its original state before changes in the output
- `pipeline`—Specifies an aggregation pipeline to filter the change stream output at the source

DOCUMENT ARRAY

You can also use the `$source` to stream data from an array of documents, which is useful when the source data is predefined in an array format:

```
{
  "$source": {                              ⬅ Timestamp, format, and override
    "timeField": {
      "$toDate": "<expression>" |
      "$dateFromString": "<expression>"     ⬅ Format expression
    },
    "tsFieldName": "<timestamp>",           ⬅ Custom timestamp field
    "documents": [{"source-doc"}] | "<expression>"  ⬅ Document array or expression as data source
  }
}
```

This configuration allows you to process an array of documents as a continuous stream, using the same pipeline processing logic as for other source types. Here are the key points of the prototype:

- `timeField`—Specifies an authoritative timestamp field for incoming documents
- `expression`—Defines the format for the timestamp by converting to a date or parsing a date string
- `timestamp`—Overrides the default timestamp field name if necessary
- `documents`—Specifies an array of documents or an expression that evaluates to an array of documents, serving as the data source for the stream

NOTE You must place the `$source` stage at the beginning of any pipeline where it is used, and only one $source stage is allowed per pipeline.

15.5.2 Using the stream processor $validate aggregation stage

A second noteworthy aggregation pipeline stage dedicated to Atlas Stream Processing is `$validate`. The `$validate` stage checks streaming documents to ensure that they conform to a specified schema, including expected ranges, values, or data types. The pipeline stage has the following prototype form:

```
{
  "$validate": {
    "validator": { <filter> },              ◄──┘ Validator filter
    "validationAction": "discard" | "dlq"   ◄──┐
  }                                            │ Validation action
}                                              │ on failure
```

This configuration enables validation of incoming streaming documents against a user-defined schema, ensuring that only data meeting specific criteria is processed further. Here are the key points:

- `validator`—Contains expressions to validate incoming messages against the schema, supporting all query operators except `$near`, `$nearSphere`, `$text`, and `$where`.
- `validationAction`—Specifies the action for nonconforming messages. Options are `discard` and `dlq` (logs to DLQ while discarding without guarantees). The default action is `discard`.

NOTE You can apply the `$validate` stage anywhere in the pipeline after the `$source` stage and before the `$emit` or `$merge` stage.

15.5.3 Viewing all supported aggregation pipeline stages

An Atlas Stream Processing pipeline is limited to 16 MB. Table 15.2 lists the aggregation pipeline stages that are unique to Atlas Stream Processing as well as those that have been modified specifically for use in Atlas Stream Processing. Some stages have been changed or adapted from their original versions to better handle the continuous data streams in Atlas Stream Processing.

Table 15.2 Atlas Stream Processing aggregation pipeline stages

Aggregation pipeline stage	Purpose
`$source`	Defines the streaming data source from which messages are consumed
`$validate`	Checks incoming stream documents against a user-defined schema to ensure that they meet the required format
`$lookup`	Executes a left outer join with a specified collection, pulling in documents from the joined collection for further processing. In this version, you must specify an Atlas collection from the Connection Registry for the `from` field.

Table 15.2 Atlas Stream Processing aggregation pipeline stages (*continued*)

Aggregation pipeline stage	Purpose
$hoppingWindow	Distributes stream documents into windows based on user-defined durations and intervals between window start times
$tumblingWindow	Segregates stream documents into nonoverlapping, continuous windows, each with a user-defined duration
$emit	Sends processed messages to a stream or time-series collection as defined in the Connection Registry
$merge	A specialized version of the $merge stage in which connectionName must refer to a remote collection in the Connection Registry

You can also use the aggregation pipeline stages that were introduced in earlier chapters. Table 15.3 shows the aggregation pipeline stages supported by MongoDB, which you can also apply in your streaming data pipelines.

Table 15.3 MongoDB aggregation pipeline stages usable with stream processing

Aggregation pipeline stage	Use condition
$addFields	Anywhere
$match	Anywhere
$project	Anywhere
$redact	Anywhere
$replaceRoot	Anywhere
$replaceWith	Anywhere
$set	Anywhere
$unset	Anywhere
$unwind	Anywhere
$group	Only within $hoppingWindow or $tumblingWindow stages
$sort	Only within $hoppingWindow or $tumblingWindow stages
$limit	Only within $hoppingWindow or $tumblingWindow stages
$count	Only within $hoppingWindow or $tumblingWindow stages
$group	Only within $hoppingWindow or $tumblingWindow stages

Stream processing extends the aggregation pipeline with stages specifically designed for continuous data streams, seamlessly integrating with standard MongoDB aggregation pipeline stages. This allows developers to perform operations on streaming data similar to the ones they would perform on static data. Unique stages such as $source, $validate, and $tumblingWindow handle stream-specific tasks. You can also use standard stages like $match and $project, though some are limited to specific contexts.

15.6 Mastering Atlas Stream Processing

Let's explore the new stream processing methods available in `mongosh` and create a stream processing instance (SPI) in an Atlas cluster, which you can think of as a logical collection of one or more stream processors. When the SPI is set up, it comes with a connection string, similar to what you would find in a standard Atlas cluster.

15.6.1 Adopting new stream processor methods

New `mongosh` methods designed to manage stream processors are available only for deployments hosted in Atlas. These methods provide a set of tools to create, manage, and monitor stream processors in an Atlas environment. Table 15.4 describes the new `mongosh` methods that you can use to manage stream processors.

Table 15.4 Atlas `mongosh` methods dedicated to Atlas Stream Processing

Name	Description
`sp.createStreamProcessor()`	Creates a new stream processor
`sp.listConnections()`	Lists all existing connections in the Connection Registry of the current instance
`sp.listStreamProcessors()`	Lists all existing stream processors in the current SPI
`sp.process()`	Creates a temporary (ephemeral) stream processor
`sp.processor.drop()`	Deletes an existing stream processor
`sp.processor.sample()`	Returns an array of sampled results from a running stream processor
`sp.processor.start()`	Starts an existing stream processor
`sp.processor.stats()`	Returns statistics summarizing a running stream processor
`sp.processor.stop()`	Stops a running stream processor

You will use these methods later in the book; they will help you build and manage stream processors, allowing precise control over their creation, execution, and termination. They will also help you monitor the state and performance of stream processors and handle connections within the system. These methods are key for interacting efficiently with SPIs and ensuring smooth operations in Atlas.

15.6.2 Using the Atlas CLI with stream processing

You can use the `atlas streams` command in the Atlas command-line interface (CLI) to create an SPI. The Atlas CLI supports creation of SPIs and management of the Connection Registry, which handles available data sources and destinations. The following listing shows the capabilities of Atlas CLI stream processing.

Listing 15.1 Managing Atlas Stream Processing via the Atlas CLI

```
atlas streams --help
The streams command provides access to your Atlas Stream
```

```
➥Processing configurations. You can create, edit, and delete
➥streams, as well as change the connection registry.

Usage:
  atlas streams [command]

Aliases:
  streams, stream

Available Commands:
  instances   Manage Atlas Stream Processing instances.
  connections Manage Atlas Stream Processing connections.
```

The `atlas streams` command provides access to your Atlas Stream Processing configurations, allowing you to create, edit, and delete streams as well as modify the Connection Registry. To create an Atlas SPI, follow these steps:

1 Use the command `atlas streams`, which will be named `MongoDB-in-Action-SPI` and located in the AWS Frankfurt region:

```
atlas streams instances create MongoDB-in-Action-SPI --provider "AWS" \
--region FRANKFURT_DEU
```

You can display the new instance with

```
atlas streams instances list
```

The output is

```
ID                          NAME                    CLOUD   REGION
66dc35fc0b97566745a8ccdb    MongoDB-in-Action-SPI   AWS     FRANKFURT_DEU
```

2 Display the details of your new instance:

   a Use `atlas streams instances describe MongoDB-in-Action-SPI` to display the details of your new instance.

   b Click Stream Processing on the left side of the Atlas UI, located on the drop-down menu below Services.

3 Connect to the new SPI by clicking the Connect button. The menu shown in figure 15.6 appears; choose Shell from this menu.

4 Copy your individual connection string to the Atlas SPI. My connection string looks like this:

```
mongosh "mongodb://atlas-stream-66dc35fc0b9cdb-nu96v.frankfurt-
➥deu.a.query.mongodb.net/"
➥--tls --authenticationDatabase admin
➥--username manning
```

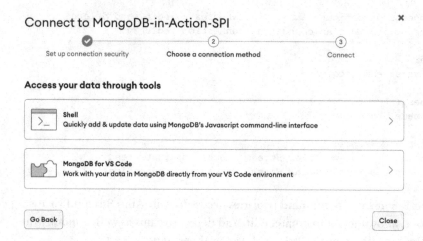

Figure 15.6 The `Connect to MongoDB-in-Action-SPI` interface includes steps for setting up connection security, choosing a connection method, and connecting. In the section Access Your Data Through Tools, you have two options. The first option is Shell, which allows you to add and update data quickly using MongoDB's JavaScript CLI. The second option is MongoDB for VS Code, which enables you to work with your data in MongoDB directly from your Visual Studio Code (VS Code) environment. (Image © MongoDB 2025)

5 Connect to the SPI instance, and execute the `sp.listConnections()` command:

```
AtlasStreamProcessing> sp.listConnections()
[ { name: 'sample_stream_solar', type: 'inmemory' } ]
AtlasStreamProcessing>
```

This command displays all existing connections in the Connection Registry of the current instance. You see that the only existing connection is `[ { name: 'sample_stream_solar', type: 'inmemory' } ]`, which is the preconfigured connection to the sample data source called `sample_stream_solar`.

15.6.3 Creating your first stream processor

The SPI comes preconfigured with a connection to a sample data source called `sample_stream_solar`. This source generates a stream of reports from various solar power devices. Each report describes the observed wattage and temperature of a single solar device at a specific point in time, as well as the device's maximum wattage. You can display a connection to a sample data source using the `atlas streams connections` command:

```
atlas streams connections list -i MongoDB-in-Action-SPI
NAME                  TYPE      SERVERS
sample_stream_solar   Sample    nil
```

The sample source in Atlas is a convenient built-in source that continuously emits a stream of sample solar generation data, which can be useful for learning, demos, and debugging. This source is configured in the Connection Registry like any other source. You can use the `sp.process()` mongosh method to create a temporary stream processor as your first exercise. Stream processors created with `sp.process()` do not persist after they are terminated. The `sp.process()` method is explained in section 15.6.4. Use it to create your first stream processor in mongosh:

```
// Create a source from the sample stream solar connection
let s = {$source: {connectionName:
 "sample_stream_solar"}} //   ◄──────┐  The source is created from the
let processor = [s] //   ◄──────────┤  sample_stream_solar connection.
// Now, run it
sp.process(processor) //   ◄────────┐  The source is added to
                                    │  the processor pipeline.
         The processor is executed
         using the defined source.
```

You should see a continuously flowing stream in your console, which might look like this output:

```
{
  device_id: 'device_1',
  group_id: 10,
  timestamp: '2024-09-07T12:32:02.717+00:00',
  max_watts: 450,
  event_type: 0,
  obs: {
    watts: 114,
    temp: 11
  },
  _ts: ISODate(<2024-09-07T12:32:02.717Z>),
  _stream_meta: {
    source: {
      type: 'generated'
    }
  }
}
{
  device_id: 'device_4',
  group_id: 1,
  timestamp: '2024-09-07T12:32:02.717+00:00',
  max_watts: 450,
  event_type: 0,
  obs: {
    watts: 129,
    temp: 20
  },
  _ts: ISODate(<2024-09-07T12:32:02.717Z>),
  _stream_meta: {
    source: {
      type: 'generated'
    }
  }
}
```

TIP Press Ctrl+C to stop the in-shell processing.

15.6.4 Learning the anatomy of a stream processor

A *stream processor* is a sequence of stages that process and route data in real time. At its core, a processor is an array of these stages, and it can be constructed incrementally using variables in the shell. Each stage serves a distinct purpose, starting with a source stage, which defines where the data originates, such as a MongoDB collection or another connected data source. After the source stage, more processing stages can be added. These stages might perform actions such as filtering, transforming, or aggregating the data as it flows through the pipeline.

NOTE The Connection Registry settings for the source and sink connections in this section, shown as the variables `let source` and `let sink`, are placeholders, not defined. These examples are provided for learning purposes and will not work unless proper connections are set up in the registry. To run these examples in a real environment, you need to configure the appropriate connections for the source and sink.

UNDERSTANDING STREAM PROCESSOR COMPONENTS

Common stages include operations such as `$match` to filter the data and `$addFields` to enhance it with new information. The final stage is a sink, where the processed data is sent. This could be another MongoDB collection, defined with a `$merge` stage, or a Kafka topic, sent using `$emit`. This ensures that the data is stored or forwarded for further use. The pseudocode in the following listing demonstrates the key components of the processor and serves as a skeleton.

Listing 15.2 The stream processor key components pseudocode

```
// A processor is essentially a sequence of stages organized in an array,
// and it can be constructed incrementally using variables within the
// mongosh shell. Right now, this is an empty processor, meaning nothing is
// defined yet.
let processor = [] //         ◄─── Empty processor array

// The first stage must always be a source. The source retrieves data from
// a connection, which is defined in the connection registry.
// For now, the source is empty.
let source = {$source:{}} //         ◄─── Source to retrieve data

// Add the source to the processor. This creates the first stage in the
// processor pipeline.
processor = [source] //         ◄─── Adds source to processor

// At this point, the processor is useful to inspect the source data.
// We can preview the data in the shell by running .process() command.
// This will display the results continuously to the shell.
sp.process(processor) //         ◄─── Runs processor to view data

// The sink is the final stage. It specifies where the data should go, such
```

```
// as sending it to a MongoDB collection using $merge or to a Kafka topic
// using $emit.
let sink = {$merge: {}} //            ◄──┐ Sink for output

// This simple processor transfers data from a source to a sink without
// modifying it.
processor = [source, sink] //         ◄──┐ Processor from source to sink

// Between the source and the sink, you can add any number of stages to
// process the data. These stages work like standard MongoDB aggregation
// stages, such as $match, $addFields, etc.
processor = [source, stageA, stageB, ..., sink] //  ◄──┐ Adds processing stages

// Finally, processors can be saved with a name for future use.
// You can start or stop them as needed.
// When started, they run continuously in the background.
sp.createStreamProcessor(
  'myProcessor', processor); //       ◄──┐ Saves processor by name
sp.myProcessor.start(); //            ◄──┐ Starts processor for
                                           continuous run
```

The source is the starting point of the pipeline, where data is ingested, and the sink is the endpoint, where the processed data is sent. Between these two stages, you can add as many intermediate processing stages as you want, such as filtering or transforming the data. When they are configured, stream processors can run continuously, making them ideal for handling real-time data flows efficiently and dynamically. Here are the key points of the prototype:

- `processor`—Initializes an empty array to hold processing stages
- `source`—Defines the starting stage, retrieving data from a connection
- `processor` *with* `source`—Adds the source as the first stage in the processing pipeline
- `sp.process`—Runs the processor, displaying source data continuously
- `sink`—Specifies the endpoint, such as MongoDB or Kafka, to which to send processed data
- `processor` *with* `source` *and* `sink`—Transfers data from source to sink without modifications
- `processor` *with* `stages`—Enables adding intermediate stages such as `$match` and `$addFields` between source and sink
- `sp.createStreamProcessor`—Saves the processor with a unique name for future use
- `sp.myProcessor.start`—Starts the processor, enabling continuous processing in the background

USING $VALIDATE STAGE

In the following listing, I add a `$validate` stage to ensure that the incoming data conforms to the required structure before it reaches the sink.

Listing 15.3 Stream processor with validation

```
// Initially, the processor is empty.
let processor = [] //                ◄──┤ Initializes an empty
                                         │ processor array

// The first stage is a source that retrieves data
// from a MongoDB connection. It's a placeholders,
// not actually defined.
let source = {
  $source: {
    connectionName: "myMongoConnection",
    // placeholder connection name for MongoDB
    db: "myDB",                          // Database name
    coll: "myCollection"                 // Collection name
  }
} //                    ◄──┤ Defines the source
                           │ to retrieve data

// Add the source to the processor.
processor = [source] //              ◄──┤ Adds source to processor

// $validate stage to check that each document has a required structure.
let validate = {
  $validate: {
    validator: {
      $and: [
        {
          name: { $exists: true, $type: "string" }
// Name must be a string and is required
        },
        {
          age: { $exists: true, $type: "int", $gte: 18 }
// Age must be >= 18 and an integer
        },
        {
          email: { $exists: true, $regex: "^.+@.+\\..+$" }
// Email must match a valid pattern
        }
      ]
    },
    validationAction: "discard"  // Discard invalid documents
  }
} //                    ◄──┤ Defines $validate to ensure
                           │ schema compliance

// Add the validation stage to the processor.    ┌ Adds validation
processor.push(validate) //              ◄───────┤ stage to processor

// The sink is the final stage. It specifies where
// the validated data should go.
let sink = {
  $merge: {
    into: {
      connectionName: "validatedDataConnection",
// Connection name for MongoDB placeholders,
// not actually defined.
      db: "validatedDB",
```

```
    // Database name for storing validated data
        coll: "validatedCollection"
    // Collection name for storing validated data
      }
    }
  } //
```
⟵ Defines sink to store validated data

```
// Add the sink to the processor.
processor.push(sink) //
```
⟵ Adds sink to processor

```
// The complete processor transfers data from a source,
validates it, and sends it to a sink.
sp.createStreamProcessor(
'validatedProcessor', processor) //
```
⟵ Saves processor as 'validatedProcessor'

```
// Start the processor, which will now run continuously in the background.
sp.validatedProcessor.start() //
```
⟵ Starts processor for continuous run

The $source stage defines where the data is ingested from, and the $validate stage ensures that the incoming data meets the schema requirements (e.g., name, age, and email). If the data fails validation, it won't proceed to the next stage. The validated data is sent to the sink, which stores the results in a MongoDB collection. With this configuration, the stream processor continuously validates data in real time, making it ideal for scenarios in which data integrity is crucial. Here are the key points of the prototype:

- processor—Initializes an empty array to hold processing stages
- source—Defines the starting stage, retrieving data from a MongoDB connection (myMongoConnection), targeting myDB and myCollection
- processor *with* source—Adds the source as the first stage in the processing pipeline
- $validate—Ensures that each document meets required schema conditions:
  - Name must exist and be a string
  - Age must exist, be an integer, and be ≥ 18
  - Email must match a valid email pattern
- validationAction—Specifies that invalid documents are discarded
- processor *with* validation—Adds the validation stage to the processor
- sink—Specifies the endpoint for storing validated data in MongoDB (validatedDB and validatedCollection)
- processor *with* source, validation, *and* sink—Creates a complete processor from source to sink, transferring only validated data
- sp.createStreamProcessor—Saves the processor as validatedProcessor for continuous use
- sp.validatedProcessor.start—Starts the processor, allowing it to run continuously in the background to process data in real time

ADDING A DEAD-LETTER QUEUE

In listing 15.4, I create a stream processor that validates incoming data against a defined schema. If the data does not match the schema, it is sent to a DLQ for further review or reprocessing. A DLQ is a designated collection that stores messages or data that could not be processed successfully, allowing troubleshooting or later reprocessing. The DLQ is discussed in detail in section 15.7.2. Valid data is passed through and saved in a MongoDB collection.

Listing 15.4 Stream processor with validation and DLQ

```
// Initially, the processor is empty.
let processor = [] //                 ◀── Initializes processor array

// The source retrieves data from a placeholder connection.
let source = {
  $source: {
    connectionName: "salesDataConnection", // source connection name
    topic: "dailySales"                    // Kafka topic as the data source
  }
} //        ◀── Source for Kafka data

// Add the source to the processor. This creates the first stage.
processor = [source] //       ◀── Adds source to processor

// Add a $validate stage to ensure the incoming data
// meets the required structure.
let validate = {
  $validate: {
    validator: {
      $and: [
        {
          productId: { $exists: true, $type: "string" }
          // productId must be a string and is required
        },
        {
          quantity: { $exists: true, $type: "int", $gte: 1 }
          // quantity must be an integer >= 1
        },
        {
          price: { $exists: true, $type: "double", $gte: 0 }
          // price must be a positive number
        }
      ]
    },
    validationAction: "dlq"  // If validation fails, send data to
    // the Dead Letter Queue (DLQ).
    // DLQ needs to be definied
  }
} //     ◀── Defines $validate for schema

// Add the validation stage to the processor.
processor.push(validate) //       ◀── Adds validation to processor
```

```
// Final stage. It specifies where the valid data should go.
let sink = {
  $merge: {
    into: {
      connectionName: "validatedSalesData",
// The destination placeholder  connection for valid data
      db: "salesDB",                    // MongoDB database
      coll: "validatedSales"            // MongoDB collection
    }
  }
} //            ◄─────┘ Defines sink for MongoDB

// Add the sink to the processor.
processor.push(sink) //   ◄─────┘ Adds sink to processor

// The complete processor transfers data from a source, validates it,
// and sends valid data to the MongoDB collection,
with invalid data sent to the DLQ.
sp.createStreamProcessor(
'salesDataProcessor', processor) //   ◄─────┘ Creates 'salesDataProcessor'

// Start the processor, which will run continuously.  │ Starts for continuous
sp.salesDataProcessor.start() //            ◄─────────┘ processing
```

Listing 15.4 shows a stream processor with validation and a DLQ. The processor starts with an empty array. The $source stage retrieves data from a connection, specifically from a Kafka topic named "dailySales" through the "salesDataConnection" connection. After the source is added, a $validate stage is introduced to ensure that the incoming data matches the required schema. This schema requires the fields productId, quantity, and price to meet the specified conditions. If the data does not meet these conditions, it is sent to the DLQ for further handling. The sink stage follows, specifying where the valid data is stored—in this case, the validatedSales collection in the salesDB database. The entire processor, now complete with the source, validation, and sink stages, is created using sp.createStreamProcessor, and once started, it continuously runs in the background, validating data in real time. Here are the key points of the prototype:

- processor *array*—Holds each stage of data processing
- source—Defines the starting stage, retrieving data from a Kafka topic specified by salesDataConnection
- validate—Ensures that each document has the required fields (productId as a string, quantity as an integer >= 1, and price as a positive number)
- sink—Specifies the final destination for valid data, sending it to a MongoDB collection in validatedSalesData
- sp.createStreamProcessor—Saves the processor with the name 'salesData-Processor' for managing the pipeline
- sp.salesDataProcessor.start—Initiates the processor, allowing it to run continuously in the background to process data in real time

412 CHAPTER 15 *Building event-driven applications*

ENRICHING DATA WITH $LOOKUP

In the next listing, I create a stream processor that retrieves messages from a Kafka topic and enriches them using a MongoDB collection via the `$lookup` stage. The enriched data is validated against a schema and stored in a MongoDB collection.

Listing 15.5 Stream processor with `$lookup` for data enrichment

```
// Initially, the processor is empty.
let processor = [] //                  ◄─── Initializes an empty
                                            processor array

// The source retrieves data from a Kafka topic.
let source = {
  $source: {
    connectionName: "inventoryKafkaConnection",
➥// placeholder Kafka connection
    topic: "inventoryUpdates"
➥// Kafka topic for inventory updates
  }
} //            ◄─── Source stage to retrieve
                    data from Kafka topic

// Add the source to the processor.
processor = [source] //                ◄─── Adds source to processor

// Use $lookup to enrich the incoming data with
➥   // information from an Atlas collection.
let lookup = {
  $lookup: {
    from: {
      connectionName: "inventoryDbConnection",
➥// pseudo Atlas connection for MongoDB
      db: "inventoryDB",                       // pseudo database in Atlas
      coll: "products"
➥// pseudo collection to join (product details)
    },
    localField: "productId",                   // Field from the source
    foreignField: "_id",
➥// Field from the products collection
    as: "productDetails"
➥// Output array field to store the results
  }
} //            ◄─── Defines $lookup to enrich
                    data from MongoDB

// Add the $lookup stage to the processor.
processor.push(lookup) //               ◄─── Adds $lookup to processor

// Use $validate to ensure the enriched data meets the required structure.
let validate = {
  $validate: {
    validator: {
      $and: [
        {
          productId: { $exists: true, $type: "string" }
➥// productId must exist and be a string
        },
```

```
      {
        quantity: { $exists: true, $type: "int", $gte: 1 }
// quantity must be an integer >= 1
      },
      {
        productDetails: { $exists: true, $type: "array" }
// productDetails must be an array from $lookup
      }
    ]
  },
  validationAction: "discard"   // Invalid documents will be discarded
 }
} //                    ◄─────┤ Defines $validate to
                              │ ensure data structure

// Add the validation stage to the processor.
processor.push(validate) //               ◄─────┤ Adds validation to processor

// The sink is the final stage. It specifies where the valid,
 enriched data should go.
let sink = {
  $merge: {
    into: {
      connectionName: "validatedInventoryData",
// placeholder connection for valid data storage
      db: "inventoryDB",                        // MongoDB database
      coll: "validatedInventory"
// MongoDB collection for storing valid data
    }
  }
} //                 ◄─────┤ Defines sink to store
                           │ data in MongoDB

// Add the sink to the processor.
processor.push(sink) //        ◄─────┤ Adds sink to processor

// The complete processor transfers data from the Kafka topic,
  enriches it with $lookup,
// validates the data, and stores the valid results in a MongoDB collection.
sp.createStreamProcessor(
 'inventoryProcessor', processor) //    ◄─────┤ Creates processor as
                                              │ 'inventoryProcessor'

// Start the processor, which will run continuously.
sp.inventoryProcessor.start() //    ◄─────┐
                                          │ Starts processor
                                          │ to run continuously
```

This example shows how to use `$lookup` within a stream processor to enrich incoming data from a Kafka topic by joining it with additional data from a MongoDB collection. The processor starts by retrieving messages from the Kafka topic `"inventory-Updates"`, using a connection to a Kafka source. Then the `$lookup` stage is applied, pulling related data from the MongoDB collection `"products"` in the `"inventoryDB"` database. The join matches the `productId` from the Kafka messages with the `_id` field in the `products` collection, adding the results to the `productDetails` field in the source messages.

After enrichment, a validation stage ensures that the resulting documents have the required fields: `productId`, `quantity`, and `productDetails`. If any of these fields is missing or invalid, the message is discarded as specified by the validation configuration. If the data passes validation, it moves to the sink stage, where it is stored in the MongoDB collection `validatedInventory` within the same database. This process runs continuously, enriching and validating the data in real time before saving it to the specified collection. Here are the key points of the prototype:

- `processor` *array*—Holds each stage in the data processing pipeline
- `source`—Defines the initial stage, retrieving data from the Kafka topic `inventoryUpdates` via `inventoryKafkaConnection`
- `lookup`—Enriches incoming data by joining it with the MongoDB `products` collection in `inventoryDB` using `inventoryDbConnection`
- `validate`—Ensures that the enriched data contains the required fields (`productId` as a string, `quantity` as an integer >= 1, and `productDetails` as an array from the `$lookup`)
- `sink`—Specifies the final destination for valid data, sending it to the MongoDB collection `validatedInventory` in `inventoryDB`
- `sp.createStreamProcessor`—Saves the processor with the name `'inventoryProcessor'` for managing this pipeline
- `sp.inventoryProcessor.start`—Starts the processor, running continuously to handle real-time data processing and validation

USING TIME WINDOWS

Listing 15.6 uses the `$hoppingWindow` command in a stream processor. In this scenario, I'm processing data from a Kafka topic that collects Internet of Things (IoT) sensor readings, and I want to calculate the average temperature from sensors in overlapping 30-second windows, starting every 10 seconds.

Listing 15.6 Stream processor with `$hoppingWindow` for IoT sensor data

```
// Initially, the processor is empty.
let processor = [] //                          ◄──── Initializes processor array

// The source retrieves data from a Kafka topic named "sensorData".
let source = {
  $source: {
    connectionName: "iotSensorConnection",
    // placeholder Kafka connection for IoT data
    topic: "sensorData"                        // Kafka topic with sensor data
  }
} //                    ◄──── Source from Kafka topic

// Add the source to the processor.
processor = [source] //                        ◄──── Adds source to processor
```

Mastering Atlas Stream Processing

```
// Use $hoppingWindow to create overlapping time windows of
  30 seconds, starting every 10 seconds.
  let hoppingWindow = {
    $hoppingWindow: {
      interval: {
        size: 30,    // Each window lasts 30 seconds
        unit: "second"
      },
      hopSize: {
        size: 10,    // Windows start every 10 seconds
        unit: "second"
      },
      pipeline: [
        {
          $group: {
            _id: "$_id",   // Use the default _id field for the window
            avgTemperature: { $avg: "$temperature" }
  // Calculate the average temperature from sensor data
          }
        }
      ]
    }
  } //                      ◀──── $hoppingWindow for time windows
                                  and average temperature

  // Add the hopping window stage to the processor.
  processor.push(hoppingWindow) //        ◀──── Adds window to processor

  // The sink is the final stage. It specifies where
  the aggregated data should go.
  let sink = {
    $merge: {
      into: {
        connectionName: "processedSensorData",
  // placeholder connection name for storing processed data
        db: "iotData",
  // MongoDB database for sensor data
        coll: "temperatureAverages"
  // Collection for storing average temperatures
      }
    }
  } //          ◀──── Defines sink for MongoDB

  // Add the sink to the processor.
  processor.push(sink) //       ◀──── Adds sink to processor

  // The complete processor pulls data from the Kafka topic,
  applies the hopping window,
  // calculates average temperatures, and stores the results
  in a MongoDB collection.
  sp.createStreamProcessor(
    'iotTemperatureProcessor', processor) //   ◀──── Creates
                                                    'iotTemperatureProcessor'

  // Start the processor, which will run continuously.
  sp.iotTemperatureProcessor.start() //    ◀──── Starts continuous
                                                 processor
```

In this example, the stream processor pulls IoT sensor data from a Kafka topic called `sensorData`. The processor uses a `$hoppingWindow` stage to create overlapping time windows of 30 seconds, starting every 10 seconds. This allows the processor to calculate average temperatures from the sensor readings within each window. The windowed aggregation pipeline groups the data by the start time of the window and computes the average temperature from the incoming sensor data. After processing, the results are stored in a MongoDB collection named `temperatureAverages` in the `iotData` database. The processor runs continuously, providing real-time monitoring of average temperatures from the IoT sensor data and saving the aggregated results for further analysis. Here are the key points of the prototype:

- `processor`—Initializes an array to hold each processing stage.
- `source`—Sets up the initial stage to pull data from the Kafka topic `sensorData`, which provides IoT sensor readings.
- `hoppingWindow`—Creates overlapping 30-second time windows with a 10-second interval. Each window computes the average temperature using the `$avg` operator.
- `sink`—Specifies MongoDB as the destination, saving the aggregated temperature data in the `temperatureAverages` collection within the `iotData` database.
- `sp.createStreamProcessor`—Names and saves the processor as `iot-TemperatureProcessor` to manage this pipeline.
- `sp.iotTemperatureProcessor.start`—Starts the processor, running it continuously to pull data, process it in time windows, and store results in MongoDB.

DEBUGGING WITH A DOCUMENT ARRAY SOURCE

You can also use a document array as a source. This allows you to provide a predefined set of data directly to a processor without relying on external systems like Kafka and MongoDB. This is especially useful for debugging and testing because it offers full control of the input and allows quick validation of your pipeline logic. By using static data, you can focus on testing how each stage of the pipeline processes the data without the unpredictability of live data sources. The following listing shows how to run this working code in your SPI.

Listing 15.7 Using a document array as a source

```
// Create a source using an array of documents.
This array simulates incoming sensor messages
let source = {
  $source: {
    "documents": [
      { sensorName: 'sensor01', temperature: 22, humidity: 55,
timestamp: new Date("2023-09-07T12:00:00Z") },
      { sensorName: 'sensor02', temperature: 45, humidity: 60,
timestamp: new Date("2023-09-07T12:01:00Z") },
      { sensorName: 'sensor03', temperature: 5, humidity: 80,
```

```
      timestamp: new Date("2023-09-07T12:02:00Z") }
    ]
  }                              ⬅ Source with static
} //                                array for sensor data

// Check for types and ranges of fields
let validate = {
  $match: {
    sensorName: { $exists: true, $type: "string" },
    temperature: {
      $exists: true,
      $type: "int",
      $gte: -50,      // Temperature range from -50 to 100°C
      $lte: 100
    },
    humidity: {
      $exists: true,
      $type: "int",
      $gte: 0,        // Humidity range from 0 to 100%
      $lte: 100
    },
    timestamp: { $exists: true, $type: "date" }
  }
} //                              ⬅ Validates stage for
                                     required fields and ranges

// Projection with transformation of warning level using proper $cond
let projectWithWarning = {
  $project: {
    sensorName: 1,
    temperature: 1,
    humidity: 1,
    timestamp: 1,
    warningLevel: {
      $cond: {
        if: { $gte: ["$temperature", 40] },
        then: "HIGH",
        else: {
          $cond: {
            if: { $lte: ["$temperature", 10] },
            then: "LOW",
            else: "NORMAL"
          }
        }
      }
    }
  }
} //                              ⬅ Projection adds warningLevel
                                     based on temperature

// Filter only sensors with warnings
let filterWarnings = {
  $match: {
    warningLevel: { $in: ["HIGH", "LOW"] }
  }
} //                              ⬅ Filters for HIGH
                                     or LOW warnings
```

```
// Combine processing stages
let processor = [source, validate,
    projectWithWarning, filterWarnings] //
```
⬅ **Combines stages into processor array**

```
// Execute the processor
sp.process(processor) //
```
⬅ **Executes processor on data**

First, a validation stage ensures that the data meets certain criteria, such as checking that `sensorName` is a string, `temperature` is between -50 and 100°C, and `humidity` is between 0 and 100%. Next, the pipeline transforms the data by adding a `warningLevel` based on the temperature: `"HIGH"` for temperatures 40°C or above, `"LOW"` for 10°C or below, and `"NORMAL"` otherwise. Finally, the processor filters out sensors without warnings, showing only those with `"HIGH"` or `"LOW"` levels. Here are the key points of the prototype:

- `processor`—Initializes an array to hold each processing stage.
- `source`—Sets up the initial stage using a static array of documents, simulating incoming sensor messages.
- `validate`—Ensures that each document meets specific criteria: `sensorName` exists and is a string, `temperature` is an integer between -50 and 100°C, `humidity` is an integer between 0 and 100%, and `timestamp` exists and is a date.
- `projectWithWarning`—Adds a `warningLevel` field based on temperature. If the temperature is 40°C or higher, the level is set to `HIGH`. If it's 10°C or lower, it is set to `LOW`. Otherwise, it is `NORMAL`.
- `filterWarnings`—Filters the data to include only documents with a `warningLevel` of either `HIGH` or `LOW`.
- `processor`—Combines these stages in an array to define the processing pipeline.
- `sp.process(processor)`—Executes the pipeline, processing data based on the defined stages.

The output displays two sensor readings:

```
{
  sensorName: 'sensor02',
  temperature: 45,
  humidity: 60,
  timestamp: ISODate('2023-09-07T12:01:00.000Z'),
  warningLevel: 'HIGH',
  _stream_meta: {
    source: {
      type: 'generated'
    }
  }
}
{
  sensorName: 'sensor03',
  temperature: 5,
```

```
      humidity: 80,
      timestamp: ISODate('2023-09-07T12:02:00.000Z'),
      warningLevel: 'LOW',
      _stream_meta: {
        source: {
          type: 'generated'
        }
      }
    }
}
```

`sensor02` has a temperature of 45°C (classified as `HIGH`), and `sensor03` has a temperature of 5°C (classified as `LOW`). These records are displayed in the console as the result of the processing pipeline.

> **TIP** Using a document array as a source is ideal for debugging because it allows you to control and define static data without relying on unpredictable live data sources. This setup makes it easy to quickly validate each stage of your pipeline and troubleshoot problems in a controlled environment.

15.6.5 Setting up a streams Connection Registry

To create a new connection for the SPI, you can use the Atlas CLI with the command `atlas streams connections create`. You can also use the Atlas UI. To add an Atlas database connection to the SPI, follow these steps:

1. In your Atlas UI, go to the Stream Processing panel, select your SPI, and click Configure in the top-right corner.

   Click Connection Registry; then click the Add Connection button. An interface like the one shown in figure 15.7 appears. I named my connection `mongodb-in-action-connection`, selected the Atlas cluster `MongoDB-in-Action`, and chose the role Read and Write to Any Database.

2. Check whether the new connection has been created using `mongosh` by running `sp.listConnections()`:

```
AtlasStreamProcessing> sp.listConnections()
[
  {
    name: 'mongodb-in-action-connection',
    type: 'atlas',
    cluster: 'MongoDB-in-Action'
  },
  { name: 'sample_stream_solar', type: 'inmemory' }
]
AtlasStreamProcessing>
```

Alternatively, you can use the Atlas CLI with the command

```
atlas streams connections list -i MongoDB-in-Action-SPI
```

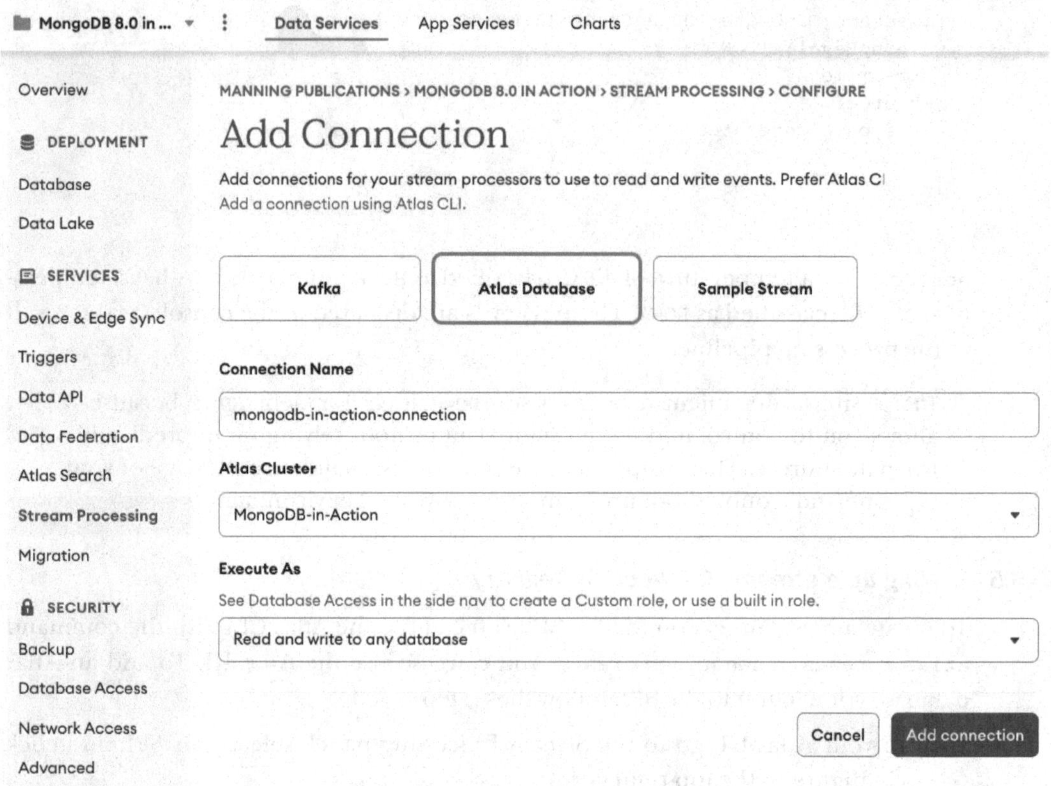

420   CHAPTER 15   *Building event-driven applications*

Figure 15.7   Add Connection interface within the Stream Processing panel in Atlas allows you to add connections for stream processors to use for reading and writing events. You have three connection options: Kafka, Atlas Database, and Sample Stream. The form includes fields for entering the connection name and selecting an Atlas cluster. You also have an option to choose the execution role, such as Read and Write to Any Database. At the bottom are buttons that cancel or add the connection. (Image © MongoDB 2025)

This command displays

```
NAME                             TYPE       SERVERS
mongodb-in-action-connection     Cluster    MongoDB-in-Action
sample_stream_solar              Sample     nil
```

The output shows two connections: `mongodb-in-action-connection`, which is a Cluster type linked to the `MongoDB-in-Action` Atlas cluster, and `sample_stream_solar`, which is a Sample type with no servers listed.

15.6.6   Ensuring persistence in stream processing

By using an aggregation pipeline, you can process and transform each document as it's being ingested. The following pipeline calculates the maximum temperature and the average, median, maximum, and minimum wattages of each solar device at 1-second intervals. The data source used is again `sample_stream_solar`, and the sink is an Atlas cluster:

1. In `mongosh`, set up a `$source` stage. The following `$source` stage pulls data from the `sample_stream_solar` source and maps the Atlas Stream Processing `time` field to the source's `timestamp` field:

   ```
   let s = {
       $source: {
           connectionName: "sample_stream_solar",
           timeField: {
               $dateFromString: {
                   dateString: '$timestamp'
               }
           }
       }
   }
   ```

2. Configure a `$group` stage. The following `$group` stage groups incoming data by `group_id`, aggregates the `obs.temp` and `obs.watts` field values for each `group_id`, and calculates the desired statistics:

   ```
   let g = {
       $group: {
           _id: "$group_id",
           max_temp: {
               $avg: "$obs.temp"
           },
           avg_watts: {
               $avg: "$obs.watts"
           },
           median_watts: {
               $min: "$obs.watts"
           },
           max_watts: {
               $max: "$obs.watts"
           },
           min_watts: {
               $min: "$obs.watts"
           }
       }
   }
   ```

3. To perform accumulations like `$group` on streaming data, Atlas Stream Processing uses windows to bound the data set. The following `$tumblingWindow` stage divides the stream into consecutive 10-second intervals. When the `$group` stage calculates a value for `median_watts`, for example, it uses the `obs.watts` values from all documents with a given `group_id` ingested in the previous 10 seconds:

```
        let t = {
            $tumblingWindow: {
                interval: {
                    size: NumberInt(10),
                    unit: "second"
                },
                pipeline: [g]
            }
        }
```

4 Configure a $merge stage. The $merge stage allows you to write your processed streaming data to an Atlas database. The connectionName for the Atlas database is "mongodb-in-action-connection", which you created in the previous section. The data will be written to the spiDB Atlas database and into the spiColl collection:

```
        let m = {
            $merge: {
                into: {
                    connectionName: "mongodb-in-action-connection",
                    db: "spiDB",
                    coll: "spiColl"
                }
            }
        }
```

5 Create the stream processor. Assign a name to your new stream processor, and define its aggregation pipeline by listing each stage in order. The $group stage is part of the nested pipeline in the $tumblingWindow stage, so it should not be included directly in the processor pipeline definition:

```
AtlasStreamProcessing> sp.createStreamProcessor
↪ ("mongodbInAction", [s, t, m])
Atlas Stream Processor: mongodbInAction
AtlasStreamProcessing>
```

6 Start the new stream processor:

```
AtlasStreamProcessing> sp.mongodbInAction.start()
{ ok: 1 }
AtlasStreamProcessing>
```

After you start the stream processor, it begins processing data in real time. The $source stage continuously ingests data from the sample_stream_solar source. The $tumblingWindow stage organizes the data in 10-second intervals, during which the $group stage aggregates the obs.temp and obs.watts values. Finally, the $merge stage writes the processed data into the spiDB database and the spiColl collection in your Atlas database. As a result, you'll have a constantly updating collection of processed streaming data stored in your database. To get the current status of your stream processor, execute the `stats()` function:

```
AtlasStreamProcessing> sp.mongodbInAction.stats()
{
  ok: 1,
  ns: '66dc35fc0b97566745a8ccdb.65d70c5bc9b5633e80a9c998.mongodbInAction',
  stats: {
    name: 'mongodbInAction',
    processorId: '66dc6a7dcf04eaa02e51e659',
    status: 'running',
    scaleFactor: Long('1'),
    inputMessageCount: Long('30'),
    inputMessageSize: 13292,
    outputMessageCount: Long('10'),
    outputMessageSize: 13560,
    dlqMessageCount: Long('0'),
    dlqMessageSize: 0,
    stateSize: 2448,
    memoryTrackerBytes: 33554432,
    watermark: ISODate('2024-09-07T15:01:04.708Z'),
    ok: 1
  },
  pipeline: [
    {
      '$source': {
        connectionName: 'sample_stream_solar',
        timeField: { '$dateFromString': { dateString: '$timestamp' } }
      }
    },
    {
      '$tumblingWindow': {
        interval: { size: 10, unit: 'second' },
        pipeline: [
          {
            '$group': {
              _id: '$group_id',
              max_temp: [Object],
              avg_watts: [Object],
              median_watts: [Object],
              max_watts: [Object],
              min_watts: [Object]
            }
          }
        ]
      }
    },
    {
      '$merge': {
        into: {
          connectionName: 'mongodb-in-action-connection',
          db: 'spiDB',
          coll: 'spiColl'
        }
      }
    }
```

```
        }
    ]
}
AtlasStreamProcessing>
```

This command provides detailed statistics about the processor, including the number of input and output messages, memory use, and the current state of the processor. The pipeline shows the stages being processed: a `$source` pulling data from `sample_stream_solar`, a `$tumblingWindow` that groups the data in 10-second intervals, and a `$merge` stage that writes the results to the `spiDb` database in the `spiColl` collection. You can also use the `sample()` method to retrieve a sample of the processed data:

```
AtlasStreamProcessing>sp.mongodbInAction.sample()
{
  _id: 5,
  max_temp: 24,
  avg_watts: 48,
  median_watts: 48,
  max_watts: 53,
  min_watts: 48,
  _stream_meta: {
    source: {
      type: 'generated'
    },
    window: {
      start: ISODate('2024-09-07T15:01:30.000Z'),
      end: ISODate('2024-09-07T15:01:40.000Z')
    }
  }
}
AtlasStreamProcessing>
```

This method returns a document with aggregated values such as `max_temp`, `avg_watts`, and `median_watts`. It includes metadata about the window of time during which the data was processed, providing insight into the stream's performance over that interval.

To stop and remove the stream processor, execute

```
AtlasStreamProcessing> sp.mongodbInAction.drop()
```

This command deletes the `mongodbInAction` stream processor. After dropping it, the output confirms with `{ ok: 1 }`. To verify that the stream processor no longer exists, you can list all stream processors with

```
AtlasStreamProcessing> sp.listStreamProcessors()
[]
AtlasStreamProcessing>
```

The empty list `[]` confirms that no stream processors are active in the instance.

15.7 Controlling the stream processing flow

In stream processing, it is vital to ensure that data flows continuously, even if some records are incorrectly formatted, delayed, or contain errors. A strong, reliable pipeline should not stop processing due to these problems but should keep the data moving while flagging and logging any problems for later investigation. This allows the main flow of data to proceed without disruption. Atlas Stream Processing helps manage such scenarios by providing a DLQ. This feature captures any problematic data, storing it separately for future review and correction, ensuring that errors don't halt the overall process.

15.7.1 Capturing the state

Atlas Stream Processing relies on checkpoint documents to monitor its progress in processing data. These checkpoints function like bookmarks, allowing the system to remember its exact position in the data stream, ensuring that it can resume processing from the correct point without missing or duplicating data.

Atlas Stream Processing uses checkpoint documents to track the state of a stream processor. These documents have unique identifiers and follow the logic flow of the stream processor. When the final operator in the processor finishes processing a checkpoint document, Atlas Stream Processing commits the checkpoint, creating two types of records:

- A record that confirms the checkpoint ID and the associated stream processor
- A series of records detailing the status of each stateful operation within the stream processor at the time of checkpoint commitment

If the stream processor is restarted after an interruption, Atlas Stream Processing retrieves the last committed checkpoint and resumes processing from the saved state.

15.7.2 Using a dead-letter queue

In stream processing systems, a DLQ is used to ensure that data the system can't process isn't lost. Instead of being dropped, it's sent to a special error or reprocessing queue. From there, it can be handled by another program, reviewed by humans, or deleted if necessary. Messaging systems including AWS EventBridge, Apache Kafka, and Solace use DLQs, and Atlas Stream Processing has this feature as well.

Atlas Stream Processing can be configured with an optional DLQ when defining a processor. The DLQ is stored in an Atlas database cluster, and the data can be saved to any MongoDB collection. This collection can be capped, sharded, and set up with any indexing strategy that MongoDB supports. The following listing shows an example.

Listing 15.8 DLQ configuration

```
// Set up a dead letter queue (DLQ) configuration
using an existing connection
let dlqConfig = {
```

```
    dlq: {
      connectionName: " mongodb-in-action-connection ",
➥ // name of the connection in the connection registry
      db: "ErrorLogs",                      // target database for the DLQ
      coll: "TransactionErrors"
➥ // collection to store failed records
    }
}

// Create a basic stream processing pipeline
let inputSource = {$source: {$kafka: {...}}}  // input from a Kafka stream
let outputSink = {$merge: {...}}    // output data to a MongoDB collection
let pipeline = [inputSource, outputSink]

// Initialize a stream processor with a pipeline and DLQ setup
sp.createStreamProcessor("TransactionProc", pipeline, dlqConfig)

// Start the processor; any problematic data is sent to the DLQ
sp.TransactionProc.start()
```

Storing data in MongoDB is powerful because it allows easy querying within the Atlas ecosystem. You can also monitor the collection to track the rate, size, and type of messages saved to the DLQ. The data can be processed later using MongoDB commands, reintroduced into the stream, or handled according to specific business needs.

By adopting a few best practices, you can ensure that your stream processors are equipped to handle a wide range of data problems without disrupting the overall flow of your system. Even in the event of malformed data, validation failures, or processing errors, your stream can continue to operate smoothly while problematic data is safely captured in the DLQ for further inspection. These best practices are

- Defining a DLQ for any processor where it's essential to ensure that all data is processed or sent to the DLQ—especially important for production-level stream processors
- Using tools such as the Atlas UI and alerts to monitor DLQ collections and track problems
- Using capped collections to prevent DLQs from growing too large in case of frequent errors
- Setting up Atlas Triggers on DLQ collections to enable automatic reprocessing and various handling options

15.8 Securing Atlas Stream Processing

Atlas offers a robust framework for managing user permissions across organization, project, and database levels (chapter 20). With Atlas Stream Processing, this framework is expanded to include roles and privileges tailored to stream processing tasks, allowing for fine-grained control. Also, user permissions can be restricted to individual SPIs, ensuring precise access control.

15.8.1 Discovering new roles

Users manage SPIs and their connection registries at the project level. Atlas Stream Processing offers the `Project Stream Processing Owner` role for this purpose. A user with this role can manage all SPIs, connection registries, and databases within the project. Assigning this role allows the user to configure everything related to Atlas Stream Processing while following the principle of least privilege, ensuring that they have only the permissions required for stream processing tasks.

15.8.2 Learning new privilege actions

You can access and manage an existing SPI as a database user, similar to how you would access an Atlas cluster. The roles and actions assigned to your database users control what operations they can perform on stream processors within the instance. Atlas Stream Processing offers several privilege actions, including

- `processStreamProcessor`
- `createStreamProcessor`
- `startStreamProcessor`
- `stopStreamProcessor`
- `dropStreamProcessor`
- `listStreamProcessors`
- `sampleStreamProcessor`
- `streamProcessorStats`
- `listConnections`

You can assign only the necessary privilege actions to a database user or custom role, ensuring that they have exactly the permissions they need for their tasks.

15.8.3 Protecting network access

Atlas Stream Processing can connect to both Atlas clusters and external data sources like Apache Kafka. Connections to Atlas clusters are set up automatically, but for external sources, you need to add Atlas IP addresses to the access list of your external data source.

When setting up a connection to an external streaming data source, you can choose to connect via public IP addresses or through a virtual private cloud (VPC) peering connection.

15.8.4 Auditing events

Atlas Stream Processing auditing allows administrators to monitor authentication and entity management events within their SPIs. Whenever an auditable event happens, it is logged for that specific instance. The log remains available for the lifetime of the SPI, and events are never deleted. If an SPI is deleted, its log is retained for 30 more days.

Summary

- Event-driven applications move away from the traditional model where tightly coupled services request data directly, leading to latency and complex dependencies. This traditional approach slows the system and limits scalability.
- Traditionally, event processing is handled in two ways: embedding the logic directly in the application code, which can make the code complex and difficult to maintain, or sending events to a database for processing. The latter approach simplifies the code but adds latency, as events need to be stored and indexed before processing.
- Event-driven architecture decouples services by using real-time events for communication, managed by platforms like Apache Kafka. This approach reduces latency, lowers overhead, and enhances system performance.
- Today, mature event streaming platforms and databases exist for managing events, but real-time processing of high-volume streams remains challenging. The differences in languages, APIs, and tools create fragmentation, slowing development and increasing complexity, time, and costs.
- Atlas offers a seamless solution in which events align naturally with flexible, JSON-like document structures. These events can be processed efficiently using MongoDB's unified Query API, which is central to its design.
- The Connection Registry stores configuration details for all connections between an SPI and external data sources or sinks. It contains information such as connection endpoints, authentication credentials, and other settings to ensure secure, reliable communication between the stream processor and external systems.
- A stream processor is a MongoDB aggregation pipeline that continuously processes streaming data from a designated source and sends the output to a specified destination.
- An Atlas SPI is a designated namespace tied to a specific connection string, cloud provider, region, and (optionally) a security context for extra protection. Stream processors created within an instance are available only in that instance.
- Atlas stream processor pipelines begin with a $source stage that connects to a data source, initiating the flow of a continuous stream of documents. These documents must be in valid JSON or EJSON format.
- The $source aggregation pipeline stage specifies a connection in the Connection Registry to stream data from, supporting the following connection types: Apache Kafka broker, MongoDB collection change stream, MongoDB database change stream, and document array.
- The $source stage must be placed at the beginning of any pipeline where it is used, and only one $source stage is allowed per pipeline.
- The $validate stage examines streaming documents to confirm that they match a defined schema, ensuring that correct ranges, values, and data types are adhered to.

- The $tumblingWindow stage divides the data stream into fixed, nonoverlapping windows based on a set time duration. Each document is processed only once because each window closes before the next begins.
- The $hoppingWindow stage creates overlapping windows with a specified duration and hop interval. Documents can appear in multiple windows, providing a sliding view of the data stream.
- A document array as a data source is perfect for debugging because it lets you control static data, avoiding unpredictable live sources. This makes validating your pipeline and troubleshooting easier.
- Atlas Stream Processing uses checkpoint documents to track its progress in processing data. These checkpoints act like bookmarks, allowing the system to resume processing from the correct point, preventing data loss or duplication and maintaining the state of a stream processor.
- In Atlas Stream Processing, a DLQ prevents unprocessable data from being lost by sending it to an error queue for further handling. You can configure an optional DLQ when defining a processor with data stored in an Atlas database cluster and saved to a MongoDB collection.
- With Atlas Stream Processing, the existing Atlas framework for managing user permissions at the organization, project, and database levels is expanded to include roles and privileges specific to stream processing tasks. This allows fine-grained control, and permissions can be restricted to individual SPIs for precise access management.

Optimizing data processing with Atlas Data Federation

This chapter covers

- Explaining the MongoDB unified Query API
- Understanding the Atlas Federated Database architecture
- Deploying a federated database instance

Atlas Data Federation serves as a distributed query engine that seamlessly integrates various data sources within and beyond Atlas, such as external cloud storage. The federation setup allows the creation of virtual databases and collections, which serve as pathways to access the stored data. It enables you to perform complex analytical queries across combined data sets from historical and live data sources, ensuring efficient data management and deep analytical insights. This setup is particularly useful when you need to maintain a consistent, comprehensive view of your data for strategic decision-making.

16.1 Querying Amazon S3 and Azure Blob Store data via the Query API

Atlas Data Federation is a powerful feature that allows users to query, transform, and analyze data across various sources in a unified way without moving or duplicating the data. It provides seamless access to data stored in different places, including MongoDB databases, cloud storage (such as Amazon S3 or Microsoft Azure Blob Store), Atlas Online Archive (chapter 17), HTTP and HTTPS endpoints, and other external sources. With Atlas Data Federation, you can run queries using the MongoDB Query API or Structured Query Language (SQL) and combine results from multiple data sources into a single consistent view. This flexibility makes it easier to work with diverse data sets while maintaining performance and efficiency, all within the Atlas environment.

Figure 16.1 illustrates Atlas data processing. The unified Query API allows you to query data from a data source such as S3 using MongoDB Query Language, the same language used for querying the database.

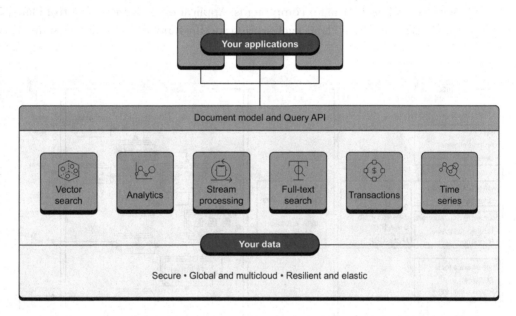

Figure 16.1 The unified Query API allows you to query workloads from S3 and Azure Blob Store. (Image © MongoDB 2024 CC BY-NC-SA 3.0)

In addition to providing seamless access to multiple data sources, Atlas Data Federation reduces the complexity of managing large data sets across storage systems. By allowing you to run real-time queries on data stored in MongoDB collections, cloud storage like S3, or even other databases, it eliminates the need for costly and time-consuming extract, transform, load (ETL) processes. The federation also enables you to create virtual databases, which means you can work with your data as though it were all in one place, even when it's spread across locations. This feature is especially useful for businesses that need to integrate and analyze data from multiple environments without moving or replicating it, thus lowering costs and simplifying data governance.

16.2 Learning Atlas Data Federation architecture

The Atlas Data Federation distributed query engine facilitates seamless querying, transforming, and transferring of data across multiple internal and external Atlas sources. Federated database instances are deployed, consisting of virtual databases and collections that map to your existing data stores. Atlas Data Federation supports a variety of data stores, including Atlas clusters, Atlas Online Archive, S3 buckets, Azure Blob Storage, and HTTP and HTTPS endpoints.

Storage configuration involves setting up mappings in JSON format between your virtual databases, collections, and data sources. By defining these mappings in the storage configuration, you can access and execute queries on your data.

Figure 16.2 displays the architecture of Atlas Data Federation. The architecture is segmented into four main components: Application & Services, Control Plane, Compute Plane, and Data Plane, each serving specific functions within the system.

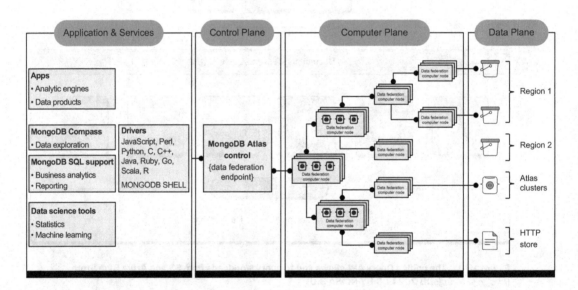

Figure 16.2 The architecture of Atlas Data Federation (Image © MongoDB 2024 CC BY-NC-SA 3.0)

Let's take a closer look at the layers. Together, they form a cohesive data federation architecture with distinct responsibilities:

- *Application & Services*—This layer includes various applications and data exploration tools such as MongoDB Compass, supports multiple programming languages through drivers (such as JavaScript, Python, and C++), and provides data science tools for statistics and machine learning. It serves as the interface for users to interact with the federation system.

- *Control Plane*—Operating similarly to the Atlas Control Plane, this layer handles the orchestration of user requests and aggregates the final results. It ensures that operations are managed efficiently and data processing workflows are optimized across the distributed environment.
- *Compute Plane*—Here, Atlas Data Federation processes all data requests. It uses an elastic pool of compute nodes strategically placed close to the data sources to minimize latency and data transfer, enhancing query response times and system performance. This plane is critical for the dynamic allocation of resources based on demand and data locality.
- *Data Plane*—This plane is where the data is stored. Configurations within this plane allow Atlas Data Federation to access a variety of storage services, including S3 buckets and Azure Blob Storage. It supports role-based access control (RBAC), ensuring that data access is secure and compliant with data governance standards. The plane is optimized for data locality, aiming to process data close to its source to reduce transmission costs and speed access.

Overall, these components work together to provide a robust, scalable, and efficient distributed query system that uses Atlas technologies to facilitate complex data operations across multiple sources and regions.

With Atlas Data Federation, you can copy data from Atlas clusters into Parquet or CSV files and store them in S3 buckets or Azure Blob Storage. You can also query multiple Atlas clusters and Atlas Online Archive to gain a comprehensive overview of your Atlas data. And you can materialize data from aggregations spanning Atlas clusters and S3 buckets, as well as read and import data from your S3 buckets into an Atlas cluster.

> **TIP** To avoid high charges, set up your Atlas Data Federation in the same Amazon Web Services (AWS) or Azure region as your S3 or Azure Blob Storage. You can query S3 only with federated database instances created in AWS and Azure Blob Storage with instances created in Azure.

> **NOTE** The Atlas SQL interface is available by default when you create a federated database instance. You can query your data using the well-known SQL language (chapter 18).

16.3 Deploying an Atlas Federated Database instance

To create an Atlas Data Federation instance, start by logging in to your Atlas account. In the left navigation pane, select the Data Federation option. In the Data Federation section, click Create New Federated Database. You will be prompted to choose how you want to set up your federated instance.

First, give your federated database a name. Then specify data sources, which could be one or multiple Atlas clusters or external data stores like S3. You can include all collections within a cluster or select specific collections. If you're using an external data store, you need to authorize the connection, such as by setting up Amazon identity and access management (IAM) roles for S3 access.

Next, configure how and when data will be queried or exported. If you're exporting to S3, for example, you can schedule recurring queries that copy data to your S3 buckets at defined intervals, transforming it into formats such as Parquet, CSV, Binary JSON (BSON), or JSON.

After you've selected your data sources and defined the connection and export settings, review your setup, and click Create to finalize the federated database instance. After deployment, you can begin running federated queries across the selected data sources, accessing, transforming, and analyzing data from various locations without moving it from its original storage environment.

> **TIP** You can find a detailed step-by-step guide in the official MongoDB documentation at https://mng.bz/DwDE.

16.4 Limitations of Atlas Data Federation

Atlas Data Federation is a powerful tool, but it has several important limitations that you need to be aware of when planning implementations. These limitations affect various functionalities, from authentication to query handling. Features not supported include the following:

- *Limited authentication methods*—Atlas Data Federation supports only specific authentication methods, including SCRAM, X.509 Certificates, OpenID Connect (OIDC), and AWS IAM. Any other forms of authentication are not supported.
- *Lack of monitoring support*—Although Atlas offers robust monitoring tools for clusters, these tools are not available for monitoring federated database instances. This limitation requires alternative methods for tracking performance or diagnosing problems in federated instances.
- *Restricted AWS S3 account use*—If you are using S3 buckets for storage with Atlas Data Federation, the federated database instance must be confined to a single AWS account. Atlas does not support federating data across S3 buckets that span multiple AWS accounts.
- *Document size limitation*—Atlas Data Federation does not support handling queries for documents that exceed 16 MB. Any queries involving such large documents will fail.
- *Inconsistent document order in queries*—The order of documents across queries is not guaranteed unless specific query operators are used. Without the appropriate operators, the order in which documents are returned may vary between queries, making consistent ordering difficult.
- *Connection limits*—A federated database instance in Atlas is limited to 60 simultaneous connections per region. Exceeding this limit may result in connection problems or degraded performance.

- *Query limitations*—Atlas Data Federation supports a maximum of 30 simultaneous queries on a federated database instance. When this limit is reached, additional queries will not be processed until other queries are completed.
- *Lack of index creation support*—Atlas Data Federation does not support creation of indexes within federated database instances. As a result, query performance may be affected when you're working with large data sets that typically benefit from indexing.

TIP Atlas Data Federation automatically terminates your cursor if it doesn't process at least 16 MB of results every minute.

These limitations are important to consider when you're designing or deploying a system that relies on Atlas Data Federation to manage and query data from multiple sources.

16.5 Charges for Atlas Data Federation

You will face charges for the following:

- Data processed by federated database instances
- Data returned by federated database instances

These charges are based on total bytes processed from your data sources, rounded to the nearest megabyte, at a rate of $5 per TB, with a minimum of 10 MB per query. Charges include costs for the data processed to execute your queries and the data returned as results. Processing a 10 GB file without partitions, for example, incurs a cost for all 10 GB, but if the file is partitioned into 10 segments of 1 GB each, and only one segment is read, the charge is for 1 GB. Implementing partitioning strategies and setting query limits can help you manage and reduce these costs.

Atlas also calculates charges based on the total bytes returned and transferred by your federated database instance, encompassing all data movements during query operations. This includes bytes returned to the client from query results, bytes transferred between Atlas Data Federation query nodes during query execution, and bytes written during $out or $merge operations. The cost of these data transfers varies with the cloud service provider's rates for data movement within the same region, between regions, or to the internet. AWS, for example, typically charges 1 cent per GB for data returned and transferred within the same region and to the client.

Summary

- Atlas Data Federation, a distributed query engine, enables seamless querying, transforming, and transferring of data across Atlas sources. It deploys federated database instances, including virtual databases and collections mapped to your existing data stores.
- The federation merges data from your Atlas clusters, HTTP and HTTPS endpoints, Atlas Online Archive, and cloud storage into virtual databases and collections. The data remains in its original location and format.

- You can build and manage Atlas Federated Database in the Atlas UI as well as the Atlas command-line interface (CLI).
- Atlas charges for data processed and returned by federated database instances. These costs are based on the volume of data handled and delivered by the system during operations.
- The Atlas SQL interface is enabled by default when you create a federated database instance, which allows you to start querying your data immediately without additional configuration.

Archiving online with Atlas Online Archive

This chapter covers
- Archiving infrequently accessed data to lower-cost storage
- Setting archiving rules based on data use and retention
- Archiving data from time-series collections
- Accessing archived and live data together
- Calculating costs associated with querying archived data
- Restoring archived data to live cluster

Atlas Online Archive is designed to help you manage data storage costs by archiving infrequently accessed data to lower-cost storage. It integrates seamlessly with Atlas, allowing you to define custom rules based on data access patterns and retention requirements. The archived data is queryable, ensuring that it remains accessible without full restoration. This service is particularly useful for long-term data storage, compliance, and historical analysis, providing a scalable solution (though one that likely sacrifices some performance).

WARNING Online Archive is not a substitute for a primary backup solution because it is designed primarily for cost-effective storage of infrequently accessed data, not for data recovery purposes. Backups, on the other hand, are comprehensive snapshots of your data intended for recovery after data loss, corruption, or other catastrophic events. Therefore, it's important to maintain a separate, robust backup strategy to ensure data integrity and availability.

17.1 Archiving your data

Atlas transfers infrequently accessed data from your primary Atlas cluster to a read-only federated database instance (chapter 16), managed by MongoDB, in cloud object storage. When the data is archived, you can access your live Atlas data and the archived data through a unified, read-only federated database instance.

The archiving process is governed by rules you establish, specifying what data should be archived. Table 17.1 outlines archiving criteria based on the type of collection to archive.

Table 17.1 Atlas archiving criteria

Criteria type	Archiving criteria	Federated database instance
Standard collection	*Date-based archiving*—A combination of a `date` field and number of days to retain data in the Atlas cluster. Data is archived when the current date surpasses the `date` field plus the specified days.	*Archive-only instance*—Allows querying of only the archived data *Combined instance*—Allows querying of the live cluster and archived data
	Custom query—Executes a specified query to determine which documents to archive	
Time-series collection	*Time-based archiving*—A combination of a `time` field and a specified number of days to keep data in the Atlas cluster. Data is archived when the current time exceeds the specified `time` field by the designated days, hours, and minutes.	*Archive-only instance*—Permits queries on archived data only *Combined Instance*—Enables querying of the live cluster and archived data
Remarks	Online Archive is available only for clusters that are M10 and higher.	

Atlas offers a single endpoint that allows you to query all databases and collections from your live cluster and archived data using the same names as in your Atlas cluster.

17.1.1 Seeing how Atlas archives data

Atlas runs a designated query within the archive's specific namespace to identify documents eligible for archiving; this query is called a *job*. By default, this job is scheduled to run every 5 minutes. Should the size of documents ready for archiving fall below the 2 GB threshold, Atlas extends the interval between job runs by 5 minutes, with a possible extension of up to 4 hours. The job restarts at 5-minute intervals when the document size meets the threshold or when the maximum time interval is reached.

To ensure the efficiency of the archival process, Atlas conducts an index sufficiency query. When the ratio of documents scanned to documents returned is 10 or higher, it triggers an `Index Sufficiency Warning` message, indicating the need for better indexing. Specifically, `date` fields in date-based archives and expressions in custom queries must be indexed appropriately.

Each archiving job can process up to 10,000 partitions and writes a maximum 2 GB of document data per run to the cloud object storage. Data is grouped efficiently to reduce partition numbers, particularly with `date` fields, and each subsequent data batch up to 2 GB continues in this manner per job execution.

> **TIP** The interval for each archival job in Atlas is 5 minutes, with the next job starting 5 minutes after the current one completes. The duration of an archival job varies based on factors such as cluster resources.

Online Archive operates within your Atlas cluster and consumes the same resources, including input/output operations per second (IOPS). To prevent excessive resource use, it imposes a default cap of 2 GB per archival job. If your cluster is already operating near its resource limits, enabling Online Archive could exceed its capacity. It's important to confirm that your Atlas cluster has additional resources available before you activate Online Archive.

With Online Archive, you choose a region to store your archived data. Table 17.2 describes these regions.

Table 17.2 Current Online Archive regions

Provider	Atlas Data Federation region	Corresponding region
Amazon Web Services (AWS)	Virginia, USA	`us-east-1`
AWS	Oregon, USA	`us-west-2`
AWS	São Paulo, Brazil	`sa-east-1`
AWS	Ireland	`eu-west-1`
AWS	London, England	`eu-west-2`
AWS	Frankfurt, Germany	`eu-central-1`
AWS	Tokyo, Japan	`ap-northeast-1`
AWS	Mumbai, India	`ap-south-1`
AWS	Singapore	`ap-southeast-1`
AWS	Mumbai, India	`ap-southeast-2`
AWS	Montreal, Canada	`ca-central-1`
Azure	Virginia, USA	`US_EAST_2`
Azure	The Netherlands	`EUROPE_WEST`

Online Archive currently has several limitations that you should be aware of:

- Writing data directly to Online Archive is not supported. Data must be archived from the primary data store according to specific archiving rules.
- Archiving from capped collections is unavailable. These collections have a fixed size and retain only the most recent data, making them incompatible with the archiving process.
- Any data that remains smaller than 5 MB after seven days will not be archived because the system prioritizes larger, less frequently accessed data to optimize storage.

NOTE Atlas uses Amazon's server-side encryption with S3-managed keys (SSE-S3) to encrypt your archived data.

17.1.2 Deleting archived documents

When it archives data, Atlas initially transfers the data to cloud object storage and subsequently removes it from your Atlas cluster. This process may temporarily result in duplicated documents appearing in your Atlas cluster and Online Archive. When the archival process is complete and Online Archive is idle, however, the previously archived documents are no longer in your Atlas cluster.

NOTE The archiving job can be initiated from any node within the cluster, but it connects to the primary replica set member for operations that involve deletion.

You have the option to set up automatic deletion of archived data after a specified period by configuring the Deletion Age Limit when creating or updating your Online Archive. When data is archived, Atlas does not synchronize Online Archive with the Atlas cluster to ensure consistency.

NOTE Online Archive is read-only. Atlas doesn't update archived data.

17.2 Initializing Online Archive

You can set up archiving for data within a collection by defining an archiving rule. In this example, I use the M10 cluster MongoDB-in-Action-M10, created in chapter 16. (M10 is the smallest cluster that has access to Online Archive.) To initiate archiving, you need to do the following:

- Define an archiving rule by specifying a namespace (database name with collection name) along with a date field and age limit or a custom query for selecting documents to archive.
- Select fields that are frequently queried to partition your archived data, ensuring optimal query performance.
- Set up Online Archive and start archiving documents that comply with your specified rule.

When they are archived, documents are removed from your Atlas cluster and cannot be modified or deleted. You have the flexibility to pause or remove the archive whenever necessary. Although Online Archive can reduce your cluster's storage expenses by archiving historical data automatically, it introduces additional costs for object storage and archive queries, which will appear as new items on your monthly bill.

Here's an archiving rule that archives documents located in the `sample_supplies` database within the `sales` collection:

```
use sample_supplies
db.sales.find({_id: ObjectId('5bd761dcae323e45a93ccfe9')})
{
  _id: ObjectId('5bd761dcae323e45a93ccfe9'),
  saleDate: ISODate('2015-08-25T10:01:02.918Z'),
  items: [
    {
      name: 'envelopes',
      tags: [ 'stationary', 'office', 'general' ],
      price: Decimal128('8.05'),
      quantity: 10
    },
    {
      name: 'binder',
      tags: [ 'school', 'general', 'organization' ],
      price: Decimal128('28.31'),
      quantity: 9
    },
    {
      name: 'notepad',
      tags: [ 'office', 'writing', 'school' ],
      price: Decimal128('20.95'),
      quantity: 3
    },
    {
      name: 'laptop',
      tags: [ 'electronics', 'school', 'office' ],
      price: Decimal128('866.5'),
      quantity: 4
    },
    {
      name: 'notepad',
      tags: [ 'office', 'writing', 'school' ],
      price: Decimal128('33.09'),
      quantity: 4
    },
    {
      name: 'printer paper',
      tags: [ 'office', 'stationary' ],
      price: Decimal128('37.55'),
      quantity: 1
    },
    {
      name: 'backpack',
      tags: [ 'school', 'travel', 'kids' ],
```

```
      price: Decimal128('83.28'),
      quantity: 2
    },
    {
      name: 'pens',
      tags: [ 'writing', 'office', 'school', 'stationary' ],
      price: Decimal128('42.9'),
      quantity: 4
    },
    {
      name: 'envelopes',
      tags: [ 'stationary', 'office', 'general' ],
      price: Decimal128('16.68'),
      quantity: 2
    }
  ],
  storeLocation: 'Seattle',
  customer: { gender: 'M', age: 50,
  email: 'keecade@hem.uy', satisfaction: 5 },
  couponUsed: false,
  purchaseMethod: 'Phone'
}
```

This rule archives documents five days after the sale date, which is recorded in the `saleDate` field. The archiving rule corresponds to this query:

```
db.sales.find({ "saleDate": { $lte: new Date(ISODate().getTime()
    - 1000 * 3600 * 24 * 5)}}).sort({ "saleDate": 1 })
```

You must index this field before the archiving process starts, which you can accomplish using the `createIndex()` method:

```
db.sales.createIndex({ "saleDate": 1 })
```

Listing 17.1 demonstrates using the Atlas command-line interface (CLI) to facilitate managing Online Archive through the command `atlas clusters onlineArchive`. The command uses the `saleDate` as the `date` field to determine when documents should be archived, which is set to occur five days after the specified date.

Listing 17.1 Initializing Atlas Online Archive with the Atlas CLI

```
atlas clusters onlineArchive create \
--clusterName MongoDB-in-Action-M10 \
--db sample_supplies --collection sales \
--dateField saleDate --archiveAfter 5 \
--partition saleDate,customer --output json
{
  "_id": "66771d91d7775c0583b47e93",
  "clusterName": "MongoDB-in-Action-M10",
  "collName": "sales",
  "collectionType": "STANDARD",
  "criteria": {
```

```
      "type": "DATE",
      "dateField": "saleDate",
      "dateFormat": "ISODATE",
      "expireAfterDays": 5
  },
  "dataProcessRegion": {
    "cloudProvider": "AWS",
    "region": "US_EAST_1"
  },
  "dbName": "sample_supplies",
  "groupId": "65d70c5bc9b5633e80a9c998",
  "partitionFields": [
    {
      "fieldName": "saleDate",
      "order": 0
    },
    {
      "fieldName": "customer",
      "order": 1
    }
  ],
  "paused": false,
  "schedule": {
    "type": "DEFAULT"
  },
  "state": "PENDING"
}
```

The command `atlas clusters onlineArchive create` configures a new online archive for the cluster named `MongoDB-in-Action-M10`. It specifies the `sample_supplies` database and `sales` collection, using `saleDate` as the key field to trigger archiving five days after the specified date. The command sets up partitioning of the archived data based on `saleDate` and `customer` to optimize access and query performance. The archive operation is set to run on Amazon Web Services (AWS) in the US East (Northern Virginia) region, which is the default.

You can also view the current status of Atlas Online Archive using the Atlas CLI:

```
atlas clusters onlineArchive list --clusterName MongoDB-in-Action-M10
ID                         DATABASE           COLLECTION    STATE
66771d91d7775c0583b47e93   sample_supplies    sales         ACTIVE
```

You can start an archive job manually using the command `atlas clusters onlineArchive start`:

```
atlas clusters onlineArchive start 66771d91d7775c0583b47e93 \
--clusterName MongoDB-in-Action-M10
Online archive '66771d91d7775c0583b47e93' started.
```

You can also use the Atlas UI to display Online Archive. In the Atlas UI, choose the Online Archive option from the drop-down menu in the Database section. This option displays the archive setup for the `sample_supplies.sales` collection, including archiving criteria and storage settings. Clicking the Connect button provides the connection string for the federated database and lets you query archived data using the Atlas SQL interface.

> **TIP** You can also query your Online Archive data with SQL (chapter 18).

17.3 Connecting and querying Online Archive

You have the option to set data processing limits for queries against archived data to manage the costs associated with Online Archive. If the processed data hits any set limit, Atlas halts new queries and issues an error notification to the client application, indicating that the limit has been exceeded. Alternatively, you can enable query termination, which stops any queries that surpass the established limit.

To access archived data via the federated database, click Connect in the Online Archive section of your cluster. A set of connection strings appears, as shown in figure 17.1. The main string allows read-only federated queries across both a live Atlas cluster and Online Archive. Two additional strings are available: one for the cluster only and another for the archive only.

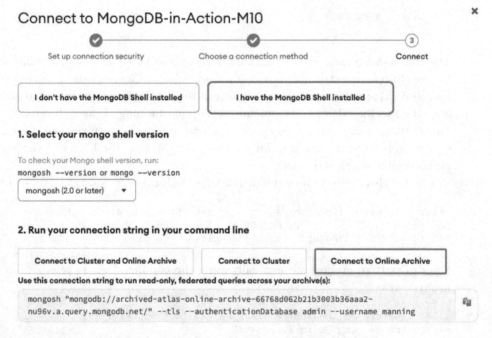

Figure 17.1 Federated database connection strings (Image © MongoDB 2025)

First, connect to the federated database, which consists of the primary Atlas cluster and Online Archive:

```
mongosh "mongodb://atlas-online-archive-
 66768d062b21b3003b36aaa2-
 nu96v.a.query.mongodb.net/" \
--tls --authenticationDatabase admin \
--username manning
Enter password: ************
AtlasDataFederation test> show dbs
admin                  0 B
config                 0 B
local                  0 B
sample_airbnb          0 B
sample_analytics       0 B
sample_geospatial      0 B
sample_guides          0 B
sample_mflix           0 B
sample_restaurants     0 B
sample_supplies        0 B
sample_training        0 B
sample_weatherdata     0 B
AtlasDataFederation test>
```

All database names and collections are available, archived and live, so you can run queries on both types of data seamlessly.

Then use the third connection string in the list—Connect to the Online Archive—which provides a connection string solely for the Online Archive instance:

```
mongosh "mongodb://archived-atlas-online-archive-
 66768d06003b36aaa2-nu96v.a.query.mongodb.net/" \
--tls --authenticationDatabase admin \
--username manning
Enter password: ************
AtlasDataFederation test> show dbs
sample_supplies   0 B
AtlasDataFederation test> use sample_supplies
switched to db sample_supplies
AtlasDataFederation sample_supplies> show collections
sales
AtlasDataFederation sample_supplies> db.sales.countDocuments()
5000
AtlasDataFederation sample_supplies>
```

The data from the sample_supplies.sales collection has been archived from the live database and is now available as read only in the Online Archive instance. All documents were transferred in this case because each of them had a saleDate older than five days, which triggered their archival according to the defined rule. This allows applications to connect and query the archived data continuously, providing cost benefits by reducing the load on the live database and using cheaper storage solutions for infrequently accessed data. Also, maintaining this separation between live and archived data improves performance and scalability, ensuring that critical operations on the live database are not affected by historical data queries.

NOTE When data is archived, it is no longer included in the backup configuration of your live Atlas cluster, but the archived data benefits from the same redundancy guarantees provided by the object storage vendor.

When you query data in your cluster and Online Archive through the federated connection string, performance varies based on the type of query:

- *Blocking queries*—These queries, such as sorts that process all input documents before returning results, are constrained by the slower speed of the archive storage. This means that sort operations wait to receive all data from the queried sources before producing results.
- *Streaming queries*—These queries, like find operations, benefit from the faster performance of the Atlas cluster. Results are returned as they become available, leading to quicker responses from the Atlas cluster compared with the archive.

Querying a federated database is associated with additional costs:

- *Data scan*—Costs are incurred when Atlas processes data from both the cluster and the archive. The system strives to minimize scans from the archive, which is more costly, by executing as much of the query as possible on the cluster. Specific match queries, for example, extract only relevant documents from the cluster to reduce costs.
- *Data access*—Each partition accessed within the archive is charged. If a query requires accessing specific partitions, each accessed partition incurs a fee.
- *Data seek*—Operations to locate necessary partitions for a query also come with costs. Atlas runs the fewest possible operations to find the required partitions—up to 1,000 partitions per operation.
- *Data transfer*—Any data transferred to or processed by the federated infrastructure results in data transfer fees.

17.4 Restoring archived data

You have the option to restore archived data to your Atlas cluster. Atlas Data Federation offers an alternative syntax for the `$merge` pipeline stage, allowing you to transfer the data back to the same or a different Atlas cluster, database, or collection within the same Atlas project. To restore the archived data, you pause it first and then restore it, following these steps:

1. Find your archive ID. You can display your archive ID using the following command:

   ```
   atlas clusters onlineArchive list --clusterName MongoDB-in-Action-M10
   ID                        DATABASE          COLLECTION    STATE
   66771d91d7775c0583b47e93  sample_supplies   sales         ACTIVE
   ```

2. Use the command `atlas clusters onlineArchive pause` to pause the archive service:

```
atlas clusters onlineArchive pause 66771d91d7775c0583b47e93 \
--clusterName MongoDB-in-Action-M10
Online archive '66771d91d7775c0583b47e93' paused.
```

3 Run the command `atlas clust:rs onlineArchive list` again to verify that the archive has been paused:

```
atlas clusters onlineArchive list --clusterName MongoDB-in-Action-M10
ID                          DATABASE           COLLECTION    STATE
66771d91d7775c0583b47e93    sample_supplies    sales         PAUSED
```

4 Use MongoDB Shell (`mongosh`) to connect to your live Atlas instance (`MongoDB-in-Action-M10`), which is the target for data restoration. Then create a unique index on the fields `saleDate` and `customer`, which Atlas requires to avoid duplicates:

```
use sample_supplies
db.sales.createIndex({ saleDate:1,customer:1}, {unique: true })
```

5 Use `mongosh` to connect your Online Archive instance. You can obtain the connection string through the Atlas UI:

```
mongosh "mongodb://archived-atlas-online-archive-
 66768d062b21b3-nu96v.a.query.mongodb.net/" \
--tls --authenticationDatabase admin \
--username manning
Enter password: ************
AtlasDataFederation test> use sample_supplies
switched to db sample_supplies
AtlasDataFederation sample_supplies> show collections
sales
```

6 Run this aggregation pipeline with the `$merge` step. Be sure to provide the correct names for the target cluster (`MongoDB-in-Action-M10`), database (`sample_supplies`), and collection (`sales`):

```
db.sales.aggregate([
  {
    "$merge": {
      "into": {
        "atlas": {
          "clusterName": "MongoDB-in-Action-M10",
          "db": "sample_supplies",
          "coll": "sales"
        }
      },
      "on": [ "saleDate", "customer" ],
      "whenMatched": "keepExisting",
      "whenNotMatched": "insert"
    }
  }
])
```

By running this aggregation pipeline, you restore data from your Online Archive instance back to the main database.

TIP Make sure that your cluster has enough capacity to handle the data being restored from your archive to avoid running out of space during or after the restoration process.

WARNING This method is not advisable for large data sets (approximately 1 TB) that have many partitions.

Summary

- Atlas Online Archive reduces storage costs by moving rarely accessed data to cheaper storage, integrating smoothly with Atlas. You can set custom archiving rules based on data use and retention needs.
- Online Archive is available only for clusters that are M10 and higher.
- Atlas moves rarely used data from your primary Atlas cluster to a read-only federated database instance, hosted on cloud object storage and managed by MongoDB. After archiving, you can access your active Atlas data and the archived data through a single read-only federated database instance.
- Atlas executes a specific query within the archive's designated namespace to select documents for archiving. This job is set to run every 5 minutes.
- During data archiving, Atlas first moves data to cloud storage and then deletes it from your cluster. This may briefly cause duplicates in both locations, but when archival is complete, these documents are only in Online Archive.
- You can access both the Atlas cluster and Online Archive to execute read-only federated queries across live and archived data. You can also connect solely to the archived data.
- You can configure data processing limits for queries on archived data to control costs related to Online Archive. When the amount of processed data reaches a specified limit, Atlas stops executing new queries and sends an error message to the client application, indicating that the limit has been exceeded.
- Costs for federated and archive-only queries in Atlas accrue from data scans, access, and transfers. These expenses are driven by the amount of data processed, the number of archive partitions accessed, and the volume of data transferred within the federated infrastructure.
- You can restore archived data to your Atlas cluster. Atlas Data Federation provides a different syntax for the `$merge` pipeline stage, enabling the transfer of data to the same or another Atlas cluster, database, or collection within the same project.

Querying Atlas using SQL

This chapter covers

- Exploring the Atlas SQL interface architecture
- Enabling Atlas SQL interface with Quick Start
- Connecting to the Atlas SQL interface with `mongosh`
- Querying with the `$sql` aggregation pipeline stage
- Operating a short-form SQL syntax with `db.sql()`

Atlas enables SQL querying through its Atlas Data Federation feature, allowing you to run SQL queries such as SELECT and WHERE statements directly on your MongoDB collections. This feature provides a unified interface for data analysis and reporting using familiar SQL syntax. This functionality also enables you to create visualizations, graphs, and reports on your Atlas data using relational business-intelligence (BI) tools such as Power BI and Tableau.

The Atlas SQL interface, along with its connectors and drivers, allows you to use your existing SQL skills to query and analyze live application data directly from your favorite SQL-based tools. Built with `mongosql`, an SQL-92–compatible dialect, this interface is designed to eliminate complex extract, transform, load (ETL) operations, enabling faster insights on Atlas data while preserving the richness of the document model.

18.1 Introducing the Atlas SQL interface

The Atlas SQL interface is exclusively for read operations. It does not support writing data back to your Atlas cluster because the interface uses Atlas Data Federation as its backend query engine, integrating data from various sources solely for querying purposes. The SQL interface is accessible only through this federated database setup, ensuring that you can perform SQL queries seamlessly across aggregated data from multiple sources. This design maintains data integrity and consistency by limiting operations to read-only, optimizing query performance, and preventing data synchronization complexities across sources.

Figure 18.1 shows the architecture of the Atlas SQL interface. Starting from the left, the Atlas data is accessed via the SQL interface, which is available through Atlas Data Federation. Each federated database instance contains virtual databases and collections that map to data in your data stores. The interface connects to SQL drivers and named connectors, facilitating seamless integration with various BI tools.

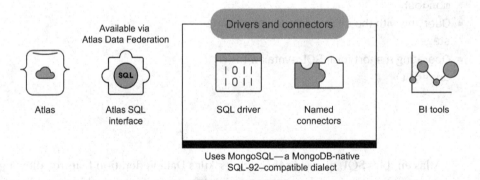

Figure 18.1   Atlas SQL interface architecture (Image © MongoDB 2024 CC BY-NC-SA 3.0)

> **NOTE** Querying your federated database instance with Atlas SQL incurs data transfer charges.

Atlas Data Federation automatically generates schemas for collections to facilitate SQL query compilation and type inference.

Atlas SQL schemas are based on JSON schemas, which define the structure of MongoDB data, including flexible and nested fields. Atlas Data Federation automatically creates these JSON schemas by analyzing a sample of documents from your collection or view, making it easier for SQL-based tools to understand and work with MongoDB data.

If you change the name of a collection or view with an existing schema, the schema is renamed accordingly. Also, Atlas Data Federation automatically creates a schema for wildcard (*) collections upon their discovery in the namespace catalog. Atlas SQL recognizes the following fields within JSON schemas: bsonType, items, properties, additionalProperties, and required.

18.2 Connecting to the Atlas SQL interface

First, enable the SQL interface by using the Atlas SQL Quick Start or configuring your own federated database instance, which automatically enables Atlas SQL. In this chapter, I cover the first method.

18.2.1 Enabling the interface

Navigate to the main view of your cluster in the Atlas UI. In this example, I use the M0 instance created in part 1 of this book, MongoDB-in-Action (figure 18.2). To connect to Atlas SQL, click the Connect button.

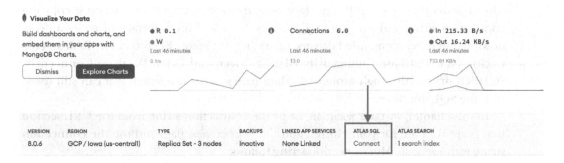

Figure 18.2 The Connect button connects to the Atlas UI in the M0 cluster. (Image © MongoDB 2025)

You see various options for connecting your application to the MongoDB cluster. Select Atlas SQL, the last option in the list. When I wrote this book, the Atlas command-line interface (CLI) did not support Atlas SQL; therefore, you must use the Atlas UI.

Figure 18.3 shows the interface that appears after you select the Atlas SQL option. This chapter focuses solely on the Quick Start option. If you are interested in advanced options, look them up in the official MongoDB documentation at https://mng.bz/Jwlv.

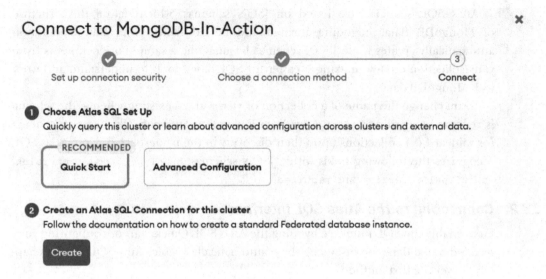

Figure 18.3 Atlas SQL Quick Start (Image © MongoDB 2025)

Click the Create button, and Atlas creates a data federation and activates the SQL interface. Atlas SQL operates on Atlas Data Federation and is free to enable.

18.2.2 Accessing the interface

After a short time, your SQL interface is ready to use. All you have to do is copy the connection string and execute SQL queries. Step 3 of the interface provides a drop-down menu of recommended drivers, including the Power BI connector, Tableau connector, Java Database Connectivity (JDBC) driver, and Open Database Connectivity (ODBC) driver. Although MongoDB Shell (mongosh) is not listed, you can still use it with the SQL interface.

In this chapter, you use mongosh. Copy the connection string from the URL section that is appropriate for your cluster, add the --username flag, and use the connection string with mongosh. My connection string follows:

```
mongosh "mongodb://atlas-sql-6658af98-nu96v.a.query.mongodb.net/" \
 --tls --username manning
Enter password: ************

Current Mongosh Log ID: 66781bda6e037b83814161ac
Connecting to: mongodb://<credentials>@atlas-sql-6658cf98-
 nu96v.a.query.mongodb.net/?directConnection=true&tls=true&
 appName=mongosh+2.1.5
AtlasDataFederation test>
```

Now that you are connected to the SQL instance, you can execute queries on MongoDB using the familiar SQL language.

18.3 Querying MongoDB using SQL

Atlas SQL offers two syntax options for formulating SQL queries: an aggregation pipeline stage syntax and a simplified short-form syntax. You can use both options to craft queries within `mongosh`.

18.3.1 Aggregation pipeline Atlas SQL syntax

The `$sql` aggregation pipeline stage allows you to craft Atlas SQL queries by processing an SQL query on the data within a collection. Key points about the `$sql` stage are

- It must be the initial stage in any pipeline.
- It supports SELECT and UNION statements.

The `$sql` stage has the following syntax:

```
{
  $sql: {
    statement: "<SQL-statement>",
    excludeNamespaces: true | false
  }
}
```

`statement` is a string, SQL query, or command to run. `excludeNamespaces` is an optional Boolean flag that specifies whether to exclude namespaces in the result set.

Let's see how to execute an Atlas SQL query that includes the `$sql` aggregation stage through `mongosh`. After logging into the Atlas SQL instance, navigate to the `sample_analytics` database:

```
AtlasDataFederation test> use sample_analytics
switched to db sample_analytics
AtlasDataFederation sample_analytics>
```

Next, run the aggregation pipeline shown in the following listing, which uses SQL to retrieve a document from the `customers` collection.

Listing 18.1 Aggregation pipeline with the `$sql` stage

```
AtlasDataFederation sample_analytics>
db.aggregate([
  {
    $sql: {
      statement: "SELECT * FROM customers WHERE
 username = 'valenciajennifer' AND
 email = 'cooperalexis@hotmail.com'",
      format: "jdbc",
      dialect: "mongosql"
    }
  }
])
```

```
[
  {
    customers: {
      _id: ObjectId('5ca4bbcea2dd94ee58162a69'),
      username: 'valenciajennifer',
      name: 'Lindsay Cowan',
      address: 'Unit 1047 Box 4089\nDPO AA 57348',
      birthdate: ISODate('1994-02-19T23:46:27.000Z'),
      email: 'cooperalexis@hotmail.com',
      accounts: [ 116508 ],
      tier_and_details: {
        c06d340a4bad42c59e3b6665571d2907: {
          tier: 'Platinum',
          benefits: [ 'dedicated account representative' ],
          active: true,
          id: 'c06d340a4bad42c59e3b6665571d2907'
        },
        '5d6a79083c26402bbef823a55d2f4208': {
          tier: 'Bronze',
          benefits: [ 'car rental insurance', 'concierge services' ],
          active: true,
          id: '5d6a79083c26402bbef823a55d2f4208'
        },
        b754ec2d455143bcb0f0d7bd46de6e06: {
          tier: 'Gold',
          benefits: [ 'airline lounge access' ],
          active: true,
          id: 'b754ec2d455143bcb0f0d7bd46de6e06'
        }
      }
    }
  }
]
```

The query runs an aggregation pipeline in MongoDB using the `$sql` stage to execute an SQL query directly on the `customers` collection. It uses a `SELECT` statement to retrieve all fields (`*`) from records in which the `username` is valenciajennifer and the `email` is cooperalexis@hotmail.com. The query format is specified as jdbc and the dialect as mongosql, which indicates the use of MongoDB's SQL-like query syntax. This approach enables complex querying capabilities within MongoDB, bridging the gap between SQL and NoSQL database interactions by using SQL syntax directly in MongoDB's aggregation framework.

> **NOTE** Atlas SQL uses the dialect mongosql.

18.3.2 Short-form Atlas SQL syntax

You have the option to use the concise db.sql method to input an Atlas SQL statemen directly, as shown in the following listing. This streamlined syntax simplifies executing SQL queries within MongoDB by allowing you to pass SQL statements directly, bypassing the more complex aggregation pipeline structure.

Listing 18.2 The short-form syntax (`db.sql`)

```
AtlasDataFederation test> use sample_analytics
switched to db sample_analytics
AtlasDataFederation sample_analytics>

db.sql(`
  SELECT username, name, address, birthdate
  FROM customers
  WHERE username = 'valenciajennifer' AND email = 'cooperalexis@hotmail.com'
`);

[
  {
    '': {
      username: 'valenciajennifer',
      name: 'Lindsay Cowan',
      address: 'Unit 1047 Box 4089\nDPO AA 57348',
      birthdate: ISODate('1994-02-19T23:46:27.000Z')
    }
  }
]
```

The `db.sql` method in `mongosh` allows direct execution of SQL queries within Atlas Federated Database. This method inputs an SQL statement that projects specific fields—username, name, address, and `birthdate`—from the `customers` collection. The query targets a customer identified by the `username valenciajennifer` and the `email cooperalexis@hotmail.com`.

18.3.3 UNWIND and FLATTEN with Atlas SQL

With Atlas SQL, you can use `UNWIND` and `FLATTEN` functions to work efficiently with complex data structures within your documents. These functions enhance your capacity to manipulate and analyze data directly in an SQL-like environment, providing powerful tools for dealing with nested arrays and semistructured data.

`UNWIND` serves to deconstruct an array field from a data source, producing a separate row for each item in the array, simplifying data manipulation and analysis of array structures. The syntax for expanding array fields involves using the `UNWIND` function within the `FROM` clause, along with a data source and various options:

```
SELECT *
FROM UNWIND(<data source>
 WITH PATH => <array_path>,
 INDEX => <identifier>,
 OUTER => <bool>
)
```

Let's see how the `UNWIND` function works in Atlas SQL, using a document from the `accounts` collection in the `sample_analytics` database:

```
AtlasDataFederation sample_analytics> db.accounts.findOne()
{
  _id: ObjectId('5ca4bbc7a2dd94ee5816238e'),
  account_id: 198100,
  limit: 10000,
  products: [ 'Derivatives', 'CurrencyService', 'InvestmentStock' ]
}
AtlasDataFederation sample_analytics>
```

This document contains an array of products associated with an account, making it a suitable candidate for demonstrating the UNWIND operation in Atlas SQL. Here's how you use the UNWIND function to expand the products array to individual rows, each containing a product and the associated account_id:

```
db.sql(`
  SELECT account_id, products AS product
  FROM UNWIND(accounts WITH PATH => products)
  WHERE account_id = 198100
`);
Note: this is an experimental feature that
⇀may be subject to
⇀change in future releases.
[
  { '': { account_id: 198100, product: 'Derivatives' } },
  { '': { account_id: 198100, product: 'CurrencyService' } },
  { '': { account_id: 198100, product: 'InvestmentStock' } }
]
```

You can use the UNWIND function in Atlas SQL to handle array fields by transforming them into a format akin to that of traditional relational database outputs, facilitating easier data analysis and manipulation.

FLATTEN transforms semistructured data such as JSON name–value pairs into distinct columns for easier analysis. This function converts document field names to column names and aligns their corresponding values in rows. It's particularly useful for flattening nested documents. You can specify the function in the FROM clause of an SQL query with options to control the depth and format of the output.

The syntax for converting nested documents to a flattened format employs the FLATTEN function, which is incorporated into the FROM clause along with a designated data source and various options:

```
SELECT *
FROM FLATTEN(<data source>
 WITH DEPTH => <integer>,
 SEPARATOR => <string>
)
```

I'll demonstrate how the FLATTEN function works in Atlas SQL using a document from the routes collection in the sample_training database. To select the relevant document, I query the `routes` collection for flights that originate from Kazan International Airport (KZN) and land at Astrakhan Airport (ASF):

```
AtlasDataFederation sample_training>
 db.routes.find({ src_airport: 'KZN', dst_airport: 'ASF' })
[
  {
    _id: ObjectId('56e9b39b732b6122f877fa3f'),
    airline: { id: 410, name: 'Aerocondor', alias: '2B', iata: 'ARD' },
    src_airport: 'KZN',
    dst_airport: 'ASF',
    codeshare: '',
    stops: 0,
    airplane: 'CR2'
  }
]
AtlasDataFederation sample_training>
```

The query returns a single document that details a flight without any codeshares and with no stops, using a CR2 aircraft. To further illustrate the use of the FLATTEN function, I ensure that the SQL query specifically targets this document by using precise conditions in the WHERE clause:

```
db.sql(`SELECT * FROM FLATTEN(routes) WHERE src_airport = 'KZN'
 AND dst_airport = 'ASF'`);
Note: this is an experimental feature that
 may be subject to
 change in future releases.
[
  {
    routes: {
      _id: ObjectId('56e9b39b732b6122f877fa3f'),
      airline_alias: '2B',
      airline_iata: 'ARD',
      airline_id: 410,
      airline_name: 'Aerocondor',
      airplane: 'CR2',
      codeshare: '',
      dst_airport: 'ASF',
      src_airport: 'KZN',
      stops: 0
    }
  }
]
```

The FLATTEN function transforms the nested structure of the document into a flat, tabular format. In this case, it extracts and lists the fields from the nested airline object and other top-level fields directly within the `routes` key, providing a simplified, more accessible view of the data.

> **Limitations of the Atlas SQL interface**
>
> Atlas SQL is built on the SQL-92 standard, but it has some limitations that prevent full compatibility:
>
> - The UNION function is not supported, though UNION ALL is available.
> - The date data type is not supported. Use timestamp instead.
> - SELECT DISTINCT is not supported.
> - Interval and date-interval arithmetic are not supported.

NOTE Atlas SQL does not support Atlas Vector Search and Atlas Search.

Summary

- Atlas enables SQL querying through Atlas Data Federation, allowing you to run SQL queries directly on your MongoDB collections.
- The Atlas SQL interface is designed solely for read operations. It can't perform write operations back to your Atlas cluster because it relies on Atlas Data Federation as its backend query engine, consolidating data from multiple sources exclusively for querying.
- Atlas Data Federation automatically generates JSON schemas for collections to aid in SQL query compilation and type inference. These schemas capture the unique characteristics of MongoDB data, including its polymorphism, sparseness, and complex nested structures.
- To use the Atlas SQL interface, activate it by using the Atlas SQL Quick Start or setting up your own federated database instance, which automatically enables Atlas SQL.
- The $sql aggregation pipeline stage enables the formulation of Atlas SQL queries through the execution of an SQL query on the data set within a collection.
- You can use the streamlined db.sql method to input an Atlas SQL statement directly. Be aware that this short-form syntax is unstable and may be subject to change.
- Atlas SQL allows you to use the UNWIND and FLATTEN functions to handle complex data structures in your documents. These functions enable effective manipulation and analysis of nested arrays and semistructured data within an SQL-like environment.

Creating charts, database triggers, and functions

This chapter covers
- Visualizing your data with charts
- Using natural language to build charts
- Discovering the Atlas billing dashboard
- Triggering server-side logic with database triggers
- Writing functions

MongoDB Atlas Charts is a powerful data visualization tool that makes it easy to analyze, explore, and interpret data. With customizable charts and dashboards, you can gain insights into data trends, detect anomalies, and effectively communicate findings to stakeholders. The intuitive drag-and-drop interface ensures that you can create detailed visualizations without going near a command-line interface (CLI). Its integration with MongoDB data makes it simple to keep information current and actionable. Atlas Charts can also help you create and customize your own billing dashboard, allowing precise tracking and visualization of your database expenses.

Atlas offers a wide range of auxiliary features to enhance database management and streamline operations. One of these features is Atlas Database Triggers, part of Atlas Application Services, which allows you to automate real-time data processing by executing server-side logic in response to specific database events. This reduces manual intervention, ensuring that workflows and data updates happen seamlessly and without human involvement. Triggers are particularly useful for applications that require immediate data synchronization, logging, or notifications based on changes within the database.

19.1 *Visualizing data with Atlas Charts*

Sometimes, you need to visualize data to gain insights or communicate complex information more effectively, particularly when dealing with cloud spending, user behavior analytics, performance metrics, and other large data sets. Effective visualization can help identify trends, anomalies, and areas for optimization, which is crucial for making informed business decisions.

Atlas Charts is a data visualization tool that allows you to create and share charts and graphs based on your MongoDB data. It provides a user-friendly, no-code interface to build visualizations such as bar charts, line graphs, and heat maps directly from your MongoDB collections. The feature is designed to work seamlessly with MongoDB, offering powerful aggregation capabilities and real-time data updates. Key features include

- *Aggregation*—It includes built-in aggregation capabilities, allowing you to analyze your collection data using various metrics. You can perform calculations such as mean and standard deviation to gain deeper insights.
- *Integration with Atlas*—It integrates with Atlas, enabling you to connect charts to your Atlas projects and visualize your cluster data.
- *Document data handling*—It can manage document-based data, including embedded objects and arrays. It supports flexible data structuring while maintaining robust visualization features.

Figure 19.1 shows a dashboard displaying multiple charts of key movie statistics from documents in a MongoDB collection.

You can embed these charts in your applications or dashboards, making it easy to analyze and present your data without moving it to another platform. The ecosystem consists of several essential elements:

- *Data source*—When creating a chart, you must select a data source that provides the fields for building your visualizations. You can connect to these data sources:
  - *MongoDB collection or database view*—Connect directly to a collection or view within your MongoDB deployment.
  - *Charts view*—Create a custom charts view from an existing collection to tailor the data specifically for visualization.
- *Chart*—A chart is a visualization built from a specific data source. Fields from the selected data source are used to construct the chart, enabling you to represent complex data sets in formats such as bar charts, scatter plots, and number charts.
- *Dashboard*—A dashboard displays one or more charts. The dashboard is the primary interface for creating, managing, and viewing your visualizations.

Visualizing data with Atlas Charts

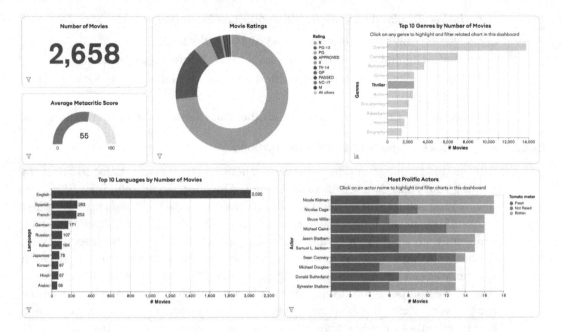

Figure 19.1 This example dashboard displays the total number of movies (2,658) and their average Metacritic score (55). The Movie Ratings pie chart breaks down films by rating categories. The Top 10 Genres bar chart highlights the most popular genres, with Drama leading. The Top 10 Languages chart shows that English dominates, and the Most Prolific Actors chart identifies actors with the most appearances, categorized by critic ratings (Fresh, Not Rated, and Rotten). (Image © MongoDB 2025)

The following chart types offer a wide range of options for visualizing your data. Each type serves a specific purpose, allowing you to analyze and present your data effectively in various formats:

- *Natural language*—Automatically generate charts based on a plain-English query using AI models.
- *Column and bar*—Compare values within categories to provide an overview of data trends.
- *Line and area*—Display data points connected by lines, showing trends over time or categories.
- *Combo*—Combine column and line views for a mixed representation of data.
- *Heatmaps*—Visualize aggregated data in a color-coded grid format.
- *Scatter*—Plot individual data points along the X and Y axes to show distribution or correlation.
- *Doughnut*—Represent data as segments of a circle, showing proportions of each category.
- *Gauge*—Show data as a percentage of a semicircle with customizable ranges and an optional target value.

- *Tables*—Display data in a spreadsheetlike tabular format.
- *Number*—Show a single aggregated value from the data.
- *Word*—Highlight key words or phrases by their frequency in the data.
- *Top item*—Show the document with the largest or smallest value for a specified field.
- *Geospatial*—Combine geospatial and other data to create map-based visualizations.

19.1.1 Using natural language to build visualizations

With natural-language mode, you can generate data visualizations instantly by querying your Atlas data sets in plain English. This functionality eliminates complex query writing and technical expertise, allowing you to interact with data intuitively. You can quickly create advanced, scalable visualizations directly within the Atlas ecosystem, significantly streamlining data analysis and reducing the time required for insights. Without knowing how to generate a chart professionally or write an aggregation pipeline, you can use a plain-English sentence like "What are the top 10 cuisines in terms of the number of restaurants in each borough?" when visualizing data from the `sample_restaurants` database and the `restaurants` collection. Atlas can generate a chart based on your request. Figure 19.2 presents the chart generated from this query.

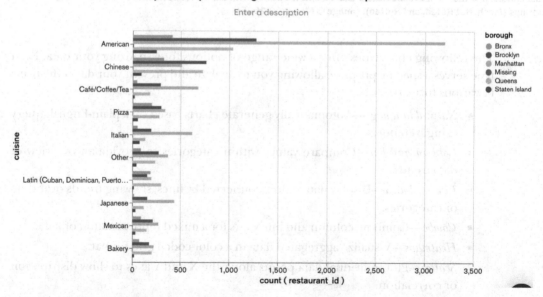

Figure 19.2 The chart generated using natural-language mode based on a plain-English query. The chart displays a boroughwise breakdown of the top 10 cuisines by number of restaurants. The y axis lists the cuisines, and the x axis shows the count of restaurants (`restaurant_id`). Each borough is represented by different colors (along with restaurants that are missing a designation). The chart shows that American cuisine has the highest presence, particularly in Manhattan. (Image © MongoDB 2025)

You can view the aggregation pipeline that was used to create the chart in figure 19.2 by accessing the chart's Options menu. The aggregation applied to the data source for this chart looks like this:

```
[
  {
    "$group": {
      "_id": {
        "__alias_0": "$cuisine",
        "__alias_1": "$borough"
      },
      "__alias_2": {
        "$sum": {
          "$cond": [
            {
              "$ne": [
                {
                  "$type": "$restaurant_id"
                },
                "missing"
              ]
            },
            1,
            0
          ]
        }
      }
    }
  },
  {
    "$project": {
      "_id": 0,
      "__alias_0": "$_id.__alias_0",
      "__alias_1": "$_id.__alias_1",
      "__alias_2": 1
    }
  },
  {
    "$project": {
      "x": "$__alias_2",
      "y": "$__alias_0",
      "color": "$__alias_1",
      "_id": 0
    }
  },
  {
    "$addFields": {
      "__agg_sum": {
        "$sum": [
          "$x"
        ]
      }
    }
  },
  {
```

```
            "$group": {
              "_id": {
                "y": "$y"
              },
              "__grouped_docs": {
                "$push": "$$ROOT"
              },
              "__agg_sum": {
                "$sum": "$__agg_sum"
              }
            }
        },
        {
          "$sort": {
            "__agg_sum": -1
          }
        },
        {
          "$limit": 10
        },
        {
          "$unwind": "$__grouped_docs"
        },
        {
          "$replaceRoot": {
            "newRoot": "$__grouped_docs"
          }
        },
        {
          "$project": {
            "__agg_sum": 0
          }
        }
]
```

This aggregation groups data by cuisine and borough, counting the number of valid restaurants. Then it projects the results into fields for visualization: `x` for the count of restaurants, `y` for cuisine, and `color` for borough. After sorting by total count, it selects the top 10 cuisines and restructures the output for display in the chart.

Natural-language charts currently rely on the Microsoft Azure OpenAI service, although this may change. When you interact with natural-language charts, Atlas transmits the following data to MongoDB's backend and/or the third-party AI provider:

- The full content of your natural-language query
- The schema of the collection used to generate the chart, including collection and field names and field data types
- Sample field values to enhance the accuracy of chart recommendations

This information is not shared with external third parties or retained by the AI provider. Database connection strings and credentials are never transmitted. By default, MongoDB retains your original query text for up to one year to support customer assistance and improve the service.

19.1.2 Using billing dashboards

You can use Atlas Charts to visualize your billing data by creating a billing dashboard. These dashboards come with prebuilt charts to help you track your Atlas use. After you import your billing data, you can add a billing dashboard and adjust it to fit your needs.

Billing dashboards offer detailed metrics and charts that show your organization's use across various categories and time frames. These insights help you manage and optimize your Atlas expenses. Billing dashboards include the following metrics and charts:

- Total spending across the organization
- Top spenders in the organization
- Total spending by instance size, project, cluster, product category, or Stock Keeping Unit (SKU), a unique identifier for each product or service)
- Total cost by product category

You can also customize your billing dashboard by applying filters and adding new charts, including those based on tags you've assigned to your billing data. Figure 19.3 shows an example of a billing dashboard.

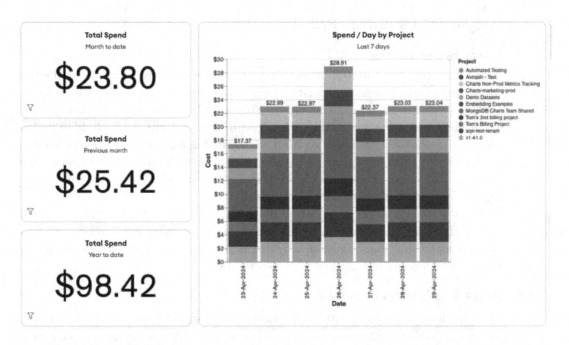

Figure 19.3 The Atlas billing dashboard with three main financial metrics on the left. Total spend for the month to date is $23.80, total spend for the previous month is $25.42, and total spend for the year to date is $98.42. The central chart visualizes daily spending across projects over the past week, with each project contributing to the total spend on each day, represented by colored bar segments. Filters on the right side allow further customization of the data displayed. (Image © MongoDB 2025)

Billing dashboards make it easy to monitor and compare costs across projects and periods. Filtering by project, team, and other criteria makes this tool flexible and enables you to drill down into specific spending patterns, which helps with budget management, cost optimization, and identifying trends in resource use across the organization.

> **NOTE** Billing dashboards always display the most recent 12 months of billing data for the selected organization.

PRICING

Billing is based on the data volume transferred from the Charts web server to clients' web browsers. Each instance comes with 1 GB of free data transfers per month. You can monitor this use on the Data Transfer page and create a billing dashboard to get a detailed view.

This free tier provides around 500,000 chart renders monthly, though the actual number depends on the chart types. Simple charts, such as number and bar charts, use less data; complex charts, such as scatter plots with numerous data points, use more.

After you exceed the 1 GB free limit, data transfer is billed at $1 per gigabyte. Additional data transfer fees may apply, as detailed in the Data Transfer Fees section of the pricing page.

> **NOTE** Atlas Charts is hosted in the Amazon Web Services (AWS) us-east-1 region, which is used for fee calculation.

SUPPORTED CLUSTER TYPES

Atlas Charts provides full support for all cluster configurations within Atlas, whether you're using flex clusters, dedicated clusters, data stored in Online Archive, or federated data through Atlas Data Federation. No matter how you set up or manage your application data, you can visualize it easily with charts. There are no hidden limitations or compatibility problems; if your data is hosted in Atlas, it can be represented in Charts, allowing you to explore and analyze it effortlessly. This flexibility ensures that as your data architecture evolves, Charts remains a powerful, reliable tool for visualizing your data without additional constraints.

If you're looking to get started with Charts, the best place to begin is the MongoDB documentation, which provides step-by-step tutorials to guide you through creating and managing your charts. You can explore all the resources and tutorials by visiting https://www.mongodb.com/docs/charts/tutorials.

19.2 Atlas Application Services

Atlas Application Services provides fully managed backend solutions in Atlas, enabling you to use database triggers and functions to build reactive, event-driven applications. Database triggers automatically execute functions when specific changes occur in the Atlas database, allowing real-time responses to data updates, inserts, deletes, and similar operations. This makes it easier to automate processes, such as sending notifications or synchronizing data across systems.

Functions, written in JavaScript, allow developers to define custom server-side logic without managing or deploying servers. These functions can handle complex operations such as data validation, transformation, and external API integration, simplifying tasks that typically require more infrastructure.

By using triggers and functions together, you can create scalable, serverless solutions that react to data changes dynamically, improving efficiency and performance. For more information about Atlas Application Services, see https://www.mongodb.com/docs/atlas/app-services.

19.2.1 Triggering server-side logic with Atlas Database Triggers

Triggers in a database are powerful tools that allow automation and enforcement of rules without manual intervention. They can respond to changes in the data and ensure that the information being stored adheres to predefined standards or business requirements. In the real world, triggers are similar to doors that open automatically when someone approaches. No one needs to push a button; the door reacts to the person's presence. In the same way, database triggers respond to changes in data automatically, performing tasks without manual input.

Triggers can facilitate complex data interactions and automate responses to data changes. When a customer's address is modified, for example, a trigger can automatically update related records, such as shipping information, to maintain consistency across the system. Triggers can also communicate with external services. Adding a new order might initiate a real-time stock update in an inventory management system, for example.

With the help of functions, triggers can automate calling external APIs, such as the OpenAI Embedding API, to generate a vector representation of a new document upon its insertion into the database. Then this vector can be stored automatically alongside the original document in MongoDB. This setup streamlines data processing and integration workflows, allowing advanced analysis and retrieval by keeping the original data and its enriched vector representation directly within the database. Triggers invoke Atlas Functions (section 19.2.2).

Figure 19.4 showcases the trigger types available for an Atlas cluster, designed to react automatically to changes, schedules, and user actions. These triggers are organized in three main types: database, scheduled, and authentication.

TRIGGER TYPES

Atlas supports three types of triggers, allowing you to automate workflows and respond to events within your system based on specific criteria or actions:

- *Database*—These triggers fire when certain operations occur in a collection, such as inserting, updating, deleting, or replacing documents. In an e-commerce application, for example, a database trigger could automatically adjust inventory levels when a new order is placed. Similarly, if a customer updates their address, the trigger ensures that the new shipping information is synced across all relevant systems, eliminating manual updates. Database triggers use MongoDB

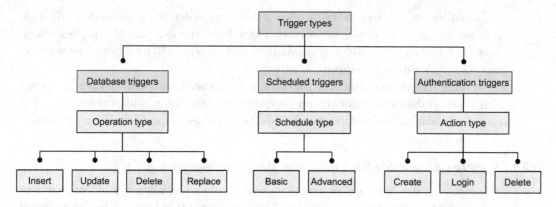

Figure 19.4 Trigger types in Atlas: database (insert, update, delete, and replace), scheduled (basic and advanced), and authentication (create, login, and delete) (Image © MongoDB 2024 CC BY-NC-SA 3.0)

change streams to monitor real-time updates in a collection. A change stream consists of a sequence of events, each detailing an operation performed on a document within the collection. For every collection with at least one active trigger, the application opens a single change stream. If a collection has multiple triggers, all of them use this shared change stream.

- *Scheduled*—These triggers enable tasks to be executed at predefined intervals. You can use scheduled triggers for daily tasks such as sending automated email reports and performing routine data analysis. You could use advanced scheduled triggers for more complex workflows, such as generating monthly financial reports or sending out seasonal promotions based on specific dates and times.

- *Authentication*—These triggers are activated by user authentication events such as login, account creation, or deletion. When a user creates an account, for example, an authentication trigger might send a welcome email or initiate a process to add the user to a mailing list. If a user deletes their account, the trigger could automatically revoke the user's access to associated services or log the event for security tracking.

NOTE Atlas Triggers are, in essence, serverless functions linked to change streams. Every trigger is associated with a specific function. When the trigger detects an event matching its configuration, it activates and sends the event object to the linked function as an argument.

TIP Atlas limits the number of database triggers based on the size of your cluster. Each trigger requires a change stream, and the total number cannot exceed the cluster's change stream limit.

CREATING A TRIGGER

Database triggers execute server-side code whenever a change occurs in a connected Atlas cluster. You can set up triggers for specific collections, whole databases, or the entire cluster. Unlike SQL data triggers, which operate directly on the database server, Atlas Triggers run on a separate serverless computing layer, which scales independently from the database server itself. Triggers can automatically invoke functions and also send events to external services using AWS EventBridge.

Database triggers use change streams to monitor real-time changes within a collection. When multiple triggers are enabled on the same collection, they all use a single change stream. You can control which operations activate a trigger and define what actions are taken when the trigger is fired. Triggers support $match expressions to filter change events and $project expressions to restrict the data included in each event. Follow these steps to create a trigger:

1. Navigate to the Atlas UI for your cluster.
2. In the left panel, expand the Services section, and click Triggers.
3. Click the Add Trigger button in the top-right corner. The menu shown in figure 19.5 appears.

Figure 19.5 The Add Trigger interface in Atlas. At the top, you can choose the trigger type: Database or Scheduled. In the Trigger Details section, you can set the trigger's name, enable or disable it, choose to skip events when reenabled, and control event ordering. (Image © MongoDB 2025)

4. In the Trigger Details section, choose Database for database triggers, and provide a name for the trigger.
5. Activate the trigger by clicking the Enable toggle switch, and choose to skip events on reenable to avoid processing events that occurred while the trigger was disabled. Enable event ordering if you want events to be processed sequentially based on their timestamps, or disable it for parallel processing to improve performance.

CHAPTER 19 *Creating charts, database triggers, and functions*

6 Configure the trigger source details:

   a Select the level of granularity for the Watch Against setting.

   b Choose Collection to trigger on changes in a specific collection, Database for changes in any collection within a specific database, or Deployment for changes across the entire cluster. Note that the deployment option is available only on dedicated tiers.

   I used `MongoDB-in-Action` as the cluster name, `sample_restaurants` as the database, and `restaurants` as the collection.

7 Select the operation types that will trigger the event, such as `insert`, `update`, and `delete`.

8 Enable the Full Document option to include the latest version of the modified document in the change events and the Document Preimage option to include a snapshot of the document before the change.

9 In the Function section, select the action to take when the trigger fires. Listing 19.1 demonstrates a function designed to log various change events, such as `insert`, `update`, and `delete`, in a separate collection for debugging and recordkeeping.

Listing 19.1 Database trigger function to log change events

```
exports = async function(changeEvent) {
  // Log the entire change event for debugging
  const fullChangeEvent = EJSON.stringify(changeEvent, null, 2);
  console.log(`Full Change Event: ${fullChangeEvent}`);

  // Check if changeEvent is empty
  if (!changeEvent || Object.keys(changeEvent).length === 0) {      ◄── Validates changeEvent
      console.error('No change event data received.');
      return; //
  }

  // Log all keys in changeEvent
  console.log(`Change Event Keys: ${Object.keys(changeEvent).join(', ')}`);   ◄── Logs changeEvent keys

  // Access the change event details
  const { operationType, documentKey, updateDescription } = changeEvent;      ◄── Extracts event details

  // Validate the existence of required fields in the change event
  if (!operationType) { //
      console.error('Missing operationType in changeEvent.');        ◄── Validates operationType
      return; //
  }
```

```
  if (!documentKey) { //                              ⎤ Validates
    console.error('Missing documentKey in changeEvent.');  ⎥ documentKey
//
    return; //
  }

  // Get a reference to the MongoDB service
  const mongodb = context.services.get("MongoDB-in-Action");
//
  const logsCollection =        ◀──── Accesses MongoDB service
mongodb.db("sample_restaurants").collection("restaurants_logs");

  // Handle different operation types
  if (operationType === 'insert') { //
    console.log('Insert operation detected.'); //

    // Create a log entry for the insert operation
    const logEntry = { //
      operation: "insert", //
      documentId: documentKey._id, //                           ⎤ Handles
      timestamp: new Date() //                                  ⎥ insert
    };                                                          ⎥ event

    // Insert the log into the "restaurants_logs" collection
    await logsCollection.insertOne(logEntry); //

    console.log(`Log entry inserted: ${JSON.stringify(logEntry)}`);
//

  } else if (operationType === 'update') { //
    if (!updateDescription || !updateDescription.updatedFields) {
//
      console.error('Missing updateDescription.updatedFields in
changeEvent.');
//
      return; //
    }

    // Get the updated fields
    const updatedFields = updateDescription.updatedFields; //
                                                                ⎤ Handles
                                                                ⎥ update
    // Log the updated fields                                   ⎥ event
    console.log(`Updated Fields: ${JSON.stringify(updatedFields)}`);
//

    // Create a log entry for the update operation
    const logEntry = { //
      operation: "update", //
      documentId: documentKey._id, //
      updatedFields: updatedFields, //
      timestamp: new Date() //
    };

    // Insert the log into the "restaurants_logs" collection
```

```
        await logsCollection.insertOne(logEntry); //         ▲ Handles
                                                             │ update
        console.log(`Log entry inserted: ${JSON.stringify(logEntry)}`); │ event
    ▶ //                                                     │

    } else if (operationType === 'delete') { //
        // For delete operations, only documentKey is available
        console.log('Delete operation detected.'); //

        const logEntry = { //
          operation: "delete", //                              Handles
          documentId: documentKey._id, //                      delete
          timestamp: new Date() //                             event
        };

        // Insert the log into the "restaurants_logs" collection
        await logsCollection.insertOne(logEntry); //

        console.log(`Log entry inserted: ${JSON.stringify(logEntry)}`);
    ▶ //

    } else { //                                                Handles
        console.error(`Unsupported operation type: ${operationType}`); │ unsupported
    ▶ //                                                       │ types
    }
};
```

The function logs the entire change event for debugging purposes and then checks whether the change event contains any data. If essential fields such as `operationType` and `documentKey` are missing, it logs an error and stops execution. It connects to the "MongoDB-in-Action" service and accesses the `restaurants_logs` collection in the `sample_restaurants` database. It handles different events based on the `operationType`. For `inserts`, it logs the event with the document ID and timestamp; for `updates`, it includes the updated fields; and for `deletes`, it logs the document ID. Then it inserts each log entry into the `restaurants_logs` collection.

The Advanced section of the interface provides optional configurations. The Match Expression field allows you to define a `$match` expression to filter which change events cause the trigger to fire, for example. For detailed information, see https://mng.bz/4n1a.

> **NOTE** Atlas Database Triggers have many uses beyond the examples listed, such as syncing databases, enforcing business rules, calling external APIs, auditing, validating data, sending alerts, aggregating in real time, maintaining views, cleaning up after deletions, and securing sensitive data. All this logic is implemented within Atlas Functions (section 19.2.2).

CONFIGURING A SCHEDULED TRIGGER

You can use scheduled triggers for recurring tasks, such as updating a document every minute, cleaning up old log entries every night, or synchronizing data with an external API on a weekly basis. Figure 19.6 shows how to create a scheduled trigger in the Atlas UI.

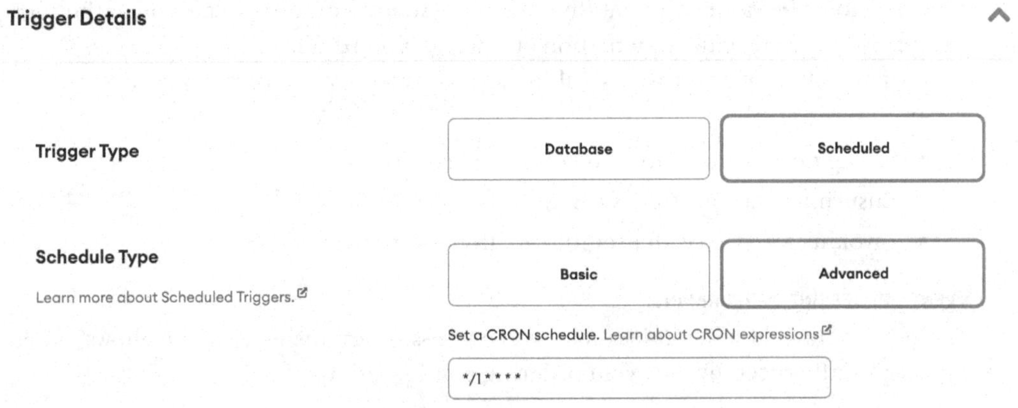

Figure 19.6 The interface for setting up a scheduled trigger. Trigger Type is set to Scheduled, indicating that this trigger will execute at regular intervals. Schedule Type is set to Advanced, which allows complex scheduling with `cron` expressions. `cron` expressions provide flexibility by allowing you to define when the trigger should run. (Image © MongoDB 2025)

To set up a scheduled trigger, select Scheduled in the Trigger Type section, ensuring that the trigger runs at specific intervals that you define. Make sure that the Enabled toggle is switched on, indicating that the trigger is active. In the Schedule Type section, select Advanced, and allow complex scheduling with CRON expressions. *CRON expressions* are strings made up of five space-separated fields, with each field defining a particular part of the schedule for the trigger:

```
*  *  *  *  *
|  |  |  |  └── weekday.......... [0 (SUN) - 6 (SAT)]
|  |  |  └───── month............ [1 (JAN) - 12 (DEC)]
|  |  └──────── dayOfMonth....... [1 - 31]
|  └─────────── hour............. [0 - 23]
└────────────── minute........... [0 - 59]
```

In this case, the CRON expression */1 * * * * is used, indicating that the trigger will execute every minute. You can customize the schedule to suit your needs, however, specifying exactly when the trigger should run, including the minute, hour, day, month, and day of the week. With this configuration, the trigger will execute the function you define at the specified times.

USING AN AUTHENTICATION TRIGGER

An authentication trigger activates when a user interacts with an authentication provider. Atlas handles user authentication by using role-based access rules to set permissions for reading and writing data. It links each request to an authenticated user and assesses permissions for every object involved. You can manage user-specific metadata and custom data through user accounts. Authentication is managed through various providers, including built-in ones like Facebook and Google, as well as custom providers for integrating other authentication systems. For more details on authentication providers, see the documentation at https://mng.bz/Qw8w.

Authentication triggers are useful for sophisticated user management tasks such as these:

- Saving new user data to your connected cluster
- Ensuring data consistency when a user is deleted
- Invoking a service with user information upon login

EVENT PROCESSING PERFORMANCE

Triggers operate in a serverless manner, processing events as capacity allows. Their capacity is influenced by the event ordering configuration:

- Ordered triggers process events sequentially from the change stream, handling one event at a time. The next event starts processing only after the previous one is fully processed.
- Unordered triggers can handle multiple events concurrently, with a default limit of up to 10,000 events. If the trigger's data source is an M10+ Atlas cluster, this limit can be increased to surpass the default 10,000 concurrent events.

It's important to note that trigger capacity doesn't translate directly to throughput or a fixed execution rate; it simply defines the maximum number of events a trigger can handle at a given moment. The actual processing rate depends on the logic within the trigger function and the volume of incoming events. To increase a trigger's throughput, you can

- Optimize the trigger function's execution, such as minimizing network calls
- Use a projection filter to reduce the size of each event object, ideally to 2 KB or less
- Apply a match filter to limit the events the trigger processes, firing only when specific conditions are met, such as changes to a particular field

> **NOTE** Defining a database trigger on a federated database instance is not possible; these instances do not support change streams.

19.2.2 Writing Atlas Functions

Atlas Functions are serverless and essential for executing logic with Atlas Triggers. When a function is called, the request is routed to a managed server that runs your code and returns the result. This serverless model eliminates the need to handle server deployment or maintenance. Functions can execute any JavaScript code you define, allowing for a variety of tasks. Typical use cases include low-latency, short-duration operations such as data transformations, validation, and data movement. They can also interact with external services, such as APIs, abstracting complex logic. Atlas Functions can invoke other functions, and they come with a built-in client for interacting with data in Atlas clusters. They also offer useful global utilities, support standard Node.js modules, and allow you to import and use external libraries from the npm registry.

When using triggers (section 19.2.1), you write functions that are executed automatically in response to specific database events. When a database trigger detects a change, for example, it calls its associated function with the change event as an argument. Then this function can access the event details and take appropriate actions, such as updating other parts of the database or sending notifications. Here's a simple function that returns a greeting:

```
exports = function(name) {
  return `Hello, ${name ?? "MongoDB-in-Action"}!`;
}
```

> **TIP** A function executes within a context that includes details about its environment, such as the calling user, the method of invocation, and the app's state at that time. This context allows you to run user-specific code and interact with other parts of your app.

You can use modern JavaScript features and import libraries to create more sophisticated functions, as shown in the following listing. This example code is provided for learning purposes; the API URL is fictional.

Listing 19.2 Example Atlas function

```
// Using ES6 arrow functions
const calculateSum = (a, b) => a + b;  //  ◀── Simple arrow function to calculate the sum of two numbers

// Using async/await for handling Promises
exports = async function fetchUserData() {  //  ◀── Defines an async function to fetch user data
  try {  //  ◀── Starts a try block for error handling
    // Retrieve user-specific information
    const userId = context.user.custom_data.id;  //  ◀── Retrieves the user ID from the context
    // Import Node.js modules and npm packages
    const { URL } = require('url');  //
    // Add an API URL. Please note that this address is fictional.
    const apiUrl = new URL('https://api.example.com/user');
    //                                                              ◀── Imports the url module and constructs the API URL
    apiUrl.pathname += `/${userId}`;  //

    // Make an HTTPS request to an external API
    const response = await context.http.get({  //
      url: apiUrl.toString(),  //                 ◀── Makes an HTTPS request to the external API
      headers: { Accept: 'application/json' }  //
    });

    // Check if the response is valid
```

```
    if (!response || response.statusCode !== 200) { //         Validates the response
      console.error('Failed to fetch user data.');              and handles errors
      return 'Error fetching user data'; //
    }

    // Parse the response body
    const userData = JSON.parse(response.body.text());   Parses the API
    //                                                   response
    const { name, email } = userData; //                      Extracts the
                                                              user's name and
    // Return the formatted user information                   email from the
    return `User Information:\nName: ${name}\nEmail: ${email}`;  response
    //                    Returns the formatted
  } catch (error) { //    user information
    console.error(`Error in fetchUserData: ${error.message}`);   Catches and
    //                                                            logs errors
    return 'Error fetching user data'; //
  }
};
```

This function uses modern JavaScript features to fetch user data from an external API. It employs ES6 arrow functions for simplicity and `async/await` for handling asynchronous operations. The function retrieves a user ID from the context, constructs a URL to request the user data, sends an HTTPS GET request, and processes the response to return the user's name and email.

Atlas Functions can interact with your MongoDB databases, perform complex queries, trigger on database events, call external APIs, and implement business logic. They are often used for tasks such as data synchronization, data validation, automation, and real-time processing while ensuring scalability and security.

Summary

- Atlas Charts is a tool for creating and sharing visualizations such as bar charts and line graphs directly from your MongoDB data. It offers a no-code interface, real-time data updates, and seamless integration with MongoDB, allowing you to embed charts in applications or dashboards for easy data analysis.
- Natural-language charts currently use Azure OpenAI. MongoDB sends your query, schema, and sample data to its backend and the AI provider without sharing credentials or data with third parties. Queries are stored for up to a year to improve service and support.
- You can create a billing dashboard to visualize your billing data. Billing dashboards include ready-made charts that help you monitor your use. After loading your billing data, you can customize a dashboard to meet your requirements.

- Atlas Application Services are managed backend services and APIs that simplify building cloud apps. They let you respond to Atlas data changes, integrate with other systems, and scale easily without server or infrastructure management.
- The three types of Atlas Triggers are database (for changes in a MongoDB collection), scheduled (for recurring tasks), and authentication (for user interactions with authentication providers). Each trigger is connected to a specific function. When the trigger detects an event that meets your defined criteria, it fires; then it passes the event object as an argument to the associated function.
- Database triggers are highly effective mechanisms for automating processes and enforcing rules without manual input. They react to data changes and ensure that the stored information adheres to established standards and complies with specific business rules.
- Triggers use MongoDB change streams to track real-time changes in a collection. A change stream is made up of a series of events, each describing an action taken on a document within the collection.
- Scheduled triggers enable you to execute server-side logic at predefined intervals. They are ideal for tasks that need regular execution, such as updating a document every hour, generating a daily performance report, or processing routine data analysis.
- Authentication triggers are triggered by events related to user authentication, such as login, account registration, or account deletion. When a user registers a new account, an authentication trigger can be used to send a welcome email or automatically subscribe the user to a mailing list.
- An Atlas Function is server-side JavaScript code that controls your app's behavior. It can be run directly from the client app or triggered automatically. These functions can call other functions, access Atlas data, and use built-in tools.
- Atlas Functions can call other functions, access data in Atlas clusters using a built-in client, and support global utilities, Node.js modules, and external npm packages.

Part 3

MongoDB security and operations

Imagine waking up to an alert that sensitive customer data has been exposed, or finding out that a misconfigured permission allowed someone to delete your production database, or realizing too late that your backups stopped running a week ago. Security and operational excellence aren't technical requirements alone; they're also the foundation of trust between your application and your users.

As applications grow more complex and teams become more distributed, keeping your data secure and your systems healthy becomes more important and more difficult. MongoDB Atlas was built with this reality in mind. It helps you develop quickly—and safely.

This part of the book focuses on the critical aspects of security, monitoring, backup, and performance optimization in MongoDB and Atlas. You'll learn how to build systems that are fast, scalable, resilient, compliant, and auditable.

In chapter 20, you'll dive deep into the security features offered by MongoDB and Atlas, from authentication and authorization to encryption at rest and in transit. You'll see how Atlas helps you enforce best practices by default. You'll explore field-level encryption, key management integration (KMS), private networking, and features such as Queryable Encryption that let you search over encrypted data while meeting strict compliance standards.

Chapter 21 shifts the focus to operational best practices. You'll learn how to monitor and alert on system health using Atlas's built-in tools. Whether you're tracking slow queries, watching replication lag, or receiving alerts when resource use spikes, Atlas gives you deep visibility into your cluster's behavior.

You'll also dive into backup and restore strategies, an essential layer of operational safety. You'll learn the differences between cloud backups and snapshots for Flex clusters. You'll see how to restore data, even to a precise point in time. You'll also see how to encrypt backups and meet compliance requirements while ensuring data durability.

The chapter ends with practical guidance on performance tuning. You'll learn how to identify and resolve common performance problems, such as slow queries, missing indexes, suboptimal schema designs, and resource bottlenecks. These techniques can dramatically improve the user experience of your application and reduce infrastructure costs.

This part is about keeping your MongoDB environment strong and secure even under pressure. Whether you're managing one cluster or an enterprise fleet, these chapters will help you stay in control, react quickly, and sleep better at night.

Understanding Atlas and MongoDB security features

This chapter covers
- Learning Atlas's shared responsibility model
- Using authentication, authorization, and auditing
- Encrypting data using customer-managed keys
- Securing network connections
- Defending Atlas in depth

In the digital age, cybersecurity is essential for protecting sensitive information from a wide range of advanced threats. Strong security measures help maintain data confidentiality (keeping information private), integrity (ensuring that data isn't altered without permission), and availability (keeping data accessible). These three elements are the foundation for building customer trust, securing personal and business data, and meeting legal requirements across industries. Without effective cybersecurity, data breaches can lead to serious financial loss, regulatory penalties, and lasting reputational damage. Also, with remote work and cloud-based systems becoming the norm, the risk of cyberattacks is higher than ever, making cybersecurity a critical priority for every organization.

Atlas offers robust security features designed to safeguard your data at every stage of its life cycle. The platform is built with strong security defaults, ensuring that your data is protected from the moment it's ingested to the time it's archived or deleted. Over the years, MongoDB has undergone extensive evaluations to meet stringent industry standards and regulatory requirements. It has achieved certifications such as the Health Insurance Portability and Accountability Act (HIPAA), General Data Protection Regulation (GDPR), International Organization for Standardization (ISO), Payment Card Industry (PCI), and FedRAMP Moderate (which certifies cloud security for US government data). These certifications highlight MongoDB's commitment to data protection and compliance across industries; they reinforce Atlas as a reliable solution for businesses handling sensitive and regulated information while adhering to data localization and security controls.

Knowing the security capabilities of Atlas will significantly help you secure your database and protect sensitive data. In this chapter, you'll learn about key features that will help you prepare your environment for security audits.

20.1 Understanding the shared responsibility model

In today's cloud computing landscape, security is a key concern for businesses migrating from on-premises systems to cloud services. Atlas operates under a shared responsibility model in which security tasks are divided among MongoDB, cloud providers (such as Amazon Web Services [AWS], Google Cloud Platform [GCP], and Microsoft Azure), and customers. This division is essential for ensuring the security of data and infrastructure.

Atlas operates under the Software as a Service (SaaS) model, in which Atlas manages platform security, database operations, and essential security controls, and cloud providers focus on physical security and infrastructure. Customers are responsible for data access, identity management, and certain security settings. Figure 20.1 shows a high-level overview of Atlas's shared responsibility model.

At the top of the hierarchy, your responsibilities focus primarily on data management and access control. You are responsible for data management, user accounts, roles, identity providers, and multifactor authentication (MFA). You also control the selection and configuration of cloud providers, geographic regions, and appropriate infrastructure tiers for their databases. Essentially, you control how data is accessed and ensure that proper authentication mechanisms are in place.

The middle layer represents shared responsibilities between the customer and MongoDB. This layer is divided into two key stages:

- *Initial configuration/setup*—At this stage, you play a central role in configuring important security and operational settings. This role includes setting up federation/Lightweight Directory Access Protocol (LDAP)/MFA for identity management, choosing data residency policies, enabling database encryption through services such as Key Management Service (KMS) and Bring Your Own Key

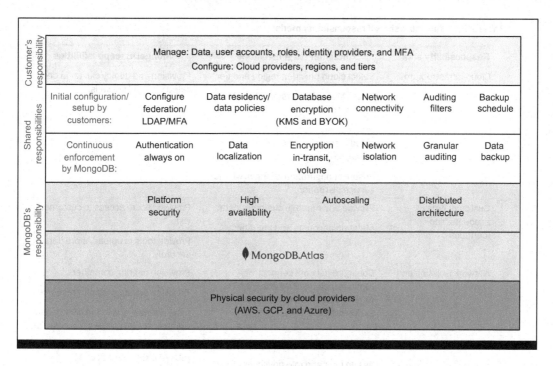

Figure 20.1 The shared responsibility model in Atlas divides security and operational tasks among customers, MongoDB, and the underlying cloud providers (AWS, GCP, and Azure). (Image © MongoDB 2024 CC BY-NC-SA 3.0)

(BYOK), configuring network connectivity, setting auditing filters, and determining backup schedules.

- *Continuous enforcement by MongoDB*—When setup is complete, MongoDB takes over continuous enforcement of essential security features. It ensures that key security mechanisms such as always-on authentication, data localization, encryption (in transit and at rest), network isolation, granular auditing, and regular data backups are operational and enforced. MongoDB is responsible for maintaining these security standards throughout the life cycle of the customer's database, ensuring ongoing protection without requiring further intervention from the customer.

The MongoDB responsibility section covers areas in which MongoDB is fully accountable. MongoDB ensures platform security, high availability, autoscaling, and a robust distributed architecture. These tasks are automated and embedded in Atlas.

At the base of the model, physical security is managed by the cloud providers themselves (AWS, GCP, and Azure). These providers are responsible for the physical infrastructure, including providing data center security, maintaining hardware, and ensuring a secure environment for MongoDB's services. Table 20.1 lists the detailed responsibilities in the shared responsibility model.

Table 20.1 The Atlas shared responsibility model

Responsibility area	Customer responsibilities	MongoDB responsibilities
Cloud infrastructure	Select cloud provider, region and tier. Select MongoDB version and auto-scaling options. Provision and deploy cluster in dedicated virtual private cloud (VPC) and firewalls. Ensure configuration changes without service disruption.	Provision and deploy cluster in dedicated VPC and firewalls.
Customer data, accounts, and identities	Provide and manage customer data. Maintain accounts and identities.	Provide secure access to customer data. Provide tools to upload/store data securely.
Network isolation and connectivity	Configure network connectivity (options include IP access list, VPC peering connections, and private endpoints).	Provision peering containers. Provision private endpoint resources. Allow connections to the cluster only from entries in a project's access list.
Database access	Configure user authentication. Assign user and role privileges. Manage certification authority. Configure AWS identify and access management (IAM) and LDAP integration. Configure Data API access keys.	Maintain always-on authentication (SCRAM, x509 certificates). Provide role-based access controls (RBAC) with predefined roles. Provide audit log access.
Atlas access	Create users and access. Configure MFA and federated authentication. Configure API keys.	Maintain always-on authentication. Provide integration interfaces with identity providers and MFA tools.
Data encryption (in transit and at rest)	Configure cloud provider (KMS). Set minimum Transport Layer Security (TLS) version.	Ensure that encryption is always on (in transit and at rest). Ensure that data is stored on encrypted volumes with cloud-provider–managed keys. Encrypt data at rest using customer-provided keys.
Data encryption (in use, BYOK)	Configure client-side field-level encryption. Configure cloud-provider KMS.	Provide tools, drivers, and shared libraries for field-level encryption. Provide drivers to communicate with KMS.
Granular auditing	Enable granular database auditing. Configure audit filters.	Maintain database access history.

Table 20.1 The Atlas shared responsibility model (*continued*)

Responsibility area	Customer responsibilities	MongoDB responsibilities
Data locality	Set up and enforce data locality rules.	Support multiple regions and global clusters.
		Ensure that cloud snapshots for backup are located in the origin regions.
Security patches and maintenance	Set maintenance window.	Apply minor version upgrades.
		Apply security patches.

20.2 *Managing authentication*

Atlas provides various authentication methods in the Atlas UI and the Atlas database clusters, ensuring secure access and flexibility:

- *Atlas UI*—You use this web interface to manage clusters, user roles, and permissions. To access the Atlas UI, you can authenticate using a username/password combination or federated authentication via external identity providers. For increased security, you can add MFA and enforce it for all users with options such as Short Message Service (SMS), voice calls, authentication apps, and hardware devices such as YubiKey.
- *Atlas database clusters*—Authentication for the actual database clusters is enabled by default, ensuring a secure environment. Administrators can define roles for users or applications to specify what data can be accessed and modified. Temporary users can be set up for specific periods, and their access is revoked automatically when the time expires.

Table 20.2 provides an overview of the key authentication features of Atlas, highlighting the various methods and tools available to ensure secure access and management of user credentials.

Table 20.2 Authentication features in Atlas

Feature	Description
Atlas Federated Authentication	Supports login through external identity providers such as Okta, GitHub, Google, Ping Identity, and Microsoft Entra ID
Database authentication	Ensures secure database access with Salted Challenge Response Authentication Mechanism (SCRAM), X.509 certificates, LDAP, OpenID Connect (OIDC), and passwordless authentication with AWS IAM
	Integrates with HashiCorp Vault for dynamic user creation

MongoDB Federated Authentication in Atlas uses the Federated Identity Management (FIM) model for authentication. Atlas is set up to authenticate users based on information provided by your identity provider (IdP). With this model, your organization manages user credentials through the IdP, enabling authentication across multiple online services. For more information, visit https://mng.bz/X75G.

20.2.1 Choosing an Atlas database cluster authentication method

You can authenticate to a MongoDB database using methods such as SCRAM, X.509 certificates, LDAP, OIDC, and authentication through AWS IAM without a password.

> **WARNING** Beginning with MongoDB 8.0, LDAP authentication and authorization are deprecated. Although LDAP functionality is fully supported and unchanged in MongoDB 8, it will be phased out in a future major release.

SALTED CHALLENGE RESPONSE AUTHENTICATION MECHANISM)

SCRAM is Atlas's default password-based authentication mechanism. It functions by ensuring that passwords are never transmitted over the network in plain text. Instead, the client and server exchange a series of cryptographic challenges to verify the user's identity securely. The process involves hashing the password with a unique, random salt and iterating the hash multiple times to enhance security. This approach effectively mitigates the risk of brute-force attacks, password interception, and replay attacks. SCRAM is widely supported across MongoDB drivers and frameworks, making it a versatile, robust choice for securing applications of all sizes.

X.509 CERTIFICATES

Atlas allows the use of X.509 certificates to authenticate clients and cluster nodes. These certificates rely on public-key infrastructure (PKI), using encryption and digital signatures to provide high levels of security. Atlas supports Atlas-managed and self-managed X.509 certificates. In high-trust environments such as finance, health care, and government, X.509 certificates are particularly valuable, as they ensure that only authenticated and trusted entities can access the system. Also, X.509 provides mutual authentication capabilities, which means that the client and server can verify each other's identities before establishing a secure connection.

OPENID CONNECT

OAuth 2.0 and OIDC are protocols that Atlas integrates with to provide secure authentication through third-party identity providers such as Google, Microsoft, and custom enterprise systems. OAuth 2.0 facilitates the delegation of access without requiring the user to share their credentials, instead using access tokens issued by the identity provider. OIDC, an extension of OAuth 2.0, adds a layer for obtaining user identity information, enabling secure and efficient single sign-on (SSO). This system simplifies identity management by providing centralized control of user access while reducing the need for users to manage multiple sets of credentials. Support for MFA further enhances security by adding a layer of protection beyond the user's password.

AMAZON WEB SERVICES IDENTITY AND ACCESS MANAGEMENT

For cloud-native applications hosted on AWS, Atlas seamlessly integrates with AWS IAM, allowing services to authenticate using IAM roles. This eliminates the need for traditional credentials such as passwords and API keys. Instead, services such as EC2 and Lambda can assume IAM roles to connect securely to Atlas, streamlining access management and reducing operational complexity. With IAM role-based authentication, organizations benefit from automatic key rotation and centralized permissions management. This approach reduces the surface area for credential exposure, making it an ideal solution for environments in which security and efficiency are critical, such as DevOps and cloud-native architectures.

LIGHTWEIGHT DIRECTORY ACCESS PROTOCOL

LDAP allows Atlas to authenticate and authorize users by connecting to an external LDAP server. This method enables centralized identity management, meaning that user credentials and access permissions are stored and managed in an LDAP directory, such as Active Directory. By using LDAP, Atlas can authenticate users via their Distinguished Names (DN) and authorize their actions based on roles mapped to LDAP groups.

LDAP operates over TLS (LDAP Secure [LDAPS]) to ensure that all communications between Atlas and the LDAP server are securely encrypted. This approach is especially useful for organizations with existing LDAP infrastructure, providing seamless integration with Atlas for managing user access and roles centrally. Through LDAP, Atlas can apply enterprise-level authentication and authorization policies, streamlining access control across teams and departments.

20.2.2 Integrating with HashiCorp Vault

Atlas integrates seamlessly with HashiCorp Vault to generate database credentials dynamically, providing a secure automated solution for managing access to Atlas databases. HashiCorp, known for its open source tools in infrastructure automation, security, and management, provides products such as Vault, Terraform, and Consul that secure and optimize cloud and on-premises infrastructure. This integration uses Vault's database secrets engine to create on-demand credentials based on predefined roles within Vault. These dynamically generated credentials have a limited lifespan, mitigating security risks tied to long-lived credentials. They can be used to grant a developer read-only access for a defined period, for example. When the time to live (TTL) expires, Vault automatically removes the associated user account from the MongoDB database, ensuring that no unauthorized access persists. This functionality is particularly beneficial for granting temporary or project-specific database access, balancing strict security measures with controlled developer access.

Using Vault, you can configure roles that map directly to Atlas permissions, allowing you to generate database credentials on demand. You can create roles with specific permissions such as `read`, `readAnyDatabase`, or `atlasAdmin` to suit various access needs. Each set of credentials is generated with a defined TTL, after which they expire automatically, enhancing security by ensuring that access is available only for the required duration. This approach provides precise control of database access and minimizes security risks associated with long-lived credentials.

To learn more, see the Vault documentation at https://mng.bz/yNdG. You can also learn about Vault and MongoDB integration at https://mng.bz/Mwl7.

20.2.3 Choosing the authentication method

When you decide which authentication method to use in MongoDB, your choice depends largely on your organization's needs and the environment in which your applications operate. SCRAM is a strong option for general-purpose applications that require password-based authentication. It's easy to configure, widely supported, and offers robust protection by hashing and salting user credentials. For environments with strict security requirements, such as financial services and health care, X.509 certificates are a better fit; they provide mutual authentication between clients and servers, using PKI for highly secure communications.

OAuth 2.0 and OIDC are ideal for organizations that integrate with third-party identity providers such as Google and Microsoft, especially when SSO is required. These protocols streamline identity management through access tokens and MFA, making them suitable for user and application authentication. If your enterprise already uses corporate identity solutions such as Okta or Entra ID, these methods can integrate seamlessly with your existing setup.

For cloud-native applications hosted on AWS, using AWS IAM roles is the most secure and efficient method. It eliminates the need to manage traditional credentials and provides a seamless way to authenticate AWS-hosted services such as EC2 and Lambda. Last, for large enterprises with an existing LDAP infrastructure, LDAP is the optimal solution. It enables centralized management of user authentication and authorization, making it particularly useful for controlling access across departments and teams.

Choosing the right authentication method requires balancing your security needs, compliance requirements, and operational environment to ensure that Atlas integrates into your infrastructure securely and efficiently. Using dynamic Vault credentials with HashiCorp Vault offers another level of security by allowing on-demand generation of short-lived database credentials, significantly reducing the risk of credential misuse. This approach is especially advantageous for organizations looking to automate and streamline credential management while ensuring that credentials are valid for only the required period. You can learn more about available authentication options at https://mng.bz/a9Mz.

20.3 Handling authorization

Authentication verifies your identity, ensuring that the user or service attempting to access the database is legitimate, typically using credentials such as a username and password, LDAP, or certificate-based authentication. Authorization, on the other hand, determines what actions you are allowed to perform when you're authenticated, defining your permissions and access levels such as read, write, or administrative privileges.

Atlas uses RBAC to manage access to its cloud resources and MongoDB deployments. Users are assigned roles that define their permissions within an Atlas organization or project. These roles control what actions they can take. Fine-grained roles can be assigned to users for specific database operations. With identity federation, access to Atlas can be managed through your identity provider, linking user groups with Atlas roles. Beyond Atlas, MongoDB clusters offer access control through their own RBAC system. They provide detailed role-based permissions for specific actions on databases and collections.

20.3.1 Understanding the principle of least privilege

The principle of least privilege (PoLP) is a security concept that recommends giving users, applications, or systems the minimum level of access necessary to perform their tasks. This reduces the risk of accidental or intentional misuse of privileges by limiting access to what is essential for completing a specific function, improving security and minimizing potential damage from breaches or human errors. If a user needs to read data from only a specific database, they should not be granted write or administrative access. Similarly, a service responsible for backups should have access to only the databases it needs to back up rather than all databases in the system. Remember to apply this principle when assigning permissions to your users in Atlas and within the MongoDB database.

20.3.2 Differentiating Atlas user roles

Atlas user roles define the actions users can perform within organizations and projects, offering granular control over access and permissions. Organization and project owners can manage user roles, ensuring that the correct permissions are assigned at both levels.

Permissions can be applied at the organization or project level, so it's essential to plan your organizational and project hierarchy carefully to ensure the correct allocation of roles and access:

- *Organization roles*—Include the organization owner, who has root access to all aspects of the organization, including management of users, settings, and projects. Other roles include organization project creator, billing admin, billing viewer, read-only, and member, each offering different levels of access and administrative capabilities.
- *Project roles*—Determine what actions can be performed within a specific project. The project owner can create clusters, manage project settings, and handle database access, for example, whereas the project cluster manager can manage clusters without creating new ones. Roles such as project stream processing owner, data access admin, data access read/write, and read-only provide varying degrees of control of data and resources.

Each role offers privileges tailored to specific responsibilities, ensuring secure and efficient management of users and resources within Atlas. For more information about user roles, visit https://mng.bz/gmJl.

20.3.3 Using MongoDB RBAC

MongoDB uses RBAC to manage access to its system. Each user is assigned roles that determine what actions they can perform on the database. Without a role, a user has no access to the system.

A role defines specific privileges, allowing the user to perform certain actions on a given resource. Privileges can be defined explicitly in a role or inherited from another role. If a user has multiple roles, the role with the greatest access level takes precedence. If a user has both the `read` role and the `readWriteAnyDatabase` role, the latter allows write access, overriding the `read` role.

Atlas provides several built-in database roles tailored to common access needs:

- `atlasAdmin`—Grants full administrative rights across the cluster. This role is suitable for administrators managing high-level tasks such as balancing and updating configurations.
- `readWriteAnyDatabase`—Allows read and write access to all databases. This role is ideal for developers and administrators who need broad data access across the cluster.
- `readAnyDatabase`—Provides read-only access to all databases. This role is designed for users or applications that need only to query data without making modifications.
- `clusterMonitor`—Enables access to various monitoring functions. This role is useful for users who need to oversee cluster performance and health without altering data or settings.
- `read`—Offers read-only access to a specific database, allowing data querying and analysis without modification. This role is ideal for applications, reporting tools, or users focused on data analysis, following PoLP by restricting access to read-only actions within a designated database.

The full list of built-in roles in Atlas, along with their specific permissions, is at https://mng.bz/5v1z.

These roles provide a foundation for managing access in a MongoDB environment, covering most standard needs, but they sometimes grant broader permissions than necessary. Custom roles provide a more tailored approach, enhancing security and efficiency by restricting permissions to only what each user or application truly requires. This aligns with PoLP, allowing administrators to set precise access levels such as permissions limited to specific collections. Custom roles are especially useful when you need temporary project-based access or when regulatory requirements demand strict control of data exposure.

When creating roles, it's important to determine whether to define them in the admin database or within a specific application database:

- *Admin database*—Roles created in the admin database are available across all databases within the MongoDB instance, making them suitable for users who need broader access, such as database administrators and developers who require permissions across multiple databases.
- *Specific database*—Roles created within a particular database are valid only within that database, making them ideal for users who need limited access to a specific database, such as an application service or user restricted to managing data within a single database. This approach aligns with PoLP by granting users only the permissions they need for their specific tasks, minimizing potential security risks associated with broader access.

Roles created outside the admin database are restricted to containing privileges specific to their own database and can inherit permissions only from roles within that same database.

To create a custom role, Atlas provides the `atlas customDbRoles create` command, enabling you to define precise permissions for each role. Begin by specifying the privilege actions the role should include, such as `find`, `insert`, or `update`, and the databases or collections these permissions will apply to. Privilege actions define the operations that a user or application is permitted to execute on a resource; each privilege in MongoDB connects a resource with its allowed actions. You can find a full list of available privileges at https://mng.bz/641y.

Here's an example of creating a custom role:

```
atlas customDbRoles create customReadUpdateRole \
--privilege 'UPDATE@sample_training.routes' \
--privilege 'FIND@sample_supplies.sales'
```

The custom role named `customReadUpdateRole` is designed to meet specific access needs. This role grants `UPDATE` permissions on the `routes` collection within the `sample_training` database, allowing the user to modify documents in that collection. Also, it grants `FIND` access on the `sales` collection in the `sample_supplies` database, providing read-only access to that collection. Including only the explicitly defined privileges allows precise control of permissions, closely adhering to PoLP.

You can also inherit privileges from other roles, default or custom, to build on existing access configurations without redundancy. Here's an example of creating a custom role that inherits privileges from an existing `read` role:

```
atlas customDbRoles create readWriteAnalyticsRole \
--privilege 'INSERT@sample_analytics' \
--inheritedRole 'read@sample_analytics'
```

`readWriteAnalyticsRole` inherits privileges from the existing `read` role on the `sample_analytics` database and adds `INSERT` permissions. This setup is useful for users who need general read access across all collections in `sample_analytics` but also require specific write permissions in certain collections. By inheriting from the `read` role and adding only the required `INSERT` action, this approach ensures efficient, straightforward access management.

The `atlas customDbRoles list` command in Atlas displays all custom roles within a project, showing each role's specific permissions, including actions and associated resources:

```
customRoleName         INSERT    N/A     sample_analytics    ALL COLLECTIONS
customRoleName         N/A       read    sample_analytics    N/A
customReadUpdateRole   UPDATE    N/A     sample_training     routes
customReadUpdateRole   FIND      N/A     sample_supplies     sales
```

The `customReadUpdateRole` has `UPDATE` permission on the `routes` collection in the `sample_training` database, allowing modifications to documents in that collection, and `FIND` permission on the `sales` collection in the `sample_supplies` database, granting read-only access to that collection. The `customRoleName` includes `INSERT` permission across all collections within the `sample_analytics` database, enabling document insertion in any collection. This role also inherits the `read` role for the `sample_analytics` database, allowing read-only access across the entire database.

You can create new users in the Atlas UI or Atlas command-line interface (CLI) by using the `atlas dbusers create` command, or you can add roles to existing users with the `atlas dbusers update` command.

> **TIP** To prevent potential security risks and enhance manageability, avoid shared accounts by creating a unique user for each application or service account per application or service. This practice allows for more granular access control, making it easier to track activity, enforce PoLP, and manage permissions independently. For more information, see https://mng.bz/oZJM.

20.4 Auditing Atlas

Atlas provides Control Plane auditing, which lets you monitor all events initiated from the Atlas UI at both the project and organization levels. These logs capture actions performed by users within the Atlas interface, helping them maintain oversight of administrative activities. You can access these logs directly within the Atlas UI or retrieve them via the Atlas API, offering flexible options for reviewing and integrating audit data into broader monitoring workflows.

You can also use MongoDB database auditing in your Atlas cluster; it allows you to monitor database activities and user actions within a project. This feature enables selection of specific actions (such as `read` and `write`), users, roles, and LDAP groups to track. Audit logs for users and modifications are not available, however, because Atlas performs these actions in the admin database.

> **NOTE** The auditing feature is unavailable for M0 and Flex clusters.

The MongoDB auditing log captures different event types to monitor database interactions, focusing primarily on authCheck and authenticate events. authenticate events track attempts to log in, recording details such as timestamp, IP addresses of local and remote systems, user information, associated roles, and authentication mechanism (such as SCRAM-SHA-256). These events document successful and failed login attempts, with the result indicating the outcome (0 for success).

authCheck events go beyond authentication to cover actions such as data access attempts, logging successful and failed reads and writes to the database. By default, only failed attempts are recorded to minimize performance effect, though you can enable full logging for successful actions by using the auditAuthorizationSuccess option. MongoDB auditing tracks specific database operations such as aggregate, insert, update, and delete. Whenever one of these actions is performed, it gets logged.

WARNING Enabling auditAuthorizationSuccess logs every successful read and write, which creates a high volume of logs in busy clusters. This extra processing can slow performance, so it's best to enable it only if necessary.

Here's an example of an authCheck event in the audit log in JSON format, referencing the sample_training database and routes collection:

```
{
  "atype": "authCheck",
  "ts": {"$date": "2024-10-28T10:15:30.123Z"},
  "local": {
    "ip": "192.168.1.1",
    "port": 27017
  },
  "remote": {
    "ip": "203.0.113.42",
    "port": 53245
  },
  "param": {
    "ns": "sample_training.routes",
    "command": "find",
    "args": {},
    "result": 0
  },
  "users": [
    {
      "user": "sampleUser",
      "db": "admin"
    }
  ],
  "roles": [
    {
      "role": "readWrite",
      "db": "sample_training"
    }
  ]
}
```

This `authCheck` log shows an access attempt on the `sample_training.routes` namespace. The server IP and port, along with the client's IP and port, are recorded while `sampleUser` attempts a `find` command successfully (`result: 0`). The user, authenticated in the admin database, has a `readWrite` role on `sample_training`.

You can limit the number of logged events by refining filter conditions to capture only essential actions or specific operations. Atlas supports a custom JSON audit filter that allows precise targeting of specific users, commands, and namespaces, granting full control of logged events. This bypasses the default UI filter builder, enabling more detailed and tailored audit configurations. Atlas checks only the JSON syntax, so the filter logic needs to be crafted carefully.

With this filter, you can include or exclude specific usernames by using conditions such as `{"users.user": { "$nin": ["backup", "admin"] }}` to omit these users from logs. You can also filter event types (`atype`) to focus on actions such as `authenticate`, `dbAccess`, and `authCheck`, and you can log specific commands such as `find`, `insert`, and `delete` selectively with `{"param.command": { "$in": ["find", "insert", "delete"] }}` to capture only relevant operations. Also, you can narrow logging to particular namespaces or databases, excluding namespaces such as `config` and `local` using `{"param.ns": { "$nin": [{ "$regex": "^config\\." }, { "$regex": "^local\\." }] }}`. Here's an example filter that combines several of these options:

```
{
  "users.user": { "$nin": ["backup", { "$regex": "^sa_" }, "__system"] },
  "$or": [
    { "atype": "authenticate" },
    {
      "atype": "authCheck",
      "param": {
        "command": { "$in": ["find", "insert", "delete", "update"] },
        "ns": { "$nin": [{ "$regex": "^config\\." }, { "$regex": "^local\\." }] }
      }
    }
  ]
}
```

This filter excludes actions from specific users such as `"backup"`, any usernames beginning with `sa_`, and the `__system` user. It logs only `authenticate` and `authCheck` events, focusing on commands such as `find`, `insert`, `delete`, and `update`, and it excludes events in the `config` and `local` namespaces. By narrowing to these conditions, the audit logs capture only relevant activities, reducing noise and enhancing audit efficiency. For a complete explanation of all terms and a detailed overview of the auditing process, see https://mng.bz/nZJK.

> **TIP** You can use `atlas auditing describe` to return the auditing configuration for the specified project or `atlas auditing update` to update the auditing configuration for the specified project. You can access audit logs by

downloading them directly from the Atlas UI or viewing them through the Atlas CLI.

20.5 Encrypting data in Atlas

Information generated, exchanged, and stored within a company is one of its core assets. Ensuring the security of this data—particularly sensitive details such as personal identifiers, financial records, health care data, and government-related information—is essential to prevent unauthorized access and breaches. Although authentication and authorization help protect data access, encryption is necessary to safeguard critical workloads. MongoDB provides advanced encryption solutions, including built-in tools within its Atlas developer data platform.

20.5.1 Encrypting data in transit

Encryption in transit is a security measure designed to protect data during transfer across networks or between devices, ensuring confidentiality and integrity throughout the process. By encoding data so that only authorized users or systems can decrypt it, encryption prevents unauthorized access and modification during transmission. This approach defends against attacks like Man in the Middle (MITM), in which an attacker intercepts or alters the data in transit. In these attacks, a third party positions itself between the sender and receiver to eavesdrop or manipulate information.

In Atlas, encryption in transit is ensured by automatically applying TLS to secure all connections with MongoDB clusters. TLS, a cryptographic protocol, protects data during transmission by establishing an encrypted channel, ensuring that data remains confidential and unaltered throughout transfer. All network traffic, including customer data sent to Atlas and data exchanged between nodes in an Atlas cluster, is protected by TLS, which is enabled by default and cannot be disabled. You can select the TLS version for your clusters; TLS 1.2 is the recommended default with a minimum key length of 128 bits. This setup guarantees that all data moving to and between cluster nodes stays encrypted, providing secure end-to-end communication.

Atlas enforces encryption in transit through strict key management practices using the OpenSSL FIPS Object Module, a cryptographic suite certified to meet Federal Information Processing Standards (FIPS). FIPS is a set of U.S. government-developed standards for protecting sensitive data in high-security environments, ensuring certified encryption and secure key handling. MongoDB uses these standards to enhance data security during transmission, with practices covering secure key generation, distribution, storage, and replacement. Detailed guidelines outline key activation and deactivation timelines, limiting access to authorized people. In a case of key compromise, MongoDB promptly revokes and replaces the affected key. TLS certificates are sourced from trusted authorities, and ephemeral session keys—generated per session during TLS negotiations—are never stored on disk. Also, keys are protected in storage by encryption and are stored separately from encrypted data, ensuring strong end-to-end protection for data in transit.

20.5.2 Encrypting data at rest

Encryption at rest protects data stored on physical media (such as disks, including data managed by databases) by encrypting it to prevent unauthorized access. This process ensures that even if the storage medium is compromised, the data remains unreadable without the correct decryption key. Commonly used in databases, filesystems, and cloud storage, encryption at rest safeguards sensitive information by keeping it secure whenever it is stored and not actively accessed or transmitted. In MongoDB, encrypted data means that the information within collections, documents, or backups is encoded to prevent unauthorized access. This encryption typically occurs at the storage level (encryption at rest); in some cases, it occurs at the individual field level (explained in section 20.5.4), adding an extra layer of security for highly sensitive data, such as credit card numbers and personal identifiers. MongoDB manages encryption and decryption automatically, allowing authorized users to access readable data while keeping it secure from unauthorized access or breaches.

20.5.3 Managing encryption keys yourself

When you create an Atlas cluster, customer data is automatically encrypted at rest using AES-256, an advanced encryption standard with a 256-bit key length that is known for strong security, securing all disk-stored data. This encryption is handled seamlessly through the cloud provider's transparent disk encryption (AWS, GCP, or Azure), with the provider also managing the encryption keys. Also, you can opt for database-level encryption through the WiredTiger Encrypted Storage Engine, which also uses AES-256. This option enables you to bring your own encryption key via AWS KMS, GCP KMS, or Azure Key Vault—secure key management tools provided by Amazon, Google, and Microsoft, respectively, that allow users to create, store, and manage encryption keys securely.

By using your own encryption key, you gain greater control of your data security, ensuring that only you have access to the key that protects your sensitive information. This capability enhances privacy and reduces the risk of unauthorized access by third parties. Being able to manage the key life cycle, including rotation and revocation, allows you to maintain compliance with regulatory standards and internal security policies. If you ever need to change providers or discontinue your service, you can easily revoke access to the key, making the data unreadable and protecting it from unauthorized access. Figure 20.2 shows the architecture for using your own encryption key in Atlas on AWS.

AWS KMS provides a customer master key (CMK), which Atlas uses to create an encrypted data encryption key (DEK) for each Atlas deployment. Each MongoDB database within the cluster has a unique encryption key (e.g., `db1` uses `key1`, and `db2` uses `key2`), and these keys are further encrypted by the MongoDB master key.

When MongoDB Server starts, Atlas's security layer communicates with AWS KMS to decrypt the DEK. Then this decrypted DEK is provided to MongoDB Server, enabling it to access the database keys for data stored in the WiredTiger Storage Engine. In a

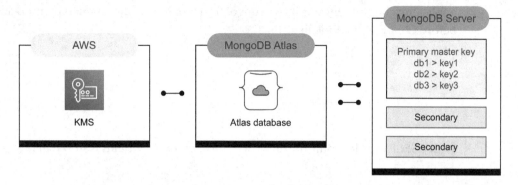

Figure 20.2 Atlas's encryption architecture shows the interaction between MongoDB Server, AWS KMS, and Atlas's internal security layers. (Image © MongoDB 2024 CC BY-NC-SA 3.0)

multinode replica set, each node has its unique DEK, stored on disk within the Atlas cluster. The DEK is decrypted at startup, ensuring that each node can access the necessary database encryption keys securely. This layered approach maintains encrypted data across primary and secondary nodes in the cluster, ensuring secure data replication. You can find more information about these products at https://mng.bz/vZ1M.

20.5.4 Encrypting during processing

Atlas In-Use Encryption ensures that sensitive fields in customer data are encrypted on the client side before they reach the database. With options like client-side field-level encryption (discussed in the next section) and Queryable Encryption, data is encrypted by the application, and Atlas never has access to the plain text. Decryption occurs only when the data returns to the client, keeping encryption keys exclusively accessible to the application.

Encryption keys are managed using strong symmetric encryption through external key management services like AWS KMS, Azure Key Vault, and GCP KMS and can also integrate with Key Management Interoperability Protocol (KMIP). KMIP is an open-standard protocol developed by the Organization for the Advancement of Structured Information Standards (OASIS), a global not-for-profit consortium that develops and promotes open standards. KMIP facilitates encryption key management across diverse systems and devices, enabling the secure exchange of keys, certificates, and other cryptographic data, especially between key management servers and applications that require these keys. For added security, you can use KMIP-compliant key managers or tools like HashiCorp Vault.

UNDERSTANDING CLIENT-SIDE FIELD-LEVEL ENCRYPTION

Client-side field-level encryption (CSFLE) allows sensitive data fields to be encrypted on the client side before being sent to the database. If an application needs to store personal data such as a Social Security number, CSFLE encrypts this field within the application before sending it to MongoDB. Here's what the unencrypted document before CSFLE might look like:

```
{
  "name": "Name Surname",
  "socialSecurityNumber": "123-45-6789",
  "email": "user@example.com"
}
```

With CSFLE enabled, only the encrypted form of sensitive fields is stored in MongoDB:

```
{
  "name": " Name Surname",
  "socialSecurityNumber": { "$binary": "AE4F0F9DE7..." },
  "email": "user@example.com"
}
```

In this encrypted document, the `socialSecurityNumber` field is encrypted on the client side, so MongoDB never sees the unencrypted value. Only authorized clients with access to the appropriate decryption keys can view or modify this field, providing enhanced security and privacy. Even database administrators with full access cannot view the encrypted data. CSFLE ensures that sensitive data remains encrypted throughout its life cycle within MongoDB, even during storage and transmission.

> **NOTE** CSFLE supports only equality queries on deterministically encrypted fields. *Deterministically* means that the same plain-text value, encrypted with the same key, always produces the same output. This enables the database to perform equality matches on encrypted data. It does not support range, prefix, suffix, or substring queries, which require comparisons beyond exact equality.

> **TIP** You can find a detailed description of CSFLE at https://www.mongodb.com/docs/manual/core/csfle.

QUERYING ENCRYPTED FIELDS WITHOUT DECRYPTING THEM

Queryable Encryption allows you to query encrypted fields without decrypting them first. It enables secure search operations, such as equality matches and encrypted range queries, on sensitive data that remains encrypted in the database. This is the biggest difference compared to CSFLE, which supports equality queries only on deterministically encrypted fields. Queryable Encryption supports prefix, suffix, and substring searches, making it more versatile for secure data searches.

Queryable Encryption is particularly useful for applications that need to protect sensitive information—such as Social Security numbers, credit card numbers, and email addresses—while allowing searches. Queryable Encryption uses advanced cryptographic techniques to index and search encrypted data, ensuring that MongoDB can execute queries on the encrypted fields without exposing the plain-text data.

Encrypting data in Atlas 499

Encryption and decryption occur on the client side, so MongoDB never has access to the unencrypted values, enhancing data security and privacy.

Figure 20.3 shows the operation flow for MongoDB's Queryable Encryption.

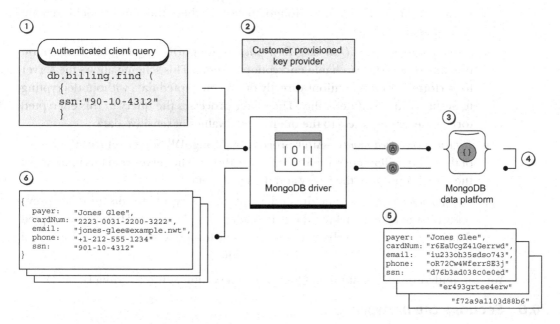

Figure 20.3 An authenticated client (1) submits a query containing sensitive information, such as a Social Security number (SSN). The MongoDB driver (2) analyzes the query and identifies that it targets an encrypted field, prompting a request for encryption keys from a customer-provisioned key provider. Using these keys (3), the driver encrypts the query and sends it to MongoDB Server (4), where it is processed without decryption, ensuring that sensitive data remains secure and hidden. The server returns encrypted results (5) to the driver, which decrypts them and provides the plain-text data to the client (6), maintaining end-to-end security throughout the process. (Image © MongoDB 2024 CC BY-NC-SA 3.0)

Let's take a closer look at figure 20.3. The process follows this flow:

1 *Query submission and analysis*—The application submits a query containing sensitive data (e.g., SSN) to the MongoDB driver. The driver begins by analyzing the query to determine whether it involves fields that require special handling due to encryption.

2 *Recognition of encrypted field and key request*—The driver determines that the query targets an encrypted field. To proceed, it requests encryption keys from a customer-provisioned key provider, which can include services like these:
   – AWS AWS KMS
   – GCP KMS)
   – Azure Key Vault

– KMIP-compliant key providers such as HashiCorp Vault, Thales CipherTrust, and IBM Key Protect

3 *Submission of encrypted query*—After receiving the necessary keys, the driver encrypts the sensitive query fields, converting them to cipher text. This encrypted version of the query is sent to MongoDB Server, where the sensitive fields remain hidden as encrypted text.

4 *Server processing with Queryable Encryption*—MongoDB's Queryable Encryption uses an advanced, searchable encryption scheme. This scheme allows the server to perform search operations directly on the encrypted data without decrypting it, ensuring full confidentiality. The server processes the query in this encrypted form; it never has access to the unencrypted values of sensitive data.

5 *Return of encrypted results*—After processing, MongoDB Server returns the results of the query, still in encrypted form, to the driver. The server remains unaware of the actual content of the query and the result data.

6 *Decryption for the client*—The driver decrypts the encrypted results using the previously obtained keys, making the data readable as plain text. Then the decrypted data is provided to the client application, ensuring that sensitive data is exposed only on the client side, not on the server side.

You can find more information on Queryable Encryption at https://mng.bz/4n1V.

20.6 Securing the network

Atlas offers strong network security through IP whitelisting, VPC peering, private endpoints, and network access controls. IP whitelisting restricts access to specific IP addresses, ensuring that only trusted networks can connect to the database. VPC peering and private endpoints allow secure private connections within your cloud environment, keeping data off the public internet. Network access controls give you detailed control of who can access the network, enabling strict security policies and enhanced monitoring.

20.6.1 Using an IP access list

Atlas clusters are initially locked down from internet access; they're deployed in a VPC with no inbound traffic allowed. To manage access, users can create IP access lists that specify which IP addresses have permission to connect to the database. Without inclusion in this list, application servers cannot reach the database, ensuring that only trusted IPs have access.

Atlas also allows temporary access entries that expire after a set time, making it convenient for users who need short-term access from temporary locations.

> **TIP** You should allow access only from small, specific IP ranges (such as individual /32 addresses) and avoid broad Classless Inter-Domain Routing (CIDR) blocks, keeping potential exposure to a minimum.

To set up an IP access list for your project via the Atlas CLI, use the following command:

```
atlas accessLists create -currentIp
```

Alternatively, you can configure the IP access list through the Atlas UI.

20.6.2 Peering networks

Network peering in Atlas lets you connect your own VPC to an Atlas VPC, allowing private routing of traffic without exposure to the public internet. Network peering is available for dedicated clusters on AWS, GCP, and Azure as well as for multicloud sharded clusters. You can enable access only via private IPs or also allow connections through public IPs as defined by the IP access list.

> **NOTE** Network peering is unavailable for clusters on the M0 and Flex tiers.

Figure 20.4 illustrates an Atlas VPC connected via VPC peering to an AWS VPC hosting a customer's application servers.

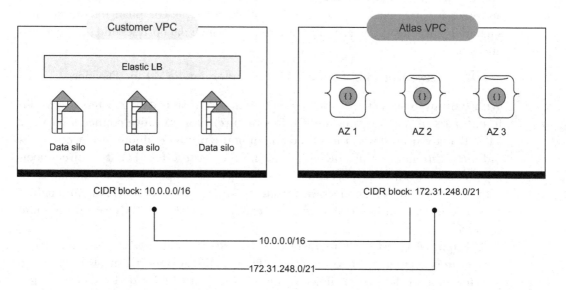

Figure 20.4 Atlas VPC peered to an AWS VPC (Image © MongoDB 2024 CC BY-NC-SA 3.0)

In figure 20.4, a customer's AWS VPC, labeled Customer VPC, is peered with an Atlas VPC in Atlas. The Customer VPC includes multiple application servers, with traffic managed by an Elastic load balancer (LB). The Customer VPC has a CIDR block of 10.0.0.0/16, which allows its internal network to route traffic securely within this range.

The Atlas VPC, on the other hand, is organized across three availability zones (AZ 1, AZ 2, and AZ 3), each containing an Atlas cluster node. The CIDR block for the Atlas VPC is set to 172.31.248.0/21, defining its network space.

Use cases for network peering include organizations that need secure direct access to Atlas from their internal applications hosted within private VPCs. It's ideal for companies handling sensitive data, as it ensures that data never traverses the public internet. Network peering is also valuable for enterprise environments with strict compliance needs; it helps them achieve regulatory standards by keeping data traffic private and controlled. It also benefits applications that require low-latency connections to the database because private routing improves network performance compared with public internet routing. To learn how to set up network peering, see https://mng.bz/Qw8j.

20.6.3 Using private endpoints

Private endpoints in Atlas allow secure one-way connections from your VPC to an Atlas VPC without exposing traffic to the public internet. This setup ensures that Atlas can receive connections from your VPC but cannot initiate connections back, which keeps your network boundary-controlled and enhances security.

By using private endpoints, you reduce the risk of data exposure to external threats because traffic remains within the internal network of your cloud provider. This approach is particularly beneficial for industries with strict compliance requirements, such as finance, health care, and government, in which data privacy and secure access are essential.

NOTE Network peering is unavailable for clusters on the M0 and Flex tiers.

With transitive connections, you can extend access to your Atlas clusters across different parts of your organization's infrastructure. In a transitive connection, other VPCs that are peered with the VPC containing the private endpoint can access Atlas indirectly through that private endpoint. In other words, if a VPC has a direct peering connection with the VPC containing the private endpoint, it can communicate with Atlas without needing its own private endpoint connection. This setup enables seamless integration between services spread across multiple VPCs within the same network.

This approach is especially useful in hybrid cloud environments because on-premises data centers connected to your cloud VPC via DirectConnect can also reach the private endpoint. This setup allows organizations that use both cloud and on-premises resources to maintain a smooth connection between systems located in different places.

Private endpoints are particularly valuable for applications that handle sensitive data because they provide secure private access to Atlas without exposing the connection to the public internet. This setup enhances data privacy and boosts performance by keeping traffic within the private network, ensuring lower latency and reducing potential bottlenecks associated with public internet traffic. To learn more about private endpoints, check out https://mng.bz/X756.

20.7 Implementing defense in depth

Defense in depth is a security strategy that layers multiple defensive mechanisms to protect data and systems. In this approach, each layer of defense is designed to slow or block an attacker, even if they breach one or more security controls.

Defense in depth in a cloud environment might include firewalls, network segmentation, MFA, intrusion detection systems, and data encryption. If an attacker bypasses one layer, they still encounter additional barriers, reducing the likelihood of full system compromise. This strategy improves resilience against attacks, as it relies on a combination of preventive, detective, and corrective controls to protect assets at various levels of the infrastructure.

Implementing defense in depth in Atlas involves layering multiple security measures to protect different aspects of the data infrastructure. Here are some specific examples:

- *Network isolation and access control*—Start by isolating your Atlas cluster in a VPC and controlling access through IP access lists. Allow traffic only from specific trusted IP addresses or network ranges, keeping unwanted traffic out. For additional isolation, enable private endpoints so that traffic between your application and Atlas remains within the cloud provider's private network, bypassing the public internet.
- *Authentication and authorization*—Use federated identity providers such as Okta and Entra ID for SSO in the Atlas UI, and enforce MFA for an added security layer. For database access, choose a strong authentication method such as SCRAM or X.509 certificates to ensure that only authenticated users can connect. Employ RBAC to assign granular permissions, ensuring that users can perform only actions relevant to their roles.
- *Data encryption*—Secure data at rest by enabling encryption through a customer-managed key using AWS KMS, GCP KMS, or Azure Key Vault (BYOK). This way, encryption keys are under the customer's control, adding a layer of security even if the storage is compromised. Also use CSFLE for highly sensitive fields, encrypting them within the application so that Atlas never sees the plain-text values. For searchable encrypted data, implement Queryable Encryption to allow secure querying of encrypted fields.
- *Intrusion detection and auditing*—Enable database auditing to monitor access and track operations on sensitive collections or actions by specific users. You can configure audit logs to capture all `authCheck` events, for example; these events include every attempt to read or write to the database, providing insight into both successful and failed access attempts. Implement Control Plane auditing in the Atlas UI to log administrative actions at the project and organization levels, enabling you to monitor activities such as user management and configuration changes.

- *Secure configuration and change management*—During initial setup, ensure that all network peering connections, IP access lists, and private endpoint configurations align with your security policies. Configure minimal TLS version requirements (preferably TLS 1.2 or later) for all cluster connections, ensuring encrypted data in transit. Use automated tools within Atlas to enforce these configurations consistently across environments, and apply security patches regularly to mitigate newly discovered vulnerabilities.
- *PoLP*—Apply this principle by creating custom database roles in MongoDB that grant only necessary permissions for specific tasks. A role limited to read-only access on a specific collection or database, for example, can be assigned to reporting tools, whereas more advanced roles with write permissions are reserved for developers who need data modification capabilities. By controlling access tightly, you limit exposure and reduce the potential effect of any compromised credentials. Carefully define each role to provide only the permissions required for specific users or applications, ensuring that no one has more access than necessary. This approach helps prevent accidental or malicious actions that could harm data security or disrupt operations.
- *Automated backups*—Implement regular automated backups to provide a reliable recovery point in case of data loss, corruption, or security breach. (Chapter 21 discusses backups.) Atlas offers continuous backups and scheduled snapshots, ensuring that you can restore your data to a previous state if necessary. By storing backups separately and securing access to them, you protect your data from potential attacks or failures, providing an essential safety layer in your defense-in-depth strategy. Atlas encrypts all snapshots using your cloud provider's standard storage encryption method, ensuring the security of cluster data at rest. Backup encryption prevents unauthorized access, ensures compliance, and strengthens security by keeping data protected even if storage is compromised.
- *Monitoring and alerting*—Implementing robust monitoring and alerting is crucial for maintaining security in Atlas. By continuously tracking database activity, you can detect and respond to suspicious behavior in real time. Set up alerts for unusual access patterns, failed login attempts, and changes to critical settings. Atlas provides built-in monitoring tools and integrates with third-party solutions, enabling you to customize alerts based on security needs (chapter 21). With proactive monitoring, you can swiftly identify and mitigate threats, ensuring the ongoing security and integrity of your data infrastructure.

By implementing defense in depth across network isolation, authentication, encryption, auditing, secure configurations, and access control, Atlas provides a layered security strategy that protects data at every stage. This structured approach makes it significantly harder for attackers to gain access or compromise data; each layer adds an obstacle that must be overcome, thereby reinforcing overall data security and resilience.

Summary

- Atlas, as a SaaS platform, relies on cloud providers for physical security and infrastructure, whereas MongoDB ensures platform security and database management. Customers manage data access, identity, and certain security settings, following the shared responsibility model.
- Atlas has two primary authentication areas: the Atlas UI and Atlas database clusters. The Atlas UI is used to manage clusters, user permissions, and configurations. Atlas database clusters handle data security by assigning roles to users or applications, controlling what actions they can perform, such as reading or modifying data.
- Federated authentication in Atlas UI uses the FIM approach to user authentication. In this setup, Atlas relies on your IdP to authenticate users. With this system, your organization controls user credentials via the IdP, allowing seamless authentication across various online platforms.
- MongoDB database clusters support multiple authentication methods for database access, including SCRAM, X.509 certificates, LDAP, OIDC, and AWS IAM for login.
- Atlas integrates with HashiCorp Vault to securely generate time-limited database credentials on demand, reducing security risks from long-lived credentials. This is part of Vault's database secrets engine, using predefined roles in Vault.
- Atlas uses RBAC to govern access to its cloud resources and MongoDB deployments by assigning roles to users, specifying their access rights within an Atlas organization or project. Similarly, MongoDB databases use RBAC to regulate specific actions on databases and collections.
- PoLP advises granting users, applications, or systems only the access they need to complete their tasks. By limiting permissions to the bare minimum, PoLP reduces the risk of misuse, enhances security, and minimizes potential damage from breaches or errors.
- MongoDB controls access to its system using RBAC; users are granted specific roles that define what they can do within the database. If a user isn't assigned any role, they have no permissions to access or interact with the system.
- MongoDB custom roles enable precise access control, enhancing security by granting only the necessary permissions, unlike default roles that may overexpose sensitive data or functions.
- To minimize security risks and streamline management, avoid shared accounts by setting up dedicated users or service accounts for each application. This approach ensures finer access control, simplifies tracking of actions, and enables enforcement of PoLP, keeping permissions well defined and isolated.
- Database auditing allows administrators to monitor system activity in deployments with multiple users. In Atlas, administrators can choose the actions, database users, and roles they want to audit.

- Atlas secures all connections with clusters using TLS, which encrypts data during transmission to maintain confidentiality and integrity. All network traffic, including data sent to Atlas and between cluster nodes, is safeguarded by TLS, enabled by default; it cannot be disabled.
- When you create an Atlas cluster, customer data is encrypted at rest using AES-256, securing all disk-stored data through the provider's transparent disk encryption. You can also use database-level encryption with the WiredTiger Encrypted Storage Engine, which allows you to bring your own encryption key via AWS KMS, GCP KMS, or Azure Key Vault for secure key management.
- CSFLE allows sensitive fields to be encrypted on the client side, ensuring that they are protected before reaching MongoDB. If an application stores an SSN, CSFLE encrypts it within the application so that only encrypted data is sent to the database.
- Queryable Encryption in MongoDB allows secure searches on encrypted fields without decryption. It's ideal for protecting sensitive data like SSN and credit card info while enabling queries such as equality matches.
- Atlas clusters are protected from internet access by default, residing in a VPC with inbound traffic blocked. Users can create IP access lists to allow only specific IP addresses to connect, ensuring that access is limited to approved sources.
- In Atlas, network peering enables you to link your VPCs directly to an Atlas VPC, allowing traffic to flow privately without being exposed to the public internet. This feature is supported for dedicated clusters in AWS, GCP, and Azure and in multicloud sharded clusters.
- Private endpoints in Atlas enable a secure private link from your VPC directly to an Atlas VPC, isolating all data traffic from the public internet. This configuration ensures that although your VPC can reach Atlas, Atlas cannot initiate connections back to your network, preserving a strict network boundary and bolstering security.
- Defense in depth is a security approach that uses multiple layers of protective measures to safeguard data and systems. With this method, each security layer is intended to deter or obstruct an attacker, ensuring that even if one control fails, additional defenses remain in place to prevent unauthorized access.

Operational excellence with Atlas

This chapter covers
- Discovering Atlas's cloud backup capabilities
- Restoring an Atlas cluster
- Monitoring Atlas database cluster metrics
- Executing MongoDB diagnostic commands
- Using Atlas alerting and logging

Atlas provides easy-to-use tools for managing databases. It includes automatic backups that protect your data and allow quick recovery if a problem occurs. Real-time monitoring and alerting tools help teams catch and fix problems early, keeping systems running smoothly without interruptions. Atlas also offers detailed health metrics, providing insights that make it easier to plan resources and improve performance over time.

For performance tuning, Atlas has tools to identify slow queries, optimize indexes, and refine database structure and schemas, making sure that it can handle heavy workloads with ease. All together, these features help companies reduce costs, comply with regulations, and ensure a smooth and reliable user experience, supporting growth and stability over the long run. Using these Atlas tools, you can manage databases securely and efficiently.

21.1 Crafting backup strategies and practices

Database backups are essential for maintaining data integrity and operational resilience, especially in unexpected situations. Suppose that someone accidentally deletes a collection containing critical customer records. Having a recent backup allows for swift restoration, minimizing disruptions and helping the business maintain continuity.

For cybersecurity, backups are equally vital. In the event of a ransomware attack, which involves malicious software encrypting files or locking systems to demand a ransom, secure offline backups offer a recovery option. These backups bypass ransom demands, ensuring data recovery and safeguarding the organization's reputation. Backups offer a safeguard against data corruption by providing a clean previous version of the data, which can be restored if the current set becomes compromised.

Regulatory compliance in many industries heightens the need for consistent backups. Financial institutions, for example, are often legally required to retain transactional records for auditing and compliance. Reliable regular backups ensure that sensitive information is preserved and accessible to meet these standards, supporting the organization's legal and operational obligations.

21.1.1 Discovering Atlas backup methods

Atlas offers a managed cloud backup service that automatically creates and stores backups of your MongoDB clusters hosted on the Atlas platform. Cloud Backup uses the native snapshot capabilities of cloud providers such as Amazon Web Services (AWS), Microsoft Azure, and Google Cloud Platform (GCP). Backups are stored in the same region as the cluster, ensuring data proximity and compliance with data residency requirements. For multiregion clusters, snapshots are stored in the cluster's preferred region. All managed snapshots and images are encrypted automatically. If encryption key management integration with AWS Key Management Service (KMS), Azure Key Vault, or GCP KMS is enabled, your AWS customer master key (CMK), Azure Key Vault Secret Key, or CCP Service Account Key and identity and access management (IAM) credentials are required to perform restores of backup snapshots. Cloud Backup also offers customizable snapshot schedules and retention policies, supporting multiyear retention to meet compliance obligations.

BACKING UP M0 CLUSTERS

Atlas Cloud Backup is not available for M0 free clusters. As an alternative, you can use your own tools, such as `mongodump` for creating backups and `mongorestore` for restoring data. `mongodump` creates a logical backup of MongoDB data, extracting the database content and saving it as Binary JSON (BSON) files instead of copying the physical data storage layer. This method is useful for transferring data between MongoDB instances or creating an external data copy, but it is not optimal for large databases because it requires significant time and processing power to export and import large amounts of data.

The `mongodump` tool has certain limitations when used in Atlas, with some options being unsupported. The `--dumpDbUsersAndRoles` option, which normally allows the export of users and roles specific to a database, is not supported, so users and roles must be handled separately if they need to be re-created. The `--oplog` option, typically used to include the oplog during the dump for point-in-time snapshots, is also unsupported. Point-in-time captures using the oplog cannot be created directly with `mongodump` in Atlas.

For detailed information on how to back up your data manually, see https://mng.bz/yNdq.

BACKING UP FLEX CLUSTERS

Atlas Cloud Backup is available for Flex clusters, but its functionality is limited. On-demand snapshots aren't available for Flex clusters. Atlas automatically captures daily snapshots for these shared clusters, starting 24 hours after the cluster's setup. These snapshots use the cloud provider's native snapshot functionality, which captures the data state at a specific moment, enabling quick restoration if necessary. To reduce effect on cluster performance, snapshots are always taken from a secondary node.

> **NOTE** The Atlas command-line interface (CLI) does not support Flex backup snapshots.

Atlas retains the eight most recent daily snapshots, providing a secure, efficient backup solution. Restoration to the point in time is not available for Flex instances.

To learn how to create a backup of these instances using the Atlas UI, see https://mng.bz/Mwln.

BACKING UP DEDICATED CLUSTERS (M10+)

Dedicated clusters (M10 and higher) offer the most advanced Cloud Backup options, providing access to a wide range of features. Cloud Backup uses the native snapshot capabilities of cloud providers to create full-copy snapshots stored locally within the same region as the cluster. These snapshots can be scheduled at regular intervals, and you can configure retention policies to meet your data protection requirements. Atlas also supports on-demand snapshots, allowing you to create backups at any time.

You can create an M10 cluster with Cloud Backup enabled by using the Atlas CLI with the flags `-backup` and `--tier M10`:

```
atlas cluster create "MongoDB-in-Action-M10" \
--backup --provider GCP --region CENTRAL_US \
--tier M10
```

The command returns the following information:

```
Cluster 'MongoDB-in-Action-M10' is being created.
```

Now your cluster has backups, which will run according to the schedule. To display the backup schedule, use the Atlas CLI and the command `atlas backup schedule describe`:

```
atlas backups schedule describe MongoDB-in-Action-M10
```

The command should return the current backup schedule:

```
CLUSTER NAME              AUTO EXPORT ENABLED     NEXT SNAPSHOT
MongoDB-in-Action-M10     false                   2024-06-22 14:49:20 +0000 UTC

ID                       Frequency Interval   Frequency Type    Retention Value   Retention Unit
6676900fe259a12fa8ccfc73 6                    hourly            7                 days
6676900fe259a12fa8ccfc74 1                    daily             7                 days
6676900fe259a12fa8ccfc75 6                    weekly            4                 weeks
6676900fe259a12fa8ccfc76 40                   monthly           12                months
6676900fe259a12fa8ccfc77 12                   yearly            1                 years
```

The output tells you that the MongoDB cluster has its next snapshot scheduled for June 22, 2024, at 14:49 Coordinated Universal Time (UTC). The backup schedule includes multiple frequencies and retention periods: hourly and daily snapshots retained for 7 days, weekly snapshots kept for 4 weeks, monthly snapshots retained for 12 months, and yearly snapshots preserved for 1 year. Each backup entry is assigned a unique ID, facilitating easy management and reference for different backup intervals and retention durations.

You can also create an on-demand backup. If necessary, you can trigger a backup immediately using the Atlas CLI command `atlas backups snapshots create`:

```
atlas backups snapshots create "MongoDB-in-Action-M10" \
--desc "Atlas on-demand"
Snapshot '66731653c782c81efb877f7e' created.
```

Next, use the command `atlas backups snapshots list` to monitor the progress of the backup process. Wait until the command returns a status-completed message:

```
atlas backups snapshots list "MongoDB-in-Action-M10"
```

The command returns a completed on-demand backup snapshot:

```
ID         TYPE STATUS         CREATED AT EXPIRES AT
66769417cca8491bfe9fa771 onDemand completed 2024-06-22
09:08:58 +0000 UTC 2024-06-23 09:10:58 +0000 UTC
```

To back up single-region M10 and higher clusters, Atlas determines the order of MongoDB nodes for snapshots based on a specific algorithm. First, it tries to snapshot a secondary node. If that is not possible, it selects the node with the lowest priority. If there is still a tie, it attempts an incremental snapshot from one node to the next, using the same storage disk if feasible. If no clear choice is made, it defaults to the node with the lexicographically smallest hostname.

When the order of nodes is set, Atlas attempts to create a snapshot. If the chosen node is unhealthy, it moves to the next preferred node. The snapshots are stored in the same cloud region as the cluster and are retained according to the specified retention policy.

If the current snapshot storage volume becomes invalid, Atlas creates a new snapshot volume within the same region as the cluster's primary node. This process includes taking a full-copy snapshot to ensure backup continuity, allowing Atlas to maintain backup availability and support incremental snapshots in the corresponding region. Figure 21.1 illustrates a single-region backup strategy.

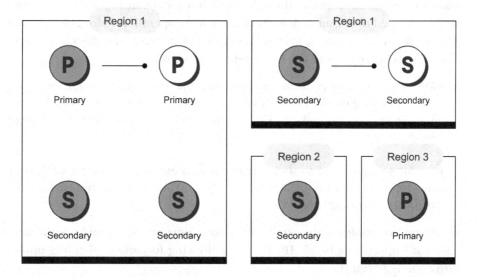

Figure 21.1 The primary node (P) and secondary nodes (S) are located within the same region (Region 1). Backups are created by taking snapshots of these nodes, prioritizing secondary nodes where possible to reduce effect on the primary node. If a new snapshot storage volume is required, it is created within the same region. This setup ensures that all backups remain in the same geographic area as the original data, following Atlas's single-region backup policy. (Image © MongoDB 2024 CC BY-NC-SA 3.0)

With multiregion cluster backups, Atlas follows an algorithm to determine the order of nodes for snapshots. First, it attempts to snapshot a node in the highest-priority region. If nodes are tied in priority, Atlas compares them in descending order to determine the preferred node. If snapshotting in the highest-priority region isn't possible, Atlas moves on to snapshot a secondary node. When there's a tie at this step, it proceeds to the next criterion. If neither attempt succeeds, it selects the node with the lowest priority, preferring nodes that allow incremental snapshots from previous ones, specifically nodes on the same disk. If there's still a tie, Atlas defaults to the node with the lexicographically smallest hostname. When the order of nodes is set, Atlas begins the snapshot on the chosen node. If the selected node is unhealthy, it moves to the next node in priority order.

> **NOTE** If a snapshot fails, Atlas automatically tries to create another one. Fallback snapshots are available for restoring a cluster, but they should be used only when necessary. Created through a different, more manual process, fallback snapshots may not be as reliable or consistent as regular snapshots, making them less accurate for data recovery.

CONTINUOUS CLOUD BACKUPS

Continuous cloud backups in Atlas provide robust data protection by allowing you to restore your clusters to any specific moment within a defined retention window. This feature continuously captures the oplog, which is a real-time log of all write operations, over a specified time frame. By storing these write operations, MongoDB enables precise point-in-time recovery, ensuring that users can revert the database to the exact state at any chosen minute within the retention period.

> **NOTE** Clusters with continuous cloud backups use object storage for oplog data, depending on the cloud provider. In AWS, this data is stored in Amazon S3; in Azure, it's kept in Azure Blob Storage; in GCP, it's maintained in Google Cloud Storage.

> **TIP** Atlas enables you to secure backups with encryption using a CMK from your cloud provider's KMS. You can set up encryption for backups via the Atlas dashboard or through the API.

If you want to enable continuous cloud backup for your Atlas cluster, see the documentation at https://mng.bz/a9MB. If you are looking for advanced config options, see https://mng.bz/gmJE.

21.1.2 Restoring an Atlas cluster

Cluster restoration is critical, ensuring that data can be recovered quickly in case of failure, data corruption, or accidental deletion.

> **TIP** Test restore procedures regularly to ensure their reliability and identify potential problems. Testing reduces the risk of data loss and downtime during an actual recovery.

> **NOTE** Restoring data to an alternative cluster is an option for handling complex scenarios, providing a valuable approach for testing setups or preparing for disaster recovery.

Restoring data in Atlas from scheduled or on-demand snapshots lets you revert a cluster to a previous state or restore to a different cluster. The process includes specific requirements and limitations depending on the cluster type, such as M0 and Flex or M10 instances.

> **Restoring data from Cloud Backup**
>
> During a restore in Atlas from Cloud Backup, the target cluster undergoes a process that ensures that it returns to the exact state defined by the chosen snapshot or backup point. To accomplish this task, Atlas first removes all existing data from the target cluster to prevent conflicts or data inconsistencies. This initial wipe prepares the cluster for an accurate restoration of data as it existed at the backup time.
>
> After clearing the data, Atlas begins loading the snapshot or replaying the oplog entries, depending on whether the restore is from a scheduled snapshot or a continuous backup. This sequential loading or replaying process rebuilds the database to reflect each operation performed up to the backup point, ensuring data accuracy. While these actions occur, the cluster is temporarily taken offline to prevent client access, which could disrupt data integrity if reads or writes occur midrestore. When the data is fully restored and verified, the cluster is brought back online, allowing normal operations to resume.

RESTORING M0 CLUSTERS

Because free M0 clusters do not offer cloud backup snapshots, the recommended method for restoring data is using the `mongorestore` tool, which restores a dump created with `mongodump`. But the `mongorestore` used in Atlas has certain limitations and does not support several options. The `--restoreDbUsersAndRoles` option, which typically restores users and roles specific to a database, is not supported, so users and roles must be re-created separately if necessary. The `--oplogReplay` option, used to replay operations from an oplog for point-in-time recovery, is also unsupported, so you cannot use it for incremental backups or changes since the last backup. Finally, `--preserveUUID`, which normally keeps the unique identifiers for collections intact during restoration, is unavailable, so restored collections are assigned new universally unique identifiers (UUIDs).

RESTORING FLEX CLUSTERS

Atlas automatically creates daily snapshots for Flex shared clusters, starting 24 hours after the cluster is created. Because Atlas CLI restoration is not supported for Flex clusters, you must use the Atlas UI to restore. Navigate to the Clusters page, select your project, and open the cluster's Backup tab. Locate the snapshot you want, choose Restore from the Actions menu, and select the target cluster. Confirm the restore, and restart your application to connect to the updated cluster.

> **NOTE** Flex snapshots can be restored only to replica sets, not to sharded clusters.

RESTORING DEDICATED CLUSTERS (M10+)

The Atlas CLI allows you to restore Atlas dedicated clusters with the `atlas backups restores start` command, which initiates a restore job for M10 or higher clusters.

When performing an automated restore, Atlas first deletes all existing data in the target cluster to ensure that it mirrors the state saved in the selected snapshot. This command has three primary options: Automated Restore, Point-in-Time Restore, and Download Restore.

Automated Restore restores a cluster to the state saved in a specific snapshot. Specify the source cluster name, the snapshot ID, the target cluster, and the project ID.

In the first scenario, suppose that you want to restore data within the same cluster. You would specify the source cluster name, snapshot ID, target cluster name, and project ID. Here's an example command:

```
atlas backups restores start automated \
--clusterName "MongoDB-in-Action-M10" \
--targetClusterName "MongoDB-in-Action-M10" \
--snapshotId 6725be13eae896510f35a553 \
--targetProjectId 65d70c5bc9b5633e80a9c998
```

This command restores the cluster `"MongoDB-in-Action-M10"` to the state of the snapshot with ID `6725be13eae896510f35a553`, retaining it as the original cluster.

In the second scenario, you may want to restore data to a different cluster, perhaps for testing or validation purposes. You still specify the source cluster and snapshot ID, but you change the target cluster and project ID to avoid overwriting the original data:

```
atlas backups restores start automated \
    --clusterName "MongoDB-in-Action-M10" \
    --snapshotId 6725be13eae896510f35a553 \
    --targetClusterName myRestoreDemo \
    --targetProjectId 1a2345b67c8e9a12f3456de7
```

In this case, `"MongoDB-in-Action-M10"` is the source cluster, `6725be13eae896510f35a553` is the snapshot ID, `myRestoreDemo` is the target cluster, and `1a2345b67c8e9a12f3456de7` is the project ID where the restored data will be directed, ensuring that the original cluster remains unchanged. The restore sets up a new cluster from the backup snapshot; this process can take some time, depending on the size of your cluster and snapshot. When the restore is complete, your restored cluster is ready for regular use.

Point-in-Time Restore restores data to a specific time within the past 24 hours by specifying the UNIX timestamp. Useful for more precise recovery needs, this option requires the cluster name, point-in-time timestamp, target cluster, and target project ID. This command is explained in the next section.

Download Restore downloads the specified snapshot data. Use the `download` option with the snapshot ID. To download a snapshot, you can run

```
atlas backups restores start download \
    --clusterName MongoDB-in-Action-M10 \
    --snapshotId 6725be13eae896510f35a553
```

In this case, `MongoDB-in-Action-M10` is the cluster from which you are downloading, and `6725be13eae896510f35a553` is the snapshot ID to download.

> **NOTE** When the restore is finished, Atlas creates a new snapshot of the restored cluster. This snapshot is retained for a period matching the continuous Cloud Backup window set for the cluster.

> **TIP** Use the Atlas CLI command `atlas backups restores watch <restore job id> --clusterName "MongoDB-in-Action-M10"` to watch the current restore status.

RESTORING FROM CONTINUOUS CLOUD BACKUP

Atlas enables precise data restoration from continuous Cloud Backup by allowing you to select an exact date and time or a specific oplog entry as the restore point. This feature provides greater flexibility and control, enabling you to recover your data to the exact moment required, which is especially valuable for resolving data inconsistencies or reverting unintended changes.

> **NOTE** This feature is available for M10 and higher dedicated clusters.

Point-in-time recovery

During a point-in-time restore, the system replays the captured oplog entries—recorded write operations—over the backup snapshot from the defined start point up to the specified moment within the retention window. The restore process begins by applying the latest snapshot as the baseline; then it sequentially replays the oplog entries to rebuild the database state exactly as it was at the chosen moment. This approach ensures that all changes up to that specific time are reflected accurately while keeping read operations unaffected. The result is a precise reconstruction of the database, aligned to the exact state required for restoration.

Recovery-point objectives (RPO) define the maximum acceptable amount of data that can be lost measured in time. With continuous cloud backup, you can achieve RPOs as short as 1 minute, providing a high level of data recovery accuracy. You can configure the continuous backup window to align with your data retention and recovery goals. Enabling this feature, however, may increase monthly costs due to the additional storage and processing needed to maintain the oplog and facilitate smooth on-demand restoration.

To restore data to a specific point in time, you can use the `atlas backups restores start pointInTime` Atlas CLI command:

```
atlas backups restores start pointInTime \
    --clusterName MongoDB-in-Action-M10 \
    --pointInTimeUTCSeconds 1588523147 \
    --targetClusterName myRestoreDemo \
    --targetProjectId 1a2345b67c8e9a12f3456de7
```

Here, `MongoDB-in-Action-M10` is the source cluster, `1588523147` is the timestamp for the desired point in time, `myRestoreDemo` is the target cluster, and `1a2345b67c8e9a12f3456de7` is the project ID of the target cluster.

Use this command to restore data to a specific point in time. This is helpful for recovering from unintended changes or data loss that happened at a specific moment. The process creates a copy of the database at that exact time on a separate target cluster, so the main live data is not affected. It's an ideal way to fix problems from accidental deletions, updates, or other mistakes, allowing you to return to a stable state safely without touching the primary database.

> **TIP** You can use the `--oplogTs` and `--oplogInc` flags together to restore data to an exact point in time, down to a specific second. The `--oplogTs` flag specifies the target time as a UNIX timestamp (in seconds), whereas the `--oplogInc` flag is a 32-bit incrementing value that identifies the precise operation within that second, allowing highly granular restoration.

To learn about advanced restore strategies, see https://mng.bz/eBJv.

21.2 Inspecting the performance of your Atlas cluster

Atlas offers built-in tools for monitoring and alerting to help you oversee your clusters and enhance performance. You can analyze slow queries using Performance Advisor, monitor collection-level query latency with Namespace Insights, and track real-time performance through the Real-Time Performance Panel. To ensure optimal cluster performance, Atlas allows you to configure alerts based on specific conditions related to your databases, users, and accounts. When these conditions are met, Atlas sends notifications via email, Short Message Service (SMS), or third-party services like PagerDuty and Slack. Atlas also provides deployment metrics for historical throughput, performance, and use, helping you with continuous improvement and capacity planning. For comprehensive monitoring, you can integrate Atlas with third-party services and access MongoDB logs for detailed insights.

21.2.1 Finding slow queries

To optimize query performance in Atlas, you can use the following built-in tools.

USING PERFORMANCE ADVISOR

Performance Advisor monitors queries that are considered slow and suggests new indexes to improve query performance. The threshold for slow queries varies based on the average time of operations in your cluster to provide recommendations pertinent to your workload. Recommended indexes are accompanied by sample queries, grouped by query shape, run against a collection that would benefit from the suggested index.

> **NOTE** Indexes improve the performance of queries. If you are trying to optimize write/insert performance, extra indexes can affect performance of those operations.

TIP By default, Atlas activates the Atlas-managed threshold for slow operations. You can disable it using `atlas performanceAdvisor slowOperationThreshold disable`. To enable it again, use `atlas performanceAdvisor slowOperationThreshold enable`. Atlas does not support the Atlas-managed slow query operation threshold for M0 and Flex clusters.

Atlas sets a dynamic slow-query threshold by default, adjusting according to operation times across your cluster. If you turn off this dynamic adjustment, MongoDB instead applies a fixed threshold of 100 milliseconds (ms) for slow queries. I generally advise that you not set this fixed threshold below 100 ms.

To use Performance Advisor with the Atlas CLI, first display the available nodes (called *processes*). With the node names, you can connect to each one with the Atlas CLI and use its capabilities for performance optimization. To list Atlas processes, use the following command:

```
atlas processes list
```

The command returns a list of processes (Atlas nodes):

```
ID                      REPLICA SET NAME    SHARD NAME          VERSION
atlas-rr5vne-shard-00-00.a7niyd4.mongodb.net:27017
 atlas-rr5vne-shard-0  8.0.4  atlas-rr5vne-shard-00-
 01.a7niyd4.mongodb.net:27017    atlas-rr5vne-shard-0  8.0.4
 atlas-rr5vne-shard-00-02.a7niyd4.mongodb.net:27017
 atlas-rr5vne-shard-0  8.0.4
```

This list of processes includes details like the ID, which is the unique identifier for each process; the REPLICA SET NAME, indicating the name of the replica set for high availability; the SHARD NAME, specifying the shard to which the process belongs if the cluster is sharded; and the VERSION, which shows the MongoDB version running on each instance. Having a list of processes rather than relying on a connection string is essential because a connection string connects to the entire cluster as a whole without allowing direct access to individual nodes.

> **Monitoring node metrics**
>
> In MongoDB, each node has a distinct role. Some nodes are part of sharding, and others function as replicas. Each node can process queries. The primary node handles reads and writes, and secondary nodes handle read operations. Performance problems can vary significantly between nodes, so analyzing performance on a per-node basis enables more precise identification and resolution of problems.
>
> With a node-specific list, you can focus on the exact node experiencing slow queries rather than query the entire cluster. This targeted approach helps you isolate performance bottlenecks more accurately; certain problems may affect only one part of the cluster rather than the system as a whole.

Now you can retrieve a list of up to 20 namespaces (in the format `database.collection`) that have slow queries for a specified node. To list these namespaces, use the following command:

```
atlas performanceAdvisor namespaces list \
    --processName atlas-rr5vne-shard-00-00.a7niyd4.mongodb.net:27017
```

This command returns a set of namespaces that are experiencing slow queries, allowing you to focus on specific areas within your database that may need optimization. The specified node name in the command, such as `atlas-rr5vne-shard-00-00.a7niyd4.mongodb.net:27017`, refers to one of the nodes listed in the previous output. You can examine each node.

You can also get a list of suggested indexes to optimize query performance for collections with slow queries. To get a list of suggested indexes, use the following command:

```
atlas performanceAdvisor suggestedIndexes list \
    --processName atlas-rr5vne-shard-00-00.a7niyd4.mongodb.net:27017
```

Each index recommendation comes with an average query targeting score, which shows the ratio of documents read to documents returned for the queries that use the suggested index. A score of 1 indicates highly efficient query patterns, in which every document read was a match and included in the results. Implementing any suggested index gives you a chance to enhance query performance.

Use the following command in the Atlas CLI to retrieve log entries for slow queries identified by the Performance Advisor and Query Profiler:

```
atlas performanceAdvisor slowQueryLogs list \
    --processName atlas-rr5vne-shard-00-00.a7niyd4.mongodb.net:27017
```

Using those commands regularly helps you stay on top of performance problems before they affect users or system stability. This approach also provides proactive database management by identifying problem areas as they arise, ensuring that your Atlas environment remains efficient and responsive. You can also use Performance Advisor with Atlas UI. Learn how in the official documentation at https://mng.bz/pZd8.

USING QUERY PROFILER

Atlas Query Profiler is designed to diagnose and monitor performance problems in your database clusters. It identifies slow-running queries and provides key performance statistics in the Atlas UI. By collecting and displaying statistics from your `mongod` instances, Query Profiler helps you pinpoint inefficient queries based on log data. This data is presented on the Query Insights tab in the Query Profiler section of an instance. It shows operations across your entire cluster by default, with options on the Host Selector drop-down menu that allow you to view operations from specific shards or nodes within a shard. The Query Insights tab reveals slow database operations over a set time frame, displaying metrics such as Operation Execution Time and Server

Execution Time in chart and table formats. You can filter this data by aspect and time frame, allowing detailed analysis.

> **NOTE** Query Profiler is available only for M10 and higher clusters. Query Profiler and MongoDB Database Profiler serve different functions. Query Profiler helps identify slow-running queries based on log data. Database Profiler captures detailed information about all database operations, depending on the profiling level set, and it works independently of Query Profiler settings.

Query Profiler organizes data with options for filtering by time frame and query type. It supports the management of slow operation thresholds, which you can adjust as necessary. Query Profiler may capture sensitive query data, so use it in alignment with your security practices. With its ability to highlight inefficient queries, Query Profiler is essential for optimizing Atlas cluster performance. To learn more about using Query Profiler with the Atlas UI, see https://mng.bz/OwpR.

VIEWING THE REAL-TIME PERFORMANCE PANEL

The Real-Time Performance Panel (RTPP) is a powerful monitoring tool that provides live insights into key operational metrics, supporting proactive management of database performance. With RTPP, you can track metrics such as CPU, memory, and disk use, which allows you to monitor resource consumption and quickly identify potential bottlenecks or capacity problems. Network metrics provide visibility into data flow, displaying incoming and outgoing traffic to help you manage load and identify spikes that could affect performance.

> **TIP** When you're working on improving performance, it's always important to know what the current bottleneck is. There's no point in making changes to reduce CPU use if your database is using all the available I/O throughput you have configured, for example.

> **NOTE** RTTP is available only for M10 and higher clusters.

RTPP offers insights into query execution times and identifies slow-running queries, providing an immediate view of performance at the query level. This enables database administrators to troubleshoot and optimize problematic queries in real time. The panel also highlights replication lag for secondary nodes in replica sets, helping ensure data consistency and smooth failover operations.

With customizable time ranges and metric charts that autorefresh, RTPP allows you to maintain continuous oversight of your database's health. This panel is invaluable for teams that need real-time monitoring to maintain high performance, optimize resource use, and address problems before they affect application performance or user experience. You can learn more at https://mng.bz/OwpR.

MONITORING COLLECTION-LEVEL LATENCY WITH NAMESPACE INSIGHTS

Namespace Insights provides detailed metrics on query latency at the collection level, allowing teams to monitor the response times and performance of specific collections within a database. This feature helps identify collections experiencing high latency or inefficient query patterns, enabling targeted optimizations to improve overall database performance.

> **NOTE** The Namespace Insights page is available only for M10 and higher clusters.

With Namespace Insights, you gain access to real-time latency data, which is especially useful for diagnosing problems related to indexes, query patterns, or data structure that could be causing delays. The tool allows granular monitoring, showing which collections require attention and providing insights into query execution times for each collection. This detailed level of visibility helps database administrators make data-driven adjustments, optimize resource allocation, and maintain consistent performance across high-traffic or complex collections. You can learn more at https://mng.bz/GwRv.

21.2.2 Improving your schema

Atlas offers schema suggestions designed to improve database structure and optimize performance. Performance Advisor analyzes high-traffic collections and those with slow-running queries, offering targeted recommendations to address inefficiencies in data modeling. By identifying patterns that contribute to performance bottlenecks, Atlas suggests schema modifications aligned with MongoDB's best practices, such as restructuring fields, optimizing indexes, and adjusting data types to suit your query patterns better.

Atlas samples documents from collections to understand their structure and suggest improvements where data organization may be inefficient. If a collection has deeply nested fields or excessive arrays, Atlas may recommend changes to flatten the structure, reducing the complexity of query execution. Similarly, if a collection has fields that vary widely in data type or size, schema suggestions might include recommendations to normalize data types, which can improve query performance and storage efficiency.

Another key aspect of schema suggestions is improving data access patterns. Atlas can detect collections in which queries frequently filter on fields that lack suitable indexes or use fields prone to high cardinality. In such cases, schema recommendations may include adding indexes on frequently queried fields or adjusting field arrangements to optimize query execution plans, thereby reducing latency and improving response times. By proactively addressing these problems, schema suggestions not only enhance performance but also reduce resource consumption, making it easier to scale applications efficiently.

These recommendations are accessible in the Atlas UI, allowing you to evaluate and implement them easily. With a focus on actionable insights, schema suggestions serve as an ongoing resource for maintaining and improving database performance, adapting as your workloads and data structures evolve. You can learn more at https://mng.bz/z2mB.

21.2.3 Using native MongoDB diagnostic commands

Apart from Atlas's built-in monitoring tools, you can use native MongoDB diagnostic commands. These commands provide direct insights into the server's performance and operational status, allowing you to track resource use, analyze query execution, and identify potential bottlenecks within your MongoDB environment. Many of Atlas's built-in tools rely on these commands, using them under the hood to gather and display critical performance metrics.

VIEWING SERVERSTATUS

The `serverStatus` command returns a document that provides an overview of the database's state. Running `db.serverStatus()` in MongoDB Shell (`mongos`) retrieves key metrics on various operational aspects of the server, including instance information (such as hostname, MongoDB version, and uptime), memory use (tracking memory allocation and use by MongoDB), connections (showing the number of active and available connections), network statistics (data on incoming and outgoing network traffic), and operation counters (counts of inserts, queries, updates, and deletes). In addition, `serverStatus` provides information on WiredTiger Storage Engine tickets, which are limits for concurrent read and write operations managed by WiredTiger. These tickets help you control the number of simultaneous operations, preventing excessive load on the server and ensuring stable performance. The WiredTiger Storage Engine has separate tickets for reads and writes. In MongoDB 7.0 and later, the storage engine dynamically adjusts the number of concurrent tickets to optimize performance under load. A ticket availability of 0 for a prolonged period does not indicate an overload because of this dynamic adjustment. In MongoDB 6.0 and earlier, a prolonged 0 ticket availability likely indicates an overload because tickets are statically configured. To check current ticket use, you can run `db.serverStatus().wiredTiger.concurrentTransactions` in the `mongosh`.

Queue metrics in `serverStatus` show the number of operations waiting for resources, indicating potential contention points. High values in `db.serverStatus().globalLock.currentQueue`, especially if read or write queues consistently exceed 100, suggest that operations are delayed due to limited resource availability, which may affect performance.

USING CURRENTOP

The `currentOp` command in MongoDB is a valuable tool for monitoring active operations on a server. It provides a snapshot of all ongoing operations, including queries, updates, inserts, and administrative tasks. It is particularly useful for identifying long-running or potentially problematic operations that may be causing performance bottlenecks or blocking other tasks.

To use `currentOp`, execute `db.currentOp()` in `mongosh`. This command returns a document containing detailed information about each active operation, such as operation type, namespace (database and collection), client details, duration, and resource use:

```
{
  "active" : true,
  "opid" : 12345,
  "secs_running" : 45,
  "ns" : "myDatabase.myCollection",
  "command" : {
    "find" : "myCollection",
    "filter" : { "status" : "active" }
  },
  "client" : "127.0.0.1:56789",
  "desc" : "conn123",
  "waitingForLock" : false
}
```

In this example, `secs_running: 45` indicates that the operation has been running for 45 seconds, and `waitingForLock: false` shows that it is not waiting for a lock.

You can also filter the output to focus on specific operations. To see only long-running operations, you can specify a threshold:

```
db.currentOp({ "secs_running" : { "$gt" : 60 } })
```

This command lists operations that have been running for more than 60 seconds, which can help you pinpoint tasks that may need attention or optimization. If you want to view only insert operations, use

```
db.currentOp({ "op" : "insert" })
```

If you identify a long-running or problematic operation using `currentOp`, you can terminate it using the `killOp` command. This command is helpful for stopping operations that are consuming excessive resources, causing bottlenecks, or blocking other tasks. To use `killOp`, retrieve the operation ID (`opid`) from the `currentOp` output. Each active operation has a unique `opid`, which you'll need to pass to `killOp`. If you see an operation with `opid : 12345` that you want to terminate, run

```
db.killOp(12345)
```

This command stops the specified operation.

> **WARNING** Use `killOp` cautiously; ending operations abruptly could lead to partial writes or incomplete tasks. It's best applied to noncritical operations, long-running queries, and maintenance tasks that have exceeded expected run times and are affecting overall performance.

EXECUTING TOP

The `top` command in MongoDB provides detailed statistics on the time spent reading and writing in different collections. This command helps you identify which collections or resources are most heavily used, offering insights into potential bottlenecks or areas that may need optimization.

The `top` command tracks the cumulative time MongoDB spends on each collection, displaying separate statistics for reads, writes, and total operations. This breakdown enables you to understand workload distribution across collections and make informed decisions on indexing, sharding, and other optimizations. To use `top`, execute

```
db.runCommand({ top: 1 })
```

The command returns a document with an entry for each database and collection, showing the time spent on each operation type:

```
sample_training.routes': {
  total: { time: 12000, count: 150 },
  readLock: { time: 7000, count: 80 },
  writeLock: { time: 5000, count: 70 },
  queries: { time: 7000, count: 80 },
  getmore: { time: 2000, count: 40 },
  insert: { time: 3000, count: 50 },
  update: { time: 4000, count: 60 },
  remove: { time: 1000, count: 20 },
  commands: { time: 500, count: 15 }}
```

In this output, `total.time` indicates that the collection `sample_training.routes` is heavily used, with high times and counts across `readLock`, `writeLock`, `queries`, `insert`, and `update`. This level of activity suggests that the collection is under substantial load, likely serving numerous read and write operations, and may require optimization to improve efficiency.

DISCOVERING DBSTATS AND COLLSTATS

The `dbStats` command provides statistics for a specific database, including its size, data and index use, and storage efficiency. To retrieve these stats, run

```
db.runCommand({ dbStats: 1 })
```

The `collStats` command offers detailed information on a particular collection, such as the number of documents, data size, index count, and index performance. To see details, run

```
db.runCommand({ collStats: "collection_name" })
```

Both commands are essential for monitoring resource use and performance, allowing administrators to optimize storage and identify potential areas for improvement at the database and collection levels.

MONITORING REPLICATION

You can use `rs.printReplicationInfo()` to check the overall replication status of a MongoDB replica set. This command provides information on the oplog, including its size and the time range of operations it holds, which is critical for understanding how long secondary members can go offline while still being able to catch up with the primary. If the oplog is too small, secondaries may fall out of sync and require a full resync after downtime.

`rs.printSecondaryReplicationInfo() also` offers insights into the status of secondary members in the replica set. This command shows details such as replication lag, which is the delay between when an operation occurs on the primary and when it is applied to a secondary. Monitoring replication lag is important because significant lag can result in secondaries serving outdated data, which can affect applications that rely on up-to-date reads. By keeping track of these metrics, you can ensure that replica set members remain synchronized, enabling consistent data availability and performance.

> **TIP** `db.runCommand({ listCommands: 1 })` returns a list of all available commands in MongoDB along with their descriptions, which is useful for exploring the full capabilities of the server.

You can read about more diagnostic commands at https://mng.bz/0zyN.

21.3 Alerting and logging

Logging and alerting are crucial for database cluster health and security. Logging tracks system activities, user actions, and application events, providing a history for troubleshooting, performance checks, and detecting security problems. Alerting notifies admins of critical events such as slow performance or security threats, preventing small problems from becoming larger problems. Together, they help you maintain performance, reliability, and security compliance by constantly monitoring and analyzing database activities.

21.3.1 Setting alert conditions

Atlas provides flexible alerts to notify you automatically if certain conditions in your cluster go outside defined limits. These alerts help you manage performance without continually checking everything manually. Alerts are automated notifications that let you know when something unusual is happening in your system. When an alert is triggered, Atlas displays a warning icon on your cluster and sends a notification (via email, SMS, webhook, PagerDuty, or other channels) based on your chosen settings. This lets you respond quickly to potential problems before they affect performance. Your site reliability engineering (SRE) team should keep close watch on those alerts and react quickly. You can set alerts for specific conditions and thresholds, each designed to monitor important performance metrics:

- *CPU steal*—This metric applies to environments such as AWS EC2 clusters with burstable performance that use shared CPU cores. It measures the percentage by which CPU use exceeds the guaranteed baseline CPU credit accumulation rate. CPU credits represent units of CPU use that accumulate at a constant rate, ensuring a guaranteed level of performance. These credits can be used to boost CPU performance beyond the baseline. When the credit balance is depleted, only the baseline CPU performance is maintained, and any additional use appears as steal percent. High CPU steal values (above 10%) indicate potential strain on the system's capability to meet demand, which can affect performance. Atlas alerts you to these conditions, prompting considerations such as scaling resources or optimizing workloads.

- *Queues*—This metric tracks operations waiting for access to resources (known as locks). If too many operations are queued (more than 100), it signals potential delays, and an alert helps you manage resource allocation.
- *Query targeting*—This metric identifies inefficient or slow database queries. Alerts at high values (50 or more) help you improve performance by highlighting queries that may require optimization.
- *Connection limits*—This metric alerts you when the cluster is nearing its connection capacity (80%–90%), letting you address scaling needs or avoid connection problems.

You can learn more about conditions that can trigger an alert and how to set them up in the Atlas UI at https://mng.bz/Kwlj and https://mng.bz/9yD7.

You can also use the Atlas CLI to create specific alerts. If you want to create an alert that triggers when the number of scanned objects per returned query exceeds a set threshold, you could use the following command:

```
atlas alerts settings create --event OUTSIDE_METRIC_THRESHOLD --enabled \
--metricName QUERY_TARGETING_SCANNED_OBJECTS_PER_RETURNED \
 --metricOperator GREATER_THAN --metricThreshold 1000 \
--metricUnits RAW --notificationType EMAIL --notificationEmailEnabled \
--notificationEmailAddress your-email@example.com \
--notificationIntervalMin 15
```

After successful creation, Atlas confirms with a message like this:

```
Alert configuration 672712f476c13d0e1dd98d28 created.
```

This alert targets the `QUERY_TARGETING_SCANNED_OBJECTS_PER_RETURNED` metric, which monitors the efficiency of query execution. Setting `--metricThreshold 1000` means that the alert will trigger if the query scans more than 1,000 objects for each object returned. This threshold helps you identify potential inefficiencies. When the scanned-to-returned ratio is high, it often points to suboptimal index use or poorly structured queries. Exceeding this threshold could lead to increased resource use (CPU, I/O) and longer query response times. Configuring this alert with a threshold enables proactive monitoring and allows adjustments to improve query performance and resource allocation.

To display information about newly created alert, you can use

```
atlas alerts settings describe 67271087cc3c1c55ff7867a1
```

You can also execute `atlas alerts settings list` to display information about all alerts currently available:

```
atlas alerts settings list
```

The following output shows a limited list of alerts:

```
ID                        TYPE                          ENABLED
67271087cc3c1c55ff7867a1  OUTSIDE_METRIC_THRESHOLD      true
65d70c5bc9b5633e80a9c99f  NO_PRIMARY                    true
65d70c5bc9b5633e80a9c9a4  CLUSTER_MONGOS_IS_MISSING     true
65d70c5bc9b5633e80a9c9b8  HOST_HAS_INDEX_SUGGESTIONS    true
65d70c5bc9b5633e80a9c9bb  HOST_MONGOT_CRASHING_OOM      true
6659e725bd53995b6b4ffd5f  SYNC_FAILURE                  true
6659e725bd53995b6b4ffd63  REQUEST_RATE_LIMIT            true
6659e725bd53995b6b4ffd67  LOG_FORWARDER_FAILURE         true
```

You can also update an alert setting with the Atlas CLI by using the `atlas alerts settings update <alert id>` command or delete an alert by using the `atlas alerts settings delete <alert id>` command.

21.3.2 Logging in Atlas

Atlas offers comprehensive logging capabilities to monitor and manage your database deployments. Logs available in Atlas include

- *Database logs*—Each `mongod` and `mongos` instance maintains its own log file, recording activities such as slow queries, connections, and system events. Atlas retains these logs for 30 days.
- *Audit logs*—For clusters with database auditing enabled, audit logs capture detailed records of database activities, including authentication attempts and data access events. These logs are essential for tracking user actions and ensuring compliance with security policies.
- *Trigger logs*—Atlas logs events related to triggers, functions, and change streams, providing insights into application-level operations. These logs are retained for 10 days.

If you want to access or manage logs in Atlas, you can do so via the Atlas UI or CLI. In the Atlas UI, navigate to your cluster's Logs tab to view and download logs. You can filter logs by type, status, timestamp, user, and request ID to focus on relevant entries.

If you want to use the Atlas CLI, the `atlas logs download` command allows you to download MongoDB logs from specific hosts in an Atlas project. The general syntax is

```
atlas logs download <hostname> <log-type> [flags].
```

Replace `<hostname>` with the hostname and `<log-type>` with the type of log file you need. Common log types include `mongodb.gz`, `mongos.gz`, `mongosqld.gz`, `mongodb-audit-log.gz`, and `mongos-audit-log.gz`. You can find the hostname with the help of the `atlas process list` command. This command lists all hostnames for the project, making it easy to find the one you need:

`atlas logs download atlas-123abc-shard-00-00.111xx.mongodb.net mongodb.gz`

> **NOTE** Downloadable logs are not available for M0 free clusters and Flex shared clusters.

Regular analysis of logs helps you identify performance bottlenecks such as slow queries or resource contention and detect potential security problems, including unauthorized access attempts. Using tools like Performance Advisor and Query Profiler can further help you optimize database operations.

Atlas also lets you send logs to other tools for better monitoring and analysis, making it easier to keep track of what's happening in your database. You can set up automatic log forwarding; logs are sent directly to other services without your having to download them manually. You could send logs to AWS CloudWatch to view them alongside other data from your AWS resources, for example. This way, you have one place for all your logs, helping you monitor everything together.

If you use Datadog for monitoring, you can also connect it to Atlas. Datadog is a monitoring and analytics platform that offers real-time visibility into your infrastructure, applications, and logs, providing comprehensive dashboards and alerting capabilities. By setting up a function in Atlas to send logs to Datadog, you'll get alerts and insights about your MongoDB database directly in Datadog's dashboard.

Atlas also allows you to store logs in Amazon S3 if you need long-term storage. By connecting Atlas to an S3 bucket, you can keep your logs in one place for as long as you need, making it easy to look back at historical data.

Another popular option is sending logs to Elasticsearch, a powerful search engine where you can analyze and search large amounts of data quickly. When your logs are in Elasticsearch, you can use Grafana to create dashboards, helping you visualize trends and spot problems in your database over time.

These integrations make it easy to monitor Atlas along with other tools you may already be using, allowing you to manage and analyze your database logs in a way that best fits your needs.

21.4 Upgrading your Atlas cluster

Regular upgrades in Atlas are crucial for maintaining security and performance and accessing new features. Atlas makes these upgrades straightforward, offering minor and major version upgrades, each with distinct purposes and effects.

Minor upgrades involve updates within the same major version (from 8.0.3 to 8.0.5, for example). These upgrades focus on security patches, bug fixes, and minor improvements, ensuring that your clusters are secure and up to date without changing core functionality. Atlas applies minor version upgrades automatically during the maintenance window, with little to no downtime, via a process called *rolling upgrades*, in which nodes are updated one at a time to maintain cluster availability. You can use the Atlas CLI and manage the maintenance window with commands like `atlas maintenanceWindows create`, `atlas maintenanceWindows update`, and `atlas maintenanceWindows delete`, or you can use the Atlas UI. To learn how to set up maintenance windows, go to https://mng.bz/jZPr.

Major upgrades, such as moving from MongoDB 7.0 to 8.0, introduce new features and significant changes to the database engine. To upgrade the major version of MongoDB in an Atlas cluster, the cluster must be in a healthy state, and any on-demand snapshots should be completed before starting. The upgrade can proceed only one major version at a time; version skipping is not allowed. MongoDB doesn't apply an upgrade to a major version of your cluster automatically; that is your responsibility.

> **NOTE** Atlas upgrades to the next major version automatically only if the current version reaches end of life. Shared tiers (M0/Flex) upgrade automatically shortly after a few patch releases of the new version.

Each new version may introduce non-backward–compatible features, so review the release notes to understand potential effects on your application. To learn how to upgrade your Atlas cluster to the latest version, see https://mng.bz/Wwza.

> **Major version upgrades**
>
> When performing a major upgrade, it's essential to verify that your MongoDB driver is compatible with the new database version. Different versions of MongoDB may introduce changes that affect how the driver interacts with the database, and outdated drivers can lead to unexpected behavior or even errors. Atlas provides documentation to help you check for any breaking changes introduced in the upgrade that might affect driver functionality. If your current driver version is incompatible, you should plan to upgrade the driver along with the database. Testing the driver and database in a staging environment before deploying to production is highly recommended. This testing phase allows you to identify and resolve any problems that might arise due to new behaviors or changes in the database performance and driver interaction. By verifying driver compatibility and reviewing any breaking changes, you can ensure a stable, seamless transition when upgrading to a new major version in Atlas.

> **NOTE** Upgrading to the latest version enhances security with critical patches and new features, keeping your data protected from vulnerabilities. Atlas clusters benefit from built-in security, such as encryption at rest and network isolation, that is updated regularly to meet standards. Staying current with minor and major upgrades ensures that your clusters are secure against new threats.

> **TIP** Using the Stable API ensures API stability, shielding applications from unexpected behavior changes.

Summary

- Database backups are crucial for data integrity and resilience. They allow quick recovery if data is accidentally deleted and maintaining business continuity in case of corruption. In cybersecurity, backups are key to recovery, especially during ransomware attacks, because secure backups can help you restore data without paying a ransom.
- Atlas Cloud Backup is a managed service that automatically stores point-in-time snapshots of clusters using AWS, Azure, or GCP. It supports scheduled and on-demand snapshots, offering options such as continuous backup with point-in-time recovery to ensure data protection and policy compliance:
  - Cloud Backup is not available for M0 free clusters. Instead, you can use tools like `mongodump` to create backups and `mongorestore` for data restoration. `mongodump` generates a logical backup by extracting database content and saving it as BSON files rather than copying the physical data layer.
  - Atlas cloud backup for Flex clusters is limited to automatic daily snapshots, starting 24 hours after setup. On-demand snapshots aren't supported, but cloud provider snapshots enable quick restoration.
  - Dedicated clusters (M10 and higher) have advanced Cloud Backup options, using cloud providers' native snapshot capabilities to create full-copy snapshots stored in the same region. Snapshots can be scheduled regularly, with configurable retention policies, and on-demand snapshots are available for backups anytime.
  - Continuous cloud backups offer robust data protection with point-in-time recovery, continuously capturing database changes for restoration at any moment within a set retention window. Available for M10 and higher clusters, this feature may increase costs due to additional storage and processing. You can configure the backup window duration to meet specific recovery needs.
  - In Atlas, `mongorestore` doesn't support `--restoreDbUsersAndRoles`, `--oplogReplay`, or `--preserveUUID`, so users and roles must be re-created manually; restored collections receive new UUIDs, and there is no point-in-time restore option.
- When you restore from a Cloud Backup, the target cluster is prepared to match the exact state of the selected snapshot or backup point. To achieve this, Atlas first clears all existing data on the target cluster, avoiding any potential conflicts or inconsistencies. This clean start ensures that the cluster can be restored accurately to reflect the data as it was at the backup time.
- Atlas offers real-time monitoring and alerting for database performance, health, and resource use. You can track metrics like CPU, memory, disk I/O, and active connections to spot problems early. Custom alerts can be set for specific thresholds, with notifications sent automatically via email, SMS, or integrations such as PagerDuty and Slack.

- Performance Advisor monitors slow queries and suggests indexes to boost performance, adjusting thresholds based on your cluster's average operation time. Each index recommendation includes sample queries that would benefit from it, grouped by query structure.
- Query Profiler helps you diagnose and monitor database cluster performance. It identifies slow queries and provides key metrics such as execution time and server processing time, allowing in-depth analysis across clusters or individual nodes.
- RTPP is a live monitoring tool that tracks key metrics such as CPU and memory, disk, and network use, helping you identify bottlenecks and manage database performance proactively.
- Namespace Insights offers detailed collection-level metrics on query latency, helping teams monitor response times and pinpoint collections with high latency or inefficient queries for targeted optimizations.
- Atlas offers schema suggestions to optimize database performance by analyzing high-traffic collections and slow queries. It recommends changes such as field restructuring, index optimization, and data type adjustments to reduce bottlenecks.
- You can also use native MongoDB diagnostic commands, which provide direct insights into server performance, resource use, and potential bottlenecks. Many Atlas tools use these commands under the hood. Key commands include `serverStatus`, `dbStats`, `collStats`, `currentOp`, `top`, and `replSetGetStatus`.
- Logging records system activities for troubleshooting and security, while alerting notifies admins of critical problems. Together, they ensure performance, security, and reliability by tracking and responding to problems proactively.
- You can set alerts for specific conditions, including CPU steal, queues, query targeting, and connection limits. Each condition monitors essential performance metrics to help you maintain cluster health.
- Enable an alert with `atlas alerts settings enable <alertConfigId>`, and delete it with `atlas alerts settings delete <alertConfigId>`. List all alerts using `atlas alerts list`, and view details with `atlas alerts describe <alertId>`.
- Atlas provides logging for effective database monitoring, including database logs for instance activities (kept for 30 days), audit logs for tracking database actions, and trigger logs for application events (kept for 10 days). Logs are accessible via the Atlas UI or CLI.
- Regular upgrades ensure security, performance, and new features. Minor upgrades are automatic during maintenance, focusing on patches and stability. Major upgrades require manual initiation and introduce significant changes, requiring a healthy cluster and completed snapshots.

index

Numbers

2d indexes 163
2dsphere indexes 162
8000 port 376

Symbols

$addFields stage 125
$addToSet operator 66
$all operator 80
$arrayElemAt 133
$currentOp pipeline stage 223
$each modifier 65
$elemMatch operator 80, 84
$emit stage 395
$graphLookup stage 99
$group stage 124, 131, 144, 421–423
$gt operator 80
$hoppingWindow command 414
$hoppingWindow stage 395
$[<identifier>] operator 69
$inc operator 62, 63, 189
$indexStats aggregation pipeline stage 172
$in operator 74
$jsonSchema operator 115
$limit operator 284
$limit stage 125, 287
$lookup operation 95, 131, 299
$lookup operator 131
$lookup stage 99, 125, 131–134, 144, 412
$match expression 469, 472
$match stage 124, 125, 131
$merge aggregation stage 118
$mergeObjects stage 133
$merge stage 130, 422–424
$meta: 282
$meta expression 319
$nin operator 74
$not operator 74
$or operator 73
$out aggregation stage 118
$out operation 130
$out stage 129
$planCacheStats stage 141
$pop operator 67
$project expression 469
$project operator 127
$project stage 319, 322, 332
$pull operator 66
$push operator 64–66
$replaceRoot stage 134
$search aggregation pipeline stage 279
$search facet operator 287, 290

531

$search fuzzy property 283
$searchMeta aggregation pipeline stage 294–297
$searchMeta stage 134, 268, 278
$search proximity search 284
$search stage 134, 268, 278, 293
$search text operator 281
$search wildcard search 286
$set operator 62, 63, 68, 127–129, 189, 330
$set stage 133, 287
$shardedDataDistribution 222
$size operator 81
$slice modifier 65
$sort modifier 65
$sort stage 124, 125, 287
$source aggregation stage 395–399
$source stage 394, 421–424
$sum operator 124
$ symbol, when not allowed 32
$text operator 159, 283
$tumblingWindow stage 395, 421–424
$unionWith operation 299
$unset operator 127–129
$unset stage 133, 287
$unwind stage 125
$validate aggregation stage 400
$validate stage 394, 407
$vectorSearch filter option 320, 322
$vectorSearch operator 323, 325, 326
$vectorSearch stage 315–319, 321, 322

A

accounts collection 131, 134, 189
accumulators 136
ACID (atomicity, consistency, isolation, and durability) 2
    multidocument transactions, executing 185
    transactions, defining 183
Active state 141
Add Connection button 419
addShard() operation 223
admin system database 172
aerocondorRoutesView 30
aggregation framework 9, 122–131
aggregation pipelines 11, 121
    accumulators 136
    Atlas SQL syntax 453

saving results of 129–131
structuring stream processor 394–400
using $set and $unset instead of $project 127–129
using MongoDB Atlas builder 137
viewing stages 124
writing 123
aggregations 388, 460
AI (artificial intelligence) applications, developing locally with Atlas CLI
    building first local Atlas cluster 340
    configuring Docker 338
    creating Atlas cluster locally with Atlas CLI 337–341
    displaying processes 349
    executing into containers 350
    local Atlas clusters 336, 341–352
AI chatbots
    AI-powered MongoDB chatbots 365
    building 362–364
    communicating programmatically with 381
    LangChain CLI 363–364
    retrieval-augmented generation, MongoDB Atlas Vector Search RAG template 362
    testing with LangServe 376
alerting 524–527
Algolia 263
analytics nodes 256–257
ANALYTICS nodes 257
analyzers, handling data using 272
analyzeShardKey command 217–219, 221
AND operator 267
ANN (approximate nearest neighbor) 355
    searches 309
anomaly detection 388
antipatterns 119
Apache Kafka 386
    broker 395
Apache Lucene 265–267
app directory 366
application and driver 7
applications, event-driven 402
Approximation pattern 102
arbiter, defined 198
archive-only instance 438
Archive pattern 103
archiving

INDEX

connecting and querying Online Archive 444–446
initializing Online Archive 440–444
restoring archived data 446–448
with Atlas Online Archive 437–440
    deleting archived documents 440
    overview of 439
arrays
    adding elements to 64
    multikey indexes with embedded fields in 158
    querying 78–81
    removing elements from 66
    returning array of all documents 89
    updating 64–69
    using array filters 68
async/await 476
asyncio 362
Atlas
    adding IP addresses to project access list 20
    alerting 524–527
    authorization, Atlas user roles 489
    backup strategies and practices 508–516
    loggin 524–527 g
    querying MongoDB using SQL 453–457
    shared responsibility model 482–485
    upgrading clusters 527–528
atlasAdmin
    permission 488
    role 21, 490
Atlas Application Services 466–476
    triggering server-side logic with Atlas Database Database Triggers 467, 469–472
    writing Atlas Functions 475–476
atlas auditing 495
atlas backup commands 510, 514, 515
Atlas CLI (command-line interface) 214, 242, 312, 335, 451, 509
    creating Atlas account 15
    creating Atlas cluster 18
    creating Atlas cluster locally with 337–341
    creating Atlas project 17
    creating organization 16
    developing AI applications locally 336, 349, 350, 352
    developing AI applications locally with, creating search indexes 352–356
    installing 15

    managing local Atlas cluster 341–345
    navigating Atlas user interface 19
    setting up first cluster using 15–19
    using with stream processing 402
atlas cluster commands 275, 277, 314, 442, 443
atlas clusters pause/start 214
Atlas command-line interface (CLI) 214, 242, 335, 451
atlas customDbRoles create command 491
atlas customDbRoles list command 492
Atlas database clusters 485
Atlas Database Triggers 10, 467–474
    configuring scheduled triggers 472
    creating 469–472
    event processing performance 474
    trigger types 467
    using authentication triggers 474
Atlas Data Federation 10, 430
    architecture of 432
    charges for 435
    deploying Atlas Federated Database instance 433
    limitations of 434
    optimizing data processing with, querying Amazon S3 and Azure Blob Store data via Query API 431
atlas dbusers create commands 492
atlas deployments commands 336, 337, 340, 342–345, 372, 375
Atlas Functions 475–476
Atlas Global Clusters 253
atlas–help command 23
atlas logs download command 526
atlas maintenanceWindows create commands 528
Atlas Online Archive 437–440
atlas organizations create command 16
atlas processes commands 517, 527
atlas process list command 527
atlas project commands 17
Atlas Search 9, 268–273, 359
    Apache Lucene 265–267
    architecture 268
    building index 274–277
    commands 297
    full-text search 262–263
    indexes 270–273
    Nodes 269

Atlas Search Playground 298
Atlas SQL Interface 10
  connecting to 451–452
  limitations of 458
Atlas Stream Processing 10, 389–393, 402
  capabilities 392
  components 391–392
  securing 426–427
atlas streams commands 403, 404, 419
Atlas Triggers 326–331, 468
Atlas UI 485
Atlas Vector Search 10, 371
  creating index 375
  embeddings with 309–314
  executing with programming languages 322–326
  improving performance of 331
  running queries 315–322
Attribute pattern 103
attributes, indexes 165–170
audio embeddings 304
auditing Atlas 492–494
audit logs 526
authCheck
  event 493
  log 494
authenticate event 493
authentication 485–488
  choosing authentication method 486–488
  integrating with HashiCorp Vault 487
  methods 434
  triggers 468, 474
authorization 489–492
  Atlas user roles 489
  MongoDB RBAC 490–492
  principle of least privilege 489
auth register command 15
autocomplete, defined 36
AUTOCOMPLETE environment 299
autoscaling
  clusters 249
  storage 251
AWS (Amazon Web Services) 9, 18, 245, 433, 443, 466, 508
  IAM (identity and access management) 434, 487
AWS IOPS (input/output operations per second) 253

AWS S3 account 434
  querying data via Query API 431
Azure Blob Store, querying data via Query API 431
Azure Key Vault 499

B

backup strategies and practices 508–516
  Atlas backup methods 508–512
  Atlas cluster restoration 512–516
backward compatibility 90
balancer 224
BaseModel 371
bash shell 350
batch document updates 205
BI (business intelligence) tools 242, 449
Bloated Documents 119
blocking queries 446
BSON (Binary JSON) 5, 29, 60, 99, 136, 167, 320, 344, 434, 509
Bucket pattern 104
builds, indexes 170–172
bulkWrite() method 86
BYOK (Bring Your Own Key) 483

C

Callback API 184
  using transactions with 187, 190, 192
callback function 187
capped collections 28
case insensitivity 159
cat command 351
chain, defined 371
chained replication 203
chain.py file 366, 369
change streams 9, 207–211
  connections for 207
  modifying output of 210
  with Node.js 209
charts 459, 460
  Atlas Application Services 466–476
  types 460–462
  view 460
  visualizing data with Atlas Charts 460–466
chatbots. *See* AI chatbots
ChatOpenAI 370, 381
ChatPromptTemplate 371, 379, 381

INDEX   535

checkpoints   181
chunks
   administrating   225, 227
   balancing   224
CIDR (Classless Inter-Domain Routing)   500
class, defined   371
classpath   350
clearJumboFlag command   228
CLI (command-line interface)   15, 248, 274, 459
client, defined   371
clusterMonitor role   490
CMK (AWS customer master key)   496, 508
collections
   managing data with   23
   resharding   222
collMod command   114, 150, 151, 168, 169, 173
COLLSCAN stage   153
column and bar, chart type, defined   461
column-oriented storage   181
combined instance   438
combo   461
commitTransaction command   184
communicating with MongoDB, MongoDB
       Compass   43–45
comparison operators   74
compound condition   282
COMPOUND environment   299
compound
   indexes   151, 15, 155
   multikey index   157
   operator   281
   query   73
compression, defined   182
config servers   8, 212
   embedding in sharded clusters   230
config shard   215
config system database   172
connect command   337
connection limits   434
   metric   525
connection properties, restoring archived data   447
Connection Registry   391
connections, establishing to MongoDB through
       MongoDB Shell   21
containers, executing into   350
contextual help   36

continuous cloud backups   512
   restoring from   515
Core API   184
cosine similarity   312
cost, defined   264
count command   195
CPU steal metric   525
cron expressions   473
CRUD (create, read, update, and delete)
       operations   11, 44, 57
   bulkWrite() method   86
   connecting to mongosh for   58
   cursors   88
   deleting documents   85
   inserting documents   58–61
   executing   77
   limiting   84, 85
   querying arrays   78–81
   querying embedded/nested documents   84
   reading documents   71–77
   regular-expression searches   77
   replacing documents   70
   skipping   84
   sorting   84
   Stable API   89
   updating, arrays   64–69
   updating documents   61–64
CSFLE (client-side field-level encryption)   498
CSRS (config server replica set)   224
curl command   344
cursors   88–89, 141, 208, 521
CUSTOM ANALYZER environment   299
customers collection   131–133, 157
custom query   438
customReadUpdateRole   491, 492
customRoleName   492

D

dashboards   46, 465–466
data
   access   446
   encryption   495–500
   loading sample data set   19
   managing with databases, collections, and
       documents   23, 24
databases

logs   526
managing data with   23–25
triggers   468
data consistency and availability, managing   233–238
Read Concern   235
Read Preference   237
Write Concern   234–235
data models, document-oriented   4–6
data reshaping   11
data scan   446
data seek   446
data source   460
data synchronization   264
data transfer   446
date-based archiving   438
dateFacet field type   279
date field   167, 168
date type   167
DBaaS (Database as a Service)   4, 243
Atlas custom Write Concerns   259
Atlas Global Clusters   253
dedicated clusters   247–253
predefined replica set tags for querying   257–259
shared clusters   244
dbAccess event   494
dbAdmin permission   114
db global variable   25
DB_NAME   371
db object   37, 38
DBRefs   100
dbStats command   523
decryption
for the client   500
querying encrypted fields without   498
dedicated clusters   247–253
autoscaling clusters and storage   249–253
for high-traffic applications   249
for low-traffic applications   248
dedicated clusters (M10+)
backing up   509–511
restoring   514
dedicated nodes, workload isolation with   331
def, defined   371
default index   375, 376
name   367

defense in depth, defined   503–504
DEK (data encryption key)   496
delete operation   470
deleting
archived documents   440
documents   85
denormalized models   98
deployment, defined   17
deployments command   337
designing schema, Polymorphic pattern   109
deterministically, defined   498
diagnostic commands, native MongoDB
currentOp   521
dbStats   523
monitoring replication   524
serverStatus   521
top   522
direct indexing   67
DLQ (dead-letter queue)   425
DNS (Domain Name System)   207
Docker, configuring   338
docker commands   346, 348–350
document
array   399
data handling   460
embeddings   304
joins   11
order in queries   434
size limitation   434
documentKey   329, 472
document-oriented data model   4–6
documents   399
deleting   85
managing data with   23–31
querying embedded/nested documents   81–84
reading   71–77
replacing   70
Document Versioning pattern   106
dot notation   82
dot product   313
doughnut, chart type, defined   461
Dremio, querying Iceberg tables in   447
drivers, defined   45
dropDatabase() operation   223
dropIndexes command   172
dynamic

mappings 270
queries 11
schema 24

E

EJSON (Extended JSON) 395
Elasticsearch 263
electable nodes, adding for high availability 256
elements
   adding to arrays 64
   removing from arrays 66
embedded documents, querying 81–84
embedded fields, multikey indexes with embedded fields in arrays 158
embedded_movies collection 310, 312, 313, 328, 330, 355
embedding
   field 375, 376
   key 374
   LangChain in RAG ecosystem 361
   vs. referencing 98–101
embeddings 303–309
   Atlas Triggers for automated embeddings creation 326–331
   converting text to 305–308
   inserting into MongoDB Atlas 367
   product 305
   vector databases 308
encryption, in Atlas 495–500
ENN (exact nearest neighbor) search 309
equality, defined 154
EQUALS environment 299
equal volumes of data deletions and insertions 205
error messages 36
error setting 117
ESR (Equality, Sort, Range) rule 154
ETL (extract, transform, load) 258, 431, 450
Euclidean distance 312
event auditing 427
event-driven applications 384
   adopting new stream processor methods 402
   Atlas Stream Processing 389–393, 402
   controlling stream processing flow 425–426
   securing 426–427
   setting up streams Connection Registry 419
   stream processors 404–407, 410, 412, 414, 416
   structuring stream processor aggregation pipeline 394–400
   using Atlas CLI with stream processing 402
   technology 385–387
event time, differentiating from processing time 387
executeTransaction function 184, 186
executionStats 143, 148
expireAfterSeconds option 167–169
explain plan 148, 155
expression, defined 399
EXPRESS stages 143–144
Extended Reference pattern 107

F

facet
   operator 279, 287, 289
   stage 291
FastAPI 362
FETCH stage 143, 148, 156
fields 312
   querying for 76
FIFO (first-in-first-out) feature 28
filtered positional operator 68
filters, array 68
FIM (Federated Identity Management) 486
FIND access 491
FIPS (Federal Information Processing Standards) 495
FLATTEN function 455–457
flex clusters
   backing up 509
   restoring 513
fragmentation, defined 231
frequent in-place updates 205
full collection scan 141
full-text search 11, 158, 262
   Atlas Search 268–273
   building Atlas Search index 274–277
   executing locally 352–355
   implementing 263
   running Atlas Search queries 278
   using Atlas Search Playground 298
fuzzy search 291

G

gauge, chart type, defined   461
GCP (Google Cloud Platform)   9, 18, 214, 508
GCP KMS   499
GDPR (General Data Protection Regulation)   482
GenAI (Generative AI)   45
general settings, restoring archived data   446
Generative Pretrained Transformer (GPT)   303
genres field   312
geospatial, chart type, defined   462
geospatial and graph-based queries   11
geospatial indexes   162, 163
getIndexes() method   147, 150
getParameter command   195
GPT (Generative Pretrained Transformer)   303
GUI (graphical user interface)   34

H

hashed
   indexes   164
   sharding   217
HashiCorp Vault   487
hasNext() method   89
heatmaps, chart type, defined   461
help command   37
helper method   147
HH:MM   225
hidden indexes   169
hidden members, defined   199–200
high availability, ensuring with replication   197–206
   distinguishing replica set members   197–200
   electing primary replica-set member   200–206
   logical initial sync process   206
   oplog size   204
   oplog window   205
hint() method   174
HIPAA (Health Insurance Portability and Accountability Act)   482
historyLength setting   41
HNSW (Hierarchical Navigable Small Worlds)   309
hopping windows   388
horizontal scaling   211
hot shard   216

I

IAM (identity and access management)   434, 484, 508
Iceberg tables
   creating BI dashboard from   448
   querying in Dremio   447
IDLE status   342
IdP (identity provider)   486
image embeddings   304
IMDb (Internet Movie Database)   151, 175, 312
Inactive state   141
index creation   12
   support   435
indexes   9, 140
   attributes   165–170
   builds   170–172
   compound   151
   creating wildcard   160
   dropping   165
   geospatial   162
   hashed   164
   managing   172–177
   multikey   156–158
   query planner   141–145
   single-field   146, 148, 150
   sorting query results   148
   text indexes   158
   types of   145
   when not to use   178
indexing
   for query performance   148, 150
   vectors   332
index prefix   152
Index Sufficiency Warning message   439
INSERT action   492
insert command   118, 470
inserting documents   58–61
insert methods   25, 26, 58–61, 115
insert operation   470
INSERT permission   492
inspections collection   275–278
integration
   complexity   264
   with Atlas   460
interacting via MongoDB Wire Protocol   35
i (operation sequence)   203

INDEX

IOPS (input/output operations per second) 244, 439
IP addresses, adding to project access list 20
ISO (International Organization for Standardization) 482
IXSCAN stage 143, 148, 156

J

JavaScript, executing vector search with 322
j:<boolean> 234
JDBC (Java Database Connectivity) driver 452
job 439
JOIN operations 1, 107, 113
journaling, defined 182
JSON schema validation 114
jumbo chunks 227
jwt (JSON Web Token) 202

K

keyFile 351
keys, shard 216
killOp command 522
KMIP (Key Management Interoperability Protocol) 497, 500
KMS (AWS Key Management Service) 483, 508
k-NN (k-nearest neighbors) 355
knnVector 355

L

LangChain
  application 366
  capabilities of 363
  CLI 364
  embedding in RAG ecosystem 361
langchain-community 363
langchain-core 363
langchain database 367, 372, 373, 375
langchain-mongodb package 362, 363
langchain_openai module 366
langchain-openai package 363
LangGraph 363
LangServe 362, 363, 376
LangSmith 364
language-specific rules 159
LB (Elastic load balancer) 501

LDAP (Lightweight Directory Access Protocol) 483, 487
limiting 84
limit parameter 322
line and area, chart type, defined 461
linearizable Read Concern 236
LLaMA (Large Language Model Meta AI) 305
LLM (Large Language Model) 305
load() method 39
LocalSearchIndex index 354, 355
local system database 172
logging 524–527
  in Atlas 526
  setting alert conditions 524–526
logical initial sync process 206
logical operators 73
login command 16
logs collection 103
logs command 337
LRU (least recently used) 145

M

M0 clusters
  backing up 509
  restoring 513
majority Read Concern 233, 235
majority Write Concern 233
major version upgrades 528
manning user 21
manual iteration 88, 89
manual references 100
Massive Arrays 119
Match Expression field 472
materialized views 31
maxWriteBatchSize 60
merge commands 228, 229
message broker 386
metadata, checking table metadata 447
MFA (multifactor authentication) 482
Missing state 141
MITM (Man in the Middle) 495
mode, defined 371
modern web applications 1–2
MongoClient 371
MongoDB
  Atlas overview of 14

communicating with
  connecting to, using drivers   45
  ecosystem   8–11
  interacting via MongoDB Wire Protocol   35
  mongosh   35–43
  Motor   51
  Node.js driver   46–49
  PyMongo   49
  PyMongo vs. Motor   53
  Python drivers   49–53
  querying using SQL   453–457
  replication, chunk balancing   224
  Ruby drivers   53
  scaling data horizontally   6–8
  sharding, chunk balancing   224
  TCMalloc   11
MongoDB Atlas
  aggregation pipeline builder   137
  connecting to   36
  creating sharded clusters via Atlas CLI   214
  creating users   21
  data platform   241
  establishing connection to MongoDB through MongoDB Shell   21
  inserting embeddings into   367
  inspecting performance of cluster   516–524
  loading sample data set   19
  overview of   14
  querying using SQL   449
  setting up first cluster using Atlas CLI   15–19
  SQL interface   450
MONGODB_ATLAS environment variables   17
MongoDB Atlas Vector Search   362, 370
mongodb collection   367
mongodb package   46
MongoDB Query API   6, 11
MongoDB Shell (mongosh)   35
  establishing connection to MongoDB through   21
MongoDB Uniform Resource Identifier (URI)   43
MongoDB Wire Protocol   35
mongod process   212, 268, 337, 350, 352
mongodump   246
mongo gem   54, 325
Mongoid, defined   55
mongo library   194

mongo-rag template   377
mongo-ra template   362
mongorestore tool   509
mongos, defined   212
mongosh   35–43, 141, 199, 225
  configuring   40
  connecting to for CRUD operations   58
  connecting to MongoDB Atlas   36
  connecting to self-hosted deployments   36
  .mongoshrc.js   42
  performing operations   36
  running scripts in   39–40
  viewing logs   38
mongosql   10
mongos (query routers)   7–8
MongotCli class   350
mongot component   350
MONGO_URI environment variable   371
monitoring support   434
Motor   51
  PyMongo vs.   53
moveChunk command   227
moveCollection command   211
movies collection   169, 174, 175, 176
MsgHeader header   35
multidocument ACID (atomicity, consistency, isolation, durability) transactions   181
  Callback API   184
  considerations for   194
  Core API   184
  executing, using transactions with mongosh   185
  single-document transactions   182
  using transactions with Callback API   187, 190, 192
  WiredTiger storage engine   181–182
multikey indexes   156–158
multiregion, workload isolation   254–256
must clause   282
MVCC (multiversion concurrency control)   181

N

namespace   27
Namespace Insights   520
natural language   461
NDJSON (Newline Delimited JSON)   38
ne operator   175

INDEX

network access, protecting 427
network security 500–502
next( ) method 89
NIN operator 175
Node.js
  changing streams with 209
  driver 46–49
  transactions 187
non-TTL indexes, converting to TTL index 168
NOT operator 175, 267
null values 76–77
number, chart type, defined 462
numberFacet field type 279
numCandidates parameter 318, 322
numDimensions 312
num_mflix_comments field 312

O

OASIS (Organization for the Advancement of Structured Information Standards) 497
ObjectId 203
OCC (optimistic concurrency control) 183
ODBC (Open Database Connectivity) driver 452
ODM (object-document mapper) 55
OIDC (OpenID Connect) 485, 486
on-demand materialized views 31
Online Archive
  connecting and querying 444–446
  initializing 440–444
OpenAIEmbeddings 370
operational excellence 507
  inspecting performance of Atlas cluster 516–524
operational overhead 264
operationType field 472
oplog (operations log) 201
OP_MSG opcode 35
ordered triggers 474
organization roles 489
ORM (object-relational mapping) layer 389
OR operator 267
OR queries 174
Outlier pattern 107
overlay2 storage driver 349

P

partial indexes 166

PATH environment variable 349
patterns. *See* schema design
pause command 337
PCI (Payment Card Industry) 482
Performance Advisor 516–518
persistence 4
  ensuring in stream processing 421
PHI (protected health information) 16
PII (personally identifiable information) 16
pip3 package manager 364
PKI (public-key infrastructure) 486
plot_embedding 312, 313, 317, 330, 355
plot_embedding 313
point-in-time recovery 515
PoLP (principle of least privilege) 489
Polymorphic pattern 109
positional operator 68
Preallocation pattern 109
predefined replica set tags 257–259
PRIMARY state 198
printMongoDBDetailsSimplified function 39
priority, defined 200
private endpoints 502
privilege actions 427
processes, displaying 349
processing time, differentiating from event time 387
programming languages, executing vector search with 322–326
  JavaScript 322
  Python 323
  Ruby 325
projections, defined 75
project roles 489
Project Stream Processing Owner role 427
prompt, defined 371
ps command 349
pub/sub (publish/subscribe) queues 386
PV1 (protocolVErsion:1) 201
pydantic 362
PyMongo 49
  Motor vs. 53
pymongo library 192, 323
PyPDFLoader 370
Python
  executing vector search with 323

542 INDEX

transactions 190
Python drivers 49–53
   Motor 51
   PyMongo 49
   PyMongo vs. Motor 53

Q

Queryable Encryption 499
Query API, querying Amazon S3 and Azure Blob Store data via 431
query
   challenge 264
   covered 177
   limitations 435
   planner 141–145
   sorting results 148
   submission 499–500
   targeting metrics 525
queryHash 148
querying
   Atlas using SQL 449
   MongoDB using SQL 453–457
   predefined replica set tags for 257–259
Query Profiler 519
Question class 371
queues metric 525

R

rag-mongo template 365, 366
RAG (retrieval-augmented generation) 10, 242, 359
   AI chatbots 358–359
      building 362–364
      communicating programmatically with chatbot 381
      creating Atlas Vector Search index 375
      embedding LangChain in RAG ecosystem 361
      inserting embeddings into MongoDB Atlas 367
      LangChain capabilities 363
      LangChain CLI 364
      MongoDB Atlas Vector Search RAG template 362
      setting up new applications 365
   model 303
range, defined 155
RANGE environment 299

RBAC (role-based access control) 207, 433, 484
   MongoDB 490–492
readAnyDatabase permission 488
Read Concern 235
README.md file 351
read-only nodes 256–257
read permission 488
Read Preference 237
read role 490–492
RecursiveCharacterTextSplitter 371
referencing, vs. embedding 98–101
regular-expression searches 77
reindexing in Atlas Search 273
replaceOne() method 61, 70, 71
replica sets
   predefined tags for querying 257–259
   secondaries 130
replication 196
   administrating chunks 225, 227
   automerging chunks 228
   choosing shard key 217
   chunk balancing 224
   creating sharded clusters via Atlas CLI 214
   ensuring data high availability with 197–206
   managing data consistency and availability 233–238
   monitoring 524
   scaling data horizontally through sharding 211
   shard key 216–219
REPL (Read-Eval-Print Loop) 21, 35
resharding collections 222, 232
restaurants collection 462, 470, 472
restoring archived data 446–448
restoring Atlas clusters 512–516
ResultsByStatus group 287
ResultsByYear group 287
Retriever, defined 378
roles, discovering new 427
ROLLBACK state 198
rolling upgrades 528
routes collection 47, 54, 71, 82, 123, 128, 129, 131, 229, 491, 492
row-oriented storage 181
RPO (recovery-point objectives) 515
RTPP (Real-Time Performance Panel) 519
Ruby

drivers   53
executing vector search with   325
transactions   192
run function   189
RunnableLambda   371
RunnableParallel   371, 381
RunnablePassthrough   371, 379, 381

S

$$SEARCH_META variable   291–294
SaaS (Software as a Service)   482
sales collection   491, 492
sample_analytics database   131, 132, 167, 492
scaling
  cluster tier and cluster storage in parallel   251
  data horizontally   6–8
scatter, graph type, defined   461
scheduled triggers   468, 472
schema design, introduction   92–93
  antipatterns   119
  Approximation pattern   102
  Archive pattern   103
  Attribute pattern   103
  Bucket pattern   104
  Computed pattern   105
  Document Versioning pattern   106
  Extended Reference pattern   107
  organizing data model   93–98
  Outlier pattern   107
  Polymorphic pattern   109
  Preallocation pattern   109
  Schema Versioning pattern   110
  Subset pattern   111
  Tree pattern   112
  validations   113–119
schemas
  embedding vs. referencing   98–101
  improving   520
SCRAM (Salted Challenge Response Authentication Mechanism)   53, 485, 486
scripting   36, 39–40
search
  Atlas Search, running queries   278
  command   338
  indexes, creating   352–356
SECONDARY state   198

SectorSummary group   287
security   479
  auditing Atlas   492–494
  authentication   485–488
  authorization   489–492
  encryption in Atlas   495–500
  features   481
  implementing defense in depth   503–504
  network security   500–502
    IP access lists   500
    peering networks   501
    private endpoints   502
  shared responsibility model   482–485
SELECT statement   449
self-hosted deployments, connecting to   36
semantic techniques   302
  embeddings   303–309
  embeddings with Atlas Vector Search   309–314
  running Atlas Vector Search queries   315–322
sentence embeddings   304
Separating Data Accessed Together   119
server processing with Queryable Encryption   500
server.py file   366
server-side logic, triggering with Atlas Database Triggers   467–474
serverStatus command   521
sessions collection   202
setDefaultRWConcern command   236
setup command   337
sharding   7, 196
  administrating chunks   225, 227
  automerging chunks   228
  choosing shard key   217
  chunk balancing   224
  creating sharded clusters via Atlas CLI   214
  detecting shard-data imbalance or uneven data distribution   222
  features in MongoDB 8.0   229–233
  resharding collections   222
  scaling data horizontally through   211
  sharded cluster architecture   212
  shard key   216
shards   197, 212
shared clusters   244
shared responsibility model   482–485
short-form Atlas SQL syntax   454

show collections command   27, 373
show dbs command   22, 216, 372
similarity, defined   312
single-document transactions   182
single-field indexes   146
   converting existing indexes to unique   150
   sorting query results   148
sink, defined   390
skip operation   84
SKU (Stock Keeping Unit)   465
slow queries   516–520
   monitoring collection-level latency with Namespace Insights   520
   using Performance Advisor   516–518
   using Query Profiler   519
   viewing Real-Time Performance Panel   519
SMS (Short Message Service)   516
Snappy library   182
snapshot Read Concern   236
snapshots   181
snippets, defined   36
Solr   263
SORT environment   299
sorting   84, 155
   query results   148
   on multiple fields   176
source, defined   390
sparse indexes   166
special collections   9
spiColl collection   422–424
split command   226
sp.process() method   405
SQL (Structured Query Language)   431
   Atlas SQL interface   450–452
   querying Atlas using   449
   querying MongoDB using   453–457
SRE (site reliability engineering) team   524
SRV (Service Record)   36
SSD (solid-state drive)   252
SSO (single sign-on)   486
Stable API   89
start command   337
startTransaction command   184
STARTUP states   198
stateful/stateless operations   394
static mappings   270

stats() function   423
sticky sessions   8
STOPPED state   342
storage capacity, changing   252
storage settings, restoring archived data   447
streaming queries   446
stream processing   12
   concepts of   387–388
   ensuring persistence in   421
   structuring stream processor aggregation pipeline   394–400
   using Atlas CLI with   402
stream processors   391, 406
   $lookup stage   412
   $validate stage   407
   adopting new methods   402
   components of   406
   dead-letter queues   410
   document array source   416
   instances   391
   time windows   414
streams Connection Registry, setting up   419
stringFacet field type   279
StrOutputParser   370, 371, 381
Subset pattern   111
switchToDatabase() function   42
SYNONYMS environment   299
syntax highlighting   36

T

tables, chart type, defined   462
TCMalloc   11
TCP/IP (Transmission Control Protocol/Internet Protocol)   35
testing
   chatbots with LangServe   376
   indexes   158
   schema validation rules   115
   search operator   282, 284
text embeddings   304
   converting to   305–308
TEXT environment   299
time-series
   analysis   12
   collections   9, 29
Time Travel, using with Iceberg snapshots   447

time windows   388, 395
TLS (Transport Layer Security)   53, 484
toArray( ) method   89
tokens   266
top item   462
transactions   185, 189, 192, 194
transactions collection   131–134, 167–168
TransientTransactionError   186
Tree pattern   112
trial phase   141
trigger logs   526
triggers, Atlas Application Services   466–476
    configuring scheduled triggers   472
    creating   469–472
    event processing performance   474
    triggering server-side logic with Atlas Database Triggers   467–474
    trigger types   467
    unordered   474
    using authentication triggers   474
    writing Atlas Functions   475–476
try block   189
ts (timestamp)   203, 399, 421
TTL (time-to-live) indexes   9, 167–169
t (transaction identifier)   203
tumbling windows   388
type check   77

U

$unwind operator   134–136
unique
    constraint   150, 165
    indexes   150
    property   164
UnknownTransactionCommitResult error   186
Unnecessary Indexes   119
unsharding collections   232–233
UNWIND function   455–457
update operation   470
UPDATE permission   491, 492
updating
    arrays   64–69
    documents   61–64
upgrading Atlas clusters   527–528
URI (MongoDB Uniform Resource Identifier)   43
uri variable   189, 192, 194

use commands/methods   25, 27, 37, 58, 310, 341, 373
user embeddings   305
user_id   202
users, creating   21
UTC (Coordinated Universal Time)   510
UTF (Unicode Transformation Format)   77
UUIDs (universally unique identifiers)   513
uvloop   362

V

validationAction   400
validations   113–119
    bypassing   118
    JSON schema validation   114
    modifying schema validator behavior   117
    testing schema validation rules   115
validator   400
vCPUs (virtual CPUs)   244
vector databases   308
vector search   11
    database   308
    executing locally   355
    executing with programming languages   322–326
    workload isolation with dedicated nodes   331
vectorSearch collection   375
vector similarity search engine   308
verbosity mode   142
vertical scaling   211
views, defined   30
visualizing data   460–466
    using billing dashboards   465
    using natural language to build visualizations   462–464
v (MongoDB oplog version)   203
votes, defined   200
VPC (virtual private cloud)   427
VS Code (Visual Studio Code)   404

W

wall (exact time of operation)   203
warn setting   117
WHERE statement   449
wildcard indexes   160
winningPlan   148

546 INDEX

WiredTiger storage engine   181–182
withTransaction method   187, 190
word, chart type, defined   462
workers, defined   391
workload isolation   331
    multiregion   254–256

Write Concern   234–235, 259
WSL (Windows Subsystem for Linux)   15

X

X.509 certificates   53, 486